From Scratch

published with a grant
Figure Foundation
within hearing muse

From Scratch
Writings in Music Theory

James Tenney

Edited by Larry Polansky, Lauren Pratt, Robert Wannamaker, and Michael Winter

University of Illinois Press
Urbana, Chicago, and Springfield

First Illinois paperback, 2019

1 2 3 4 5 C P 5 4 3 2 1

♾ This book is printed on acid-free paper.

Library of Congress Control Number: 2015944784
ISBN 978-0-252-03872-3 (hardcover)
ISBN 978-0-252-09667-9 (e-book)
ISBN 978-0-252-08437-9 (paperback)

CONTENTS

NOTES ON THE EDITION

All dates in the table of contents indicate when the articles were written and completed, not necessarily when they were published.

Each article in this edition has been checked against published and original sources. Substantive changes in Tenney's writing are few and are noted. Minor spelling corrections and grammatical changes have been made by the editors, all of whom worked closely with Tenney for many years.

All editors' notes are indicated as such by square brackets and "—Ed."

Robert Wannamaker had conferred extensively with Tenney on the content of three of the mathematically intensive articles ("The Structure of Harmonic Series Aggregates," "An Experimental Investigation of Timbre—the Violin," and "The Several Dimensions of Pitch"), and he has served as technical editor for them in consultation with the other editors. Their content was nearly (but not completely) finalized at the time of Tenney's death. Certain corrections, derivations, and clarifications have been supplied by the editors in the notes. Only "The Several Dimensions of Pitch" was ever published in a version different from the one included here.

In a few cases, figures have been located or redone to complete an unpublished essay. Most figures and examples have been left in Tenney's own hand. We have cleaned up some of them, visually clarifying a few lines and words. In general, though, we have left the figures alone, avoiding the temptation to regenerate them with modern technology.

ACKNOWLEDGMENTS

We thank Clarence Barlow, who made the original transcription of Tenney's lecture "The Several Dimensions of Pitch." We extend our appreciation to Jim Fox and Nicolás Carrasco Diaz, who assisted in the preparation of the graphic examples. Thanks also to two musicologists, Amy Beal (ex camera) and Bob Gilmore (ex patria), for important contributions to this project. The index was prepared by Amy Beal.

For previous publication of works reprinted in this volume, see Publication History on page 437.

Introduction

> A new kind of music theory is needed which deals with the question of what we actually hear when we listen to a piece of music, as well as how or why we hear as we do. To the extent that music theory involves the development and application of a descriptive language for music, this means that both the things named and the relations between things described by such a language must be much more precisely correlated than they are now with the things and relations actually perceived or experienced.
>
> James Tenney, "Review of *Music as Heard*, by Thomas Clifton"

> We must all be reduced to an attitude of humility that may once have been associated with the word "theory."
>
> Tenney, "Contributions toward a Quantitative Theory of Harmony"

The theoretical writings collected here were selected, sequenced, edited, revised, and titled by James Tenney near the end of his life. Lauren Pratt, Robert Wannamaker, Michael Winter, and I have edited this book into its final form based on consultation with Tenney himself and the extensive notes he left for the treatment of each essay in this collection. We believe this collection constitutes one of the most important bodies of music-theoretical thought of the twentieth century.

Tenney sometimes described himself as a "composer/theorist" despite his understated claim in "The Several Dimensions of Pitch" that he was "first of all a composer, and only secondarily and occasionally a theorist." He nurtured a synergistic and ineluctable connection between explanation and creation. While his music has become better known in the last twenty years, his writings have remained relatively unavailable, and his ideas, consequently, are not well known or understood. This book represents the denominator of his self-description.

Tenney wrote prolifically. The articles in this volume are just a part of his output, describing the most important theoretical ideas of his music. He also wrote a great deal about the work of other composers, including writings on Charles Ives and Conlon Nancarrow not reprinted here, as well as the theoretical essays about John Cage, Carl Ruggles, and Arnold Schoenberg included in this collection. Interestingly, he wrote sparingly about his own music, some important exceptions being "Computer Music Experiences," "About *Changes: Sixty-Four Studies for Six Harps*," "Reflections after *Bridge*," and "About *Diapason*." When he *did* write about his music, compositional ideas are clearly explained in fine detail with transparency. These articles are invaluable resources for understanding Tenney's compositions.

The articles in this collection are the most abstract and *fundamental* of his prose, perhaps the musical embodiment of his occasional self-description as "amateur cosmologist." He is trying to get to the bottom of things. Tenney often stressed his concern for "what the ear hears." He is less interested in style, history, and culture than he is in acoustics and perception. Each article in this collection asks: How might new and radical musical ideas emerge from how we hear?

Tenney's writings are foundational. As a composer he was faithful to his own theories. His theory became practice. The absence of the arbitrary in his music is reflected in the elegance of his theory. He didn't waste ideas, and he embraced Cage's dictum about "possibility" ("nothing is necessary, everything is possible") by explaining it. The poetry of Tenney's music (what Cage might have called its "form") is always partnered in a subtle dance with his speculative theoretical designs.

The twenty-one writings included in this book span the years from 1955 to 2006. They include both previously published and unpublished texts. In this introduction, I first describe what seem to me to be Tenney's major theoretical concerns (sound, cognition, form, and harmony). Next, I discuss the articles in more detail, often highlighting specific ideas. I try to elucidate the relationships among the articles by grouping them in three general categories (not delineated by Tenney himself) that I hope will be helpful. Those groups are *Meta ≠ Hodos* and the writings directly related to it; writings on harmony; and those on specific pieces.

Sound, Cognition, Form, Harmony

Tenney's central concern was not only "How do we hear music?" but also "How might we hear and then make new music?" There is a grand design in the chronological trajectory of this work—a lifelong attempt to explain *everything* about sound, musical perception, and composition. Knowing such an agenda was endless didn't make him any less enthusiastic about the trying.

Tenney first needed to consider the idea of a sonic *parameter*, both acoustically and psychoacoustically. The next step, his groundbreaking work in *hierarchical and temporal formal organization*, deals with higher-level cognition and, by extension, models of form. The basic mechanisms of these ideas (making distinctions, organizing things distinguished in time) are fundamental to perception, perhaps some of the "oldest" cognitive mechanisms we possess.

Some of the articles in this collection have a somewhat narrower focus, as in the highly detailed "On 'Crystal Growth' in Harmonic Space" and the article on Ruggles. Yet most of the articles refer to each other in a variety of ways, gaining richness in the intersection of their ideas.

Much of his early writing deals directly with acoustics, psychoacoustics, and the phenomenological bases of cognition. There is a rough chronological division between the earlier writings and his later writings on harmony (pitch perception and tuning theory). The early articles, written before 1970, include, in chronological order, "Pre–*Meta ≠ Hodos*," "On the Development of the Structural Potentialities of Rhythm, Dynamics, and Timbre in the Early Nontonal Music of Arnold Schoenberg," "On Musical Parameters," *Meta ≠ Hodos*, "Computer Music Experiences," "On the Physical Correlates of Timbre," "An Experimental Investigation of Timbre—the Violin," and "Form in Twentieth-Century Music."

Later work, beginning in the 1970s, often explores Tenney's reawakened interest in harmony. In much of this work, the concept of *harmonic space* is central—frequency and pitch relations are considered mathematically based on perceptual assumptions (mostly about the ear itself). These articles include "Introduction to 'Contributions toward a Quantitative Theory of Harmony,'" "The Structure of Harmonic Series Aggregates," "The Several Dimensions of Pitch," and "On 'Crystal Growth' in Harmonic Space." Once Tenney solved some basic (but difficult) problems of harmony, he quickly began to integrate harmonic ideas with his earlier work on form. Some good examples are found in articles like "John Cage and the Theory of Harmony" and in pieces like *Bridge* (1982–84) and *Changes* (1985).

When Tenney wrote about cognition, as far back as the earliest essay in this collection ("Pre–*Meta ≠ Hodos*"), he did so in an unusual way. Most of his work predates a more recent explosion of experimentally and heuristically based research in psychoacoustics, perception, music cognition, and neurocognition. Tenney read widely on all aspects of music, the ear, and cognition, but he seldom utilized experiment- or evidence-based arguments. By nature a scientific and exacting musical thinker, he nonetheless felt strongly and clearly that he was not a scientist. Early on, while at Bell Labs, he learned to trust the primacy of his listening experience as a composer and musician over the data of the "laboratory":

> It is questionable whether such tests as the one described, carried out in very artificial laboratory conditions and divorced from any musical context, can ever be of much use to the composer. And for this reason, primarily, I have not done any more experiments of this kind. Instead, I have tried to gain an understanding of such physical-to-psychological correlations more directly—by listening to the sounds in a musical context. What this approach lacks in precision (and sometimes, unfortunately, communicability), it more than makes up for in efficiency. Only after giving up all intentions of dealing with these problems in the strict ways of the psychophysical laboratory has it been possible for me to produce compositions with any degree of fluency. ("Computer Music Experiences")

Freed from the cumbersome burdens of formal science—extreme specificity, hypothesis testing, statistical analysis of experimental data, and institutions like the academic laboratory—Tenney's theoretical and musical ideas were able to bloom. His methodology consisted of reading, a great deal of thought, self-critique, and then *even more* thought (a recipe repeated until he felt he had gotten it right). His laboratory subjects were his own ears, his statistical analyses his own exacting logical criteria, and his experiments often simple computer simulations of his models. The approach was that of a humanist skilled in the logic of science and the clarity of mathematics.

This methodology and trust in his instincts found a natural rationale in the work of the gestalt theorists. It is worth noting that since its early days, gestalt theory has primarily dealt with the visual domain, even though several of its pioneers were musicians themselves and often used music examples (such as the transposition of melodies as an illustration of gestalt invariance). Tenney was one of the first to apply these principles to *auditory perception in time*, making important analogies between, for example, spatial and temporal proximity, as well as visual and acoustic similarity.

Recently, I heard an anecdote from a psychologist who had been a student of a well-known early gestalt theorist. A student had discovered an optical illusion demonstrating a gestalt principle. When he asked his mentor if he should run a subject-based experiment, the reply was: "No need. If I can see it, it's a phenomenon." In his review of Thomas Clifton's *Music as Heard* (which, as Michael Winter points out, is not only an excellent review of someone else's work but an extraordinary articulation of his own), Tenney cites C. S. Peirce: "This effort must 'not . . . be influenced by any tradition, any authority, any reason for supposing that such and such ought to be the facts.'" Confidence in the *veracity* of one's own experience, only (and this is important) *if* that experience is rigorously questioned, unbiased, and deeply explored, is central to the phenomenological approach.

Tenney was rigorous in assuring the consistency and completeness of his models of "the things themselves." I and others know all too well that when he encountered a problem in a model, no matter how small, he battled it until there was a clear winner. In one particular case—the unfinished late paper called "Multiple Pitch Perception Algorithm" (around 2005, intended as an appendix to the larger book manuscript "Contributions toward a Quantitative Theory of Harmony")—a small problem finally doomed the idea to incompletion.

Meta ≠ Hodos and Its Allies

> The necessary thing now is to start if possible at the very beginning, to clear the mind of loose ends whose origins are forgotten; loose ends and means become habits. What do we hear when we listen; if we really listen, what do we really hear when listening. This means too, what do we hear first and what later after learning after words. (1) *The substance of it is SOUND, the essence, TIME*. Sound and Time. Sound in time sounding time.
>
> "Pre–*Meta ≠ Hodos*"

Meta ≠ Hodos (*MH*), despite its importance to Tenney's work and wide influence since the 1960s, was first published in book form only in the early 1980s. *MH* is typical, perhaps archetypical, of Tenney's writing. It attempts to explain the *why* and, perhaps, the *how* of his own understanding. His aim was to articulate a new formal theory that might shed light not only on the composers who interested him (like Varèse, Ives, Webern, Ruggles) but, more generally, on all music.

In *MH* he sought fundamental precepts using simply stated assumptions. First, we make perceptual distinctions by simple mechanisms of *similarity/difference*, with a resultant mental representation of *distance*. Second, sound events are *grouped* in time using various types of similarity and temporal proximity, and third, this is done *hierarchically*. Applying those gestalt psychological principles to music, Tenney wrote a short book that is now considered to be one of the most important and radical explanations of formal perception in music. That it was written as a master's thesis should inspire graduate students everywhere, or perhaps make them weep.

After leaving Illinois for Bell Labs, Tenney immediately began to apply the ideas of *MH* to generate his computer music pieces. In "Computer Music Experiences" he documents the application of the gestalt formation ideas to the remarkable pioneering computer music pieces he wrote there. In the personal introduction to that article, he provides an outline for the work he would accomplish not just at Bell Labs but for the rest of his life.

> I arrived at the Bell Telephone Laboratories in September 1961 with the following musical and intellectual baggage:
>
> 1. numerous instrumental compositions reflecting the influence of Webern and Varèse;
> 2. two tape-pieces, produced in the Electronic Music Laboratory at the University of Illinois—both employing familiar, "concrete" sounds, modified in various ways;
> 3. a long paper ("*Meta ≠ Hodos*, a Phenomenology of Twentieth-Century Music and an Approach to the Study of Form," June 1961), in which a descriptive terminology and certain structural principles were developed, borrowing heavily from gestalt psychology. The central point of the paper involves the clang, or

primary aural gestalt, and basic laws of perceptual organization of clangs, clang-elements, and sequences (a higher-order gestalt unit consisting of several clangs);

4. a dissatisfaction with all purely synthetic electronic music that I had heard up to that time, particularly with respect to timbre;
5. ideas stemming from my studies of acoustics, electronics and—especially—information theory, begun in Lejaren Hiller's classes at the University of Illinois; and finally
6. a growing interest in the work and ideas of John Cage.

A number of other ideas are first discussed in the article that follows. One such idea is the formal discussion of the "avoidance of repetition," which became central to his work beginning in the 1980s. Further on in this same article, Tenney presages the emergence of his focus on pitch and harmony beginning in the 1970s in works like "Postal Pieces" (1965–99), *Clang* (1972), *Chorales for Orchestra* (1974), and *Quintext* (1972): "Accordingly, I no longer find it necessary to avoid any pitch, at the same time that I intend never to leave undisturbed—even when working with instruments—the traditional quantized scale of available pitches. It is not too difficult to get around this with instruments (except for such as the piano)—it's mainly a matter of intention and resolve." "Form in Twentieth-Century Music," written ten years later, allowed Tenney to restate some of *MH*'s ideas more concisely and expand upon others. But he went further in this article, including a variety of important twentieth-century compositional ideas into the larger schema developed in *MH* and focusing on the varieties of compositional techniques that may occur at various hierarchical levels. Some of his already stated musical/formal/aesthetic ideas, such as *ergodicity* (see "Computer Music Experiences"), are discussed at length. Newer ideas, like those associated with early musical minimalism, are theoretically considered here for perhaps the first time.

"Form in Twentieth-Century Music" led to the short speculative marvel "META *Meta ≠ Hodos*" (*MMH*, 1975). *MMH* is a distillation of *MH* with some additional new ideas. *MMH*'s style, consisting of a series of logical propositions, recalls, in its prose and organizational style, Wittgenstein's *Tractatus Logico-Philosophicus*. A wonderful and occasionally confounding read, it is sprinkled with elusively suggestive phrases like "nothing is yet known about structural entropy" (one is tempted to respond: "You said it!"). Its introduction is a bit ironic—"The intent was therefore to make it as concise as possible, even if at the expense of comprehensibility, and I am aware that the result is probably not easily penetrated by someone not already familiar with *Meta ≠ Hodos*"—in that few people at the time even knew of *MH*'s existence. Tenney seems to have been confident that this would change.

Around 1975, perhaps stimulated by *MMH*'s reformulation of the ideas in *MH*, Tenney developed a simple algorithm to determine temporal gestalt (TG) boundaries, furnishing the central but not yet specified "engine" of temporal gestalt formation. *MH* postulates that gestalt formations are made on one level on the basis of some kind of distinction at the next lower level but does not say precisely how. Tenney introduces the problem in "Hierarchical Temporal Gestalt Perception in Music" (1978–80):

> Many of the questions which might be the most relevant to *musical* perception have not even been asked by perceptual psychologists, much less answered. How, for example, are the perceptual boundaries of a TG determined? To what extent are the factors involved in temporal gestalt perception *objective*, bearing some measurable relation to the acoustical properties of the sounds themselves? Assuming that there are such objective factors, is their effect strong enough that one might be able to *predict* where the TG boundaries will be perceived, if one knows the nature of the sound-events that will occur?

The TG initiation mechanism is easy to understand. Gestalts at a given level are initiated by *peaks* in series of parametric differences, or *disjunction measures*, at the next lower level. A "peak" is a greater difference surrounded by lesser differences. In other words, given four TGs: *a, b, c, d*, a peak occurs if diff(*b*,*c*) is *greater than* both diff(*a*,*b*) and diff(*c*,*d*). Thus four TG (three differences) is the minimum needed for a peak to occur. It follows, interestingly, that the highest level of gestalt organization is the first that contains fewer than four gestalt units. With fewer than four "things," there are fewer than three "changes," and, excluding groupings of one, we don't have enough information to make a subgrouping.

Tenney implemented the TG initiation algorithm in software (with my assistance, starting in 1975) as a "working model" or "proof of concept" of the mechanism. This algorithm, implemented in a short FORTRAN program, uses a simple, parametrically weighted, multidimensional representation of *similarity/difference* (a metric). The experimental data consisted of a few monophonic scores and reductions of scores (by Ruggles, Varèse, Debussy, and Wagner). Given the powerful idea involved (a model of formal perception), the goal (a "reasonable" segregation of monophonic input), and 1970s computer technology, I was amazed that the program actually worked!

This research posed as many questions as it answered. How does our musical perception navigate these hierarchies: processing one level at a time in a kind of multipass behavior, or more *heterarchically*, moving fluidly between hierarchical levels in real time? (The program did the former after attempts to model the latter proved unwieldy.) How do we weight different parameters and adaptively modify those weights? How should "morphology," including things like motivic repetition and thus memory, be integrated into the model? It is a testament to Tenney's early vision that these questions still concern musical thinkers and composers.

Three early articles add to our understanding of *MH*. They predate *MH* and are published here for the first time (two of them as appendixes). The first appendix, called "Pre–*Meta ≠ Hodos*" (at Tenney's suggestion), from 1959, introduces Tenney's theoretical and phenomenological ideas in a prose style indebted to Gertrude Stein. (Tenney: "To go back. It is necessary now to go back"; "To continue. It is necessary to continue.") Though this style all but disappears in later writing, the seeds of his later, highly refined, economic prose are evident here, as is the focus on acoustic and perceptual fundamentals. ("We may say that the measure *large-small* must correspond to the primary character of the sound and that further differentiations will all derive from this.") Tenney's early interest in Cage is also evident, especially in the repeated concern with silence (although the book *Silence* had not yet been published).

"Pre–*Meta ≠ Hodos*" raises, for the first time, many questions that would continue to concern him. These include

- the relationship of *shape* to *state* ("The exact pitch-relations may be altered, without substantially altering the 'shape' of the figure");
- the theoretical, cultural, and perceptual bases of *harmony* ("It is in this respect that our pitch-perception is 'most refined,' and the capacity to hear subtle relationships has been the basis for much of the development of Western music"); and,

- the establishment of *phenomenologically based parametric descriptors* ("The reciprocal of Duration is SPEED [or Temporal Density]").

Definitions and concepts that we now recognize from *MH* are first articulated, for example: "Another basic aspect of sound—(5) *SHAPE*—the clang has a certain shape in time (this should really precede questions of individual parameters). And if it has no particularly articulate shape in time (i.e., if it is 'rectilinear'), it will at least have *QUALITY*, which might be understood as 'shape' independent of time." The complex idea of multidimensional parametric disjunction and distinction is also hinted at: "There is little consistency in differentiability of these different features." This is fascinating in light of how early this article was written. Perceptual parameters have independent scales. The relationship of scales of measurement between different parameters (e.g., what would a durational "octave" be?) are still not well formulated or quantified. To understand multifeatured data we need to resolve features, understand their relatedness and dependencies, and try to integrate them into a more general distance-function (as Tenney did later in "Hierarchical Temporal Gestalt Perception in Music"). Contemporary methods, such as machine learning, neural networks, genetic algorithms, hidden Markov models, and other nondeterministic analyses, can do this in sophisticated ways, but these processes often lack transparency. We get an answer but don't always know how we got it. These techniques were not attractive to Tenney. While yielding results, they are less able to provide the kind of clear *models* of perception that Tenney sought. Even at the time of writing "Pre–*Meta ≠ Hodos*" he was interested primarily in those models—the phenomenology of his own perception.

The second appendix, "On Musical Parameters" (a title that Tenney may have affixed at a much later date), is the first example of what became one of Tenney's central concerns: What to talk about if not pitch? He knew that the musical forms employed by twentieth-century musical innovators who interested him were based not only on pitch but also on "other things": loudness, temporal features (density and regularity, or "tempo" and "pulse salience," being perhaps the two most obvious), and most of all "timbre" (or some aggregation of time-variant spectral features). These parameters, discussed here for the first time, are more fully and formally explored in later articles also included in this volume, such as "On the Physical Correlates of Timbre," "Computer

Music Experiences," and "An Experimental Investigation of Timbre—the Violin."

The third early article in this collection, "On the Development of the Structural Potentialities of Rhythm, Dynamics, and Timbre in the Early Nontonal Music of Arnold Schoenberg," is of unknown provenance. It may have been written for a graduate seminar at the University of Illinois. Its connection to *MH* is clear: it is a study of Schoenberg's atonal music without focusing on pitch relations. This was unusual at a time when much of American academia, even in the nascent field of electronic music, focused musically and pedagogically on serial and atonal theory. As Tenney pointed out, "Schoenberg himself gave little theoretical consideration to what might be called the nonharmonic aspects of music—i.e., rhythm, dynamics, timbre, etc.—and most traditional methods of analysis have practically ignored them." Tenney's article is an implicit critique of the overemphasis on atonal and serial systematization, similar to "Pre–*Meta ≠ Hodos*" but in a more conventional scholarly style. Looking at the "other factors" in Schoenberg's music, he sets harmony aside in favor of a deeper and less stylistically based idea of "music theory."

> With the gradual dissolution of the tonal system in the music of this period, we are faced with a situation in which harmonic-melodic analysis is obviously inadequate to describe the actual formal processes in the music. It is no longer possible to ignore the rhythmic and other nonharmonic aspects, because it is frequently these very aspects that are the most potent shaping forces or that give a piece its particular form and character. Indeed, the results of the various attempts at harmonic analysis should have led to this conclusion, unless one assumes either that new harmonic "laws" may yet be discovered, more or less analogous to the old laws, which can account for the musical facts, or alternatively, that the music of this earlier period only represents a transitional or incipient stage in a longer development—that is, in the development toward the twelve-tone technique. The first assumption seems highly unlikely (though certainly not impossible), considering the fact that analysts have been looking for such laws almost exclusively these last fifty years, and consequently these should have been the first to be found, if they exist at all. But the second assumption, it seems to me, overlooks

> the real integrity and completeness—the relative perfection—of this music.

"Rhythmic and other nonharmonic aspects" are crucial in *MH* and its related theoretical explorations. "Unlikely" but "certainly not impossible" "new harmonic 'laws'" would occupy Tenney's music and thinking for much of the rest of his life.

Harmony

> Clearly, a new theory of harmony will require a new definition of "harmony," of "harmonic relations," etc., and I believe that such definitions will emerge from a more careful analysis of the "total sound-space" of musical perception.
>
> Tenney, "John Cage and the Theory of Harmony"

Beginning in the late 1970s and in this volume with "Introduction to 'Contributions toward a Quantitative Theory of Harmony,'" Tenney began *writing* about harmony. His music had, from the beginning, been concerned with pitch in a variety of ways. Pieces like *Seeds* (1956; rev. 1961) and the *Stochastic String Quartet* (1963) used pitch systems inspired by the dissonation methods of Varèse, Ruggles, and Ruth Crawford Seeger. *For Ann (rising)* (1969) might be said to be about nothing *but* pitch. Other pieces from various times in his life, like the *Three Piano Rags* (1969), *Listen* (1981), and *Hey When I Sing . . .* (1971), evince his virtuosity and imagination within more conventional harmonic traditions.

But in the early 1970s Tenney became *explicitly* interested in harmony and tuning (and in the work of Partch, with whom he'd had a difficult relationship at the University of Illinois). Harmony became integral to the form and intent of the majority of Tenney's pieces. *Clang* (1972), *Chorales for Orchestra* (1974), *Spectral CANON . . .* (1974), the "Postal Pieces" (1965–71), and *Quintext* (1972) are important early examples of this new focus, as are the seven "Harmonium" pieces (beginning in 1976).

In the 1980s, exemplified by *Bridge* and *Changes* (1985), Tenney began to deliberately and explicitly *reconcile* formal and harmonic ideas. The compositions from the last twenty or so years of his life make use of almost every one of his major ideas. The naturalness of their combination bespeaks the culmination of a lifetime's work: "To go back. It is necessary now to go back" ("Pre–*Meta ≠ Hodos*").

In "Computer Music Experiences" Tenney writes about his primary relationship to pitch:

> If I had to name a single attribute of music that has been more essential to my esthetic than any other, it would be variety. . . .
>
> . . . Since my earliest instrumental music (*Seeds*, in 1956), I have tended to avoid repetitions of the same pitch or any of its octaves before most of the other pitches in the scale of twelve have been sounded. This practice derives not only from Schoenberg and Webern, and twelve-tone or later serial methods, but may be seen in much of the important music of the century (Varèse, Ruggles, etc.).

At the time (1964), Tenney referred to equal temperament, which he used freely throughout his life. The method for achieving what, at that time, he called "variety" but what was in fact a sophisticated way of ensuring random selection with a minimum of bias (using what I and my coauthors Michael Winter and Alexander Barnett have elsewhere called the "dissonant counterpoint algorithm") was later integrated with harmonic space and with temporal gestalt structures in later pieces like *Changes* and the "Spectrum" series (beginning in 1995).

In the introduction to the never-completed "Contributions toward a Quantitative Theory of Harmony" (1979), Tenney described the chronology of his harmonic concerns, inaugurating the next stage of his work:

> Until a few years ago, my own work in composition was such that questions of harmony seemed completely irrelevant to it. Timbre, texture, and formal processes determined by the many musical parameters *other* than harmonic ones still seemed like unexplored territory, and there was a great deal of excitement generated by this shift of focus away from harmony. Harmonic theory seemed to have reached an impasse sometime in the late 19th century, and the innovations of Schoenberg, Ives, Stravinsky, and others in the first two decades of the twentieth century were suddenly "beyond the pale" of *any* theory of harmony—or so it seemed. I was never really comfortable with this situation, but there was so much to be

> done—so many other musical possibilities to be explored—that it was easy to postpone questions of harmony in my own music.

The writings about harmony are about *fundamentals*. Harmony could not be understood until words and concepts like "consonance" and "dissonance" were clarified with respect to their historical, cultural, stylistic, acoustical, semantic, emotive, narrative, and perceptual connotations. Harmony had to be quantifiable—what happens. In "John Cage and the Theory of Harmony" (1983), one of Tenney's "bridges" between musical worlds, he draws a blueprint for a new theory:

> It seems to me that what a true theory of harmony would have to be now is a theory of *harmonic perception*. . . .
>
> First, it should be descriptive—not pre- (or pro-)scriptive—and thus, aesthetically neutral. That is, it would not presume to tell a composer what should or should not be done, but rather what the results might be if a given thing is done.
>
> Second, it should be culturally/stylistically general—as relevant to music of the twentieth (or twenty-first!) century as it is to that of the eighteenth (or thirteenth) century, and as pertinent to the music of India or Africa or the Brazilian rain forest as it is to that of Western Europe or North America.
>
> Finally—in order that such a theory might qualify as a "theory" at all, in the most pervasive sense in which that word is currently used (outside of music, at least)—it should be (whenever and to the maximum extent possible) quantitative. Unless the propositions, deductions, and predictions of the theory are formulated quantitatively, there is no way to verify the theory, and thus no basis for comparison with other theoretical systems.

"Contributions . . . ," as its working table of contents shows, was meant as a comprehensive work. The broadly envisioned scope assumed greater depth as several distinct, self-contained projects grew out of it. The first was a fascinating and essential detour: *A History of 'Consonance' and 'Dissonance'* (published in 1988).[1] In that (now out-of-print) book Tenney described the historical progression of cultural and musical classifications of consonance and dissonance.

Several of the articles in this current volume, like "John Cage and the Theory of Harmony," "On 'Crystal Growth' in Harmonic Space," and "About *Changes: Sixty-Four Studies for Six Harps*," utilize the concept of *harmonic space*. This is Tenney's term for the computational model and geometrical visualization of rational tuning spaces, a conceptual expansion of what Ben Johnston and others have called *harmonic* or *prime lattices*. In harmonic space, frequency ratios are organized along prime axes (2, 3, 5, 7, . . .). Harmonic space is highly structured: we can navigate it quantifiably and intuitively: "There is one simple generalization that can be applied to nearly all of these different conceptions of consonance and dissonance, which is that tones represented by *proximate* [italics added] points in harmonic space tend to be heard as being in a consonant relation to each other, while tones represented by more widely separated points are heard as mutually dissonant" ("John Cage and the Theory of Harmony").

One of Tenney's key harmonic ideas was the *harmonic distance* (*HD*) *function*. First published in "John Cage and the Theory of Harmony," it was originally defined in "The Structure of Harmonic Series Aggregates" (begun in 1979), the previously unpublished second section of "Contributions." The HD function measures movement in harmonic space, enabling a formal concept of *distance* (something like "dissonance"), or its inverse, *proximity* (something like "consonance"), as well as an infinite set of possibilities for harmonic invention. The HD function has become well known among composers and theorists and was central to Tenney's musical thinking from about 1980 on.

Tenney's HD function is the logarithm of the product of two (relatively prime) numbers in a frequency ratio:

$$HD(a/b) = \log_2(a) + \log_2(b) = \log_2(ab)$$

Most nonheuristic measures of consonance, dissonance, and roughness are based on frequency ratios of positive integers. "Dissonance" is usually thought to relate proportionally to the *complexity* of those numbers. Complexity itself is a result of the magnitude and number of prime factors of those integers, which have naturally become the ingredients of most perceptual, theoretical, mathematical, mystical, numerological, and historical recipes for "consonance and dissonance." Specific quantifiable definitions of "harmonicity" vary by the quantities of the recipe's ingredients—the different weightings of exponents and primes. What are the relative importances of smaller primes, smaller exponents, and fewer distinct primes? And if "more important," how to measure that "importance"? There are thus many ways to construct such a function. In most, like Leonhard Euler's *gradus suavitatis* or Clarence Barlow's *harmonicity*, these components are *explicit* in the formal statements of the functions. Tenney's HD function is unusual in that the factorization of integers is not obvious in the function itself, whose appearance is elegantly but deceptively simple: just the logarithm of the product of two numbers. "The Structure of Harmonic Series Aggregates" provides a detailed explanation of its genesis.

Perhaps the most mathematical article in this volume, "The Structure of Harmonic Series Aggregates" describes, through first principles (perception, simple mathematics), what happens when "two or more compound tones are sounded simultaneously." Using simple properties of relatively prime (reduced) ratios, the harmonic series, and least common multiples and greatest common divisors, Tenney approaches *harmony* in the way he had suggested some thirty years earlier (in "Pre–*Meta ≠ Hodos*"): "to start if possible at the very beginning, to clear the mind of loose ends whose origins are forgotten; loose ends and means become habits." In this article, Tenney laid the groundwork for much of his compositional work of the next twenty-five years. At the same time, he convinced himself that, at a basic level, he knew what he was doing. If he was going to write harmonic music, he needed to be sure what harmony was. Tenney never quite finished this article. He enlisted the aid of Robert Wannamaker to check and clarify some of the mathematics (Wannamaker served as the technical editor for this article and two others in this publication). Tenney may not have felt a pressing need to publish it during his lifetime. I like to think that a work of this importance had partly a hermetic function, serving invaluably as a composition lesson in which he was both teacher and student.

The other projected sections of "Contributions" remain unwritten or unfinished. It is unclear what became of part III ("Problems of Tonality"), but those ideas most likely emerged in later articles on harmonic space such as "John Cage and the Theory of Harmony" and "Darmstadt Lecture" and, finally, in the major theoretical contributions of "The Several Dimensions of Pitch" and "On 'Crystal Growth" in Harmonic Space." As for the proposed "epilogues," I noted above that near the end of his life,

Tenney worked on a multiple pitch-detection algorithm that grew naturally out of "The Structure of Harmonic Series Aggregates." He developed an ingenious notion of "fuzzy" intersection between simultaneous compound tones, which facilitated the determination of multiple fundamentals from a compound source. As also noted above, this work was never completed to Tenney's satisfaction and is not included in this volume.

"The Several Dimensions of Pitch" is an intersecting and complementing companion to "The Structure of Harmonic Series Aggregates." The title contains a typical Tenney-esque double entendre referring not only to the several dimensions of harmonic space but also to two different pitch percepts: *contour* (shape, melody) and *harmony*. In the consideration of consonance and dissonance, the difference between *simultaneous* and *consecutive* relationships between pitches is often ignored. In "The Several Dimensions of Pitch" Tenney attempts to explain, using ideas from evolution and neurocognition, the different mechanisms behind the two percepts. One of the most important things about this article is the attempt itself. Tenney tries to unravel large and multifaceted concepts that have become confused, entangled, and misunderstood and in doing so clarifies their discussion. There are some alarmingly beautiful insights here, often made almost as asides, such as what amounts to a quantitative definition of the idea of *skip and step*, making use of a fundamental similarity measure (in this case, what I would call the *intersection over the union*) on the amplitude skirts of excitation functions. In other words, Tenney proposes a psychoacoustic explanation for contour formation based on the ear's temporal processing.

The other articles on harmony ("On 'Crystal Growth' in Harmonic Space" and "Darmstadt Lecture") are self-explanatory. Tenney's "crystal growth" algorithm has already influenced a number of composers. This idea suggests a new "harmonic syntax" (or perhaps "functional harmony") for harmonic space. As a quantitative model, it is both suggestively rich for future composition and plausible as a description of the history of tonal expansion. This is one of Tenney's models that causes you to slap your head and yell "Why didn't I think of that?"

"Darmstadt Lecture" is an invaluable, accessible introduction to Tenney's thinking. As one of the few published examples of his public lectures, it is an important addition to this collection. I appreciate its depiction of the kinds of interactions he had with friends, composers, and musicians—interactions that largely wove the fabric of his daily life. His responses to audience questions are characteristic of how he spoke to me or anybody—always with respect and thoughtfulness. He was sincerely interested in the ideas of others, even if, as should be obvious, he had plenty of his own.

Pieces

Several of the articles included here are about Tenney's own pieces or those of other composers (Schoenberg, Cage, and Ruggles). The majority of Tenney's compositional methods, especially after about 1980, are still largely undocumented. The few articles about his own work in this collection offer rare insight into the musical implementations of his theoretical ideas.

Many of Tenney's pieces after about 1980 were written with the assistance of his own computer programs. Scholars, most notably Michael Winter, have studied and documented this software in detail and, consequently, Tenney's compositional processes. In some cases, pieces have been completed or re-created primarily from the programs themselves. It is possible that to Tenney the computer code served as a "sketchbook." The software is an accurate, complete, and unambiguous document of how pieces were composed. For this reason he may have felt it less urgent to write in detail about his algorithms and techniques—they are in his software.

But the writings that do exist are a rich source of ideas. In "The Chronological Development of Carl Ruggles's Melodic Style" Tenney develops a computational analysis of Ruggles's pitch usage in an early example of what is now called "computational musicology." He postulated that it was possible to know what Ruggles was *trying to do* from what he *did* and how what he *did* evolved over time. The computer analysis demonstrates that Ruggles chronologically refined his aesthetic of "nonrepetition" of intervals and pitches toward what Tenney referred to in "Computer Music Experiences" as a greater musical "variety." This study, I believe, was a kind of pilot project toward Tenney's own reconsideration (both pedagogically and compositionally) of Seegerian dissonation. As such, this computational musicology project not only contributed to our understanding of Ruggles's music but became foundational for much of Tenney's later work.

"About *Changes: Sixty-Four Studies for Six Harps*" is unusual in Tenney's prose output as the most detailed explanation of any of his pieces. It was written for an edition of *Perspectives of New Music* about Tenney's music. Seldom has a composer explained a work so clearly and completely: "My intentions in this work were both exploratory and didactic. That is, I wanted to investigate the new harmonic resources that have become available through the concept of 'harmonic space' much more thoroughly than I had in any earlier work. At the same time I wanted to explore these harmonic resources within a formal context which would clearly demonstrate certain theoretical ideas and compositional methods already developed in my computer music of the early 1960s." *Changes* is one of Tenney's largest and most complex works. In it he combined two of his main theoretical/compositional ideas mentioned earlier: *hierarchical temporal gestalt formation* and *distance in harmonic space*. The piece integrates some other important techniques, such as Cagean-style choice procedures; the use of *tolerance* (approximation of rational relationships by large-number equal temperaments) to practically achieve complex harmonic spaces; the *half-cosine function* (a way of getting from point A to point B that "takes off and lands smoothly"); and the "dissonant counterpoint algorithm."

Tenney describes this algorithm in print for the first time, I believe, in this article, though it is informally mentioned elsewhere, most notably in "Computer Music Experiences," some twenty-five years earlier. Pitches in *Changes* were chosen by a multiplication of two probabilities—one having to do with aggregate harmonic distance, and the other dealing with the stochastic control of nonrepetition, modeling the 1930s American "ultramodernist" style:

> Just after a pitch is chosen for an element, [the probability of] that pitch is reduced to a very small value, and then increased step by step, with the generation of each succeeding element (at any *other* pitch), until it is again equal to 1. The result of this procedure is that the immediate recurrence of a given pitch is made highly unlikely (although not impossible, especially in long and/or dense clangs, and in a polyphonic texture), with the probability of recurrence of that pitch gradually increasing over the next several elements until it is equal to what it would have been if it had not already occurred.

In other words, harmonic space is navigated via both a harmonic distance function and a purely melodic one, the latter derived from some of the music that first fascinated Tenney when he was young.

The articles on *Bridge* and *Diapason* were program notes for music festivals where it may have seemed prudent for Tenney to explain his work to an audience largely unfamiliar with it. Both are nontechnical explanations of why he wrote each piece. "Reflections after *Bridge*" (1984) clearly states Tenney's aesthetic at the time, the "reconciliation" of two musical worlds: formal and aesthetic ideas inspired by Cage; harmonic possibilities suggested by Partch. *Bridge* marked a return (not made explicit in the article) to Tenney's use of the computer as a compositional partner. The computer facilitates more evolved notions of intentionality (the Cagean part) and naturally motivated a return to the formative gestalt ideas of *Meta ≠ Hodos*.

The last article in this volume, "About *Diapason*" (1996), is a fitting conclusion. Its tone is again that of Tenney the teacher. At the time, Tenney had taught for over thirty-five years, and he would continue to teach. He told me once, when I began my own teaching, that his pedagogical philosophy was not to tell the student *what* to do but to help her do what she *wanted* to do ("not presume to tell a composer what should or should not be done, but rather what the results might be if a given thing is done"). He taught at a high level and with a palpable enthusiasm for ideas. His tone is faithfully rendered in both of these articles (*Bridge* and *Diapason*), as in the almost Socratic rhetorical device anticipating a student's question:

> Why do I correlate new developments in harmony with the design of new tuning systems? Consider the history of musical innovations in the early twentieth century. ("Reflections after *Bridge*")

> One might well ask why we should go to such extraordinary lengths to produce these unusual pitches, and my answer is that I believe we have entered a new music-historical era during which there will be a resumption of the evolutionary development of harmony. ("About *Diapason*")

From Scratch

There are a number of books that I like to recommend to my students, ones that I believe are essential to an understanding of twentieth-century American music: Cage's *Silence*, Partch's *Genesis of a Music*, Ives's

Essays before a Sonata, Cowell's *New Musical Resources*, and Tenney's *Meta ≠ Hodos*. To me, all these composers started "from scratch" in wonderfully different ways, asking deep and liberating questions about aesthetics, establishing their own theoretical foundations with unique and individual relationships to history. Often they accomplished these things by returning to an earlier fork in the road and taking a new path or by reexamining fundamental assumptions buried under layers of historic stylistic development.

These composers not only rethought some central idea in what "music theory" might be but also reformulated that idea in prose. These writings are our roadmaps for the future of music, a set of hypotheses and experimental designs. Others will have their own lists. This current collection of Tenney's writings, in my opinion, belongs on any such list.

Tenney felt strongly that he was part of the "American experimental tradition," a tradition that he himself helped define. Fundamental to that tradition is, I think, an enthusiasm for starting "from scratch," as Tenney has done here. Only by doing so can the language of our musical conversation and the ideas of our new music be radically reformulated, and for the better.

Larry Polansky
Hanover, New Hampshire
December 2012

Note

1. [*A History of 'Consonance' and 'Dissonance'* was published in 1988; an excerpt appears in appendix 3.—Ed.]

From Scratch

CHAPTER 1

On the Development of the Structural Potentialities of Rhythm, Dynamics, and Timbre in the Early Nontonal Music of Arnold Schoenberg (1959)

Introduction

Beginning with the Three Piano Pieces, op. 11, and continuing through *Pierrot Lunaire* and the Four Songs with Orchestra, opp. 21 and 22, Arnold Schoenberg developed a style that he later characterized as one based on "the emancipation of the dissonance," which "treats dissonances like consonances and renounces a tonal center"—and his further descriptions of the developments of this period are almost exclusively in terms of harmonic innovations.[1] Analytical writings by others have reflected this same concern with the harmonic (and, to a lesser extent, the melodic) aspects of the music.[2] Although anyone who is familiar with the music of this period must be aware of the innovations in other areas, little attempt has been made to study these innovations in detail or to incorporate them into a consistent analytical or descriptive method. Schoenberg himself gave little theoretical consideration to what might be called the nonharmonic aspects of music—i.e., rhythm, dynamics, timbre, etc.—and most traditional methods of analysis have practically ignored them. This may have been justified, insofar as most of the music to which these methods were applied (music of the late baroque, classic, and romantic periods) was primarily conditioned by structural potentialities inherent in the system of tonality. That these methods do not thoroughly describe the music is undoubtedly true, but they do perhaps describe adequately the most important structural forces involved. Nevertheless, this single-mindedness is surprising. With the gradual dissolution of the tonal system in the music of this period, we are faced with a situation in which harmonic-melodic analysis is obviously inadequate to describe the actual formal processes in the music. It is no longer possible to ignore the rhythmic and other nonharmonic aspects, because it is frequently these very aspects that are the most potent shaping forces or that give a piece its particular form and character. Indeed, the results of the various attempts at harmonic analysis should have led to this conclusion, unless one assumes either that new harmonic "laws" may yet be discovered, more or less analogous to the old laws, which can account for the musical facts, or, alternatively, that the music of this earlier period only represents a transitional or incipient stage in a longer development—that is, in the development toward the 12-tone technique. The first assumption seems highly unlikely (though certainly not impossible), considering the fact that analysts have been looking for such laws almost exclusively these last fifty years, and consequently these should have been the first to be found, if they exist at all. But the second assumption, it seems to me, overlooks the real integrity and completeness—the relative perfection—of this music, which stands on its own, in terms of formal coherence and stylistic consistency, without any justification through reference to later developments. It is true that the 12-tone method represents a logical development of certain procedures employed earlier in a spontaneous or even perhaps unconscious way (and thus, unsystematically), but I should like to emphasize the qualification "certain procedures" in the above statement: only *some* of the many innovations in the earlier music actually became an explicit part of the 12-tone technique; others remained as *implicit* elements in the style; still others seem to have been abandoned; while certain aspects of the later method can hardly have been derived from the earlier music at all but seem rather to have been "grafted on" from the outside or to have been conceived simultaneously with the codification of the 12-tone method in the 1920s. That this method is a partial systematization of procedures that Schoenberg had already used (and that had been, as he said, "conceived as in a dream") is one of the points I hope to demonstrate in this paper. Eventually, there might be possible a broader generalization of the basic ideas underlying this same method, which could account for many more of the earlier procedures, and at the same time include the propositions of the 12-tone technique as a special case. I have not attempted to do this here, of course, but it is to be hoped that the observations made in this paper might later serve as the basis for such a generalization.

I. Rhythm

I said above that the nonharmonic elements of music are often the strongest shaping forces in Schoenberg's works of this period. That this should have happened simultaneously with or immediately following the breakdown of the system of tonality seems inevitable. Something was needed to replace the older structural functions of harmony, and it is obvious that Schoenberg did not wait for the 12-tone method to restore these functions (although this is what is implied in most accounts of his development). If we are to accept the pieces from op. 11 through op. 22 as self-sufficient and "perfect," we must try to find the forces that actually were called into play in the absence of the traditional harmonic functions, and in many cases these will be found in the development of the other attributes or parameters of sound—duration, intensity, timbre, etc.—as well as pitch. It will be seen that one of the most significant characteristics of the music of this period is that it greatly extended the structural potentialities of *all* the attributes of sound.

The third of the Three Piano Pieces, op. 11, is an example of a kind of musical development in which harmonic-melodic elements are so constantly varied that there is virtually no thematic relationship between different parts of the piece—at least not in any commonly accepted sense of the word "thematic," implying more or less invariant interval-relations among the constituent tones of a melodic line. There are no motives subject to variation and development—again in the harmonic-melodic sense. I must emphasize this qualification, "harmonic-melodic," because if the terms "motive" and (more especially) "theme" are defined more broadly to include other attributes of sound, we may find them here and in similar pieces. Conversely, if we are to demonstrate thematic correspondence in such pieces, it will be necessary to include all parameters in our definitions. The motivic or thematic organization of this piece is primarily in terms of rhythmic patterns. There are two (or perhaps three) basic rhythmic ideas heard simultaneously at the beginning of the piece, and while the pitch patterns undergo a constant, kaleidoscopic process of alteration, these rhythmic patterns remain relatively invariant—or rather, certain relations within the patterns remain invariant, while the ideas themselves are subjected to more or less straightforward techniques of variation. In example 1,[3] the various forms of one of these rhythmic ideas are superposed in such a way that one may see the correspondences between the different versions, as well as the variation-processes to which they have been subjected.

In addition to this thematic or motivic use of rhythm, another aspect of the duration-parameter, namely tempo, or *temporal density* (to distinguish between the tempo as notated and the actual "speed" of the music, which involves both the tempo and the note-values), is one of the most important means of marking structural divisions within the piece. There are three main sections in the piece, and the divisions between these sections (at measures 10 and 24) are both marked by a significant slowing of the tempo, followed by a faster tempo. The same is true of most of the smaller sections and subordinate groups. In fact, changes in temporal density (along with other factors that will be described in a moment) actually serve to *create* these divisions, not merely to emphasize them. The other factors that participate here in the creation of structural divisions—sometimes paralleling the effect of tempo, sometimes independently of this—are dynamic level, and a factor that is related to this, conditioning the dynamic level to a great extent, which might be called vertical- or pitch-density, i.e., the number of simultaneously sounding tones at any given moment. In measure 9, the dynamic level is *pianissimo*, the pitch-density decreases from five to three tones (or less, since the F and G♭ will have partially died away by the time the A is played), and the second section follows with a sudden *forte-crescendo* and a pitch-density of six or seven. Similarly, the third section is separated from the second by a change in level from *ppp* to *f*, although there is little significant change in pitch-density at this point. Such general (or even "statistical") aspects of sound do not fully account for the formal structure of the piece, which will also depend upon the more specific thematic relations, but it is clear that they do have a powerful effect in the articulation of the form and that they can, to some extent, replace the earlier harmonic functions.

The relatively independent development of rhythmic ideas in this piece is somewhat rare in Schoenberg's work: usually the rhythmic patterns are treated as subordinate features of an idea that is primarily characterized by melodic or harmonic relations. This approach was implied by Schoenberg when he said: "In every composition preceding the method of composing with twelve tones, all the thematic and harmonic material is primarily derived from three sources: the tonality, the *basic motive* which in turn is a derivative of the tonality, and the rhythm, which is included in the basic motive." Here, the basic motive—from which the "thematic material" is derived—is primarily a melodic unit that includes, as one of its features, the rhythm. (I am assuming that his statement also refers to his own pre-12-note music, in spite of the reference to tonality.) In most cases this description would be appropriate, but in op. 11, no. 3, the rhythm *is* the "basic motive," while the pitch-elements might almost be considered as derivatives of the rhythm. With this interpretation, the roles of the rhythmic and melodic ideas are seen to be reversed, and his description is not applicable. Another statement by Schoenberg, however, is relevant to the problem here, in which he says, regarding the Rondo of the Wind Quintet, op. 26: "While rhythm and phrasing significantly preserve the character of the theme so that it can easily be recognized, the tones and intervals are changed through a different use of BS (the 'Basic Set') and mirror forms." In this case, as in the piano piece, the rhythm is relatively independent of pitch-relations as a thematic *determinant* (by which I mean that attribute—or those attributes, since there may be several operating at once—that is the most effective shaping factor in a sound-idea and is thus the one by which later variations of an idea may be recognized). Rufer calls this use of rhythm the "isorhythmic principle,"[4] and it has certainly had an important place in musical composition prior to Schoenberg, although there would seem to be a significant difference between the use of invariant rhythmic relations as a *thematic* feature and the original isorhythmic devices employed by early Renaissance composers. In the latter case, the rhythmic pattern functions in a way similar to that of the *cantus firmus* in the harmonic-melodic field, providing a kind of unifying "base" to the flow of the music. That it did not have a thematic function is indicated by the fact that the actual phrase-structure often did not coincide with the isorhythmic patterns but overlapped these in various ways. Furthermore, the very idea of thematic development—implying thematic recognition—was relatively unimportant in Renaissance music, and we should not expect that the rhythmic patterns have any such thematic functions. Nonthematic isorhythmic procedures, however, do constitute an important structural force to be acknowledged along with the other potentialities of the rhythmic factor, but I have not yet found an example in Schoenberg's music of this period of the use of rhythm in this particular way. Nevertheless, in their use of specific rhythmic patterns as thematic determinants, and in their use of changes in temporal density to mark structural divisions within a piece, Schoenberg's works of this period show that the duration-parameter is capable of manifold structural functions at both the smaller and larger formal levels.

II. Dynamics

Dynamic level has already been referred to as an effective means of delineating different sections of a piece, but this parameter can operate in other ways, too. As accent, it can create a rhythmic shape in an otherwise undifferentiated succession of sounds. In the form of gradual changes of intensity—*crescendo* and *diminuendo*—it can give shape to a motive, phrase, section, or even sometimes an entire piece. A difference in dynamic level can serve to emphasize certain parts in a complex texture, or simply to separate or distinguish two individual lines in a polyphonic passage. An interesting use of the last effect can be found in Schoenberg's Six Short Piano Pieces, op. 19, in the third piece (see example 2) where the right-hand part is to be played *forte*, the left-hand part *pianissimo*, and the difference being clearly not intended for the purpose of bringing out the upper part. Here also, the dynamic distinction may be considered an important feature of the thematic idea, and this is similar in some respects to another effect of relative loudness, which is used in the last piece in this same set (example 3). The difference between the *pppp* of the highest part and the *p* of the D♯ in the next lower octave produces a unique "coloration" of the sound.

These various functions of the intensity-parameter might be summarized as follows: (1) the delineation of successive musical ideas and sections within a piece; (2) the separation of simultaneous lines in a polyphonic texture (simple emphasis of one part over another being a special case of this); (3) the creation of a rhythmic pattern through accent; (4) a kind of "color-effect" that gives a sound a unique quality or timbre; and (5) the shaping, in time, of a structural unit from the level of a single motive up through sections or entire pieces. There may be others, but these five are perhaps the most important, and of the five, only the last two indicate the possibility for independent development, or the kind of thematic significance that I have attempted to describe in the case of rhythm. There are two apparent reasons for this limitation, the most important one arising from a phenomenon that I call "parametric transference." In (2) above (separation of lines), the dynamic factor will tend to be absorbed into the pitch-factor by either focusing the attention on a particular melodic configuration or else conditioning the harmonic effect of the texture. In (3) (accent), there will be a similar transference to the rhythmic field whenever the accents superimpose larger duration-relations upon a series of undifferentiated note-values. Although superficially it might appear that (4) (the "color-effect") would also be a case of transference (to the field of timbre), it is rather more clearly a dynamic effect, as such, than (2) and (3); and of course the first of our five functions does not raise the question of "thematic significance" at all.

The second reason for the limitation of the dynamic factor in its possibilities for thematic determination is the fact that intensity is not, like pitch and rhythm, a *periodic* function of time. It is this periodicity that makes it possible to perceive precise proportional relations within the pitch- and duration-parameters. Without this periodicity there could never have been a tonal system like the one developed in Western music since the Renaissance, nor could there have been such a high development of purely rhythmic organization as may be found in certain Asian and African cultures. But before it begins to seem that I am contradicting some of my own earlier assertions, let it be noted that in these works of Schoenberg, periodicity has retained little of the importance it had in earlier music. The most effective procedures by which the tonal system was suspended or dissolved were procedures that controverted the older proportional relations by obscuring this very periodicity in both pitch and duration—i.e., through highly complex dissonances and asymmetrical rhythmic structures. And as pitch- and duration-relations become less and less proportional—and thus more and more "statistical"—the importance of the other, nonproportional parameters becomes correspondingly greater. The dynamic "coloration" or characterization and the dynamic shaping of a sound-idea can actually function as a thematic determinant in addition to the other, relatively more subordinate functions of intensity. I suggest that this attribute of sound can be—and is, in many of these works of Schoenberg—of much greater structural importance than has previously been admitted in analytical writings.

At this point I must backtrack a moment to explain something about my use of the word "structure" and perhaps forestall certain objections to my argument that can be anticipated. I do not assume any fundamental distinction between the "structural" and the "expressive" features in a piece of music—none, at least, from the standpoint of what might be called a *functional* analysis as opposed to a *historical* analysis. A rather superficial distinction does appear in the latter context, in that technical and stylistic innovations often seem to occur at first spontaneously, unconsciously, and thus "expressively"—only later becoming consciously used, deliberately planned, etc., and thus, in a way, "structural." The argument is tautological to some extent and dependent upon the way the words are defined, but there is at least a grain of truth in it. There seems to be a historical process involved by which those elements that are the least consciously controlled—one might say, the least predictable—are also the elements most subject to the expressive fantasy of the composer, especially in periods of relative stylistic stability, when a body of technical devices is more or less commonly used and consciously understood. This stylistic stability begins to break down when these same "expressive" elements develop an importance out of proportion with that of the "structural" elements: that is to say, when the expressive elements begin to affect the structure significantly and thus actually to acquire structural functions. This process can be clearly seen in these works of Schoenberg, and unless the process is understood, there will continue to be made what I consider a drastic misinterpretation of the music of this period, a misinterpretation that is reflected in the label that has been attached to the style—"expressionism." This term refers, at best, to only one aspect of the artistic tendencies of the period, namely, the concern with the subjective qualities of experience, with emotional and psychological "inner reality," as opposed to objective, materialistic "outer" reality. As such, it is hardly more than an intensification of the first term in the old "romantic vs. classic" dichotomy, and the word simply adds another to the list of such labels that only serve to obscure the real complexity of forces involved in any historical period. The term might more appropriately be used to describe the period immediately preceding Schoenberg. His work was not only a consequence of this "protoexpressionism" but a reaction against it as well. The so-called expressionist period was as much characterized by a concern with formal problems as was any other period in the history of the arts and probably no more involved with "expression" for its own sake than any other. It was the period of the birth of cubism in painting, surely one of the most "formally" oriented approaches in the history of painting; James Joyce's *Ulysses* was written, again manifesting a vigorous concern with structure; Schoenberg himself wrote the *Harmonielehre* at this time (1911); and so on. Curiously, and in seeming contradiction to my argument, Schoenberg's painting and literary works (such as *Die glückliche Hand*) are perhaps truly "expressionistic," as are also the texts that he borrowed from other writers for musical settings (*Erwartung*, *Pierrot Lunaire*), but there is a substantial difference between his essays in other media and his work in music and also a difference between the nature of the texts he chose to set and the musical settings themselves. In any case, whether or not my argument here is convincing from a historical standpoint, it will perhaps be agreed that those characteristics of Schoenberg's music of this period that give it enduring value will not be those associated with the particular expressive attitudes of that period, which can too quickly become "dated," but rather those characteristics that provide structural coherence and formal unity in the pieces.

III. Timbre

A third nonharmonic attribute of musical sound remains to be considered, and that is timbre, or "tone-color." Schoenberg has written: "My concept of color is not the usual one. Color, like light and shadow in the physical world, expresses and limits the forms and sizes of objects . . . [and] lucidity is the first purpose of color in music, the aim of the orchestration of every true artist." The "usual" concept of color, with which he contrasts his own, can be assumed to be one in which color is merely a superficial aspect of the music, and in this contrast we can see an example of the historical process described above. And yet, even this description of the importance of "color" in his music does not go far enough. Again, as with rhythm, there is some disparity between Schoenberg's statement and his actual musical achievement, or perhaps the disparity is between an earlier and a later attitude. His concept of the *Klangfarbenmelodie*, for example, which was first described in the *Harmonielehre* (1911) but already applied in the Five Pieces for Orchestra, op. 16 (1909), assigns a greater role to timbre than that of mere "lucidity" or of simply "expressing and limiting the forms and sizes of objects." In this work, tone-color frequently *creates* the "forms and sizes" of the musical "objects." In another context—his essay on Mahler—he does accord this factor a more independent significance when he writes about

> the middle movements of the Seventh Symphony, with their sonorities of guitar, harp, and solo instruments. This guitar in the Seventh is not introduced for a single effect, but the whole movement is based on this sonority. It belongs to it from the very beginning, it is a living organ of the composition: not the heart, but perhaps the eyes, whose glance is so characteristic of its aspect. This instance is very close—in a more modern way, naturally—to the method of the

> classical composers, who built whole movements or pieces on the sonority of a specific instrumental group.[5]

In this last quotation, a particular "sonority" is described as being the basis for a whole movement. From this it is not a long step to a situation in which a movement, section, or even shorter unit is based on certain *changes* in sonority, and if the articulation of the other parameters, particularly pitch, is reduced to the extent that timbre becomes the most effective *determinant*, we shall have a real "melody of tone-colors." So defined, the only clear-cut example I have found in Schoenberg's music is the third of the Five Pieces for Orchestra, op. 16, subtitled "Farben." In this piece, timbre does become the most effective shaping factor, and the degree of articulation of all the other parameters is correspondingly reduced to a minimum. There is some change in the harmonic (i.e., intervallic) structure of the five-note chord, but the actual effect of these changes is also one of a change in timbre. The harmonic factor is absorbed or transferred into the factor of timbre, or alternatively, one might say that the distinction between the two factors is neutralized—an interpretation that has important implications in relation to harmonic events in most of Schoenberg's music, as well as in that of many other composers of the twentieth century. A succession of chords, in the absence of the clear-cut relations of traditional functional harmony, is often heard as a succession of timbres, colors, or sonorities, the nature of which is primarily dependent upon the constituent intervals, the actual instrumental timbres involved, the manner of articulation, pitch registration of the chord, etc.

The last piece in the same set ("Das obligate Rezitativ") has also been associated with this concept of the *Klangfarbenmelodie*, and certainly we have here an example of an orchestral technique in which timbre plays a much greater role in the articulation of the musical ideas than it had previous to Schoenberg, although it is questionable whether this piece can be called an example of a real "melody of tone-colors," since the pitch-melody is so highly developed. Two more examples will be given, however, in which the factor of timbre is at least as important as the pitch-factor and that show that timbre is capable of relatively independent functions in the musical structure.

The first example is another of the Five Pieces for Orchestra, the fourth in the set, entitled "Peripetie" (example 4). The sudden, unpredictable "reversals in dramatic action," implicit in the title are reflected in the music by violent contrasts in dynamic level, tempo, pitch-density, and, of course, timbre. But timbre has another function here in addition to this—that is, it does not function only on this one structural level. If one examines each of the contrasting sections separately—sections within which there is a certain homogeneity due to similarities in tempo and dynamic level—it will be seen that certain changes of timbre are an inherent feature in the particular shaping of the thematic ideas. In the very beginning, the five-note upbeat figure in unison woodwinds leads to a sustained six-note chord in the cellos and basses, the woodwinds providing only an accentuated attack to the string sonority. While the strings hold the chord, the phrase itself continues almost immediately in the brass (the effect being similar to that obtained with the piano by the use of the pedal to sustain earlier tones of a melodic pattern through the sounding of later tones), then it passes to the woodwinds again, this last part of the phrase being "capped" by the *pizzicato* in the upper strings. That this three-part structure actually constitutes a single phrase is perhaps open to question, but the overlapping or dovetailing of its various parts and the singularity of gesture—an upward movement—indicate that it is to be considered a single musical idea, or to use Schoenberg's term, a "basic shape." A singular (though complex) "line" passes from woodwinds to strings, brass, woodwinds again, and finally plucked strings, all within a span of about three seconds. There can be little doubt that the essential nature of this line is intimately connected with the particular sequence of timbres involved and that an alteration in this respect would affect the character of the line as much as, say, an alteration of its interval-structure.

In measures 5 and 6 of the same piece (example 5), the repeated chord in trumpets and strings is echoed by the woodwinds, and this effect is developed later in the alternation between violas and oboes (measures 291 to 294 of the full score, and anticipated in measure 290 by the brass) and again (in measures 296 to 298) by the alternation between woodwinds (1st and 2nd flutes and oboes) and trumpets (see examples 6 and 7). In these two versions, the pitch structure of the two members of the alternating pairs is not the same as it was in the original, "echoing" version, but the effect is similar, and the difference actually serves to underline the importance of the timbre-change to the motivic or thematic character. Thus, the pitch-relations can be considerably altered without much changing the *basic shape*—as long as the timbre shape is retained (as also, of course, the rhythmic shape, which is perhaps the primary determinant here). Here it is not the specific timbres that are involved but the more general effect of timbre change—a distinction that should be made in regard to the third piece in the set, too.

A last example pertinent to the question of timbre is the fourth piece in *Pierrot Lunaire,* "Eine blasse Wäscherin." In the first eight measures, the instrumental part consists of a simple, almost chorale-like texture in three voices, but the individual instruments constantly cross each other so that each successive chord has a sonority slightly different from the previous one. The effect is similar to that in op. 16, no. 3, and this piece is an extraordinary example of compositional economy, achieving with three instruments an effect that would seem to require a whole orchestra! There is here, of course, more harmonic and melodic shaping, as such, than in the orchestra piece, but it is obvious that Schoenberg has here taken great care to superimpose a timbre-pattern upon the pitch-pattern, the two remaining relatively independent of each other.

So far in this paper I have been considering those attributes of sound not included in the realm of pitch-relations, thus avoiding the usual harmonic and melodic aspects of the music. I have done this deliberately in order to point up the importance of factors that are too often overlooked or ignored or perhaps simply taken for granted in musical analysis. I do not intend to undervalue the pitch-factors, but I believe that a fuller understanding of the music of Schoenberg (and many other significant twentieth-century composers) can only be gained after all the various shaping forces are seen to be of more nearly equal importance. That they function differently there is no doubt, and that some are more effective than others in particular situations is quite obvious, but none of them can be ignored in any reasonably adequate analysis of the music. We have seen that each of the nonharmonic parameters may attain structural importance at various levels, from that of the individual motivic and thematic ideas to that of the larger formal units. It seems not unreasonable to believe that these parameters could be controlled in ways comparable to those exercised over pitch in the 12-tone method—though these need not necessarily be identical to the pitch-controls, as they seem to be in more recent "total serialization" procedures. The mere fact that each parameter can function as an effective shaping factor does not mean that all such parametric shapes can be treated in the same way, since they may not be *heard* in the same way. Nevertheless, the possibility remains that all these factors might be brought into one comprehensive system that would be based on realities of musical perception rather than arbitrary and quasi-mathematical assumptions.

CHAPTER 2

*Meta ≠ Hodos**

A Phenomenology of Twentieth-Century Musical Materials and an Approach to the Study of Form

(1961)

Publisher's Introduction

Meta ≠ Hodos was originally written by James Tenney as his master's thesis at the University of Illinois at Champaign-Urbana in 1961. It was published in a limited edition by Gilbert Chase some years later but has been difficult to obtain since its creation. Yet it has had a wide and powerful impact on music theory and composition in the past twenty-five years to a degree greatly disproportionate to its availability. "META *Meta ≠ Hodos*," written in 1975, was first published in the *Journal of Experimental Aesthetics* 1, no. 1 (1977). The present Frog Peak Music edition of *Meta ≠ Hodos* and "META *Meta ≠ Hodos*" marks an attempt to make these seminal theoretical documents available to a larger community of artists.

This second edition includes corrections and revisions by the author.

Larry Polansky
Oakland, 1988

* "meth-od, n. [F. *méthode*, fr. L. *methodus*, fr. Gr. *methodos*, method, investigation following after, fr. *meta* after + *hodos* way]."

Meta ≠ Hodos

June 1961

Section I. The New Musical Materials

> A good description of a phenomenon may by itself rule out a number of theories and indicate definite features which a true theory must possess. We call this kind of observation "phenomenology," a word which means . . . as naive and full a description of direct experience as possible.
>
> Kurt Koffka, *Principles of Gestalt Psychology*, 73

> One must be convinced of the infallibility of one's own fantasy and one must believe in one's own inspiration. Nevertheless, the desire for a conscious control of the new means and forms will arise in every artist's mind, and he will wish to know consciously the laws and rules which govern the forms which he has conceived "as in a dream." Strongly convincing as this dream may have been, the conviction that these new sounds obey the laws of nature and our manner of thinking . . . forces the composer along the road of exploration.
>
> Arnold Schoenberg, *Style and Idea*, 218

> The first step in the direction of beauty is to understand the frame and scope of the imagination, to comprehend the act itself of esthetic apprehension.
>
> James Joyce, *A Portrait of the Artist as a Young Man*, 208

The increased aural complexity of much of the music of the twentieth century is such an evident characteristic that it should need no demonstration. Nevertheless, an examination of the many factors that produce this complexity and of some of its effects in our perception of the music will be necessary before we can hope to describe the musical materials in a really meaningful way. The complexity is not merely of structure but also of substance. That is, it is not simply the result of a new arrangement of traditional materials or elements. (I shall use the word *element* in this book in the sense of "part" or "portion" rather than "aspect" or "factor.") The elements themselves have changed, and the changes affect not only the musical structure but our way of listening to the music as well. And the problems that arise from this seem to go beyond the mere question of the amount of time required for the ear and mind to assimilate the novelties of a new style until they no longer have what Schoenberg once described as a "sense-interrupting effect." Time has given us some degree of familiarity with even the most advanced musical achievements of the early twentieth century, and yet our descriptive and analytical approaches to this music are still belabored with negatives—"atonal," "athematic," etc.—that tell us what the music is *not* rather than what it is. The narrowness of the traditional musical concepts is manifested by this very negativism and by the fact that many significant works of this earlier period are too often relegated to the realm of "exceptions," "deviations," or "interesting experiments." And the disparity between the traditional concepts and the actual musical "object" becomes even greater with the more recent (noninstrumental) electronic and tape music. But even here, the problem is not really one of a lack of familiarity but of a nearly complete hiatus between music theory and musical practice. Thus, even when the novelties of the various styles and techniques of twentieth-century music have become thoroughly familiar, certain "complexities" will still remain outside of our present conceptual framework, and it is clear that this conceptual framework is in need of expansion.

EXAMPLE 1. Charles Ives, *Scherzo: Over the Pavements* (mm. 93–94). All instruments sound as written in these examples.

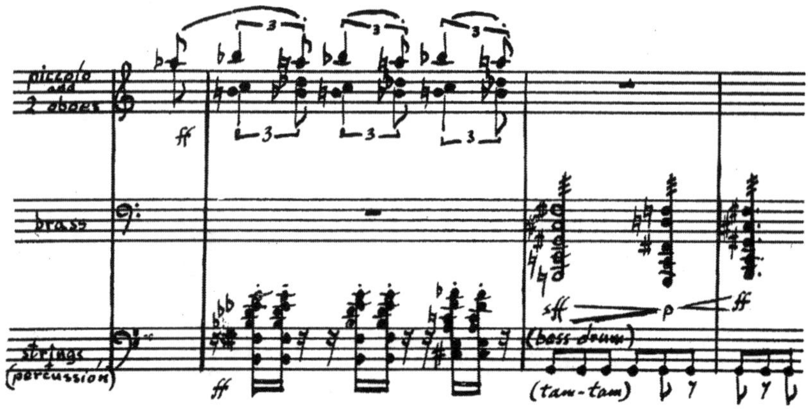

Example 2. Anton Webern, op. 6, no. 2 (mm. 17–19).

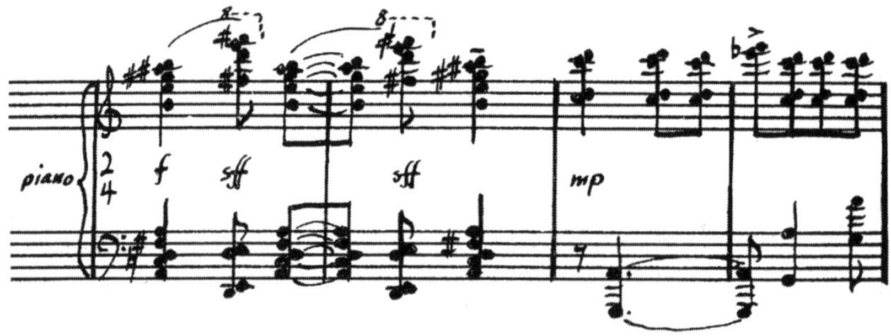

Example 3. Béla Bartók, Sonata (piano) (p. 18).

I have said that the materials of the music have changed, and this is to be seen in countless examples in which the primary musical ideas are highly complex sound-configurations whose basic elements are themselves more or less complex structures rather than single tones. Typical configurations of this kind are shown in examples 1–3. Such elemental sound-structures occur in a great variety of forms with respect to both their vertical structure and their changes in time. I shall examine them first from the standpoint of their vertical structure, with particular attention to elements in which the vertical structure is a more noticeable characteristic than any temporal form they may have.

The clearest examples of such complex sound-elements are tone-clusters and other highly dense and dissonant chords, as in these first three examples—sound-structures that seem relatively "opaque" to the ear. Such chords cannot usually be analyzed by the ear into constituent tones, and

I think they are not intended to be so analyzed. They are seldom subject to harmonic orientation, because one's perception of pitch in these dense sound-complexes is limited, at best, to the pitch of their highest or lowest tones, or to a mean pitch-level, when no more than the approximate range and register of the chords can be recognized. Their similarity to percussive sounds is very close, and it is significant that the use of such complex sound-elements coincides historically with an increasing exploitation of the percussion instruments of the orchestra and that they are frequently to be found in music of an intentionally "rhythmic" or motoric character, such as the Bartók sonata from which example 3 is taken. Such chords represent, in fact, a kind of bridge between more traditional harmonic structures and purely percussive sounds and noises, and it would be difficult to find any clear-cut line of distinction between any two of these three types of sound-elements. They are distinguished from each other only in the relative difficulties they present to the ear's power of pitch analysis, and thus in their relative specificity of pitch-definition, and in the possibility of harmonic orientation, which depends on such pitch-definition. The percussion battery itself includes both instruments of definite pitch and ones of indefinite pitch, and the sounds produced by the latter instruments are nothing more than "tone-clusters" of a higher degree of complexity.

There is thus a continuous "spectrum" of composite sound-elements, ranging from simple chords whose constituent tones can be analyzed by the ear—through more complex and opaque sounds whose pitch-characteristics are more or less indefinite or only partially perceptible—to sounds without any definite pitch, which we characterize as noise. But in spite of the breadth of this spectrum, examples can be found of the use of each of these three types of composite sounds as essentially *irreducible elements* of musical ideas—examples in which such sound-complexes are substantially *equivalent* to single tones.

One manifestation of the gradual use of more and more complex sound-units in place of single tones is to be seen in the expansion of the very concept of "melodic line" by way of various kinds of doublings. This concept had already been somewhat complicated in pre-twentieth-century music by the frequent doublings in thirds and sixths and in the late nineteenth century by the use of parallel seventh and ninth chords. These devices were intended to enrich the sonority of a single melodic line without adding any really independent lines to the texture, and the intervals and chords so used can fairly be said to be equivalent to single tones, with

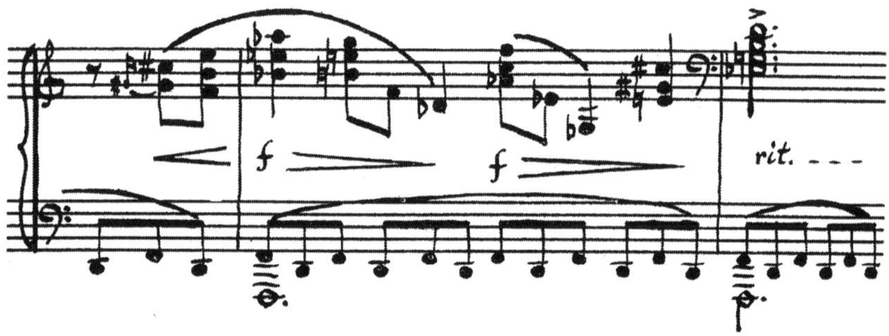

EXAMPLE 4. Arnold Schoenberg, op. 11, no. 2 (p. 7).

respect to most of the formal functions. But by about 1910, these devices had been considerably extended to include not only other, more dissonant intervals and chords but also more complex "doublings" in which the intervals change in the course of a single line, or in which the number of tones in each element is varied from one to the next, and often both types of variation are employed within the same line, as in example 4.

There was a time when theorists could refer to noises as "nonmusical sounds," and this attitude still exists to some extent. But it is clearly unrealistic to make such a distinction now in the light of musical developments in the twentieth century. The elemental building materials of this music are no longer limited to "musical" tones but may include other, more complex sounds, which in an earlier music would have seldom functioned as elements, if they occurred at all. *The substance and material of this music is sound*—this definition is inescapable—and it is of secondary importance whether this material is in the form of a tone with clearly defined pitch or of the highly complex and indefinitely pitched sound of a cymbal. *Any sound might occur* at some point in a piece of music with a function there that is virtually independent of the constitution or structure of the sound itself, being determined instead by the larger musical context in which it occurs. Once this is acknowledged, it becomes evident that the first requisite of an expanded conceptual framework for the music of our time will be a principle of *equivalence*, by which recognition is made of the equal potentiality of any sound being used as a basic element in a musical idea.

The full implications of this principle will become more clear in the course of the book, but here it may be noted that there is a close parallel to this idea of equivalence in Schoenberg's arguments about consonance and dissonance, and an examination of this parallel may help to elucidate the idea being presented here. In *Style and Idea* Schoenberg says:

> What distinguishes dissonances from consonances is not a greater or lesser degree of beauty, but a greater or lesser degree of *comprehensibility*. In my *Harmonielehre* I presented the theory that dissonant tones appear later among the overtones, for which reason the ear is less intimately acquainted with them. This phenomenon does not justify such sharply contradictory terms as concord and discord. Closer acquaintance with the more remote consonances—the dissonances, that is—gradually eliminated the difficulty of comprehension and finally admitted not only the emancipation of dominant and other seventh chords, diminished sevenths and augmented triads, but also the emancipation of Wagner's, Strauss's, Moussorgsky's, Debussy's, Mahler's, Puccini's, and Reger's more remote dissonances.
>
> The term *emancipation of the dissonance* refers to its comprehensibility, which is considered equivalent to the consonance's comprehensibility. A style based on this premise treats dissonances like consonances and renounces a tonal center.[1]

Now there is an apparent inconsistency in this argument—that is, if we understand the word "equivalent" (in the second paragraph) in an unnecessarily restricted way—because he has not established a real equivalence of comprehensibility as such but simply a *relativity* of consonance and dissonance and a lack of any clear-cut distinction or opposition between them. I suggest that he means a different sort of equivalence, and one that is analogous to the *principle of equivalence* I am proposing here. It is a functional equivalence that Schoenberg is describing, which postulates the equal potentiality of both consonances and dissonances being used as material in the musical texture—in spite of their differences with respect to "comprehensibility." In other words, the relative consonance or dissonance of a sound is no longer considered to be a functionally relevant characteristic of that sound, and two sounds that differ only in their relative degrees of consonance (or dissonance) are therefore functionally equivalent, or potentially so. This interpretation is consistent with our understanding of the meaning of dissonance in traditional harmonic practice and with the fact that the music of Schoenberg and the other composers with whom we will be concerned here represents a more or less complete suspension of traditional harmonic procedures. The functional distinction between consonance and dissonance was one of the essential features of the tonal system of the eighteenth and nineteenth centuries, and one natural result of the suspension of that system would be the breakdown of this functional distinction.

The parallel between this equivalence of consonances and dissonances (as I interpret Schoenberg's statement) and my own principle of equivalence involves more than the idea of equivalence that is common to both. There is a further similarity in that Schoenberg's "consonances" are analogous to the simpler, aurally analyzable ("comprehensible") chords mentioned earlier, and his "dissonances" correspond to the more complex sound-elements, or the indefinitely pitched noises. One of my first descriptions of the latter types of sound referred to "tone-clusters and other highly dense and dissonant chords," and indeed there is an obvious relationship—both acoustically and psychologically—between dissonance, complexity, and noise.

The kind of equivalence I am suggesting, however, is perhaps not a "functional" one in quite the same sense as is the equivalence of consonances and dissonances described by Schoenberg. It might rather be called a "substantial" or "material" equivalence, meaning not that these different kinds of sound necessarily have equivalent functions or musical effects but simply that they have an *equal potentiality* for use as elemental building materials in music. Thus the conceptual framework proposed here will not begin with *tones* as the primary units of the material—even though this might seem to be the logical starting point from an acoustical point of view. Rather, it will postulate *sounds* and *sound-configurations* as its primary units, deriving this premise from psychological or more directly musical assumptions.

So far, we have been considering sound-elements of varying degrees of complexity in the vertical dimension, with no reference to their possible changes in time. But such sound-elements must also be examined in relation to the time-dimension, since they all have some extension in time, and their vertical characteristics usually vary with respect to time. This will lead to an expansion of the principle of equivalence to include sounds with considerable variation in time, and it will be seen that these, too, can function as basic elements in the larger sound-configurations or musical ideas.

But first, it should be noted that although no sound is time-independent in its acoustical features, we are not always aware of the changes that may actually take place in a sound. Even the simplest tone has a characteristic *time-envelope* consisting of three different stages: an attack, a steady-state portion, and a decay in amplitude. But whether or not we actually perceive such changes is strongly determined by the musical context in which the sound occurs and to some extent by conventions and listening habits. It is well known, for example, that the tone of the piano begins to decrease in amplitude almost immediately after the hammer strikes the string—piano tone has, in fact, no steady-state stage at all—and yet we are virtually unaware of this when we listen to most piano music. This is strikingly demonstrated by reversing the direction of a recorded tape of piano music. The whole gestalt-character of the sound is altered quite drastically and seems to bear not the slightest relation to the character of the original sound. During such an experiment one suddenly becomes intensely aware of the envelope of each tone, though it is merely the same envelope in reverse. In the case of piano tone, it would seem that our awareness has been dulled by familiarity, but of course musical context has played its part here too. Most music for the piano has been written as though the tone did *not* fade away immediately, or it has been composed in such a way as to disguise this fact as much as possible. Playing techniques have been conditioned by this fact too, as, for example, the technique of overlapping successive tones in a line in order to simulate a *legato* that is only really possible on instruments that can sustain a tone at a given dynamic level.

In some cases, however, the musical context does encourage an awareness of the envelope or variations in dynamic shape of the sounds by the exploitation of the various possibilities of "touch" with the piano, for example, or of different kinds of articulation in other instruments. Such varieties of "touch" or articulation are—physically—nothing more than ways of varying the time-envelope of the sound. But if they are perceived at all, it is usually as differences in the "quality" of the sound rather than as dynamic variations per se. The time-envelope may become quite perceptible (whether apprehended as variations in loudness or as tone quality) when the perceptual scale of the music is reduced in such a way as to encourage the perception of smaller details, as it is in much of Webern's music and in certain pieces by John Cage (particularly those for "prepared piano"). But there are cases where even this reduction in scale in not necessary. In the example from the Ruggles piece (example 5), the listener is

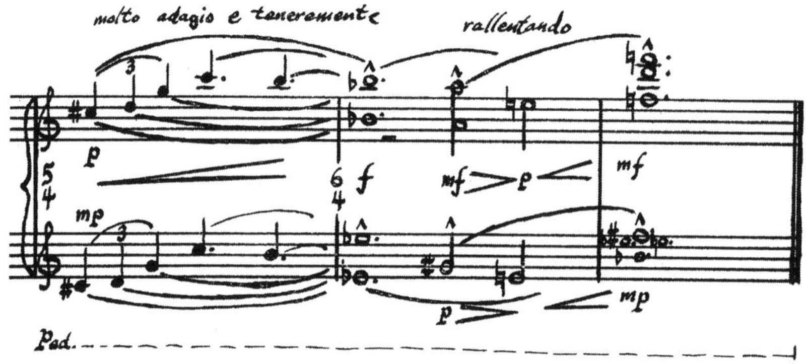

Example 5. Carl Ruggles, *Evocation IV* (mm. 30–32).

clearly intended to hear not only the fading away of the sound after the last chord has been struck but also a kind of play of interference among several tones in the chord, whereby they seem to swell and fade and swell again, each at a different rate, so that now one is the loudest, now another, resulting in an effect of internal melodic movement. The sound is very much like that of a bell whose inharmonic upper partials "beat" with one another in a similar way, so that what one hears are changes in the pitch-structure of the sound with time, as well as the change in dynamic level.

While the variations in amplitude mentioned previously were on the borderline between the realms of perceptibility and imperceptibility, the time-variations in the Ruggles example are clearly perceptible. And we can move gradually and by degrees into situations in which there can be no doubt that a sound's variations in time are no longer "subliminal" but in which the sound may still only have the character and function of a basic *element* in the larger configuration or sound-idea. Trills, tremolos, and fast repeated notes fall into this category, as do certain kinds of arpeggiations, repeated figures, fast scale-passages, and the like (see examples 6–8). They will have the "character and function" of basic elements when—because of the musical context—they are effectively "absorbed" into a larger configuration, or when their function within the configuration is made to be similar to that of their more static counterparts (i.e., trills and repeated notes like sustained tones, tremolos and arpeggios like sustained chords, etc.). Now it must be said that these sounds that vary so with time are *not* identical to their "static counterparts," since there is always some reason (usually rhythmic) why one form of the sound, rather

Example 6. Béla Bartók, Fourth String Quartet, I (p. 10).

Example 7. Arnold Schoenberg, op. 11, no. 2 (p. 10).

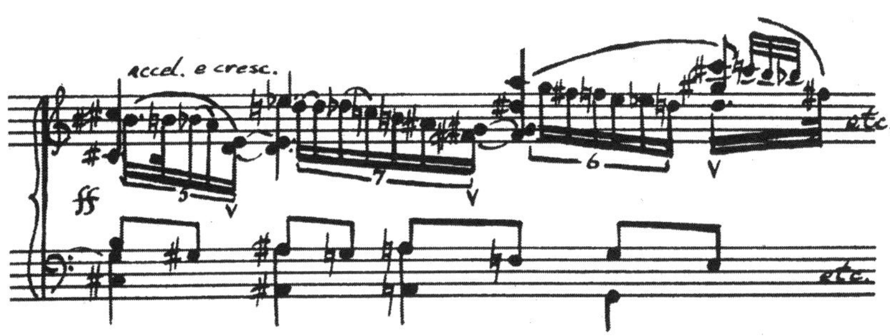

Example 8. Charles Ives, "Concord" Sonata ("Emerson") (p. 17).

than another, is used in a particular passage—they are not interchangeable. But I suggest that they may be considered "materially equivalent," in the sense defined earlier, as having equal potentiality of serving as basic elements in the larger sound-configurations that constitute the musical ideas of a piece of music.

If we shift our attention now from the basic elements to the larger configurations themselves—configurations that would approximately correspond, in length, to the motives and phrases of an earlier music—it becomes apparent that the nature of such sound-ideas will be affected by the variety and complexity of the materials of which they are composed, as well as by the variety and complexity of arrangement or organization of these materials. Before examining such sound-ideas, it seems advisable to review some of the many factors that contribute to this "variety and complexity" in a more general way.

There are two factors that are particularly important in this respect: these are (1) the extension of the gamut or range of possibilities within nearly every one of the various parameters (i.e., pitch, loudness, timbre, temporal density, etc.),[2] and (2) a faster rate of change in parametric values.[3] These two factors are related, in that a faster rate of change will generally mean the coverage of a greater range within a given time-span. With respect to certain parameters there has been both an extension of the range and an increase in the rate of change, while in others only the latter has taken place in any very significant way. The dynamic range, for example, can hardly be said to have been extended in any absolute sense—at least not since Beethoven, whose highest and lowest dynamic levels are comparable to those in twentieth-century music. But there was surely never as high a rate of change of dynamic level as we find in the music of our time. The situation is similar for the time-dimension, too. Contrasts of temporal density have become a prominent feature of music, and again it is the increased rate of change in temporal density that is most noticeable, rather than the absolute range of differences between the slowest and the fastest extremes.

The asymmetrical phrase-structure that is so characteristic of twentieth-century music can be viewed in this light, as well as the more prose-like rhythmic development that it engenders. These are partially the result of the often-noted tendency to avoid exact repetitions and of a desire to replace the measured simplicity of verse and dance-rhythms with the freer rhythms of speech—and thus represent to some extent developments of rhythm for its own sake. But these asymmetries are also determined by the generally increased rate of change in other aspects of the music. That is, they are determined by the great variety, in both shape and substance, of the successive sound-elements and configurations in the music. There is often a continual change in the vertical density (e.g., a two-part texture may be followed by one of six or eight parts; a narrow spacing may suddenly be replaced by a wide distribution of tones, etc.), and this variety seems to necessitate a corresponding variety in length. It finally becomes difficult or even meaningless to speak of "phrase-structure" at all, and new terms will be needed for these sound-configurations that will make allowance for this greater variety in length, as well as in shape and "substance" or material.

Like loudness and density, pitch and timbre have also undergone a development in the direction of increased rate of change in parametric values. A characteristic feature of the melodic writing of many twentieth-century composers—the use of wide skips or larger intervals at the expense of the smaller diatonic intervals—can be interpreted in this way. This, and the general tendency to employ the full range of a given instrument or voice, means covering more of the pitch-compass in a shorter span of time—and thus an increased rate of change in the pitch-parameter.

But in addition, the absolute ranges of both pitch and timbre have been extended considerably. With regard to pitch, for example, it may be noted that the instruments sounding in the extreme high or low registers are now less often used merely to "double"—at a higher or lower octave—parts principally carried by the more standard instruments of the middle range of the pitch-compass. These previously "auxiliary" instruments have acquired a much greater independence within the total ensemble, and there is thus a widening of the effective "field" of pitch-events as such (as distinct from such elaborations of sonority as these doublings).

The use of the full range of an instrument—and, more specifically, the use of the extreme registers of an instrument—is also one of the ways in which the timbre-range has been extended. Other extensions include the employment of special techniques such as *sul ponticello* and *col legno* in the strings, flutter-tongue in the winds, brass mutes, trombone *glissandi*, etc., as well as an increased use of the percussion battery of the orchestra.

An increased rate of change of timbre has also become a common feature of the music of our time, and the following statement by Schoenberg is instructive in this respect: "It is true that sound in my music changes with every turn of the idea—emotional, structural, or other. It is furthermore true that such changes occur in a more rapid succession than usual, and I admit that it is more difficult to perceive them simultaneously. . . . But it is not true that the other kind of sonority is foreign to my music."[4]

By "sound" he means what I am calling *timbre*—instrumental tone-quality—and the "other kind of sonority" would refer to a kind of musical texture in which the timbre does *not* change "with every turn of the idea." The comparison is with an earlier music and a more conventional instrumental style, and the question arises here whether the difference between the two kinds of "sonority" is simply a difference in degree or one in kind. I think it is a difference in kind and that the distinction he makes is fully justified. A nineteenth-century orchestral piece may show a great variety in timbre and even perhaps a relatively fast rate of change in this respect, but the changes are seldom "with every turn of the idea"—which I take to mean *within a single idea*—but occur, instead, *with the appearance of each new idea*, in most cases. There is usually a high degree of timbral homogeneity within the limits of a single musical idea, and this is because the primary shaping-factor in these configurations is usually pitch, not timbre. If these represent, then, two different kinds of "sonority," it is nevertheless true that the development from the earlier one to the later one was a gradual process, moving by degrees, and that it would be difficult if not impossible to find any sharp line of division between the two stages of that process. But there are surely many natural processes that show a complete metamorphosis from one form to another, yet in which there is no perceptible break in the process itself or in its evolution.

With this interpretation of Schoenberg's statement, we perhaps have a key to the solution of a problem that is raised by all these innovations that have been described here under the general categories of extensions of range and increased rate of change in the music. "I admit that it is more difficult to perceive them simultaneously," says Schoenberg about the fast changes in "sound" in his music, and it might be said not only of timbre but of all the other parameters of musical sound in which there has been this expansion of the range of possibilities—and not just about Schoenberg's music but about twentieth-century composers in general. One result of these innovations is the impression of discontinuity that the listener often receives on the first hearings of a piece, and an important question is raised: How or where is one to find that thread of continuity that we assume to inhere in every integral work of art? I think the answer to this question involves the ways in which the ear and mind organize the component sound-elements into larger units or gestalts, and this will depend upon both the way one listens and the actual configurations in the music.

The last problem of the "actual configurations" will be studied in more detail in section II, but here a few things might be said about "the way one listens." It seems to me that the first step in the direction of finding continuity amid the apparent discontinuity produced by these extensions of range is the acceptance of the wider gamuts as in some way normal, admitting the new events occurring in the extreme "registers" of each parameter to be within the "range of possibilities" rather than outside of it. This may seem to involve nothing beyond the assimilation of the "novelties of a new style" mentioned at the beginning of the book, but it is more than that and is a factor that must be considered in our attempts to arrive at a meaningful basis for musical description and analysis. The second step involves an understanding of the relative nature of continuity and discontinuity and of some of the factors causing this relativity.

The relativity of continuity and discontinuity might best be illustrated by an analogy with a similar situation in the realm of vision. It often happens that one's first impressions of a modern painting do not correspond with one's later impressions or with the intentions of the painter. At first one may see an apparently random distribution of colors, shapes, or lines, only later discovering a figure perhaps, or objects of a still-life, or elements of a landscape. At some point in the process of studying the painting the seemingly random elements are subjectively integrated, making perceptible the configurations that are essential to one's understanding of the work. In the terms of the previous discussion, we can say that a continuity has been found within what at first seemed a condition of discontinuity; relations are perceived among elements that had seemed disconnected and unrelated.

Now what are the factors leading to the discovery of continuity—factors whose negative effect is to prevent this discovery? One such factor has already been discussed—the "mental set" that can cause events occurring in the extreme ranges of each parameter to interrupt the sense of continuity. But there are two other factors that are even more important than this one, and these are the factor of *scale* and that of *focus*. There are at least two forms of the latter, and I will consider these first before examining the question of scale. The two forms are (1) *textural focus* and (2) *parametric focus*. The first is the most obvious, and little need be said about it, except that if one's attention is directed toward one or more of the *less* essential parts in a complex texture, the *more* important structural features of the larger configurations may be missed. This assumes, of course, a situation in which there *is* a hierarchy of more and less essential elements—which may not always be so—but the situation does occur often enough to make this a factor worth considering. In the final analysis, perhaps, the very richness of a work of art—in any medium—may be due to the ambiguities it allows in this respect and to the possibility of directing the attention toward the secondary elements and finding these meaningful. But in the beginning, at least, there must be some reckoning of what the most important parts might be.

Parametric focus is analogous to textural focus in many ways, but it is something different and perhaps not so obvious as the latter. In the course of this book, an attempt is made to demonstrate the greater importance that has been given in twentieth-century music to *all* the parameters of musical sound; that whereas in earlier music the responsibility for the articulation of musical ideas was mainly given to the pitch-parameter, the other parameters have begun to carry more and more of this responsibility, sometimes even to the extent of replacing the function of pitch altogether. It is further suggested that the relative *degree of articulation* in the several parameters (one manifestation of the rate of change discussed earlier) may vary—and with that, the parametric focus will vary—not only from one piece to another but within the same piece or even within a single passage in a piece. If this is so, "the way one listens" to the music is certainly going to be affected. Such changes in parametric focus will require a corresponding flexibility on the part of the listener, and it will be necessary to acknowledge the possibility of these changes of parametric focus or parametric articulation and to allow for them in our conceptual approach to the music. It is partially the failure to do this that has led to the attitude so often encountered in criticisms of some twentieth-century techniques, which would reduce them to "mere color-effects," or "purely rhythmic experiments," etc. The listener who can accept only pitch as a primary shaping factor in the articulation of musical ideas is bound to hear "empty spaces" in much of the music of the twentieth century and may eventually have to reject altogether some of the more advanced expressions of the musical art, such as Varèse's *Ionisation* for percussion instruments, the pieces for "prepared piano" of John Cage, electronic and tape music, etc. This is unfortunate and unnecessary when all that is required to include such music within the larger "main stream" of musical development is a broadening of our conceptual framework so as to include such phenomena as this change of parametric focus.

That factor in the creation of apparent discontinuity that I have called *scale* is even more important than either textural or parametric focus and will lead us more directly to the essential point of this section of the book. I am not using the word *scale* in the ordinary musical sense here but rather in the sense a draftsman or map-maker might use the word and, more generally, as it is used in the visual realm, from which the best illustration may again be taken. We know from our visual experience that a change in scale of a picture of a thing, or a change in the distance from which we view a thing—whether it be a picture, a landscape, or the figure of a person—can substantially alter the total impression we will have of it. The overall gestalt-character of the thing seen is thus to a great extent determined or conditioned by the scale on which we view it, and this depends not only on physical conditions such as size and distance but also on the mental set and purposive attitudes of the viewer. If we imagine again the situation described before—a person whose impressions of a painting are still disconnected and unrelated—it is apparent that the configurations he does perceive may be only the *details* of a larger configuration and that his attention to these smaller units may actually prevent his perception of the larger and more essential configuration. The process also works in the reverse direction—the larger units being mistaken for detail—in which case the whole structure must inevitably seem incomplete. The full range of this process might be illustrated by imagining a scene—say, a field of wheat—that from a certain distance will appear continuous, having a homogeneous texture that is unbroken by contrasting elements. If one moves closer, this texture will gradually become less and less homogeneous, until at last the distance is so shortened that one's field of vision can only encompass a few of the elements—the stalks of wheat. At this point, those elements that before had been absorbed into the larger unit—perceived as texture, but not distinguishable separately—become whole units in their own right, and the spaces between them are seen as real breaks in continuity. Similarly, if one starts from the original vantage-point and increases the distance from the field, one will eventually reach a point where the whole field is only an element in a larger scene—a larger gestalt—that includes houses and a road perhaps and other fields of a different color or texture. Again, a continuity has been replaced by a relative discontinuity.

If we transfer this now to the realm of musical perception, it should be evident how it applies to the problem of apparent discontinuity in music and of the relativity of continuity and discontinuity. If the scale on which the listener is prepared to grasp successive sound-configurations is not commensurate with the scale on which the music is actually organized, there will be a greater sense of discontinuity than is actually implicit in the music. If the music is highly complex, with many and variegated elements contained within the limits of each musical idea, such a listener will be in the position of the viewer described above whose attention is fixed on the details, being thereby unable to see the larger configurations of the picture. Or he will be like a person learning a new language who misses the sense of a sentence heard in that language because his mind has "stopped" to translate the first or second word of the sentence. Here again, an undue attention to the elements has prevented the apprehension of the larger configuration as a singular gestalt. This kind of situation is most likely to arise in music like that of Schoenberg or Ives, which usually requires the simultaneous perception of far more elements than does the music of most other composers. But in general, twentieth-century music is far more demanding in this way than earlier music was.

In much of the music of Webern, however, we find just the reverse situation. Here there is a very different scale of musical organization demanding a different scale of perception, in that small sound-structures—which in most other music would be no more than elements that are not intended to be heard separately—become with Webern the essential musical ideas, primary musical gestalts that must be perceived as relatively complete or self-sufficient in themselves. Here the result of a disparity between the scales of the composer (i.e., of the music) and of the listener will be a sense of incompleteness, if not of discontinuity.

Finally, and no less important than the above, it should be noted that the scale of organization of the successive musical configurations in any single piece of music may change considerably from one to the next, and this requires a greater flexibility of the listener's scale of perception. The difference between twentieth-century music and earlier music, with respect to this variability of scale, is similar to the difference between the two kinds of "sonority" described earlier. The development has been a gradual one, but it becomes a thing of a different kind in the music of this later period. In eighteenth- and nineteenth-century music such variations could generally be referred to some approximate standard or norm, and in fact, the important structural potentialities of such variations owe their strength to the very existence of such a norm. These norms no longer function in contemporary music, however, and the range of variation is much greater, so that *variability itself* must be recognized as a kind of norm. This last statement obviously applies not only to variability of scale but to the other innovations discussed so far as well—change of textural and parametric focus, the faster rate of change of parametric values, and the extension of the ranges in the various parameters. To a great extent, the impression of discontinuity and other "sense-interrupting effects" may be reduced or neutralized by the mere acceptance of such variability as normal. And, as it is with perception, so it must be with analysis and description, and a conceptual framework is needed that will allow for all these new possibilities. Only with such a broad conceptual framework as a basis can we proceed to an analysis of the specific structural forces that are active in twentieth-century music.

The recognition of the variability of scale with respect to the larger sound-configurations or musical ideas leads to a final extension of the principle of equivalence to make it applicable now not only to the component elements of sound-configurations but to these larger configurations themselves. That is, we must admit a "material equivalence"—with respect to their potential function (as musical ideas)—of a much greater variety of sounds and sound-configurations than would have been justified or necessary in pre-twentieth-century music. I say "sounds and sound-configurations" here advisedly, because—as was pointed out about the reduced scale of organization in the music of Webern—relatively simple sounds, which in another music might be only elements, are sometimes capable of functioning as musical ideas in their own right. Recalling now what has already been said about the greater range of complexity of sound-elements, it should be apparent that there is some degree of overlapping between the range of elements and the range of sound-ideas, and the principle of equivalence must now be understood to include this ambivalent potentiality of sounds and sound-configurations that fall within the overlapping portions of their respective ranges.

Whether a given sound or sound-configuration is to be considered merely as an element or as a more self-sufficient musical idea depends almost entirely upon the musical context in which it is heard. There is virtually no objective characteristic of the sound itself (except duration) that can show the analyst in which of these two categories it ought to be placed. Only its function within the larger design can reveal this—its relation to other sounds and sound-configurations. But the study of such relations, and thus the study of function, cannot begin without some definition of the *things* involved in the relations, the entities that are functioning—the sounds and sound-configurations themselves.

As a result of this last extension of the principle of equivalence, the distinction between element and "idea" has been relegated to the realm of context. The distinction thus qualified, the question arises as to what characteristics are held in common by all these sounds and sound-configurations that have been the subject of our analysis so far. It will be seen in the course of this book that there are many specific features that may be involved in an answer to this question, but the most general characteristic common to them all—one that has always been at least implicit in the previous discussions—is the fact that they are *perceived as units*. Almost by definition, the sounds and sound-configurations we have been dealing with here exhibit that unity or singularity that—in the visual domain—is characterized by the term "gestalt," and it is evident that some consideration ought to be given to the principles of gestalt perceptual psychology in our search for an expanded conceptual framework for twentieth-century music. In his *Principles of Gestalt Psychology* Kurt Koffka says: "The laws of organization which we have found operative explain why our behavioral environment is orderly in spite of the bewildering spatial and temporal complexity of stimulation. Units are being formed and maintained in segregation and relative insulation from other units. . . . [W]ithout our principles of organization . . . the phenomenal changes produced by these changes of stimulation would be as disorderly as the changes of stimulation themselves. . . . [O]rder is a consequence of organization, and organization the result of natural forces."[5]

This statement has an obvious relevance to the musical problems we have been considering here, and in the next section of the book I shall try to demonstrate the applicability of some of these same "laws of organization" to musical perception. At this point, however, I want to emphasize that the first condition mentioned by Koffka for the appearance of order within a "bewildering complexity of stimulation" is the perceptual formation of *units*, "maintained in segregation and relative insulation from other units." This will be a basic assumption in all the arguments that follow. And one of the first questions that must be asked about the various sounds and sound-configurations that occur in music is: What factors are responsible for their unity or singularity, and what factors effect their "relative insulation from other units"?

To facilitate the examination of such questions, I shall introduce here a few basic definitions—or rather, some new terms that may serve as points of departure for further definitions and distinctions. The continued use of such terms as "sound-configuration," "musical idea," etc. seems to me unsatisfactory, the former being too general, the latter too specific, and it would be misleading to try to adapt familiar terminology to the purposes of this investigation. Words like "phrase," "theme," "chord," and "chord progression," and even "melody" and "harmony," would have to be so reinterpreted that they would cease to have much meaning. I have instead attempted to develop a terminology that would be specific enough to make significant distinctions possible and yet remain general enough to allow for some degree of inner expansion.

In place of "sound," "sound-configuration," or "musical idea" (as these have been used up to this point in this book), I propose the word *clang* to be understood to refer to any sound or sound-configuration that is perceived as a primary musical unit—a singular aural gestalt. For the subordinate parts of a clang, I shall continue to use the word *element*, whether these parts are articulated in the vertical dimension as "linear" or *concurrent* parts or in the time-dimension as *successive* parts—i.e., tones, chords, or sounds of any kind. Finally, some term is needed to designate a succession of clangs that is set apart from other successions in some way so that it has some degree of unity and singularity, thus constituting a musical gestalt on a larger perceptual level or temporal scale—though it will not be as "strong" a gestalt (a term used by Köhler) as is the clang.[6] For this larger unit I shall use the word *sequence*, and further distinctions as to type and function will be made after an examination of its most general characteristics in sections II and III of this book.

I have adopted this word clang for several reasons, and some explanation of these reasons may help to clarify for the reader my understanding of the term. First, its only current meaning in English ("a loud ringing sound, as of metallic objects struck together"—Webster) suggests a kind of sound or sonority—complex and dissonant—that is frequently to be heard in twentieth-century music and the consideration of which first led me to the reexamination of musical materials and formal factors as outlined in this book. Second, although the word has had some currency in English (British, not American) writings on acoustics, it does not seem to have been used very widely or over a very long period of time with any single meaning. It is sometimes used in such writings on acoustics to mean a compound tone (i.e., one composed of several harmonic partials), but at other times it is used to mean the sound of an interval or chord. My definition of the word might be considered an extension of these meanings to include *any* singular sound or sound-configuration. Third, its derivation from or association with the German word *Klang*—meaning both "sound" and "tone"—carries with it some implication of the notion of equivalence described earlier. And finally, *clang* is a word that refers specifically to *auditory* perception and has not been borrowed—like so many others that we use or may be tempted to use (such as "configuration," "pattern," "object," "idea," etc.)—from the visual or other perceptual realms.

The distinction between *clang* and *sequence* is intended primarily to be a generalized functional distinction and will not always be entirely clear-cut or unambiguous in actual musical examples. But in general, the clang is a sound or sound-configuration that is more or less immediately perceptible as an aural gestalt, while the sequence—being apprehended in a less immediate way than the clang—would be what Köhler called a "weak gestalt." Similarly, the distinction between an element and a more complete or self-sufficient clang will always be a relative matter—the element being, in a sense, a "smaller" clang that is effectively absorbed into a larger clang, thereby losing much of its individuality as a musical gestalt.

It should be evident, then, that although the clang may often correspond in length or character to the motives or the phrases of traditional music, the word is not meant to define a structural or formal type at this perceptual level, as do the words "motive" and "phrase," but rather a kind of musical event and perceptual situation that may involve many other types of sound-structure than these. The only thing that is common to them all is their perceptual immediacy and their singularity, i.e., their character as aural or musical gestalts. The principle of equivalence may now be understood to mean that virtually any sound or sound-configuration—no matter how simple or complex it may be from an acoustic point of view—may function within the larger musical context as a clang if only it is *perceived* in that context as a primary musical gestalt.

There are some important similarities between this concept of the clang or aural gestalt and Pierre Schaeffer's "*objet sonore*" (or, more specifically, the kind of sound-object he calls the "*cellule*"), and I must acknowledge here my indebtedness to the writings of Schaeffer in the initial development of the ideas presented in this book.[7] The *objet sonore* is defined as practically any sound or series of sounds recorded on disc or tape (within certain obvious limits of duration, of course), so that the compositional process automatically involves the "potential equivalence" of various elements as this has been described here, as well as certain implications of gestalt-character with respect to the sounds.

But there are also some significant differences between Schaeffer's ideas and my own, and these should be noted here along with the similarities. Schaeffer's definitions are generally "operational" definitions to an extent that tends to restrict their applicability to the particular medium with which he is working: *musique concrète*, the compositional organization of recorded sounds on tape. The techniques of "transmutation and transformation" that he employs clearly involve the possibility that the same "sound-object" may function at one place in a composition as a clang, at another as an element or even as a sequence, and it may be split up or rearranged in ways that completely alter its original gestalt-characteristics. Thus Schaeffer's definitions refer less to the perceptual events in the music (or rather, in the musical experience) than to the physical or acoustic materials that are manipulated in the process of composition. And it is for this reason, perhaps, that he has emphasized the differences between the "abstract" music of the past—including even most twentieth-century music—and his own *musique concrète*. I think the essential difference between them is not a musical difference, however, but a *technical* one and—from the purely musical standpoint—hardly justifies such a distinction in name as between "abstract" and "concrete."

From a broader point of view, it has always seemed to me that the major innovations in twentieth-century music have tended from the very beginning to involve something like the "sound-object"—if this is interpreted as an "object" of perception rather than an object of technical manipulation. The concept of the clang, therefore, might be considered an outgrowth of Schaeffer's "*objet sonore*" but directed toward the perceptual event itself rather than the acoustic source of that event. Thus, the clang-concept should be applicable to music in any medium, whether instrumental or electronic, whether it employs natural or synthetic sounds, whether its psychological implications are "abstract" or "concrete."

Beginning, then, with the definitions of *element*, *clang*, and *sequence*, and particularly the definition of the clang as *a sound or sound-configuration that is perceived as a primary musical unit or aural gestalt*, I shall try in the next section of the book to answer the following questions: (1) What factors are responsible for the unity or singularity of the clang?—and the necessary corollary to this—(2) through what factors is one clang "segregated" from another in the sequence?

Section II. Gestalt-Factors of Cohesion and Segregation

> The two-or-more-dimensional space in which musical ideas are presented is a unit. . . . All that happens at any point of this musical space has more than a local effect. It functions not only in its own plane, but also in all other directions and planes, and is not without influence even at remote points. . . . The elements of a musical idea are partly incorporated in the horizontal plane as successive sounds, and partly in the vertical plane as simultaneous sounds. . . . Every musical configuration . . . has to be comprehended primarily as a mutual relation of sounds, of oscillatory vibrations, appearing at different places and times.
>
> Arnold Schoenberg, *Style and Idea*, 220–23

> The first phase of apprehension is a bounding line drawn about the object to be apprehended. An esthetic image is presented to us either in space or in time. . . . But temporal or spatial, the esthetic image is first luminously apprehended as selfbounded and selfcontained upon the immeasurable background of space or time which is not it. You apprehend it as *one* thing. You see it as one whole. You apprehend its wholeness.
>
> James Joyce, *A Portrait of the Artist as a Young Man*, 212

> The form, then, of any portion of matter . . . and the changes of form which are apparent in its movements and in its growth, may in all cases alike be described as due to the action of force. In short, the form of an object is a "diagram of forces," in this sense, at least,

> that from it we can judge of or deduce the forces that are acting or have acted upon it.
>
> D'Arcy Wentworth Thompson, *On Growth and Form*, 16

In 1923 Max Wertheimer published a paper entitled "Laws of Organization in Perceptual Form" in which he demonstrated certain factors of unit formation and segregation operating within systems of points and lines in the visual field.[8] This paper has since become one of the cornerstones of gestalt psychology. Wertheimer's procedure was simple but nonetheless elegant in the way each of the various cohesive factors was isolated from the others and shown to be capable of functioning independently. In the course of the demonstration, frequent analogies were suggested to auditory configurations, but no attempt was made to analyze this realm of perception in any thoroughgoing way. And in general, the gestalt psychologists' studies of perception have been directed primarily to visual problems, probably owing to the greater directness and immediacy with which visual forms may be presented, perceived, and described. Nevertheless, many of the principles of organization of visual forms may be shown to be involved in auditory perception, often with no more than a simple translation of terms. In other cases, the problems are not so simple, but the writings of the gestalt psychologists, Wertheimer, Koffka and Köhler in particular, can still serve us as a guide and precedent.[9]

The first factor demonstrated by Wertheimer was called the *factor of proximity* and might be stated as follows: in a collection of similar visual elements, those that are close together in space will naturally or spontaneously tend to form groups in perception, other factors being equal. A very simple example showing the effect of relative proximity on visual grouping is shown in figure 1.

The analogy in musical perception is obvious when we substitute time for space and sound-elements for visual elements in the statement given above. In example 9, for instance, the sounds that are separated by the shortest intervals of time (including those sounding together, of course) tend to form units or groups, while the longer time-intervals (in this case, the silences) cause unit segregation. It can be seen from this example that

00 000 00 0000 00 000

FIGURE 1.

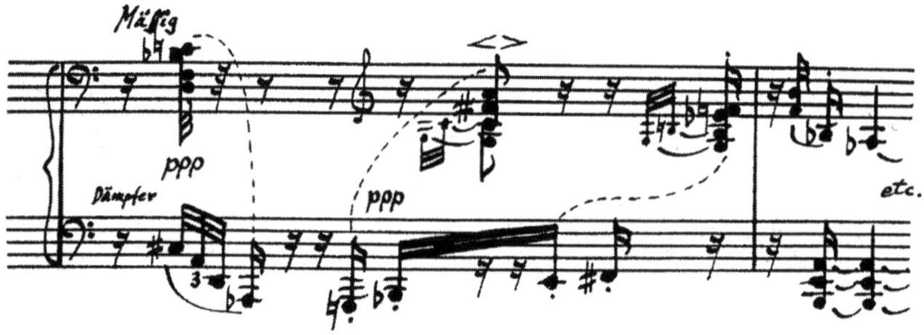

EXAMPLE 9. Arnold Schoenberg, op. 11, no. 3 (m. 22).

temporal proximity may be manifested in either (or both) of two ways—as *contiguity* or as *simultaneity*. The essential principle is the same in either case. Applied to auditory or musical perception, the *factor of proximity* might be formulated as follows: *in a collection of sound-elements, those that are simultaneous or contiguous will tend to form clangs, while relatively greater separations in time will produce segregations*, other factors being equal. (The "other factors being equal" clause is very important, as will soon become apparent.)

A second factor in the formation of visual groups Wertheimer designated as the *factor of similarity*. In a collection of visual elements, those that are similar will tend to be grouped by the eye, as is shown in figure 2, in which the elements are equally spaced so that the proximity-factor can have no effect on the grouping.

The same principle in musical perception relates to the fact—well understood by any musician, at least implicitly—that sounds played on the same instrument (i.e., of similar timbre) or in the same pitch register (of similar pitch) tend to seem "connected" and to form groups more easily than sounds that are relatively dissimilar in these respects. Examples 10 and 11 represent two typical configurations in which relative similarity of pitch (ex. 10) and of timbre (ex. 11) is the primary determinant of coherence within each clang. In the Varèse example, the pitch-similarity between the F in the trumpet and the E$\flat$–D in the clarinet is such a strong cohesive factor in this linear element of the larger clang that it overcomes the segregative influence of timbre-difference between the two instruments. Thus,

0 0 0 # # # 0 0 0 0 # #

FIGURE 2.

Example 10. Edgard Varèse, *Octandre*, II (mm. 50–53).

one does not hear as a unitary element the F–F♯–F–F♯ . . . being played by the trumpet but rather a single line that passes from trumpet to clarinet. In the Webern example, on the other hand, the effect of pitch-similarity is much less powerful than the timbre-similarity that unifies each of the two instrumental lines (i.e., E♭ clarinet and violin) into singular units and the difference in timbre that keeps them separate and distinct from each other even though the parts cross melodically. And it is the change in timbre—from clarinet to oboe—that will effect the perceptual separations between clangs 1 and 4, in spite of the pitch-similarity between the end of the clarinet line and the beginning of the oboe part. Thus, one parameter may run

Example 11. Anton Webern, op. 10, no. 2 (beginning).

counter to another with respect to the operation of this factor of similarity. But it is the existence of a relatively higher degree of similarity in some parameter that is the unifying force in such clangs.

Note also that the cohesive force of the similarity-factor implies—as its necessary corollary—the segregating effect of dissimilarity, just as, with the factor of proximity, a greater separation in time (i.e., relative "non-proximity") will tend to cause segregation. The very process of unit formation necessarily implies relative separation from other units—or from other parts of the perceptual field—and this fact will become more and more significant when we begin to analyze the possibilities for gestalt-formations on various perceptual levels or temporal scales.

The factor of similarity applies not only to pitch and timbre but also to the other parameters—dynamic level, envelope, temporal and vertical density, etc.—and in fact it may be said to function with respect to any attribute of sound by which we are able, at a given moment or within a given time-span, to distinguish one sound or sound-configuration from another. Thus, for example, morphological similarity or similarity of form among the component clangs of a sequence constitutes a powerful factor in the unification of that sequence.

Finally, it should be noted that the cohesive and segregative forces of relative similarity and dissimilarity apply not only to successive groupings—where, for example, one clang is segregated from the next clang in a sequence—but also to concurrent configurations in which one clang is distinguished from another that is sounding at the same time (as was the case in example 11). The effects of the similarity-factor may thus run counter to those of the proximity-factor—and indeed, true polyphony would be impossible if the only conditions leading to clang-formation and segregation were contiguity and simultaneity.

We may now formulate the *factor of similarity*, with specific reference to musical perception, as follows: *in a collection of sound-elements (or clangs), those that are similar* (with respect to values in some parameter) *will tend to form clangs (or sequences), while relative dissimilarity will produce segregation*, other factors being equal.

Thus far in the analysis of these factors of cohesion and segregation it has been necessary to isolate each of them and consider its effects separately. This is an abstraction, of course, and it should not be forgotten that in every real musical configuration both of these factors (and others, to be described in a moment) are operating simultaneously, although they do not usually exert equal force in any given configuration. In addition, they may be more or less cooperative, their results in perceptual organization varying over a wide range from complete congruency or mutual reinforcement, through partially ambiguous, overlapping effects, to completely ambivalent, multistructural configurations produced by antithetical relationships between the two factors. In the latter case (which is not by any means an exceptional one, even in pre-twentieth-century music), a given collection of elements may be perceived in two or more different and distinct configurations, yielding, that is, two or more clangs simultaneously, each of which may be equally important in the larger musical context.

Although the factors of proximity and similarity are not the only ones involved in the organization of perceptual units, they are the most basic—i.e., the most effective—and the most frequently decisive in the determination of clang- and sequence-unity. For this reason, I shall refer to them as the *primary* factors of cohesion and segregation. In addition to these, there are four *secondary* factors, which will be considered here. These are (1) the factor of *intensity*, (2) the *repetition-factor*, (3) *objective set*, and (4) *subjective set*. Before describing these, however, I want to introduce a very simple graphic representation that can help to illustrate the factors of proximity and similarity and perhaps also to clarify some points in the arguments that follow.

As shown in figure 3, the horizontal axis of the graph represents time, and the vertical axis represents an ordinal scale of values in one of the various parameters, i.e., in *any* parameter; it does not matter here which parameter is involved.[10] If one plots, on such a graph, the variations in some parameter with time, the result will be what I shall call a *parametric profile* of the element, clang, or sequence involved, which gives a general picture of the configuration with respect to that particular parameter. For example, if the vertical ordinate is pitch, such a plot will show melodic contour (but note that with the present definition of the vertical scale, the plot cannot tell one anything about the actual pitches or intervals in the configuration). If the vertical axis is made to represent loudness, one might plot the time-envelope of the attack and decay of a simple element or the dynamic shape of some larger clang or sequence. Thus, such a graphic representation might be considered a kind of two-dimensional perceptual "model" (albeit a very primitive one), which can be used to depict one aspect of the perception of a given configuration—that aspect that corresponds to the variations in time of one parameter.

It will be evident that distances between individual elements in such a graph, when measured along the horizontal axis (or, more precisely, distances between their respective projections onto the horizontal axis), will show their relative proximity in time. Similarly, distances measured in the vertical direction will indicate, in a general way at least, relative similarity or dissimilarity between these elements with respect to the parameter designated in the graph. Thus, proximity in time is represented by proximity in space, measured horizontally, while parametric similarity is

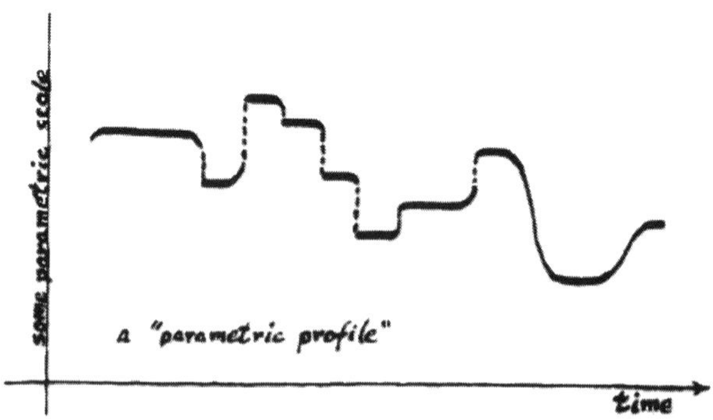

FIGURE 3.

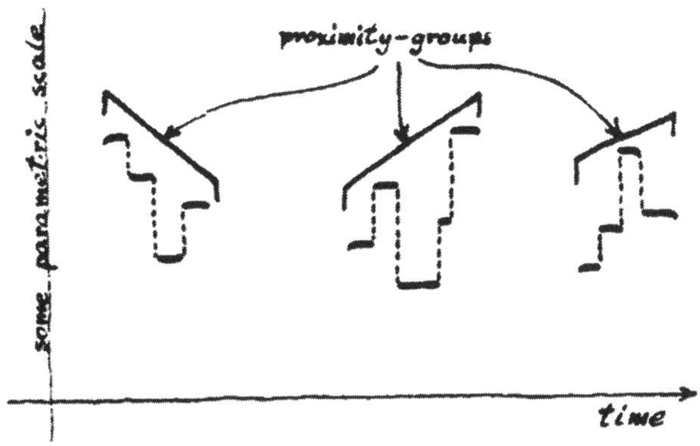

FIGURE 4.

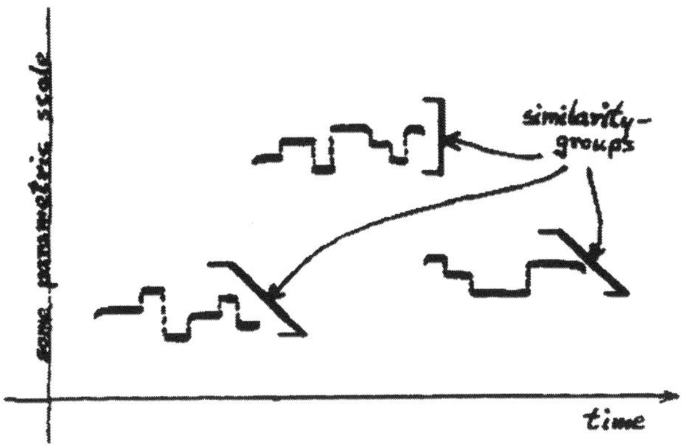

FIGURE 5.

represented by proximity (in a sort of one-dimensional "attribute-space"), measured vertically. In figures 4 and 5, two hypothetical configurations are plotted, the vertical axis being left unspecified as to the particular parameter intended, merely representing (as in figure 3) any distinctive attribute of sound in terms of which such an ordinal scale might be constructed. The configuration in figure 4 would correspond to a situation in which proximity is the principal factor in the formation of groups, whereas figure 5 shows unit-formations primarily determined by the factor of similarity.

The inherent two-dimensionality of such graphs imposes certain limitations on this "perceptual model," since the perceived form of every real musical configuration will involve an interaction of all parameters, not just one, and these parameters may not always be perceived independently, as this method of analysis of single parametric profiles might seem to imply. But by isolating the various parameters in this way and considering each profile separately, it becomes possible to formulate certain general principles that will still be valid in more complex conditions that result from the simultaneous influences of several parameters in a clang or sequence.

The first of the secondary factors of cohesion and segregation—the factor of intensity—relates to the singular directionality of the parametric scales employed in the graphs. That is, we generally assume an absolute "up" and "down" on these scales, a higher and lower parametric value that is somehow related to what might be called *musical* or *subjective intensity*. I say "somehow related" because although this "directionality" is understood and utilized by the musician in practice—and is implicit in most of the devices employed by both the composer and the performer in creating climaxes, building up musical tensions, intensifying or activating a passage of music, etc.—I know of no attempt to define these conditions explicitly, much less to explain them in nonmusical terms. It is a common fact of musical experience that a greater subjective intensity is usually associated with a rise in pitch, an increase in dynamic level or in tempo, etc. Similarly, a change from a "smooth" or "mellow" timbre to a "harsh" or "piercing" timbre or from a more consonant to a more dissonant interval is felt as an increase in subjective intensity.

An explanation of these conditions might eventually be derived from certain concepts of *information theory*, beginning with measures of the information transmitted in the form of neural discharges in the "communication channel" between the ear and the brain. Such measures have been made, at least for frequency and amplitude, and these indicate that a higher rate of transmission of neural information is indeed associated with both a higher pitch and a greater loudness, and some inferences from these data might be made in regard to timbre, vertical density, and perhaps other parameters as well.

But this can be no more than a beginning of an explanation, because many more strictly psychological factors may be involved, and if we had to wait for conclusive evidence in the form of physiological data, we would probably never be in a position to describe this factor of subjective intensity in a satisfactory way. I shall, therefore, simply define an upward displacement on a parametric scale as a change in value in that parameter that produces or is associated with an increase in the subjective intensity of the sensation. In addition, I shall call the measure of relative height on such a scale *parametric intensity*. Parametric intensity is thus to be understood as an approximate measure—in one "dimension"—of the more inclusive musical or subjective intensity of a perceived sound.

Consider, then, what happens when listening to a moderately complex clang. It may be observed that one's attention is not usually distributed evenly among the component elements but is focused more sharply on certain elements than on others. For example, in a clang with several concurrent elements—delineated, let us say, by separate instrumental parts—the attention is likely to be directed to that element that is loudest, or (if they are all equally loud) to the one with the most intense timbre, or (supposing all elements to be equal in both loudness and timbre) to the one that is highest in pitch, etc. In each case the attention will tend to be directed toward—and more sharply focused upon—the element that exhibits the highest values on some parametric scale. If the difference in parametric intensity between one such element and the others is not too great, the result will be a variation in focal "resolve," with the most intense element being heard more clearly, seeming more immediately "present" in perception, while the less intense elements will be more or less "blurred," more or less "remote" as perceptual objects. In this situation, I am assuming that all the elements are heard as parts of a single clang in spite of the dissimilarities between them, but of course, if there is too great a difference in parametric intensity between one such element and others, a subdivision may occur—as a result of our second factor of cohesion and segregation, the factor of similarity—so that one will hear two separate clangs instead of one.

So far, we have found nothing new in the way of grouping tendencies, but if the analysis of the intensity-factor is transferred now from the vertical to the horizontal dimension, it will be found that this factor by itself can produce unit-formations in time (independently of the factor of proximity and in a way that is not accounted for by the similarity-factor as this has been formulated), although parametric intensity is obviously related to the question of similarity and dissimilarity of parametric values. I am referring here to what we call *accent* and, more specifically, to the *group-initiating tendency* associated with the accent. I suggest that similar conditions hold for the effects of intensity-differentiations *in time* as were observed above in the case of vertical differentiations and that the same terms might be used to describe the perceptual results, if not to explain them. That is, in a succession of sound-elements showing marked variations in intensity (in some parameter), the attention will be more sharply caught by the more intense, accented elements, while the less intense elements will be relatively blurred, and—by way of memory, or perhaps through some kind of kinesthetic response-process—the attention at certain moments may actually be directed *backward* in time, toward the most recent accented element, until a fresh accentuation redirects the attention into the more immediate, present moment.

Such a process might be illustrated graphically as in figure 6, where each arrow represents a kind of "attention vector" associated with each successive element in the graph. The length of such a vector would indicate relative clarity, focal resolve, etc., while the direction of the vector would represent the direction or displacement in time of the perceptual attention at each occurrence of a new element. I have placed the origin of each vector at a point on the time-axis corresponding to the beginning of each new element. If one now drops vertical projections from the upper terminals of each vector, marking off the points of intersection of these projections with a third horizontal axis, the groupings resulting from the factor of intensity alone are again shown by the relative proximity of the points in space (measured horizontally), just as actual proximity in time would be. Whether or not this corresponds to some kind of distortion or "clustering" of successive moments in subjectively experienced time I have no way of knowing—and such an interpretation is not really necessary to the argument, although it does represent an intriguing possibility.

Although the above description of the grouping tendency of the intensity-factor has several advantages, it is not altogether satisfactory because of the speculative character of the subjective process represented by the "vectors." Consequently, I shall offer two alternative hypotheses—equally speculative—that might account for the group-initiating effect of accentuation either singly or in combination. The first relates the intensity-factor to the factor of proximity, interpreting it, in fact, as a special case of simultaneity, while the second would represent a special manifestation of the similarity-factor.

The first hypothesis is based on the assumption that sounds evoke kinesthetic responses in the listener, the relative *durations* of which are in some way directly proportional to the parametric intensity of these sounds—the response to a more intense sound thus lasting longer than

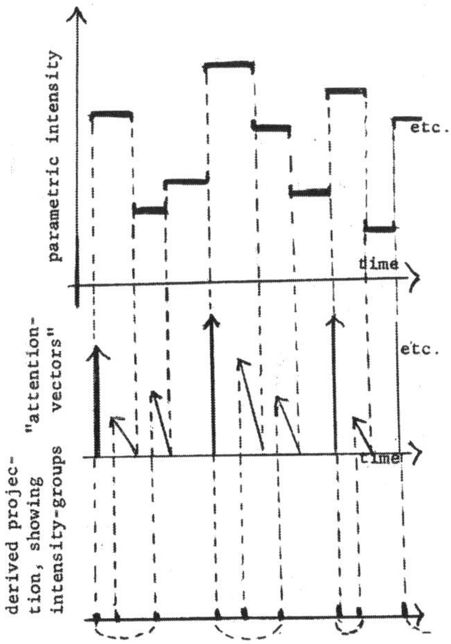

FIGURE 6.

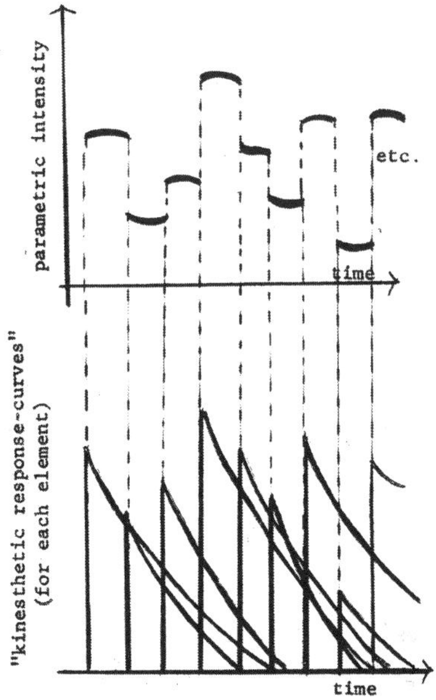

FIGURE 7.

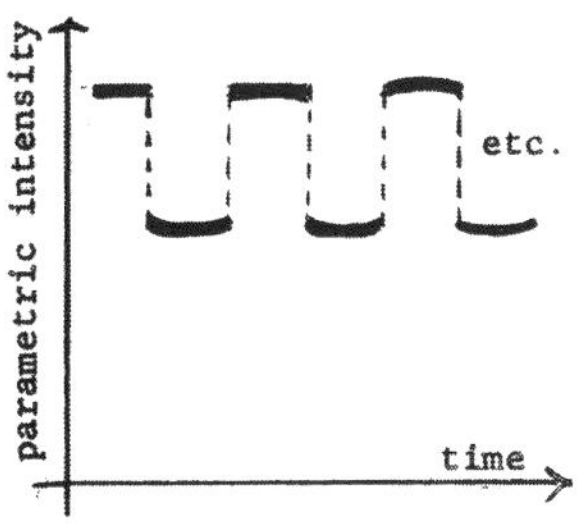

FIGURE 8.

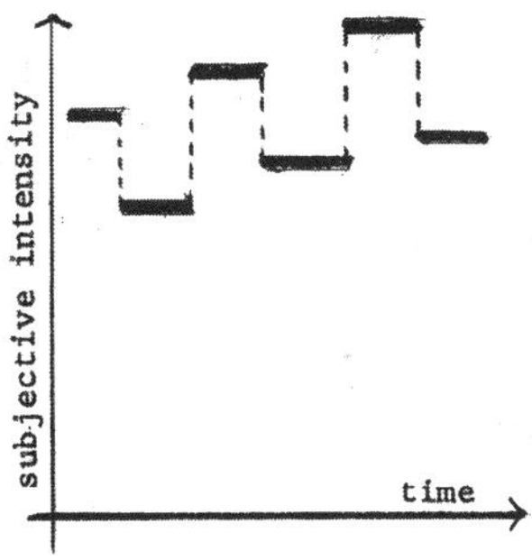

FIGURE 9.

the response to a less intense sound. This may be represented graphically by means of a plot of the subjective intensity (or the magnitude of the kinesthetic response) versus time-arranged, as before (in figure 6), "in parallel" with the plot of parametric intensity versus time. This is shown in figure 7 (using the same parametric profile as in figure 6), and it will be seen that the appropriate unit-formations are indicated in the lower plot by the way in which the response-curves for the more intense elements tend to overlap and "absorb" those for less intense elements. The perceptual result of such a situation would be a degree of subjective "simultaneity" that would tend to favor groupings initiated by the accented elements.

The second alternative hypothesis is this: it would seem, intuitively, that a change of parametric value in the upward (increasing) direction might produce a greater change in subjective intensity than would a corresponding decrease in parametric value. Thus, such a simple alternation between equal increasing and decreasing parametric intervals as that shown in figure 8 might really be responded to as though it were something like the plot of figure 9, with a greater separation associated with the ascending interval. In this case, the factor of similarity would play a decisive role in the perceptual organization of the series into three sets of two elements, whereas, in the first plot, no influence of the similarity-factor in this particular grouping could have been apparent.

A comparison of the three hypotheses suggested above reveals the fact that each of them represents the intensity-factor as a special case of either proximity or similarity. This can be taken to mean either that the latter factors are really the more basic—the intensity-factor being reducible to one of these—or, alternatively, that the analysis (and thus the analyst) is so biased in favor of the factors of proximity and similarity that a more fundamental aspect of the intensity-factor remains in obscurity. Doubts about this may perhaps be removed in the later course of this book, during which proximity and similarity (and especially the latter) will be found to be of unique significance in the unification of musical forms on all perceptual levels. The grouping force of the accent is limited in its effectiveness to relatively short time-spans, serving primarily to articulate successive clangs or shorter elements of clangs, whereas the factor of similarity produces grouping tendencies throughout much longer periods of time, affecting the formation not only of clangs but also of sequences, longer sections, and even entire pieces. It is for this reason that it has seemed appropriate to distinguish between "primary" and "secondary" factors of cohesion and segregation, as defined earlier.

What has already been said about the uneven distribution of attention in the vertical dimension, produced by differences in intensity among concurrent elements, brings up another point that should be mentioned here, although it is not directly related to the question of unit-formation per se. When the attention is focused upon one element or group of elements more directly than it is upon others in a clang, the relative musical importance of the various elements must obviously be different, with the less intense elements taking a subordinate role in the total configuration. This will still be the case when the intensity-differences are great enough to produce subdivision into two or more concurrent clangs (as long as we are considering only one parameter at a time), the result being typified (in conventional musical terms) by the distinctions between principal and secondary voices, main melodic part versus accompaniment-figures, etc. It should be evident that such distinctions are generally produced by differentiations in parametric intensity, either by the composer or by the performer, or both.

The situation here is analogous in many respects to the distinctions between *figure* and *ground* in visual perception—the figure generally being distinguished by what Koffka calls a greater "energy density" and by a higher degree of "internal articulation" than the ground.[11] The analogy between these characteristics and what I have called parametric intensity is obvious, particularly in view of the generality of the definition of the vertical ordinate of the graphs given earlier ("any distinctive attribute of sound in terms of which an ordinal scale might be constructed"). Vertical and temporal density have already been mentioned as two such attributes, and the more general notion of *degree of articulation*—the rate of change in parametric values discussed in section I—can also be considered a parameter to be ordered in a scale of intensity-values like the others.

At this point I want to summarize what has been said so far about the factor of intensity with respect to both the vertical and the horizontal dimensions of the perceptual model. (1) In a collection of sound-elements, the vertical distribution of attention *at any moment* will be such that, if the differences in the intensity of the various elements are not too great, the more intense elements will tend to be in sharper focus than those of less intensity. On the other hand, if the differences in parametric intensity are considerable, subdivisions (into separate clangs) are likely to arise as a result of the cohesive and segregative effects of the similarity-factor. (2) In a collection of sound-elements, the temporal distribution of perceptual attention—*from moment to moment*—will be such that, if the differences in the parametric intensity of the elements are considerable, successive clangs will tend to be formed that are *initiated* by the more intense, accented elements.

These two statements might be combined in a general formulation of the *factor of intensity* as follows: *in a collection of sound-elements, among which there are considerable differences in parametric intensity, clangs will*

EXAMPLE 12. Edgard Varèse, *Octandre*, III (mm. 56–58).

tend to be formed in which the more intense elements are (1) the focal points and (2) the starting-points of these clangs, other factors being equal.

A fourth factor that can influence clang-formation is the *factor of repetition*. If a repetition of parametric profile is perceived within a series of sound-elements, this alone may produce a subdivision of the whole series into units corresponding to the repeated shape, the perceptual separation between the units occurring at the point just before the first repeated element. That this is a relatively independent factor is indicated by the fact that it can determine perceptual organization even when most of the other factors would tend to produce different groupings, as in example 12.

I am not prepared to offer any explanation of the way in which this factor might function nor even such hypotheses as were suggested to account for the intensity-factor. It is evident, however, that the factor of repetition involves memory and, more specifically, a process of comparison of what is being heard with what has already been heard. Why this should result in unit-formations in the case of repetition is not so evident. The condition described does suggest, however, that there may exist in the listener a positive tendency to group successive sounds into more or less circumscribed units—a tendency that is independent of or prior to the objective conditions given in the music. The factors of cohesion and segregation that have been analyzed here would thus turn out to represent not so much active "forces" but rather facilitating conditions—i.e., objective conditions that facilitate the listener's perceptual organization of the sound-elements into clangs. In any case, whether one wishes to consider these factors as causal forces or simply as "facilitating conditions" really makes little difference from a musical point of view as long as one's primary interest is in their actual *effects* in musical perception.

We come now to a consideration of those factors of cohesion and segregation that I designated earlier as *objective set* and *subjective set*. The word *set* is used to mean, in general, a prior psychological attitude involving expectations or anticipations that may effectively determine or alter the perception of present and future events in the perceptual field. The term *objective set* is borrowed directly from Wertheimer, who used it to describe a factor influencing visual groupings that has an analogous counterpart in musical perception. The term *subjective set* is adopted here as an extension of the implications in the first term and refers to a whole group of factors such as past experience, learning, habit, association, etc., which Wertheimer mentions, but in a somewhat negative way because of the overvaluation such subjective factors had received in psychological theories whose basic premises the gestalt psychologists were opposing. The general theoretical situation at the time (1923) involved an active conflict between older, "elementaristic," and "associational" theories of perception and the newer concepts of gestalt psychology, resulting in what may seem to us now to be an undue neglect of such subjective factors in the writings of the gestalt theorists. It is evident now that any really complete evaluation of the various forces involved in musical perception will have to take into account such factors as earlier musical training, cultural orientation, familiarity with the style of the period or of the composer of the work being listened to, etc. And yet one will find a similarly disproportionate treatment of the objective versus the subjective factors in this book, although for somewhat different reasons. Some limitations had to be imposed from the beginning, and I have attempted to restrict my field of inquiry to the more objective side of the musical experience—i.e., to those aspects that may be referred directly to the sounds and sound-configurations that are the materials of the music.

It is quite impossible to make any absolute distinction between the objective and the subjective aspects of the musical experience—and similarly, it is often difficult to decide where to draw the line between the factors of objective set and subjective set, since both of them are "subjective" conditions in some sense, and any distinction we might make would probably seem arbitrary to a psychologist. However, I shall adopt the following heuristic definitions of the two factors in order to facilitate the analysis and incidentally to define more explicitly what is to be considered outside of the self-imposed boundaries of the present investigation. *Objective set* refers to expectations or anticipations arising during a musical experience that are produced by previous events occurring *within the same piece*, while *subjective set* refers to expectations or anticipations that are the result of experiences *previous* to those that are occasioned by the particular piece of music now being considered. By definition, then, objective set should be less variable from one listener to another than subjective set, because the former will always have specific analogs or correlates in the musical configurations themselves, while the latter may not.

It will readily be seen that, even after restricting the field to a factor of objective set defined in this way, an enormous number of musical relationships will still be involved. In the most general terms, the factor of objective set will relate to every way in which the perception of an earlier musical event has some effective influence upon the perception of a later event in a given piece of music. But even within a short composition, such influences are so numerous as to seem virtually infinite to a perceptive listener, and I cannot hope to define or describe completely all of the different forms in which this factor manifests itself.[12] Here I shall mention only three typical ones, with the understanding that there may be others that are just as important to the musical experience.

One of the most common examples of objective set takes a form that might be called *rhythmic inertia* and is the source of the perception of syncopation, where an accent or metrical impulse is perceived in some way that does not correspond to the actual accentuation in the music at a given point. What seems to be involved here is a psychological or kinesthetic tendency toward rhythmic repetition—the maintenance of a previously established rhythmic structure—which can determine the perceptual organization of a neutral or ambiguous structure (giving it the form of what has already been heard) or introduce new ambiguities in an otherwise unambiguous structure, thus sometimes causing the rhythmic interpretation of a clang to be very different from what it would be if the clang were heard by itself—out of the particular context.

A traditional musical device that takes advantage of this form of objective set is the baroque and classic *hemiola*, in which it may be observed that the subjective rhythmic impulse that is perceived at one moment is a carry-over from the impulse established in preceding measures and that the new rhythmic structure is often perceived as such a measure or two later than it actually occurs in the music. The strength of such devices depends, as does that of most of the other forms of the factor of objective set, on the establishment of some more or less constant or recurrent condition, and for this reason they are often much less important in twentieth-century music than they were in earlier music. But even in twentieth-century music, some degree of rhythmic inertia is probably always involved, although its relative effectiveness may be slight by comparison with other factors.

Similar to the above but not identical to it is the more general condition whereby the establishment of specific referential norms—whether tonal, metrical, or other—provides a standard of comparison for later events with more or less specific implications as to the interpretation of these events. Here again, the most obvious examples would come from earlier tonal music, one of the principal characteristics of the traditional tonal system being just this establishment of a referential pitch-level, with respect to which all other pitches receive a specific interpretation. Similarly, when a particular meter is established and maintained throughout a piece of music or a section of a piece, subsequent events acquire specific rhythmic implications by virtue of their position within that metrical structure (e.g., upbeat vs. downbeat), the syncopations mentioned above being a special case of such implications. It might be noted here that although it is *objective set* that makes these implications specifiable in the first place, the question as to what particular interpretation will be given to them depends largely on *subjective set*. Thus, for example, the existence of a clear tonal center on C makes the meaning of every other pitch potentially specific, but whether a G is to serve as a "dominant" in that context depends on other factors that include musical conventions that have been learned.

Again, it may be said that the importance of objective set has diminished in twentieth-century music but that it must still be present, if only on a smaller scale. That is, the very perception of pitch-intervals represents a sort of primitive form of the same factor. At the lowest level of the perceptual timescale, each sound represents a "referential norm" with respect to the sound that follows it, so that the conditions of objective set can never really be absent from the musical experience.

The third example of this factor—singularly important in most music, though perhaps somewhat less so now than in the past—involves thematic reference, recurrence, or recall. This condition depends, more than do the first two, on the longer-range faculty of memory and is thus less immediate than the others, but it is also capable of altering or determining the perceptual organization of later configurations that are similar or otherwise related to configurations that have already been heard. That is, a given configuration may have a very different significance when it is perceived as "a variation of" some earlier one than when it is heard as an entirely new configuration. And, as with the first two examples of objective set, the best sources of examples of this type of relation will be in pre-twentieth-century music.

It will be apparent from what has already been said that the more radically the new music departs from the conventions of the tonal system and traditional methods of thematic development, the less active do many of these manifestations of objective set become. It might be noted however, that the 12-tone technique and many of the more recent serial procedures seem to be at least partly motivated by a desire to reinstitute the cohesive forces of this factor in some new and different way. This is especially clear in the early propositions of the 12-tone method, where the tone-row is treated both as a thematic entity and as an ever-present referential norm of pitch-interval relations and thus represents an attempt to combine into one form what had previously been two separate sources of cohesive force. Whether the 12-tone technique does this successfully or not is another question; the point here is that the intention behind it can be understood in this way, and it is quite possible that still other means may be found to restore these forces. On the other hand, it may be that the use of these various forms of the factor of objective set corresponds to a more specialized musical attitude characteristic of one particular historical and cultural milieu and is becoming less and less prevalent in our own time. As I have tried to show here, the factor of objective set is by no means the only powerful force active in the perceptual organization or unification of musical configurations.

About the factor of subjective set, very little will be said here, except to note that there is one class of musical phenomena whose effects are closely related to those of thematic reference described above under the category of objective set but that result from experiences previous to the piece of music in which they exert their effect. I refer to the use of familiar sounds or sound-configurations in a new context—whether these are in the form of more or less exact quotations or of more general stylistic features. Typical examples of the former may be found in works by Charles Ives and of the latter in the music of Berg and Bartók, and it is important to note that such devices can have very powerful structural functions in the articulation of the larger form of a piece of music. In any

Example 13 [part one]. Charles Ives, "Concord" Sonata ("Emerson") (p. 3).

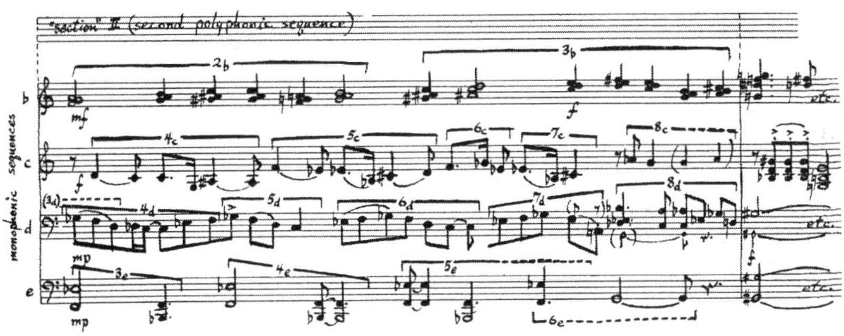

Example 13 [part two]. Charles Ives, "Concord" Sonata ("Emerson") (p. 3).

very long work, thematic references between more remotely separated points in time must partake of some of the characteristics of such references to musical ideas already familiar to the listener, and the distinction between objective and subjective set must be understood to include this region of ambiguity in such cases.

In my remarks about the factor of repetition on page 50 I mentioned that a process of comparison was involved—a comparison of what was being heard at a given moment with what had already been heard. To some extent, the factors of proximity, similarity, and intensity would also involve such comparisons, though in none of these instances is the process necessarily conscious. Now the factors of objective set and subjective set may be said to involve a comparison-process also, but in this case it is of a different sort. These factors depend upon the perceptual comparison of what the listener hears at a given moment to what he *expected* to hear at that moment rather than simply to what he has *already* heard. Again, the most appropriate theoretical definition of these factors would probably involve the concepts of information theory and, more specifically, the theory of "semantic information" based on "inductive probabilities" proposed by Bar-Hillel and Carnap.[13] Unfortunately, it is not within the scope of the present book to elaborate on these relationships to information theory, but I mention them as fruitful possibilities for further investigation.

In order to review some of the principles developed in this section of the book, I have selected for analysis a more extended musical example (example 13) in which nearly all of the gestalt-factors of cohesion and segregation may be seen in operation. This passage—taken from the first movement ("Emerson") of Charles Ives's "Concord" sonata for piano—deserves very careful study, because it represents a highly refined application of numerous devices by means of which clangs and sequences may be compositionally organized to achieve a truly polyphonic musical texture. At least two and more often four separate distinct lines are here developed simultaneously with a high degree of rhythmic independence (from the standpoint of the phrase-structure—corresponding to the durations of the successive clangs—delineated within each of the individual sequences). This results in a complex polyrhythm that could never be perceived as such if the several (sequential) lines were not heard as separate strands in the total musical fabric. And this means, of course, that each of these simultaneously developing sequences must be, in some way, both internally unified by some cohesive force that connects the successive clangs into one larger configuration and, at the same time, that each sequence must be differentiated from the other sequences by a segregative force that maintains some boundaries between them. It will be instructive to analyze the passage in order to determine specifically how this *polyphonic differentiation* is achieved here—what factors are involved and in what way they are manifested at any given moment.

In example 13 I have rearranged the notation of the music in such a way that the individual parts can be seen more clearly as separate lines, or what will be called *monophonic sequences*. These will be designated as sequences *a* to *e*, according to their predominant pitch-register—from high to low. The successive clangs in each monophonic sequence are shown bracketed, with arabic numerals corresponding to their order of occurrence in each sequence. When individual clangs are mentioned in the text, they will be designated by this number, with a subscript to indicate the sequence in which they occur—thus 3_a, 5_c, etc. The passage constitutes two successive *polyphonic sequences*, which will be referred to as "sections" I and II, respectively, their boundaries being given in the example by the three bar-lines (there are no bar-lines in the original notation). The portions of music that precede the first bar-line and follow the third bar-line are shown to help illustrate certain observations that will be made about aspects of one's perception of the main body of the example that are influenced by conditions outside of it, i.e., in connection with objective set and subjective set.

It should be noted first that the factor of proximity can have very little influence in the polyphonic differentiation of the several monophonic sequences in an example of this kind. Polyphony involves the independent development of *simultaneous* parts, whereas the effect of the proximity-factor is to neutralize the independence of simultaneous parts—to "fuse" them into a single gestalt. Thus, polyphony is only possible when other factors are made to function in opposition to the factor of proximity. Within each of the individual monophonic sequences, however, the proximity-factor may be involved in the articulation of the boundaries of successive clangs, as it is in this example, between clangs 1_c and 2_c, or from clangs 2 to 3, 5 to 6, and 6 to 7 in sequence *d*.

The most effective factor in the creation of polyphonic differentiation in a passage like this is of course the factor of similarity. The internal coherence of sequences *a*, *b*, and *c* at the beginning of section I is the result, in each case, of a characteristic *loudness* (*piano*, *forte*, and *mezzo forte*, respectively), *vertical density* (single tone, tone-cluster, single tone), and, to a lesser extent perhaps, *temporal density*. Conversely, the three sequences are "maintained in relative insulation" from one another by their differences with respect to these same parameters. It is noteworthy that the parameter in which the similarity factor manifests itself here is *not* pitch. Indeed, if sequence *a* had been marked *forte* or had comprised tone-clusters, the pitch-differences between sequences *a* and *b* would not be sufficient to distinguish the two lines—their elements would be perceived as parts of one clang at any given moment, rather than two distinct clangs. The C♯ in 1_b, for example, would then be heard as a continuation of the melodic movement at the beginning of 1_a (i.e., one would hear A♭–G–E–C♯ . . . instead of A♭–G–E–(low) D . . . etc.) rather than as part of a clang beginning with B (the upper tone of the first element in 1_b), as it is now perceived.

But after the entrance of sequences *d* and *e*, similarity of pitch-register becomes much more important as a factor of cohesion and segregation in the music. From that point on, each sequence remains within a relatively circumscribed range and register of the pitch-compass, and this is an effective determinant of both their internal coherence and their mutual separation.

But loudness and temporal density still remain important factors. Differentiation in the latter parameter is the primary source of the separation between sequences *d* and *e*, and if the distinction between the *mezzo forte* of sequence *c* and the *piano* of sequence *a* is not maintained in the performance of the latter half of section I, these two lines will surely fuse into one (as shown by the smaller notes in the notation of *a* at this point). The same general relationships can be seen to apply to the remainder of the example, where parametric similarities always constitute the primary cohesive force within each of the monophonic sequences, parametric dissimilarities being the primary segregative force exerted between them.

The factor of similarity is thus by far the most important factor in the vertical articulation of the passage into separate linear parts, and yet it is of almost no importance at all in the horizontal organization—i.e., the temporal articulation of successive clangs within any one sequence. It has already been mentioned that the proximity-factor plays a part in this temporal articulation, but much more important in this respect are the other factors—intensity, repetition, and objective set.

The factors of intensity and repetition usually function cooperatively in this example. That is, the temporal boundaries defined by these two factors are nearly always congruent or synchronous—as at the beginnings of clangs 2_a and 4_a, clang 2_c (by a repetition of the rhythmic pattern, dotted eighth to sixteenth to half note), and 5_c, and finally, in clangs 2 and 5 of sequence *d*. In clangs 6_d and 7_d, on the other hand, the factors of intensity and repetition may be seen to function independently—noncongruently—with the predominant grouping being determined by the repetition-factor (in cooperation with the factor of proximity, already mentioned as influential at these points).

Objective set is involved in the perceptual organization of this passage in two ways: that is, it influences the grouping of both melodic and rhythmic structures. The previous occurrence of the descending melodic pattern, minor second to minor third to major second, as shown in the introductory measure (the part that precedes the first bar-line), facilitates the perceptual integration of the low D in clang 1_a with the three preceding tones in the higher register (and thus, in cooperation with the similarity-factor as it is manifested in the two parameters, loudness and vertical density, but in opposition to the pitch-dissimilarities that would tend to separate these elements).

In the form of rhythmic inertia, the factor of objective set is clearly involved in many of the metrical ambiguities in this passage. A temporal progression in quarter notes has already been firmly established in earlier passages, and this pulse is maintained consistently only in sequence *b*, so that the groupings of five and seven eighth notes in duration, which occur frequently in the other sequences, create a complex polyrhythmic relationship among the several lines.

Thus, five of the six gestalt-factors of cohesion and segregation are more or less actively involved in the perceptual organization of this one passage, with each of the factors of similarity, intensity, repetition, and even objective set being manifested in two or more parameters. The only parameters that are not involved in this example are time-envelope (since a *legato* technique is the only manner of playing that is appropriate here—there are no *staccato* indications), and—for obvious reasons—timbre. It is likely that some of the differentiations intended here might have been more easily realized in an orchestral or other medium in which a diversification of timbres is possible. And yet Ives has achieved an amazingly high degree of polyphonic differentiation here without this resource—almost in spite of the medium.

The factor of subjective set has not been mentioned in the foregoing analysis, since it does not play any apparent part in the perceptual organization of these sequences. But I have included—at the very end of the example—the beginning portion of the sequence that follows the passage we have been considering because it shows one of the versions of the opening motive from Beethoven's Fifth Symphony that is used in one form or another throughout the entire "Concord" sonata. And while it cannot be said that subjective set modifies the interpretation of the clangs at this point in the music, there are many other places in the piece where the listener's familiarity with the motive does make his perceptual organization of a clang or sequence somewhat different from what it would be otherwise (i.e., if the only factors involved were the more objective ones). I mention this only as a reminder that musical configurations may not always be so amenable to an analysis in terms of such objective factors as have been shown to be responsible for the perceptual organization of this particular example.

In answer to the questions put at the end of section I, six gestalt-factors have been found to be operative in the unification and segregation of clangs and in the perceptual organization of musical configurations in general. These are the two primary factors of *proximity* and *similarity* and the four secondary factors of *intensity*, *repetition*, *objective set*, and *subjective set*. One or more of these factors will be decisive in the delineation of the boundaries of any clang or sequence, and the composer—whether he does so consciously or not—must inevitably bring these factors into play in the organization of his sound-materials. It can surely be no disadvantage to him to be able to exert that "conscious control over the new means and forms" that Schoenberg held to be the desire of every artist. And I believe that a more explicit awareness of the gestalt-factors of cohesion and segregation outlined in this section of the book might go a long way toward the formulation of a meaningful and realistic technical basis for such compositional controls. An understanding of these cohesive factors is only a beginning, however, and in the next section I try to carry the clang-concept a few steps further—into the realm of musical form.

Section III. Formal Factors in the Clang and Sequence

> Then—said Stephen—you pass from point to point, led by its formal lines; you apprehend it as balanced part against part within its limits; you feel the rhythm of its structure. In other words, the synthesis of immediate perception is followed by the analysis of apprehension. . . . You apprehend it as complex, multiple, divisible, separable, made up of its parts, the result of its parts and their sum, harmonious.
>
> James Joyce, *A Portrait of the Artist as a Young Man*, 212

> Now the state, including the shape or form, of a portion of matter is the resultant of a number of forces, which represent or symbolize the manifestations of various kinds of energy; and it is obvious, accordingly, that a great part of physical science must be understood or taken for granted as the necessary preliminary to the discussion

> on which we are engaged. But we may at least try to indicate, very briefly, the nature of the principal forces and the principal properties of matter with which our subject obliges us to deal.
>
> D'Arcy Wentworth Thompson, *On Growth and Form*, 16–17

> It is certain that this aspect of pure theater, this physics of absolute gesture which is the idea itself and which transforms the mind's conceptions into events perceptible through the labyrinths and fibrous interlacings of matter, gives a new idea of what belongs by nature to the domain of forms and manifested matter.
>
> Antonin Artaud, "On the Balinese Theater," in *The Theater and Its Double*, 62

The proposed foundation for a new conceptual framework for musical description and analysis has been based on the premise that musical perception is organized in terms of aural gestalts of great variety and potential complexity and that the question of musical coherence and formal "continuity" must inevitably revolve around the more basic question as to the essential factors responsible for the perceptual organization of any musical configuration—any clang or sequence. A first step was taken in the preceding section by isolating these factors and defining the specific conditions that lead to unification and relative segregation of musical gestalts in general—but this is only a first step. The description of a piece of music must do more than simply draw the "bounding-lines" around successive clangs and sequences. We will want to be able to describe the characteristic features of the clangs and sequences thus delimited and—more specifically—those features that are in one way or another essential to the development of the music and to the musical experience itself. This means that our concern must ultimately be with musical *form* in all its multifarious aspects and at all relevant perceptual levels or temporal scales. But in order to describe the form of a given configuration, it will be necessary to take into account certain other attributes of the component materials of the configuration—attributes that are not strictly "formal" but pertain rather to some general condition or state of these component materials. I shall refer to such nonformal aspects of the sounds or sound-configurations as *statistical* features and to their formal characteristics as *morphological* features, postponing for the moment any more specific definition or justification of these terms.

Consider first what is meant when we speak of the *form* of any sound or sound-configuration. In musical discussions the word is sometimes used to mean something that would more properly be termed "formal unity," or coherence, and is said to depend on such devices as repetition, recapitulation, "return," etc. But this is a highly specialized and I think misleading use of the word. The devices mentioned above are means toward the unification of a piece of music, or a section or part of it—they do not in themselves give it its form. They are, in fact, large-scale manifestations of the factor of similarity, or a kind of attenuated form of the factor of objective set, both defined in section II as factors of cohesion and segregation. But although the very existence of a formal unit or gestalt is obviously contingent upon the existence of *unity*—and therefore presupposes the operation of some cohesive factor—this unity is not synonymous with the actual *form* of the gestalt thus produced.

A second use of the word that is, again, often encountered in musical discussions is illustrated by such terms as "sonata form," "ABA form," "rondo form," etc., which refer to specific *formal types* generally associated with particular styles or historical periods. And although each of these formal types may be characterized by certain intrinsic formal features, common to all examples of the type, and constituting the original basis for classification, they tend to represent, in each case, not so much a form, but a *formula,* and are not, therefore, relevant to the problems I am concerned with here.

I shall not, then, use the word *form* in this book in either of the above ways. That is, it will be used neither as a substitute for *unity* or *coherence* (which ought to be designated as such in any case) nor in the sense of "a form" or *formal type*, whether classified or not. The word has another, much more general connotation that is consistent with the meaning it has in other (i.e., extramusical) fields, namely, *shape* or *structure*, and it is in this sense that it will be used in the discussion of musical form that follows—never forgetting, however, that the application of a concept borrowed from other realms of experience may be no more than a useful analogy, with all the dangers that attend any process of extrapolation from one field to another.

I shall follow the analogy one step further, however, and note that, according to the most common definitions of the terms *shape* and *structure*, the former generally implies a more superficial (i.e., pertaining to "surface") or *external* aspect of form (relating to profile or contour), while the latter (structure) usually refers more to an *internal* aspect, "connections" or interrelations among component parts that (interrelations) are not necessarily apparent "on the surface" of the form—i.e., in its *shape*.

I invoke such standard definitions merely to serve as a starting-point in the task of clarification of terms, which must precede any adequate analysis of the problem of musical form. But they are, at best, of only limited use to us, because they relate more to the visual and intellectual "fields of perception" than to the aural. What must be done now is to discover what these terms may actually mean in musical perception. That is, how are shape and structure manifested in the clang or sequence and in our perception of such configurations? To begin with, we must ask what happens when we transpose these concepts from realms whose primary dimensions are *spatial* into a realm that is essentially *temporal*. The following observations on temporal structure will easily be seen to apply as well to temporal shape and thus to temporal form in general.

I have defined *structure* as involving the "interrelations among component parts," so that the existence of structure in the first place is contingent upon the existence of subordinate parts within a given gestalt. But even at the most immediate perceptual level, a thing can be resolved into parts only when there are *differences* of some kind between one point or region in the perceptual field and another.[14] For a structure that is perceived in *time*, this will mean differences between one *moment* and another—changes in some attribute of sound from one moment to the next in time. It should be evident that, unless such changes occur within a clang, no "subordinate parts" (i.e., successively articulated elements) will be perceived and that if no parts are perceived, there can be no "interrelation of parts" and, thus, no *structure*—in the sense defined above. The very existence of structure in a temporal gestalt would depend, therefore, upon changes that occur within its boundaries and the perception of differences between one part and another that result from these changes.

But although there can be no perceptible parts where there is no change, there *can* be perceptible change without any resultant subdivision into parts, i.e., when all the changes that do occur are *continuous*. And in such situations, though we may not be able to speak of *structure* as such, we shall still perceive a *form* that can only be defined in terms of the parametric changes that occur from one moment to the next in time. What we perceive in this case is that other aspect of form—*shape*—whose temporal manifestation is again based on change, the perception of differences, etc., just as with structure, and which we can (to some extent) represent graphically as an "outline" or "profile" of the variations of some parameter with time.

Thus, it is the differences between the successive elements of a clang (and between the successive clangs of a sequence) that determine the form of the clang (or sequence), not the similarities, although the latter usually constitute the primary factor of *cohesion* in the clang or sequence, as was shown in section II. In the case of a relatively simple clang, the morphological features may be defined in terms of the *parametric intervals* and/or *gradients* between its successive elements, although with more complex clangs, and with sequences, the measure of "perceptible differences" is not so simple and may involve both the statistical and the morphological features mentioned at the beginning of this section.[15] But it will be seen that, even here, the same basic principle is still applicable, namely, that *the form of a musical configuration is primarily determined by the effective differences between its successive parts.*

An accounting of the number of distinct ways in which two elements of a clang may be perceived as *different* practically amounts to a listing of the various parameters of sound—by the very definition of the word *parameter*: "any attribute of sound by which we are able . . . to distinguish one sound or sound-configuration from another." The method of graphic representation of parametric profiles used in the last section should therefore be useful to us in analyzing the form of a clang, and perhaps we can learn something about the musical form in general by applying this method to a specific example. Let us consider a very simple clang—that heard at the beginning of Varèse's piece for solo flute, *Density 21.5*, shown in musical notation in example 14.

Conventional methods of analysis would note first of all the melodic-harmonic aspects of such a clang, which are so simple in this case that a plot of the pitch-shape hardly seems necessary. Such a plot is shown in figure 10, however, in order to illustrate some of the observations that will be made later. As is obvious even without the aid of the graph, there is very little pitch-variation within this clang, the range being only a major second, and the changes that do occur are all clustered near the beginning, the rest of the clang appearing quite static—in terms of this pitch-profile.

A more complete description of the clang might refer to its rhythmic characteristics—two short tones followed by one long tone. Whereas in the pitch-shape there were three different levels (E, F, and F♯), here there are

EXAMPLE 14. Edgard Varèse, *Density 21.5*, first clang.

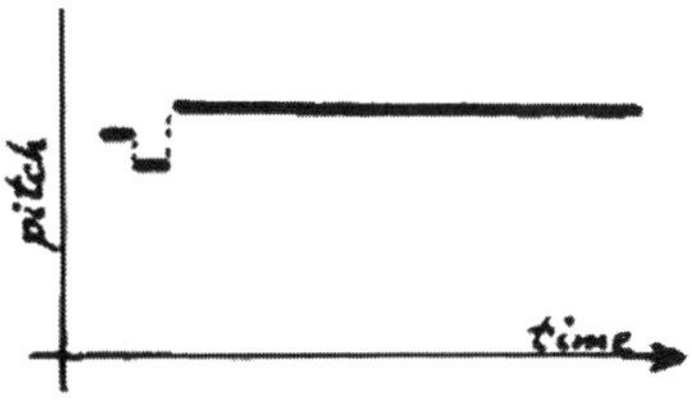

FIGURE 10.

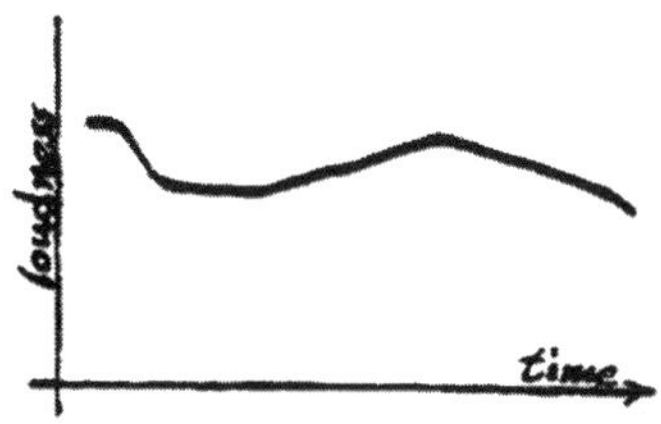

FIGURE 11.

only two, the short tones both having a duration of one-sixteenth of a whole note, but the range of variation between the lowest and highest parametric values here is much greater than in the pitch-profile. Still, the clang would appear to be rather static, the major portion of the clang showing no formal features at all—at least in terms of pitch and duration relations.

But when one listens carefully to a good performance of this piece, the first clang is heard very differently—it has a profile that permeates the whole clang, extending from the beginning to the very end and giving it a very palpable form, which is never static. Obviously, we have still not accounted for the form of this clang as it is actually perceived. And it is probably perfectly evident to the reader that the factor that is responsible for giving shape to the latter portion of the clang—a factor that has been left out of account till now—is the variation in *loudness* that is indicated for the long-held F♯. The loudness-profile of this clang might be graphed somewhat as in figure 11, where the slight accentuation of the first tone—indicated by the dash under the note in the score—is also represented.

It might be objected here that the fluctuations between *mezzo forte* and *forte* in this example are only barely perceptible to the ear, or that the extent of dynamic variation is well within the range of "expressive shadings" normally realized by a performer even in the absence of such explicit directions in the score. But this is precisely the important point—that in spite of the small magnitude of these variations in loudness, the form of the clang as a whole can be profoundly affected by them, acquiring a truly "dynamic" character, a sense of direction, forward impetus, etc., where no other parameter is actively involved. If we are to assume that the perceived form of a clang is a singular, integrated aspect of our apprehension of the clang itself, as I believe we must, we will have to admit that an adequate description of the morphological features of a clang may involve several different parametric profiles—that it will, in fact, involve *every* parameter in which some perceptible change occurs in the course of the clang. And although it means that our description of a clang's form will not have the singularity—as a description—that is a characteristic of our perception of that form, any description will be hopelessly incomplete if it does not at least begin with the simultaneous consideration of all these separate parametric profiles, not just one of them. This does not mean, of course, that all parameters will necessarily be of equal importance in the shaping of a given clang. On the contrary, one of the first things we may discover about the form of a particular clang by such an analysis is which parameter is the most effective in its formation at any one moment or for the clang as a whole. In the example given previously, the most effective shaping parameter at the beginning of the clang is pitch, but this is clearly not so in the remainder of the clang, where loudness becomes the shaping parameter.

When the formal determinant shifts in this way from one parameter to another within a clang, it becomes especially imperative that more than one parametric shape be included in the description of the clang. And this is true not only when we are concerned with the "total form" of the clang as it might be perceived but also when our interest is centered on one aspect of that form, such as, for example, the *rhythm* of the clang. Here a distinction must be made between what I shall call the *explicit rhythm* of the clang, which is associated with the relative durations of distinct elements (whose boundaries are delineated by discrete changes in parametric values), and an *implicit rhythm*, which is determined by the durations from one "peak" to another in the various parametric contours of the clang. When the formative parameter in one part of a clang is not the same as that in another part—as is the case in the Varèse example (where first it is pitch, then loudness)—either the explicit or implicit rhythm of the clang, or both, may become apparent only by means of the simultaneous comparison of the several parametric shapes involved. This is done in figure 12, where the pitch- and loudness-plots are arranged one above the other with parallel time-axes for convenient comparison.

In addition to the accentuation at the beginning, the implicit rhythm of this clang includes a loudness peak (i.e., a point of highest intensity in that parameter), occurring about halfway through the sustained F♯. If the passage is properly played, one should hear some degree of rhythmic impulse at that point, even though there is no break in the continuity of this element.

Another example of implicit rhythm, though it involves only one parameter, is the third clang of the same piece (see example 15). Here again, there is an internal impulse to be heard in the clang—a characteristic implicit rhythm—even though the clang consists merely of a single tone, a continuous *crescendo-diminuendo* being its only "articulate" shape and form.

We have so far dealt with an example in which the determination of formal profile shifts from one parameter to another within the same clang. In many clangs, this form-determining function is given to one parameter only, and it is possible to speak then of a primary formal

EXAMPLE 15. Edgard Varèse, *Density 21.5*, first sequence.

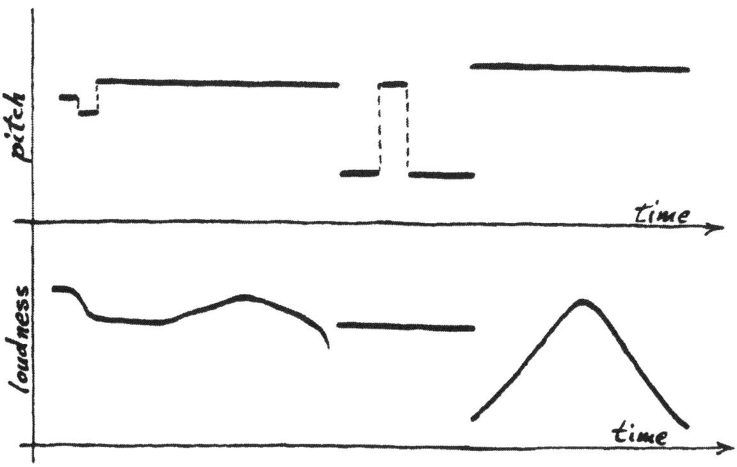

FIGURE 12.

determinant—or *formative parameter*—for the clang as a whole. This will generally be the parameter that shows the greatest amount of variation within the clang—the fastest rate of change—although other, contextual factors may exert an influence that modifies the relative effectiveness of the various parametric shapes from the standpoint of the actual musical impression of clang-form. The thing to be noted here especially, however, is that *any* parameter may function as the primary formal determinant in a clang, given certain conditions that may be illustrated by example 15—the whole first *sequence* of the Varèse piece from which the previous example was taken.

Without resorting to the graphic representation used before, it should be evident that these three clangs represent three different situations with respect to the question of parametric determination of formal profile. The formative parameter in the second clang is clearly pitch, since there is no effective change in dynamic level and very little variation in element-durations (yielding a relatively flat [explicit] rhythmic shape, in addition to the neutral loudness-profile). In clang 3, the determinant of shape is obviously loudness, since there is no variation whatsoever in either of the other parameters, and the objection that might have been raised against my interpretation of the first clang can hardly be maintained in this case. The importance here of the loudness-profile cannot be ignored, not only because the other parameters are constant (or nearly so) but because the variation in dynamic level covers a major portion of the total range of possibilities in that parameter—from *piano* to *forte*—and is no longer commensurate with the ordinary "expressive shadings" of a performer.

The observations that have been made so far in reference to the formal factors at work in the Varèse example relate specifically to shape or profile—and thus to only one of the two aspects of form involved in our initial definition. That is, nothing has been said about *structure*. But it can easily be shown that the same principles apply to structure that have been deduced for shape—i.e., all parameters may be involved in the determination of structure in a musical configuration. Thus, in describing the structure of the Varèse sequence, we would have to note the obvious similarity-relations between the third clang and the second part of the first clang with respect to dynamic shape (*crescendo-diminuendo*), duration (both being long, sustained), and pitch-region (comprising a half-step relation, which is clearly heard as a melodic movement in itself, bridging the gap created by the C♯s in the second clang).

The conclusions to be drawn from the foregoing are inescapable. Not only is it necessary to include all parameters in any adequate description of clang-form; in addition we must assume that *any parameter may function as the primary determinant of form in a clang*, if only because it is possible to reduce to zero the degree of articulation of every other parameter within the clang.

In section II, I tried to show the great functional importance of *similarity* as a factor of cohesion within a clang or sequence. In most musical configurations, one or more parameters change relatively little within the boundaries of any one configuration, and it is these parameters that do *not* change that give the clang or sequence its unity and singularity, the duration of this relative constancy in these cohesive parameters actually establishing the boundaries of each gestalt. If we compare this with the observations that have been made about the determination of *form* in a clang or sequence, some very interesting relationships become apparent. I have said that the formative parameter in a configuration is usually the parameter that changes the most—exhibits the fastest rate of change—so that it can hardly be, at the same time, the parameter that unifies the configuration because of a relative constancy of values. That is, *the formative parameter in a given configuration is generally distinct from the cohesive parameter in that same configuration*.

Furthermore, since the morphological outline of a sequence is determined by parametric differences between the successive clangs in that sequence, a rather surprising relationship emerges between parametric functions in a sequence and in its component clangs. That is, *the determinant of morphological outline in the clang will usually be a different parameter from the one that determines the morphological outline of the sequence of which that clang is a constituent part*. This follows from the principle formulated in the previous paragraph, if the latter is combined with certain other principles developed in section II. There, it was shown that the unity and singularity of a given clang necessarily implied the relative segregation of that clang from others adjacent to it in time and that these two functions (i.e., unification and segregation) are usually served by one and the same parameter—similarities in that parameter providing the force of internal coherence *within* the clang, and dissimilarities (in the same parameter) creating the points of division *between* successive clangs. Thus, the differences between clangs, which determine the morphological outline of the sequence, will generally be manifested in the same parameter that serves as the determinant of *cohesion* within each individual clang. And since the determinant of cohesion—or cohesive parameter—within each clang must be (according to the first of the two principles stated on the previous page) a different parameter from the one that serves as the determinant of form in the same clang, the formal determinant for the sequence as a whole is not likely to be the same parameter that determines the form of each of its component clangs.

Of course, all of the above remarks apply only to clangs and sequences in which the primary factor of cohesion and segregation is the *factor of similarity*. Thus, they would not apply to cases in which the clangs were organized mainly by the factors of proximity, intensity, repetition, objective set, or subjective set.

Finally, one obvious exception to these principles must be mentioned. This is the case in which the formal determinant in each clang of a sequence is pitch, but the range of variation within each clang is limited enough to allow for effective changes of register from clang to clang, the shape of the sequence being thereby determined by these changes of pitch-register. But this is only possible because the total potential range of perceptibly different values in this parameter is very great—greater perhaps than in any other parameter—and, in any case, it can only happen when the range of variation within each clang is relatively circumscribed. The more extensive the range covered within each clang in the sequence, the less perceptible will such changes of register from clang to clang become, until pitch is no longer an effective parameter in the process of formal determination at the level of the sequence.

I have repeatedly stressed the fact that the form of a configuration on one perceptual level is the result of changes or differentiations of some kind from one element (or smaller component) to the next within the configuration, because it is of very general significance in the definition of form at any level—not just at the level of the clang—and is manifested in ways that may not be obvious in the more limited discussion of clang-form. For in the first place, only by defining the form of a configuration in terms of parametric intervals and gradients, rather than parametric values themselves, can we account for the phenomenon of *transposability*, which is a unique characteristic of perceptual forms in general and of sound-forms in particular. With respect to the pitch-parameter at least, it is evident that a clang can maintain its morphological identity after transposition—even though the original and the transposed versions have no single element in common.[16] Similarly, within a certain limiting range at least, rhythmic shapes are subject to "transpositions" (i.e., augmentations and diminutions) in which only the relative *proportions* between the parametric values are maintained, not the values themselves (i.e., the element-durations). And I think it possible that such morphological invariance or recognizability after transposition might be found to hold for the other parameters as well, given as great a precision of control over these parameters as we have had in the past over pitch and duration (a precision only recently made possible for these other parameters by developments in the electronic means for generating and recording sounds), and a reasonable amount of time for our perceptive faculties to be conditioned to such relationships.

I do not suggest here that it will ever be possible to perceive *precise* differences or exact "proportions" between loudness—or timbre—levels. These very concepts may be utterly meaningless from an *aural* standpoint, since the perception of proportional relations in pitch and rhythm is only possible in that they are *periodic* phenomena. But such precision is not necessary to support my assertion here about the transposability of all parametric profiles—if only one is prepared to include less detailed morphological features within the class of transpositional invariants. For example, the *crescendo-diminuendo*, such as occurred twice in the Varèse sequence (example 15), is a recognizable shape, whether it moves from *ppp* to *p* and back to *ppp* or from *mf* to *ff* to *mf*. (In the example from the flute piece, an interval-expansion is also involved, in addition to transposition, but the conclusions will be the same in either case.) This is surely a manifestation of morphological invariance—just as much as is the recognition of a specific melodic gestalt in different registers. The only really essential difference between the two situations is in the relative range of variation in the two parameters involved—the number of different parametric levels that can be perceived, remembered, and correlated in a specific way. But this difference in no way contradicts the general principle suggested earlier—a principle that might be abbreviated as *perceived form a function of perceived differences*.

The definition of form in terms of intercomponent differences has a second application that was not explicitly apparent in the earlier considerations of clang-form. The perception of differences involves a higher-order perceptual process than mere sensation—namely, *comparison*—so that the question as to what factors may be involved in musical form can be translated: What are the essential ways in which we are able to compare two sounds or sound-configurations, either on an immediate perceptual level or on a larger temporal scale, where memory, imagination, reflection, etc. may be at work? When an attempt is made to define the essential morphological characteristics of sequences in these terms, two basic factors are encountered, whereas in the problem of clang-form, one factor seems to suffice. One of these factors corresponds very closely to that which is involved in clang-formation. That is, one aspect of sequence-form (the *morphological outline*, already referred to) can be defined in terms of the changes of *parametric state* (i.e., mean parametric levels) and other statistical features from clang to clang in a way that is quite analogous to the definition of clang-form in terms of the changes in parametric values from element to element. But in the sequence another factor emerges, resulting from the fact that we are able to compare clangs with respect to their *morphological* features, not just their statistical features, and the similarities or differences perceived in this way are an essential aspect of our total impression of form at the sequence-level. I shall return to this in a moment, but first some clarification seems desirable regarding my use of the term *statistical*.

When we speak of the *pitch* of a tone in a piece of music—say, for example, the F♯ in the first clang of the Varèse flute piece—what is it, objectively, that we are referring to? A physicist might answer that this F♯ is a vibration with a fundamental frequency of 370 cycles per second. The instrumentalist who plays the piece might say that it is the sound produced by a certain fingering on the flute and a certain tension of the lips, diaphragm, etc. in playing the tone. Obviously, the instrumentalist is not describing the sound itself but the manner of producing the sound. But neither is the physicist's answer any real description of the sound. If we tell him that "370 cycles per second" is an abstraction and press him further, he might admit that his answer referred to a measurement he might make with a suitable frequency-counting device that registers the *average* number of vibrations per second in the signal resulting from such a tone. Minor fluctuations in pitch, such as constitute *vibrato*, small variations in pitch that often occur at the beginning and at the end of a tone (*portamento*), and (as may happen in a tone played by an instrumental or vocal *choir*) vibrations whose frequency is very near but not identical to that of the average mean frequency—none of these "details" is taken into account in the designation "370 cycles per second," nor is it indicated by the musical notation for "F♯" in the score itself.

If, now, one looks at the very interesting "performance scores" in Seashore's *Psychology of Music* (pages 35–41, 48–49, 200–203, and 256–272), it becomes clear that the "pitch of a tone" is no simple thing in most music and can only be defined as some kind of statistical average or mean value of a continuously variable quantity. In these figures it can be seen that the same thing is true of the dynamic level of a tone. And yet we are generally content to represent these variable quantities by a single quantity—a constant—that is nothing but a statistical measure of the sound in some parameter, and we employ this representation both in our notation system and in our verbal descriptions of musical events.

It might be said that we cannot hear these smaller fluctuations in pitch or loudness, but this is manifestly not so. If our listening is such that we do not hear them, it is not because we cannot do so but rather because *our attention is focused on a different perceptual level*—a different temporal scale—at which these smaller variations are not relevant in the determination of a parametric profile. Such fluctuations in pitch and loudness influence the timbre or tone-quality of the sound, but they do not affect the pitch- and loudness-contours as such. The latter are determined by the large-scale changes that occur and are to be defined in terms of the successive values of the averages or means in each parameter. In general, then, it may be said that the *morphological* features of a clang will be perceived as a function of the differences between the *statistical* features of its component elements.

I suggest now that this relation between the morphological on one level and the statistical on the next lower level is also applicable to the sequence. That is, the morphological profile of a sequence is primarily determined by certain statistical measures of the clangs in the sequence. These measures would include the changes in *parametric state*, or mean parametric values (pitch-register, mean tempo or temporal density, average dynamic level and vertical density, etc.) from one clang to the next, as well as the total duration of each clang, the extent of the range covered in each parameter, etc. The fact that we have no practical way to measure some of these things precisely is unfortunate, but it in no way argues against their potential importance for musical analysis, nor their significance in actual musical perception—and this is the most important

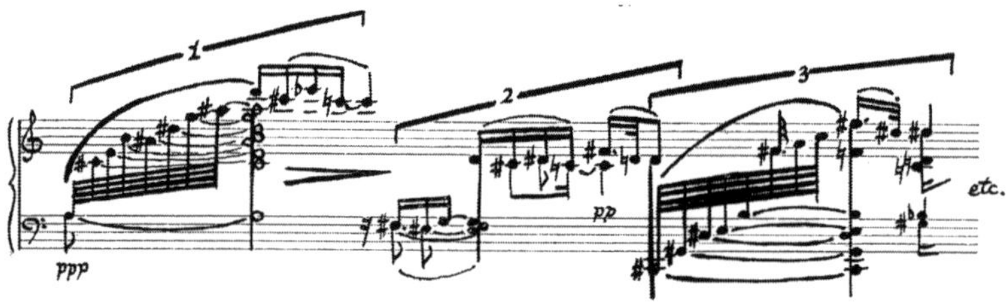

EXAMPLE 16. Charles Ives, "Concord" Sonata ("Thoreau") (beginning).

point, of course. The musical ear *can* "measure" the clangs in this way—and obviously does so—even when the mind of an analyst cannot.[17]

Example 16 should help to clarify these last remarks. It is the first sequence of the fourth movement ("Thoreau") of Ives's "Concord" sonata, the same work from which example 13 was derived (for the analysis at the end of section II of this book). The primary determinant of morphological profile in each of these three clangs (indicated again by brackets) is pitch, but how shall we go about describing the profile of the sequence as a whole? Or, rather, is there a shape to this sequence that is distinct from the clang-shapes themselves—more than simply the "sum" of these smaller shapes? The changes of pitch-register from the first clang to the second constitute one determining factor that is immediately perceptible when we listen to the sequence—a change from a higher register in the first clang to a medium register in the second and third clangs. Another important factor in the shaping of this sequence is the distinction in pitch-*range* or compass between the first and second clangs and the second and third clangs—first a contraction, then an expansion of range—so that the upper and lower boundaries of pitch in the three clangs describe a movement in the pitch-space even when (as between clangs 2 and 3) an "average" or mean pitch-level might not show any such movement. A secondary determinant of form in this sequence is temporal density, in which parameter the shape of the sequence is represented by the change from faster to slower to faster (i.e., from higher to lower to higher densities) in the three clangs.

Each of these clang-characteristics (namely, pitch-register and range, and temporal density)—in terms of which we are able to compare one clang with another and thus describe the changes that occur within the sequence, giving it its morphological outline—is clearly a statistical feature of the clangs, and each is a very real aspect of one's immediate and spontaneous perception of the music. Furthermore, it would not be difficult to find examples of sequences in which marked changes in timbre from clang to clang or in loudness, vertical density, or some other parameter would be the factor responsible for the characteristic profile of the sequence as a whole. Rather than pursue this aspect of the problem any further, however, it should be noted that there is another factor involved in our perception of form in the sequence from the Ives piece—a factor that is quite distinct from and independent of any of the statistical features of these clangs. Each of the three clangs shows a subdivision into two or three parts, and it can be seen that the second parts of clangs 1 and 2, respectively, are identical in *form*, though they differ considerably in pitch-register. Similarly, the last parts of clangs 2 and 3 are nearly identical in shape, and the first parts of clangs 1 and 3 are quite similar in their general upward motion, if not in the particular interval-relations they involve. These morphological relations (in this case, of identity or similarity) between component clangs (or parts of clangs) in a sequence constitute another important factor in its formal characterization and must be considered in any satisfactory analysis of sequence-form.

We find, therefore, that the form of a sequence may be conditioned by two distinct and independent factors, which correspond to the two basic ways in which we may perceive differences between clangs—that, is, to the ways in which we can *compare* them. Two clangs may be compared with respect to both their statistical and their morphological features, and an adequate description of the form of a sequence may have to include both kinds of differentiation, although one or the other of these might be the more important formal factor in a particular sequence. As for the statistical variations between successive clangs, little more needs to be said, since the same observations that were made about clang-form will also apply to the morphological profile of the sequence. I shall merely repeat here the most basic of the principles established earlier in connection with the clang—that all parameters must be considered and that any parameter may serve as the primary determinant of form in a musical configuration.

The morphological relations between clangs, mentioned on the previous page, are the source of a kind of formal characterization that is unique to the sequence, since it is not encountered at the level of the clang to any great extent. One can distinguish three basic types of morphological relationship possible between any two clangs: (1) they may be identical (or nearly, i.e., effectively identical) in form with respect to one or more parameters; (2) they may be entirely dissimilar and unrelated in form (again—in one or more parameters); and (3) they may be partially similar or related in form, revealing or implying some kind of morphological *transformation* by means of which one clang was (or might have been) derived from the other. I shall call the first of these an *isomorphic* relation, the second *heteromorphic*, and the last *metamorphic*, each of these terms being understood to refer to specified parametric shapes, except perhaps in the exceptional cases in which all of the several parametric profiles of the two clangs exhibit the same relation or in which it is clear that only one parameter is being considered.

These designations can be applied not only to successive clangs but to any two clangs, regardless of where they happen to occur in a piece of music. In addition to this, they can often be used to characterize a whole sequence, defining what might be called its *morphological type*—whenever the sequence involves internal relationships of one kind consistently. Many sequences, of course, will include more than one type of morphological relation between their component clangs, and these we might call *compound types*—although a meaningful description of this aspect of sequence-form in such cases would still require specification of the particular relations included in that sequence.

In terms of the above definitions, the baroque sequence would be an *isomorphic* sequence—with respect to pitch, at least. By contrast, most sequences in the early "athematic" music of Schoenberg and Webern are, of course—and by intention—*heteromorphic* in most parameters, though not always. In Schoenberg's piano piece op. 11, no. 3, for example, the pitch-contours and dynamic shapes are nearly all heteromorphic—throughout the whole piece, not just in one sequence—and yet the rhythmic relations (i.e., the morphological relations between the various profiles of the duration-parameter) are nearly all isomorphic or metamorphic, since they can all be related (by way of various kinds of transformations) to two or at most three "basic shapes" heard in the first few bars of the piece. (See example 17 for the transformations of one of these shapes.)

Finally, it is evident that isomorphic relations with respect to that aspect of the pitch-parameter that is independent of octave-transposition (i.e., *pitch-chroma*, as opposed to the more indefinite *pitch-height*), are bound to occur very often in the systematic 12-tone music of Schoenberg, Webern, Berg, and others, although the situation

Example 17. Arnold Schoenberg, op. 11, no. 3, transformations of a rhythmic shape.

is considerably complicated here by the fact that the actual boundaries of the clang in this music do not necessarily coincide with identical portions (or forms) of the series (so that it would be quite possible, in 12-tone writing, to avoid isomorphic relations altogether). For the same reason, the *isorhythmic* devices of early Renaissance music *may* result in isomorphic sequences with respect to the duration-parameter, although they need not. Very often they do not do so, and this is simply because the rhythmic patterns do not always coincide with the gestalt groupings (clangs) that are actually perceived but instead overlap these in various ways.

Isomorphic and heteromorphic relationships represent two extreme poles—two outer limits—of complete similarity and complete dissimilarity between clangs, and it is to be expected that the largest number of actual sequences, and the most commonly occurring morphological relation between clangs, would fall somewhere between these two extremes—within the class of *metamorphic* relations. Different types of metamorphic relation might be defined by reference to the various kinds of morphological transformation that can be applied to a clang, yielding a new and different clang that still bears enough resemblance to the original to be perceived as a variation of the first clang. Such transformations would include, for example, (1) expansions or contractions of the intervals between the elements of a clang (without altering its essential "topological" features—i.e., the distribution of relative maximum, minimum, and intermediate parametric values in the profile); (2) mirror-forms (inversion, retrogression, and retrograde inversion) of one or more of the parametric shapes of a clang; (3) clang-extension or compression by way of (*a*) the interpolation or elision of elements (i.e., *internal* extension or compression) or (*b*) the addition or superposition of elements, or the subtraction of elements (i.e., *external* extension or compression); and (4) permutations of the vertical order or distribution of concurrent elements and even perhaps permutations of the temporal order of elements or larger parts within a clang—although this last is not strictly a morphological transformation, unless the parts thus permuted represent substantial and morphologically definitive portions of the original clang and thus constitute, in themselves, actual clangs.

Examples of such morphological transformations are so numerous in the literature of musical analysis that it should not be necessary to illustrate them here. I have listed them merely to give an indication of the great variety of transformations that may be included in the single category of metamorphic relations—and my list is probably not complete. My primary intention, however, is not to classify but to *clarify*, and the first step in the direction of clarity is the differentiation of a large field of possibilities into its real and relevant parts—which means here the definition or delineation of all essential and independent factors that may be involved in the larger field of musical form.

There is another side to the relation between the form of a sequence and the forms of its component clangs that is not yet accounted for by the above definitions of morphological relations and transformations. The perceptual process presupposed there was—as in the case of clang-form—a process of comparison, but it is clearly a rather abstract, intellectual faculty that is involved, one that is dependent upon memory and imagination. For a given clang to be heard as morphologically related to another clang in these terms means that they must both be "present" to the mind in their more or less complete forms; i.e., they must already have occurred and passed (become *past*) and must be, at the moment of comparison, stored images that are independent of the temporal order in which they originally occurred. This is not, however, the only way in which the form of a clang is perceived, nor is it the only way in which the morphological features of a series of clangs can affect the form of the sequence containing them. This might perhaps be clarified by the following considerations.

The perceived form of a clang must include both a "dynamic" and a "static" aspect according to whether we view it from the standpoint of the immediate, progressive temporal experience we have of this form or in terms of the above-mentioned memory-comparison—which is of necessity independent of the original temporal experience. The first is related to one's direct kinesthetic response, always more or less sharply focused on the immediate present. Each moment defines only itself, and yet each is continually giving way to the next moment in time. On the other hand, although each momentary event passes away to be replaced by a new event, those in the past are not thereby lost to us irretrievably. They may be retained and stored in the memory for indefinite periods of time, during which they remain more or less available for comparison with later events—a process that transcends the purely temporal aspects of the original experience. What this amounts to is a kind of "detemporalization" of the musical images, and—although one should hesitate before calling it therefore a "spatialization" of these images—it has certain features in common with spatial perception. Only in memory can we truly perceive any moderately complex or extended clang "all at once" as a whole—and yet we *are* able to do this in a way that is similar to our perception of visual gestalts. For this reason it does not seem entirely inappropriate to employ such terms as are derived from visual or other realms of experience, such as shape, structure, profile, etc., so long as we recognize that these represent, at best, merely *one* aspect of our perception of temporal gestalts.

For that other aspect of perceived clang-form that is specifically related to immediate, temporal progression, we need other terms that—although they too may have to be borrowed from extramusical fields—will at least relate to the dynamic aspect of the musical experience in the same way that

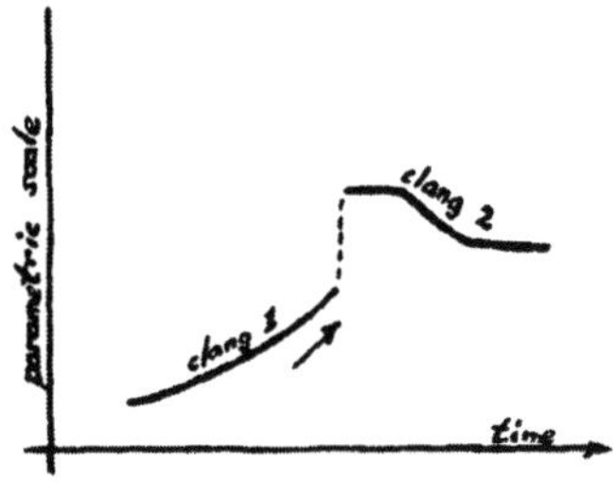

FIGURE 13.

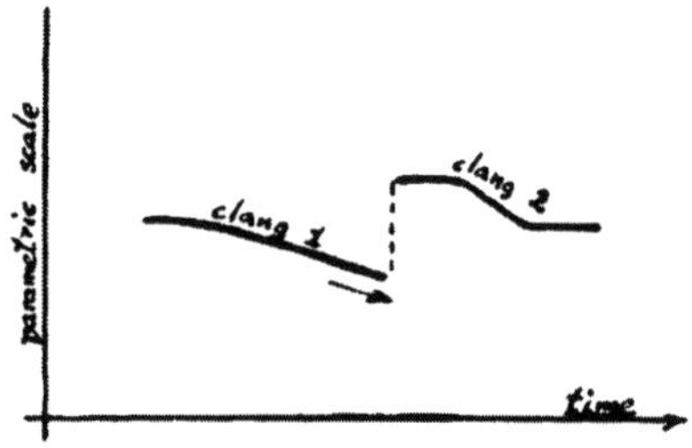

FIGURE 14.

shape and *structure* relate to the static aspect. For this dynamic characteristic of clang-form, the words *gesture* and *movement* seem appropriate. The concept of clang-form would include, then, both shape and gesture, structure and movement, the static and the dynamic—like positive and negative poles of a descriptive field, neither of which can fully represent the total field, although they are both necessary to any full description.

The relevance of all this to the problem of sequence-form may be illustrated by considering one manifestation of the dynamic aspect of clang-form—namely, the *directionality* implicit in a gesture. A conjunction of two clangs in which their gestural characteristics (symbolized by the arrow under clang 1) are related, as in the idealized plot in figure 13, will have a very different effect on the perceived form of the sequence than would the one shown in figure 14. In the first case, the direction of movement in clang 1 will considerably mitigate the discontinuity that marks the break between the two clangs, while the effect in the second case will be to emphasize the contrast between the two—even though the differential intervals between the clangs are the same in both instances (as measured from the end of the first clang to the beginning of the second; if mean parametric values are used as a measure, the interval-magnitudes would actually be in an *inverse* relation to the perceived discontinuities). The essential difference between the two situations resides in the relations between the direction of the *gradient* in the first parametric profile (in each example) and the direction of the *interval* between the profiles of clangs 1 and 2. And in general, it can be said that the degree of effective contrast between two clangs (with respect to a given parameter) depends as much upon the direction of the initial gradient as it does upon the magnitude of the interval separating the two clangs. And this "degree of effective contrast" between two successive clangs in a sequence is the proper measure of sequential profile at that point—supplementing or replacing the simpler measure of the change in parametric state.

I have related this factor of directionality to the matter of clang-morphology, although it seems also to partake of some of the characteristics of clang-statistics—and here perhaps we have a borderline phenomenon for which my earlier distinctions between the morphological and the statistical begin to break down. However, these distinctions have proved useful up to this point in helping to uncover several different factors that contribute to the formal characteristics of the sequence, and I see no reason to abandon them because of the appearance of a factor that pertains to both categories. Such dynamic aspects of clang- and sequence-morphology may, in fact, be interpreted as transitional factors, which bridge the gap that would seem to fall between the temporal, more purely sensory aspects of musical perception and the "detemporalized," mnemonic, more intellectual aspects that are involved in the musical experience. The hiatus between these two realms, which seems to arise so inevitably in most psychologies and philosophies, is perhaps something that is in the nature of the basic attitude toward experience that is involved in such disciplines rather than in the nature of experience itself.

Two further distinctions must now be made with regard to the basic types of sequence. The first of these involves the perception of sequences with respect to the time-dimension, the second relating more to the vertical characteristics of sequence-structure. In section I, the sequence was defined as "a succession of clangs . . . constituting a musical gestalt on a larger perceptual level or temporal scale." Implicit in this definition are (1) some degree of *unity*, though the sequence will be less unified than the clang in perception, and (2) a temporal articulation into distinct parts—the successive clangs—whose own unity and relative segregation within the sequence are determined by the gestalt-factors described in section II. For the most part, the factors responsible for clang-delineation are "objective" in the sense that they can be referred to perfectly objective characteristics in the music itself. That is, they are not arbitrary, and one could predict with reasonable accuracy just where the boundaries of the clangs will be perceived by most listeners. There are certain significant exceptions to this, however, which I shall call *monomorphic sequences*, and these exceptions constitute a class of musical configurations at this level that must be distinguished from the *polymorphic sequences* we have been dealing with so far.

One of the assumptions that must be made in any attempt to describe musical organization and perception in terms of the gestalt-concept is that there are some approximate durational limits beyond which a sound or sound-configuration will no longer be heard as an immediate aural gestalt—that is, it will not be perceived as a *clang*. If the duration of a sound is too short—say, less than one-half second—the sound is not likely to be heard as an individual clang but will become simply an *element* within a larger clang.[18] Similarly, a sound-configuration lasting longer than a few seconds is likely to be resolved into several shorter clangs by the listener and so be heard as a *sequence*. These durational limits obviously vary depending upon such factors as the relative simplicity or complexity of the configurations themselves and upon all the gestalt-factors discussed in section II, so that there would be no point in trying to attach any absolute values to the upper and lower boundaries of this range. But it is evident that, variable as they may be, there *are* limiting regions to the range, and these must be recognized in our definitions.

Consider, then, the following examples, which represent two kinds of monomorphic sequence. In the first, example 18, the sound designated as c (on the third staff) is maintained so long that it cannot be called simply a clang—though the term *resonant clang* would seem to be an appropriate description of its musical character. Its function, as well as its duration, is commensurate with that of a sequence, shaped only by changes in timbre and loudness (changes in the former parameter only occurring several pages later in the score). It is, of course, a subordinate part of the total musical fabric, but this does not concern us here, since the original definitions of clang and sequence did not involve the question of the relative importance of parts but simply the delineation of such parts within the texture of a piece of music.

Example 19 shows another kind of monomorphic sequence in which the changes in sonority are so continuous that the "boundaries" of unit-formations on the order of the clang may occur almost anywhere; i.e., perceptual organization does not seem to be determined by any objective characteristic of the music itself. Yet the configuration is so long that subdivision must occur somewhere, and the groupings that do result will probably be coincident with the rise and fall of each listener's acuity of attention. The musical structure of such sequences is as though composed of an extended succession of elements rather than a succession of clangs, though this is no more than a very imprecise way of describing

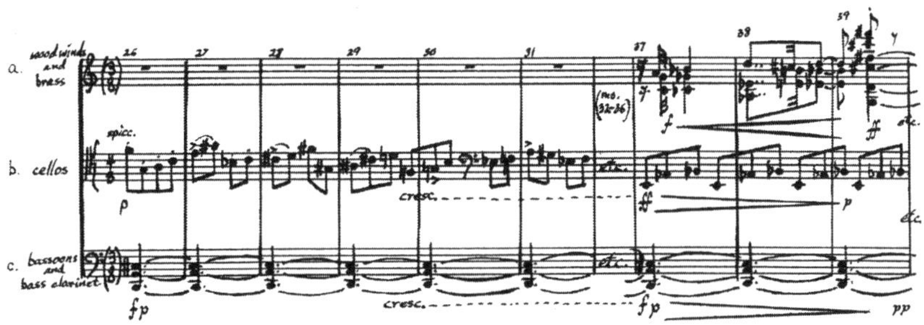

EXAMPLE 18. Arnold Schoenberg, op. 16, no. 1 (mm. 26–39).

EXAMPLE 19. Charles Ives, *Three Places in New England*, III ("The Housatonic at Stockbridge").

the process and does not apply to the type of monomorphic sequence that results from clang-resonance, as in example 18.

In any case, both the Ives and the Schoenberg examples have this much in common at least: they are extended sound-configurations of the durational order of the sequence, in which any perceptual grouping or subdivision into clang-like units is almost entirely arbitrary or subjective, not depending upon any clear-cut objective characteristics of the configurations themselves. This last statement may be taken as the definition of *monomorphic sequence*—a type of configuration to be considered as an exceptional or special case of the more general class of sequences. The typical case, on the other hand, would be the *polymorphic sequence*, and the definition of *sequence* given in section I should be understood to apply only to the latter type.

Obviously, the form of a monomorphic sequence will not involve the morphological relations between component clangs described earlier—but such a sequence will still have an overall *morphological outline* or *profile* determined by the changes in parametric values from one moment (or element) to the next in the sequence.

The second distinction with respect to type and function at the sequence-level has already been made or implied in an earlier part of this book—during the analysis of the Ives passage (example 13) at the end of section II. There a distinction between *monophonic* and *polyphonic sequences* was employed in the discussion, though I did not give any explicit definitions of the terms, assuming that the intended meanings could easily be deduced from the musical example itself. Here I shall try to define these two terms in a way that is consistent with my earlier usage of them, and it will be seen that I interpret them somewhat more broadly than is common in traditional music theory.

By *monophonic sequence* I mean one in which the clangs are perceived one at a time—even when successive clangs are not simply connected end to end but are dovetailed or overlapped to some extent. In a monophonic sequence, such overlapping connections between clangs serve primarily to provide greater continuity to the configuration—to mitigate the otherwise mechanical effect of simple juxtaposition. The sequence is still monophonic, however, so long as the attention is directed essentially to one clang at any given moment.

But if the degree of overlapping of the component clangs is increased to the point where the sequence is no longer heard in this singular way—the attention now being divided or distributed among two or more clangs simultaneously at certain moments—then the sequence becomes *polyphonic*, as in the Ives example studied at the end of section II or the last Schoenberg passage shown (in example 18), where three distinct strata sometimes sound simultaneously. It is not simply a question of increased complexity of the sound-materials that is involved here but rather the use of certain techniques of polyphonic differentiation of these materials by way of the same gestalt-factors of cohesion and segregation described in section II.

A truly polyphonic situation is not necessarily created by the addition of new parts to a texture, because these may simply be absorbed by the others in a succession of clangs that become more and more complex but no less singular. There must be strong differentiations among the various parts for a polyphonic texture to be perceived as such, and since the factor of proximity can play no role here (polyphony implies an independence of parts sounding simultaneously, as was noted earlier), the *factor of similarity* is virtually the only one that can effect such polyphonic differentiations. That is, there must be clearly perceptible parametric differences between the individual monophonic sequences and a relatively high degree of parametric similarity *within* each one before the sequence as a whole can be heard polyphonically.

Twentieth-century music furnishes many examples of this kind of complex polyphony—a polyphony in which each of the individual lines (i.e., monophonic sequences) is itself complex by comparison with earlier music. And yet polyphonic sequences are not to be found quite as easily as one might imagine, considering the prevalence of more complex textures in the music of our time. Ostensibly polyphonic music is often quite monophonic in effect, in spite of its complexity—or, as it sometimes appears, because of it—since what one actually perceives in listening to the music is essentially a succession of single clangs, some more complex (in their vertical structure) than others, but one at a time, nevertheless, as in example 20. Here, the new parts introduced in contrapuntal imitation (in measures 3 and 4) are not likely to be apprehended as distinct clangs. Rather, what will be perceived at each of these entrances is simply an intensification—by means of an increase in vertical density—of the sonority of a single clang.

I do not mean to imply here that such monophony is undesirable, nor even that polyphony as I have defined it is desirable or necessary in music, but simply that one should be prepared to distinguish the one from the other in a way that is more consistent with actual musical experience. I do believe, however, that the developments of a higher-order polyphony of the kind I have been describing constitute one of the most significant characteristics of early twentieth-century music and that the almost limitless possibilities for further development in this direction represent one of the most exciting aspects of music in our own time, the mid-twentieth century.

Unfortunately, a thorough examination of these possibilities would carry me far beyond the limits of this book—as would a more detailed study of many other problems of musical form. A beginning is all that has been attempted here and a provisional outline of possible solutions to the most immediate problems that arise in the study of form in music.

EXAMPLE 20. Anton Webern, op. 5, no. 1 (beginning).

It is probable that many of the most important questions have not even been asked yet, much less answered. And there is no doubt in my mind that some of the ideas presented here will not stand the more severe tests of practical application without at least some modification or revision. It seems to be in the very nature of musical experience to resist our attempts at rationalization and to contradict our theories.

But the final test of any concept—and the only valid source of any rationale—must be experience itself, and a musical theory that does not maintain a direct and vital connection with musical experience cannot be expected to survive for very long. I only hope that the observations made in this book may prove helpful in clarifying some of the problems that concern the musician of today and that they will provide a conceptual framework that is sufficient, in breadth and depth, to form the basis for more refined techniques of musical description and analysis—and eventually perhaps, of musical composition itself.

Glossary

A review of some of the more important terms and definitions.

CLANG. A sound or sound-configuration that is perceived as a primary musical unit or aural gestalt. The clang-concept constitutes the nucleus and core—in fact, the essential "heart and soul"—of the entire "conceptual framework" proposed in this book.

CLANG-RESONANCE. The sustention or repetition of a clang beyond the normal limits of clang-duration (i.e., lasting longer than a few seconds), resulting in one type of monomorphic sequence.

COHESION AND SEGREGATION, GESTALT-FACTORS OF. Forces (or "facilitating conditions") that determine the perceptual organization—i.e., the internal unification and mutual separation—of clangs and sequences. The primary factors are *proximity* and *similarity*; the secondary factors are *intensity*, *repetition*, *objective set*, and *subjective set*.

COHESIVE PARAMETER. See DETERMINANT OF COHESION.

DENSITY, TEMPORAL. One of the seven musical parameters most frequently referred to in this book; a measure of the relative speed of parametric alteration in a clang (or sequence), or the number of successive elements distinguishable per unit time.

DENSITY, VERTICAL. The number of simultaneous elements perceptible at a given moment in a clang.

DETERMINANT OF COHESION. The parameter (or parameters) in which the factor of similarity is manifested in a given clang or sequence; usually the parameter that varies least—maintaining relatively constant parametric values—within the boundaries of the configuration.

DETERMINANT OF FORM. Generally, the parameter (or parameters) undergoing the fastest rate of change—the highest degree of articulation—in a given clang or sequence, being thus the subject of the listener's most direct and acute parametric focus. This form-determining parameter is usually distinct from the determinant of cohesion in the same clang or sequence, since the latter is necessarily constant or nearly so.

DIRECTIONALITY. That aspect of clang- and sequence-morphology relating to a continuous increase or decrease in values in some parameter, yielding an impression of movement up or down in pitch, loudness, tempo, etc.—i.e., on some parametric scale. The term "singular directionality" was also used in section I to refer to the fact that each parametric scale is assumed to have an implicit and "absolute" upward and downward direction associated with it corresponding to an increase or a decrease in parametric intensity.

DYNAMIC. This word has been used here in two different ways. I have sometimes used the term "dynamic level"—instead of "loudness level"—to refer to some value in that parameter, in accord with conventional musical usage. In section III, however, it is also used in the more general sense, vis-à-vis "static," to describe that aspect of musical perception that is immediately bound to the temporal order of the musical experience, thus involving *gesture* and *movement* (as opposed to *shape* and *structure*).

ELEMENT. A component part of a clang that may be either one of several *successive* parts—corresponding to the internal articulation of the clang in time—or one of a number of linear, *concurrent* parts—coextensive with the clang as a whole. Thus, an element might contain smaller elements. In addition, an element is assumed to be an aural unit, as is the clang, the only basic difference between the two being the degree to which an element is "absorbed" into the larger configuration of which it is a part.

ENVELOPE or TIME-ENVELOPE. The shape of the attack and decay forms of a sound with respect to changes in amplitude. As a musical parameter, however, the perception of the time-envelope of an elementary sound relates to the impression of tone-quality or timbre more than it does to the loudness-parameter.

EQUIVALENCE and the "PRINCIPLE OF EQUIVALENCE." These terms are used in section I in reference to the "equal potentiality of any sound being used as a basic [or irreducible] element of a musical idea" (i.e., of a *clang*). It does not mean an equivalence of musical effect or character but a "material equivalence," in the sense that any sound might occur within a clang as an element.

EXPLICIT RHYTHM. The duration-relations within a clang that derive from discrete changes in parametric values from element to element, being measured, therefore, from one *attack* to the next.

FOCUS, PARAMETRIC. The directing of the attention toward a particular parameter—generally the parameter with the highest rate of change or degree of articulation within a given clang or sequence.

FOCUS, TEXTURAL. The directing of the attention toward a particular (linear) part or element within a clang (or a particular monophonic sequence within a polyphonic sequence), usually that element that is the most intense in one or more parameters.

FORM. That aspect of our perception of musical gestalts (whether these be clangs, sequences, or larger configurations) that involves *shape* and *structure*, and *gesture* and *movement*, as its "static" and "dynamic" attributes, respectively. In section II, the statement is made that "the form of a musical configuration is primarily determined by the effective differences between its successive parts." At the perceptual level of the clang, this means the changes in parametric values from one element to the next. For the sequence, two factors are involved, because "effective differences" between successive clangs may be perceived in two different ways. These are (1) as changes in the statistical features of the clangs from one to the next and (2) morphological relations (similarity, partial similarity, and dissimilarity of form) between clangs, yielding in some cases distinct sequence-types.

FORMATIVE PARAMETER. See DETERMINANT OF FORM.

GESTALT-FACTORS. See COHESION AND SEGREGATION, GESTALT-FACTORS OF.

GRADIENT. An approximate measure of the rate of change of values in some parameter when the changes are continuous rather than discrete. A parametric gradient would be specified by a magnitude ("high" or "low") and a direction (positive or negative on the parametric scale).

HETEROMORPHIC RELATION (AND SEQUENCE). The morphological relation of complete dissimilarity of form between two clangs. A sequence in which all the clangs were different in form would thus be a HETEROMORPHIC SEQUENCE.

IMPLICIT RHYTHM. The duration-relations within a clang that derive from the impulses created by "peaks" of intensity in the various parametric profiles of that clang. Since these peaks may occur during continuous changes of parametric values—and thus in the "internal" portions of an element, as well as at its beginning (in the attack)—the implicit rhythm of a clang will be a more inclusive attribute than the explicit rhythm, which is measured from one *attack* to the next.

INTENSITY, PARAMETRIC. In each parametric scale (as described and employed in section II), the higher of two values is assumed to be the one that produces or corresponds to a greater musical or subjective intensity. The measure of relative height on such a scale is then an indication of parametric intensity.

INTENSITY-FACTOR. One of the secondary gestalt-factors of cohesion and segregation described in section II, referring to the tendency of an accented sound to be heard as the beginning of a grouping. The relative intensities of several concurrent elements in a clang (or of several monophonic sequences in a polyphonic sequence) are also a determinant of textural focus. (See page 49 for a more complete statement of the effects of this factor.)

INTERVAL. A measure of the difference between two (discrete) values in some parameter—a meaningful concept even when this difference cannot be specified in any precise, quantitative way but merely in such approximate terms as "large" or "small," "wide" or "narrow," etc. In addition to a magnitude, an interval will also (like the gradient) have a direction (up or down) on the parametric scale.

ISOMORPHIC RELATION (AND SEQUENCE). The relation of complete similarity or identity of form between two clangs (with respect to a given parameter). A sequence in which all the clangs were identical in form would be termed an ISOMORPHIC SEQUENCE.

METAMORPHIC RELATION (AND SEQUENCE). The relation of partial similarity of form between two clangs, "revealing or implying some kind of morphological *transformation*, by means of which one clang was (or might have been) derived from the other." A sequence in which all the clangs were interrelated in this way would be a METAMORPHIC SEQUENCE—probably the most frequently occurring sequence-type to be found in music.

MONOMORPHIC SEQUENCE. A special case of sequence-structure that is not perceived as a "succession of clangs" because "any perceptual grouping or subdivision into clang-like units is almost entirely arbitrary and subjective." This type of configuration is often produced by clang resonance, though not always, and it usually plays a secondary role in the musical texture as an accompaniment or "background."

MONOPHONIC SEQUENCE. A sequence in which the clangs are perceived one at a time.

MORPHOLOGICAL FEATURES. Those aspects of a clang (or sequence) that relate specifically to its form, as distinct from its parametric state or other statistical features.

MORPHOLOGICAL OUTLINE or PROFILE. These terms have been used here to refer to that aspect of form that derives from the changes in parametric values from element to element in a clang, or the changes in parametric state from clang to clang in a sequence. It is assumed to be a kind of synthesis of all the various (single) parametric profiles of a clang or sequence and—for the sequence—is meant to be distinguished from the *morphological type*, which refers to the specifically formal relations between the component clangs.

MORPHOLOGICAL RELATIONS (between clangs) and SEQUENCE-TYPES. General terms that involve the isomorphic, heteromorphic, and metamorphic relations between clangs and the types of sequence-structure that derive from the consistent use of one or another of these relations in a given sequence.

OBJECTIVE SET. One of the secondary gestalt-factors of cohesion and segregation, defined in section II as "expectations or anticipations arising during a musical experience that are produced by previous events occurring *within the same piece*." One of the most effective manifestations of this factor is in the form of *rhythmic inertia*.

PARAMETER. Any distinctive attribute of sound in terms of which one (elementary) sound or sound-configuration may be distinguished from another. Seven parameters have been referred to more or less frequently, namely, *pitch*, *loudness*, *timbre*, *duration*, *temporal density*, *vertical density*, and *time-envelope*. Although these are the parameters most often involved in musical analysis (as in musical composition), the more generalized definition given above leaves room for others that may be relevant in certain cases, such as pitch-range, degree of parametric articulation, etc. These are all what I have called "musical parameters," to distinguish them from the "acoustic parameters" (frequency, amplitude, wave-form, etc.) that are their physical counterparts and source. When the terms themselves do not imply any distinction between the "objective" and the "subjective" correlates of a parameter (as is the case with "duration," "density," and "time-envelope"), it is still the specifically *musical* parameter that is intended—i.e., an attribute that is actually perceived as a part of the musical experience, not simply subject to measurement or abstract determination of some kind.

PARAMETRIC FOCUS. See FOCUS.

PARAMETRIC PROFILE or SHAPE. That aspect of the perceived form of a clang or sequence that is the result of the changes in a particular parameter from one moment to the next in time. Also, the graphic representation of these changes, as employed in section II and section III.

PARAMETRIC SCALE. An ordinal scale—i.e., one that gives a "rank ordering of relative magnitudes of some attribute [involving] the distinctions 'greater than' and 'less than' (indicated on the scale by displacements up or down, respectively), but does not show how much greater or how much less one point on the scale may be, relative to another point."

PARAMETRIC STATE. An approximate measure of the average or mean value of all those in a parametric profile of a clang. It is thus one of the main statistical features of a clang, changes in parametric state from one clang to the next constituting the basis of the morphological outline of the sequence.

PERCEPTUAL LEVEL. This term has been used synonymously with TEMPORAL SCALE to refer to distinctions between the gestalt-organization and perception of configurations of the order of a few seconds or less in duration (for the clang), and those that span longer periods of time and must be much less immediately apprehended as gestalts (viz., the sequence, as well as longer sections and even entire pieces)—though they may be apprehended thus nevertheless, if only by way of higher-order intellectual faculties such as memory.

POLYMORPHIC SEQUENCE. The kind of sequence-structure assumed to be "typical" by comparison with the monomorphic sequence. (See the definition of SEQUENCE.)

POLYPHONIC SEQUENCE. A sequence composed of two or more monophonic sequences. More precisely, a sequence is called polyphonic when "the attention is divided or distributed among two or more clangs simultaneously at certain moments." Thus, the mere existence of two or more instrumental parts in a contrapuntal passage, for example, does not necessarily mean that the passage is polyphonic. By this definition, "there must be clearly perceptible parametric differences between the individual monophonic sequences—and a relatively high degree of parametric similarity *within* each one—before the sequence as a whole can be heard polyphonically."

PRINCIPLE OF EQUIVALENCE. See EQUIVALENCE.

PROXIMITY-FACTOR. One of the primary gestalt-factors of cohesion and segregation described in section II and formulated there as follows: "In any collection of sounds (elements or clangs), those that are simultaneous or contiguous [in time] will tend to form perceptual groups (clangs or sequences), while relatively greater separations in time will produce segregation, other factors being equal."

REPETITION-FACTOR. One of the secondary factors of cohesion and segregation: "If a repetition of parametric profile is perceived within a series of sound-elements, this alone may produce a subdivision of the whole series into units corresponding to the repeated shape, the perceptual separation between the units occurring at the point just before the first repeated element."

RESONANT CLANG. A sort of borderline phenomenon—between the clang and the sequence—similar to the clang in many respects but lasting so long that it functions as a (monomorphic) sequence rather than as a real clang.

RHYTHM. See EXPLICIT and IMPLICIT RHYTHM.

RHYTHMIC INERTIA. A special form of the factor of objective set. It was said, in section II, to involve "a psychological or kinesthetic tendency toward rhythmic repetition—the maintenance of a previously established rhythmic structure," etc.

SCALE, PARAMETRIC. See PARAMETRIC SCALE.

SCALE, TEMPORAL. See PERCEPTUAL LEVEL.

SEQUENCE. Generally, "a succession of clangs that is set apart from other successions in some way so that it has some degree of unity and singularity, constituting a musical gestalt on a larger perceptual level or temporal scale—though it will not be as 'strong' a gestalt as is the clang." This definition refers to the *polymorphic sequence*, (the *monomorphic sequence* being considered an exceptional case, not justifying the more generalized definition of *sequence* that would be necessary to include it). All sequences may be assumed to be comparable, however, with respect to *duration*, if only in that they tend to be longer than the clang, or longer than the normal range of durations within which it is possible to perceive an aural gestalt in one "grasp" of the attention.

The gestalt-character of the sequence must therefore depend upon memory for its apprehension.

SEQUENCE TYPES. See MORPHOLOGICAL RELATIONS.

SET. A psychological condition that may alter or modify the perception of a thing as a result of previous experience. See OBJECTIVE SET and SUBJECTIVE SET.

SHAPE. An aspect of the form of a clang or sequence that is produced by the changes in parametric values from one moment to the next within the configuration. It has sometimes been used synonymously with such words as "profile," "contour," "outline," etc., even though there are obvious differences in the meanings of each of these terms in the realm of visual perception, from which they are borrowed. And none of them can mean quite the same thing there as they do in music—or as they are intended to mean in this book. But it is hoped that they will all connote approximately the same thing to the musician—that "aspect of form" referred to in the definition given above.

SIMILARITY-FACTOR. One of the primary gestalt-factors of cohesion and segregation described in section II and formulated there as follows: "In any collection of sound-elements (or clangs), those that are similar (with respect to values in some parameter) will tend to form clangs (or sequences), while relative dissimilarity will produce segregation, other factors being equal." The factor of similarity is probably the most important of all the gestalt-factors described, because (1) it applies to all parameters (the one in which this factor is manifested being called the *cohesive parameter*) and even to higher-order "attributes" such as shape or form; (2) it is effective at many perceptual levels or temporal scales, from element and clang to whole movements and pieces; and (3) it can function in both the horizontal (i.e., the temporal) and the vertical dimensions and is the most effective factor in the differentiations necessary to any polyphonic texture.

STATISTICAL FEATURES. Overall or "average" characteristics of a clang, such as parametric state, range (in each parameter), and duration of the clang as a whole—to be distinguished from the more specific, formal, or morphological features of the clang.

SUBJECTIVE SET. Another of the secondary gestalt-factors—"expectations or anticipations [arising during a musical experience] that are the result of experiences *previous* to those occasioned by the particular piece of music now being considered."

TEMPORAL SCALE. See PERCEPTUAL LEVEL.

TIME-ENVELOPE. See ENVELOPE.

Bibliography

Artaud, Antonin. *The Theater and Its Double*. New York: Grove Press, 1958.

Cherry, Colin. *On Human Communication*. Cambridge, MA: MIT Press, 1978.

Ellis, Willis D., ed. *A Source Book of Gestalt Psychology*. New York: Humanities Press, 1967 (contains papers by Wertheimer and Köhler).

Joyce, James. *A Portrait of the Artist as a Young Man*. New York: Viking Press, 1968.

Koffka, Kurt. *Principles of Gestalt Psychology*. London: Routledge & Kegan Paul Ltd., 1962.

Köhler, Wolfgang. *Introduction to Gestalt Psychology*. New York: New American Library, Mentor Books, 1959.

Schaeffer, Pierre. *À la recherche d'une musique concrète*. Paris: Éditions du Seuil, 1952.

Schoenberg, Arnold. *Style and Idea*. Edited by Leonard Stein. London: Faber & Faber, 1975.

Seashore, Carl. *Psychology of Music*. New York: Dover Publications, 1967.

Thompson, D'Arcy W. *On Growth and Form*. Cambridge: Cambridge University Press, 1968.

Musical Works Cited and Their Publishers

Bartók, Béla. Fourth String Quartet. Vienna: Universal-Edition, 1939.

———. Piano Sonata. Vienna: Universal-Edition, 1976.

Ives, Charles. Scherzo ("Over the Pavements") (chamber orchestra). New York: Peer International Corporation, 1954.

———. Second Pianoforte Sonata ("Concord. Mass., 1840–60"). New York: Associated Music Publishers, 1947.

———. *Three Places in New England*, an Orchestral Set. Bryn Mawr: Mercury Music Corporation, 1976.

Ruggles, Carl. *Evocations ("Four Chants for Piano")*. New York: American Music Edition, 1957.

Schoenberg, Arnold. *Drei Klavierstücke*, op. 11. Vienna: Universal-Edition, 1910.

———. *Five Pieces for Orchestra*, op. 16. New York: Peters Corp., 1952.

Varèse, Edgard. *Density* 21.5 (flute solo). New York: Colfranc Music Publisher, 1966.

———. *Octandre* (chamber ensemble). New York: Colfranc Music Publisher, 1980.

Webern, Anton. *Fünf Sätze fur Streichquartett*, op. 5. Vienna: Universal-Edition, 1949.

———. *Fünf Stücke für Orchester*, op. 10. Vienna: Universal-Edition, 1951.

———. *Sechs Stücke* (orchestra), op. 6. Vienna: Universal-Edition, 1961.

CHAPTER 3

Computer Music Experiences, 1961–1964

(1964)

I. Introduction

I arrived at the Bell Telephone Laboratories in September 1961 with the following musical and intellectual baggage:

1. numerous instrumental compositions reflecting the influence of Webern and Varèse;
2. two tape-pieces produced in the Electronic Music Laboratory at the University of Illinois—both employing familiar, "concrete" sounds, modified in various ways;
3. a long paper ("Meta ≠ Hodos: A Phenomenology of Twentieth-Century Music and an Approach to the Study of Form," June 1961), in which a descriptive terminology and certain structural principles were developed, borrowing heavily from gestalt psychology. The central point of the paper involves the clang, or primary aural gestalt, and basic laws of perceptual organization of clangs, clang-elements, and sequences (a higher-order gestalt unit consisting of several clangs);
4. a dissatisfaction with all purely synthetic electronic music that I had heard up to that time, particularly with respect to timbre;
5. ideas stemming from my studies of acoustics, electronics, and—especially—information theory, begun in Lejaren Hiller's classes at the University of Illinois; and finally
6. a growing interest in the work and ideas of John Cage.

I leave in March 1964 with:

1. six tape compositions of computer-generated sounds, of which all but the first were also composed by means of the computer, and several instrumental pieces whose composition involved the computer in one way or another;
2. a far better understanding of the physical basis of timbre and a sense of having achieved a significant extension of the range of timbres possible by synthetic means;
3. a curious history of renunciations of one after another of the traditional attitudes about music due primarily to a gradually more thorough assimilation of the insights of John Cage.

In my two and a half years here I have begun many more compositions than I have completed, asked more questions than I could find answers for, and perhaps failed more often than I have succeeded. But I think it could not have been much different. The medium is new and requires new ways of thinking and feeling. Two years are hardly enough to have become thoroughly acclimated to it, but the process has at least been begun.

I want to express my gratitude to Max Mathews, John Pierce, Joan Miller, and all my friends and coworkers who have done so much to make my stay here not only instructive but pleasant. My questions and requests for assistance have always been responded to with great generosity, and I shall not soon forget this.

II. The *Noise Study*, November–December 1961

My first composition using computer-generated sounds was the piece called *Analog #1: Noise Study*, completed in December 1961. The idea for the *Noise Study* developed in the following way: For several months I had been driving to New York City in the evening, returning to the Labs the next morning by way of the heavily traveled Route 22 and the Holland Tunnel. This circuit was made as often as three times every week, and the drive was always an exhausting, nerve-wracking experience: fast, furious, and "noisy." The sounds of the traffic—especially in the tunnel—were usually so loud and continuous that, for example, it was impossible to maintain a conversation with a companion. It is an experience that is familiar to many people, of course. But then something else happened that is perhaps not so familiar to others. One day I found myself listening to these sounds instead of trying to ignore them as usual. The activity of listening, attentively, to "nonmusical" environmental sounds was not new to me—my esthetic attitude for several years had been that these were potential musical material—but in this particular context I had not yet done this. When I did, finally, begin to listen, the sounds of the traffic became so interesting that the trip was no longer a thing to be dreaded and gotten through as quickly as possible. From then on, I actually looked forward to it as a source of new perceptual insights. Gradually, I learned to hear these sounds more acutely, to follow the evolution of single elements within the total sonorous "mass," to feel, kinesthetically, the characteristic rhythmic articulations of the various elements in combination, and so on. Then I began to try to analyze the sounds, aurally, to estimate what their physical properties might be, drawing upon what I already knew of acoustics and the correlation of the physical and the subjective attributes of sound.

From this image, then, of traffic noises—and especially those heard in the tunnel, where the overall sonority is richer and denser, and the changes are mostly very gradual—I began to conceive a musical composition that not only used sound elements similar to these but manifested similarly gradual changes in sonority. I thought also of the sound of the ocean surf—in many ways like tunnel traffic sounds—and some of the qualities of this did ultimately manifest themselves in the *Noise Study*. I did not want the quasi-periodic nature of the sea sounds in the piece, however, and this was carefully avoided in the composition process. Instead, I wanted the aperiodic, "asymmetrical" kind of rhythmic flow that was characteristic of the traffic sounds.

The actual realization of this image in the *Noise Study* took place in three stages: first, an "instrument" was designed that would generate bands of noise, with appropriate controls over the parameters whose evolution seemed the most essential to the sonorities I had heard; second, the large-scale form of the piece was sketched out in terms of changing mean-values and ranges of each of the variable parameters; third, the details—the actual note-values in each parameter—were determined by various methods of random number selection, "scaled" and/or normalized in such a way that the note-values fell within the "areas" outlined in step 2; fourth, these note-values, in numerical form, were used as the input "score" for the music program, containing the "instruments" designed in the first step, and a digital tape was generated and converted into analog form; fifth, this tape was mixed with the same tape rerecorded at one-half and double speeds for reasons—and in a way—that will be described below.

1. *The instrument* (see figure 1). The instrument is designed to produce noise-bands by random amplitude-modulation of a sinusoidal carrier, with provisions for continuous, linear interpolation between an initial and a final value (for each "note") in amplitude, bandwidth, and center frequency. (The possibility of varying the form of the carrier wave was not used in the *Noise Study* because I found that the sounds resulting from modulation of other waveforms (richer in harmonics) had a peculiar quality—more like radio "static" than the sounds I was after.) In addition, for the generator controlling the amplitude envelope (U1), functions other than the linear interpolation function could be specified (in which case the C4 input to U2 was set to zero). In the second half of the tape, two such functions are used, shown in figure 2.

Five of these instruments were used in the "orchestra" for this piece—all of them sounding simultaneously (though they were rhythmically independent) on each tape. Thus, after the three versions of the tape (at three speeds) had finally been combined, the density of independently varying noise-bands was as high as fifteen. Because of the diffuse quality

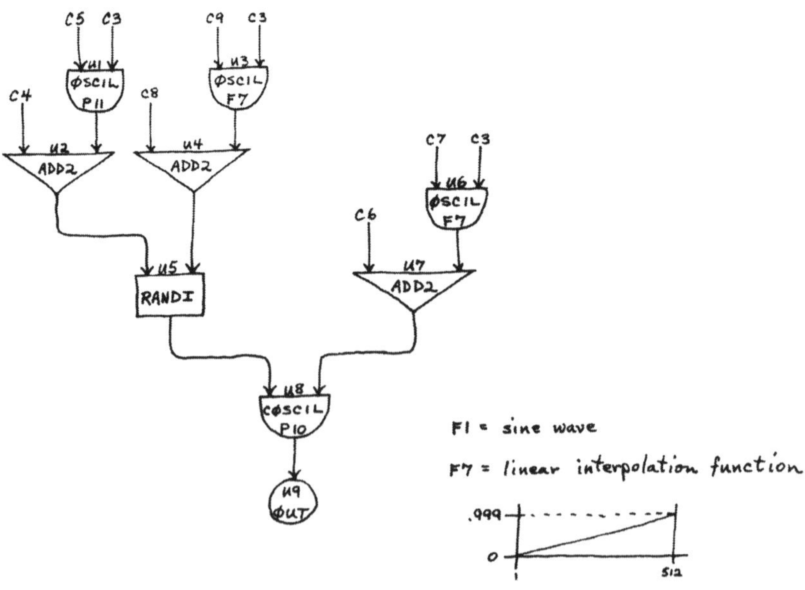

Figure 1. Instrument for Analog #1 — Noise Study.

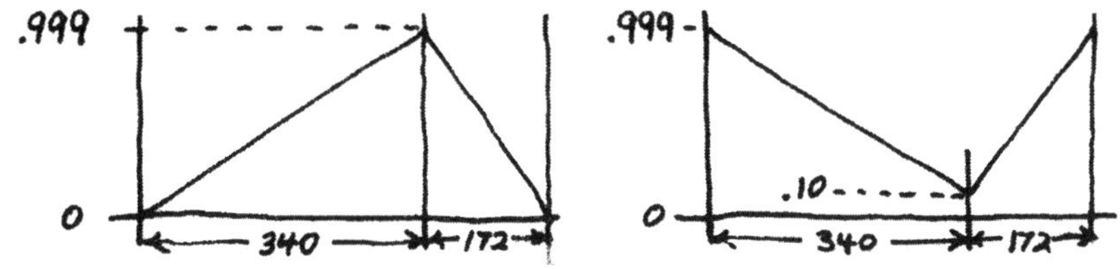

Figure 2. Amplitude-envelope functions for the Noise Study.

of most of the sounds, it is not possible (nor was it expected) that each of these fifteen "voices" could be heard separately. The high density is nevertheless essential to the total sonority, which would (and does) sound perceptibly different with fewer voices sounding (this is one of the reasons why I mixed the three tapes in the final version).

2. *The formal outline* (see figure 3). The piece is divided into five sections, the durations of the sections decreasing, progressively, from the first to the fifth. The piece begins slowly, softly, with relatively wide noise-bands whose center frequencies are distributed evenly throughout the pitch range, approximating a white noise. As the average intensity and temporal density increase (in the second and third sections) the noise bandwidths decrease, until the sounds of each instrument are heard as tones with amplitude fluctuations rather than as noise-bands. The beginning of section 4 is marked by a sudden change to a lower temporal density (i.e., longer note-durations) and wider bandwidths, and a new amplitude envelope is introduced, with percussive attack followed by a decreasing, then increasing, amplitude. During this fourth section the average intensity is maintained at a high level. The fifth section begins at a lower intensity, which decreases steadily to the end of the piece. This return to the conditions of the beginning of the piece is manifested in the other parameters also, except for temporal density, which increases during the last two sections from a minimum (like the beginning) to a maximum at the end. Thus, except for this note-duration parameter, the overall shape of the piece is a kind of arch.

3. *Determination of the "details."* Various means of random number selection were used in this stage, the method used depending on the number of quantal steps in each parametric scale and/or (what amounts to about the same thing) the number of decimal points of precision wanted in the specifications of parametric values. For center frequency, the toss of a coin was used to determine whether the initial and final

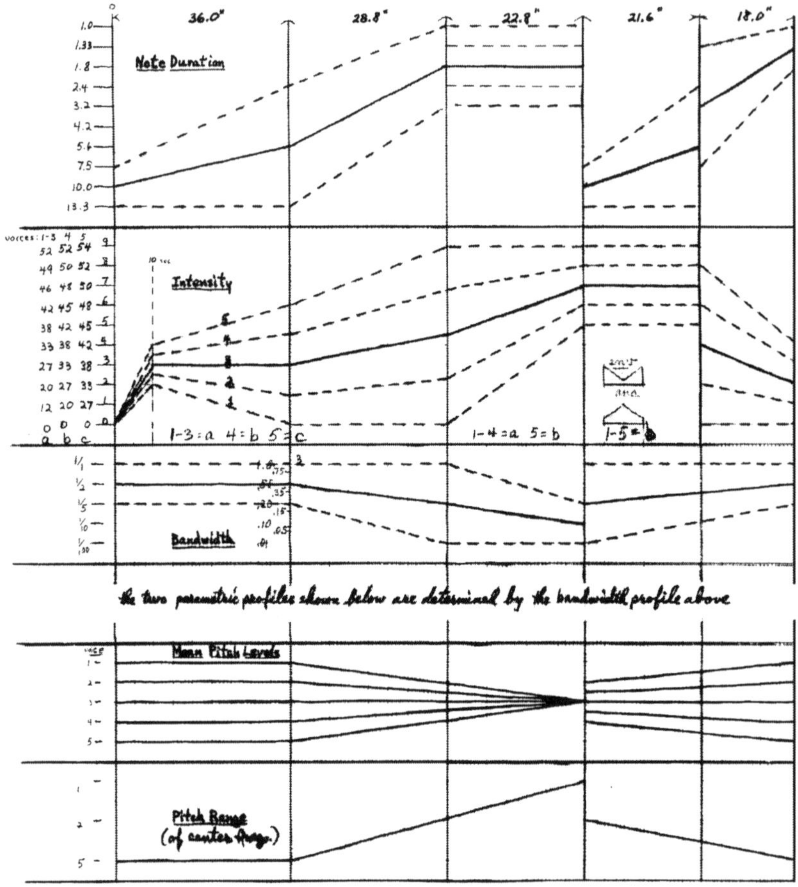

Figure 3. Parametric Means and Ranges in the *Noise Study*

values for a given note were to be the same or different (i.e., whether the pitch of the note was constant or varying). In order to realize the means and ranges in each parameter as sketched in the formal outline, a rather tedious process of scaling and normalizing was required that followed their changes in time. A more detailed description of this does not seem of much interest here, however.

4. and 5. The fourth stage involved the standard procedures for generating the sounds specified by the "score" (as described in my article in the *Journal of Music Theory*, published by Yale University).[1] The resulting analog tape seemed "successful" on first hearings, but later I began to feel somewhat dissatisfied with it in two respects: first, I would have liked it

to be denser (vertically) or cover a wider range of vertical densities; and second, the range of temporal densities (speeds, note-durations) seemed too narrow—the slow sections did not seem slow enough nor the fast sections fast enough. (I was to continue to make this mistake—especially the underestimation of the average note-durations needed to give the impression of "slowness"—for several months. Only in the most recent compositions have I finally adjusted my sense of the correlation here between the numbers representing note-duration and my subjective impression of temporal density.)

After some consideration of these problems, a very simple solution occurred to me that corrected both conditions in one stroke, though it introduced some new conditions that deviated from the original formal outline. The original analog tape was rerecorded at half speed and at double speed, and these were mixed with the original. The entrances of the three tapes were timed in such a way that the points of division between sections 3 and 4 were synchronized, thus disturbing the general shape of the piece as little as possible in the mixed version (see figure 4, showing the temporal-density and intensity graphs of the three strata as they would appear in time). This device, while sure to antagonize certain purists and undertaken with some hesitation on my part, seemed to give me more nearly what I was after—to correspond more closely to the original image—than the first analog tape

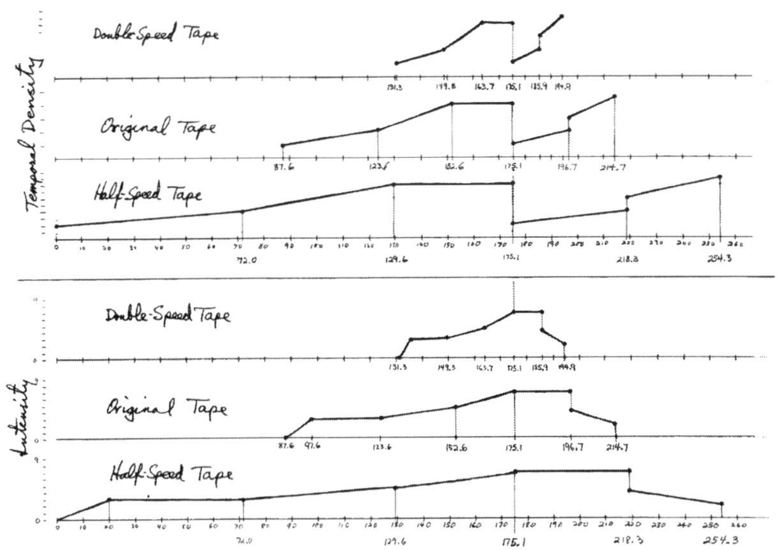

Figure 4. Superimposition of the three analog tapes in the Noise Study.

by itself, and this is its final form. So far, no one listening to the piece has even noticed the repetitions (at different speeds and in different octaves) that resulted from the overlay—though they are plain to my ear and will surely be heard by anyone told about them in advance.

When the *Noise Study* was put on the *Music from Mathematics* record, the recording engineers put it through the artificial reverberation process that is used (with such bad effect, usually) on most commercial recordings.[2] Here, to my surprise, the added reverberation had a very good effect, so I intend one day to add reverberation to the original tape itself.

III. Psychoacoustic Experiments

Between the *Noise Study* and the *Four Stochastic Studies* described in section IV, there was a period of more than a year during which no compositions were completed; a number of pieces were begun or planned, but all were abandoned before they were finished. Most of the time was spent in experiments and tests of various kinds, which will be described here under two headings: modulation and rise-time.

1. Modulation

Early tests served very quickly to establish approximate limits of the rate and range of a periodic frequency modulation corresponding to the vibrato in conventional musical instruments and the voice. I found that, with sinusoidal modulation of a simple tone in the midrange of the frequency scale, ranges of from about ±.25% to ±2.0% (times the center frequency) at rates of 6.5 to 9.0 cycles per second were usable, with mean (or "modal") values for these parameters at about ±1.0% at 7.5 to 8.0/sec. These define the "limits" for the vibrato in this sense: a deviation from the center frequency of less than .25% is hardly perceived at all, while one greater than 2% sounds "rough" (at the fastest vibrato rates) or "wobbly" (at slower rates). At a rate slower than 6.5/sec., the successive vibrato swings are heard as "changes in frequency" as such, rather than "fusing" together into a homogeneous sound (Seashore's "sonance"), while at rates higher than 9.0/sec., the sound is (again) "rough," if the range is wide enough to be perceived at all.

The "optimum" values for range and rate of the vibrato seem to be somewhat different for different people; however, "good vibratos" used by others here at the Labs usually sound either too slow or too wide to my ears, and a comparison of my results with Seashore's measure of average rates and ranges of vibratos in tones of singers shows the same disparity. That is, his singers' vibratos are nearly all either slower or wider (or both) than a vibrato that would sound best to me with the synthetic tones. In this case, the disparities may be due simply to differences of taste (I haven't heard the tones he measured, so I don't know whether they would actually sound poor to me), but it might also be due to differences in other attributes of the tones (the singers' tones were richer in harmonics and had more or less constant formant frequencies, while the synthetic tones I had been working with were usually simpler, and their spectra were modulated as a whole, "in parallel," any formant peaks changing along with the fundamental).

The tones produced with such a periodic frequency modulation were still not very interesting, however (and the reason for studying modulation in the first place was precisely to enrich the quality of the tone in a way suggested by conventional musical sounds). Consideration of the way "natural" tones were shaped (e.g., by a singer) led to redesigning the test instruments in such a way that the vibrato parameters themselves could be made to vary in time during the course of the tone instead of remaining constant. Of the various possible ways of doing this, the one that seemed to correspond most closely to a conventionally "good musical tone" was the result of enveloping the vibrato range so that it built up to its maximum toward the middle of the tone and then decreased again toward the end, as shown in figure 5. Corresponding envelopes on the vibrato rate did not seem to be of much interest, probably because the range of usable vibrato rates is so much narrower than that of usable (vibrato) ranges.

A sort of "mechanical" quality still persisted in these tones, however, and in order to overcome this I began to experiment with random frequency modulation, both with and without some amount of periodic modulation. The nature of the interpolating random number generator is such that, in order to give the impression of a modulation of a range and rate similar to the periodically modulated tone, higher values in both parameters are necessary (±.5 to 2.0% at 16 to 20/sec.). Using random modulation by itself produces an interesting tone, but it does not sound like a conventional "musical tone" with normal vibrato. The combination of random and periodic modulation, with enveloping on

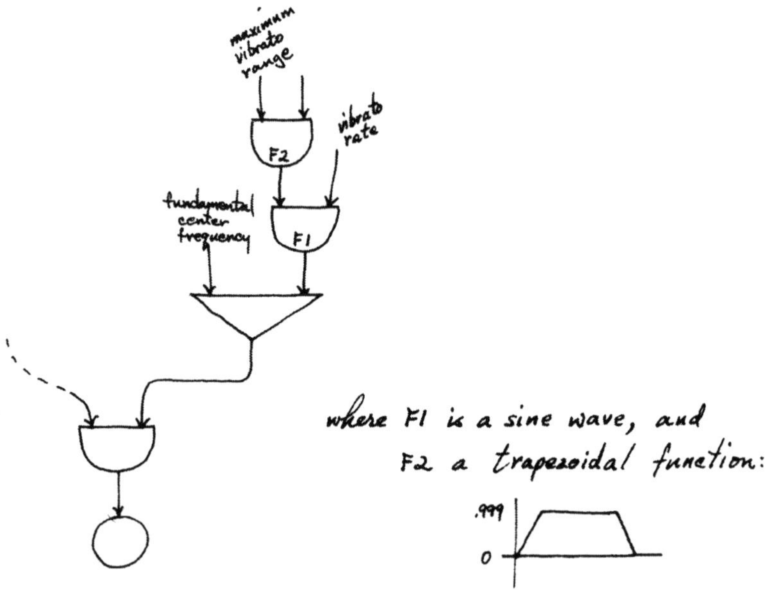

Figure 5. Enveloped vibrato-range

the ranges of each (as described above), does, however, produce an effect so "realistic" that I felt I had achieved one of the partial goals I had set for myself in these tests when I heard the results. The relative proportion of the range allotted to the two modulation sources does not seem to make very much difference, just so long as there is a "perceptible" amount of each and the sum of the two ranges does not exceed the range considered "good" for a periodic modulation above (about .5 + .5 = 1.0% in my work).

With amplitude modulation, I found that the effect of a periodic modulation was not very interesting and did not even seem to be needed with the more interesting random amplitude modulation to simulate the kind of fluctuations of amplitude that give "life" to most instrumental and vocal sounds. Only with such sounds as those of the flute, vibraphone, and bell does a periodic modulation of amplitude seem perceptually important.

The useful ranges and rates of random amplitude modulation are from about ±15 to ±50% (times the mean amplitude) at rates of from about 4 to 30 per second. The wider ranges given reflect the greater size of the DLs for amplitude (by comparison with those for frequency), but the greater range of AM *rates* requires some explanation.[3]

Our perception of amplitude apparently differs from the perception of frequency in such a way that the condition of "fusion" or "sonance" does not apply here. That is, the very slow rates (4 to 6/sec.) are heard simply as a kind of amplitude envelope on the tone, giving it shape, not felt as a "deviation" in its primary characteristics. The faster rates (12 to 30/sec.) are, at the same time, quite usable for the production of "good" tone, provided that the range of AM used is small enough to avoid "roughness." Thus, there is a kind of reciprocal relation between the range and rate of amplitude modulation that will produce a tone of ordinary "musical" character: narrow ranges with faster rates, and slower rates with wider ranges. (This reciprocal relation was later built into the PLF 3 composing program, described in section IV.) Since the AM range is automatically enveloped in the computer instrument, along with the main amplitude of the tone, it was not found necessary to envelope the AM range in any additional way (corresponding to that used with FM).

When random amplitude modulation is applied to the synthesized tone along with the combination of periodic and random frequency modulations already described, the result is a quality of tone that compares very favorably with that of a tone produced by a conventional musical instrument; it no longer seems "mechanical," "lifeless," "electronic," and so on, adding that element of richness to the computer sounds that I had so long felt necessary. Since these experiments, every instrument I have designed—with the intention of producing interesting tones—employed these modulations. Figure 6 shows a typical instrument in which these modulations are all used.

The modulations effected by such an instrument (as diagrammed in figure 6) are applied to the signal waveform as a whole, so that all spectral components will be modulated together, synchronously. This is an artificial condition, and I was interested to discover whether independent modulations of spectral components would enrich the tones still further. This was found to be so, but the differences were really quite small, while the generating time was considerably increased, and I have not used such independent modulations in actual compositions primarily for this (economic) reason.

Among the various ways that spectral components may be made independent with respect to modulation, the simplest one to work with breaks

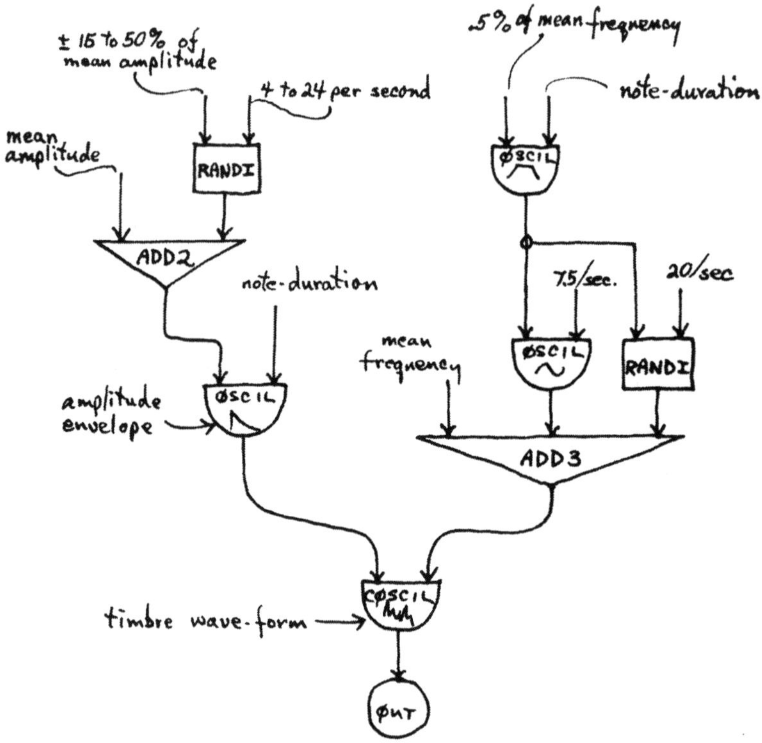

Figure 6. Instrument with slight random modulations.

the tone up into two parts, one including odd partials only, the other even partials. The periodic frequency modulation is common to both, but the random modulations are independent. Such a tone sounds as rich as one divided into three groups of partials in various ways, so I conclude that no more than two groups are necessary. Care must be taken, though, that the range of the random frequency modulations is not too wide, because this can result in a sound like the "mistuned unison" of two instruments playing together but only approximately in tune. (Of course, if such an effect is wanted, this is a relatively easy way to get it.)

With larger values of range and/or rate for the random generators in figure 6, the result will be a band of noise, with relative amplitude and bandwidth depending on the input parameters. Thus, increasing the AM rate will produce a noise-band of increasing bandwidth that is centered at the tonal frequency and superimposed on the tone, as shown in figure 7,

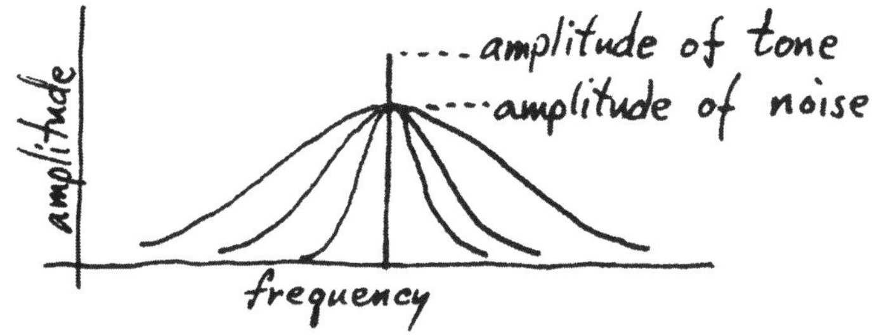

Figure 7. Noise spectra produced by random amplitude modulation.

where the relative amplitude of the noise is determined by the right-hand or "M" input to the random generator U1 in figure 6. If A1 of U2 is set to zero, this pure tonal component is removed, and only the noise-band remains.

With frequency modulations, the relations between the input settings and the characteristics of the noise-band are different, as described in my *Journal of Music Theory* article. Here, the bandwidth of the noise depends primarily on the range of the FM (rather than on the rate, as with AM), while the rate of the FM has an effect on the quality of the sound that is difficult to describe, though the differences are quite perceptible, at least among the relatively slower rates (at fast rates they are not so easily perceptible). Roughly, however, they are this: for a given random FM range (= bandwidth), the slower rates (30–100) result in a greater "roughness," the sound becoming "smoother" (more homogeneous) as the rate is increased.

Acoustic analyses of both speech and singing have shown that there are irregular fluctuations of period-length (frequency) at rates as high as the mean fundamental frequency of the tone itself, though these fluctuations may cover only a very narrow range. In addition, experiments have shown that such fluctuations—in the case of speech at least—are essential to "naturalness" of the speech sounds. They contribute a kind of "noisy" character to the sounds, but the noise is of a very narrow bandwidth, and it is very probable that the timbres of many conventional musical instruments are characterized by similar, fast, narrow, quasi-random modulations. For reasons of economy, again, I have not made use of such modulations in my compositions yet, but I suspect that any attempts to simulate the sounds of conventional musical instruments would find these necessary, in addition to the slower modulations I have described (and used).

The noises that can be produced by an instrument like that drawn in figure 6 are centered around the frequency of the tone, as specified by A1 of U7, or around integral multiples of that frequency (harmonics). In order to generate sounds in which the noise component has a center frequency different from that of the tone, a more complex instrument design would be necessary.

2. *The Rise-Time of a Tone*

Instead of describing this work here, I am including, among other articles I have written here at the Labs, the paper given at a meeting of the Acoustical Society in May 1962.[4] The following remarks will assume a reading of that paper or at least of the conclusions.

In retrospect, several things need to be said about the rise-time experiment. It has gradually become evident that musical context has such a powerful effect on the differential perception of rise-time and other parameters that the results of an experiment like this one are of very little use musically. I find that in most actual musical situations, I can distinguish—at most—about three rise-times: "short," "medium," and "long." Furthermore, I find the use of a scale of discrete steps in any parameter no longer necessary and of much less interest than the use of a continuous scale, letting the ear of the listener do the "quantizing." This the listener's ear will do anyway, so it is a question simply of lessening the disparity between the process of composition and that of listening. One result of the experiment is useful, however: the implication of an approximately logarithmic (rather than linear) spacing on the continuum of perceived rise-times. Nearly all the parametric continua relevant to sounds show this logarithmic condition, and my later composing programs have treated them in this way.

It is questionable whether such tests as the one described, carried out in very artificial laboratory conditions and divorced from any musical context, can ever be of much use to the composer. And for this reason, primarily, I have not done any more experiments of this kind. Instead, I have tried to gain an understanding of such physical to psychological correlations more directly by listening to the sounds in a musical context.

What this approach lacks in precision (and sometimes, unfortunately, communicability), it more than makes up for in efficiency. Only after giving up all intentions of dealing with these problems in the strict ways of the psychophysical laboratory has it been possible for me to produce compositions with any degree of fluency.

IV. *Four Stochastic Studies* and *Dialogue*

If I had to name a single attribute of music that has been more essential to my esthetic than any other, it would be variety. It was to achieve greater variety that I began to use random selection procedures in the *Noise Study* (more than from any philosophical interest in indeterminacy for its own sake), and the very frequent use of random number generation in all my composing programs has been to this same end. I have tried to increase this variety at every gestalt "level"—from that of small-scale fluctuations of amplitude and frequency in each sound (affecting timbre), to that of extended sequences of sounds—and in as many different parameters of sound as possible (and/or practicable). The concept of entropy has been extremely useful as a descriptive "measure" of variety, and several important laws of musical structure have been derived in terms of entropy relations (see the memo "On Certain Entropy Relations in Musical Structure" included with my articles).[5] The composing programs described below represent various attempts to combine the clang concept developed in "Meta ≠ Hodos" with more recent ideas about these entropy relations and stochastic processes in general.

During the spring and summer of 1962 I designed several very elaborate instruments that generated, automatically, random sequences of tones. This was done by means of the RANDH noninterpolating random number generator, modulating very long "notes."[6] Figure 8 shows such an instrument, in which note-duration, amplitude, and frequency are all varying randomly (on linear scales, note!). Tests with these instruments produced results that were quite interesting to me, but it was not very efficient to use the compiler itself for these operations. It became clear that programming facilities were needed that would make it possible to derive a computer "score" from another *composing* program, maintaining a separation between the compositional procedures and the actual sample-generation. In October 1962, Max Mathews

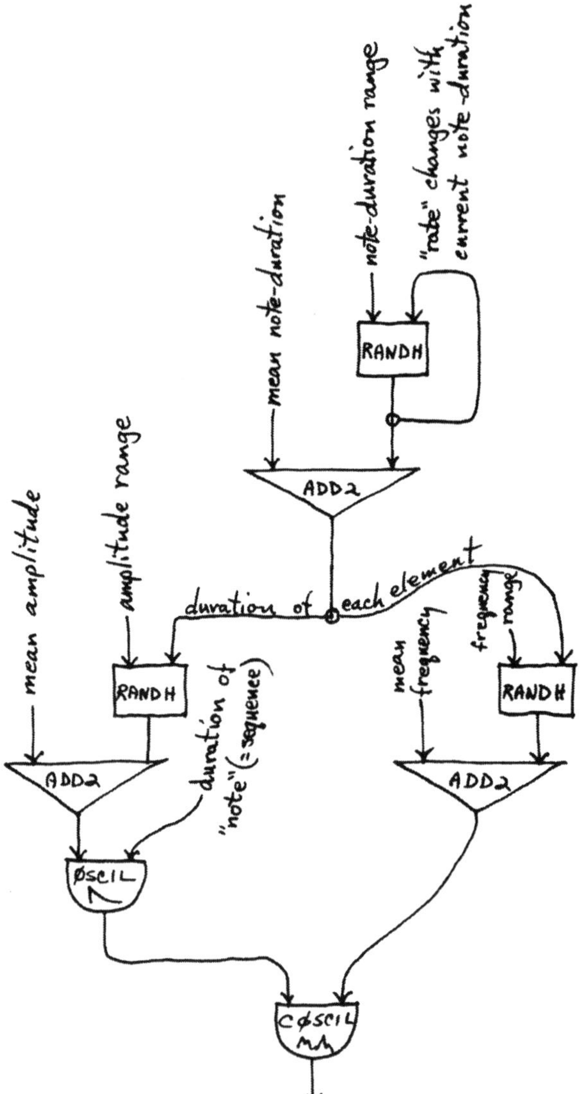

Figure 8. Instrument for generating random sequences.

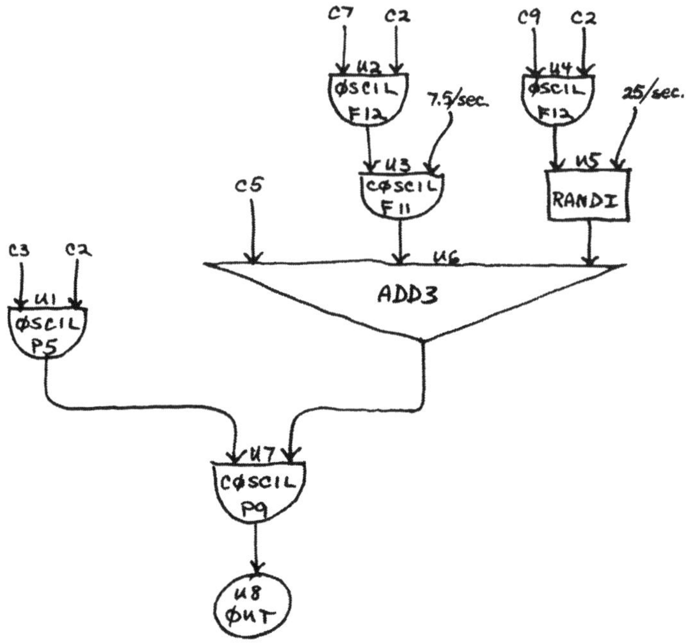

Figure 9. Instrument-design for use with PLF-2 ("Four Stochastic Studies").

completed the subroutines necessary for linking such composing programs to the compiler and helped me write my first "Stochastic Music" program (PLF 2).[7]

The conditions I wanted to be incorporated into this program were these: three parameters (note-duration, amplitude, and frequency) were to vary randomly from note to note, but the mean-value and range of deviation around this mean was to change (also in a quasi-random way) after every second or two (i.e., from clang to clang). In addition, in each clang, at least one of the three parameters should be variable over its entire range, whereas the other parameters might be varying (temporarily) over a narrower range. No further constraints were placed on the process.

Accordingly, the input data to this program included lists of nine "states"—means and ranges (on log scales)—for each parameter, the first state listed being the one with maximum range. In addition, the following data were specified: the number of clangs to be generated in the computer run; the minimum and maximum durations of clangs

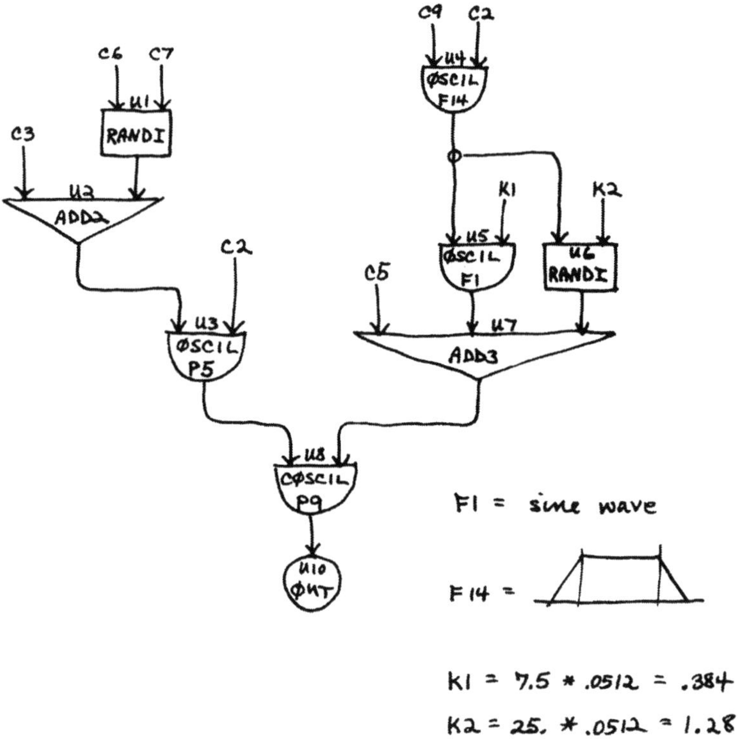

Figure 10. Instrument-design for use with PLF-3 ("Dialogue" and "Ergodos I").

(actual durations of successive clangs varied randomly within these limits); the number of voices to be generated in the clang; the probability of notes (vs. rests) occurring in each voice; and the range of frequency modulation for each voice. The instrument used is shown in figure 9.

The program was run with various settings for clang-duration, number of voices, and note-probability, and these tapes were later edited, becoming the *Four Stochastic Studies*. Much was learned from this first program, and each later program became more elaborate as it incorporated more refinements—greater flexibility, more precise controls, and so on. However, these stochastic studies are remarkably interesting considering the simplicity of the program itself. I was well pleased with the results while anxious to experiment with more elaborate compositional procedures.

One refinement, especially, seemed desirable. This was to make it possible to vary the large-scale mean-values in each parameter so that some sense of "direction" could be given to longer sequences while still allowing the smaller details to vary randomly. In order to do this and other things to be mentioned later, a new program (PLF 3) was written whose input data included, for each section, initial and final values of the mean and two ranges in each parameter. The program first interpolates between the two values for the mean, according to the starting time of the clang in the section, then computes the clang-mean by adding to or subtracting from this mean a random number within the (first) specified range, and finally computes the successive note-values within the (second) range (around the clang-mean). The instruments used with PLF 3 were as diagrammed in figure 10 and were designed to produce either tones or noise-bands. The probability of a sound being a noise (vs. a tone) is given among the input data. Three more parameters are variable in PLF 3 besides duration, amplitude, and frequency. These are amplitude-modulation rate (which becomes noise bandwidth for faster rates), amplitude-envelope function-number, and waveform function-number. The two types of stored functions are arranged in arbitrary "scales" and controlled in essentially the same way the other parameters are. (The arrangement of the function-number scales is not entirely arbitrary: for waveform, the spectra with more energy in the lower harmonics were given the lower scale-values, and for amplitude-envelope, those with the shorter rise-times were given the lower values. Thus, a sequence could change, gradually, from less to more "penetrating" and/or "percussive" timbres, for example.) The PLF 3 subroutine was written in December 1962, but the first composition (*Dialogue*) employing it was not completed until April 1963, because another project was begun that had to be finished very quickly. This was the string quartet program, described in section V. *Dialogue* was originally planned as a two-channel piece, with tones in one channel and noise-bands in the other. When the two tapes had been generated, however, I found the fixed correlation between timbre and stereophonic position disturbing, so the two tapes were rerecorded into a single channel. The form of the piece is graphed in figures 11a and 11b, which show the evolution of the large-scale mean-values in each of the six parameters, as well as rest- and noise-probabilities and vertical density (number of voices generated per clang).

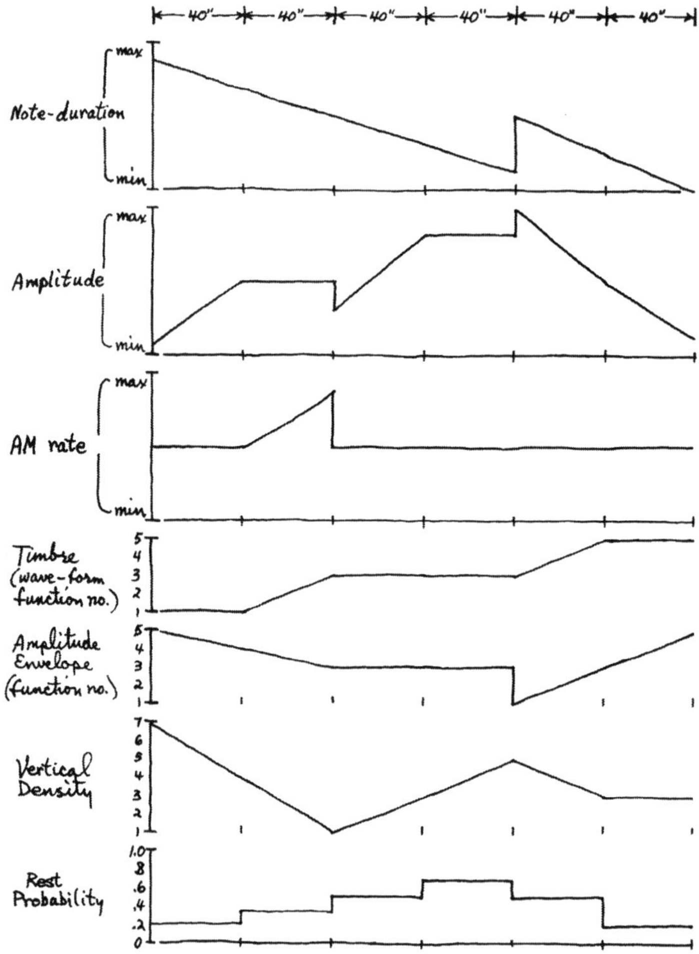

Figure 11a. Parametric Means for "Dialogue" (tonal stratum).

V. The *Stochastic String Quartet*

In December 1962 I received a request for a computer-composed piece to be played by instruments (the request came from the Paganini String Quartet in Los Angeles, who were to play the music on a special program celebrating "Science and Music" in February 1963). Previously, such a use of the computer had only been attempted by Hiller at the University of Illinois (the *Illiac Suite*).

One problem was involved that had not arisen in my earlier work with tape: how to quantize the various parameters of the sounds and

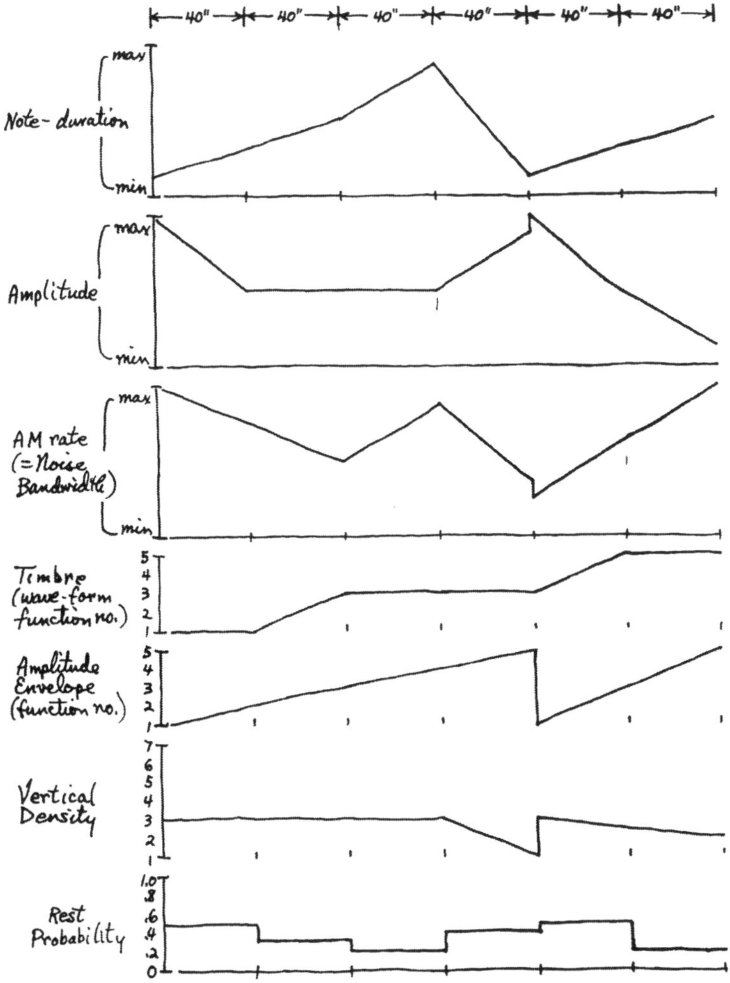

Figure 11b. Parametric Means for "Dialogue" (noise stratum).

print out the information in a way that could be transcribed into conventional musical notation. For most parameters, this problem was not great: pitches could be represented by integral numbers (of semitones, from the cello's low C), dynamic levels by numbers from 1 (*ppp*) to 8 (*fff*), and other parameters could be encoded similarly. The real problem was time. With computer-generated sounds, I could deal with seconds and fractions of a second on a virtually continuous scale, with no necessary "rational" relationship between one note-duration and another. Conventional musical notation does not deal with time in this way, however, but rather in terms of measures that are integral multiples of a basic metrical unit duration, which may be subdivided, in turn, into various integral numbers of smaller units.

In order to achieve as much variety as possible within this system, I used the following procedure:

1. the duration of the metrical unit for the section is read from a card (giving the "tempo");
2. the duration of each clang is computed as some integral multiple of this metrical unit duration (random within certain limits);
3. this clang-duration is next divided into some (limited random) number of "gruppetto" units,[8] which may or may not equal the number of basic "metrical" units;
4. each of these secondary gruppetto units is further subdivided into from one to three or four parts, yielding the (current) minimum possible note-value;
5. from the mean-value and range of note-durations (computed along with corresponding values in other parameters for the clang as a whole earlier in the program), a minimum and a maximum note-duration are computed;
6. for each note, the program steps through the smallest units, increasing the note-duration accumulatively, from the beginning to the end of the clang, testing the new duration after each addition; if the duration of the note is less than the minimum duration (described in number 5 above), another increment is added to it, and it is tested again; if the duration is equal to or greater than the minimum but less than the maximum duration for a note in that clang, the duration may be incremented or not (randomly, but with equal probability of either); if it is incremented, an indication that the note is "tied over" to the next unit is printed out; if it is not, the parameters for that note are printed out, and the program begins to compute a new note; finally, if the duration is equal to or greater than the maximum duration, the note-parameters are of course printed out, as above. This process continues until all the subdivisions of each gruppetto unit, and all the gruppetto units themselves, for the clang have been used up for a given voice, and the next voice in the clang is computed.

The printout showed the number of metrical units in the clang, the number of gruppetto units, and of the smaller unit in that gruppetto unit on which the note ended, and the transcription into musical notation was made using this information.[9] Transcription turned out to be an exceedingly tedious process, however. In addition, the music was quite difficult to play (though no more difficult than some of Schoenberg's or Ives's music), and the Paganini Quartet ended up playing only a few pages of it. Later, the piece received a "reading" at the Bennington Composers' Conference, though the players refused to play the piece on the program it had been scheduled for. In the course of writing this program, another program was written that enabled the computer to read the "score" of the quartet and generate a tape version of the piece. The design of the computer "instruments" was done too quickly to make possible any very convincing simulation of the sounds of the ("real") stringed instruments, but the general rhythmic and textural character of the piece can be judged from this synthesized tape.

Since this first quartet was completed I have twice begun a new program for instrumental music and twice abandoned the work before a piece was finished. The reasons for this were not clear to me until recently and involve not only the experiences in writing the programs and listening to the (synthetic) results on tape but also the experiences in trying to get string players to play the first quartet and other, more general changes in my musical attitudes in these last several months.

In the first quartet the complexities of the notated parts were such that a string player would have had to practice his or her part diligently, and even then the ensemble would probably have needed a conductor to keep it together. Now if every detail in the score were part of some "musical idea" (in a nineteenth-century sense) that needed to be realized precisely, such a situation might be justified. But this was not the case. Each detail in the score was the result of a random selection process that was being used only to ensure variety and might thus have been—within limits—anything else than what it was and still have fulfilled the conditions I had set up in the beginning. (At Bennington, I tried to explain this and to assure the players that their "best approximation" to the part as notated was really sufficient. But the very appearance of the score itself contradicted me!) Thus, it began to be clear to me that there was an enormous disparity between ends and means in such a piece, and I have more recently tried to find a way to get that variety—in the "human," instrumental situation—in ways more appropriate to the situation itself, in terms of the relationship between what the player sees and what he or she is expected to do.

Another problem arose with this quartet that has led to changes in my thinking and my ways of working and may be of interest here. Since my earliest instrumental music (*Seeds*, in 1956), I have tended to avoid repetitions of the same pitch or any of its octaves before most of the other pitches in the scale of twelve have been sounded. This practice derives not only from Schoenberg and Webern and twelve-tone or later serial methods but may be seen in much of the important music of the century (Varèse, Ruggles, etc.). In the programs for both the *Stochastic String Quartet* and *Dialogue*, steps were taken to avoid such pitch repetitions, even though this took time and was not always effective (involving a process of recalculation with a new random number when such a repetition did occur, and this process could not continue indefinitely). In the quartet, a certain amount of editing was done, during transcription, to satisfy this objective when the computer had failed.

But several things about all this began to bother me: (1) it represented a kind of negative aspect of a process that was supposed to make "everything" possible; (2) it was a constraint applied only to one parameter—pitch—whereas almost all the other operations in the program were common to all parameters; and finally, (3) it used up a lot of computer time that might have been used to make more music rather than less. Also, I had noticed that in the *Dialogue*, where the pitches are selected from a continuous scale (as opposed to the quantized scale of the *Stochastic String Quartet*), the pitch repetitions (two pitches within a very small interval of each other or of one's octave) that got by the exclusion-process in the program did not seem to decrease the variability of the music or interrupt the flow in the way they did in the quartet. This suggested that the unison-octave avoidance was needed only when the pitch-scale was quantized as traditionally—only, that is, when the entropy of the pitch distribution had already been severely limited by such quantization. Accordingly, I no longer find it necessary to avoid any pitch, while at the same time I intend never to leave undisturbed—even when working with instruments—the traditional quantized scale of available pitches. It is not too difficult to get around this with instruments (except for such as the piano)—it's mainly a matter of intention and resolve.

VI. *Ergodos I*

Both the *Stochastic String Quartet* and *Dialogue* made use of programming facilities that enabled me to shape the large-scale form of a piece in terms of changing means and ranges in the various parameters in time. Now my thoughts took a different turn—an apparent reversal—as I began to consider what this process of "shaping" a piece really involved. Both the intention and the effect here were involved in one way or another with "drama" (as in Beethoven, say)—a kind of dramatic "development" that inevitably reflected ("expressed") a guiding hand (mine) directing the course of things now here, now there, and so on. What seemed of more interest than this was to give free rein to the sounds themselves, allowing anything to happen within as broad a field of possibilities as could be set up. One question still remained as to the possible usefulness of my controls over the course of parametric means and ranges: Are there ways in which the full extent and character of the "field" may be made more perceptible—more palpable—by careful adjustments of these values?

In later pieces, I was to test this question in various ways: by shaping only the beginning and the end of a piece, leaving the longer middle section "free" (*Ergodos I*), and by imposing a set of slowly oscillating functions on several parameters, with changing phase-relations between them in time (*Phases*). Finally (in *Music for Player Piano* and *Ergodos II*), even these last vestiges of external "shaping" have disappeared, resulting in processes that evolve as freely as possible within the field of possibilities established for each one in the program itself. It is still often necessary to allow for a variable specification of parametric means and ranges (though these no longer need to change in time), simply because it is still difficult to estimate the settings for these values that will result in the greatest variety and interest (while remaining within the practical limits imposed by the medium itself).

Ergodos I used the same composing program (PLF 3) and the same orchestra of computer instruments as *Dialogue*, but the nature of the music is very different. The composition consists of two ten-minute monaural tapes that may be played either alone or together, either forward or backward. For each tape, only the first and last two minutes of the sound were subjected to any of the "shaping" of parametric means made possible by the composing program, and then only in a very simple way: the mean intensity begins (and ends) at a low level and increases to midrange toward the middle of the tape, while the mean tempo increases toward midrange at one end of the tape (the beginning, say) and increases away from the midrange at the other (the end; if a tape is played in the reverse direction, the tempo decreases toward midrange from the beginning, then decreases further away from midrange at the end). During the middle six minutes of sound on each tape, all the parametric means are constant near the middle of their respective scale-ranges, and these ranges are at their maximum. Thus, the sounds on each tape are nearly ergodic, and thus the title—*Ergodos*.

In order to make possible so many different versions of this piece—so many alternative ways of performing it—it was necessary, first of all, to ensure a certain temporal symmetry with respect to the amplitude envelope functions, for example. That is, first, there would have to be an equal probability of envelope forms and their own "retrogrades." And second, the average density of the sounds on each tape had to be great enough that a tape could be interesting when played by itself and yet not so great that the two tapes could not be played together without losing clarity.

After preliminary tests to ascertain optimum settings of all parameters, and after generating the first two minutes of the first tape (the section with changing parameters), the program was run in one-minute segments. Each new segment on analog tape was then added to what had already been done, and I listened to the whole to determine whether more of these internal (constant) segments should be run before generating the final two minutes. My criterion was a subjective one that is not easy to define but that was quite easily employed: Does the "field of possibilities" seem to have been "used up"? Does it seem that anything more can happen in this field that has not already happened? After I had heard the sixth of these constant, one-minute segments, it seemed to my ear that this criterion had been satisfied, and the final sections were generated.

For the second tape, the same number of sections was generated so that both tapes would be of the same length. Before the second tape was begun, however, a few slight changes were made in certain parameters, adjustments that seemed needed after several hearings of the first. (My reactions were different when there were ten minutes of material from what they had been in the testing period.) The final analog tapes were made by alternating between the sequence of digital tapes generated first and the second sequence in order that the differences between the two series might be "balanced out" in the long run. Thus, the sounds on each tape are not truly ergodic, though my intention had been to make them as nearly so as possible (in the longer middle sections, at least), and they do approach this condition quite closely.

It may be of interest here to describe the changes that were made for the second set of digital tapes as an example of the kind of values in various parameters that seem to approach the "midpoint" of the range and of the extent of these ranges, but also to give an idea of the (small) magnitude of changes in statistical conditions that may have a perceptible musical effect. In the first set of digital tapes, the lower limit of the range of note-durations was 1/16 of a second, the upper limit 4 seconds. In the second set, this upper limit was increased to 5.3 seconds. In both cases, the overall mean-values were close to 1/2 second (log scales were used in nearly all parameters). In the first set of digital tapes, the note-rest probability (for the middle section) was .33, and four voices were generated per clang (average vertical density < 3). In the second set, this probability was increased to .5, and there were six voices per clang (average vertical density = 3, slightly greater than the density in the first set). Finally, the probability of a sound being a noise (rather than a tone) was .5 in the first set, .67 in the second. Settings in all other parameters were the same for the two series of digital tapes.

VII. *Phases* and *Ergodos II*

In *Dialogue* and *Ergodos I* the variable parameters of the sounds were frequency, amplitude, AM rate (= noise bandwidth), waveform, and amplitude envelope form. The range of different timbres was thus relatively limited. In addition, each sound was either a tone or a noise-band, depending on the noise-probability specified for a sequence. In the next composing program, an attempt was made to extend the range of timbres as far as possible and to achieve a continuous range of sound qualities between these two extremes of tone and noise. I spent a great deal of time listening to all kinds of natural and mechanical sounds as these occur in the environment, trying to determine their acoustical properties and, especially, the kinds of fluctuations in various parameters that were most often taking place within each sound. The whole "world" of environmental sounds (including sounds of musical instruments but no longer limited to these) became a kind of "model" for the range of sounds I wanted to be able to generate with the computer.

One of the most obvious aspects of many of these environmental sounds was their frequency instability—"glissandi" and "portamenti," as well as faster modulations. The sounds in *Dialogue* and *Ergodos I* had some frequency modulation but no frequency "enveloping," and this now seemed a necessary extension of the list of variables. Filling in the gap between tones and noise-bands was achieved simply by allowing intermediate values to occur in the parameters affecting the noise—the range and rate of random amplitude modulation. In addition, it seemed desirable to envelope the AM rate so that the bandwidth of the noise could vary within each sound.

In earlier orchestras, I had used a set of waveform functions whose spectra contained formant peaks at different positions. The sounds of my "model" usually showed spectral variations independent of their fundamental frequency, which was not possible to achieve using such a fixed set of waveform functions. What was clearly needed was the possibility of modifying the spectrum of each sound by means of a formant (bandpass) filter with continuously variable controls over center frequency and bandwidth, and the new instrument was designed accordingly. Since the current digital filter unit in the music compiler has a positive gain-factor greater than 1, varying as a function of both center frequency and bandwidth, it was necessary to compensate for this gain in the course of sample-generation. A FORTRAN function (RMSG) was written (based on computations made for me by Max Mathews and Jim Kaiser) that computes the root mean square (rms) gain of the filter (i.e., the ratio of the rms amplitude of the output to that of the input to the filter), and this function is "called" by the amplitude conversion functions (the CVTs) used by the instrument.[10] Figure 12 shows a block-diagram of the instrument incorporating these changes; it is the instrument design that was used for the piece called *Phases*.

The composing program for *Phases* (PLF 5) also incorporated some new features. Whereas PLF 3 used random numbers to compute parametric values at two gestalt levels (the means of each clang and of elements in a clang), the parameters of each sequence (clang-group, the next larger gestalt unit) could only be specified at the input. Since the input data usually referred to relatively long time-segments (30 to 90 seconds), gestalt units of the order of the sequence (as perceived) were not actually being produced by the program. In the new program, this was accounted for by including sequence-generation in the program in a way precisely

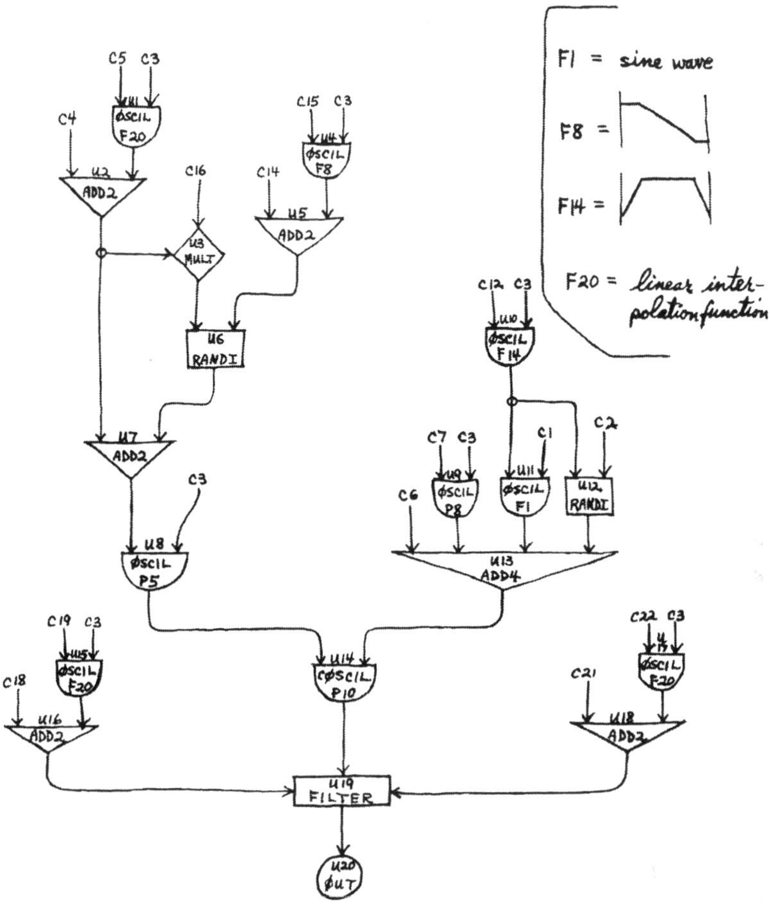

Figure 12. Instrument-design for "Phases."

analogous to the way clangs and elements were generated—via random numbers within a specified range above and below a larger mean-value (in each parameter). The mean duration of clangs (and sequences) and a range of variability for these durations were specified in terms of a logarithmic time-scale (whereas in earlier programs, a minimum and maximum clang-duration had been specified in terms of a linear time-scale). Parametric means and ranges were specified (for a section) using Mathews's CON function so that fluctuations in these values could more easily be represented by straight-line segments than in earlier programs.[11] Finally, no attempt was made to exclude unison or octave repetitions of pitch.

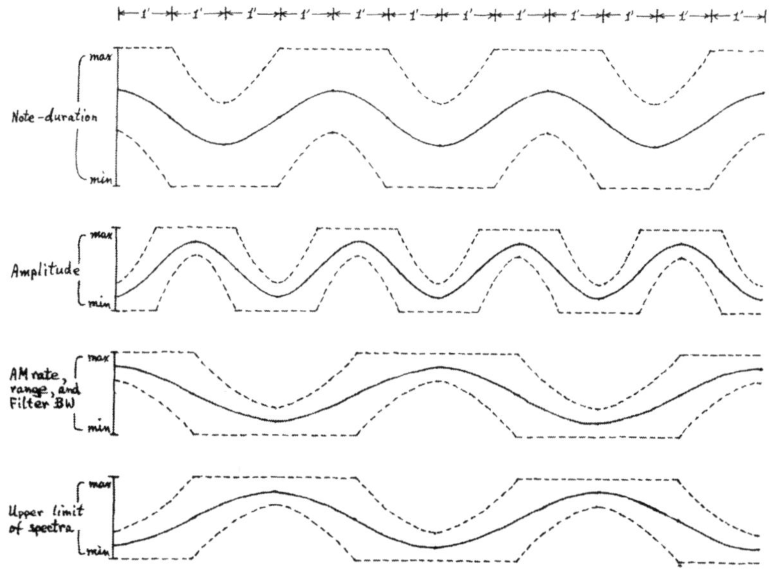

Figure 13. Parametric Means and Ranges (dotted lines) for "Phases".

Figure 13 shows a graphic description of the most important variable parameters in *Phases*. The title *Phases* derives from the form of the piece, in which amplitude, note-duration, and the noise-parameters were varied sinusoidally, oscillating around the midpoints of their respective scales at different rates so that continually changing phase-relations between their mean-values resulted in the course of the piece. By comparison with the ergodic form of *Ergodos I*, this was a small step backward—an experiment, really, to determine whether this kind of variation might produce a larger form more interesting than the ergodic one without sacrificing much in the way of variety. At this moment, the experiment remains inconclusive—I have not yet lived with these pieces long enough to be sure of my own reactions to them in these large-formal terms.

Phases was completed in December 1963, and I began almost immediately to work on what was to become *Ergodos II*. Although provisions for stereophonic output have been incorporated in the music compiler since the summer of 1963, I had not yet made use of them.[12] The need for stereophonic distribution of sounds had been apparent for a long time, however, and I was determined to add this to the list of variables already active. Otherwise, the orchestra used for *Ergodos II* was almost identical to the one for *Phases*, with some minor revisions to improve the signal-to-noise ratio of the output (a problem caused by the digital filter). The form of the piece is ergodic again without even the shaping of the beginning and end of the tape that was done in *Ergodos I*. The settings of the means and ranges of the various parameters were nearly the same as for *Ergodos I* and (the average means of) *Phases*, except that the rest-probabilities are higher—and there is thus a greater proportion of silence on the tape than in previous pieces. The final tape is eighteen minutes long and may be played in either direction, beginning and ending at any points (i.e., a performance need not last the whole eighteen minutes). In addition, the tape may be subdivided into two or more segments of approximately equal length, and these segments may be played simultaneously (over one to *N* pairs of loudspeakers for *N* segments). *Ergodos II* is the last composition I completed during my term at the Labs. Another piece was begun after its completion but abandoned when my dissatisfaction with the early test results made it clear that I would not have time to complete it before leaving.

CHAPTER 4

On the Physical Correlates of Timbre

(1965)

There are essentially two ways the problem of timbre may be studied—by analysis and by synthesis. Each will involve the other to some extent, but they remain distinct points of departure. My approach has been by synthesis, using the digital computer technique developed at the Bell Telephone Laboratories. The intention was not to "simulate" particular, known sound qualities but rather to synthesize a large class of timbres, attempting to achieve as great a variety and richness in this respect as possible. With this intention, I have been led repeatedly to a consideration of the physical properties of natural sounds, and sounds produced by conventional musical instruments. With these as a kind of *model,* I have asked the following questions: In how many different ways may the quality or timbre of a sound be made to vary perceptibly, and in how many ways may the quality of one sound be distinguished from that of another, given that the perceived pitch, intensity, and duration are held constant?

Various answers have been given to these questions in the past, mostly referring to the waveform or the spectrum of the sound, assuming a steady-state condition. We know, however, that it is not the waveform as such that is perceived, since drastic differences of waveform produced by shifting the phases of harmonics are only perceptible in special laboratory conditions, if at all. But even the steady-state spectrum cannot serve by itself as our point of reference; many sounds do not even have a "steady state," and yet we still ascribe characteristic timbres to them. And even during what we would perceive as a steady state, there are often fluctuations in the signal that cannot be described simply in terms of a spectral analysis. What must be accounted for are certain *transient phenomena* and various kinds of quasi-steady-state *modulation* processes. These, along with the spectrum, constitute what I shall call the three basic parameters of timbre. Each of these three parameters may, in turn, be analyzed into several *subparameters*.

Here, I will give a brief outline of these subparameters as I have found them operative in my work with computer-generated sounds. First, the spectrum: in attempts to synthesize vowel sounds in speech research, the most essential features of the steady-state spectrum have been found to be the *center-frequencies*, *bandwidths*, and *relative amplitudes* of from two to perhaps four *formant peaks*. The variety of timbres articulated and distinguished in speech communication is great enough that it seems highly unlikely that very many more parameters would be needed to describe, uniquely, the discriminable aspects of the steady-state spectrum of *any* sound. However, at least two more factors must be considered. One is the bandwidth of the spectrum *as a whole*—especially the magnitude of the *upper limit* of the spectrum (or the number of harmonics)—and the other is the presence and nature of any noise components in the spectrum. These noise components—which are present in some degree in virtually every natural sound we hear, including the sounds of conventional musical instruments and the human voice—add three more subparameters to the list: the center-frequency, bandwidth, and relative amplitudes of perhaps two or three noise bands.

As for what I have called "quasi-steady-state modulation processes," the most familiar are those fluctuations of frequency and amplitude that constitute the *tremolo* and *vibrato* in musical instruments. Here, both the *rate* and the *range* of modulation are of importance in determining the quality of the tone. And although descriptions of the vibrato by Seashore and others have usually called it a sinusoidal modulation, it is never more than *approximately* sinusoidal, except perhaps in certain electromechanical instruments such as the vibraphone and the electric organ. In fact, I have found it absolutely essential, in synthesizing what I would call "rich" timbres, to use *random modulation* of frequency and amplitude, sometimes with and sometimes without a simultaneous periodic modulation. Here, too, both the *rate* and the *range* of the modulation process are determining factors in the resulting timbre. Thus, considering these relatively slow, quasi-steady-state modulation processes, we find it necessary to add eight more variables to our list of the subparameters of timbre. These are the rates and ranges of both periodic and random modulations of the frequency and amplitude of the tone. Even this is not a really exhaustive list, however; the waveform of the periodic modulation could very well be other than sinusoidal. I have not yet studied the effects of such variations in the waveform, however, so I cannot say anything about it except that it is probably of importance in many familiar sounds (especially "noises") in our environment.

The number of subparameters in this list is now fifteen, and this number refers only to the steady-state portion of a sound! I have not even begun to describe the transient phenomena mentioned earlier. Instead of extending the list even further, however, I will suggest a more convenient way of describing these transient effects, namely, as progressive, "unstable" variations in time of one or more of the fifteen subparameters already named—*envelopes*, in effect, of any or all of the steady-state parameters. The specification of each envelope would require a description of its shape, with the rate of change at the beginning being especially significant. The precise mode of specification is of less importance than the fact that such progressive changes be specified in some way, because they are of crucial importance in the determination of the perceived timbre. Finally, various partial components of a sound, such as formant bands and noise bands—sometimes even single harmonics—may need to be varied, by means of these parametric envelope functions, quite independently in time. Naturally, all possible variations of all such components are not going to be equally distinguishable, and the limits of our perception here need further study, but my experience has been that many such variations *are* perceptible and, in fact, *necessary* for the impression of timbral "richness."

The fifteen subparameters of timbre and the varieties of "enveloping" I have been describing were derived from an original set of three factors: the steady-state spectrum; quasi-steady-state modulation processes; and non-steady-state transient phenomena. It would be gratifying if we could simplify this formulation still further, subsuming all these different and disparate "physical correlates of timbre" under one definition. The definition that has served us for so long—for better or worse—is clearly inadequate. I am referring here to Ohm's famous "law of acoustics," which stated (and here I'm quoting from Dayton C. Miller in *The Science of Musical Sounds*): "All musical tones are periodic [phenomena]; the human ear perceives pendular vibrations alone as simple tones; *all varieties of tone quality are due to particular combinations of a larger or smaller number of simple tones*."[1] The inadequacies of this formulation will be evident in the light of my earlier statements.

Now each of the three basic parameters may be described—in terms of the signal itself—as a departure, in varying degrees and at various levels of perceptual integration—from a *simply periodic* or *sinusoidal* oscillation—from what the textbooks call "simple harmonic motion" (Ohm's "pendular vibration"). And these departures are *not* simply the results of an additive process, as Ohm's law implies. Amplitude modulation, for example, is essentially a *multiplicative* operation, as is "enveloping" (this also is a kind of modulation). Following this line of reasoning, I would like to propose the following tentative definition of the physical basis of timbre, designed to take into account the manifold ways in which "varieties of tone quality" may actually be produced and discriminated: *Timbre is that attribute of sound perception that is determined by the nature and extent of the departures from "simple harmonic motion" in the acoustical signal.*

Such departures from simple harmonic (sinusoidal) motion are of three kinds, corresponding with the three basic parameters mentioned in the beginning:

1. the waveform may be nonsinusoidal (the signal still remaining periodic), resulting in the elaboration of harmonic partials in the spectrum;
2. the signal may be subjected to relatively slow modulations, more or less periodic in themselves, but assumed to be in a quasi-steady state; and
3. the various parameters of the steady state may change in a progressive way with time, manifesting an "envelope" of some form.

Such a redefinition of the physical correlates of timbre seems necessary today. Whether it is also sufficient is a question that can be answered only in the light of analytical work yet to be done. In the meantime, it may serve as a useful working hypothesis in the study of timbre.

CHAPTER 5

Excerpts from "An Experimental Investigation of Timbre—the Violin" (1966)

Preface

This report covers the research that has been completed to date on the project "An Experimental Investigation of Timbre," although certain aspects of this work have already been described in published papers (Mathews et al. 1965; Tenney 1965). The result has so far been limited to a single instrument—the violin—although the concepts and methods used here are entirely applicable to other musical instruments as well. A description of the equipment and computer programs used in the investigation is given in section 1 of this report. The description is brief, since most of the techniques are relatively standard. More detailed descriptions are readily available in the literature on speech analysis and computer systems. The experimental results of the research are dealt with in section 2.

[These are excerpts from an unapproved proposal to the National Science Foundation dated June 30, 1966. The proposal was in three sections. Tenney originally planned to publish only the third of those sections in this volume. He later decided that some information from the first two sections should be included for context, but he left no prescription for how this material was to be chosen or incorporated. We have decided to preface the third section with selected excerpts from the first two sections that we believe may provide clarifying context.—Ed.]

In the course of the investigation, new methods have been developed, though some of the most interesting of these emerged too late to be put into practice. Because of this, and because of the need to extend the investigation to other musical instruments, the last section of this report is in the form of a proposal for further research and a request for continued support by the National Science Foundation.

The work described here was done at the School of Music and the Computation Center at Yale University, with frequent consultations with and valuable assistance from former colleagues at Bell Telephone Laboratories. I have recently been appointed an associate professor of electrical engineering at the Polytechnic Institute of Brooklyn, and I anticipate that this new affiliation will provide much more in the way of laboratory facilities and technical assistance than have been available to me at Yale.

Excerpts from Section 1. Equipment and Procedures

[. . .]

The basic approach to sound analysis and synthesis described in this report was, in fact, originally developed in speech research (David, Mathews, and McDonald 1958, 1959; Mathews, Miller, and David 1961; David 1961) and employs a digital computer with peripheral equipment for translating a signal from "analog" to digital form (for analysis) and from digital to analog form (for synthesis). Sounds are first recorded on ordinary magnetic tape. From this tape, a second recording is made on digital tape in a format that can be read by the computer. The computer is then used to carry out various kinds of mathematical analysis of the signal, printing out the results in numerical and graphic form. From these results, parameters are derived for the sound-synthesis program. Using this information as input, the computer produces another digital tape from which, finally, another analog tape recording may be made. A comparison of this tape with the original recording then provides a direct aural test of the success of the analysis. In addition, manipulation of the parameters used in the computer synthesis may indicate the relative importance of each parameter in the perception of timbre.

[. . .]

Analysis Programs

The analysis programs used in this study comprise a "pitch-synchronous" system (Mathews, Miller, and David 1961). That is, the computer steps through the signal period by period, carrying out all the primary analytical operations on a given period and printing out the results of these operations before proceeding to the next period. Some of the information is stored in the memory so that after the last period of a given tone has been analyzed, certain averaging operations may be carried out. . . .

Since the program deals with the signal one period at a time, the first thing that must be done is to measure the period-length, defined in this program as the number of samples between successive signal amplitude peaks. This requires that the computer search for the point of maximum amplitude within a predetermined range of probable sample-distances. . . . In the course of this frequency-measuring process, peak and RMS amplitudes are also determined for the period, and this information is printed out along with the frequency information.

[. . .]

Fourier series coefficients are next computed for the period. . . . Amplitudes and phases of the harmonics are printed out, and a printer-plot is made of the amplitude spectrum. In addition, a spectral envelope is computed by interpolation through all the harmonic amplitude values, and the frequency-position of all relative maxima and minima are determined. These positions are assumed to represent possible "poles" and "zeros" of the waveform function and turn out to be important in the later synthesis of the tones.

At this point, the program shifts to the next period, and the whole process is repeated until the end of the tone has been reached. The program then produces two printer-plots showing, respectively, the changes of peak amplitude and frequency in the course of the tone. These amplitude and frequency-envelope plots are used later to determine the nature of various types of modulation such as vibrato and tremolo.

Synthesis Program

The sound-generating program used in this study to synthesize violin tones is Max V. Mathews's "Music IV Compiler" (Mathews 1961; Tenney

1963). This program allows for the precise specification of all parameters of a sound. In addition, provision is made for altering the structure of the sound-generating program itself in order to simulate musical instruments of any degree of complexity. . . . From the user's point of view, the computer-simulated "instrument" to be designed will consist of a configuration of "unit generators," each of which performs some function that has an easily understandable physical or acoustical analog. These unit generators include, for example, the periodic function generator (oscillator), the random function generator, the adder (mixer), the multiplier, the bandpass filter, etc. Each unit generator has a single output and a number of control inputs, one or more of which are generally taken from the outputs of another unit generator. . . .

Excerpts from Section 2. Experimental Results

[. . .]

Summary

[. . .] By way of summarizing these results, the data will be recast in the form of a description of the temporal evolution of the violin tone itself. That is, I shall describe first the initial transient portion of the tone and then the steady-state and decay portions in terms of all the parameters that appear to be significant in the determination of timbre.

The initial buildup in amplitude during the attack segment, while quite irregular in shape, approximates an exponential curve. . . .

During this initial buildup of the amplitude of the tone, the fundamental frequency is very unsteady. This unsteadiness is generally of two kinds. If the tone is within a legato-group (thus following immediately a tone of another pitch), there is nearly always a glide ("portamento") from the frequency of the previous tone to that of the current tone. This glide is not usually a simple interpolation between the two frequencies, however, but generally includes some degree of "overshoot"—which may occur more than once, and thus in both directions—before the frequency settles down to what will be the central frequency of the steady-state portion of the tone. . . .

The second kind of unsteadiness in the fundamental frequency during the initial transient portion of the tone is a random frequency modulation, the bandwidth of which is relatively wide at the beginning, thereafter decreasing more or less gradually toward the steady-state bandwidth. This kind of fluctuation is of very great importance in the determination of violin timbre (or, more generally, of bowed-string timbre).

During the buildup of the tone, the amplitude spectrum varies irregularly, though it already shows many of the characteristic features of the steady-state spectrum.

At some 120 to 180 milliseconds after the beginning of the tone, there begins a quasi-periodic frequency modulation (the *vibrato*) that continues throughout the steady-state portion of the tone (in all tones except those played on an open string). . . . A corresponding amplitude modulation is sometimes evident at the same rate as the frequency modulation but with very variable ranges and in varying phase relationships with the frequency modulation from one tone to another.

[. . .]

In addition to these more nearly periodic modulations during the steady-state portion of the tone, there are random modulations in both frequency and amplitude. . . .

The spectrum does not become absolutely constant during the steady-state portion of the tone, though the fluctuations from one period to the next are not as great as during the initial transient portion. The spectral envelopes exhibit formant peaks at approximately 500, 1,700, and 3,000 cycles per second, and, in addition, antiresonances or zeros appear at approximately periodically spaced intervals along the frequency axis. Whereas the peaks in the spectral envelopes reflect fixed resonances in the instrument, the zeros reflect discontinuities in the excitation waveform due to the mechanism of bowed-string oscillation. The frequency locations of those zeros depend primarily on the distance of the bow from the bridge and secondarily on bow-speed and pressure.

The experimental data did not show any very important differences between conditions during the decay portion and those during the steady-state portion of the tones analyzed. The form of the amplitude envelope during the decay segment was clearly linear, however. . . .

One of the most noticeable characteristics of the tones is the high degree of fluctuation that takes place in the course of their evolution in time. This fluctuation is only slightly less prominent during the steady-state region than it is during the initial transient period, so that the very term "steady state" begins to seem inappropriate. That such fluctuations are an essential aspect of the timbre of instruments like the violin may easily be demonstrated by synthesizing tones without them. By comparison with other synthetic tones in which such fluctuations are included, the former seem quite lifeless and mechanical. And though the experiments in synthesis that have been carried out so far have not yet resulted in a fully successful simulation of the timbre of the violin, they have provided a great deal of insight into the question of what it is that characterizes the timbre of a musical instrument played by a human being.

[. . .]

Section 3. Proposal for Continued Research

Introduction

In order to synthesize the tone of a musical instrument on the basis of data derived from computer-analysis, these data need to be in the form of a set of parameters representing inputs to an "instrument" in the sound-generating program. Thus, the design of a computer-instrument to simulate the real instrument must be done *before* the computer-analysis, rather than after it, as was done previously. Such a computer-instrument actually constitutes a kind of "model" of the real musical instrument whose tones we want to synthesize, and its design will be determined by all *a priori* knowledge we have or may gain about the instrument's physical structure and mode of operation and about the way in which the instrument is played. In the case of the violin (and other bowed-stringed instruments), for example, we know that the spectrum of the tone will be conditioned by a number of fixed resonances, that there will generally be a set of slowly varying antiresonances in addition to the resonances, that there will be a quasi-periodic frequency-modulation (and perhaps also a similar amplitude-modulation) whenever the player is producing the tone with vibrato, etc.

The need for physical analysis of the instrument had not been anticipated at the beginning of the work described in earlier sections of this report, only becoming apparent as the work progressed. Now it is evident that this kind of analysis should be done at the very beginning of the study of an instrument.

The complete analysis of the sounds of a given musical instrument will thus involve several stages, as outlined below:

1. a physical (and/or mathematical) analysis of the mechanical action of the instrument and of the "system" comprised of instrument and player;
2. the design of a computer-instrument to simulate this instrument-player system;
3. a *complete* computer-analysis of recorded tones of the real instrument;
4. the computer-synthesis of these tones, using the "instrument" designed in stage 2, with input parameters derived from stage 3; and
5. listening tests comparing the original recorded tones with the synthesized tones to evaluate the relative success of the analysis.

With regard to the way in which the computer is used to carry out the analysis of a tone (stage 3, above), certain revisions seem to be called for. First, Fourier series analysis assumes perfect periodicity in the tone being analyzed, and since no real tone produced by a musical instrument is ever perfectly periodic, Fourier analysis ought to be applied only to that part of the signal that *is* truly periodic—or to a truly periodic function that may be derived from the signal in some meaningful way. The presence of a salient pitch in musical tones indicates that such signals are at least approximately periodic, and the procedure to be outlined here assumes, in fact, that there is an essential periodicity in the signal that is "perturbed" in various well-defined ways. That is, the deviations from strict periodicity are assumed to be due to a set of modulating and additive functions that can be isolated from the signal along with the periodic function. This possibility of isolating various aspects of the signal would be extremely useful later also, because it would make it possible to study the subjective effect of each such single aspect separately.

Second, if the computer-analysis is to provide data that are immediately applicable to the synthesis of the tones—without "interpretation"—an analysis program must be written that does much more than simply compute Fourier coefficients, plot amplitude-spectra, and plot amplitude- and frequency-envelopes. It will have to compute, for example, rates and ranges of the various kinds of modulation present in the signal.

The kinds of data required of the program thus depend on the design of the computer-instrument that will be used for synthesis.

In order to illustrate the procedures proposed for the analysis program itself, a computer-instrument has been designed to simulate the tones of the violin and other bowed-stringed instruments (figure 1). It is based on what is already known about these instruments, but in fact it would probably be adequate to simulate the tones of most of the more common instruments of the orchestra (*more* than adequate for some, since they might not require such an elaborate model). The computer-instrument shown in figure 1 would generate each tone in three segments (representing the attack, steady-state, and decay regions of the tone, respectively), with linear interpolations between an initial and a final value for all parameters except the formant-filter parameters (1 through 6) that determine center frequencies and bandwidths, which remain constant during the tone. The design of this instrument assumes, further, that the actual fluctuations of amplitude and frequency in the course of the (real) tone

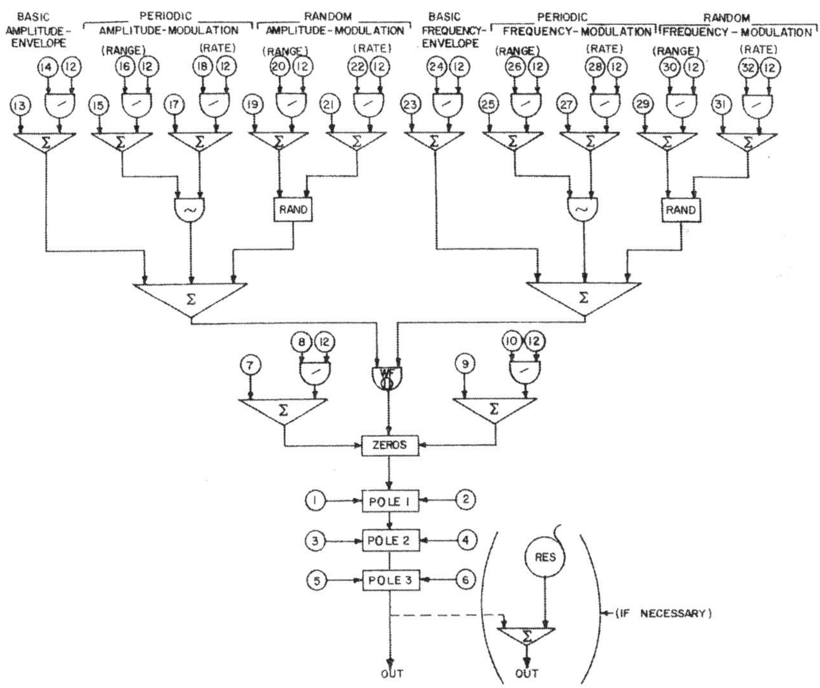

FIGURE 1. Model computer-instrument representing generalized musical sound-source.

can each be replaced by a combination of one periodic and one random modulation-function with simplified parameters and that the more slowly varying amplitude- and frequency-envelopes can be effectively approximated by linear (ramp) functions (in three segments).

The process of analysis now involves simply the derivation of appropriate values for all the external input-parameters in our model instrument (the points numbered from 1 through 32 in the diagram, figure 1). It is not possible to derive all these values directly, however. A step-by-step procedure is necessary that gradually isolates each of the major kinds of variation in the signal, subjecting these to further, information-reducing analytical operations, employing simplifying approximations whenever possible. It will be seen in the outline that follows that the analytical process moves, essentially, from the bottom of the computer-instrument ("OUT") to the top, in a stepwise progression that gradually fills in the various control parameters.

Spectral Parameters

We define the original recorded signal, $S(t)$, as composed of several functions, as listed below:

1. a basic waveform, $WF(t)$, which is a single-period function assumed to be repeated periodically in the course of the tone. The spectrum of this is assumed to have been altered by two kinds of filters, symbolized by the transfer functions . . .
    a. P, representing a set of (three) resonances or poles ("formant filters"), and
    b. Z_t, representing a set of slowly varying antiresonances or zeros, periodically spaced in frequency. In addition, the signal includes
2. a frequency modulating function, FM_t;
3. an amplitude modulating function, $AM(t)$;
4. a low-frequency additive function, $LF(t)$, which will include inharmonic, "DC," and noise components generally lower in frequency than the fundamental of the tone; and finally
5. a higher-frequency additive function, $HF(t)$, which may include some low-frequency components but will involve mostly higher-frequency inharmonic and noise components, appearing as fine-

structure fluctuations in the waveform from period to period in the original signal. (Note: $LF(t)$ and $HF(t)$ are not represented in figure 1.)

The combination of these various functions in the signal is then represented by the following expression:[1]

$$S(t) = P\big[Z_t[FM_t[LF(t) + AM(t) \times (WF(t) + HF(t))]]\big].$$

As each of these component functions is extracted from the signal, the values of the function will be stored on digital tape for later use. The steps in the analysis of the signal are as follows:

1. Find P (thereby determining parameters 1–6 in figure 1) and inverse-filter to obtain a new function

$$S_1(t) = P^{-1}[S(t)] = Z_t\big[FM_t[LF(t) + AM(t) \times (WF(t) + HF(t))]\big].$$ [2]

2. Find Z_t (parameters 7–10) and inverse-filter to obtain

$$S_2(t) = Z_t^{-1}[S_1(t)] = FM_t[LF(t) + AM(t) \times (WF(t) + HF(t))].$$ [3]

Steps 1 and 2 together are intended to isolate any constant or slowly varying spectral-envelope characteristics (i.e., those that are varying independently of the fundamental frequency of the signal) before the frequency-demodulation (step 3, below) is carried out, since spurious spectral characteristics may then be introduced if this "prewhitening" has not been done. In addition, it should lessen the effect of phase-shifts in adjacent harmonics that sometimes cause artifactual discontinuities in the frequency-measuring program.

3. Find FM_t and frequency-demodulate (i.e., resample, with polynomial interpolations—a quadratic should be sufficiently precise here) to obtain

$$S_3(t) = FM_t^{-1}[S_2(t)] = LF(t) + AM(t) \times (WF(t) + HF(t)).$$

$S_3(t)$ will now be a signal with constant fundamental frequency throughout, or at least constant time-intervals between successive amplitude-peaks.

4. Find $LF(t)$ and subtract to obtain

$$S_4(t) = S_3(t) - LF(t) = AM(t) \times (WF(t) + HF(t)).$$

This first additive function, $LF(t)$, will be the mean value of the positive and negative peak-amplitude envelopes of $S_3(t)$. These envelopes would be computed by polynomial interpolations through the points representing peak amplitudes on the positive and negative sides of the zero-axis.

5. Find $AM(t)$ and amplitude-demodulate (i.e., divide) to obtain

$$S_5(t) = S_4(t) \,/\, AM(t) = WF(t) + HF(t).$$

$S_5(t)$ will now be a signal with a relatively constant amplitude-spectrum, constant peak-amplitudes, and constant period-lengths. The signal is still not perfectly periodic, however, since the waveforms will generally be slightly different in different periods. We must derive from $S_5(t)$ a single waveform that represents an average of the periods in its steady-state region (the boundaries of which will have been determined in a preliminary run).

6. Find $WF(t)$ (parameter 11), by averaging corresponding samples in successive periods of the steady-state region of the tone and subtract to obtain $HF(t)$. $HF(t)$ is only part of the total inharmonic, DC, and noise components in the tone and should be recombined with $LF(t)$, as in step 7 below.

7.1. Remodulate (in amplitude) $HF(t)$ to obtain

$$S_6(t) = AM(t) \times HF(t).$$

7.2. Remodulate (in frequency) $S_6(t)$ and $LF(t)$ to obtain

$$S_7(t) = FM_t[LF(t) + AM(t) \times HF(t)].$$

7.3. Filter $S_7(t)$ with Z_t to obtain

$$S_8(t) = Z_t[FM_t[LF(t) + AM(t) \times HF(t)]].$$

7.4. Filter $S_8(t)$ with P to obtain a "residue" function

$$S_r(t) = P[Z_t[FM_t[LF(t) + AM(t) \times HF(t)]]].$$

This "residue" function, $S_r(t)$, is now in the same form it is assumed to have in the original function, $S(t)$, being the difference between $S(t)$ and a quasi-periodic function, $S_q(t)$, where

$$S_q(t) = S(t) - S_r(t) = P\big[Z_t[FM_t[AM(t) \times WF(t)]]\big].$$

Both $S_q(t)$ and $S_r(t)$ should be generated as sound so they can be listened to. ($S_r(t)$ should be of very small amplitude, so it may be useful to amplify it digitally.) If the process has failed to keep any true harmonic components out of $S_r(t)$, this should be immediately *audible*. In addition, listening to $S_q(t)$ should indicate how important $S_r(t)$ may be in determining or conditioning the timbre of the tone. If $S_r(t)$ does seem to be important, it will have to be analyzed by some other method—perhaps by that used for the preliminary run or by that used to analyze the random modulations in the amplitude- and frequency-envelopes (see step 5, below). $WF(t)$ is now only a single-period function, and this, of course, may be Fourier-analyzed and its spectrum compared to P and Z_t.

We have now isolated each of the several functions assumed to compose the signal. In addition, we have another signal, $S_r(t)$, which will contain much of the random noise in the tone, and a more nearly periodic signal, $S_q(t)$, representing the original signal with $S_r(t)$ removed. To help make clear what will have been achieved by the analysis so far, a second diagram is shown in figure 2, representing schematically the nature of our analytical results at this intermediate stage in the whole process. Several functions ($AM(t)$, FM_t, etc.) will have been stored on digital tape (denoted by the circular symbols in the diagram). The inputs to the formant filters will have been reduced to six constants (determining the center frequencies and bandwidths of the three filters), and a basic (excitation-function) waveform will have been stored (in sampled form). Thus, the major spectral parameters have been derived, but the various enveloping and modulating functions have yet to be reduced to their final (simplest) form. Although some of the noise in the tone will be contained in $S_r(t)$, there will generally be random fluctuations in $AM(t)$ and FM_t that may produce perceptible noise in the tone. And these two modulating functions will usually exhibit some quasi-periodic fluctuations too whose parameters need to be determined. The following procedure also requires that a preliminary run on the computer has been made, producing amplitude- and frequency-envelope plots.

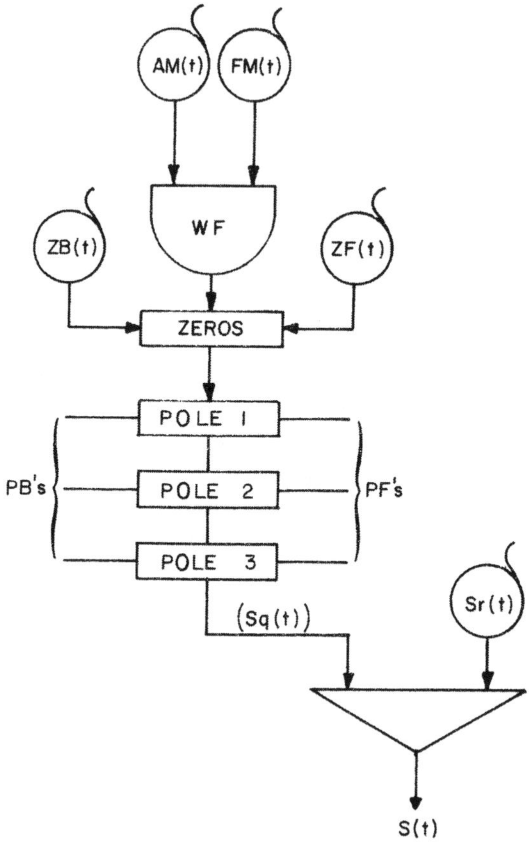

FIGURE 2. Data representation at intermediate stage of analysis.

Envelope and Modulation Parameters

Let $E(t)$ represent either of the modulation functions (FM_t or $AM(t)$) extracted from the signal by the foregoing analysis. We assume that $E(t)$ is composed of several functions (as with the signal itself, in the earlier stages of the analysis) such that

$E(t) = L(t) + C(t) + R(t)$, where

$E(t)$ is the original envelope function,

$L(t)$ is the best-fitting (least-squares) linear function (in three segments),

$C(t)$ is a quasi-periodic (cosinusoidal) modulation, and

$R(t)$ is a random modulation (to be simulated by the random function generator in the music compiler).

1. After visual inspection of plots produced in the preliminary run, divide $E(t)$ into three segments (whose durations will specify parameter 12 in figure 1) and estimate the rate of $C(t)$.

2. Compute $L(t)$ (parameters 13–14 and 23–24) for each of the three segments and subtract (thus removing this "basic envelope") to obtain a modulation function

$$M(t) = E(t) - L(t) = C(t) + R(t).$$

3. Determine $C(t)$ (by peak-detection and cosine interpolation) and subtract to obtain the random modulation by itself,

$$R(t) = M(t) - C(t).$$

$C(t)$ is assumed to be a sequence of ramp-modulated cosines, each quasi-period of which has the form

$$C_i(t) = \left(a_{1_i} + \frac{t - t_i}{T_i}\left(a_{2_i} - a_{1_i}\right)\right)\cos\left[\phi + 2\pi\left(f_{1_i} + \frac{t - t_i}{T_i}\left(f_{2_i} - f_{1_i}\right)\right)t\right]$$

or

$C_i(t) = A_i \cos\left(\phi + 2\pi F_i t\right)$, with

$A_i = a_{1_i} + \frac{t - t_i}{T_i}(a_{2_i} - a_{1_i})$ and

$F_i = f_{1_i} + \frac{t - t_i}{T_i}\left(f_{2_i} - f_{1_i}\right)$, where

the index, i, denotes successive cycles of the cosine modulation, the subscripts 1 and 2 indicate initial and final values, ϕ is a constant (phase) determining starting position only, t_i is the time at the beginning of each cosine period, T_i is the duration of the period, $a_{1_i} = a_{2_{i-1}}$ and $F_{1_i} = F_{2_{i-1}}$.[4]

But we want to simulate $C(t)$ more simply, as a cosine-function with both rate and range enveloped by single ramp-functions for each of the three segments of the tone. This simpler function, $Q(t)$, may be derived as follows:

4. Compute best-fitting linear functions (in three segments) for a_i and f_i. These will then reduce to one initial and one final value for each, A_1 and A_2, F_1 and F_2 (parameters 15–18 and 25–28). We can now represent the simplified quasi-periodic modulation, $Q(t)$, as follows:

$$Q(t) = \left(A_1 + \frac{t}{T}(A_2 - A_1)\right)\cos\left[\phi + 2\pi\left(F_1 + \frac{t}{T}(F_2 - F_1)\right)t\right],$$

where T is the duration of the whole segment of the function.[5]

5. Simulate $R(t)$ as the output of the random function-generator in the music compiler, with rate and range enveloped as for $Q(t)$ (i.e., by linear functions in three segments). This means (for the range) finding straight-line segments on both positive and negative sides of the zero-axis that contain all peaks inside them. But in order that their slopes be correct, a least-squares fit to relative peaks on each side should be found first and then shifted outward. For the rate, we can assume that the output of the random function-generator changes slope from positive to negative or from negative to positive at about half the rate at which new values are generated. Thus (for rate),

5.1. locate points in $R(t)$ where the slope changes from positive to negative or from negative to positive;

5.2. store a function representing time-intervals between these successive points of change of slope; and

5.3. compute a best-fitting straight line through this function. Initial and final *rates* for the random function-generator (parameters 21–22 and 31–32) will be double the values at each end of the line derived in step 5.3. Then (for range),

5.4. select from the points derived in step 5.1 those that change from positive to negative and from negative to positive;

5.5. compute a best-fitting straight line through each (positive and negative) set of points from step 5.4; and

5.6. add a (positive or negative) constant to each of these straight lines so they are shifted just outside (or touching?) the outermost points on their respective sides of the zero-axis. Initial and final *ranges* for the random function-generator (parameters 19–20 and 29–30) will be the average of the two functions at each end (or one-half the distance between them at each end).

Discussion

The analytical procedure outlined above has the obvious advantage that the results will be in a form that makes them immediately applicable in synthesizing the sound of the instrument being analyzed. A direct link is thus provided between the analysis and the synthesis programs, so that the entire process could eventually be carried out in a single computer run (or at most, two, if we include the preliminary run needed to estimate certain parameters). The procedure has another advantage, however, perhaps more important than the first one. This was mentioned earlier, but it should be considered here in more detail. This second advantage has to do with the fact that the various component functions isolated from the original signal can be used to test the relative importance of different aspects of the signal—different components and types of variation—in the perception of timbre. This, in turn, would make possible an approach to an optimal information-reduction in the numerical description of the sounds. The successful synthesis of a given sound—in itself—does not guarantee that any such optimal description has been found. That is, while it does indicate that our analysis has provided a numerical description that is sufficient, it does not prove that this description is *necessary* in all its details. The only way to be sure that a particular component in a signal makes a real difference in the perception of the tone is to synthesize the tone with that component eliminated or replaced by some other component.

Such a strategy becomes very simple with the analytical procedure outlined here. For example, it has already been mentioned that $S_r(t)$ and $S_q(t)$ should be generated as sound and listened to, but many other possibilities emerge at that same intermediate stage of the analysis at which these two functions have been derived. Referring to figure 2, tones could be generated with other waveforms substituted for $WF(t)$, with $AM(t)$ replaced by simple linear functions (while FM_t remains unchanged) and vice versa, etc. At the end of the analysis, it would be possible to make direct aural comparisons between the final synthesized tones and tones employing one or more of the original (unsimplified) modulating functions ($AM(t)$ or FM_t). By such means as these, then, it would become possible to make meaningful evaluations of the aural effects of the various simplifications, substitutions, and other operations that occur at the several stages in the analysis and synthesis of the tone.

Equipment, Facilities, and Personnel Costs

The equipment necessary for this project is already available at the Polytechnic Institute of Brooklyn, where the proposed research will be done. In addition to the principal investigator, two half-time graduate assistants will be needed to carry out some of the detailed work on certain aspects of the research. One of these will assist in problems of mathematical analysis and computer operations, the other in problems of physical analysis and electronic instrumentation. Funds are also being requested to pay for the use of the computer facilities. The research would be carried out over a period of two years, beginning in September 1966.

Principal Investigator

The principal investigator will be James C. Tenney. Since February 1959 he has been engaged in both experimental studies and practical utilization of various techniques of electronic music. His musical training previous to that time had been as a composer, pianist, and conductor, and he has remained active in these areas up to the present time (for further information on these activities, see the résumé attached to this report). But his interest in the new musical possibilities of electronic media began as early as 1952, when he first entered college. He became convinced that the fullest realization of the enormous resources of these new media would require more than a passing knowledge of mathematics, acoustics, and electronics, though these would be of little use until he had acquired a firm musical foundation. Accordingly, his studies have always included as much that was of a technical nature as was possible while still pursuing the ordinary musical curriculum. Thus, he holds the degree of master of music from the University of Illinois, while his schooling has also included two years in the engineering school of the University of Denver. He received additional training in acoustics and electronics at the University of Illinois and was laboratory assistant in the Electronic Music Laboratory there for two years.

From September 1961 through March 1964 he was an associate member of technical staff at the Bell Telephone Laboratories, doing research in physical acoustics, psychoacoustics, and electronic music, employing a digital computer for the generation of the sounds and sound-sequences used in these studies. During this time he became a proficient computer-programmer and gained additional training and experience in mathematics, electronics, and sound analysis.

Since April 1964 he has been research associate in the theory of music at Yale University, engaged in the two-year research project "An Experimental Investigation of Timbre" described in sections 1 and 2 of this report on a grant from the National Science Foundation.

References

David, E. E. 1961. "Digital Simulation in Research on Human Communication." *Proceedings of the Institute of Radio Engineers* 4(9): 319–29.

David, E. E., M. V. Mathews, and H. S. McDonald. 1958. "Description and Results of Experiments with Speech Using Digital Computer Simulation." In *Proceedings of the 1958 National Electronics Conference*, 766–75. New York: Institute of Radio Engineers.

———. 1959. "A High-Speed Data Translator for Computer Simulation of Speech and Television Devices." In *Proceedings of the Western Joint Computer Conference*, 354–57. New York: Institute of Radio Engineers.

Mathews, M. V. 1961. "An Acoustic Compiler for Music and Psychological Stimuli." *Bell System Technical Journal* 40: 677–94.

Mathews, M. V., J. E. Miller, and E. E. David. 1961. "Pitch Synchronous Analysis of Voiced Sounds." *Journal of the Acoustical Society of America* 33(2): 179–86.

Mathews, M. V., J. E. Miller, J. R. Pierce, and J. Tenney. 1965. "Computer Study of Violin Tones." *Journal of the Acoustical Society of America* 38(5): 912–13.

Tenney, J. C. 1963. "Sound-Generation by Means of a Digital Computer." *Journal of Music Theory* 7(1): 24–70.

———. 1965. "The Physical Correlates of Timbre." *Gravesaner Blätter* 26:106–9.

CHAPTER 6

Form in Twentieth-Century Music (1969–70)

FORM. In the most general sense: *shape* (contour, the variation of some attribute of a thing in space or time) and *structure* (the disposition of parts, relations of part to part, and of part to whole). In music, shape is the result of *changes* in some attribute or parameter of sound in time, while structure has to do with various relations between sounds and sound-configurations at the same or at different moments in time. The word is often used in the more restricted sense of a fixed or standard scheme of relationships (e.g., "sonata form"), but this definition of *form* is of little use in a study of music in the twentieth century, which has tended to break away from such fixed patterns, yielding a fantastic variety of new forms. In order to deal with this variety, our basic definition of *form* must be as broad as possible, and a number of new terms will have to be developed.

Shape and structure imply at least two *hierarchical levels* of organization and perception ("whole" and "part") and usually more than two (since relations between sound-configurations that are themselves parts of the larger whole must involve the internal structure of each configuration and thus subordinate "parts of parts"). Any thorough description of the form of a piece of music must therefore include descriptions at several of these hierarchical levels. This is true of pre-twentieth-century music as well but has been obscured by the fact that much of the detailed "infrastructure" of that music was conventionally given, culturally "pre-programmed," and consequently taken for granted. Since 1900, however, changes have occurred at all hierarchical levels, and we can no longer afford to ignore the infrastructure.

In addition to shape and structure, there is a third factor that determines form. A description of the shape (or sometimes the structure) of a formal unit at one of these hierarchical levels frequently involves certain *statistical* characteristics of the formal units at the *next lower level*, for example, the average value and range of each important parameter. We thus have three aspects of form to consider at each hierarchical level: the *structural* (internal relations), the *morphological* (shape), and the *statistical* (state, condition). It will be found, as we proceed, that shape at a given hierarchical level depends on statistical properties at the next lower level, while structure at a given level depends primarily on the morphological properties at the next lower level and secondarily on the structural and statistical properties at the next (or several) lower level(s).

These relations between state, shape, and structure at adjacent hierarchical levels are, incidentally, relevant to the old problem of "form versus content." A little reflection will show that the "content" of a formal unit at a given hierarchical level is determined by the structural, morphological, and statistical properties—that is, the *form*—of each of its component units at the next lower level. Conversely, formal properties at one hierarchical level become the "content" of formal units at the next *higher* level. This is not always obvious at intermediate levels, but what we do finally call "content" is the result of "forms" at a level below the first one we have decided to deal with formally. ("Form versus function" posits a similarly artificial distinction—the reverse of the form/content distinction, but one that may also be resolved via the concept of hierarchical levels.) These various relations between the three aspects of form at several hierarchical levels of organization and perception are represented schematically in figure 1. We shall still find inconsistencies in the historical development of new forms at various levels simultaneously ("old wine in new bottles" and vice versa), but it is no longer necessary to treat form and content as fundamentally different things.

Implicit in all the above is the importance of *perception* in the matter of form. We might say that form is equally dependent on the thing-in-itself and on perceptual processes. Actually, the "thing-in-itself" doesn't even exist in music apart from our perception of it. All that may be said to "exist" are various partial manifestations or symbolic representations of it, and even these must be mediated by perception. So it is really the form of the *musical experience* that must be dealt with.

In what follows, new formal conditions in twentieth-century music will be described at each of these hierarchical levels. For the smallest, "indivisible" sound units at the first hierarchical level, the word *element* will be used. Singular configurations of elements, forming units at the second hierarchical level, will be called *clangs*. For a unit at the third hierarchical level, consisting of a cohesive group of clangs, the word *sequence* will be used. Whether a given sound or sound-configuration is to be considered an element, a clang, or a sequence depends on many variable factors, both objective and subjective. Most commonly, an element will be a single tone, but it might be a trill, a chord, a glissando, or a more complex noise. Perhaps the most important variable factor is the musical context itself. In a very dense texture, an "indivisible element" might actually be a complex sound-configuration. On the other hand, in a very sparse texture—especially at a slow tempo—a single tone might be perceived as a clang. Although the clang is often equivalent to the "motive" or "phrase" of traditional musical analysis, it should be understood here to include *any* collection of sound elements perceived as a primary aural gestalt.

Within each level, distinctions will be made, where appropriate, between the two aspects of form: the *structural* (involving internal relations between parts) and the *morphological* (involving shape or changes in some parameter with time). Finally, the form of whole sections, movements, and pieces is considered, and a provisional typology of large forms is suggested.

The First Hierarchical Level: Sound Elements

Changes have occurred in the larger framework within which pitches are selected and interrelated (scales and tuning systems). After two centuries of a music whose elements consisted of tones and chords based on a diatonic/triadic, twelve-tone, tempered tuning system, we have

1. chromatic and other nondiatonic pitch scales (still within the tempered tuning system) (Debussy, Scriabin, Schoenberg);
2. different tuning systems, for example, quarter-tone and sixth-tone temperaments (Hába, Ives), simple-ratio ("just") scales (Partch), and free, indeterminate pitch "gamuts" (Cage, *musique concrète*); and
3. harmonic (i.e., chordal) structures based on no. 1 or 2 above (or otherwise nontriadic).

In addition, there have been important changes at the element-level with respect to timbre, including

1. an increased use of new timbres produced by unusual playing techniques on conventional instruments (e.g., *sul ponticello,* flutter-tongue, etc.) (Schoenberg, Webern);
2. further extensions of the range of timbres via the development of new instruments, including electronic devices (Russolo, Varèse, Partch, Cage);
3. the use of tone-clusters and other dense, "dissonant" chords (Ives, Cowell, Bartók) and complex "aggregates" (Cage); and
4. a more frequent use of noises (i.e., sounds without salient pitch) as elements structurally equivalent to tones and chords rather than as secondary, supportive, or merely "background" elements (Varèse, Cage, *musique concrète,* etc.).

In some cases (e.g., *musique concrète* and much of Cage's later work), the elements so frequently lack pitch-saliency that the very notions of "scale" and "tuning system" become irrelevant. Here, the conventional distinction between "musical" and "nonmusical" sounds breaks down completely. In the light of the changes that have taken place in music since 1900, it is evident that *any* sound is potentially "musical"—that is, any sound may function as an element in the musical fabric and in a way that is structurally equivalent to any other sound.

It is of interest to note here that formal changes at this first level have profoundly influenced, and been influenced by, changes in the *medium* (the development of new instruments, playing techniques, and notation systems). The most obvious example of this, of course, is electronic music, but this is only the latest of a series of changes in the medium that began as early as 1910.

The Second Hierarchical Level: The Clang

At the next higher level, at which the smaller sound-elements are grouped into what I call *clangs* (meaning any collection of sound-elements perceived as a primary aural gestalt), important structural changes have occurred with respect to both tonality and rhythm. It is at this level that key-defining pitch-relations would begin to be manifested in pre-twentieth-century (as well as later tonal) music, and the avoidance or "transcendence" of such pitch-relations is characteristic of much of the new music since 1900. This is of structural (as distinct from merely textural) significance, if only because it removes one of the most powerful means of relating one part to another and of providing both continuity (via similarity) and variety among musical configurations at the clang level and higher. One example of this tendency to avoid key-defining pitch-relations is found in the early melodic writing of Schoenberg, Berg, and Webern and later in the work of Ruggles—the avoidance of an early repetition of a previously heard pitch or its near octaves. In the later twelve-tone method of Schoenberg, the "tendency" actually became a systematic *procedure* that, together with a number of others, was intended to replace the cohesive and structural functions of the earlier tonal system.

With regard to rhythm, after several centuries of a music based on periodic and divisive rhythms organized primarily in multiples of two and three, we have

1. higher-order periodicities (five, seven, etc.);
2. additive rhythmic processes;
3. polymetric and otherwise polyrhythmic structures and compound or "irrational" gruppetto subdivisions; and
4. aperiodic and indeterminate rhythms.

In general, there has been an increase in rhythmic complexity, often to the very limit of human playability.

In addition to these structural changes at the clang-level, there have been other changes of both a morphological and a statistical nature. First, there has been a greater use of parameters other than pitch (and time) to give shape to a clang (e.g., intensity, timbre, etc.). Second, there has been a tendency for the shaping parameters of the clang to vary over a wider range of values than in pre-twentieth-century music. And finally, clang-durations tend to vary more widely than before.

The Third Hierarchical Level: The Sequence

At the next higher level—that of groups of clangs, or what I call *sequences* (meaning a series of several clangs perceived as a larger, if looser, gestalt)—quite a number of new formal conditions have arisen. It is at this third hierarchical level that structure in its fullest sense—relations among parts that are themselves complex—first becomes really important. Among the new developments are the following:

1. new (and some very old) kinds of shape-variations of the basic "thematic" clangs (e.g., inversion, retrograde, octave-transposition, etc.);
2. a new importance of parameters other than pitch (and time) in determining shape-relations between the clangs in a sequence (which follows from their use in giving shape to each clang, as noted earlier);
3. completely *heteromorphic* and completely *isomorphic* sequences (implicit in nos. 1 and 2 above is the assumption that one clang is, in fact, *related* to another by some process of shape-variation). I call sequences with this kind of relationship between clangs *metamorphic* sequences. An *isomorphic* sequence, then, is one in which all the clangs have the *same* shape (with respect to some variable parameter); a *heteromorphic* sequence is one in which no two clangs have (or are derived from) the same shape;
4. the variability of clang-durations mentioned earlier is manifested at this third hierarchical level as a lack of *periodicity* with respect to clang-durations; in addition, sequence durations tend to vary more widely, leading to a similar lack of periodicity at the next higher level; and
5. the absence—in nontonal music—of conventional cadence-formulae to define the end of a sequence. Just how the perceptual boundaries of the sequence are created in the absence of tonal conventions is a problem of gestalt-perception ("closure") and will not be dealt with here, except to say that, in general, the same gestalt-factors of cohesion and segregation are involved at the sequence-level as are involved at the clang- and element-levels, primarily temporal *proximity* and parametric *similarity*. The above all refer to structural changes at the sequence-level. In general, no new morphological or statistical characteristics seem to have emerged at this level beyond those already noted at the clang-level (i.e., the remarks there about the use of new shaping-parameters, varying over wider ranges, apply also to the sequence).

It was noted earlier that the medium influences—and is influenced by—formal conditions at the first hierarchical level. At the clang- and sequence-levels it is compositional *method* that seems to play a similar role. Nos. 1 and 2 above will be recognized as two aspects of serial technique, and it is at these levels that the effects of serial methods have been most noticeable. This applies to other methods too, including those based on chance (indeterminacy, aleatoric procedures, stochastic processes, etc.).

Higher Levels of Organization: Sections, Movements, the Whole Piece

Between the sequence and the whole piece, the question arises as to the actual number of hierarchical levels that are relevant to the musical experience, and this depends on the piece itself. In much earlier music there are well-defined sections and often movements, thus interposing two distinct hierarchical levels between those of the sequence and the whole piece. In much twentieth-century music, on the other hand, there is no reason to consider any intermediate levels between these two—that is, the next larger grouping of sequences that is relevant to perception and analysis is the whole piece itself. In general, however, it may be said that where there *are* intermediate levels, their formal characteristics will be similar to those of the sequence or of the whole piece. More specifically, what has already been said about sequences will apply also to sections, and the observations that follow on whole pieces will apply to movements. The next hierarchical level I shall deal with here, then, is that of the whole piece—*large-form*.

The absence—in nontonal music—of conventional cadence-formulae to effect closure, mentioned earlier with respect to sequences, applies to large-form as well (and to any intermediate levels). The whole piece, of course, has its "boundaries" defined automatically simply by virtue of its starting and stopping (though just how coherent a gestalt it is will depend on many other factors as well). Again, the same gestalt-factors of cohesion and segregation will be involved at this large-formal level as at all lower levels. But in addition, a number of other devices have been used by twentieth-century composers to effect or reinforce this sense of closure. These include

1. a *return* to some point of departure and/or a *resolution* of some kind of tension: these are equivalent to conventional formal situations when the point of departure and return is a key-center and the resolution is achieved harmonically, but both "return" and "resolution" may be realized in a number of other ways not involving conventional tonality;
2. *reaching a limit* beyond which the preceding process cannot continue: this is usually an upper or lower limit of some parametric scale and might be called an *intrinsic limit* to distinguish it from no. 4, below;
3. an abrupt *decrease in complexity*—a "settling down" to a more static condition—or a sudden and usually abbreviated *recall* or "flashback" to an earlier condition or thematic "idea" (not necessarily that of the beginning); and

4. the *arbitrary stopping* of a process, which might also be called "reaching an *extrinsic* limit" (i.e., the time allotted for a particular performance of a piece of indeterminate duration): the effect here is as though looking at a landscape through an open window—the perceptual boundaries are defined "arbitrarily" (by the window frame) rather than being inherent or "intrinsic" to the process ("landscape") itself; music that ends this way often begins this way also, and we might call it a "windowed" form of closure (or gestalt boundary-definition in general).

The first of these four types of closure assumes that the piece has begun by establishing some clear point of departure, which is then followed by an excursion or deviation. This suggests a kind of "arch" form (either structural or morphological) that is familiar to us in pre-twentieth-century music. The second implies that most of the piece has been "moving" in a given direction, which has finally brought it to some intrinsic limit, and we might call this a "ramp" form. The fourth, on the other hand, assumes the precedence of a relatively static—or statistically homogeneous—condition, creating a large-formal shape that I shall call *ergodic* (borrowing a term from mathematics), which I am using to mean a process in which the statistical properties of each part at the next lower hierarchical level are the same as those of every other part at that same (lower) level and of the whole. The arch and ramp forms are thus *nonergodic*, but they are only two especially clear and simple examples of nonergodic shapes. There are surely others of importance, though these can usually be heard as combinations of arch and ramp forms. Among the ergodic forms, we may further distinguish two types. In one, the statistical homogeneity is the result of the constant use of the entire range of possibilities in each parameter—often by way of chance methods, though sometimes via serial methods also. In the other, the statistical homogeneity is the result of what are often severe restrictions of parametric ranges, within which "all possibilities" are still made use of. Note that, while the arch form may be realized either structurally or morphologically, the ramp and ergodic forms are uniquely morphological.

The most important morphological distinction here is that between ergodic and nonergodic forms. But these terms refer to the shape of a piece in some parameter, as distinct from relations between the parts of a piece. They may thus serve to describe the morphological aspect of a whole piece, but they tell us nothing about *structure*. For this, other terms will be needed that can distinguish among various types of large-formal structure. Returning to the original definition of structure as "relations between sounds and sound-configurations," let us consider how many different kinds of relationship are possible. There are, first of all, simple parametric relations—higher/lower, louder/softer, faster/slower, and so on. But these have already been subsumed in our definition of *shape*. The simplest kind of relation that is uniquely structural would involve comparisons between two or more shapes at the next *lower* hierarchical level and specifications of their relative positions in time. The first question in the determination of structure would thus be: Is this clang (or sequence, or section) identical in shape to some previous clang (or sequence, or section), or is it of a different shape? If the two gestalt units thus compared are not identical, are they still morphologically similar in some way or in some degree? That is, are they "related" by some perceptible process of transformation, by which one might be considered to have been derived from the other? And finally, if they *are* so related, what type of transformation or variation is involved in this apparent derivation?

In answering these questions, the three terms that were used to describe types of structure at the sequence-level will be found useful: *isomorphic* (identity of shape), *heteromorphic* (complete dissimilarity of shape), and *metamorphic* (partial similarity of shape—relation via transformation). These terms may be applied, in fact, to structure at *any* hierarchical level beyond the first (since structure only exists—by definition—when the parts of a thing themselves contain parts). We may begin with the following breakdown of structural types applied to the highest level. When no morphological similarities at all are perceptible in a piece of music (as in some of the earlier works of Schoenberg and Webern, as well as many of the more recent works of Cage), the structure may be called heteromorphic. When there *are* perceptible morphological relations of various kinds in a piece (as in *most* music), the structure may be called metamorphic. And if a piece consists of nothing but the repetition of one morphological entity—at whatever level—it may be called isomorphic (with respect to that level, and with respect to the parameter that determines the shape of the repeated unit). This last is obviously rare, though Ravel's *Bolero* provides one example, at least, of a structure that is essentially isomorphic at the section level and with respect to pitch and note-duration, if not other parameters. And other manifestations of such a structure—at other levels and in other parameters—are certainly conceivable, if not common, occurrences in twentieth-century music.

We thus have, as our starting-point, three types of structure at the large-formal level (as well as at lower levels): isomorphic, metamorphic, and heteromorphic. By far the most common type of structure is the metamorphic, and within this type there are obviously a very large number of possible structures, reflecting the multiplicity of types of morphological transformation that can be perceived. A partial list of such transformations would have to include *permutations* of the temporal order of the gestalt units at the next lower hierarchical level, whether elements, clangs, or sequences, perhaps even sections: *interval expansions* and *contractions*; *extensions* and *truncations* (both "horizontal" and "vertical"); *insertions* and *deletions* of lower-level gestalt units (again, both horizontally and vertically), including all varieties of "ornamentation"; the *mirror-transformations* (inversion, retrogression, etc.) of twelve-tone and later serial music; and finally, various less systematic distortions or *parametric shifts* of lower-level gestalt units, which preserve only the general topological features of the larger unit's shape.

In most cases, a combination of several of these types of transformation will be heard in any given piece of music, so they do not provide a basis for characterizing the structure of a whole piece—with the possible exception of permutation. Many of the works of Stravinsky, for example, seem to involve little more than permutations of the temporal order of a relatively fixed set of clangs (e.g., the "Danse sacrale" in *Le sacre du printemps* or the second of the *Three Pieces for String Quartet*). Sometimes this kind of permutation process is applied to sequences rather than clangs, as in the same composer's *Symphonies of Wind Instruments*. Such a process is analogous to a kaleidoscope, in which all of the perceived forms are the result of the continually varied juxtaposition of a fixed set of gestalt units at the next lower level. The fact that so many pieces in the repertoire of twentieth-century music proceed in this way suggests that the permutational structure should be considered a basic structural type within the larger category of metamorphic structures (e.g., Messiaen, *Catalogues des oiseaux*; Cage, *Music of Changes*).

There is another large class of structures: those that use a much wider range of transformations (though also including permutation). These will be called *developmental* structures, and whereas the permutational structures were compared to a kaleidoscope, the developmental structures might be compared to the growth of a flower or a tree. More generally, these developmental structures proceed rather like some natural process in which the gestalt units at the lower level undergo perceptible changes also, as well as creating changing shapes at the higher level. Among such developmental structures, we might further distinguish two basic types, according to the apparent *direction* of the morphological changes, whether essentially from simple to complex (as in the sonata-allegro form, for example, or in fact so much music of the eighteenth and nineteenth—and even the twentieth—centuries) or in some other direction, including no direction at all. The "Emerson" movement of the "Concord" Sonata (as Henry Cowell points out)[1] seems to begin with everything at once in a deliberately not-so-clear profusion, followed by a progressive clarification of this initial material, in which one after another of a set of four or five basic thematic ideas is singled out—extricated from the more complex fabric—and subjected to transformations of various kinds. The process seems to involve a kind of *extractive* variation in contrast to the *expansive* variation of, say, Beethoven or Brahms or Bartók. I call the first of these two types of developmental structure the "classical" type, while the second might be called the "kitchen sink" type.

The third of the four types of closure described earlier ("an abrupt *decrease in complexity*") assumes nothing about the form of the music that precedes it, but the other three either imply or are generally associated with specific ways of beginning and/or continuing at the large-formal level. This, in turn, suggests the possibility of a more general typology of large-forms, and this will be attempted later. But first, let us consider some of the various ways pieces begin and proceed. In addition to (1) the "classical" and (2) the "kitchen sink" types, these include (3) a *serial* type, beginning with one of the many variants of a single *Grundgestalt* that will be the basis of everything that follows. Whereas the first two structural types involve *developmental* structures, I would call this third type *permutational* rather than developmental. In addition, this serial type is what we might call *monomorphic*—that is, all the specific forms in the piece (at one level, at least) are derived from one "basic shape." And there is a second permutational type, which I call (4) the *polymorphic-permutational*, involving a larger number of "basic shapes" whose forms are never varied but whose sequential ordering in time is subjected to continual variation.

Note that, in no. 1 above, there is always the sense that the initial statement of the idea is the "canonic" form of it—the true starting point—whereas in no. 2 the canonic form of a given thematic idea seems rather to occur sometime later in the piece, when it is finally "clarified." In no. 3, on the other hand, *any* variant of the *Grundgestalt* could be taken as the starting-point, and the canonic form, if indeed there *is* one, might occur anywhere. In addition, the first two types involve what the mathematician might call an "open" or "infinite" set, because there is no limit on the number of potential variants of the basic "idea," whereas in no. 3 there is often a "closed" or "finite" set, with a limited number of variants. There is, finally, (5) the *windowed* type, mentioned earlier, which arbitrarily begins a process that could be imagined to have begun at some earlier point in time; the music thus initiated is invariably ergodic, as defined earlier, and usually—though not always—heteromorphic in structure.

At this highest of our several hierarchical levels of organization and perception, in place of medium or method, certain *esthetic* concerns seem to have the most influence on musical form—or, rather, one aspect or manifestation of esthetic concerns that might be called the *experiential model*, by which I mean conscious and unconscious assumptions about the *function* of a piece of music and about the nature of the musical experience itself. The model, of course, affects musical form at other, lower levels, too, but it is at this large-formal level that the *idea* of a model underlying musical forms becomes most useful. In pre-twentieth-century music, the model often has to do with *song and dance* forms—the "colloquial language" of folk music. In addition, there is a large body of music whose overall form suggests—explicitly or implicitly—a *rhetorical* model (often superimposed upon or incorporating the basic elements of the song and dance model).

At the large-formal level, the song and dance model is manifested primarily in the *orderly recurrence of sections* (supported, of course, at the lower levels by all of the basic conventions of pre-twentieth-century music mentioned earlier). With a few notable exceptions, there has been a tendency to avoid the repetition or recurrence of whole sections in the new music since 1900, even when there is a clear-cut sectional structure. The song and dance model, therefore, has not survived very well the changes that have occurred in twentieth-century music. The same cannot be said of the rhetorical model, however, even though a number of new models have emerged. The rhetorical model, of course, is most clearly expressed in traditional sonata form, with its exposition, development, and recapitulation and its excursion away from and back to a tonic (both structural arch forms). Again, this large-formal model is supported, at lower levels, by variation-processes and by tonal conventions. In later nineteenth-century program music and impressionism, certain new models began to be used (natural processes or events, life situations, place characteristics, etc.). But these tended to be completely conscious and explicit and to be superimposed upon or assimilated within the conventions of the traditional song and dance and rhetorical models.

New experiential models in twentieth-century music include the following:

1. *subconscious, irrational thought processes* (Viennese "expressionism"): while still related to the older rhetorical model in its implication that some kind of idea (or "thought process") is being communicated, the actual form is radically changed by the shift from "rational" to "irrational." (It is significant that this development in music coincides, historically, with Freud's work in psychology, including the psychoanalytic technique of free association, and James Joyce's stream-of-consciousness prose.) Among the formal manifestations of this model were the heteromorphic ("athematic") sequence-structure mentioned earlier and the development of what might be called the *short-form*, involving extreme condensation and often (though not always) extreme complexity, by comparison with earlier music;

2. *memory-processes* (Ives): similar in many ways to no. 1 but involving the "irrational" juxtaposition and superimposition of otherwise "rational" clangs and sequences, or fragments of these, and a deliberate stylistic eclecticism (Ives used many other models, of course, including the song and dance and rhetorical models, and perhaps no single piece expresses only the memory-process model, but such a model is nevertheless relevant to many of his pieces);

3. the *machine*, or the idea of mechanism in general: involving both an overall effect of mechanical drive, precision, or rigidity and the *premise* that the whole piece somehow unfolds inevitably or "logically" from a given set of initial conditions; and

4. *physical processes* (Varèse, Cage): related to no. 3 somewhat as the statistical branches of physical science are related to the older mechanical laws of Galileo and Newton. Since Cage's work in the 1950s, this model often involves chance methods and situations that are *indeterminate* in various ways and to varying degrees. Among the formal manifestations of this model are the *ergodic* form (with windowed boundaries) mentioned earlier and a kind of *environment music* (Cage, Alvin Lucier) in which some physical process is not only the model but actually becomes the *source* or *controlling agent* of the sounds themselves. The first two of these new models usually give rise to structures that are developmental, even when they are *nonrhetorical*—with the exception of a few cases in which the structures are completely heteromorphic (e.g., Schoenberg's op. 19, no. 1). The last two models, on the other hand, most often give rise to permutational

structures, since they often involve a situation in which—in some sense, at least—all the possibilities are *given at the outset*, and what happens later results simply from the permutation of this set of possibilities.

Although the song and dance model has virtually disappeared from Western "art music" in the twentieth century (it is still very much in evidence in popular music, of course), much otherwise new music has been written that is still based on the old rhetorical model. Such music is not new, however, with respect to its form at this level. The listener is still having an initial set of "ideas" presented to him, the ideas are then "developed" or otherwise elaborated upon, and finally, the ideas are summarized or "recapitulated"—tensions are "resolved," and the communication process has been completed (one-way as this process of "communication" may be). The form here—and all of its associated devices—comprises, essentially, a *strategy of persuasion* within a situation assumed to involve, in a fundamental way, the communication of ideas. It should be obvious by now, however, that this is not all that music can be—indeed, it is not what music *was* until late in the Baroque period, that is, relatively recently in the long history of music. And yet, it is interesting to note that of the three extra-formal factors that have been mentioned as contributing to, and resulting from, changes of form at various hierarchical levels (*medium*, *method*, and *model*), this last was actually the *first* to change (in late nineteenth-century program music and impressionism). This was followed by the changes in method (resulting from the breakdown of the tonal system around the turn of the century) and finally by the changes in the medium (beginning around 1910). The major changes in these broad, form-influencing factors have thus been—from the standpoint of our hierarchical levels—*from the top down*. The reason for this order of events is probably that, as we move from higher to lower hierarchical levels, we move from musical realms that were more consciously controlled, subject to individual stylistic variation, and less predetermined culturally, toward realms that were more highly predetermined, less subject to individual stylistic variation, and therefore less consciously controlled in pre-twentieth-century music.

The preceding observations may be summarized, in a very abbreviated way, in the following suggested typology of large-forms, based on the distinctions that have already been made between the structural versus the morphological aspects of form in general, rhetorical versus nonrhetorical models, developmental versus permutational structures, and ergodic versus nonergodic morphological conditions.

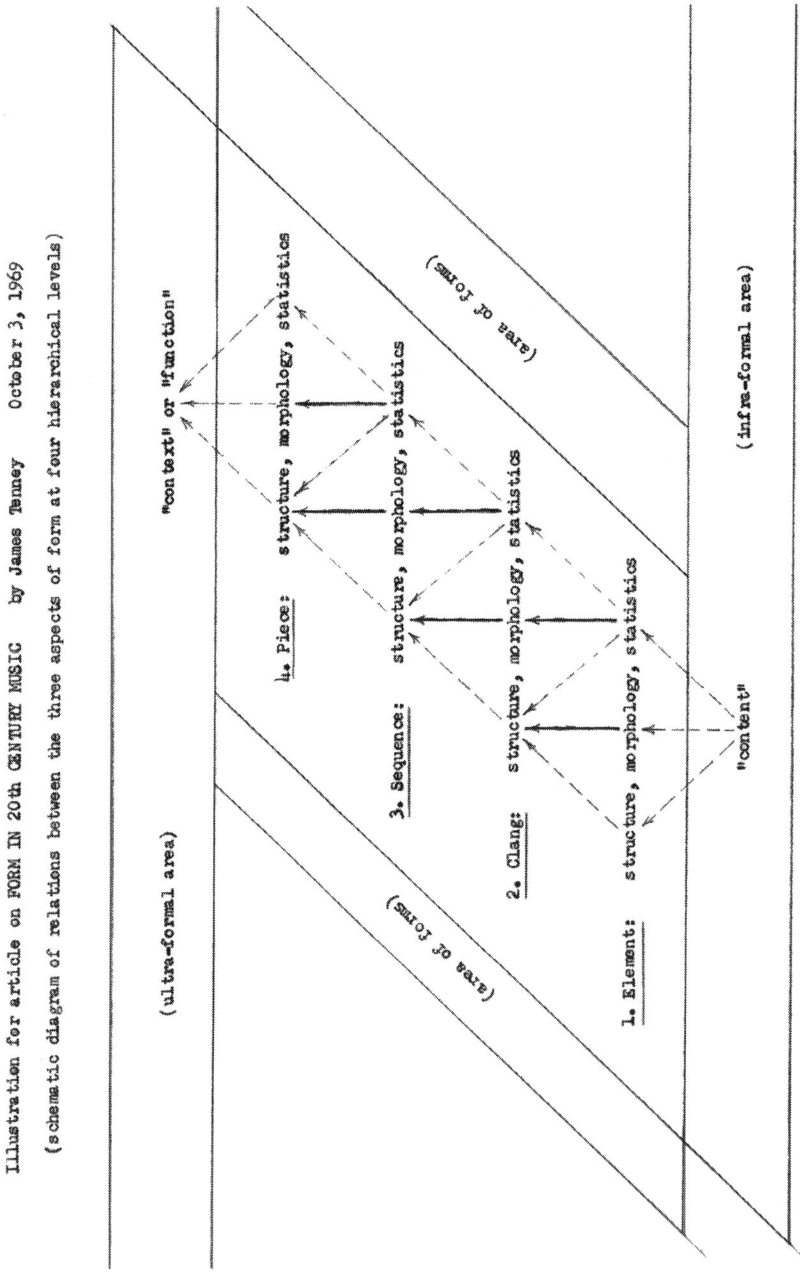
Illustration for article on FORM IN 20th CENTURY MUSIC by James Tenney October 3, 1969
(schematic diagram of relations between the three aspects of form at four hierarchical levels)
"context" or "function"
(ultra-formal area)
4. Piece: structure, morphology, statistics
3. Sequence: structure, morphology, statistics
2. Clang: structure, morphology, statistics
1. Element: structure, morphology, statistics
(area of forms)
(area of forms)
(infra-formal area)
"content"

Structural

1. Developmental
    a. rhetorical (generally bithematic and metamorphic, with a kind of additive or expansive variation)
    b. nonrhetorical (generally polythematic and metamorphic, with a kind of subtractive or extractive variation)
2. Permutational
    a. monomorphic or serial (all forms derived from one "basic shape")
    b. polymorphic (variable ordering of a fixed set of "basic shapes")
3. Heteromorphic (athematic)

Morphological

1. Nonergodic
    a. arch-form
    b. ramp-form
    c. (others?)
2. Ergodic ("windowed" closure)
    a. using "all possibilities" (wide parametric ranges)
    b. with imposed restrictions (narrow parametric ranges)

CHAPTER 7

META *Meta ≠ Hodos*

(1975)

Preface

"META *Meta ≠ Hodos*" represents an attempt to organize certain ideas first presented in *Meta ≠ Hodos* in 1961, incorporating insights and revisions that have emerged since then. The writing was initially motivated by the desire to provide an outline of my ideas and terminology for use by students in a class in formal perception and analysis at the California Institute of the Arts. The intent was therefore to make it as concise as possible, even if at the expense of comprehensibility, and I am aware that the result is probably not easily penetrated by someone not already familiar with *Meta ≠ Hodos*. Nevertheless, I am pleased with the form it has taken and hope that others may find it of interest in spite of its difficulties.

James Tenney, November 1975

A. On Perceptual Organization

Proposition I: In the process of musical perception, *temporal gestalt-units* (TGs) are formed at several different hierarchical levels (HLs).

Comment I.1: The number of hierarchical levels in a given piece and the relative durations of the TGs at adjacent hierarchical levels vary, depending on such things as style, texture, tempo, the duration of the piece, etc.

Comment I.2: TGs at a given hierarchical level are not always or necessarily disjunct—i.e., there are frequent intersections and ambiguities in their perceptual formation.

Definition 1: A TG at the lowest (or first) hierarchical level will be called an *element*.

Comment 1.1: An element is a TG that is perceived as (temporally) *singular*, i.e., not divisible into lower-level (shorter) TGs. (See Comment IV.1.3, below, for a further description of element characteristics.)

Definition 2: A TG at the next higher (second) hierarchical level will be called a *clang*.

Comment 2.1: A clang is a TG at the lowest hierarchical level within which still-lower-level TGs are perceived.

Definition 3: A TG at the next higher (third) hierarchical level will be called a *sequence*.

Comment 3.1: A clang thus consists of a temporal succession of two or more elements; a sequence consists of a temporal succession of two or more clangs. Note that a combination of two or more elements occurring simultaneously does not necessarily constitute a clang. (For the case of simultaneous TGs, see Definitions 5 through 8, below.)

Definition 4: The TG at the highest hierarchical level is the *piece* as a whole (but see Proposition V and Comment V.1, below).

Comment 4.1: The number of intermediate hierarchical levels (between those of the sequence and the piece) is variable (cf. Comment 1.1, above).

Definition 5: A TG whose component, next-lower-level TGs are perceived one at a time will be called *monophonic*.

Definition 6: A TG whose component, next-lower-level TGs are perceived two or more at a time will be called *polyphonic*.

Definition 7: A TG whose component TGs at all lower levels are monophonic will be called *simple*.

Definition 8: A TG whose component TGs at any lower level are polyphonic will be called *compound*.

Comment 8.1: These terms will frequently be combined to describe four types of "vertical" construction or texture:

(1) a *simple-monophonic* TG (at a given hierarchical level) is one whose component TGs are monophonic (at all lower levels) and are perceived one at a time (at the given level);

(2) a *simple-polyphonic* TG (at a given hierarchical level) is one whose component TGs are monophonic (at all lower levels) but perceived two or more at a time (at the given level);

(3) a *compound-monophonic* TG (at a given hierarchical level) is one whose component TGs are polyphonic (at any lower level) but are perceived one at a time (at the given level);

(4) a *compound-polyphonic* TG (at a given hierarchical level) is one whose component TGs are polyphonic (at any lower level) and are perceived two or more at a time (at the given level).

Comment 8.2: The relationships among these four types of texture at three adjacent hierarchical levels are shown schematically in figure 1.

Proposition II: The perceptual formation of TGs at any hierarchical level is determined by a number of factors of cohesion and segregation, the most important of which are *proximity* and *similarity*; their effects may be described as follows:

Proposition II.1: Relative temporal *proximity* of TGs at a given hierarchical level will tend to group them, perceptually, into a TG at the next higher level.

Proposition II.2: Relative *similarities* of TGs at a given hierarchical level will tend to group them, perceptually, into a TG at the next higher level.

Proposition II.3: Conversely, relative temporal *separation* and/or *differences* between TGs at a given hierarchical level will tend to segregate them into separate TGs at the next higher level.

Comment II.3.1: The perceptual formation of *lower-level* TGs is also affected by several secondary factors of cohesion and segregation, including *accent*, *repetition*, *objective set*, and *subjective set* (see *Meta ≠ Hodos*), but these will not be dealt with here.

B. On Musical Parameters

Definition 9: A *parameter* will be defined here as any distinctive attribute of sound in terms of which one sound may be perceived as different from another, or a sound may be perceived to change in time.

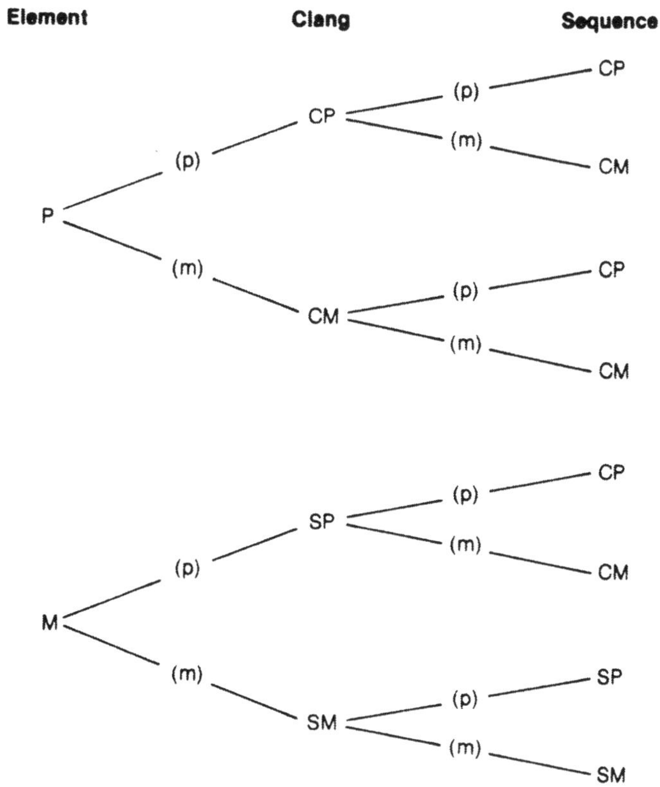

FIGURE 1. Relationships among simple, compound, monophonic, and polyphonic TGs at three HLs (M = monophonic, P = polyphonic, S = simple, C = compound, (m) = perceived one at a time, (p) = perceived two or more at a time).

Comment 9.1: This definition refers to "subjective" or *musical* parameters (e.g., pitch, loudness, etc.) as distinct from "objective" or *acoustical* parameters (frequency, amplitude, etc.).

Comment 9.2: There is not, in general, a one-to-one correspondence between musical and acoustical parameters. Where there *is* such a correspondence, the relation is more nearly logarithmic than linear.

Proposition III: Pitch, timbre, and (musical) time are not simply one-dimensional parameters, because each includes at least two relatively independent "subparameters."

Comment III.1: Similarities and differences between any two pitch *intervals* are perceived in two different ways, depending on their relative magnitudes and their interval qualities. These, in turn, result from differences in what will be called (1) *pitch-height* and (2) *pitch-chroma.*

Definition 10: *Pitch-height* refers to that aspect of pitch-perception that depends on the existence of a continuous range of pitches from low to high.

Definition 11: *Pitch-chroma* refers to that aspect of pitch-perception that depends on the phenomenon of "octave equivalence" and the fact that the continuous range of pitches is also *cyclic*, virtually returning to its starting point in each transition from one octave to the next.

Comment 11.1: These two subparameters may be related to the fact that there are two distinct mechanisms of pitch-perception involved in hearing—a "place" mechanism (determining pitch-height) and a "time" mechanism (determining pitch-chroma). The place mechanism is most effective for high frequencies, the time mechanism for lower ones, but the two overlap over a fairly broad range in the middle register, and it is here that our pitch-perception is the most acute (and the most bidimensional).

Comment 11.2: The multidimensionality of *timbre* is due to the fact that it is determined in a complex way by our perception of a large number of acoustical features, which may be subsumed under three categories:

(1) the steady-state *spectrum*,

(2) various kinds of steady-state *modulations*, and

(3) transient modulations or *envelopes.*

Comment 11.3: The subparameters of (musical) *time* will be called (1) *epoch*, (2) *duration*, and (3) *temporal density.*

Definition 12: *Epoch* refers to the moment of occurrence—in the ongoing flow of experienced time—of any musical "event," compared to some reference moment such as the beginning of the piece.

Definition 13: The *temporal density* of a TG is the number of its component, next-lower-level TGs per unit time; ("*duration*" will be used in its usual sense).

Comment 13.1: The average temporal density of a TG at a given hierarchical level will thus be equal to the reciprocal of the average duration of its component TGs at the next lower level.

Comment 13.2: "Tempo" is a special case of temporal density, referring to an expressed or implied pulse or "beat" rather than to actual durations, and it is only relevant to *lower-level* TGs.

Definition 14: Pitch-height and epoch (which correspond most closely to the acoustical parameters, log-frequency and "real" time) will be called *distributive* parameters, because a difference in at least one of these is necessary for two sounds to be perceived as *separate*.

Definition 15: All other parameters (including loudness, pitch-chroma, duration, temporal density, and the several subparameters of timbre) will be called *attributive* parameters. Note that a difference in any of these is insufficient, by itself, for two sounds to be perceived as separate—there must *also* be a difference in one of the distributive parameters.

C. On Formal Perception and Description

Proposition IV: The perception of form at any hierarchical level involves the apprehension of three distinct aspects of form at that and all lower levels. These three aspects of form will be called *state*, *shape*, and *structure*.

Definition 16: *State* refers to the statistical and other "global" properties of a TG, including the *mean values* and *ranges* in each parameter and its *duration*.

Definition 17: *Shape* refers to the "profile" of a TG in some parameter, determined by *changes* in that parameter with respect to either of the distributive parameters, epoch and pitch-height (or their acoustical correlates, "real" time and log-frequency).

Definition 18: *Structure* refers to *relations between subordinate parts* of a TG, i.e., relations between its component TGs at the next (or several) lower level(s). (See also Definition 19 and its Comments, below.)

Proposition IV.1: A complete description of a monophonic TG at any hierarchical level requires descriptions of state, shape, and structure for every parameter with respect to *time*.

Comment IV.1.1: In this context (i.e., that of monophonic TGs), shape is time-dependent, while state and structure are "out-of-time" characteristics (but see Comment IV.2.1, below).

Comment IV.1.2: The state of a monophonic TG simply depends on lower-level *states*; shape is determined by *changes of state* at the next lower level; structure depends on *relations among states, shapes, and structures* at the next (or several) lower level(s) (see figure 2).

Comment IV.1.3: Since, by Definition 1, Comment 1.1, an element is not perceived as "divisible into lower-level TGs," the structure of an element is not perceived directly—i.e., element-"structure" is located in the "infraformal" area of figure 2, below the "threshold of formal perception." Element-"shape" is sometimes above, sometimes below this threshold.

Comment IV.1.4: The various state-descriptions of an element are equivalent to the set of parametric values needed

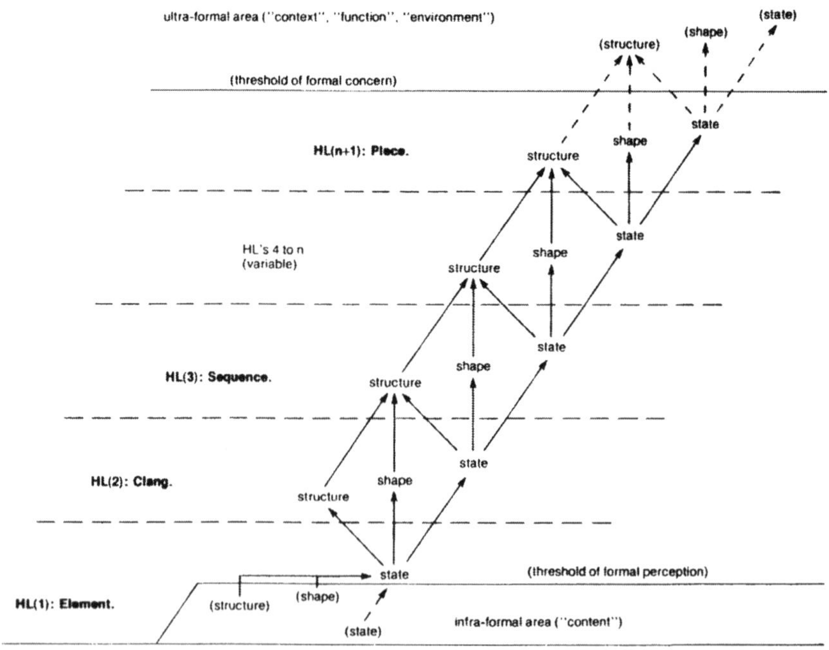

FIGURE 2. Relationships among the three aspects of form at several hierarchical levels (HLs).

to describe the element (except when aspects of element-shape are also reduced to parameters, e.g., amplitude-envelope shape).

Comment IV.1.5: The "similarities" and "differences" of Propositions II.2 and II.3 may be of all three kinds: state, shape, and structure.

Definition 19: There are three basic types of structure (corresponding to the three connecting lines to "structure" in figure 2). These will be called

(1) *statistical structure* (i.e., relations between lower-level states),

(2) *morphological structure* (relations between lower-level shapes), and

(3) *cascaded structure* (relations between lower-level structures).

Comment 19.1: Each of these three types of structure may be specified by showing the relations between each lower-level TG and *every other TG* at that level. For a given set of relations (limited in such a way that there is only one relation between each pair of TGs), this might be done by arranging them in a square array or matrix. In the case of statistical structure, such a matrix might show, for example, the set of *intervals* between the parametric mean values of each pair of TGs.

Comment 19.2: For morphological structure, the relations included in such a matrix might be as few as three (e.g., =, ≠, and T, for "identical to," "unrelated to," and "related via some transformation," respectively), or the "T" might be expanded into a longer list such as the following:

E/C (for expansion/contraction of intervals),
X/L (extension/elision at the ends of a TG),
I/D (interpolation/deletion into or from within a TG),
I (inversion),
R (retrogression),
W ("warping" or distortion of shape, still preserving its essential topological features),
P (permutation of the order of component TGs), etc.

Comment 19.3: For cascaded structure, the only relations needed for such a matrix might be = and ≠.

Definition 20: In addition to the three basic types of structure listed in Definition 19, there is still another type that is relevant to musical perception, one involving relations between *relations*, rather than relations between (various aspects of) the TGs themselves. These will be called *relational structures* and may be of three kinds: (1) *state-relational* structure, (2) *shape-relational* structure, and (3) *structure-relational* structure.

Proposition IV.2: A complete description of a polyphonic (or compound-monophonic) TG at any hierarchical level requires descriptions (in addition to those listed in Proposition IV.1) of state, shape, and structure for each of the *attributive* parameters with respect to *log-frequency*.

Comment IV.2.1: In this context, although shape is not time-dependent, it still involves the sequential order of states in the frequency domain; state and structure do not.

Comment IV.2.2: For polyphonic TGs, the relationships between state, shape, and structure (with respect to frequency)—such as those described in Comment IV.1.2, above—are not yet known.

Proposition V: Formal properties at a given hierarchical level determine the (nonsemantic) "content" of the TGs at the next higher level; they also determine the "context" (or "function" or "environment") of TGs at the next lower level.

Comment V.1: What we do finally *call* (nonsemantic) "content" is the result of "forms" at a level below the first one we are able to perceive "formally"; what we call "context" (or "function" or "environment") is determined by formal conditions at a level above the largest one we *choose to deal with* "formally."

Proposition VI: As we move from the infraformal area up into and through the first few specifically formal hierarchical levels, new parameters emerge.

Comment VI.1: Even *within* the infraformal area there is a similar "emergence," e.g., the transition from the basic physical nature of the signal as (simply) amplitude vs. time to the (acoustical) parameter *frequency*. Examples above the threshold include the *timbre*-effects of rise-time and vibrato (at HL(1) in figure 2) and *temporal density* (at HL(2)).

Proposition VII: There is a close correlation between what may be called *parametric focus* and the relative *range of variation* of next-lower-level states within a TG; that is, the greater the range in a given parameter, the more one's attention will be focused on the changes in that parameter and the more prominent will be the shape determined by those changes.

Definition 21: A parameter whose variation (over a relatively wide range) at the next lower level thus focuses the attention on the shape of a TG in that parameter will be called a *formative* parameter.

Definition 22: A parameter whose relative constancy (or variation over a *narrow* range) at the next lower level is thus significantly responsible for its unity as a gestalt (via the similarity-factor of Proposition II.2) will be called a *cohesive* parameter.

Proposition VIII: The formative parameters of a TG are generally different from the cohesive parameters of that same TG.

Comment VIII.1: This follows almost simply "by definition," but its implications are important enough to justify it as a separate Proposition.

Proposition IX: The formative parameters of a TG at a given hierarchical level are generally different from the formative parameters of the next-higher-level TG that contains it.

Comment IX.1: One obvious exception to Propositions VIII and IX may occur when the formative parameter of a TG is pitch, but this is only possible because the number of distinguishable values in this parameter is very great—and it can only occur when the range of pitch-variation within the next-lower-level TGs is relatively limited. The more extensive the range covered within each lower-level TG, the less perceptible will be the changes of pitch-state from one TG to the next, and thus the less effective will pitch be as a formative parameter at the next higher level. This adjacent-level "trade-off" relation is made more explicit and precise in the following Proposition:

Proposition X: For any parameter with respect to time, the greater the range of variation at a given hierarchical level, the smaller the range of variation possible at the next higher level, and vice versa.

Comment X.1: For a given parameter, and under the special condition that the ranges are identical for all TGs at a given hierarchical level, the following relations will hold:

For the first hierarchical level, considered by itself, the maximum range available is $N_{max}(1) = N_t$, where N_t is the total number of distinguishable values in that parameter. When two hierarchical levels are considered, the maximum range at the second level is

$$N_{max}(2) = N_t - [N(1) - 1].$$

For a third level, the maximum range will be

$$N_{max}(3) = N_t - [N(1) - 1] - [N(2) - 1].$$

More generally, the maximum range available at a given level (L) is

$$N_{max}(L) = N_t - [N(1) - 1] - [N(2) - 1] - \ldots - [N(L - 1) - 1], \text{ or}$$
$$N_{max}(L) = N_t - N_L + L - 1.$$

Finally, the total available range (N_t) may be distributed equally among some number of levels (L), so that

$$N(1) = N(2) = \ldots = N(L), \text{ and } N_{max}(L+1) = 0,$$
by setting each N at $N = N_t / L+1$.

Definition 23: A TG whose component, next-lower-level TGs all have the *same state* in a given parameter will be called *ergodic* with respect to that parameter.

Comment 23.1: The shape of an ergodic TG is thus "flat" in that parameter.

Comment 23.2: An ergodic TG has the same parametric state as each of its component, next-lower-level TGs.

Definition 24: A TG whose component, next-lower-level TGs have *different states* in a given parameter will be called *nonergodic* with respect to that parameter.

Comment 24.1: The *shape* of a TG may thus be either ergodic or nonergodic with respect to a given parameter.

Definition 25: A TG whose component, next-lower-level TGs all have the *same shape* in a given parameter will be called *isomorphic* with respect to that parameter.

Definition 26: A TG whose component, next-lower-level TGs all have *different* (or, more precisely, *unrelated*) *shapes* in a given parameter will be called *heteromorphic* with respect to that parameter.

Definition 27: A TG whose component, next-lower-level TGs have shapes that are related to each other via some process of *transformation* will be called *metamorphic* with respect to that parameter.

Comment 27.1: The *morphological structure* of a TG may thus be either isomorphic, heteromorphic, or metamorphic with respect to a given parameter.

D. On Entropy as a Measure of Variation

Definition 28: One of the most important aspects of musical experience is the perception of variation, and a useful measure of variation is *entropy*. In information theory, the entropy of a "message" consisting of a series of *n* discrete "symbols" drawn from an "alphabet" of *N* equally probable symbols is

$$H = n \log_2 N \quad \text{(bits per message).}$$

The entropy of each symbol is

$$H = \log_2 N \quad \text{(bits per symbol).}$$

Comment 28.1: The most important variable here is N, the number of symbols available. In the special case where $N = 1$, $H = 0$.

Comment 28.2: When the available symbols are not equally probable—i.e., when they do not occur with the same relative frequencies (p_i)—then

$$H = -\sum p_i \log_2 p_i \quad \text{(bits per message).}$$

Definition 29: We may define as many different types of entropies as there are different types of structures. Thus, we may distinguish between *statistical*, *morphological*, and *structural entropies*, according to whether the "symbols" considered are lower-level *states*, *shapes*, or *structures*. In addition, there will be three *relational entropies*—those involving state-relations, shape-relations, and structure-relations.

Definition 30: The entropies of a TG at a given hierarchical level may be measured either in terms of component TGs at the lowest (i.e., element-) level or in terms of component TGs at the next lower level. The first kind of measure (which has been the usual procedure in most applications of information theory) will be called an *additive* measure, the second (which will be used most often here) will be called an *adjacent-level* measure of entropy.

Definition 31: Since a TG at every hierarchical level except the lowest and highest (i.e., any except an element or the whole piece) may be considered *both* a message (containing lower-level symbols) *and* a symbol (contained within a higher-level message), the various entropies may be defined for a TG either as *message-entropies* or as *symbol-entropies*.

Comment 31.1: The following Propositions refer to adjacent-level message-entropies of a TG:

Proposition XI: The statistical entropy of an ergodic TG is zero.

Proposition XII: The state-relational entropy of an ergodic TG is zero.

Proposition XIII: The statistical entropy of a nonergodic TG at a given hierarchical level depends on

(1) the number of its component, next-lower-level TGs,

(2) the number of their distinguishable states, and

(3) the relative frequencies of these states.

Proposition XIV: The state-relational entropy of a nonergodic TG at a given hierarchical level depends on

(1) the number of its component, next-lower-level TGs,

(2) the number of the distinguishable differences between their states, and

(3) the relative frequencies of these differences.

Proposition XV: The maximum statistical entropy attainable in a TG at a given hierarchical level is *inversely related* to the statistical entropy of its component TGs at the next lower level. (This is a consequence of Proposition X.)

Proposition XVI: The morphological entropy of an isomorphic TG is zero.

Proposition XVII: The shape-relational entropy of an isomorphic TG is zero.

Proposition XVIII: The morphological entropy of a heteromorphic TG is maximal (for a given number of next-lower-level TGs).

Proposition XIX: The shape-relational entropy of a heteromorphic TG is zero.

Comment XIX.1: There must be a meaningful way to define the morphological entropy of a metamorphic TG, but this has not yet been found.

Comment XIX.2: Nothing is yet known about structural entropies.

CHAPTER 8

The Chronological Development of Carl Ruggles's Melodic Style (1977)

The music of Carl Ruggles has recently become a subject of theoretical interest again after a long period of neglect. In particular, Steven E. Gilbert has pointed out certain features of Ruggles's later works that are amenable to "trichordal" analysis.[1] In this paper I shall report the results of some statistical analyses of Ruggles's melodic lines, carried out with the aid of a computer.

Certain aspects of Ruggles's music—the general shape of the lines, the ever-present dissonant sonorities—are so consistent throughout all of his pieces that one can easily get an impression of singular stylistic homogeneity, as though there were no significant changes or developments in style from 1919 (*Toys*) through 1944 (*Organum*). My results suggest just the opposite conclusion—at least with respect to his melodic writing—and lend support to a statement he made in a letter to Henry Cowell in January 1926: "More and more I'm gaining that complete command of line which, to me, is the basis of all music. There is absolutely no comparison between that which I've done [and] that which I'm doing now."[2]

Significant changes in Ruggles's melodic style are manifested in my statistical results in three ways: (1) a gradual shift in the distribution of melodic-interval frequencies; (2) a more and more effective avoidance of early pitch-class recurrences; and (3) an increase in the frequency and proximity of dissonant relations within his melodic lines.[3]

Interval Frequencies

Tables and graphs of interval-frequency distributions for each piece and for certain groups of pieces are shown in figures 1 through 23; in figures 24 and 25 the relative frequencies of various intervals and interval-sets are shown as a function of their chronological sequence. For these latter, the information has been grouped into six data-points, as follows: (1) *Toys*, *Angels*, and the three movements of *Vox Clamans in Deserto* (1919–23); (2) *Men and Mountains* ("Men," "Lilacs," and "Marching Mountains") (1924); (3) *Portals* (1925); (4) *Sun Treader* (1931); (5) *Evocations* I–IV (1937–43); and (6) *Organum* (1944).[4] From these graphs we can get a very clear picture of certain developmental aspects of Ruggles's melodic style. First of all, there is a decisive trend from a relatively diatonic to a highly chromatic idiom, shown by the increased use of minor seconds and major sevenths and a corresponding decrease in the use of major seconds and minor sevenths. In addition, there is a significant increase in the frequency of tritones and (to a lesser extent) perfect fourths and fifths, with a decrease in the frequency of minor thirds, major thirds, and major sixths—all of which suggest a progressive elimination of triadic/tonal implications.

In many ways (note especially the graphs for minor seconds, tritones, major seconds, minor thirds, and major sevenths in figure 24) there is a radical change between *Portals* (1925) and *Sun Treader* (1931), and it was during just this period that Ruggles made the statement to Cowell quoted earlier. By the same token—according to the same criteria—his last completed work, *Organum* (1944), marks a return to some of the conditions characteristic of the earlier works (see these same interval-plots [figure 24] and also the superimposed graph for *Organum* versus earlier groups of pieces [figure 21]). In a sense, of course, *Portals* is a transitional work between two fairly distinct style periods. Whether it should be considered the last of the early works or the first of the later works would depend on many factors not considered here, but the superimposed plot (figure 22) of interval-frequency distributions for *Portals*, the pieces preceding *Portals* (i.e., 1919–24), and those following it (1931–44) clearly suggests that it belongs to the early group, at least in terms of melodic-interval statistics.

Figure 23 shows superimposed plots of interval-frequency distributions for the early versus the later periods, and here the trends mentioned above can be seen quite clearly—the increase in the use of minor seconds, tritones, fourths, fifths, and major sevenths and the decrease in the frequencies of most of the other intervals—especially major seconds, minor and major thirds, major sixths, and minor sevenths. The interval-frequency distribution for all of Ruggles's pieces together is shown in figure 20. As in the plots for individual pieces, these are graphed in two ways, one distinguishing between ascending and descending forms of each interval, the other combining these into one plot of "absolute intervals." It is of interest to note that there are rather significant differences between ascending and descending interval frequencies for certain intervals—most importantly, I think, perfect fourths and fifths. What this plot tells us about these two intervals is that ascending fourths (and descending fifths) occur much less often in Ruggles's work than descending fourths (and ascending fifths). In the first case, descending fourths are used 1.75 times as often as ascending fourths. In the other, ascending fifths occur 2.17 times as often as descending fifths. This discrepancy is found in most of the individual pieces (though there are some exceptions—most notably *Organum*) and in the overall statistics, and it seems to constitute an important tendency in Ruggles's melodic writing. An explanation of the discrepancy suggests itself immediately. Both the ascending fourth and (even more) the descending fifth can easily imply or evoke a V–I cadential sense, "rooting" the melodic line (harmonically) at the second tone and thus obstructing the ongoing momentum of the line.

Another sort of asymmetry between ascending and descending interval frequencies can be seen in figure 25: The smaller intervals (up to and including the tritone) occur most often in descending form, while intervals larger than the tritone tend to occur most frequently in ascending form.[5] The shape of the larger melodic gestures implied by this asymmetry is one involving a faster ascent and a slower descent, thus: 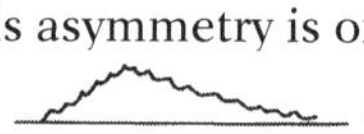 . I have no way of knowing whether this is a distinctive feature of Ruggles's style, or whether it is, in fact, typical of other styles as well (though I suspect it is). In any case, it might be an interesting line of investigation for someone involved in comparative studies of musical style.

Pitch-Class Repetition and Dissonant Relations

Ruggles's intention to avoid early pitch-class recurrences in his melodic lines has often been mentioned. In *New Musical Resources* (first published in 1930), Henry Cowell described Ruggles's procedure as follows:

> Carl Ruggles has developed a process for himself in writing melodies for polyphonic purposes which embodies a new principle. . . . He finds that if the same note is repeated in a melody before enough notes have intervened to remove the impression of the original note, there is a sense of tautology, because the melody should have proceeded to a fresh note instead of to a note already in the consciousness of the listener. Therefore Ruggles writes at least seven or eight different notes in a melody before allowing himself to repeat the same note, even in the octave.[6]

And in 1932 Charles Seeger wrote:

> The determining feature or principle of the melodic line is that of non-repetition of tone (either the same tone or any octave of it) until the tenth progression. This applies rigidly to the leading melody and characterizes the other parts to a surprising extent, though in *Portals* many repeated notes may be found at the fourth, fifth, and sixth progression. . . . Reiteration (immediate repetition) is occasionally effective, but only occasionally. The repetition of tones resulting from reiteration of phrase (as in the 6th and 7th measures of *Portals* and again in the 9th and 10th) constitutes, I believe, almost the only exception to the principle.[7]

The similarity of this "principle" to analogous procedures in the works of Schoenberg, Berg, and Webern is obvious, but it is important to note that there may have been a slightly different reason for it in Ruggles's case. Schoenberg has written: "The construction of a basic set of twelve tones derives from the intention to postpone the repetition of every tone as long as possible. I have stated in my *Harmonielehre* that the emphasis given to a tone by a premature repetition is capable of heightening it to the rank of a tonic. . . . It seemed in the first stages immensely important to avoid a similarity with tonality."[8]

Although Ruggles undoubtedly shared this desire to avoid giving any pitch "the rank of a tonic," this was not his only reason, or even his main one. I believe that what he was primarily concerned with was *freshness* (newness, maximal variety of pitch-content) and the sustaining of a high degree of atonal or atonical (but nevertheless *harmonic*) tension. As Seeger observed: "The harmonic variety, added to the extreme floridity of the melodic and contrapuntal fabric, gives one a feeling of having heard a great deal in a very short time."[9] This is reminiscent of Schoenberg's remarks about Webern's brevity and perhaps tells us something about the brevity of most of Ruggles's pieces, as well as their small number in his total oeuvre.

The fact that it was Ruggles's intention to postpone pitch-class repetitions as long as possible (whether this be after "seven or eight different notes," as Cowell wrote, or "until the tenth progression," as Seeger described it) is thus well documented. To my knowledge, however, no systematic effort has yet been made to determine precisely to what extent this intention was actually realized in the finished works. In order to investigate this aspect of Ruggles's melodic style, the computer program kept a running count of lengths of strings of different pitch-classes (LSDP) and computed overall averages (ALSD) of these string-lengths for the primary melodic line in each of Ruggles's pieces. In *Toys* and *Vox Clamans in Deserto*, the "primary melodic line" was simply the voice part. In the other pieces, it was generally taken to be the highest part, although secondary, contrapuntal parts were sometimes included when there was a temporary cessation of activity in the upper part. Immediately repeated pitches (or, as Seeger refers to them, "reiterated tones") were treated as a single occurrence of that pitch.

In addition to his tendency to avoid early pitch-class recurrences, there is another characteristic of Ruggles's melodic writing that has not been dealt with in the analytical literature. I referred to this earlier as "the frequency and proximity of dissonant relations within his melodic lines." That is, even in the absence of such interval-relations between consecutive pitches, some such relation will generally be found between each new pitch and one of the several immediately preceding pitches. To provide information on this feature, the program was designed to keep a running count of lengths of strings of consonant intervals (LSCI) and to compute overall averages of these (ALSC) for each piece.

In order to clarify the nature of the statistical measures involved here, let us consider the following example—the first long phrase in *Portals*. The twenty-four consecutive pitches in this initial phrase are shown in figure 26. The numbers immediately above the staff (LSDP) show the lengths of strings of different pitch-classes preceding (and including) each element in the line. The numbers immediately below the staff (LSCI) indicate the lengths of strings of pitches preceding each element that are consonant with respect to that element ("consonant" being defined here as any interval *except* the minor second and its derivatives). Consider, for example, the D (element 12) that marks the high-point and approximate midpoint of the phrase. The value of LSDP is 9, meaning that this D is the ninth element in a string, all of whose pitch-classes are different. The value for LSCI is 2, meaning that this D is preceded by only two pitches in consonant relation to it, the *third* preceding pitch—the E♭ of element 9—being in a dissonant relation to it. Note the sudden change in both values at element 13—the B♭ immediately following this high D. The value of LSDP drops from 9 to 3, while that of LSCI jumps from 2 to 8. I now suggest that these two measures, averaged over the total length of each piece, can provide useful indices of an important aspect of Ruggles's melodic style—its "atonal chromaticism"—a part, at least, of what Gilbert calls Ruggles's "twelve-tone system." Other measures are certainly conceivable, but these—especially ALSD—are particularly significant in Ruggles's case because they relate so closely to his declared intentions.

The values for ALSD and ALSC are shown graphically in figure 27, and it will be seen that there is a nearly perfect correlation between ALSD and the chronological sequence in which Ruggles's pieces were written.[10] The correlation between chronological sequence and LSCI is only a little less perfect, reaching its lowest point with *Sun Treader* and then increasing again (though only slightly) in the later works. Consider for a moment what is meant by the incredibly high values for ALSD reached in *Sun Treader*, the *Evocations*, and *Organum*. It is, in each case, almost 9, which means that at every moment in the process of composing these melodic lines there were only *four* pitch-classes remaining to choose from for the next tone—and not even all of these four would necessarily satisfy certain other conditions, such as the desire for dissonant relations in close proximity. Very severe constraints indeed for a music that sounds so free!

At this point I almost feel compelled to apologize for using statistics in a study of Carl Ruggles's music—or at least to make some effort to justify it. Carl was a friend and mentor to me early in my own musical life, and I know well the disdain he had for theoretical constructs detached from the expressive, intuitive core of the musical process. And yet, as Charles Seeger says so perceptively "in memoriam," although "Carl was no theorist . . . he admired it in others, especially when they worsted him in argument or brought some point to support his contention."[11] I would like to think that the statistical results reported here may indeed support his "contention," quoted earlier: "More and more I'm gaining that complete command of line which, to me, is the basis of all music."

	<-13	-13	-12	-11	-10	-9	-8	-7	-6	-5	-4	-3	-2	-1	0	1	2	3	4	5	6	7	8	9	10	11	12	13	>13	n
Toys (1919)	0	2	0	0	2	2	1	0	3	1	2	0	4	3	0	4	4	5	2	0	0	1	0	1	2	3	1	1	0	44
in %	0.	4.5	0.	0.	4.5	4.5	2.3	0.	6.8	2.3	4.5	0.	9.1	6.8	0.	9.1	9.1	11.4	4.5	0.	0.	2.3	0.	2.3	4.5	6.8	2.3	2.3	0.	
	ALSD = 4.17				ALSC = 3.32			absolute-interval frequencies:							0.	15.9	18.2	11.4	9.1	2.3	6.8	2.3	2.3	6.8	9.1	6.8	2.3	6.8	0.	

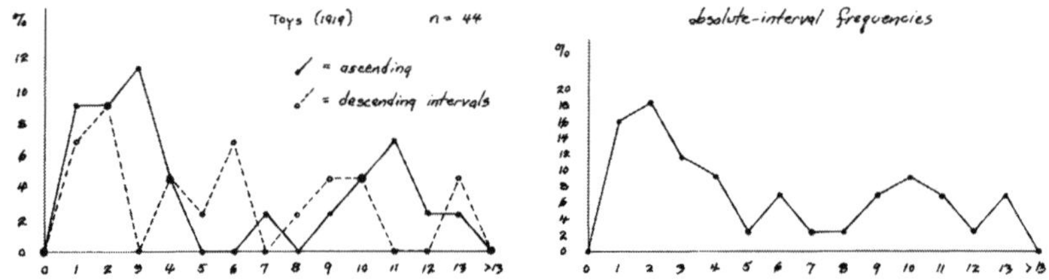

FIGURE 1. Melodic-interval frequency-distributions for *Toys* (1919).

	<-13	-13	-12	-11	-10	-9	-8	-7	-6	-5	-4	-3	-2	-1	0	1	2	3	4	5	6	7	8	9	10	11	12	13	>13	n
Angels (1920)	0	0	0	0	2	1	0	1	0	2	1	4	44	6	0	10	5	13	7	4	4	2	0	1	1	0	0	0	0	108
in %	0.	0.	0.	0.	1.9	.9	0.	.9	0.	1.9	.9	3.7	40.7	5.6	0.	9.3	4.6	12.0	6.5	3.7	3.7	1.9	0.	.9	.9	0.	0.	0.	0.	
	ALSD = 5.18				ALSC = 5.45			absolute-interval frequencies:							0.	14.9	45.3	15.7	7.4	5.6	3.7	2.8	0.	1.9	2.8	0.	0.	0.	0.	

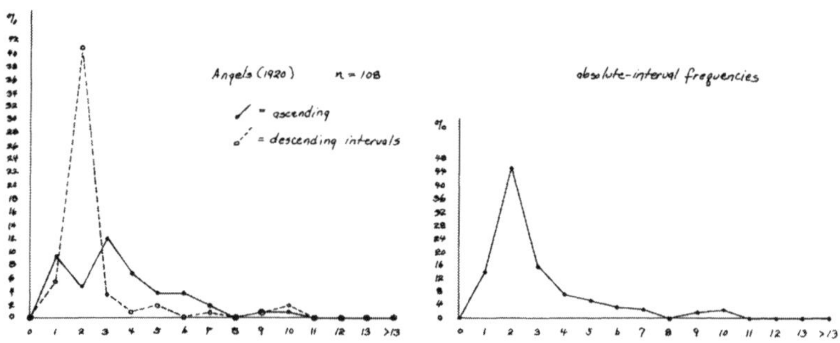

FIGURE 2. Melodic-interval frequency-distributions for *Angels* (1920).

(1923)	<-13	-13	-12	-11	-10	-9	-8	-7	-6	-5	-4	-3	-2	-1	0	1	2	3	4	5	6	7	8	9	10	11	12	13	>13	n
Vox Clamans in Deserto	1	1	0	7	2	8	0	2	5	4	11	9	11	10	0	22	11	16	2	3	4	6	6	1	3	3	0	5	1	154
in %	.6	.6	0.	4.5	1.3	5.2	0.	1.3	3.2	2.6	7.1	5.8	7.1	6.5	0.	14.3	7.1	10.4	1.3	1.9	2.6	3.9	3.9	.6	1.9	1.9	0.	3.2	.6	
	ALSD= 6.51				ALSC= 2.69			absolute-interval frequencies:							0.	20.8	14.3	16.2	8.4	4.5	5.8	5.2	3.9	5.8	3.2	6.5	0.	3.9	1.3	

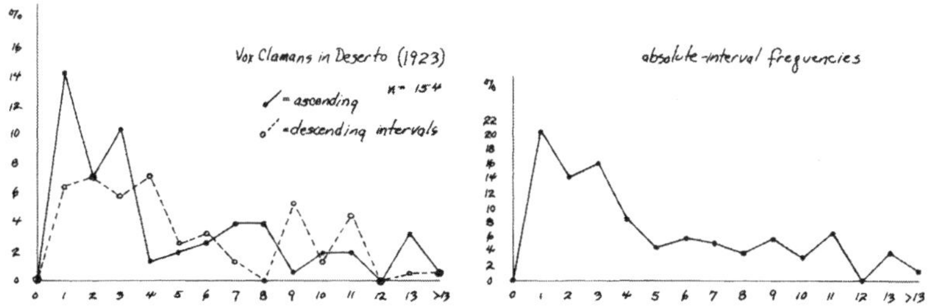

FIGURE 3. Melodic-interval frequency-distributions for *Vox Clamans in Deserto* (1923).

1919–1923 sub-totals	<-13	-13	-12	-11	-10	-9	-8	-7	-6	-5	-4	-3	-2	-1	0	1	2	3	4	5	6	7	8	9	10	11	12	13	>13	n
	1	3	0	7	6	11	1	3	8	7	14	13	59	19	0	36	20	34	11	7	8	9	6	3	6	6	1	6	1	306
in %	.3	1.0	0.	2.3	2.0	3.6	.3	1.0	2.6	2.3	4.6	4.2	19.3	6.2	0.	11.8	6.5	11.1	3.6	2.3	2.6	2.9	2.0	1.0	2.0	2.0	.3	2.0	.3	
	ALSD= 5.70				ALSC= 3.78			absolute-interval frequencies:							0.	18.0	25.8	15.4	8.2	4.6	5.2	3.9	2.3	4.6	3.9	4.2	.3	2.9	.7	

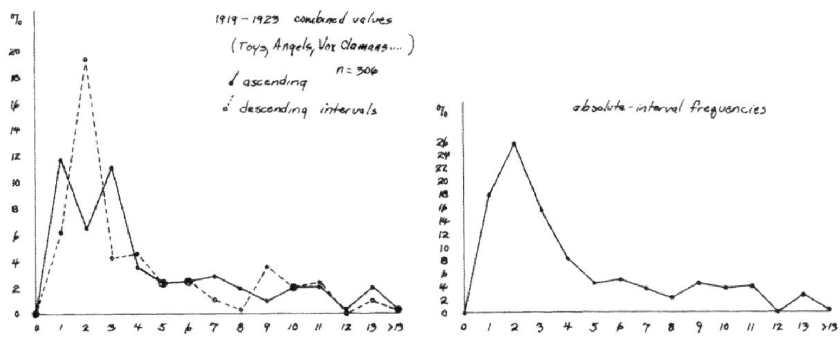

FIGURE 4. Melodic-interval frequency-distributions for the period 1919–23.

Men & Mtns:	<-13	-13	-12	-11	-10	-9	-8	-7	-6	-5	-4	-3	-2	-1	0	1	2	3	4	5	6	7	8	9	10	11	12	13	>13	n
I "Men" (1920–1924)	6	4	1	6	3	2	0	1	8	25	5	14	22	25	0	17	10	14	6	9	4	4	3	12	2	5	0	6	7	221
in %	2.7	1.8	.5	2.7	1.4	.9	0.	.5	3.6	11.3	2.3	6.3	10.0	11.3	0.	7.7	4.5	6.3	2.7	4.1	1.8	1.8	1.4	5.4	.9	2.3	0.	2.7	3.2	
	ALSD= 6.49				ALSC= 3.07			absolute-interval frequencies:							0.	19.0	14.5	12.7	5.0	15.4	5.4	2.3	1.4	6.3	2.3	5.0	.5	4.5	5.9	

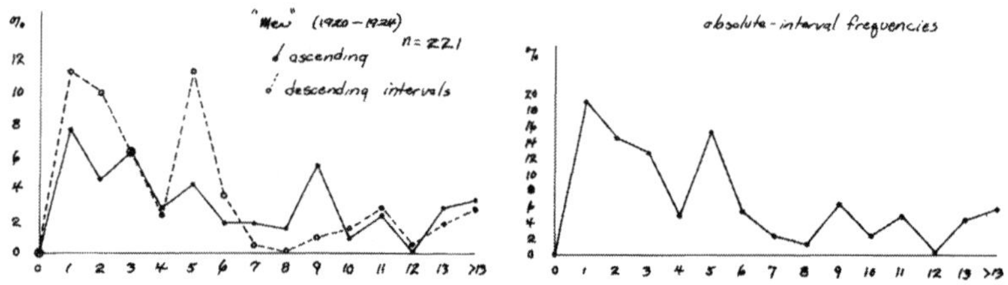

FIGURE 5. Melodic-interval frequency-distributions for *Men and Mountains* I ("Men," 1920–24).

Men & Mtns:	<-13	-13	-12	-11	-10	-9	-8	-7	-6	-5	-4	-3	-2	-1	0	1	2	3	4	5	6	7	8	9	10	11	12	13	>13	n
II "Lilacs" (1924)	0	0	0	0	0	0	2	3	5	4	5	7	8	3	0	2	6	10	10	6	4	0	0	0	0	1	0	0	0	76
in %	0.	0.	0.	0.	0.	0.	2.6	3.9	6.6	5.3	6.6	9.2	10.5	3.9	0.	2.6	7.9	13.2	13.2	7.9	5.3	0.	0.	0.	0.	1.3	0.	0.	0.	
	ALSD= 7.69				ALSC= 3.29			absolute-interval frequencies:							0.	6.6	18.4	22.4	19.7	13.2	11.8	3.9	2.6	0.	0.	1.3	0.	0.	0.	

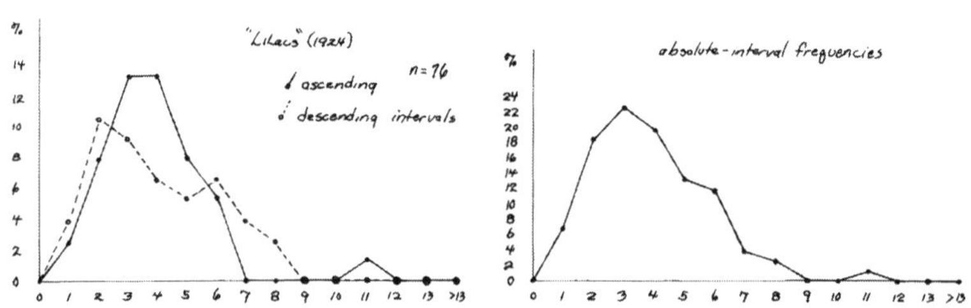

FIGURE 6. Melodic-interval frequency-distributions for *Men and Mountains* II ("Lilacs," 1924).

Men & Mtns.:	<-13	-13	-12	-11	-10	-9	-8	-7	-6	-5	-4	-3	-2	-1	0	1	2	3	4	5	6	7	8	9	10	11	12	13	>13	n
III "Marching Mountains" (1924)	1	0	0	4	4	1	2	1	24	10	6	36	21	32	0	21	38	7	3	4	11	10	2	0	1	8	0	5	2	254
in %	.4	0.	0.	1.6	1.6	.4	.8	.4	9.4	3.9	2.4	14.2	8.3	12.6	0.	8.3	15.0	2.8	1.2	1.6	4.3	3.9	.8	0.	.4	3.1	0.	2.0	.8	
	ALSD = 7.28(7.52)			ALSC = 2.79				absolute-interval frequencies:							0.	20.9	23.2	16.9	3.5	5.5	13.8	4.3	1.6	.4	2.0	4.7	0.	2.0	1.2	

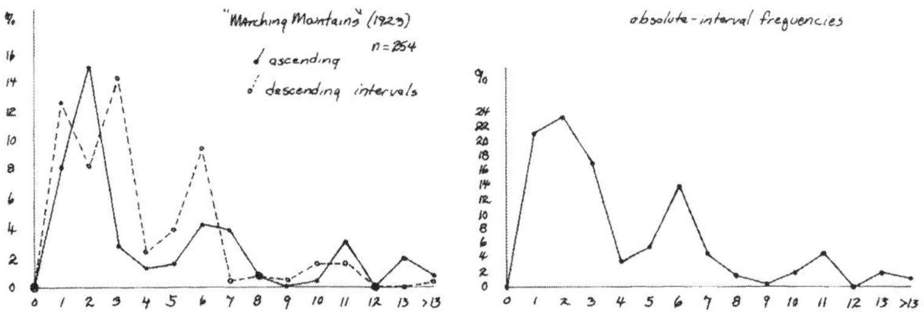

FIGURE 7. Melodic-interval frequency-distributions for *Men and Mountains* III ("Marching Mountains," 1924).

Men and Mountains I–III (1920–24)	<-13	-13	-12	-11	-10	-9	-8	-7	-6	-5	-4	-3	-2	-1	0	1	2	3	4	5	6	7	8	9	10	11	12	13	>13	n
	7	4	1	10	7	3	4	5	37	39	16	57	51	60	0	40	54	31	19	19	19	14	5	12	3	14	0	11	9	551
in %	1.3	.7	.2	1.8	1.3	.5	.7	.9	6.7	7.1	2.9	10.3	9.3	10.9	0.	7.3	9.8	5.6	3.4	3.4	3.4	2.5	.9	2.2	.5	2.5	0.	2.0	1.6	
	ALSD = 6.98			ALSC = 2.98				absolute-interval frequencies:							0.	18.1	19.1	16.0	6.4	10.5	10.2	3.4	1.6	2.7	1.8	4.4	.2	2.7	2.9	

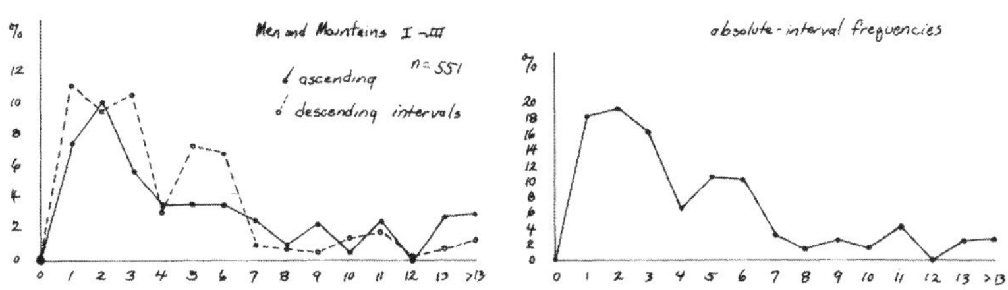

FIGURE 8. Melodic-interval frequency-distributions for *Men and Mountains* I–III (1924).

	<-13	-13	-12	-11	-10	-9	-8	-7	-6	-5	-4	-3	-2	-1	0	1	2	3	4	5	6	7	8	9	10	11	12	13	>13	n
Portals (1925)	6	9	0	4	0	8	4	3	22	12	20	23	44	50	0	33	26	34	23	13	14	8	9	4	4	11	0	11	3	398
in %	1.5	2.3	0.	1.0	0.	2.0	1.0	.8	5.5	3.0	5.0	5.8	11.1	12.6	0.	8.3	6.5	8.5	5.8	3.3	3.5	2.0	2.3	1.0	1.0	2.8	0.	2.8	.8	
	ALSD = 8.04(8.08)				ALSC = 2.92				absolute-interval frequencies:						0.	20.9	17.6	14.3	10.8	6.3	9.0	2.8	3.3	3.0	1.0	3.8	0.	5.0	2.3	

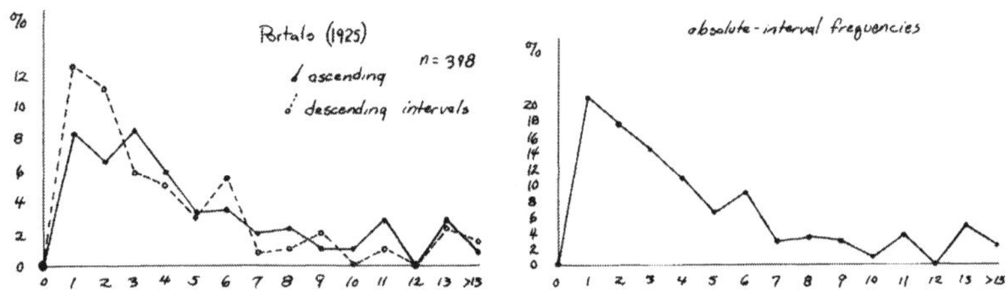

FIGURE 9. Melodic-interval frequency-distributions for *Portals* (1925).

	<-13	-13	-12	-11	-10	-9	-8	-7	-6	-5	-4	-3	-2	-1	0	1	2	3	4	5	6	7	8	9	10	11	12	13	>13	n
1919–1925 sub-totals	14	16	1	21	13	22	9	11	67	58	50	93	154	129	0	109	100	99	53	39	41	31	20	19	13	31	1	28	13	1256
in %	1.1	1.3	.1	1.7	1.0	1.8	.7	.9	5.3	4.6	4.0	7.4	12.3	10.3	0.	8.7	8.0	7.9	4.2	3.1	3.3	2.5	1.6	1.5	1.0	2.5	.1	2.2	1.0	
	ALSD = 7.0				ALSC = 3.16				absolute-interval frequencies:						0.	19.0	20.2	15.3	8.2	7.7	8.6	3.3	2.5	3.3	2.1	4.1	.2	3.5	2.2	

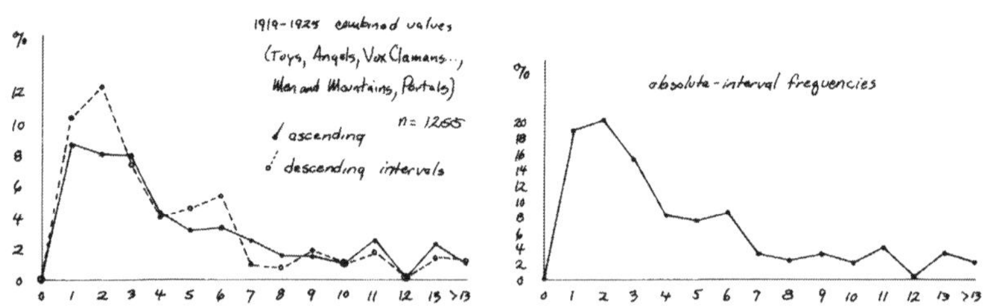

FIGURE 10. Melodic-interval frequency-distributions for the period 1919–25.

Sun Treader (first half) 1926–31	<-13	-13	-12	-11	-10	-9	-8	-7	-6	-5	-4	-3	-2	-1	0	1	2	3	4	5	6	7	8	9	10	11	12	13	>13	n
	21	8	0	24	0	5	4	14	59	19	32	14	9	127	0	83	16	12	11	17	44	25	3	2	1	51	0	16	10	627
in %	3.3	1.3	0.	3.8	0.	.8	.6	2.2	9.4	3.0	5.1	2.2	1.4	20.3	0.	13.2	2.6	1.9	1.8	2.7	7.0	4.0	.5	.3	.2	8.1	0.	2.6	1.6	
	ALSD = 8.81 (9.31)				ALSC = 2.02			absolute-interval frequencies:							0.	33.5	4.0	4.1	6.9	5.7	16.4	6.2	1.1	1.1	.2	12.0	0.	3.8	4.9	

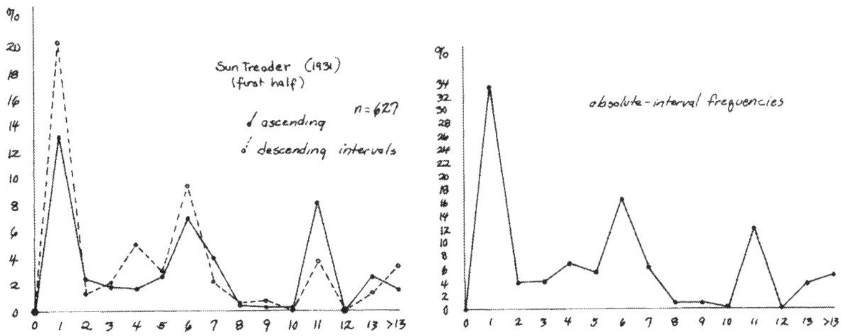

FIGURE 11. Melodic-interval frequency-distributions for *Sun Treader* (1931).

Evocation I (1937)	<-13	-13	-12	-11	-10	-9	-8	-7	-6	-5	-4	-3	-2	-1	0	1	2	3	4	5	6	7	8	9	10	11	12	13	>13	n
	3	0	0	4	0	0	0	0	10	8	0	2	0	3	0	15	11	5	3	4	7	10	3	1	1	0	0	2	0	92
in %	3.3	0.	0.	4.3	0.	0.	0.	0.	10.9	8.7	0.	2.2	0.	3.3	0.	16.3	12.0	5.4	3.3	4.3	7.6	10.9	3.3	1.1	1.1	0.	0.	2.2	0.	
	ALSD = 8.91 (9.13)				ALSC = 2.42			absolute-interval frequencies:							0.	19.6	12.0	7.6	3.3	13.0	18.5	10.9	3.3	1.1	1.1	4.3	0.	2.2	3.3	

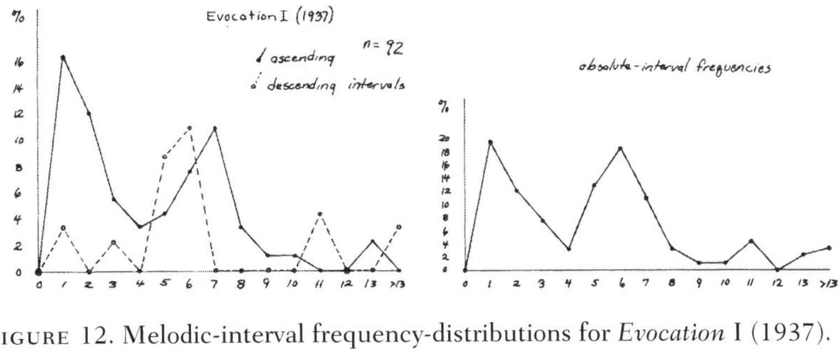

FIGURE 12. Melodic-interval frequency-distributions for *Evocation* I (1937).

	<-13	-13	-12	-11	-10	-9	-8	-7	-6	-5	-4	-3	-2	-1	0	1	2	3	4	5	6	7	8	9	10	11	12	13	>13	n
Evocation III (1940)	5	0	0	4	0	0	4	12	9	26	0	0	0	31	0	22	0	4	0	6	14	17	1	3	0	9	0	3	4	174
in %	2.9	0.	0.	2.3	0.	0.	2.3	6.9	5.2	14.9	0.	0.	0.	17.8	0.	12.6	0.	2.3	0.	3.4	8.0	9.8	.6	1.7	0.	5.2	0.	1.7	2.3	
	ALSD=8.14(9.24)				ALSC=2.14			absolute-interval frequencies:							0.	30.5	0.	2.3	0.	18.4	13.2	16.7	2.9	1.7	0.	7.5	0.	1.7	5.2	

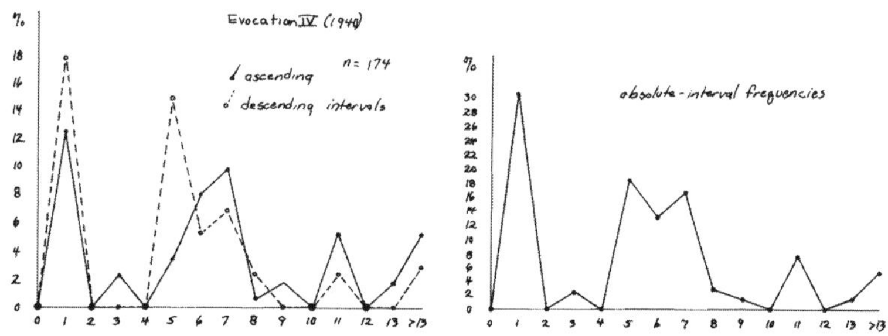

FIGURE 13. Melodic-interval frequency-distributions for *Evocation* IV (1940).

	<-13	-13	-12	-11	-10	-9	-8	-7	-6	-5	-4	-3	-2	-1	0	1	2	3	4	5	6	7	8	9	10	11	12	13	>13	n
Evocation II (1941)	2	1	0	10	4	6	3	5	14	27	0	8	12	48	0	48	17	7	10	4	20	15	3	6	1	6	0	2	2	281
in %	.7	.4	0.	3.6	1.4	2.1	1.1	1.8	5.0	9.6	0.	2.8	4.3	17.1	0.	17.1	6.0	2.5	3.6	1.4	7.1	5.3	1.1	2.1	.4	2.1	0.	.7	.7	
	ALSD=9.16(9.62)				ALSC= 2.50			absolute-interval frequencies:							0.	34.2	10.3	5.3	3.6	11.0	12.1	7.1	2.1	4.3	1.8	5.7	0.	1.1	1.4	

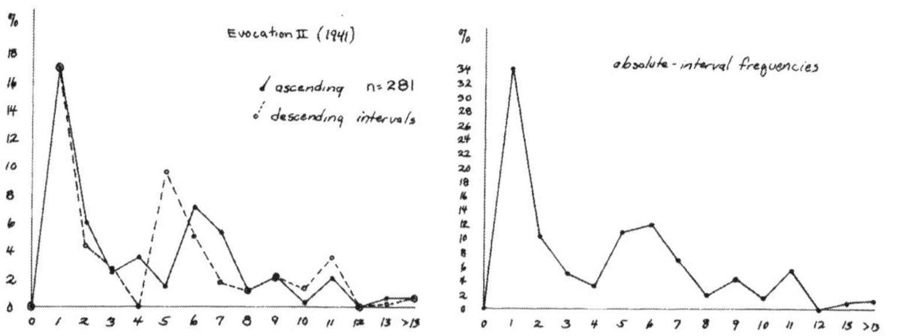

FIGURE 14. Melodic-interval frequency-distributions for *Evocation* II (1941).

	<-13	-13	-12	-11	-10	-9	-8	-7	-6	-5	-4	-3	-2	-1	0	1	2	3	4	5	6	7	8	9	10	11	12	13	>13	n
Evocation III (1943)	5	3	0	12	0	0	1	4	11	15	5	11	7	17	0	26	2	5	4	10	12	9	6	3	1	5	0	6	5	185
in %	2.7	1.6	0.	6.5	0.	0.	.5	2.2	5.9	8.1	2.7	5.9	3.8	9.2	0.	14.1	1.1	2.7	2.2	5.4	6.5	4.9	3.2	1.6	.5	2.7	0.	3.2	2.7	
	ALSD = 8.78 (8.85)				ALSC = 2.46			absolute-interval frequencies:							0.	23.2	4.9	8.6	4.9	13.5	12.4	7.0	3.8	1.6	.5	9.2	0.	4.9	5.4	

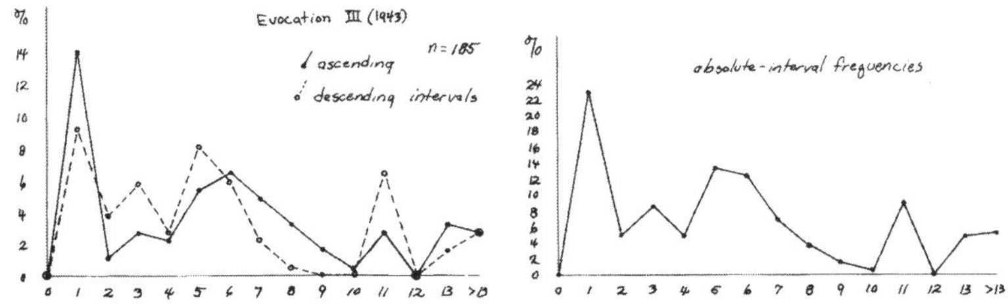

FIGURE 15. Melodic-interval frequency-distributions for *Evocation* III (1943).

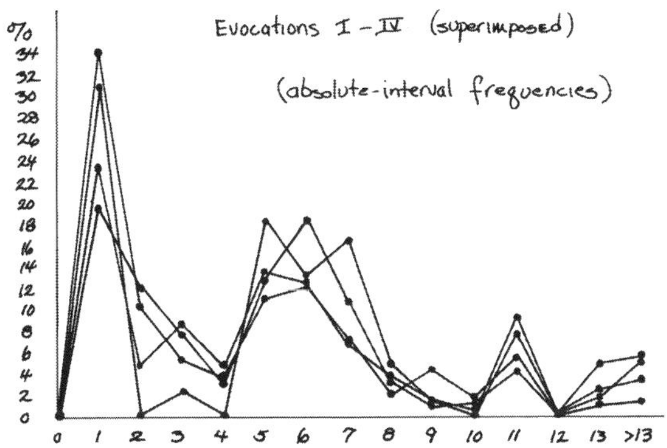

FIGURE 16. Superimposed plot of melodic-interval frequency-distributions for *Evocations* I–IV (1937–43).

	<-13	-13	-12	-11	-10	-9	-8	-7	-6	-5	-4	-3	-2	-1	0	1	2	3	4	5	6	7	8	9	10	11	12	13	>13	n
Evocations I–IV (1937–43)	15	4	0	30	4	6	8	21	43	76	5	21	19	99	0	111	30	21	17	24	53	51	13	13	3	20	0	13	11	732
in %	2.0	.5	0.	4.1	.5	.8	1.1	2.9	5.9	10.4	.7	2.9	2.6	135	0.	15.2	4.1	2.9	23	3.3	7.2	70	1.8	1.8	.4	2.7	0.	1.8	1.5	
	ALSD = 8.90 (9.30)				ALSC = 2.39			absolute-interval frequencies:							0.	28.7	6.7	5.7	3.0	13.7	13.1	9.8	2.9	2.6	1.0	6.8	0.	2.3	3.6	

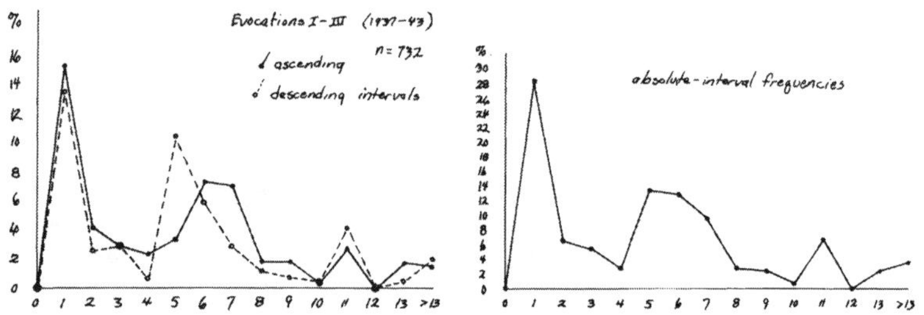

FIGURE 17. Melodic-interval frequency-distributions (average values) for *Evocations* I–IV (1937–43).

	<-13	-13	-12	-11	-10	-9	-8	-7	-6	-5	-4	-3	-2	-1	0	1	2	3	4	5	6	7	8	9	10	11	12	13	>13	n
Organum (1944)	3	0	0	6	0	3	6	6	26	13	5	16	18	59	0	49	15	29	15	14	14	7	11	6	2	5	0	3	2	333
in %	.9	0.	0.	1.8	0.	.9	1.8	1.8	7.8	3.9	1.5	4.8	5.4	17.7	0.	14.7	4.5	8.7	4.5	4.2	4.2	2.1	3.3	1.8	.6	1.5	0.	.9	.6	
	ALSD = 8.89 (9.77)				ALSC = 2.79			absolute-interval frequencies:							0.	32.4	9.9	13.5	6.0	8.1	12.0	3.9	5.1	2.7	.6	3.3	0.	.9	1.5	

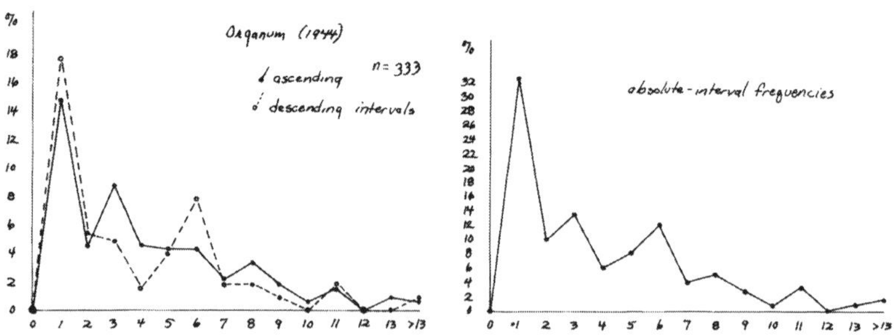

FIGURE 18. Melodic-interval frequency-distributions for *Organum* (1944).

	<-13	-13	-12	-11	-10	-9	-8	-7	-6	-5	-4	-3	-2	-1	0	1	2	3	4	5	6	7	8	9	10	11	12	13	>13	n
1931–1944 sub-totals	39	12	0.	60	4	14	18	41	128	108	42	51	46	285	0	243	61	62	43	55	111	83	27	21	6	76	0	32	23	1692
in %	2.3	.7	0.	3.5	.2	.8	1.1	2.4	7.6	6.4	2.5	3.0	2.7	16.8	0.	14.4	3.6	3.7	2.5	3.3	6.6	4.9	1.6	1.2	.4	4.5	0.	1.9	1.4	
								absolute-interval frequencies:							0.	31.2	6.3	6.7	5.0	9.6	4.1	7.3	2.7	2.1	.6	8.0	0.	2.6	3.7	

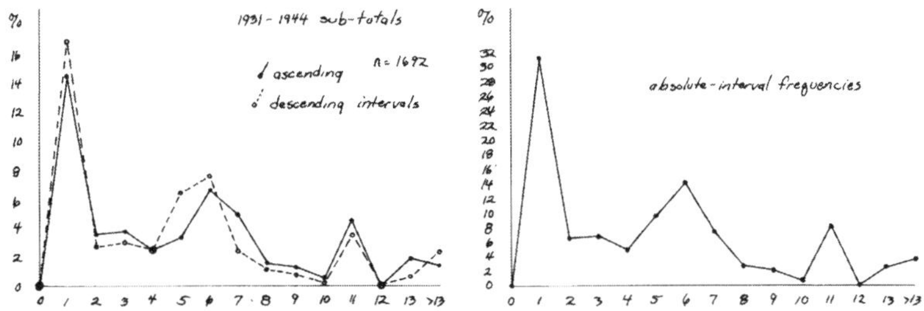

FIGURE 19. Melodic-interval frequency-distributions for the period 1931–44.

	<-13	-13	-12	-11	-10	-9	-8	-7	-6	-5	-4	-3	-2	-1	0	1	2	3	4	5	6	7	8	9	10	11	12	13	>13	n
All pieces 1919–1944	53	28	1	81	17	36	27	52	195	166	92	144	200	414	0	352	161	161	96	94	152	114	47	40	19	107	1	60	36	2947
in %	1.8	1.0	0.	2.7	.6	1.2	.9	1.8	6.6	5.6	3.1	4.9	6.8	14.0	0.	11.9	5.5	5.5	3.3	3.2	5.2	3.9	1.6	1.4	.6	3.6	0.	2.0	1.2	
								absolute-interval frequencies:							0.	26.0	12.2	10.3	6.4	8.8	11.8	5.6	2.5	2.6	1.2	6.4	.1	3.0	3.0	

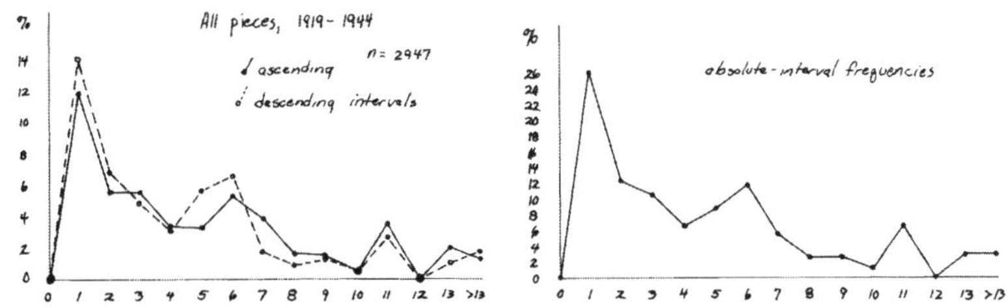

FIGURE 20. Melodic-interval frequency-distributions for all pieces, 1919–44.

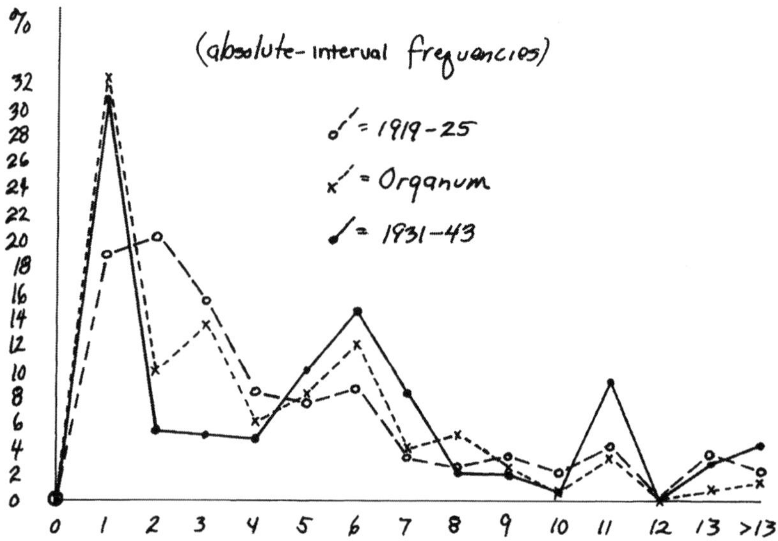

FIGURE 21. Melodic-interval frequency-distributions for *Organum* versus the periods 1919–25 and 1931–43.

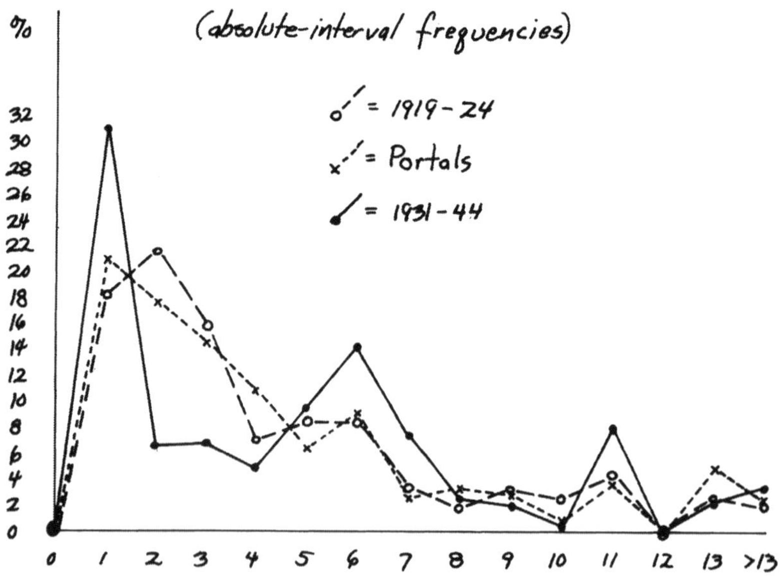

FIGURE 22. Melodic-interval frequency-distributions for *Portals* versus the periods 1919–24 and 1931–44.

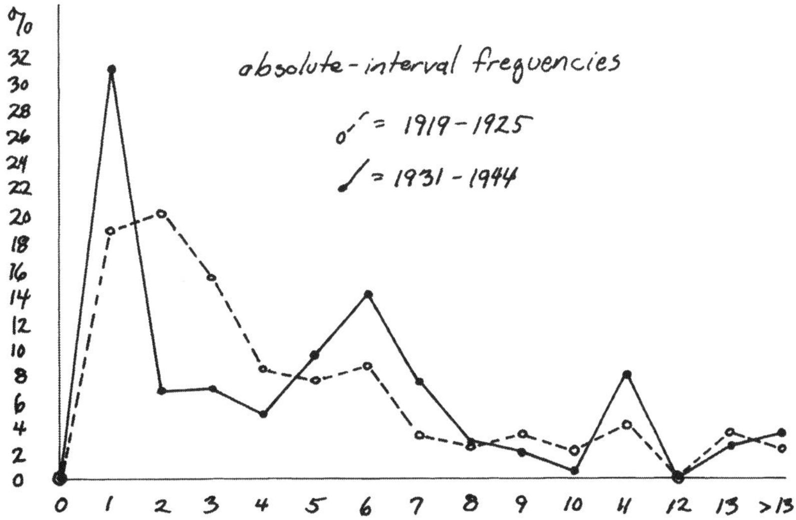

FIGURE 23. Melodic-interval frequency-distributions for the early versus the later works (1919–25 and 1931–44).

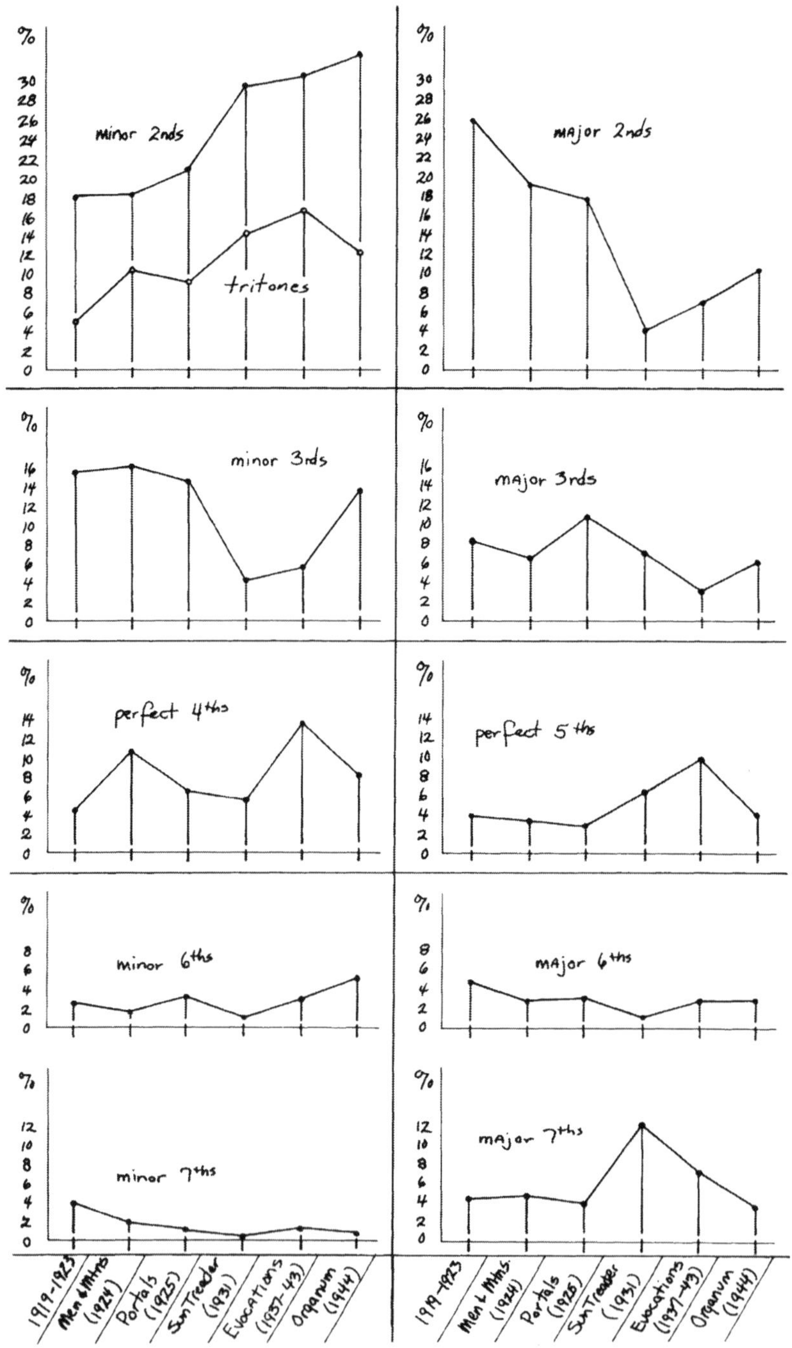

FIGURE 24. Absolute-interval frequencies as a function of chronological sequence.

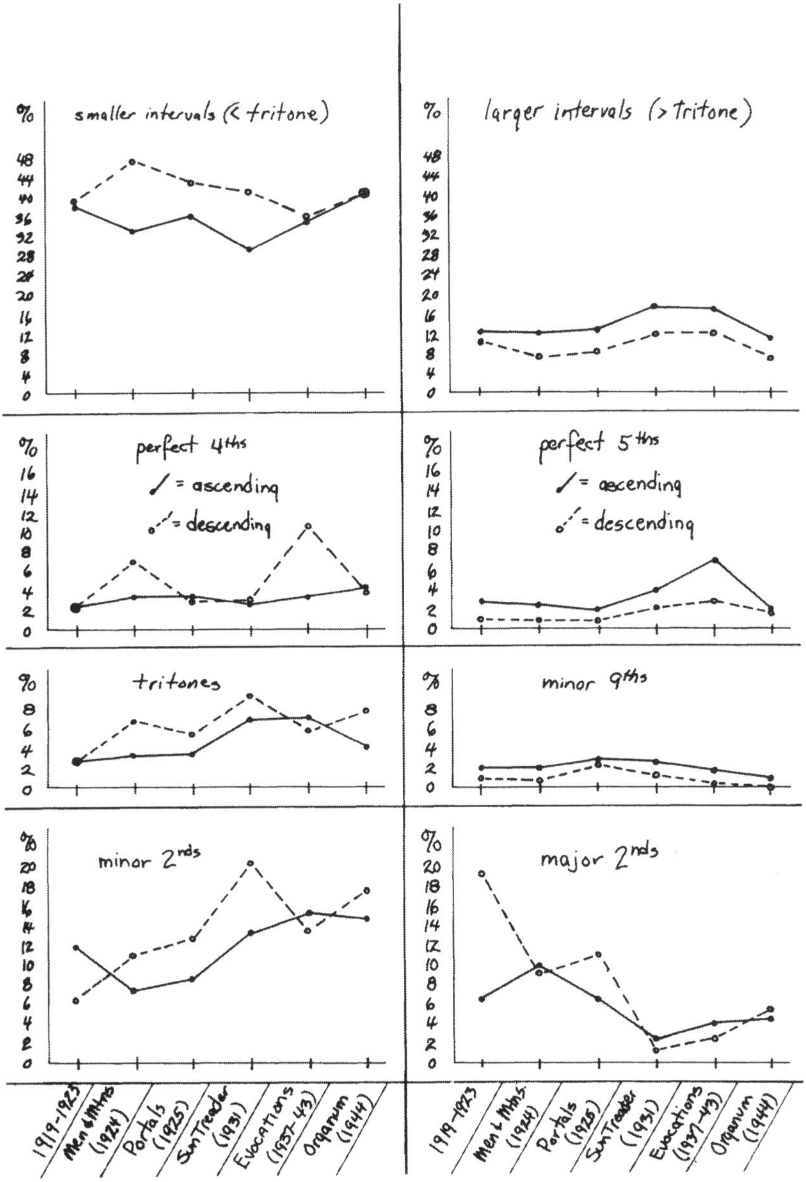

FIGURE 25. Ascending versus descending interval frequencies.

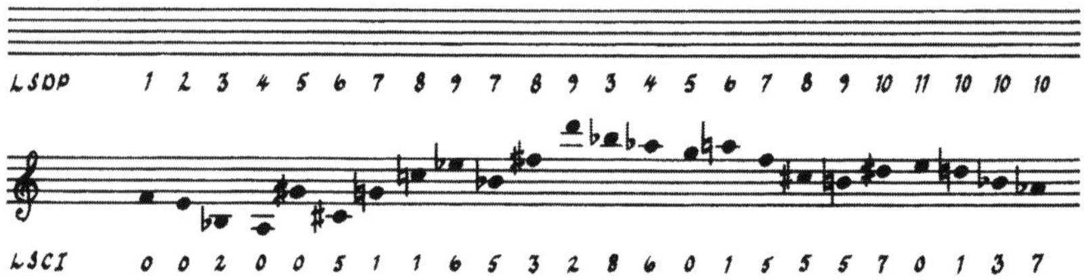

FIGURE 26. Values for LSDP and LSCI at the beginning of *Portals*.

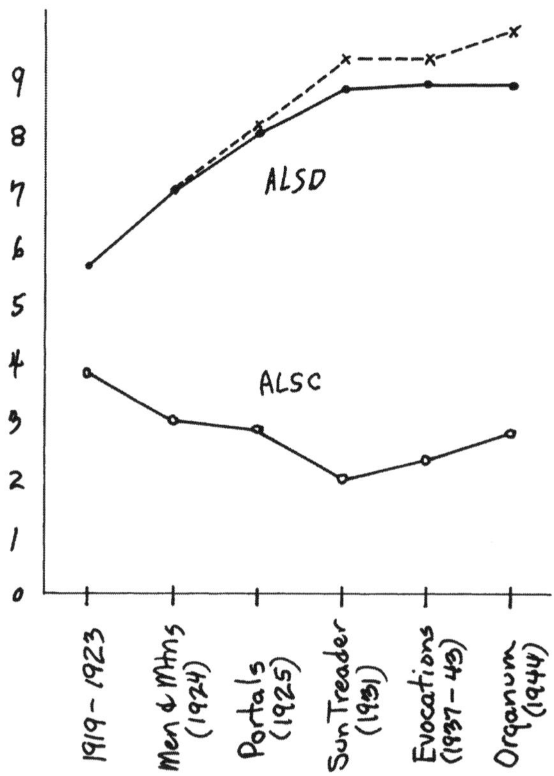

FIGURE 27. ALSD and ALSC as a function of chronological sequence.

CHAPTER 9

Hierarchical Temporal Gestalt Perception in Music

A Metric Space Model (with Larry Polansky)

(1978)

Introduction

For the historian, *time* is not the undifferentiated "continuum" of the theoretical physicist but a hierarchically ordered network of moments, incidents, episodes, periods, epochs, eras, etc.—i.e., time-spans whose conceptual "boundaries" are determined by the nature of the events or processes occurring within them (or of the historian's interpretation of these events or processes). Similarly for the musician, a piece of music does not consist merely of an inarticulate stream of elementary sounds but a hierarchically ordered network of sounds, motives, phrases, passages, sections, movements, etc.—i.e., time-spans whose *perceptual* boundaries are largely determined by the nature of the sounds and sound-configurations occurring within them. What is involved in both cases is a conception of distinct spans of time at several hierarchical levels, each of which is both internally cohesive and externally segregated from comparable time-spans immediately preceding and following it. Such time-spans (and the events or processes that define them) will here be called *temporal gestalt-units* (or TGs).

In the years that have elapsed since the early papers on gestalt perception by Wertheimer, Köhler, and others,[1] a considerable body of literature has accumulated that deals with the visual perception of *spatial* gestalt-units, although some of this literature remains highly speculative. Much less has been written (even of a speculative nature) about the perception of *temporal* gestalt-units. Some useful analogies have been drawn between visual and auditory perception, but such analogies provide little insight into the basic mechanisms of temporal gestalt perception, and many of the questions that might be the most relevant to *musical* perception have not even been asked by perceptual psychologists, much less answered. How, for example, are the perceptual boundaries of a TG determined? To what extent are the factors involved in temporal gestalt perception *objective*, bearing some measurable relation to the acoustical properties of the sounds themselves? Assuming that there are such objective factors, is their effect strong enough that one might be able to *predict* where the TG boundaries will be perceived if one knows the nature of the sound-events that will occur?

In an effort to provide some tentative answers to such questions, a hypothesis of temporal gestalt perception will be proposed in section 1 of this paper, and section 2 will present some results of a computer analysis program based on this hypothesis. The program represents a simplified *model* of this aspect of musical perception, and some of the implications, limitations, and possible extensions of this model will be considered in section 3. Although the hypothesis on which the model is based is very simple, it involves some unfamiliar concepts and terms that will have to be explained before the hypothesis will be comprehensible. Some of these concepts were first stated—albeit in rather embryonic form—in an earlier paper,[2] though these have evolved considerably in the intervening years.[3] Others have emerged more recently in the effort to organize the more general music-theoretical ideas into an explicit "algorithmic" form. Though I will not recount the history of the development of the model, I will try to describe the conceptual transformations of these earlier ideas in a way that parallels their actual historical development.

1. The Fundamental Hypothesis

As in my earlier writings, I shall use the terms "element," "clang," and "sequence" to designate TGs at the first three hierarchical levels of perceptual organization. An element may be defined more precisely as a TG that is not temporally divisible, in perception, into smaller TGs. A clang is a TG at the next higher level, consisting of a succession of two or more elements. A succession of two or more clangs—heard as a TG at the *next* higher level—constitutes a sequence. In the earlier writings, names were not given to TGs at levels higher than that of the sequence, but recently we have been using the terms "segment" and "section" for units at the next two higher levels. The TG at the highest level normally considered is, of course, coextensive with the *piece* itself, although situations are certainly conceivable where still larger gestalt-units might be of interest—e.g., the series of pieces on a concert, or the set of all pieces by a particular composer.

In *Meta ≠ Hodos* (1961), I designated *proximity* (in time) and *similarity* (with respect to any or all other parameters) as the two "primary factors of cohesion and segregation" involved in musical perception (or, more specifically, in clang-formation) as follows: "*In a collection of sound-elements, those that are simultaneous or contiguous will tend to form clangs, while relatively greater separations in time will produce segregations*, other factors being equal. . . . *Those that are similar* (with respect to values in some parameter) *will tend to form clangs . . . , while relative dissimilarity will produce segregation*, other factors being equal." Aside from certain other differences between these early formulations and my more recent ideas (e.g., that two or more simultaneous elements do not necessarily constitute a clang but more likely what I would now call a "compound element"), several problems had to be solved before the current algorithm could be designed.[4]

First, the principles, as stated, were not "operational" but merely descriptive. That is, although they were able to tell us something about TGs whose boundaries were already determined, they could say nothing about the process by which that determination was made. They described the *results* of that process but not its *mechanism*.

Second, "similarity" was not defined in any precise way, except by reference to "values in some parameter." The assumption here, of course, was that the similarity of two elements is an inverse function of the magnitude of the *interval* by which they differ in some parameter. This remains a plausible assumption, though it was never made explicit, but even such a correlation of similarity/dissimilarity with interval-magnitude does not, by itself, allow for the simultaneous consideration of more than one parameter at a time. This rather profound difficulty was implicit in the "other factors being equal" clause appended to the two statements. At the time, this qualification seemed necessary in order to rule out cases where two or more parameters vary in conflicting ways or where two or more "factors" function independently. Although this was a useful device for isolating and studying some important aspects of temporal gestalt perception, it imposed a very severe limitation on the range of musical examples whose gestalt structure might be predicted. In most real musical situations, other factors are manifestly *not* equal, and our perceptual organization of the music is a complex result of the combination and interaction of several more or less independent variables.

Third (and finally), these early formulations referred to *one* hierarchical level only—the grouping of elements into clangs—although it was obvious to me even then that the similarity-factor, at least, was of great importance in the perceptual organization of TGs at all higher levels. In a later paper,[5] an attempt was made to generalize these principles, restating them in a way that would be applicable to all hierarchical levels. Thus, from Proposition II of "META *Meta ≠ Hodos*":

> The perceptual formation of TGs at any hierarchical level is determined by a number of factors of cohesion and segregation, the most important of which are *proximity* and *similarity*; their effects may be described as follows: . . . relative temporal *proximity* . . . [and] relative *similarities* of TGs at a given hierarchical level will tend to group them, perceptually, into a TG at the next higher level. . . . Conversely, relative temporal *separation* and/or *differences* between TGs . . . will tend to segregate them into separate TGs at the next higher level.[6]

Although these later "propositions" served to extend the earlier formulations to higher levels, they suffered all of the other deficiencies of the earlier formulations: they were nonoperational in character, imprecise with respect to the concept of "similarity," and restricted to one parameter (or factor) at a time.

The first of these problems has been solved by a shift of emphasis from the unifying effects of proximity and similarity to the segregative effects of temporal separation and parametric dissimilarity and by a more careful consideration of these effects as they must occur in real time. In the ongoing process of perception in time, TG-boundaries are determined by successive *TG-initiations*. This obviously applies to the beginning of a TG but also to the *end* of it, since the perception that it has ended is determined (in the monophonic case, at least) by the perception that a *new* TG at that same hierarchical level has *begun*. In this new light, the effect of the proximity-factor (at the element/clang level) might be restated as follows:

> In a monophonic succession of elements, a clang will tend to be initiated in perception by any element that begins after a time-interval (from the beginning of the previous element, i.e., after a *delay-time*) that is *greater than those immediately preceding and following it*, other factors being equal.

Thus, in mm. 24–28 of Varèse's *Density 21.5* (example 1), where clang-initiations are determined almost entirely by the proximity-factor, it can be seen that the elements that initiate successive clangs are, in fact, invariably those whose delay-times are "greater than those immediately preceding and following" their own (the delay-times associated with each element are indicated in the example by the numbers below the staff in triplet sixteenth-note units; those that are circled are for the clang-initiating elements). Note that the first occurrence of D (at the end of m. 25) does not initiate a new clang, in spite of its fairly long delay-time (12 units), because the delay-time that follows it is still longer (19 units). As stated above, the proximity-factor begins to take on a form that *is* "operational." In a musical situation where no other parameters are varying (say, a drum solo at constant dynamic level), this principle can provide an unambiguous procedure for predicting clang-boundaries.

In an analogous way, the effect of the similarity-factor (at the element/clang level) may be reformulated as follows (and note that this statement can actually include the previous one as a special case if the parameter considered is time and the "interval" is a delay-time):

> In a monophonic succession of elements, a clang will tend to be initiated in perception by any element that differs from the previous element by an interval (in some parameter) that is *greater than those* (inter-element intervals) *immediately preceding and following it*, other factors being equal.

This, too, is "operational" in that it suggests an unambiguous procedure for predicting clang-boundaries, though it is limited to special cases where only one parameter is varying at a time. Consider, for example, the first twelve measures of Beethoven's Fifth Symphony. Example 2 shows the melodic line, abstracted from all contrapuntal/textural complications—as it would be heard, say, in a piano transcription. Because of the considerable difference in tempo here compared to the Varèse example—and thus in the actual duration of notated time-values—relative weights are used that give the value of 1 to the eighth note (as well as to the semitone, as before). The clang-initiations during the first six bars are obviously determined by the proximity-factor alone, but beginning in m. 6, the proximity-factor can have no effect on the clang-organization (except in m. 9), because the delay-times are all equal. This passage is not heard simply as two clangs, however, but as a succession of clangs (indicated by the brackets above the staff), each consisting of four elements. And note that, for every clang-initiating element, the pitch-interval associated with it is greater than those immediately preceding and following it.

The parallelism of the proximity- and similarity-factors, as restated above—and the fact that the second statement can be considered to include the first one as a special case—is extremely important. In both, it is the occurrence of a *local maximum in interval magnitudes* that determines clang-initiation. An *interval* is simply a *difference*, and whether this is a difference in starting-times, or pitch, or intensity—or any other attribute of sound—is not what is important. Rather, it is *relative differences* (in *any* parameter) that seem to be crucial. We live in a "universe of change," but whether a particular change marks the beginning of a new temporal gestalt-unit or simply another "turn" in the *shape* of the current

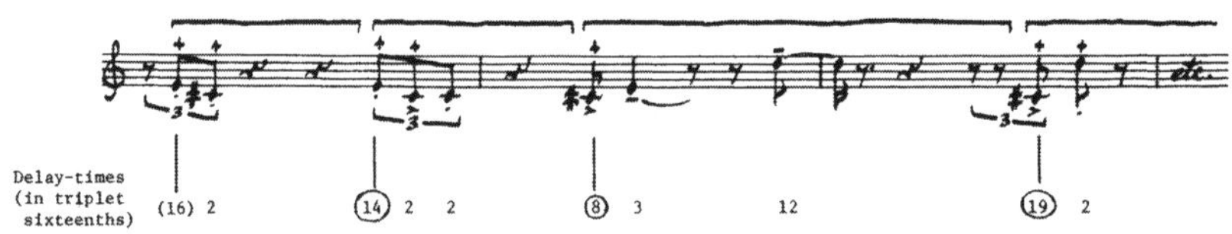

EXAMPLE 1. Clang-initiations determined by delay-times.

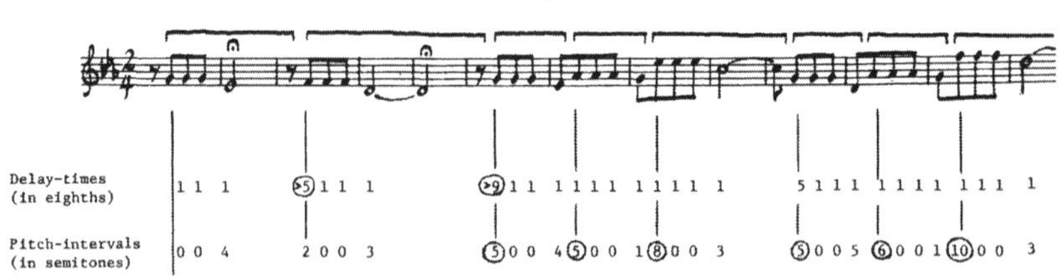

EXAMPLE 2. Clang-initiations determined first by delay-times (mm. 1–5), then by pitch-intervals (mm. 6–12).

one depends not only on its absolute magnitude but on the magnitude of the changes that precede and follow it.

The restriction to one parameter (or factor) at a time, still implicit in the last formulation, remains to be overcome before our principle can be of much use in predicting clang-initiations in any but a very limited set of musical situations. What is needed is some way to combine or integrate the interval-magnitudes of *all* parameters into a single measure of change or difference. The solution to this problem involves a concept that has been employed by experimental psychologists for several decades now—that of a *multidimensional psychological or perceptual "space."*[7] The "dimensions" of this space are the several parameters involved in the perception and description of any sound, i.e., time, pitch, and intensity. Other parameters (e.g., timbre) could be added to this list if they satisfy certain conditions, but I shall limit my discussion here to these three basic ones. The set of parametric values characterizing an element serves to locate that element at some "point" in this multidimensional space, and we can consider not only the intervals between two such points (one along each separate axis) but also a *distance* between those points, which takes into account the contribution of intervals in each individual parameter but effectively combines these into a single quantity. Such a distance, or distance-measure—what a mathematician would call a "metric"—may now be used in place of the less precise notions of "similarity" and "proximity."[8] In order to do this, however, two further questions had to be answered: first, how to *weight* the several parameters relative to each other (thereby "scaling" the individual dimensions) in a way that is appropriate to musical perception, and second, what kind of function to use in computing these distances.

The weightings referred to above are necessary for two reasons: first, because quantitative scales of values in the several parameters—and thus the numbers used to encode these values as input data to a computer program—are essentially arbitrary, bearing no inherent relation to each other; and, second, because we have no way of knowing, a priori, the relative importance of one parameter versus another in its effects on TG-formation. As yet, no clear principle has been discovered for determining what the weights should be. The current algorithm requires that they be specified as input data, and the search for "optimum" weightings has so far been carried out purely on a trial-and-error basis. It now appears that such optimum weightings are slightly different for each piece analyzed, which suggests that there might be some correlation between these optimum weightings and statistical (or other) characteristics of a given piece, but the principles governing such correlations have yet to be determined.

Regarding the type of distance-measure to be used, there are many different functions that can satisfy the mathematical criteria for a metric and therefore many distinct measures that might be used. A definitive answer to the question as to which of these metrics is the most appropriate to our musical "space" would depend on the results of psychoacoustic experiments that, to my knowledge, have never been done, although studies of other multidimensional perceptual or psychological spaces provide a few clues toward an answer.[9] The best-known metric, of course, is the Euclidean, but after trying this one and noticing certain problems that seemed to derive from it, another was finally chosen for the algorithm. This second distance measure is sometimes called the "city-block" metric, and an example of this metric versus the Euclidean is shown graphically in figure 1 for the two-dimensional case. When three or more dimensions are involved, the relations become difficult or impossible to represent graphically in two dimensions, but the relationships are the same. In the Euclidean metric, the distance between two points is always the square root of the sum of the squares of the distances (or intervals) between them in each individual dimension (in two dimensions, this is equivalent to the familiar Pythagorean formula for the hypotenuse of a right triangle). In the city-block metric, on the other hand, the distance is simply the sum of the absolute values of the distances (or intervals) in each dimension.[10]

One of the most important steps in the development of our model involved the decision to treat musical space as a metric space within which all the individual parametric intervals between two points might be integrated into a single measure of distance and to use this distance, in turn, as a measure of relative "cohesion" (or "segregation") between two musical events. This made it possible to reformulate the basic principle of TG-initiation in a new way that can be applied to virtually any musical situation, without the old restriction to variations in just one parameter at a time (though it is still limited to the element/clang level and to monophonic textures), as follows:

> A new clang will be initiated in perception by any element whose distance from the previous element is greater than the inter-element distances immediately preceding and following it.

Euclidean metric:

$$d = \sqrt{(y_2 - y_1)^2 + (x_2 - x_1)^2}$$

"City-block" metric:

$$d = |y_2 - y_1| + |x_2 - x_1|$$

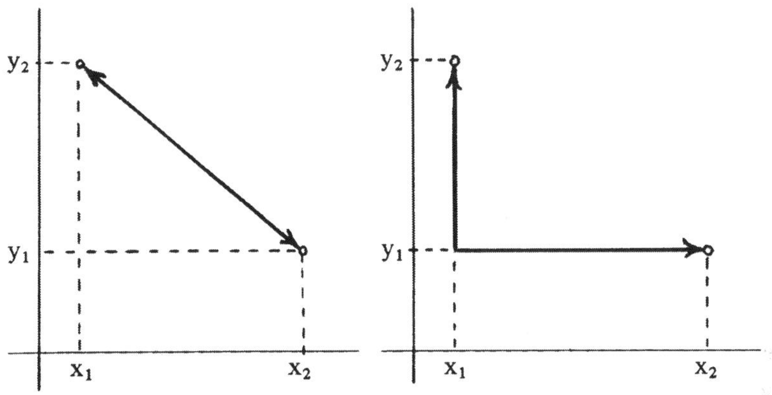

FIGURE 1. Euclidean versus "city-block" distances.

If we now apply this principle to the Beethoven example considered earlier, using (again) relative weights for duration and pitch that give values of 1 for both the eighth-note duration and the semitone (example 3), we see that this simple principle serves to predict or locate all of the clang-initiations involved in the passage (note that each inter-element distance, listed in the bottom row of figures, is simply the sum of the two (weighted) intervals associated with each element). As a second example, consider the Varèse passage quoted earlier (example 4). Although in this case delay-times alone were sufficient to determine clang-initiation, we see that maxima in the distance-function will still predict the same boundaries. Again, our simple principle of clang-initiation seems to determine clang-boundaries in a reasonable way.

One final problem remained to be solved, before the current algorithm could be realized—that of extending this basic principle of clang-formation to higher levels. The discussion so far has been limited to TG-initiations at the element/clang level because the notion of a "distance" in the musical space can only be used properly as a difference between two *points* in that space. How might the "differences" between two clangs, sequences, or still higher-level TGs—which would correspond to clusters or *sets* of points—be defined? It has seemed to me that such differences are of three basic kinds, corresponding to three distinct aspects of our perception (and/or description) of these higher-level TGs, namely, differences of *state*, *shape*, and *structure*.[11] By "state" I mean the set of average or *mean values* of a TG (one for each parameter except time), plus its *starting-time*. The state of a TG might thus be compared to the "center of gravity" of an object in physical space, except that the temporal counterpart to mean parametric value is the *beginning* of the TG rather than its "center." "Shape" refers to the contour or profile of a TG in each parameter, determined by changes in that parameter with time, and "structure" is defined as "relations between subordinate parts" of a TG—i.e., relations between its component TGs at the next lower level (or at several lower levels). Thus, the differences between any two TGs may be differences between their states, or between their shapes, or between their structures, or any combination of these. At the element level, however, the differences that are reflected in the measure of distance are of the first kind only (differences between states) because we are not yet dealing with shape at the element-level, and because structure is assumed to be imperceptible at this level, by the very definition of "element" as "not temporally divisible, in perception, into smaller TGs" (see above).

It is not yet clear what role similarities and differences of shape and structure might have in temporal gestalt perception, but it is quite clear that state-differences have virtually the same effects at the higher levels

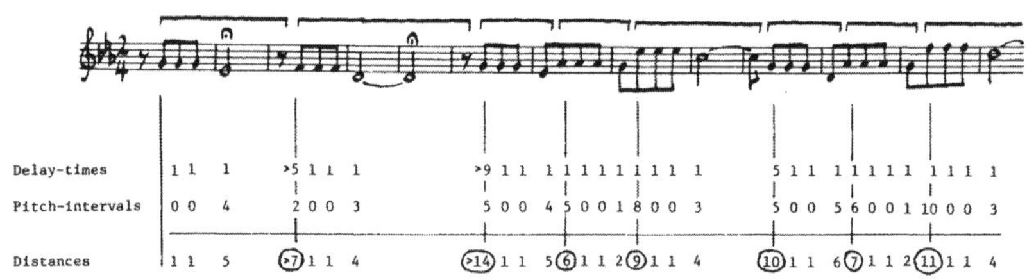

EXAMPLE 3. Clang-initiations determined by inter-element distances.

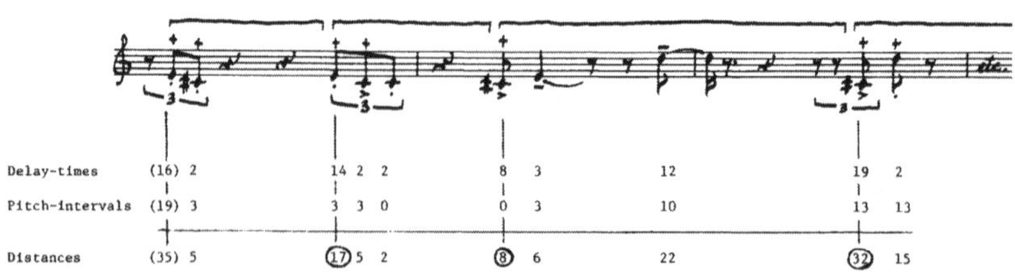

EXAMPLE 4. Clang-initiations determined by inter-element distances.

that they have at the element-level. Consequently, shape and structure play no part in the current model, but state-differences (i.e., intervals and distances) are treated essentially the same way at all hierarchical levels, with just one additional refinement not mentioned previously. Although the magnitude of change perceived when one element follows another is well represented by the distance-measure defined above, the magnitude of change perceived in the succession of two clangs, sequences, or higher-level TGs is only partially accounted for by this distance. In addition, the changes perceived *at the boundary* between two TGs have an important influence on TG-initiation at higher levels. In order to deal with this, a distinction is made between "mean-intervals" and "boundary-intervals," as follows:

> A *mean-interval* between two TGs at any hierarchical level, in any parameter except time, is the difference between their *mean values* in that parameter; for the time-parameter, a mean-interval is defined as the difference between their *starting-times*. A *boundary-interval* between two TGs is the difference between the mean values of their *adjacent terminal components* (i.e., the final component of the first TG and the initial component of the second).

Note that a boundary-interval at one hierarchical level is a mean-interval at the next lower level. An analogous distinction is made between "mean-distances" and "boundary-distances," as follows:

> The *mean-distance* between two TGs at any hierarchical level is a weighted *sum of the mean-intervals* between them, and the *boundary-distance* between two TGs is a weighted *sum of the boundary intervals* between them.

Finally, mean- and boundary-distances are combined into a single measure of change or "difference" that we call "disjunction," defined as follows:

> The *disjunction* between two TGs, or the disjunction of a TG with respect to the preceding TG (at a given hierarchical level), is a weighted *sum of the mean-distance and the boundary-distances between them at all lower levels.*

Note that, whereas the weightings referred to in the definitions of mean- and boundary-distances are weightings across *parameters*, the weightings used in the definition of disjunction are weightings across *hierarchical levels*. In the program, these are set to decrease by a factor of two for each successively lower level considered. The disjunction between two sequences, for example (or the disjunction of the second sequence with respect to the first), involves—in addition to the mean distance between them—one-half of the mean-distance between their adjacent terminal clangs and one-fourth of the mean-distance between the adjacent terminal elements of those clangs.[12]

Now, at last, it becomes possible to state the fundamental hypothesis of temporal gestalt perception, on which the current model is based, as follows:

> *A new TG at the next higher level will be initiated in perception whenever a TG occurs whose disjunction (with respect to the previous TG at the same hierarchical level) is greater than those immediately preceding and following it.*

2. The Model

A computer analysis program based on the hypothesis developed in the previous section has been written by Larry Polansky and used to obtain hierarchical segmentations for several pieces.[13] It is beyond the scope of this paper to describe this program in any detail, but a few points must be noted before its results can be appropriately evaluated. The model has certain limitations in terms of the kind of music it can deal with, as well as the musical factors it considers, and it is essential that these limitations be clearly understood. First of all, it can only work with *monophonic* music. Although in principle the same concepts and procedures should be applicable to polyphonic music, there are certain fundamental questions about how we actually *hear* polyphonic music that will have to be answered before it will be possible to extend the model in that direction. In addition, and for the same reason, the algorithm is not yet able to deal with what might be called "virtual polyphony" in a monophonic context—that perceptual phenomenon that Bregman has called "stream segregation."[14] Real as this phenomenon is, I think it can only be dealt with, algorithmically, by a more extended model designed for polyphonic music.

The next two limitations of the algorithm are related to each other in that both have to do with factors that are obviously important in musical perception but that the current model does not even consider, namely, *harmony* (or harmonic relations between pitches or pitch-classes) and *shape* (pattern, motivic/thematic relations). What the algorithm is capable of doing now is done entirely without the benefit (or burden) of any consideration of either of these two factors. Thus, although it is by no means a comprehensive model of musical perception, the very fact that it does so much without taking these factors into account is significant.

Still another type of limitation is inherent in certain basic procedures used by the program. For one thing, all higher-level TGs must contain *at least two* TGs at the next lower level (thus there can occur no one-element clangs or one-clang sequences, etc.). Furthermore, no *ambiguities* regarding TG-boundaries are allowed: a terminal element might be the initial element in a clang *or* the final element in the preceding clang, but it cannot be both. A different approach to this problem, involving the notion of a "pivotal" TG (i.e., a TG that might function as *both* an initial component of a TG at the next higher level *and* as the final component of the preceding TG at that same higher level has recently been sketched but has not yet been implemented.

Finally, the reader should be warned that the output of this program says absolutely nothing about the musical *function* of any of the TGs it finds. It merely partitions the overall duration of the piece into component TGs at several hierarchical levels. Questions of function are left entirely up to us to interpret as we will. What the algorithm *does* purport to tell us is where the temporal gestalt boundaries are likely to be perceived—surely a prerequisite to any meaningful discussion of the musical "function" of the TGs determined by these boundaries.

Input data to the program are numbers representing the pitch, initial intensity, final intensity, duration, and rest-duration of each element in the score, plus weighting factors for each parameter and certain constants for the particular piece or run (e.g., the total number of elements, the tempo of the piece, etc.). Numerical values for these parameters are encoded as follows: in order to avoid "roundoff" errors, the value of 1.2 (rather than 1.0) is used for the quarter note at the specified tempo for the piece, with other note-values proportional to this. Thus, an eighth note equals .6, a triplet-eighth equals .4, etc. These values are rescaled, internally, to units of one-tenth of a second. Pitches are represented by integers, with the value of 1 usually assigned to the lowest pitch in the piece (although this is entirely arbitrary, since the program's operations involve only the intervals between pitches, not the pitches themselves). For intensity, integer values from 1.0 through 8.0 are used for the notated dynamic levels, *ppp* through *fff*, with decimal fractions for intermediate values, as during a gradual crescendo or diminuendo. In transcribing the score, these fractional values are derived by simple linear interpolations between the integer values.

At the element-level, then, three basic parameters are involved: time (or "delay-time," determining "proximity"), pitch, and intensity, and weights must be input for each of these. At the clang-level, and carrying through to all higher levels, a new parameter emerges that I considered important in musical perception, namely, *temporal density* (or, more strictly, element-density as a function of time). Provision was therefore made in the program for this parameter, although it has turned out to be unnecessary. Our best results on the pieces analyzed so far have been obtained with a weight of zero for temporal density. The program also allows for input data (and a weighting-factor) to be given for one more parameter, which we call "timbre" but which could be used for any other attribute of sound that seemed appropriate in a particular piece. It should be noted, however, that meaningful results can only be expected if this additional parameter is one in which values may be specified (or at least approximated) on what S. S. Stevens has called an "interval scale."[15] So far, it has only been used in a very primitive way, with scale values of either 0 or 1 to represent the "key-clicks" in mm. 24–28 of Varèse's *Density 21.5*. Provision was originally made for specifying the weights in each parameter for mean- and boundary-intervals independently. As it turned out, however, the optimum weightings seemed to be the same in any given parameter for both types of interval, so they are now both given the same value.

The parametric weights used for the results shown in examples 5–7 are as follows:

	duration	*pitch*	*intensity*	*timbre*
Varèse	1.0	0.67	6.0	20.0
Webern	1.0	0.5	6.0	0.0
Debussy	1.0	1.5	2.0	0.0

An input weight of 1.0 implies a time-unit of one-tenth of a second, a unit-interval of one semitone or of one dynamic-level-difference (as between *mf* and *f*), depending on the parameter involved. The set of weights listed above may thus be taken to imply certain equivalences between intervals in the several parameters, at least with respect to their effects on TG-initiation. In the Debussy piece, for example, a delay-time of one-tenth of a second is equivalent to a pitch-interval of two-thirds of a semitone and to one-half of one dynamic-level-difference. In the Varèse piece, on the other hand, a delay-time of one-tenth of a second is equivalent to a pitch-interval of 1.5 semitones and to one-sixth of one dynamic-level-difference. The relatively large intensity-weights for both the Varèse and the Webern pieces confirm what one would already have expected—that both of these composers were using dynamics as a structural (rather than merely "expressive") parameter in these pieces. The differences between the pitch-weights for the three pieces are more difficult to explain. As noted earlier, it seems likely that correlations may eventually be found between these "optimum" weightings and some statistically measurable aspect of the pieces themselves, but no such correlations have yet been found.

The input data described above are used in a first "pass" through the program to compute inter-element intervals, distances, and disjunctions, and the latter are tested to determine the points of initiation of successive clangs, according to the fundamental hypothesis described in the previous section of this paper. The beginning of each new clang is assumed to define the end of the preceding clang, and when that clang's boundaries have thus been determined, the program computes and stores its starting-time, average pitch, and average amplitude—i.e., values that represent what I have called its "state." When there are no more elements to be considered, the program returns to the (temporal) beginning of the piece, but one hierarchical level higher. It then goes through successive clangs, computing and storing sequence-initiations and states. This procedure continues "upward" through progressively higher hierarchical levels until a level is reached at which there are not enough TGs to make a next-higher-level grouping possible (i.e., fewer than four). The program's architecture is thus hierarchically recursive; the computations are *essentially identical* at every level of TG organization, and this is one of the most attractive features of the model.

Results of the program for three pieces—Varèse's *Density 21.5*; Webern's Concerto, op. 24, second movement; and Debussy's *Syrinx*—are displayed in the form of graphically annotated scores in examples 5 through 7. The segmentation given by the algorithm for each piece is indicated by the vertical lines above the staff-notation, each extending to a horizontal line corresponding to the hierarchical level of the largest TG initiated at that point. For the first two pieces, these results may be compared with analogous segmentations to be found in the analytical literature. In the case of *Density 21.5*, a segmentation both explicit and complete is available in a monograph by Jean-Jacques Nattiez, and it will be used for comparison.[16] For the Webern example, an analysis of the first "period" by Leopold Spinner will be compared to the results of our program.[17] The results for Debussy's *Syrinx* are given without any such comparisons because we have not found any published analyses of this piece in which the segmentation is sufficiently explicit to justify a comparison.

Edgard Varèse, Density 21.5

The segmentation given by Nattiez for this piece is shown in the lower portion of example 5 so that a direct, point-by-point comparison can be made. Here the correlations between the two partitionings are quite close—especially at the clang- and sequence-levels—although the two are not identical, of course, and the similarities diminish at higher levels. In fact, some 81 percent of the clang-initiations in our results and 85 percent of the sequence-initiations (but only 44 percent of the segment-initiations) coincide with the corresponding boundaries in Nattiez's segmentation. There are no coincidences at any higher level. Some of the discrepancies between the two segmentations are fairly trivial, as where one of the two "models" simply interpolates an extra clang-break between two otherwise coincident boundaries (as at elements 8, 25, 54, 109, 117, 118, 140, 179, 224, 226, 233, and 241). A few differences result from the fact that Nattiez does not prohibit one-component TGs, as our model does. These occur in his segmentation in the form of "one-element clangs" beginning at elements 109, 117, and 118 and as sequences containing only a single clang beginning at elements 22, 52, 74, and 97.

Even if we disregard such discrepancies as these, however, there will still remain a number of places where the two segmentations differ. Some of these probably have to do with the fact that neither harmonic nor motivic factors are considered by our algorithm. For example, the high-level TG-initiation that Nattiez locates at element 188 is clearly determined by the fact that the initial motivic idea of the piece suddenly returns at this point, and a model that included some consideration of motivic relations might well yield a result here more like Nattiez's. On the other

EXAMPLE 5. Edgard Varèse, *Density 21.5*.

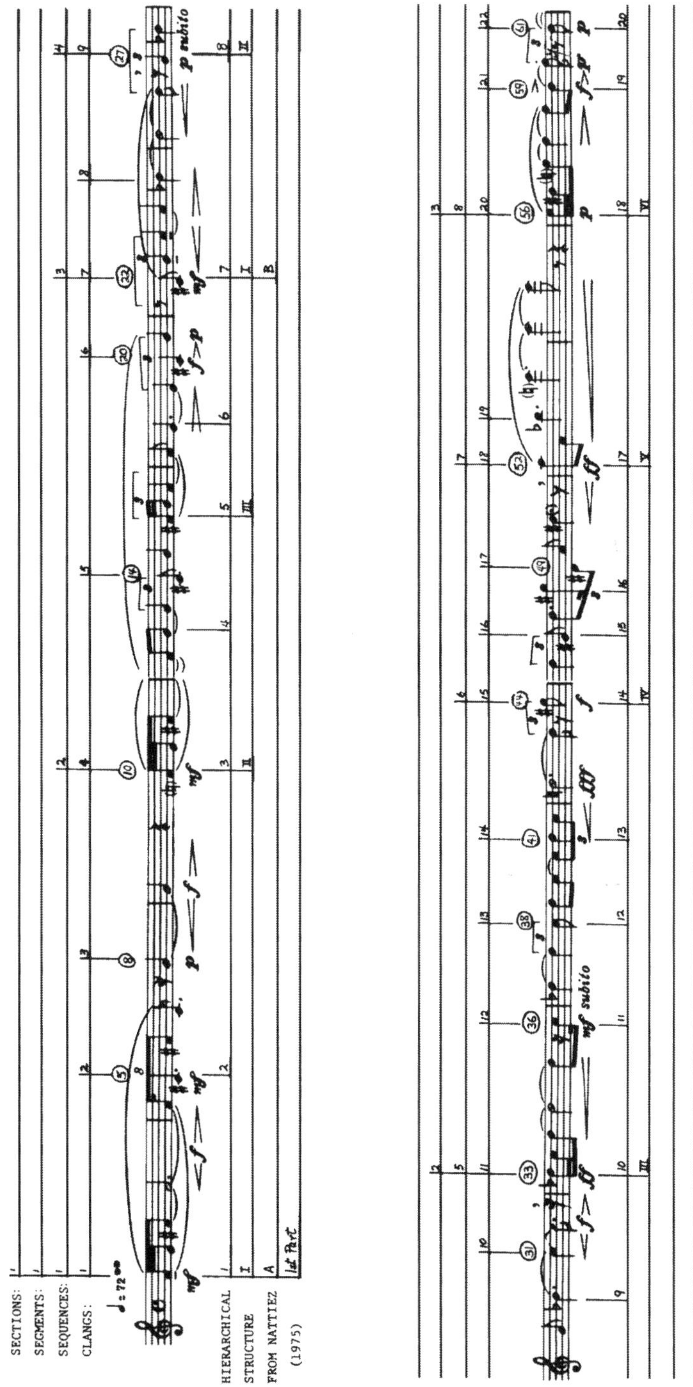

(Ex. 5, cont.)

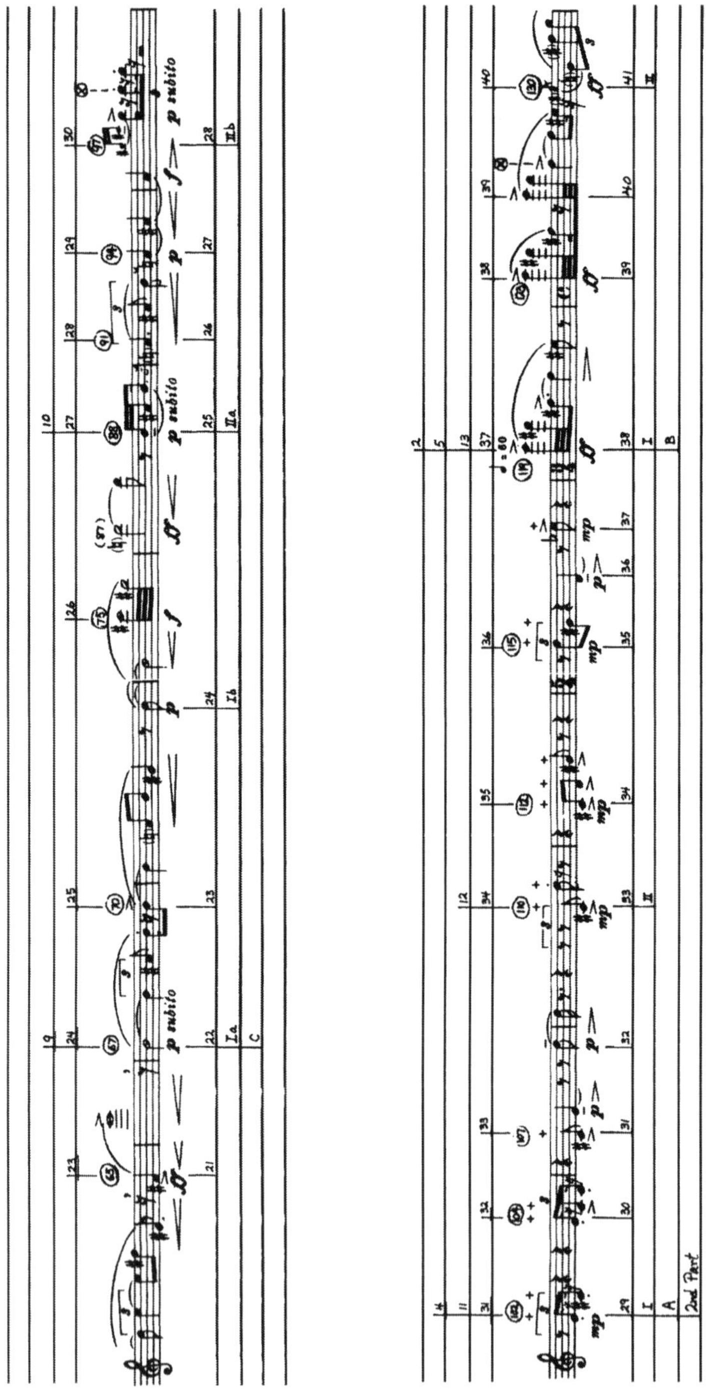

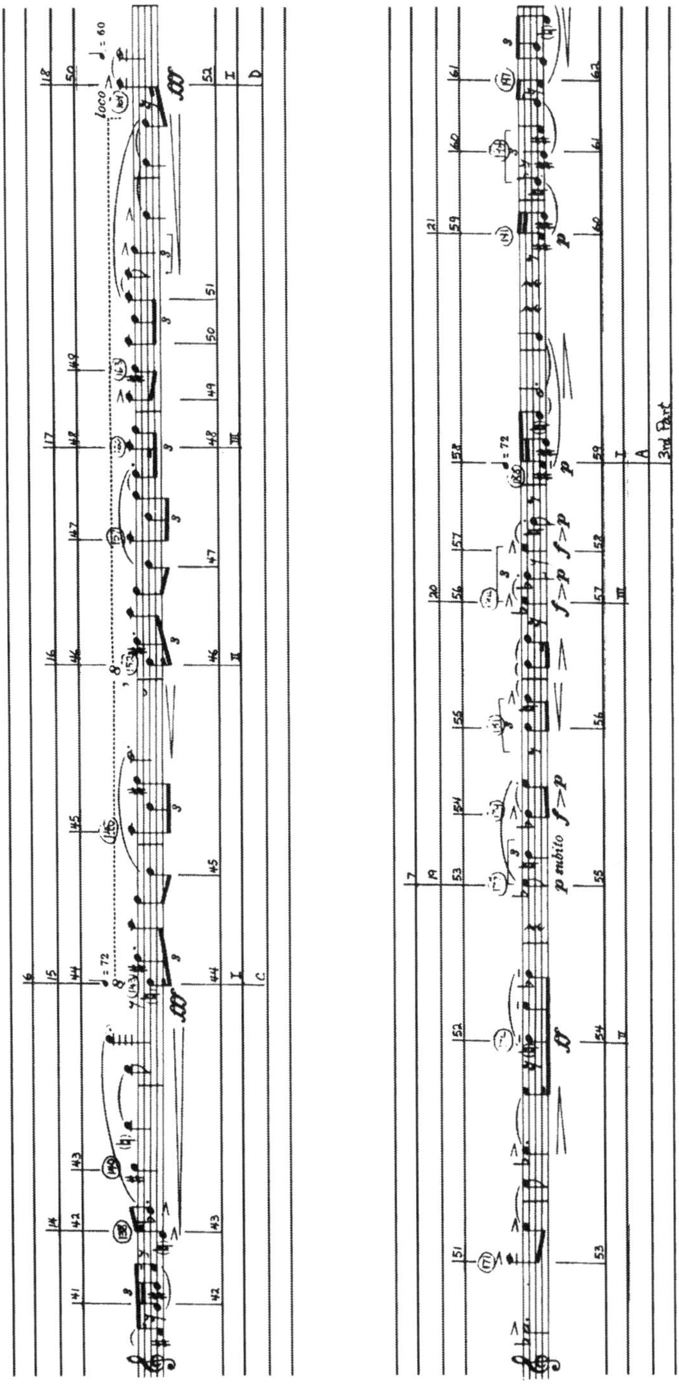
loco
p subito
3rd Part

(Ex. 5, cont.)

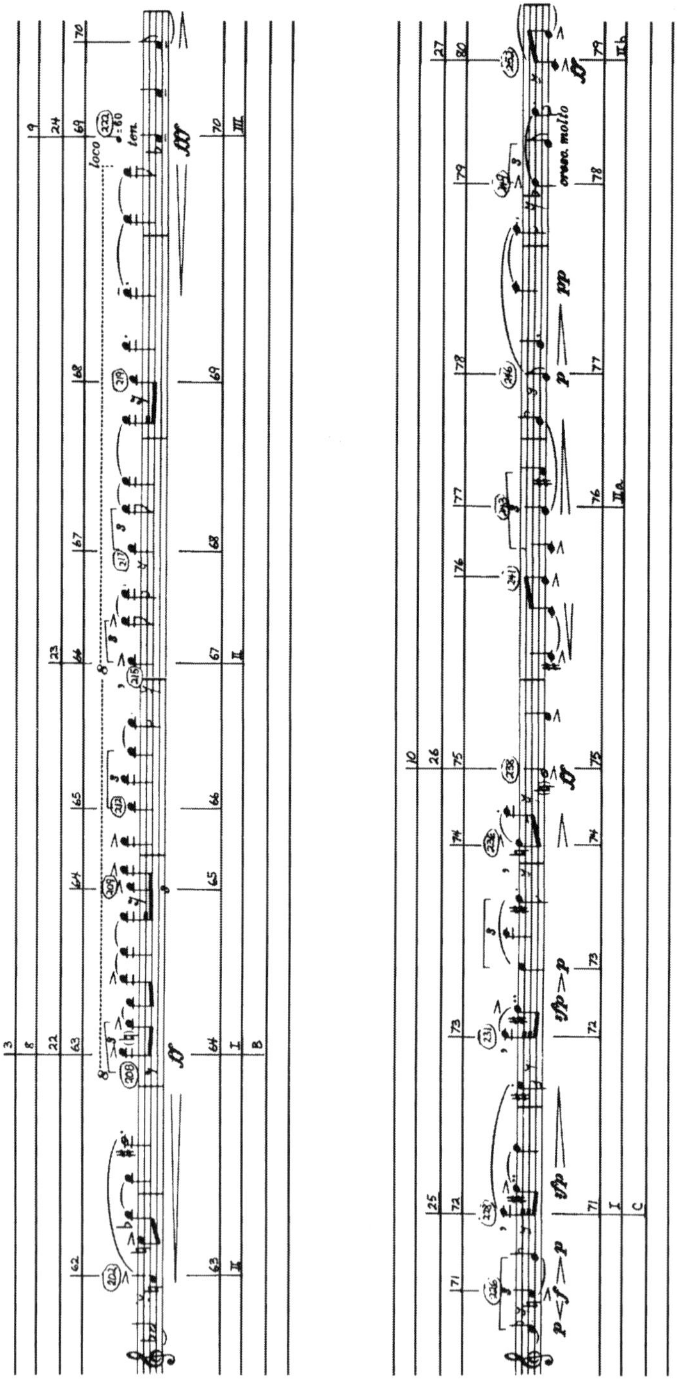

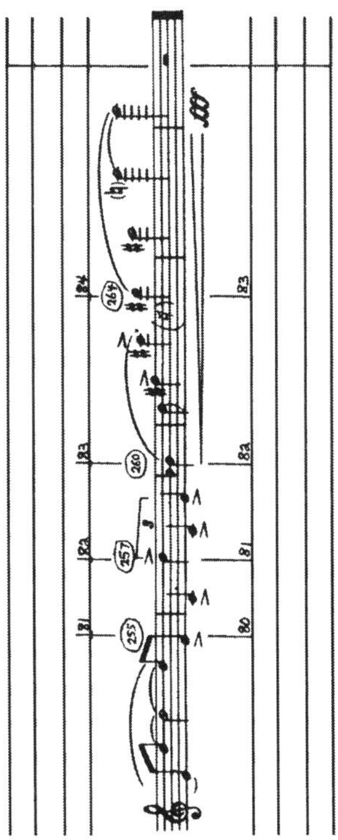

hand, the strong element of surprise that this return of the initial motive evokes in my perception of the piece suggests that this motivic factor is here working very much "against the grain" of most of the other factors of TG-organization and that an important part of the musical effect of this event in the piece depends on the fact that the motive recurs at a point that would *not* otherwise be a high-level boundary.

After all of the foregoing reasons for the differences between the two segmentations have been accounted for, a few discrepancies will remain that suggest that our weightings may not be quite "optimum" after all, or that they are simply different from those unconsciously assumed by Nattiez, or even that some aspect of our algorithm may need refining. Finally, however, I must say that I think our segmentation represents the perceptual "facts" here more accurately than Nattiez's at certain points. These would include the clang-initiations at elements 13, 20, and 75 and the sequence-initiations (and perhaps even the segment-breaks) at 177 and 238.

Anton Webern, Concerto, op. 24, second movement (melodic line only)

The segmentation given by our program for the first twenty-eight bars of this piece is identical at every point but two with that assumed by Leopold Spinner in his "Analysis of a Period" (see example 6). Spinner's first "period" is equivalent to our first segment, and each of the three parts into which he divides this period ("antecedent," "consequent," and "prolongation of the consequent") begins at a point that coincides with one of our sequence-breaks (although the program further divides Spinner's "consequent" into two sequences). Our clangs are coincident with his "phrases" everywhere except at elements 31–34 (marked x in the lower part of line 2 of the annotated score), but the discrepancy here is easily explained. Spinner's concern in the analysis is to demonstrate a cohesive unity in the music resulting from the recurrences of a limited set of rhythmic motives in addition to that deriving from serial pitch-relations. At the point in question, he notes the equivalence of a three-note motive beginning in m. 25 (element 31) with the motive that begins the movement (𝅗𝅥 ♩ ♩). To my ear, however, the oboe's high C in m. 25 sounds like the final element in the three-element clang beginning in m. 23 (element 29), as our program determines it, rather than an initial element, as Spinner would have it.

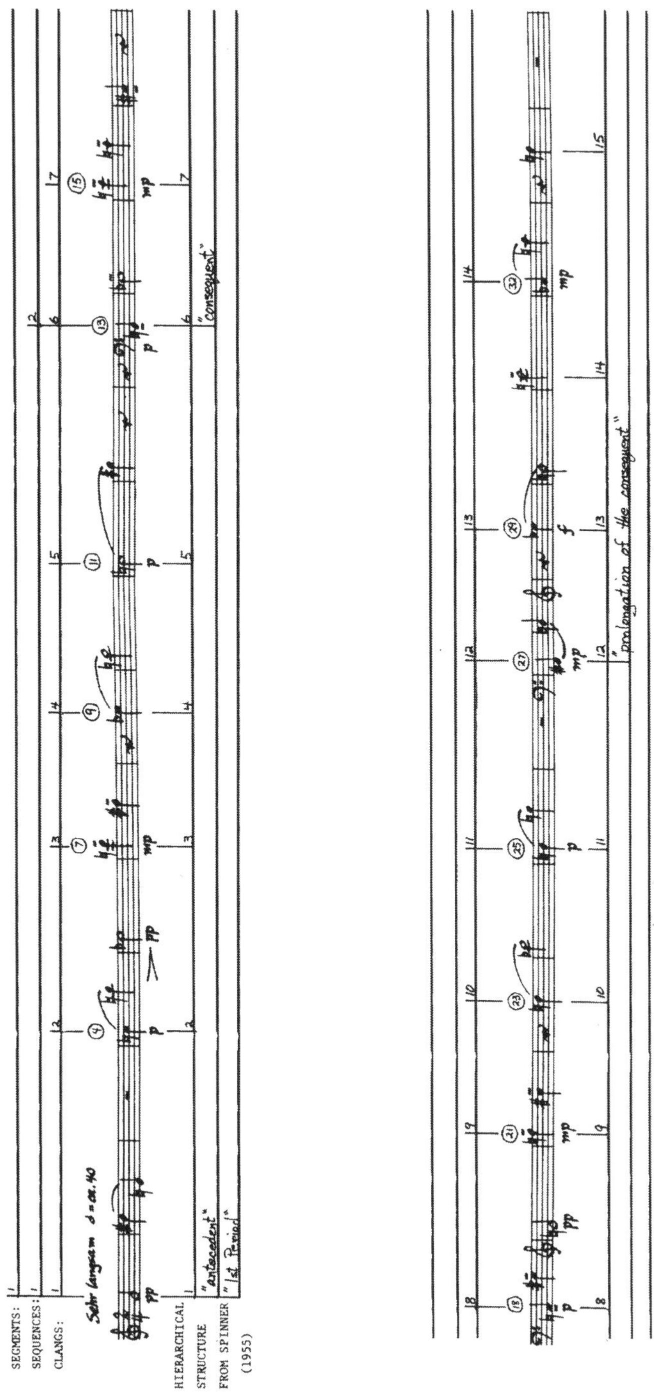

EXAMPLE 6. Anton Webern, Concerto, op. 24, II (melodic line only).

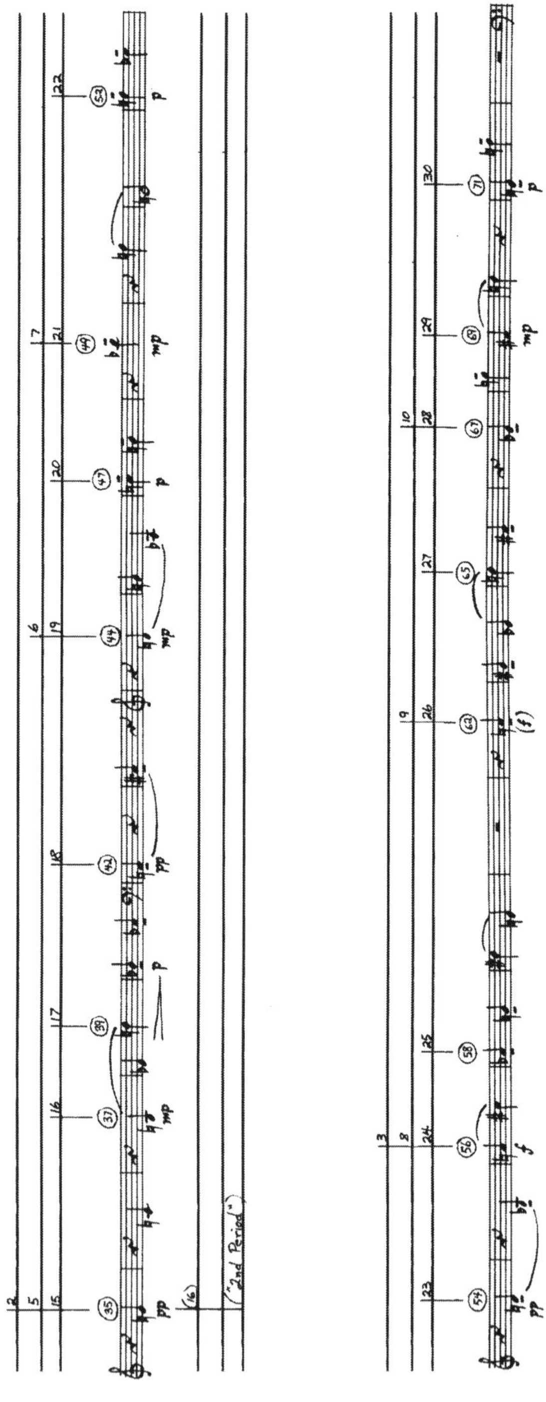

(Ex. 6, cont.)

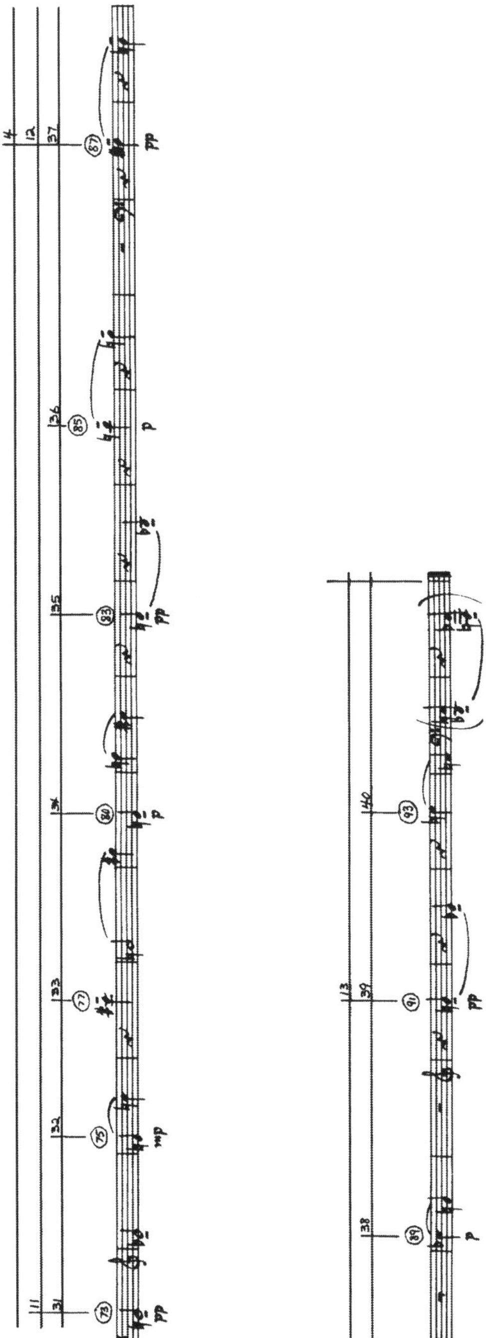

Claude Debussy, Syrinx

Our best results for this piece, using the parametric weights listed earlier, are shown in example 7. In the absence of any other analysis with which these results might be compared, I shall leave it to the reader to decide whether—and to what extent—they correspond to the temporal gestalt organization he or she might make of this piece "spontaneously." I should point out, however, that the intention behind these analyses (at this stage in the development of the model) has not been to demonstrate a segmentation that is more accurate or "correct" than another derived by alternative means—"spontaneous" or systematic. The music has been used primarily to *test the model*, and the only claim that might reasonably be made at this point is that our algorithm is remarkably effective, considering the simplicity of the hypothesis on which it is based. What the results of the model seem to show are aspects of the structure of these pieces that we all more or less take for granted. We have proceeded on a sort of faith in the commonality of our (*all* of our) perceptual "structurings" in this respect, and the validity of our model may ultimately stand or fall according to whether this faith was justified or not.

3. Applications, Implications, and Possible Extensions of the Model

In spite of the rather severe limitations of this model, the degree to which its results correspond to segmentations arrived at by other means suggests that the "fundamental hypothesis of temporal gestalt perception" on which the model is based is at least a plausible formulation of an important principle of musical perception. As such, it may have useful applications for the composer as well as the theorist, since it can be used to create perceptually effective formal structures without recourse to traditional devices, "tonal" or otherwise. For example, serial, aleatoric, and stochastic compositional methods frequently result in textures that are *statistically homogeneous* at some fairly low hierarchical level. A typical negative response to this kind of formal situation (which I have elsewhere called "ergodic") is that although "everything is changing, everything remains the same."[18] Whether this is to be considered undesirable or not obviously depends on a number of purely subjective factors, including the expectations of the listener, the intentions of the composer, etc., none of

EXAMPLE 7. Claude Debussy, *Syrinx.*

(Ex. 7, cont.)

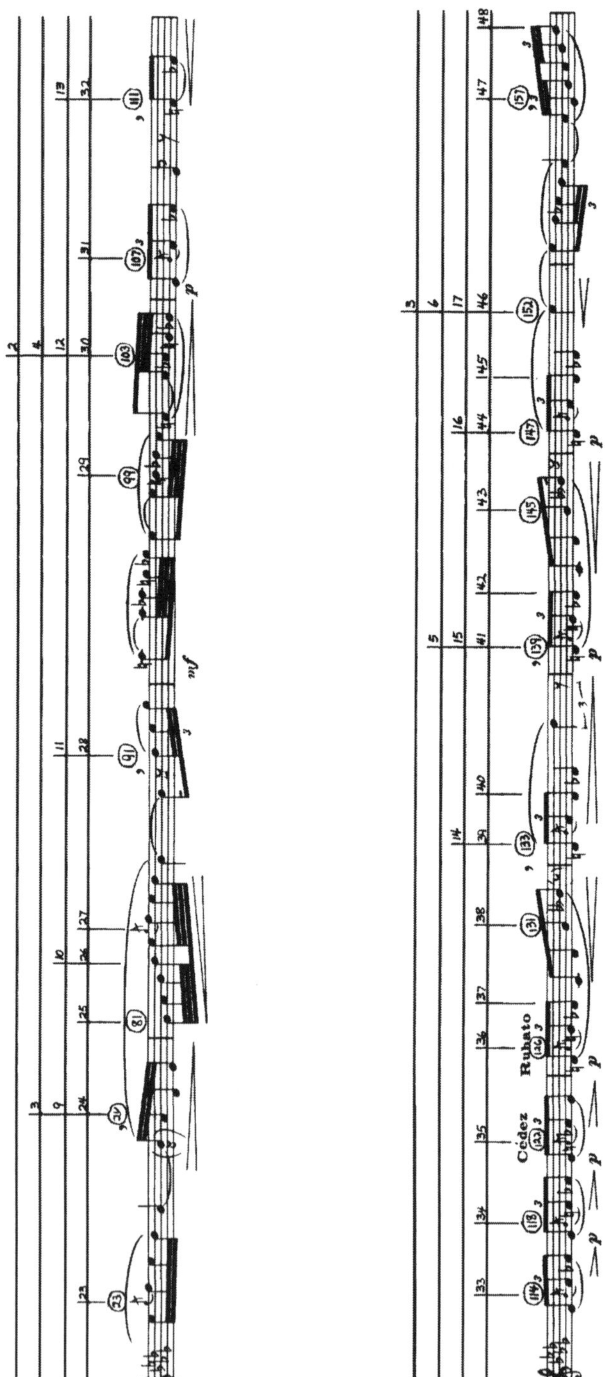

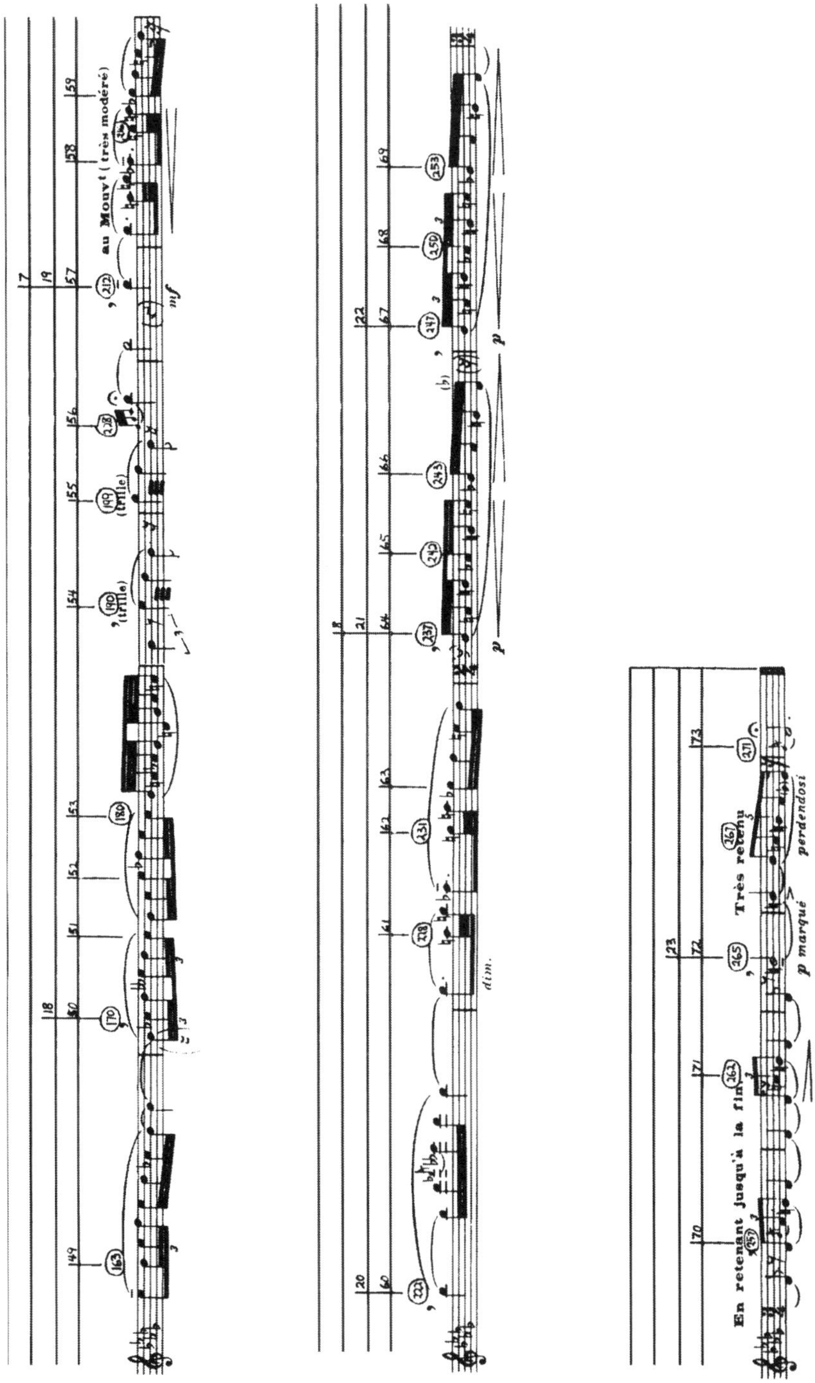
au Mouvt (très modéré)
(trille)
mf
dim.
En retenant jusqu'à la fin
Très retenu
p marqué
perdendosi

which are of concern to me at the moment. What is of concern, however, is the fact that the model outlined in this paper suggests a technique for *controlling* this aspect of musical form when the composer's intentions make such control desirable. A piece becomes "ergodic" (with respect to some parameter) as soon as a hierarchical level is reached at which the *states* of successive TGs are indistinguishable—i.e., at that level at which the mean-intervals between successive TGs (in that parameter) are all effectively zero. In general, this can be shown to depend on the degree to which parametric ranges are *constrained* at the lower levels. That is, the more the total available range in some parameter is "used up" at a given level, the smaller will the average effective differences be *between* TGs at that level, and the more quickly will the texture approach "ergodicity" at the next higher level. The technical remedy for this is simply to *distribute* the total available ranges more evenly over as many hierarchical levels as needed to achieve the formal structure intended.

The model also has certain interesting implications regarding the nature of musical perception. One of the most surprising of these involves what might be called the "decision-delay" between the moment of initiation of a TG at any level and the moment at which this TG-initiation can be perceptually determined or "known." This is the result of several basic conditions inherent in the model, including (1) the fact that the TG-initiating effect of a given disjunction is dependent upon the disjunction that *follows* it (as well as the one that precedes it); (2) the fact that the measure of disjunction involves intervals between *mean* parametric values (i.e., "states") of those TGs and that these mean values can only be determined after that TG has *ended*; and (3) the fact that this, in turn, is determined by the perception that a *new* TG has begun at that level. The decision-delays resulting from these various conditions are shown schematically in figure 2, where it can be seen that the delays are *cumulative* at progressively higher levels and become quite long fairly quickly. The implications of this for musical perception are significant, especially for what they tell us about the importance and function of *memory* and *anticipation*. Clearly, the higher the level concerned, the greater will be the demands on short-term memory, if the TG-boundaries are to be determined at all, and the less certain these boundary determinations must be on a first hearing. On second and later hearings—i.e., with gradually increasing familiarity with a piece—these delays may be diminished or finally eliminated altogether, to the extent to which TGs that have not

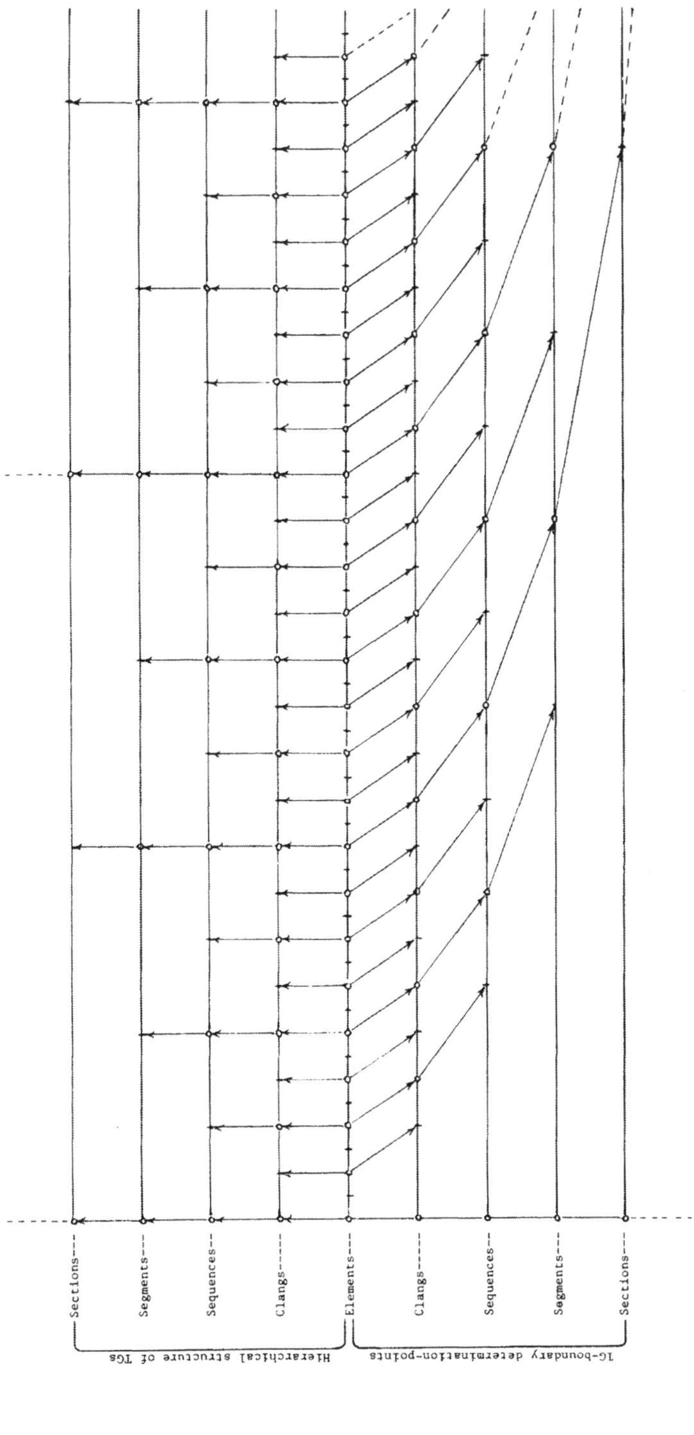

FIGURE 2. Schematic diagram of decision-delays implied by the model.

yet occurred can be anticipated via longer-term memory. Thus, while the indispensable importance of memory to musical perception is a matter of common agreement, and the anticipation of what is about to be heard in a familiar piece is surely a common experience, our model goes one step farther and suggests that the primary *function* of both memory and anticipation is *to diminish the delay between the moment of occurrence of a TG and the moment of recognition of its gestalt boundaries and eventually to bring these into synchrony.*

The extent to which our temporal gestalt perception might be confused, if not utterly confounded, by these phase-shifting "decision-delays" might appear to throw into question the efficacy of the model described here if it were not for the very considerable *information-reduction* implicit in the model. That is, the information that is retained at a given hierarchical level for determining TG-initiations at that level is always less than (or at most, equal to) *half* of the information that was needed at the next lower level. The ratio of information-reduction here depends on the average number of components per higher-level TG, which is by definition at least two. In fact, the average for the pieces analyzed so far turns out to be slightly larger than three.

The algorithm described here obviously needs to be tested with other musical examples, so considerable work remains to be done with the program in its present form. In addition, there are several extensions of the model that ought to be possible and that promise to be important to the growth of our understanding of musical perception and perceptual processes in general. One area in which such extensions are most immediately needed would involve the incorporation of harmonic and motivic factors in the workings of the algorithm. Another area would include whatever elaborations might be necessary to enable it to deal with polyphonic music. Still another would involve some method of dealing with ambiguous TG-boundaries in a more flexible and musically realistic way (perhaps using the notion of "pivotal" TGs, mentioned earlier).

Finally, it should be possible to extend the model "downward" to subelement levels, which would not only eliminate the tedious process of transcription now required to specify input data to the program but also be far more *accurate* than this process can ever be in representing the sounds as we actually hear them. Such an extension would involve analog-to-digital conversion of the acoustical signal into numerical "samples" suitable for input to the computer program. These samples would then constitute the "elements" (or microelements) whose parameters would be subjected to computational procedures essentially the same as in the current algorithm. Element states (sample amplitudes and starting-times) and inter-element disjunctions would be computed and used to determine the points of initiation of micro-TGs at the next higher level. Microclangs would probably correspond to individual periods of the original signal and microsequences to groups of these periods delimited by the on-off behavior of the amplitude-envelopes and/or other modulation processes that might be present (vibrato, tremolo, etc.). Eventually, TGs will be found (probably at the microsequence or microsegment level) whose boundaries correspond to those of the elements whose parameters are now given as input to the program. In the course of such a process, new "parameters" would emerge—pitch and perhaps timbre—in the form of additional "states" not definable at the lowest level (where the only parameters were amplitude and time).

Many of the details of any "downward" extrapolation of the current model are still unclear, but I am convinced that such an extension to sub-element levels is an area of investigation well worth pursuing. Moreover, the conclusion seems justified that the basic procedures in this model will work, with perhaps only minor revisions, at *any* level of perceptual organization and with "elements" whose description might involve other "parameters" than those relevant to sound. Thus, extrapolations of the model "upward" to TGs larger than individual pieces should be possible, as well as what might be described as extrapolations "outward" to temporal gestalt-units involving other modes of perception or several different modes of perception simultaneously.

CHAPTER 10

Introduction to "Contributions toward a Quantitative Theory of Harmony" (1979)

Introduction[1]

I have always thought of myself primarily as a composer and performer rather than as a theorist, and yet there have been several periods in my musical life when I found my energies devoted almost exclusively to theoretical questions. At such times I have drawn courage from the words of one of the greatest of all composer-theorists, Arnold Schoenberg:

> One must be convinced of the infallibility of one's own fantasy and one must believe in one's own intuition. Nevertheless, the desire for a conscious control of the new means and forms will arise in every artist's mind, and he will wish to know consciously the laws and rules which govern the forms which he has conceived "as in a dream." Strongly convincing as this dream may have been, the conviction that these new sounds obey the laws of nature and our manner of thinking . . . forces the composer along the road of exploration.[2]

Until a few years ago, my own work in composition was such that questions of harmony seemed completely irrelevant to it. Timbre, texture, and formal processes determined by the many musical parameters *other* than harmonic ones still seemed like unexplored territory, and there was a great deal of excitement generated by this shift of focus away from harmony. Harmonic theory seemed to have reached an impasse sometime in the late nineteenth century, and the innovations of Schoenberg, Ives, Stravinsky, and others in the first two decades of the twentieth century were suddenly "beyond the pale" of *any* theory of harmony—or so it seemed. I was never really comfortable with this situation, but there was so much to be done—so many other musical possibilities to be explored—that it was easy to postpone questions of harmony in my own music. This situation began to change, however, in about 1970, when I wrote the first of a series of instrumental pieces that were to become more and more involved with specifically harmonic relationships. Then it was no longer the questions that seemed irrelevant but the "answers" offered by the available theories of harmony—both "traditional" and otherwise. The inadequacies of these theories were not confined to their inabilities to deal with twentieth-century music. On closer inspection, it turned out that they had not really answered many of the questions that arise even in the consideration of music of the seventeenth and eighteenth centuries. Considerable confusion and disagreement still existed regarding such fundamental questions as the nature of consonance and dissonance and the origin and status of the minor triad—among others. Though it was clear that pedagogical expediency had dictated the textbook evasions of these problems, the viability of the speculative theory *behind* the textbook pronouncements became that much less convincing.

I finally resolved to attack these problems myself, and the approach I have taken is twofold. On the one hand, I have tried to analyze some of the important factors of harmony from a historical point of view in an attempt to determine what the principal "facts" of harmonic perception might be and what approaches might be appropriate to an explanation of these facts. On the other hand, I have tried to apply acoustical and psychoacoustical considerations to those aspects of harmonic perception that seem amenable to such an approach. That is, I have asked these questions: *Are* there purely acoustical correlates of the principal facts of harmonic perception? And if so, what are they, and can they be used as a basis for a *quantitative* description of harmonic phenomena in music? By "harmonic perception" I mean simply the perception of varying *relations* between tones of definite pitch and of varying *qualities* or *conditions* that arise when two or more tones are heard together—either simultaneously or successively. The principal facts of harmonic perception I take to be those implied by the terms "consonance" and "dissonance," on the one hand, and "tonic" or "root," on the other. Together, these seem to be the most important variables in terms of which various harmonic styles—both of individual composers and of entire periods or cultures—may be described and compared. They are also the outstanding unsolved problems of harmonic theory vis-à-vis "common practice harmony." I will deal with each of these first from a historical viewpoint—in an effort to clarify the nature of the problems involved and to define more precisely the questions that a "quantitative" theory should answer—and then from an acoustical viewpoint.

In choosing this acoustical approach, I was under no illusion that *all* of the problems of harmony could be solved in this way. Obviously, many other factors—emotional, intellectual, and sociological—have influenced the historical evolution of harmonic practice in music and will continue to influence our harmonic perception. But although these may well have determined the *choices* that composers have made—and the responses to these choices by their audiences—the acoustical nature of the tonal materials must always have played a very large part in determining what options were available to them *from which to choose*. Similarly, although an acoustically based theory of harmony cannot (and, indeed, *should* not) presume to tell a composer what choices "ought" to be made, it *can* (and should be able to) say what the most immediate perceptual effects are likely to be if a certain choice *is* made.

While thus acknowledging the obvious limitations of a theory of harmony based primarily on acoustical considerations, I will nevertheless maintain that the most crucial problems regarding harmonic perception—and those that are now most urgently in need of solution—are precisely those to which meaningful answers *can* be provided by an acoustically based theory. I am quite aware that the very idea that the evolution of harmonic practice—or the realities of harmonic perception—might be "explained" primarily on the basis of the acoustical nature of tonal materials has recently fallen into some disrepute. The evident failure of earlier efforts of this kind to account for even some of the most common musical "facts" (like the normative autonomy and definitional power of the minor triad, for example) has led to a disillusionment—if not actual despair—with this whole approach. And yet it is inconceivable to me that the obvious correlations that *do* exist between the structure of a single compound tone and certain other harmonic-perceptual phenomena could be merely coincidental, and the fact that a satisfactory theory has not yet been formulated does not, in itself, prove the impossibility of doing so. It simply proves that the task is a difficult one, beset with logical and epistemological dangers on every side—not the least of which is the danger of molding a theory to fit a set of cultural and personal biases. Thus, for example, Rameau's undisguised intention in the *Treatise on Harmony* to demonstrate that the music of his own era was "more perfect" than that of any earlier generation and Hindemith's evident (though unacknowledged) intention in chapter 2 (volume 1) of *The Craft of Musical Composition* to prove the 12-tone tempered scale the best of all possible solutions to the problems of scale-building, and so on.

It would clearly be naive of me to contend that I am without any such biases, no matter how objective I might wish to be. The most dangerous of these will undoubtedly be those of which I am quite unaware. Among those of which I *am* aware, the most important seem (to me) to be a number of beliefs I have about the needs, limits, and proper *function* of any new theory of harmony. These are, first of all, that such a theory should be *descriptive*—not pre- (or pro-)scriptive—and thus *aesthetically neutral*.

Second, it ought to be culturally/stylistically *general*—as relevant to music of the twentieth (or the thirteenth) century as it is to eighteenth- and nineteenth-century music, and as pertinent to the music of India or Africa as it is to that of western Europe or North America. Third—and in spite of such "generality"—it must be *informative* when applied to a particular work or body of works (this may seem obvious, but the difficulty of satisfying this condition is likely to be directly related to that very same generality). Fourth, it ought to be *consistent*—not only internally, among its own propositions and conclusions, but "externally" as well vis-à-vis other relevant disciplines, including acoustics, psychoacoustics, psychology, anthropology, sociology, and history (this is not to suggest that a mere "theory of harmony" must encompass or embrace the whole content of these disciplines but simply that it should not *contradict* that content). And finally, in order that such a theory might qualify as a "theory" at all in the most pervasive sense in which that word is currently used, I believe that it should be (whenever and to the maximum extent possible) *quantitative*.

Regarding this last condition (which is reflected in the title of this paper), it seems to me that any serious attempt to develop a theory of harmony on a scientific basis (whether the science involved be physical, psychological, or sociological) is bound to come up against the necessity of quantifying its results. Unless the propositions, deductions, and predictions of the theory are formulated quantitatively, there is no way to *verify* the theory and thus no basis for comparison with other theoretical propositions. Such quantification has seldom even been attempted in the past beyond the use of numerical ratios to represent intervals or scale degrees and the ubiquitous "rank orderings" of intervals with respect to consonance and dissonance. In most cases, the efforts by musicians to develop a "scientific" theory of harmony have been as fraught with difficulties as the efforts by scientists to construct a truly "musical" one. As a result, harmonic theory—in the first case—has seldom been a true "theory" at all but more often a bewildering pastiche of recipes, prescriptions, and moral rationalizations for a particular method or style, more akin to alchemy than to chemistry, astrology than astronomy, numerology than mathematics, religion than science. The contributions by scientists, on the other hand, while frequently including valuable observations, deductions, and speculations, betray at least as much cultural bias as do those by musician-theorists when inferences are drawn regarding musical practice.

Having thus stated my beliefs concerning the needs and requirements of any new theory of harmony—and some opinions regarding the inadequacies of most earlier theories—I should hasten to add that I do not imagine that the "contributions" offered herein are likely to completely satisfy such stringent criteria. The most that I would hope to have done is to have scratched the surface of a sphere whose radius is virtually infinite and to have revived an interest in a method of approaching these problems that I consider fruitful. In the end, we must all be reduced to an attitude of humility that may once have been associated with the word "theory"—though this association has long since been forgotten. Both "theory" and "theater," I am told, derive from a common etymological root—the Greek verb "theasmai," which—in Herodotus, the *Iliad*, and the *Odyssey*—was used to mean "to gaze at or behold with wonder."[3]

CHAPTER 11

The Structure of Harmonic Series Aggregates (1979)

1. Harmonic Intersection and Disjunction

When two or more compound tones are sounded simultaneously, their combined spectra form a *harmonic series* (or *HS*) *aggregate*, the structure of which depends on the relative frequencies of their fundamentals.[1] When these frequencies are related to each other by integer ratios, certain pairs of harmonics coincide or intersect, and these points of harmonic intersection occur *periodically* throughout the spectrum—as can be seen for a set of rational dyads in figure 1. The frequencies of the points of harmonic intersection are equal to each *common multiple* of the fundamental frequencies of the constituent tones, and the first (or lowest) of these points will be at a frequency equal to their *least common multiple*. Because of this periodicity, and because the "distances"—or frequency differences—between all adjacent pairs of these points are equal to the frequency of the first intersection point, we can define what will here be called the *harmonic period* of a simultaneous dyad, f_a/f_b (where f_a and f_b represent the fundamental frequencies of the two tones, and the diagonal slash is used to indicate simultaneity), as follows:[2]

$$HP(f_a/f_b) = [f_a, f_b] = \frac{f_a f_b}{(f_a, f_b)} \quad \text{(in Hz)}, \qquad (1.1)$$

where $[f_a, f_b]$ and (f_a, f_b) denote the least common multiple (LCM) and greatest common divisor (GCD), respectively, of f_a and f_b.[3] When these

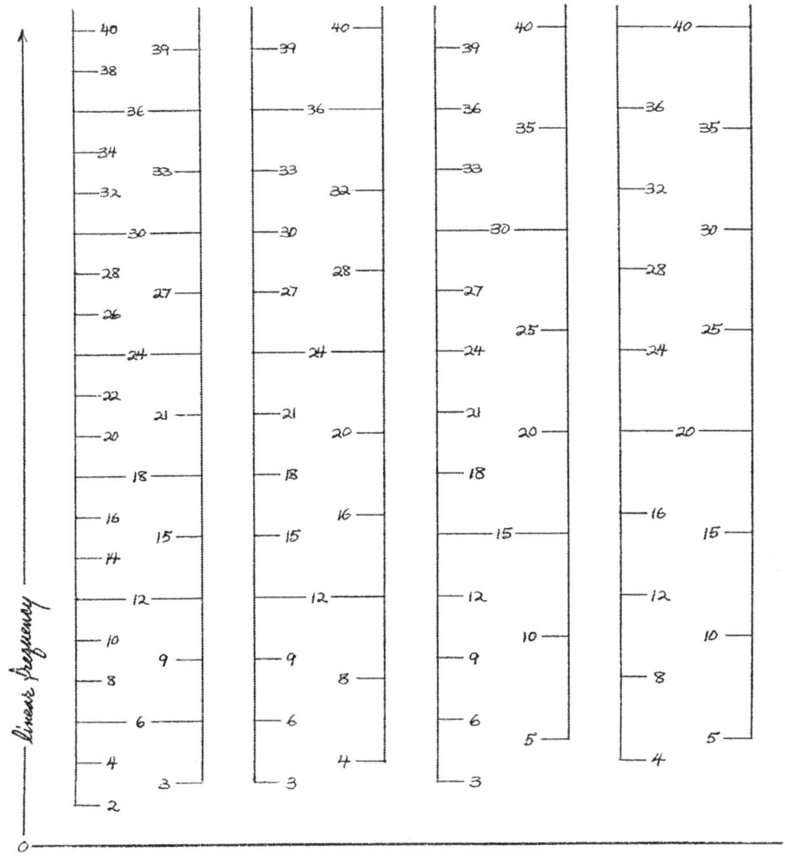

FIGURE 1. Harmonic series aggregates for four rational dyads.

frequencies are reducible to some simpler ratio-terms, a and b, that are relatively prime to each other (such that $a = f_a / (f_a,f_b)$, $b = f_b / (f_a,f_b)$, and $(a,b) = 1$), a *relative harmonic period* can be defined more simply as the product of a and b. That is,

$$HP(a/b) = ab.^{4} \quad (1.2)$$

In the discussion that follows, such reduced ratio-terms will be used whenever possible in the equations describing HS aggregate structure.

From one harmonic period of an HS aggregate to the next, the *pattern* of frequency differences between adjacent harmonics is also periodic, and this periodicity considerably facilitates the analysis and description of their structure, since certain generalizations can be made about the spectrum of the aggregate as a whole on the basis of features found within its first harmonic period. For example, the number of harmonics in one of the tones that are intersected by the HS of the other can be expressed as a fixed fraction of the total number of harmonics in the first tone, and vice versa. This fraction will be called the *intersection ratio* of one tone with respect to the other and—for any reduced rational dyad, a/b—may be expressed as follows:[5]

$$I(a:b) = \frac{1}{b} \quad \text{(to be read "the intersection ratio of tone } a \text{ by tone } b\text{") and} \tag{1.3}$$

$$I(b:a) = \frac{1}{a} \quad \text{(the intersection ratio of tone } b \text{ by tone } a\text{).} \tag{1.4}$$

The fraction of a tone's HS that is *not* intersected by that of the other tone will be called the *disjunction ratio* of the first tone with respect to (or "by") the second, and vice versa, and is simply

$$Dsj(a:b) = 1 - I(a:b) = 1 - \frac{1}{b} = \frac{(b-1)}{b}, \tag{1.5}$$

and

$$Dsj(b:a) = 1 - I(b:a) = 1 - \frac{1}{a} = \frac{(a-1)}{a}. \tag{1.6}$$

Such intersection and disjunction ratios (and more complex ones, which will be introduced later) will be shown to have important applications to the problems of consonance and dissonance and of the harmonic roots of intervals and chords.[6] In addition, it will be useful to have expressions for the number of different harmonics in various HS aggregates. Again, the spectral periodicity mentioned above can be used to derive such expressions, as shown in the following paragraphs.

The number of harmonics in each tone within a harmonic period of a dyad is

$$N(a) = \frac{ab}{a} = b, \tag{1.7}$$

and

$$N(b) = \frac{ab}{b} = a, \tag{1.8}$$

but the number of *different* harmonics in each harmonic period of a dyad is equal to the sum of the number of harmonics in each tone, minus one (for the intersected harmonic in each period). That is,

$$N(a/b) = a + b - 1. \tag{1.9}$$

Within a given frequency range up to and including some upper cut-off frequency, f_{max} (assumed to equal some integer multiple of the harmonic period), the total number of harmonics in each tone (considered by itself) is simply

$$NH(f_a) = f_{max} / f_a, \tag{1.10}$$

and

$$NH(f_b) = f_{max} / f_b, \tag{1.11}$$

and the number of harmonic intersections within that same range is equal to the number of harmonic periods in the dyad within that range, which is

$$NHP(f_a/f_b) = \frac{f_{max}}{[f_a, f_b]}. \tag{1.12}$$

Finally, the total number of different harmonics in a dyad, within the range from zero to f_{max}, can be derived in either of two ways, as follows: first, it is equal to the number of different harmonics in each harmonic period of the dyad, multiplied by the number of harmonic periods within the range, thus:

$$NH(f_a/f_b) = N(a/b)NHP(f_a/f_b) = (a+b-1)\frac{f_{max}}{[f_a, f_b]}, \tag{1.13}$$

but it is also equal to the sum of the number of harmonics in each tone (within the range) minus one for each intersected harmonic (and thus, for each harmonic period within the range), that is,[7]

$$NH(f_a/f_b) = NH(f_a) + NH(f_b) - NHP(f_a/f_b) = \frac{f_{max}}{f_a} + \frac{f_{max}}{f_b} - \frac{f_{max}}{[f_a, f_b]}$$
$$= f_{max}\left(\frac{1}{f_a} + \frac{1}{f_b} - \frac{1}{[f_a, f_b]}\right) = f_{max}\left(\frac{f_a + f_b - (f_a, f_b)}{f_a f_b}\right) = \frac{f_{max}}{(f_a, f_b)}\left(\frac{a+b-1}{ab}\right). \tag{1.14}$$

A continuous graphic representation of points of harmonic intersection is shown in figure 2. Here the fundamental frequencies of the two tones forming the dyad are represented by the darker lines at the bottom, passing continuously through every interval from a unison to a double octave. Points of harmonic intersection are indicated by the circled crossover points within the pattern of upper partials, shown by the lighter lines in the figure. Note that the vertical distance between the lowest of these intersection-points for a given dyad and the dashed horizontal line representing the geometric mean of the two fundamental frequencies is an increasing function of the magnitude of the numbers, *a* and *b*, used to define the interval—the larger these numbers, the higher the first point of harmonic intersection will be found in the spectrum.[8] (This relationship will be used later to define a measure called "harmonic distance.")

The discussion so far has been based on several implicit assumptions, which must now be stated explicitly. First, I have been assuming that the harmonic partials of each tone in an aggregate are indeed "harmonic"—i.e., that their frequencies are *integral multiples* of the fundamental frequency of the tone. Second, I have been assuming that the spectrum of each tone is fairly *extensive*, including harmonics at least as high as the first point of harmonic intersection in the HS aggregate, and that this spectrum is *complete* within that range—i.e., that it contains no "gaps." This means, among other things, that the equations given here do not apply to "odd-only" spectra like that of a square wave (or any other waveform exhibiting what is called "half-wave symmetry"). These two assumptions taken together imply certain limitations regarding the generality of the equations, but I believe that less restrictive conditions—e.g., slightly inharmonic or less extensive spectra—can eventually be dealt with by minor modifications of these equations, and I will not attempt to develop such modifications in this paper.

A third implicit assumption in the preceding discussion is one that has caused considerable difficulty in all earlier theories using ratios to represent intervals and deriving their "measures" from these ratios. This is the assumption that harmonic intersection occurs at discrete "points" in the spectrum, at which the frequencies of two intersecting harmonics are precisely equal. This would mean that any description of harmonic relations or conditions based on the pattern of these intersections would only be applicable when the ratios involved were correspondingly precise, since even the smallest deviation from precise intonation would lead to

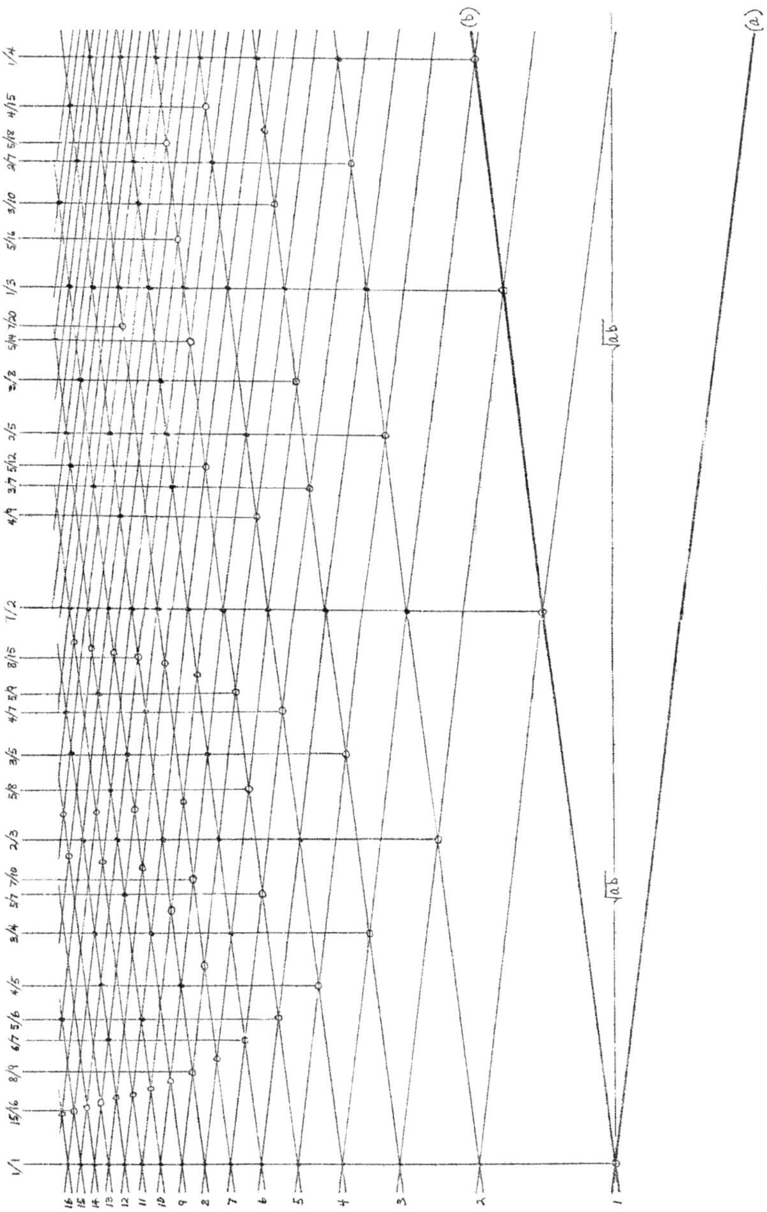

FIGURE 2. Patterns of harmonic intersection for dyads from the unison through the double octave.

very different results. Our musical experience tells us immediately, however, that such small deviations from the simpler "just" ratios (and, to some extent, even fairly large deviations, as in the 12-tone equal-tempered scale) do *not* always or necessarily have such a strong effect on perception. This third assumption is therefore not a realistic one. Here again, I do not think it necessary to incorporate into the equations the modifications that would be necessary to get around this problem. I will, however, describe the basic form that I believe the appropriate modifications would take.

The more realistic assumption—with respect to the actual *perception* of the structure of HS aggregates—would be that harmonic intersection is effective within a certain *region* around such a point, delimited by some small but finite interval, r, where

$$r = k \log_2(q/p) \tag{1.15}$$

above and below the "ideal" point of harmonic intersection. Here, q and p are ratio-terms appropriate to the interval, and k simply determines the unit of measurement (cents, semitones, etc.). Now, for any measure of HS aggregate structure based on harmonic intersection—given some chosen value for r—we would define the *effective value* of that measure for *any* dyad, u/v, as equal to that of the interval with the *minimum value* for that measure within the range from $(k \log_2(u/v) + r)$ to $(k \log_2(u/v) - r)$. Thus, for example, although the ideal value for the number of different harmonics in each harmonic period of the dyad a/b = 64/81 (the Pythagorean major third) is 144, its effective value might be reduced to N(4/5) = 8 if we assume a value for r greater than 408 – 386 = 22 cents. The actual value chosen for r might depend on some sort of psychoacoustic experiment designed to determine the smallest difference between two intervals that has any effect on harmonic perception, or it might simply be chosen in a way that achieves results that seem consistent with musical experience. For example, if we wish to consider the 12-tone tempered scale as an effective approximation of the basic "5-limit" just intervals (using Partch's terminology) from which it was derived, historically—or with respect to which it was, in fact, developed as an "approximation"—we would have to choose a value of r slightly larger than about 17 cents, thus "equating" the measures associated with the tempered minor third and the just ratio, 5/6, which differ by about 16 cents. This is a very small interval—about one-twelfth of a "tone"—and would still allow for a distinction between the just and Pythagorean major thirds (4/5 vs. 64/81—a difference of 80/81 = 22 cents). Leaving open the question of the appropriate size of *r*, I shall assume in all that follows that harmonic intersection should be understood to be effective within some such finite region, rather than simply at a "point," and corresponding modifications (or more precisely, substitutions) are to be made for any measure of HS aggregate relationships based on the phenomenon of harmonic intersection.[9]

For HS aggregates containing three tones, the equations corresponding to those already presented for dyads become more complicated, as it is always necessary to use terms representing least common multiples and greatest common divisors, because—in general—even when the simplest ratio-terms are relatively prime to each other, they may not be so when taken in pairs. When *more* than three tones are involved, these increases in complexity are compounded at each step until the equations become so unwieldy that only a computer program could make use of them in any practical way. Consequently, I shall present here only the equations for triads on the assumption that the principles involved will have been made clear enough to allow for subsequent extensions to more complex HS aggregates.[10]

The *harmonic period* of a triad with fundamental frequencies f_a, f_b, and f_c is equal to their least common multiple, just as with dyads. That is (Griffin 1954, 33),[11]

$$HP(f_a/f_b/f_c) = [f_a, f_b, f_c] = \frac{f_a f_b f_c (f_a, f_b, f_c)}{(f_a, f_b)(f_a, f_c)(f_b, f_c)}. \tag{1.16}$$

Again, when these frequencies are reducible to simpler ratio-terms, *a*, *b*, and c (such that $a = f_a / (f_a, f_b, f_c)$ etc., and $(a,b,c) = 1$), we can define a *relative harmonic period*,[12]

$$HP(a/b/c) = [a,b,c] = \frac{abc}{(a,b)(a,c)(b,c)} = \frac{[f_a, f_b, f_c]}{(f_a, f_b, f_c)}. \tag{1.17}$$

The *intersection ratios* for each tone of a triad, with respect to the dyad formed by the other two tones, are[13]

$$I(a:b/c) = a\left(\frac{1}{[a,b]} + \frac{1}{[a,c]} - \frac{1}{[a,b,c]}\right) = \frac{b(a,c) + c(a,b) - (a,b)(a,c)(b,c)}{bc}, \tag{1.18}$$

$$I(b:a/c)=b\left(\frac{1}{[a,b]}+\frac{1}{[b,c]}-\frac{1}{[a,b,c]}\right)=\frac{a(b,c)+c(a,b)-(a,b)(a,c)(b,c)}{ac},\tag{1.19}$$

and

$$I(c:a/b)=c\left(\frac{1}{[a,c]}+\frac{1}{[b,c]}-\frac{1}{[a,b,c]}\right)=\frac{a(b,c)+b(a,c)-(a,b)(a,c)(b,c)}{ab}.\tag{1.20}$$

The corresponding *disjunction ratios* for each tone of a triad, with respect to the dyad formed by the other two tones, are therefore

$$Dsj(a:b/c)=1-\frac{b(a,c)+c(a,b)-(a,b)(a,c)(b,c)}{bc},\tag{1.21}$$

$$Dsj(b:a/c)=1-\frac{a(b,c)+c(a,b)-(a,b)(a,c)(b,c)}{ac},\tag{1.22}$$

and

$$Dsj(c:a/b)=1-\frac{a(b,c)+b(a,c)-(a,b)(a,c)(b,c)}{ab}.\tag{1.23}$$

Equations 1.20 and 1.23 are of particular interest in the special case when $c = (a,b) = 1$—i.e., when we consider the degree to which a dyad, a/b, intersects its own greatest common divisor. In this case, equations 1.20 and 1.23 reduce to the following:

$$I((a,b):a/b)=\frac{a+b-1}{ab},\tag{1.24}$$

$$Dsj((a,b):a/b)=1-\frac{a+b-1}{ab}=\frac{ab-a-b+1}{ab}.\tag{1.25}$$

Note that the expression on the right side of equation 1.24 has already been encountered—in equation 1.14. Another implication of this expression will be discussed later, after the presentation of a few more of the basic structural relations in triadic aggregates.

The intersection ratios for each *dyad*, with respect to the third tone in a triad, are[14]

$$I(a/b:c)=\frac{ab}{a+b-(a,b)}\left(\frac{1}{[a,c]}+\frac{1}{[b,c]}-\frac{1}{[a,b,c]}\right), \qquad (1.26)$$

$$I(a/c:b)=\frac{ac}{a+c-(a,c)}\left(\frac{1}{[a,b]}+\frac{1}{[b,c]}-\frac{1}{[a,b,c]}\right), \qquad (1.27)$$

and

$$I(b/c:a)=\frac{bc}{b+c-(b,c)}\left(\frac{1}{[a,b]}+\frac{1}{[a,c]}-\frac{1}{[a,b,c]}\right). \qquad (1.28)$$

The corresponding disjunction ratios for each dyad, with respect to the third tone in a triad, are then simply

$$Dsj(a/b:c)=1-I(a/b:c), \qquad (1.29)$$

$$Dsj(a/c:b)=1-I(a/c:b), \qquad (1.30)$$

and

$$Dsj(b/c:a)=1-I(b/c:a). \qquad (1.31)$$

Again, equations 1.26 and 1.29 are of interest in the special case when $c = (a,b) = 1$, as they reduce to the following:

$$I(a/b:(a,b))=\frac{ab}{a+b-1}\left(\frac{1}{a}+\frac{1}{b}-\frac{1}{[a,b]}\right)=1, \qquad (1.32)$$

and

$$Dsj(a/b:(a,b))=1-I(a/b:(a,b))=0. \qquad (1.33)$$

Thus, any rational dyad is completely intersected by a HS on its own GCD, but the latter is intersected by the dyad in varying degrees, as given by equation 1.24.

The number of harmonics in each tone within the harmonic period of a triad, $a/b/c$, is

$$N(a) = \frac{[a,b,c]}{a}, \tag{1.34}$$

$$N(b) = \frac{[a,b,c]}{b}, \tag{1.35}$$

and

$$N(c) = \frac{[a,b,c]}{c}, \tag{1.36}$$

but the number of *different* harmonics in the triad—within each of its harmonic periods—is equal to the sum of the number in each tone, minus one for each singly intersected harmonic, plus one for the doubly intersected harmonic in each harmonic period. That is,

$$N(a/b/c) = [a,b,c]\left(\frac{1}{a} + \frac{1}{b} + \frac{1}{c} - \frac{1}{[a,b]} - \frac{1}{[a,c]} - \frac{1}{[b,c]} + \frac{1}{[a,b,c]}\right). \tag{1.37}$$

The number of harmonics in each tone of a triad within the range from zero to f_{max} inclusive (where, again, f_{max} is an integer multiple of the HP) is

$$NH(a) = \frac{f_{max}}{f_a}, \tag{1.38}$$

$$NH(b) = \frac{f_{max}}{f_b}, \tag{1.39}$$

and

$$NH(c) = \frac{f_{max}}{f_c}, \tag{1.40}$$

and the number of harmonic periods of the triad within that same range is

$$NHP(a/b/c) = \frac{f_{max}}{[f_a, f_b, f_c]}. \tag{1.41}$$

Thus, the number of different harmonics in a triad, within the range from zero to f_{max}, is

$$NH(a/b/c) = N(a/b/c)NHP(a/b/c)$$
$$= \frac{f_{\max}[a,b,c]}{[f_a,f_b,f_c]}\left(\frac{1}{a}+\frac{1}{b}+\frac{1}{c}-\frac{1}{[a,b]}-\frac{1}{[a,c]}-\frac{1}{[b,c]}+\frac{1}{[a,b,c]}\right)$$
$$= \frac{f_{\max}}{(f_a,f_b,f_c)}\left(\frac{1}{a}+\frac{1}{b}+\frac{1}{c}-\frac{1}{[a,b]}-\frac{1}{[a,c]}-\frac{1}{[b,c]}+\frac{1}{[a,b,c]}\right). \quad (1.42)$$

A comparison of this last equation for the number of different harmonics ($\leq f_{\max}$) in a triad to the corresponding equation (equation 1.14) for dyads will bring out some important features, especially if equation 1.14 is rewritten in one of the forms it would take if we did not assume the ratio-terms, *a* and *b*, to be relatively prime.[15] In that case,

$$NH(a/b) = N(a/b)NHP(a/b)$$
$$= \frac{f_{\max}[a,b]}{[f_a,f_b]}\left(\frac{1}{a}+\frac{1}{b}-\frac{1}{[a,b]}\right)$$
$$= \frac{f_{\max}}{(f_a,f_b)}\left(\frac{1}{a}+\frac{1}{b}-\frac{1}{[a,b]}\right). \quad (1.43)$$

Comparing this to the last form of equation 1.42, it becomes clear that the expressions in parentheses are simply *intersection ratios*, specifying the fraction of a complete HS on its own GCD actually present in the HS aggregate. Thus, equations 1.43 and 1.42 may be rewritten as follows:

$$NH(a/b) = \frac{f_{\max}}{(f_a,f_b)} I((a,b):a/b), \quad (1.44)$$

and

$$NH(a/b/c) = \frac{f_{\max}}{(f_a,f_b,f_c)} I((a,b,c):a/b/c), \quad (1.45)$$

where

$$I((a,b):a/b) = \frac{1}{a}+\frac{1}{b}-\frac{1}{[a,b]} = \frac{a+b-1}{ab},$$

this last form as already given in equation 1.24, and

$$I((a,b,c):a/b/c) = \frac{1}{a}+\frac{1}{b}+\frac{1}{c}-\frac{1}{[a,b]}-\frac{1}{[a,c]}-\frac{1}{[b,c]}+\frac{1}{[a,b,c]} \quad (1.46)$$
$$= \frac{ab+ac+bc-a(b,c)-b(a,c)-c(a,b)+(a,b)(a,c)(b,c)}{abc}.$$

The disjunction ratio for triads (corresponding to that for dyads given in equation 1.25) is thus

$$Dsj\big((a,b,c):a/b/c\big) = 1 - I\big((a,b,c):a/b/c\big) = 1 - \left(\frac{1}{a} + \frac{1}{b} + \frac{1}{c} - \frac{1}{[a,b]} - \frac{1}{[a,c]} - \frac{1}{[b,c]} + \frac{1}{[a,b,c]}\right). \quad (1.47)$$

Earlier, it was pointed out that any rational dyad is completely intersected by an HS on its own GCD, but the latter is intersected by the dyad in varying degrees. The same is true for any rational *aggregate*, no matter how many tones it contains. Thus, an HS aggregate whose constituent tones are rationally related to each other in frequency could be considered an incomplete HS on a "fundamental" whose frequency is equal to their GCD, and the intersection ratios of the form *I*(GCD:aggregate) could then be interpreted as measures of the completeness or wholeness of *that* HS—as it is actually manifested by the harmonics in the aggregate.

It turns out that intersection ratios of this form have very interesting properties with respect to what—in *A History of 'Consonance' and 'Dissonance'* (Tenney 1988)—I called CDC-2, which is associated with early polyphony and has to do with the sonorous quality of simultaneous dyads.[16] For example, these intersection ratios increase as the ratio-terms decrease, reaching a maximum value whenever $a = 1$. Conversely, they decrease as the ratio-terms increase, approaching (though never quite reaching, as long as we are dealing with "rational" aggregates) a value of zero for very large values of the ratio-terms. Since the consonance of an interval or chord (in CDC-2) is generally understood to decrease—and its dissonance to increase—as the ratio-terms become larger, such intersection ratios might be considered as a possible correlate of the consonance of an HS aggregate and the corresponding disjunction ratios as a measure of relative dissonance.

Values of the disjunction ratios of the form $Dsj\big((a,b):a/b\big)$ for certain rational dyads are listed in the table at the end of this paper and plotted as a function of interval size in figure 3. Here it can be seen that there is, indeed, a close correlation between this function and traditional estimates of dissonance. Values of the corresponding disjunction ratios for certain *triads* are also to be found in that table, and these are plotted in figures 4 through 6 as a function of the size of the interval formed between a variable tone (b) and the lowest of the two tones of

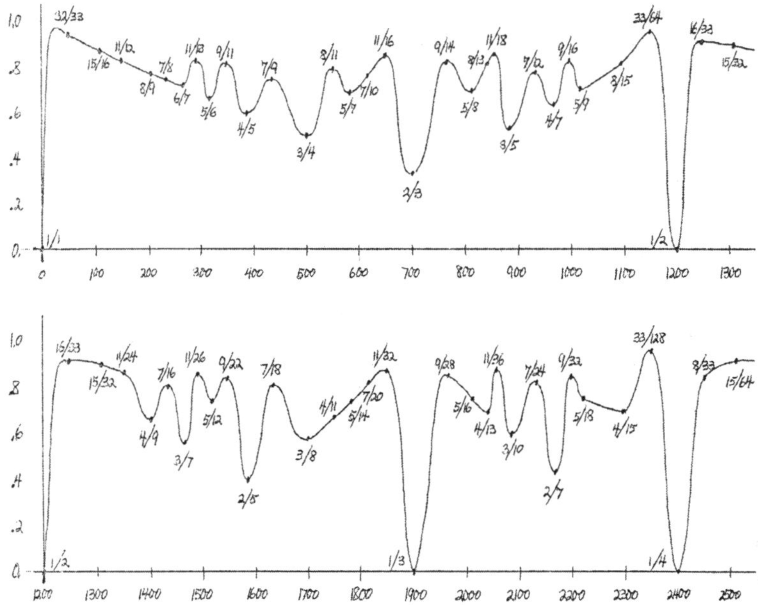

FIGURE 3. Harmonic disjunction ratios for certain rational dyads, *a*/*b*.

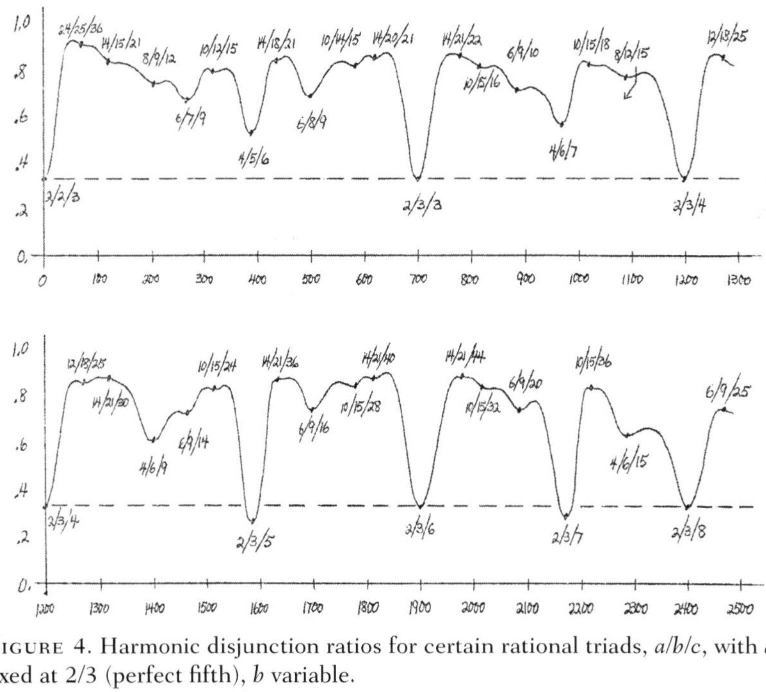

FIGURE 4. Harmonic disjunction ratios for certain rational triads, *a*/*b*/*c*, with *a*/*c* fixed at 2/3 (perfect fifth), *b* variable.

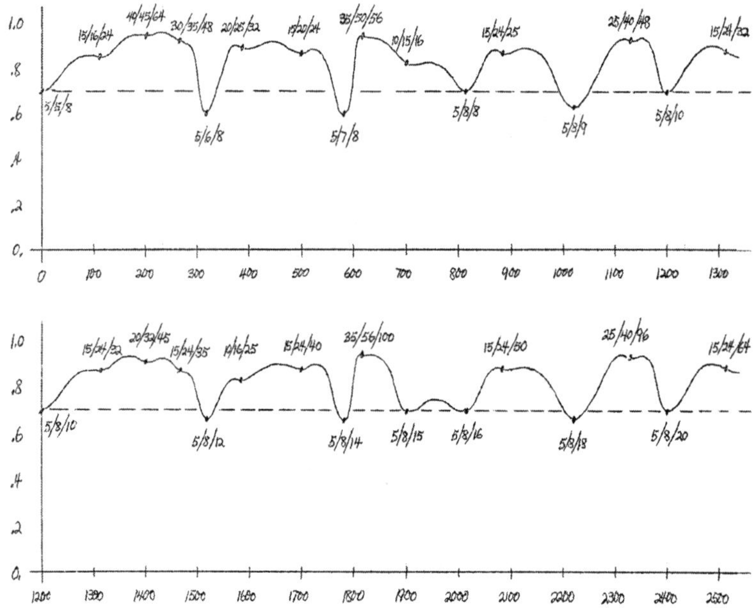

FIGURE 5. Harmonic disjunction ratios for certain rational triads, *a/b/c*, with *a/c* fixed at 5/8 (minor sixth), *b* variable.

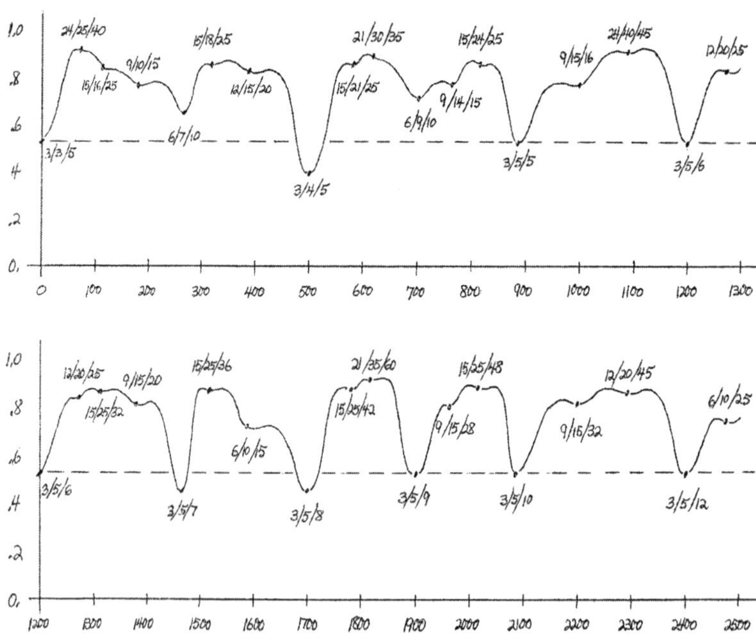

FIGURE 6. Harmonic disjunction ratios for certain rational triads, *a/b/c*, with *a/c* fixed at 3/5 (major sixth), *b* variable.

a dyad (a/c) that is held constant for a given plot. Not surprisingly, the function reaches a local minimum value whenever the variable tone is in unison with one of the tones of the fixed dyad, or when it forms an interval of an octave or twelfth (or *any* higher "harmonic" interval) with either of the lower tones. In addition, however, the disjunction ratio for certain triads is *less* than that for the fixed dyad—and this result *is* surprising. What it means is that—in certain cases—the addition of a third tone to a dyad can yield a lower disjunction ratio (and thus less "dissonance"?) than is manifested by the dyad alone. This was for me an entirely unexpected result—though not, in retrospect, an unreasonable one—a result that might play a crucial role in any future efforts to determine the connection between intersection and disjunction ratios and CDC-2.

The formula given in equation 1.25 for the dyad disjunction ratio,

$$Dsj\left(\left(a,b\right):a/b\right)=\frac{ab-a-b+1}{ab},$$

is equivalent to one to be found in an article by K. Schügerl (1970), where it is described as a measure of the "incompleteness" of an HS aggregate. Schügerl defines it as "the ratio of the number of eliminated harmonics to the total number of harmonics before elimination, calculated under the assumption that the [GCD of a and b] has a large number of harmonics."[17] He notes the (inverse) correlation of this ratio with relative degrees of perceptual "fusion" for various dyads, which is, in turn, a concept that has been suggested as a correlate for consonance (Stumpf 1898).

2. Harmonic Distance and Pitch Mapping

The standard measure of pitch-distance constitutes one type of "relation between pitches," where the pitch-parameter is conceived as a one-dimensional continuum in which two points are separated by a distance that is proportional to the (absolute value of) the logarithm of the frequency ratio of the tones represented by those points.[18] That is, for two tones whose fundamental frequencies are in a ratio of a to b, the pitch-distance between them may be defined as

$$PD\left(a,b\right)=\left|\log_2\frac{a}{b}\right| \text{ (in octave units).} \qquad (2.1)$$

But pitch-distance is not the only relationship commonly perceived between two tones. The earliest sense of consonance and dissonance—CDC-1—implies that at the octave and perfect fifth, for example, two tones seem much more closely related to each other than at immediately adjacent though smaller intervals (the major seventh and augmented fourth), and this has given rise to numerous attempts to order or "map" pitches in a way that somehow represents these other relations by proximities in a "space" of two or more dimensions while still preserving the relations of pitch-distance. What is implied here is a conception of *harmonic space* and a measure of the *harmonic distance* between any two points in that space that is distinct from—but not inconsistent with—the measure of pitch-distance. In what follows, I shall propose such a measure of harmonic distance based on certain physical properties of the spectra (and waveforms) of any two compound tones, which may then be applied to tones heard successively as well as simultaneously. The way in which this measure will be developed here is only one of several different ways in which it might be derived, and there are therefore several different physical and psychoacoustical interpretations that might be given to it, some of which will be described later, but it is presented here as a possible physical correlate of CDC-1.

It has often been noted by others—and even suggested (though I think erroneously) as the primary basis for *all* aspects of harmonic perception—that the combined waveform of two tones whose fundamental frequencies are rationally related to each other is periodic in time. That is, a resultant "common long pattern" is produced that repeats itself at equal time intervals, and the duration of this period depends not only on the absolute frequencies, f_a and f_b, but also on their relative frequencies, a and b. The duration of this period in seconds is equal to the reciprocal of the greatest common divisor of the two fundamental frequencies. That is,

$$Dur\left(f_a / f_b \right) = \frac{1}{(f_a, f_b)}, \tag{2.2}$$

and the frequency represented by this periodicity is simply equal to the greatest common divisor itself. That is,

$$F\left(f_a / f_b \right) = (f_a, f_b). \tag{2.3}$$

We might wish to define a *relative* duration for this period length, using the reduced ratio-terms a and b, as

$$Dur\left(\frac{a}{b}\right) = \frac{1}{(a,b)}, \tag{2.4}$$

and a relative frequency corresponding to this periodicity as

$$F\left(\frac{a}{b}\right) = (a,b), \tag{2.5}$$

but since, by definition, $(a,b) = 1$ and $1/(a,b) = 1$, we gain nothing by this maneuver. Of more interest is the *ratio* between the frequency of each tone and the frequency of their common periodicity, or, alternatively, the ratio between the corresponding period lengths. These ratios are the same whether expressed in terms of the actual frequencies or their reduced ratio terms, since

$$\frac{f_a}{(f_a, f_b)} = \frac{a}{(a,b)} = a, \tag{2.6}$$

and

$$\frac{f_b}{(f_a, f_b)} = \frac{b}{(a,b)} = b, \tag{2.7}$$

and the absolute values of the logarithms of these ratios are the same for both frequencies and durations. That is,

$$|\log_2 a| = \left|\log_2 \frac{1}{a}\right|, \tag{2.8}$$

and

$$|\log_2 b| = \left|\log_2 \frac{1}{b}\right|. \tag{2.9}$$

What these last equations represent is the pitch-distance between each of the tones of the dyad and the greatest common divisor of their frequencies. I now propose, as an appropriate measure of the *harmonic distance* between two tones—and thus of the relation between pitches earlier referred to as CDC-1—the *sum* of these two pitch-distances. That is, for two tones whose fundamental frequencies are in the ratio of a to b

(where a and b are relatively prime), I shall define the harmonic distance between them as follows.

$$
\begin{aligned}
HD(a,b) &= PD(a,(a,b)) + PD(b,(a,b)) \\
&= \left|\log_2 \frac{a}{(a,b)}\right| + \left|\log_2 \frac{b}{(a,b)}\right| \\
&= \log_2(a) + \log_2(b) \\
&= \log_2(ab).
\end{aligned}
\tag{2.10}
$$

(Note that it is no longer necessary to use the absolute-value function here, since a, b, and ab are always equal to or greater than 1, and their logarithms are therefore always either positive or zero, never negative.)

It seems reasonable that the GCD of a set of frequency components input to the ear would be intimately involved in the process of pitch-perception—and at a very primitive level. The interpretation given above to the measure of harmonic distance as involving the GCD of two frequencies is thus not without some plausible neurophysiological bases, even when applied to simple tones, and thus even in the absence of intersecting harmonics. When compound tones are involved, several other physical interpretations of the measure are possible, and this variety of possible interpretations should lend additional credibility to it as a correlate of this important aspect of musical perception. To help clarify these interpretations, HS-aggregates for some simple rational dyads are shown graphically in figure 7. Here a logarithmic frequency scale is used, and HS components are shown up to the first point of harmonic intersection—i.e., through the first harmonic period. There are some remarkable symmetries in these structures, such that, for example,

$$\frac{a}{(a,b)} = \frac{[a,b]}{b},$$

$$\frac{b}{(a,b)} = \frac{[a,b]}{a},$$

and

$$\log_2\left(\frac{[a,b]}{(a,b)}\right) = 2\log_2\left(\frac{[a,b]}{\sqrt{ab}}\right) = 2\log_2\left(\frac{\sqrt{ab}}{(a,b)}\right),$$

Note that, in each case, $\log\left(\frac{a}{(a,b)}\right) = \log\left(\frac{[a,b]}{b}\right)$,

$\log\left(\frac{[a,b]}{a}\right) = \log\left(\frac{b}{(a,b)}\right)$, and

$\log\left(\frac{[a,b]}{a}\right) + \log\left(\frac{[a,b]}{b}\right) = \log\left(\frac{[a,b]}{(a,b)}\right) = \log(ab)$.

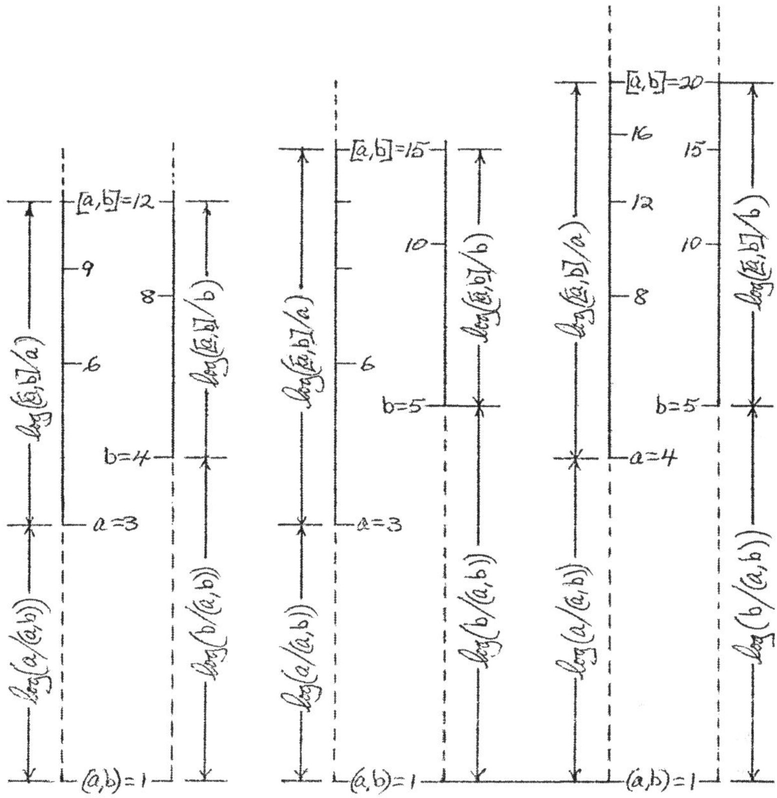

FIGURE 7. Harmonic series aggregates for three rational dyads.

and these symmetries allow for the following equivalent interpretations of the measure of harmonic distance, as defined in equation 2.10:

1. It is the sum of the pitch-distances between each tone and the least common multiple of their frequencies (i.e., the first point of harmonic intersection); that is,

$$HD(a,b) = \log_2\left(\frac{[a,b]}{a}\right) + \log_2\left(\frac{[a,b]}{b}\right). \qquad (2.11)$$

2. It is the pitch-distance between the GCD and the LCM of the two fundamental frequencies; that is,

$$HD(a,b) = \log_2\left(\frac{[a,b]}{(a,b)}\right). \tag{2.12}$$

3. It is twice the pitch-distance between the geometric mean of the two fundamental frequencies ($\sqrt{ab}$, which represents their "average pitch" on a logarithmic scale) and both their GCD and their LCM; that is,

$$HD(a,b) = 2\cdot\log_2\left(\frac{[a,b]}{\sqrt{ab}}\right) = 2\cdot\log_2\left(\frac{\sqrt{ab}}{(a,b)}\right), \text{ and thus,} \tag{2.13}$$

4. it is proportional to the pitch-height of that interval in the HS of a single compound tone—a measure of its (average) pitch-distance from the fundamental. (Here again, we can dispense with the absolute-value function if we take care to express the frequency-ratios as a larger value divided by a smaller—the higher frequency over the lower.)

This measure of harmonic distance seems to satisfy the conditions we would intuitively apply to such a measure. The values are smaller for intervals in which the tones seem to be more closely related to each other and larger for intervals in which the relationship seems more remote. Furthermore, it is an *objective* measure—i.e., it describes certain real, physical characteristics of the acoustic signals. However, it also has another attractive feature: it fulfills the mathematical criteria for a *distance function*; these criteria, in turn, determine what is called a "metric space." These mathematical criteria are the following:

1. symmetry—$HD(a,b) = HD(b,a)$,
2. nonnegativity—$HD(a,b) \geq 0$,
3. nondegeneracy—$HD(a,b) = 0$ if and only if $a = b$, and
4. the "triangle inequality"—$HD(a,b) \leq HD(a,c) + HD(c,b)$, where c is some third "point" in harmonic space.[19] A consideration of the nature of the metric or harmonic space implied by our distance function will provide some useful insights into harmonic relations in general and—a matter that will be of importance to us later in this paper—tuning systems.

The more familiar measure of pitch-distance defined in equation 2.1 constitutes a distance function by these same criteria, and, partly because the "triangle inequality" is always expressible for this measure as a strict *equality* (i.e., $PD(a,c) = PD(a,b) + PD(b,c)$ whenever point b is between points a and c), the metric space defined by the pitch-distance function is one-dimensional. That is, pitches may be ordered (or "mapped") in a way that preserves all of their relations with respect to pitch-distance, along a single line. With the harmonic distance function, however, this is not always the case. The value for harmonic distance associated with certain composite or resultant intervals is sometimes *less* than the sum of these values for its constituent intervals. This is not inconsistent with condition 4—the "triangle inequality"—since that merely states that the distance function for the resultant interval must be *less than or equal to* the sum of the distance functions for its constituent intervals. What it means, however, is that a spatial mapping of pitches that preserves their appropriate harmonic distances from each other will, in general, require more than a single dimension. As it turns out, such a mapping is possible only if a multidimensional space is assumed, with a number of dimensions equal to the number of distinct *prime numbers* involved in the ratio-terms, a and b. Thus, while it is possible to represent by points on a single line pitches represented by ratios involving *only* powers of two (the octave) or *only* powers of three (the twelfth), a two-dimensional space is required to represent the harmonic distance relations among all of the pitches in *both* sets simultaneously, as shown in figure 8. Here, pitches are represented by their frequency ratios with respect to a reference pitch ("1/1," as in Partch's method of labeling his scale degrees). The length of any line joining two adjacent points in the diagram is proportional to the harmonic distance between those pitches, and the harmonic distance between any two *nonadjacent* points is equal to the sum of the lengths of the line-segments traversed on a minimal path connecting them. Our distance function is thus of the type that mathematicians call a "city-block metric." As an example, the harmonic distance between 1/1 and 2/3 may be found by adding the lengths of the line-segment, (1/1, 1/3) and (1/3, 2/3), *or* (1/1, 2/1) and (2/1, 2/3), since these both represent minimal paths between the two terminal points, and the result is the same in both cases. Note that pitch-distances are represented in figure 8 by their positions with respect to the horizontal axis alone (imagine individual pitches projected onto the x-axis).

Figure 8 may be taken to represent the relations—with respect to harmonic distance as defined here—among the pitches in a Pythagorean

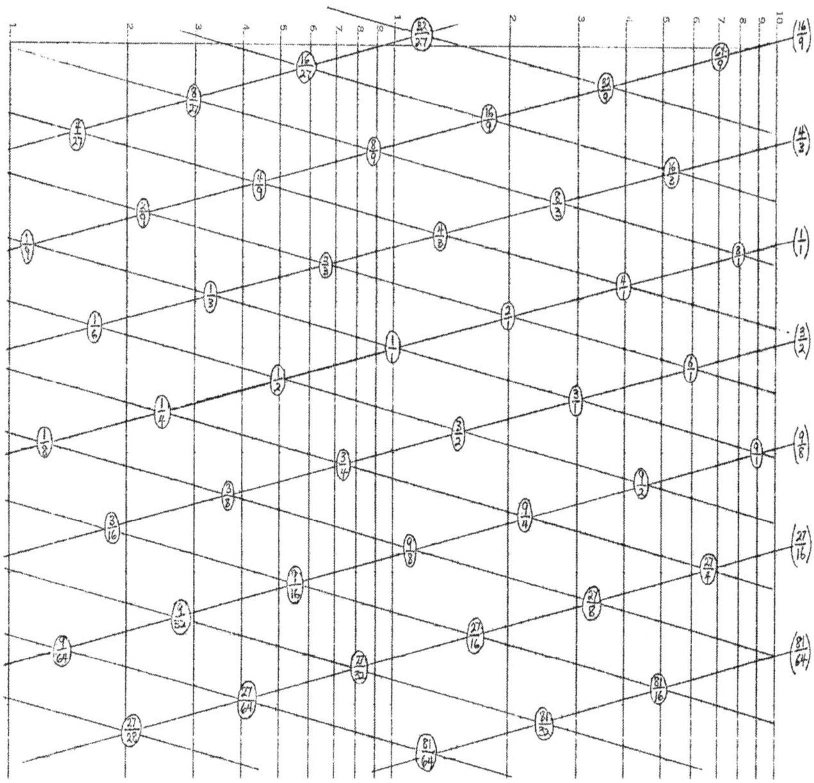

FIGURE 8. Harmonic-distance pitch-map for ratios involving powers of 2 and 3 (i.e., within the 3-limit; Pythagorean).

tuning system, based as it is on combinations of only two intervals—the octave and the perfect fifth (and thus on ratios involving the prime factors 2 and 3 only). In order to represent ratios involving the prime factor 5 (and thus to include the intervals of a "5-limit" just tuning system), a three-dimensional graph would be required. However, instead of grappling with the problem of trying to display such a three-dimensional structure on the two-dimensional surface of the page, I will introduce here an abbreviated form of harmonic distance that takes advantage of the musically familiar notion of octave-equivalence and incidentally makes it possible to display certain aspects of the harmonic distance relation among pitches whose ratios do include the prime factor 5. In figure 8, the pitches represented by the ratios on any of the right-ascending diagonals are all members of the same pitch-class. For example, if 1/1 is taken to represent the note "middle C," then all the other ratios on the right-ascending diagonal that includes 1/1 are also Cs, all the ratios on the next-lower diagonal represent Gs, etc. Thus, if we are willing to consider only harmonic distance relations among pitch-*classes*, we can collapse all the elements along any one of these diagonals into a single point, representing any (or all) member(s) of that pitch-class, and what remains is an ordered set of different pitch-classes but now reduced again to one dimension.

The algebraic correlate of this dimensional "collapse" is the elimination of any power of two in the ratios, or the maximal reduction of each ratio-term by as many divisions by two as are possible, while still leaving an integer. Thus, this "abbreviated" or octave-generalized form of harmonic distance can be expressed as

$$GD(a,b) = HD(a', b') = \log_2(a'\,b'), \tag{2.14}$$

where *GD* stands for *octave-generalized harmonic distance* and $a' = a/2^{m_a}$, $b' = b/2^{m_b}$ with maximal integer values of m_a and m_b such that a' and b' remain integers.[20] Still another way of representing this octave reduction or generalization is as follows: any positive integer product, such as *ab*, can be expressed as the product of a series of prime numbers with integer exponents greater than or equal to zero of the form

$$ab = 2^i \cdot 3^j \cdot 5^k \cdot 7^m \cdot 11^n \ldots . \tag{2.15}$$

The measure of harmonic distance can therefore take the form

$$HD(a,b) = \log_2(ab) = i \cdot \log_2(2) + j \cdot \log_2(3) + k \cdot \log_2(5) + \ldots . \tag{2.16}$$

The values *i*, *j*, *k*, etc., thus represent the number of line-segments traversed in the appropriate dimension along a minimal path connecting two pitches in the diagram. What we are doing when we invoke "octave-equivalence" in harmonic theory (and practice) is simply subtracting this term, $i \cdot \log_2(2) = i$, from the complete expression for harmonic distance, as

$$GD(a,b) = HD(a,b) - i \cdot \log_2(2) = HD(a,b) - i . \tag{2.17}$$

There are at least two possible physical interpretations of generalized harmonic distance, depending on whether the tones involved are simple or compound. With simple tones, it can be considered as the sum of pitch-distances between the GCD of their frequencies and the lowest whole-number octave-equivalents of each of those tones (which still have the *same* GCD; figure 9 provides an example).[21] With compound tones, it might be interpreted in the same way, but—in addition—it is the sum of the pitch-distances between each of the two octave-reduced fundamentals and the first (i.e., lowest) octave-equivalent of the point of harmonic intersection in the combined spectrum. That is, when either of the terms, *a* or *b*, is thus octave-reducible to some lower integer value, *a*' or *b*' (or when, in other words, there is a *difference* between *HD* and *GD*, which is not always the case), then the point of harmonic intersection represented by the product *ab* is some integral number of octaves above a lower frequency-component actually present in the HS aggregate, and the relative frequency of *this* component is equal to the product *a*'*b*'. This component is thus the lowest

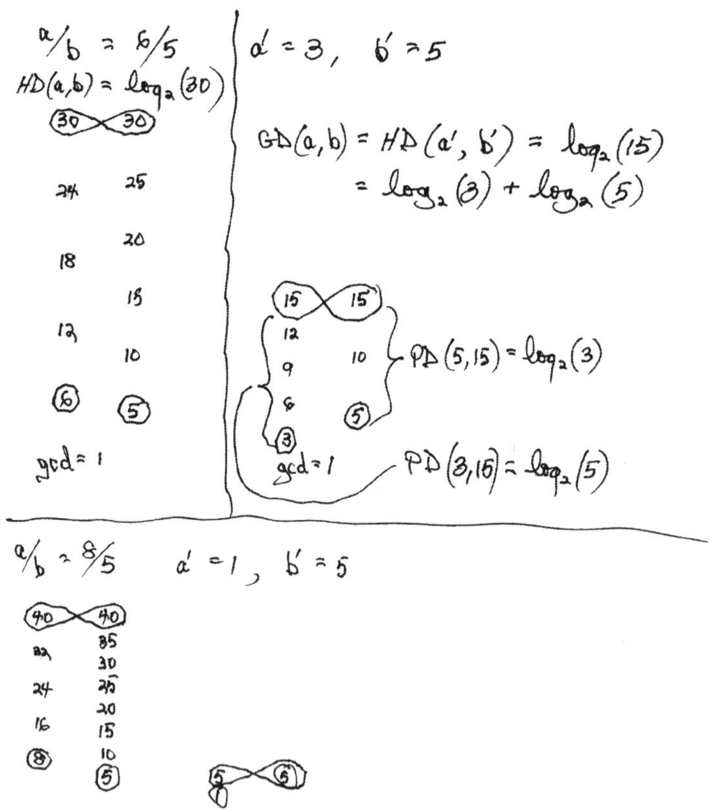

FIGURE 9.

member of the pitch-class represented by the point of harmonic intersection—its lowest octave-equivalent in the HS aggregate.[22]

Values of harmonic distance and generalized harmonic distance for various rational dyads are listed in the table, and the former are plotted as a function of interval size in figure 10. Again, there is some correspondence between these functions and traditional estimates of the dissonance of a dyad (in the sense of CDC-2), but I think they are more appropriately correlated with the earlier sense of *relations between pitches*, which I have called CDC-1 in its historical/musical manifestation.

Although the octave-generalized form of harmonic distance has been introduced here as though it were a mere convenience, it is much more than that. It could, in fact, be taken as a kind of formal recognition of this important aspect of our perception of harmonic relations between pitches—that aspect implied by the terms "octave-equivalence," "octave-generalization," "pitch-class membership," etc.—and thus deserves

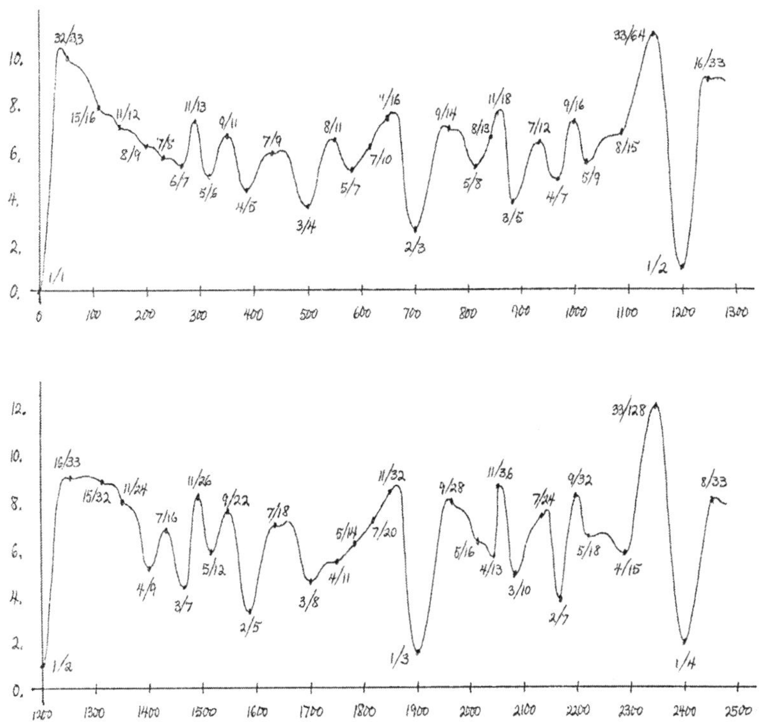

FIGURE 10. The harmonic distance between pitches at certain rational intervals.

further serious consideration. As far as I have been able to determine from my readings in the literature of music theory, musical acoustics, psychoacoustics, and perceptual psychology, *no one* has yet formulated a theoretical explanation of the phenomenon of octave equivalence in any other way than via the argument that the octave is the "first" (or "most," or "best," etc., with respect to some property) among the set of rational intervals. It has been pointed out, for example, that the octave is the *first* interval found between adjacent harmonics in the HS, that it is the *most consonant* of all the intervals, that it is the *smallest* of the intervals at which the fundamental of one tone intersects an upper partial of another tone, that it is represented by the *simplest* of all frequency-ratios other than 1/1, that this ratio involves the *smallest* prime number, etc. Such "explanations" have never seemed convincing to me, however, because of what I perceive as a *categorical* difference—a difference in *kind*, not just in degree—between the octave-relation and all other harmonic relations. A tone at the perfect fifth (or twelfth) above another is not just "a little less equivalent" to it than the octave is. The former is not "equivalent" at all, even though it is, say, only a little less consonant, its frequency ratio only a little less simple, etc. The failure of any theorist to really explain this categorical difference between the octave-relation and other interval-relations suggests that the answer to the question must ultimately come from the discipline of neurophysiology—that it will finally be found to be implicit in some peculiar aspect of the particular transduction mechanisms of the ear and the auditory portion of the nervous system. The reason the question has not yet been answered by auditory researchers is perhaps simply that they haven't yet asked the question. In a later paper, an explanation of the octave-equivalence phenomenon will be proposed on the basis of a model of pitch-perception in the auditory system. Until the details of that model have been presented, however, octave-equivalence must continue to be taken as axiomatic.[23]

Figure 11 presents a mapping of pitch-classes represented by ratios with prime factors less than or equal to 5—ratios within what Partch called the "5-limit"—showing the *generalized* harmonic distance relations among them. Here, the lengths of the connecting lines have been made to correspond to the minimum possible harmonic distance between pitch-class members, but the points in the diagram have been *labeled*

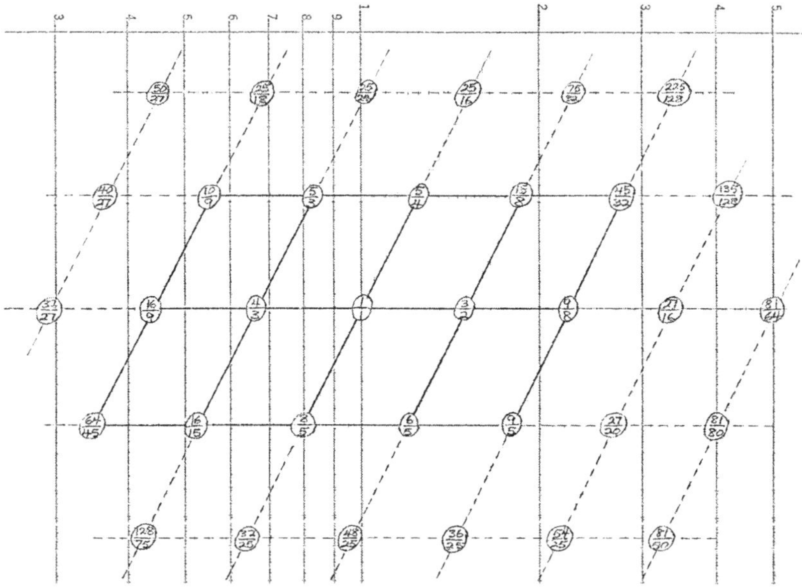

FIGURE 11. Generalized harmonic-distance pitch-map for ratios within the 5-limit (just).

by the more familiar ratio that a given pitch-class member has when it occurs within the range of one octave above the reference pitch, 1/1 (thus using Partch's labeling convention for pitch-classes; note here also that the *angle* of the connecting lines in the 5 dimension has no significance).[24] It should be noted that the structure of this mapping is equivalent to similar constructions to be found in the literature. For example, Alexander Ellis (in his appendixes to Helmholtz's *On the Sensations of Tone* [1954]) uses this construction—which he calls a "duodenarium" (see figure 12)—to describe modulations in tonal music, based on an assumption of degrees of relationship between pitches (or key-centers) that is essentially equivalent to (though less precisely defined than) the measure of harmonic distance proposed here. In *The Myth of Invariance* by Ernest G. McClain (1976), we find similar constructions in support of some interesting speculations regarding connections between ancient tuning systems, number theory, and myth. As precedent for the ideas presented here, however, the work of H. Christopher Longuet-Higgins must be acknowledged as corresponding so closely in concept that the two are virtually identical. In 1962 he wrote:

18. *The Duodēnārium.*

The large figures give the cyclic cents in the interval of each note from *C*. See Table p. 440. The small figures give the corresponding numbers of the cycle of 53 with the nearest whole number of cents. See Table p. 439.

	1 −1·26	2 −·94	3 −·63	4 −·31	5 0	6 +·31	7 +·63	8 +·94	9 +1·26	
−·32	B^4♭♭ 970 47 974	D^3♭ 156 11 158	F^2 542 28 543	A^1 928 45 928	C♯ 114 9 113	E_1♯ 500 26 498	G_2♯♯ 886 43 883	B_3♯♯ 72 7 68	D_4♯♯♯ 458 24 453	−·32
−·27	E^4♭♭ 268 16 272	G^3♭ 654 33 657	B^2♭ 1040 50 1042	D^1 226 14 226	F♯ 612 31 611	A_1♯ 998 48 996	C_2♯♯ 184 12 181	E_3♯♯ 570 29 566	G_4♯♯♯ 956 40 951	−·27
−·23	A^4♭♭ 766 38 770	C^3♭ 1152 2 1155	E^2♭ 338 19 340	G^1 724 36 725	B 1110 53=0 1109	D_1♯ 296 17 294	F_2♯♯ 682 34 679	A_3♯♯ 1068 51 1064	C_4♯♯♯ 254 15 249	−·23
−·18	D^4♭♭ 64 7 68	F^3♭ 450 24 453	A^2♭ 836 41 838	C^1 22 5 23	E 408 22 408	G_1♯ 794 39 792	B_2♯ 1180 3 1177	D_3♯♯ 366 20 360	F_4♯♯♯ 752 37 749	−·18
−·14	G^4♭♭ 562 29 566	B^3♭♭ 948 46 951	D^2♭ 134 10 136	F^1 520 27 521	A 906 44 906	C_1♯ 92 8 91	E_2♯ 478 25 475	G_3♯♯ 864 42 860	B_4♯♯ 50 6 45	−·14
−·09	C^4♭♭ 1060 51 1064	E^3♭♭ 246 15 249	G^2♭ 632 32 634	B^1♭ 1018 49 1019	D 204 13 204	F_1♯ 590 30 589	A_2♯ 976 47 974	C_3♯♯ 162 11 158	E_4♯♯ 548 28 543	−·09
−·05	F^4♭♭ 358 20 362	A^3♭♭ 744 37 747	C^2♭ 1130 1 1132	E^1♭ 316 18 317	G 702 35 702	B_1 1088 52 1087	D_2♯ 274 16 272	F_3♯♯ 660 33 657	A_4♯♯ 1046 50 1042	−·05
0	B^4♭♭♭ 856 42 860	D^3♭♭ 42 6 45	F^2♭ 428 23 430	A^1♭ 814 40 815	C 0 4 0	E_1 386 21 385	G_2♯ 772 38 770	B_3♯ 1158 2 1158	D_4♯♯ 344 19 340	0
+·05	E^4♭♭♭ 154 11 158	G^3♭♭ 540 28 543	B^2♭♭ 926 45 928	D^1♭ 112 9 113	F 498 26 498	A_1 884 43 883	C_2♯ 70 7 68	E_3♯ 456 24 453	G_4♯♯ 842 41 838	+·05
+·09	A^4♭♭♭ 652 33 657	C^3♭♭ 1038 50 1042	E^2♭♭ 224 14 226	G^1♭ 610 31 611	B♭ 996 48 996	D_1 182 12 181	F_2♯ 568 29 566	A_3♯ 954 46 951	C_4♯♯ 140 10 136	+·09
+·14	D^4♭♭♭ 1150 2 1155	F^3♭♭ 336 19 340	A^2♭♭ 722 36 725	C^1♭ 1108 53=0 1109	E♭ 294 17 294	G_1 680 34 679	B_2 1066 51 1064	D_3♯ 252 15 249	F_4♯♯ 638 32 634	+·14
+·18	G^4♭♭♭ 448 24 453	B^3♭♭♭ 834 41 838	D^2♭♭ 20 5 23	F^1♭ 406 22 408	A♭ 792 39 792	C_1 1178 3 1177	E_2 364 20 362	G_3♯ 750 37 747	B_4♯ 1136 1 1132	+·18
+·23	C^4♭♭♭ 946 46 951	E^3♭♭♭ 132 10 136	G^2♭♭ 518 27 521	B^1♭♭ 904 44 906	D♭ 90 8 91	F_1 476 25 475	A_2 862 42 860	C_3♯ 48 6 45	E_4♯ 434 23 430	+·23
	−1·26 1	−·94 2	−·63 3	−·31 4	0 5	+·31 6	+·63 7	+·94 8	+1·26 9	

FIGURE 12. Alexander Ellis's "Duodenarium," from (Helmholtz 1954, 463). Note here that the 3-dimension is vertical, the 5-dimension horizontal.

> The most important generalization which one can make about the intervals of tonal music is that every standard interval can be expressed *in one and only one way* as a combination of perfect fifths, major thirds and octaves. . . . Thanks to its specially primitive character, however, we can take the octave for granted . . . and order the intervals systematically in an only *two-dimensional* array. . . . [A]ll that I have tried to do is to stress the two-dimensional character of musical space (three-dimensional if one gives due respect to the octave) and to demonstrate the need to use two-dimensional maps for exploring it. (1962b, 280)

In a later paper, he writes: "In the formal theory [of tonality] every musical note is assigned coordinates (x,y,z) in a 'tonal space' of three dimensions, corresponding to the perfect fifth, the major third and the octave, respectively" (Longuet-Higgins 1976, 648). His own interpretation of the construction (like that shown in figure 11) as relevant to modulation in tonal music is similar to Ellis's interpretation of the "duodenarium." In this connection, he says (again, in 1962): "Harmonic relationships in general, and key relationships in particular, can only be understood by thinking in two dimensions, by recognizing the major third as a basic interval independent of the perfect fifth and the octave . . . [and] . . . (together with the octave) the perfect fifth and the major third provide the musician with a *sufficient* basis for connecting the notes of a given key with one another and with the notes of neighbouring keys" (Longuet-Higgins 1962a, 248).

I stated earlier that it is possible to map pitches in a way that preserves all of their harmonic distance relations if a multidimensional space is assumed, with a number of dimensions equal to the number of distinct prime numbers involved in the ratio terms, *a* and *b*. This applies to prime numbers beyond 5, of course—as well as those within the 5-limit—so that a mapping of pitches whose ratio-designations include 7 or 11 would require "spaces" of four or five dimensions, respectively (three or four dimensions, in the case of *generalized* harmonic distance). This association of the number of dimensions in harmonic space with the number of prime factors in the ratio is also implied by Longuet-Higgins when he says: "There is, actually, one class of intervals [not dealt with by him] . . . namely intervals involving the natural seventh harmonic of a note. If this ever comes into common use we shall have to extend the table of notes, and of intervals, into three dimensions" (Longuet-Higgins 1962b, 274). Figure 13 shows an attempt at such a mapping for certain pitches within the 7-limit by way of an illusory projection of a pair of parallel plane surfaces in front of and behind the surface of the page. The limitations of this graphic method are obvious, however, and it must be left to the reader's imagination to visualize such higher-dimensional harmonic spaces.

The pitch mappings of figures 8, 10, 11, and 13 have been presented here as applications (or "implications") of the concept of harmonic distance, but one might also say the musical relevance of such constructions *implies* a concept of harmonic distance, although this in itself does not necessarily mean that the definition proposed herein is the most useful one. It does have the advantages of simplicity, precision, and

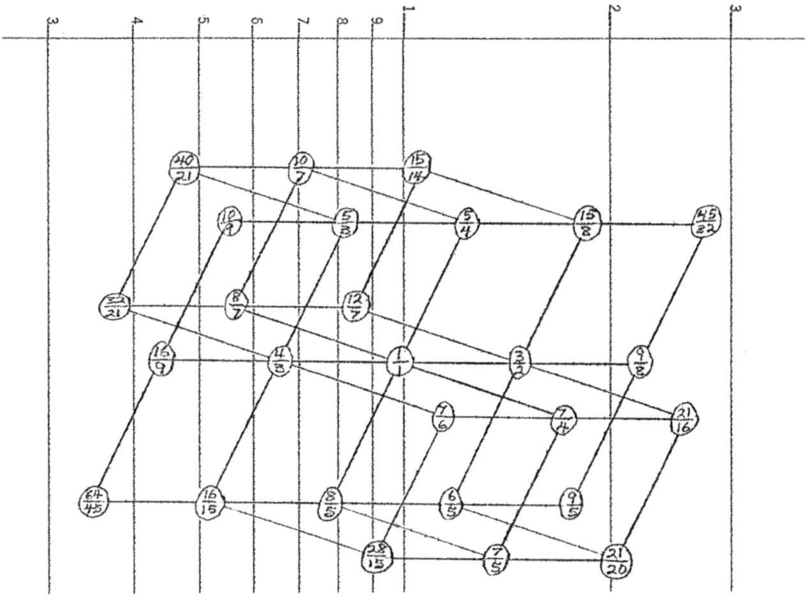

FIGURE 13. Generalized harmonic-distance pitch-map for ratios within the 7-limit.

objectivity, however, which make it extremely attractive as a measure of this important aspect of musical perception—and of that sense of consonance and dissonance designated CDC-1 in *A History of 'Consonance' and 'Dissonance.'*

A very curious property of constructions similar to that of figure 11 remains to be described—the fact that "tempered" versions of such pitch-sets may be mapped on the surface of a *torus*. Whether this is of any unusual significance or not I don't really know. It may simply be a mathematically "trivial" result of the assumptions on which the construction is based, but it is interesting, nevertheless. Figure 14 shows such a tempered version of the construction (equivalent to that in Longuet-Higgins 1972), and here the *periodic* nature of the mapping is more easily noticeable. Clearly, the region outlined by the rectangle can be folded or "rolled" in such a way, first, that the corners marked X1 and X2 are joined to the corners marked Y1 and Y2, respectively, and second, that the two ends of the cylinder thus formed can be joined so that the (now-coincident) point X1 = X2 is connected to the point Y1 = Y2, forming a torus. The result is sketched roughly in figure 15. While still reserving judgment as to the potential significance of this

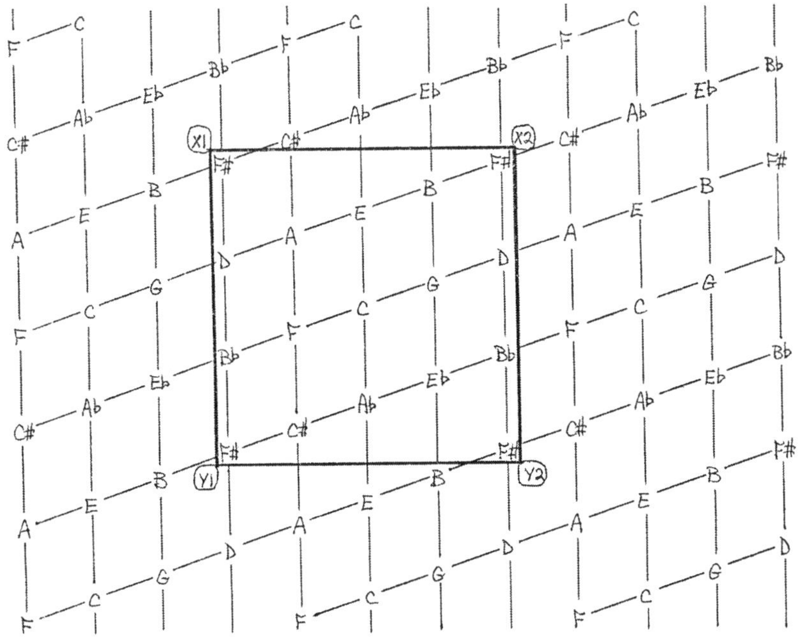

FIGURE 14. Tempered version of the pitch-map of figure 11.

toroidal mapping, we might at least consider it a welcome refinement of the various circular, spiral, or helical models that have been proposed in the past to give some geometrical representation of harmonic relations between pitches (e.g., Drobisch, Révész, Rumick, Westergaard, Cogan and Escot, et al.), because it maintains the proximity-relations (in the form of immediate adjacencies) of the fifth and the major third, which are *not* preserved in the other models mentioned above—in addition to the relation of octave-equivalence.

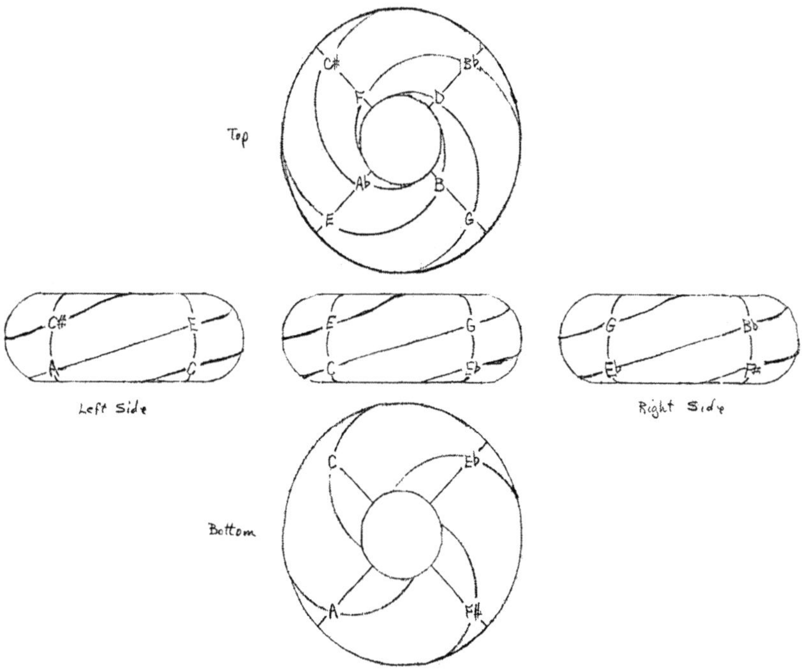

FIGURE 15. Pitch-mapping on the surface of a torus.

TABLE 11.1

a/b	PD(a,b)	HD(a,b)	GD(a,b)	Dsj(a/b)	Dsj(a/b/c)		
					a/c = 2/3	a/c = 5/8	a/c = 3/5
1/1	0	0.	0.	0.	.33	.70	.53
80/81	22	12.66	8.66	.98			
32/33	53	10.04	5.04	.94			
24/25	70	9.23	6.23	.92	.91		.91
20/21	85	8.71	6.71	.90	(.89)		
15/16	112	7.91	3.91	.88		.86	.85
14/15	119	7.71	6.71	.87	.85		
11/12	151	7.04	5.04	.83			
9/10	182	6.49	5.49	.80			.78
8/9	204	6.17	3.17	.78	.75	.94	
7/8	231	5.81	2.81	.75			
6/7	267	5.39	4.39	.71	.67	.92	.66
11/13	289	7.16	7.15	.84			
27/32	294	9.75	4.75	.93			
5/6	316	4.91	3.91	.67	.80	.60	.86
9/11	347	6.63	6.63	.81			
4/5	386	4.32	2.32	.60	.53	.90	.83
64/81	408	12.34	6.34	.97			
11/14	417	7.27	6.27	.84			
7/9	435	5.98	5.98	.76	.86		
16/21	471	8.39	4.39	.89			
3/4	498	3.58	1.58	.50	.69	.87	.40
20/27	519	9.08	7.08	.91			
8/11	551	6.46	3.46	.80			
5/7	583	5.13	5.13	.69	.81	.60	.87
32/45	590	10.49	5.49	.95	.94		

TABLE 11.2

a/b	PD(a,b)	HD(a,b)	GD(a,b)	Dsj(a/b)	Dsj(a b/c)		
					a/c = 2/3	a/c = 5/8	a/c = 3/5
45/64	610	11.49	5.49	.96			
7/10	617	6.13	5.13	.77	.86	.94	.90
11/16	649	7.46	3.46	.85			
27/40	680	10.08	7.08	.94			
2/3	702	2.58	1.58	.33	.33	.82	.71
21/32	729	9.39	4.39	.92			
9/14	765	6.98	5.98	.83			.78
7/11	782	6.27	6.27	.78	.87		
81/128	792	13.34	6.34	.98			
5/8	814	5.32	2.32	.70	.82	.70	.87
8/13	841	6.70	3.70	.81			
11/18	853	7.63	6.63	.86			
3/5	884	3.91	3.91	.53	.71	.87	.53
16/27	906	8.75	4.75	.90			
7/12	933	6.39	4.39	.79			
4/7	969	4.81	2.81	.64	.57		
9/16	996	7.17	3.17	.83			.79
5/9	1018	5.49	5.49	.71	.82	.62	
6/11	1050	6.04	5.04	.76			
8/15	1088	6.91	3.91	.82	.78		.92
21/40	1115	9.71	6.71	.93			
25/48	1129	10.23	6.23	.94		.92	
33/64	1147	11.04	5.04	.96			
81/160	1178	13.66	8.66	.98			
1/2	1200	1.0	0.	0.	.33	.70	.53
40/81	1222	11.66	8.66	.96			

TABLE 11.3

a/b	PD(a,b)	HD(a,b)	GD(a,b)	Dsj(a/b)	Dsj(a/b/c) a/c = 2/3	a/c = 5/8	a/c = 3/5
16/33	1253	9.04	5.04	.91			
12/25	1270	8.23	6.23	.88	.85		.85
10/21	1285	7.71	6.71	.86	.83		
15/32	1312	8.91	3.91	.90		.88	.88
7/15	1319	6.71	6.71	.80	.88		
11/24	1351	8.04	5.04	.87			
9/20	1382	7.49	5.49	.84			.81
4/9	1404	5.17	3.17	.67	.61	.91	
7/16	1431	6.81	2.81	.80			
3/7	1467	4.39	4.39	.57	.73	.88	.46
11/26	1489	8.16	7.16	.87			
27/64	14.94	10.75	4.75	.95			
5/12	15.16	5.91	3.91	.73	.83	.67	.88
9/22	15.47	7.63	6.63	.85			
2/5	15.86	3.32	2.32	.40	.27	.83	.73
32/81	16.08	11.34	6.34	.96			
11/28	16.17	8.27	6.27	.88			
7/18	1635	6.98	5.98	.81	.88		
8/21	1671	7.39	4.39	.83			
3/8	1698	4.58	1.58	.58	.74	.88	.47
10/27	1719	8.08	7.08	.87			
4/11	1751	5.46	3.46	.68			
5/14	1783	6.13	5.13	.74	.84	.66	.89
16/45	1790	9.49	5.49	.92	(.90)		
45/128	1810	12.49	5.49	.97			
7/20	1817	7.13	5.13	.81	.88	.95	.92

a/b	PD(a,b)	HD(a,b)	GD(a,b)	Dsj(a/b)	Dsj(a/b/c) a/c = 2/3	a/c = 5/8	a/c = 3/5
11/32	1849	8.46	3.46	.88			
27/80	1880	11.08	7.08	.95			
1/3	1902	1.58	1.58	0.	.33	.70	.53
21/64	1929	10.39	4.39	.94			
9/28	1965	7.98	5.98	.86			.81
7/22	1982	7.27	6.27	.82	.89		
81/256	1992	14.34	6.34	.98			
5/16	2014	6.32	2.32	.75	.84	.70	.89
4/13	2041	5.70	3.70	.69			
11/36	2053	8.63	6.63	.88			
3/10	2084	4.91	3.91	.60	.74	.89	.53
8/27	2106	7.75	4.75	.84			
7/24	2133	7.39	4.39	.82			
2/7	2169	3.81	2.81	.43	.29		
9/32	2196	8.17	3.17	.86			.82
5/18	2218	6.49	5.49	.76	.84	.67	
3/11	2250	5.04	5.04	.61			
4/15	2288	5.91	3.91	.70	.63		.87
21/80	2315	10.71	6.71	.94			
25/96	2329	11.23	6.23	.95		.93	
33/128	2347	12.04	5.04	.96			
81/320	2378	14.66	8.66	.98			
1/4	2400	2.0	0.	0.	.33	.70	.53
8/33	2453	8.04	5.04	.85			
6/25	2470	7.22	6.22	.80	.75		.75

Editors' Appendix

Listed below for ease of reference are selected notations, identities, and definitions used in this essay.

1. Conventional Notations

Let p, q, and r represent arbitrary positive integers.

Least common multiple (LCM) of two integers	$[p,q]$
Greatest common divisor (GCD) of two integers	(p,q)
Least common multiple (LCM) of three integers	$[p,q,r]$
Greatest common divisor (GCD) of three integers	(p,q,r)

2. Identities

Let p, q, r, and m represent arbitrary positive integers.

$$[p,q] = \frac{pq}{(p,q)}$$

$$[mp,mq] = m[p,q]$$

$$(mp,mq) = m(p,q)$$

$$[p,q,r] = \frac{pqr(p,q,r)}{(p,q)(p,r)(q,r)}$$

$$[mp,mq,mr] = m[p,q,r]$$

$$(mp,mq,mr) = m(p,q,r)$$

3. Definitions (specific to this essay)

Let f_a, f_b, f_c represent arbitrary integer-valued fundamental frequencies and a, b, and c their respective reduced values.

For dyads:

$$a = \frac{f_a}{(f_a,f_b)} \qquad b = \frac{f_b}{(f_a,f_b)}$$

For triads:

$$a = \frac{f_a}{(f_a, f_b, f_c)} \qquad b = \frac{f_b}{(f_a, f_b, f_c)} \qquad c = \frac{f_c}{(f_a, f_b, f_c)}$$

4. Notations (specific to this essay)

For dyads:

Tone dyad with fundamental frequencies f_a and f_b	f_a/f_b
Tone dyad with reduced fundamental frequencies *a* and *b*	*a*/*b*
Harmonic period of dyad *a*/*b*	*HP*(*a*/*b*)
Intersection ratio of tone *a* by tone *b*	*I*(*a*:*b*)
Disjunction ratio of tone *a* with respect to tone *b*	*Dsj*(*a*:*b*)
Number of harmonics in tone *a* within *HP*(*a*/*b*)	*N*(*a*)
Number of distinct harmonics in dyad *a*/*b* within *HP*(*a*/*b*)	*N*(*a*/*b*)
Number of harmonics between zero and f_{max} in tone with fundamental f_a	$NH(f_a)$
Number of HPs between zero and f_{max} in dyad f_a/f_b	$NHP(f_a/f_b)$
Number of harmonics between zero and f_{max} in dyad f_a/f_b	$NH(f_a/f_b)$
Pitch distance between tone *a* and tone *b*	*PD*(*a*,*b*)
Period of combined waveform of dyad	$Dur(f_a/f_b)$
Frequency corresponding to period of dyad waveform	$F(f_a/f_b)$
Harmonic distance between tone *a* and tone *b*	*HD*(*a*,*b*)
Octave-generalized harmonic distance between tone *a* and tone *b*	*GD*(*a*,*b*)

For triads:

Tone triad with fundamental frequencies f_a, f_b, f_c	$f_a/f_b/f_c$
Tone triad with reduced fundamental frequencies *a*, *b*, *c*	*a*/*b*/*c*
Harmonic period of triad *a*/*b*/*c*	*HP*(*a*/*b*/*c*)
Intersection ratio of tone *a* with respect to dyad *b*/*c*	*I*(*a*:*b*/*c*)
Disjunction ratio of tone *a* with respect to dyad *b*/*c*	*Dsj*(*a*:*b*/*c*)
Intersection ratio of dyad *a*/*b* with respect to tone *c*	*I*(*a*/*b*:*c*)
Disjunction ratio of dyad *a*/*b* with respect to tone *c*	*Dsj*(*a*/*b*:*c*)

Number of harmonics in tone *a* within *HP*(*a*/*b*/*c*)	N(*a*)
Number of distinct harmonics in triad *a*/*b*/*c* within *HP*(*a*/*b*/*c*)	*N*(*a*/*b*/*c*)
Number of harmonics between zero and f_{max} in tone with fundamental *a*	*NH*(*a*)
Number of HPs between zero and f_{max} in triad *a*/*b*/*c*	*NHP*(*a*/*b*/*c*)
Number of distinct harmonics between zero and f_{max} in triad *a*/*b*/*c*	*NH*(*a*/*b*)

References

Griffin, Harriet. 1954. *Elementary Theory of Numbers*. New York: McGraw Hill.

Helmholtz, Hermann. 1954. *On the Sensations of Tone*. New York: Dover.

Longuet-Higgins, H. Christopher. 1962a. "Letter to a Musical Friend." *Music Review* 23: 244–48.

———. 1962b. "Second Letter to a Musical Friend." *Music Review* 23: 271–80.

———. 1976. "The Perception of Melodies." *Nature* 263: 646–53.

McClain, Ernest G. 1976. *The Myth of Invariance: The Origin of the Gods, Mathematics and Music from the Rig Veda to Plato*. York Beach, MN: Nicholas-Hays.

Schügerl, K. 1970. "On the Perception of Concords." In *Frequency Analysis and Periodicity Detection in Hearing: Proceedings of the International Symposium Held at Driebergen, the Netherlands June 23–27, 1969*. Ed. Reiner Plomp and G. F. Smoorenburg. Leiden: Sijtthoff.

Stumpf, C. 1898. "Konsonanz und Dissonanz." *Beitr. Akust. Musikwiss.* 1: 1–108.

Tenney, James. 1988. *A History of 'Consonance' and 'Dissonance.'* New York: Excelsior Music Publishing.

CHAPTER 12

John Cage and the Theory of Harmony

(1983)

Part I

> Many doors are now open (they open according to where we give our attention). Once through, looking back, no wall or doors are seen. Why was anyone for so long closed in? *Sounds one hears are music*. (1967b)*

Relations between theory and practice in Western music have always been somewhat strained, but by the early years of this century they had reached a breaking point. Unable to keep up with the radical changes that were occurring in compositional practice, harmonic theory had become little more than an exercise in "historical musicology" and had ceased to be of immediate relevance to contemporary music. This had not always been so. Not only had most of the important theorists of the past—from Guido and Franco through Tinctoris and Zarlino to Rameau (and even Riemann)—been practicing composers, their theoretical writings had dealt with questions arising in their own music and that of their contemporaries. Arnold Schoenberg (one of the last of the great composer-theorists) was acutely aware of the disparities between what could be

*A list of Cage's writings referred to in this text may be found in chronological order at the end. Quotations are identified by date within the text in order to clarify the evolutionary development of his ideas. Any emphases (italics) are my own. Other sources are referenced in footnotes, indicated by superscripts.

said about harmony (ca. 1911) and then-current developments in compositional practice. Near the end of his *Harmonielehre* he expresses the belief that "continued evolution of the theory of harmony is not to be expected at present."[1] I choose to interpret this statement of Schoenberg's as announcing a *postponement* of that evolution, however—not the end of it.

One of the reasons for the current disparity between harmonic theory and compositional practice is not hard to identify: the very *meaning* of the word "harmony" has come to be so narrowly defined that it can only be thought of as applying to the materials and procedures of the diatonic/triadic tonal system of the last two or three centuries. The word has a very long and interesting history, however, that suggests that it need not be so narrowly defined and that the "continued evolution of the theory of harmony" might depend on—among other things—a broadening of our definition of "harmony."

. . . and perhaps of "theory" as well. By "theory" I mean essentially what any good dictionary tells us it means: "The analysis of a set of facts in relation to one another . . . the general or abstract principles of a body of fact, a science, or an art . . . a plausible or scientifically acceptable general principle or body of principles offered to explain phenomena,"[2] which is to say, something that current textbook versions of "the theory of harmony" are decidedly *not*—any more than a book of etiquette, for example, can be construed as a "theory of human behavior" or a cookbook a "theory of chemistry."

It seems to me that what a true theory of harmony would have to be now is a theory of *harmonic perception* (one component in a more general theory of musical perception) consistent with the most recent data available from the fields of acoustics and psychoacoustics but also taking into account the greatly extended range of musical experiences available to us today. I would suggest, in addition, that such a theory ought to satisfy the following conditions:

First, it should be *descriptive*—not pre- (or pro-)scriptive—and thus, *aesthetically neutral*. That is, it would not presume to tell a composer what should or should not be done but rather what the results might be if a given thing *is* done.

Second, it should be culturally/stylistically *general*—as relevant to music of the twentieth (or twenty-first!) century as it is to that of the eighteenth (or thirteenth) century and as pertinent to the music of India or Africa or the Brazilian rain forest as it is to that of western Europe or North America.

Finally, in order that such a theory might qualify as a "theory" at all in the most pervasive sense in which that word is currently used (outside of music, at least), it should be (whenever and to the maximum extent possible) *quantitative*. Unless the propositions, deductions, and predictions of the theory are formulated quantitatively, there is no way to verify the theory and thus no basis for comparison with other theoretical systems.

Is such a theory really needed? Perhaps not—music seems to have done very well without one for a long time now. On the other hand, one might answer this question the way Gandhi is said to have done when asked what he thought of Western civilization: "It would be nice" (1968).

Is such a theory *feasible* now? I think it is, or at least that the time has come for us to make some beginnings in that direction—no matter how tentative. Furthermore, I believe that the work of John Cage, while posing the greatest conceivable *challenge* to any such effort, yet contains many fertile seeds for theoretical development, some of them not only useful but *essential*.

Such an assertion may come as a surprise to many—no doubt including Cage himself, since he has never shown any inclination to call himself a theorist nor any interest in what he calls "harmony." The bulk of his writings—taken together—sometimes seem more like that "thick presence all at once of a naked self-obscuring body of history" (to quote his description of a painting by Jasper Johns; 1964) than a "body of principles" constituting a theory. But these writings include some of the most cogent examples of pure but practical theory to be found anywhere in the literature on twentieth-century music. His work encourages us to reexamine all of our old habits of thought, our assumptions, and our definitions (of "theory," of "harmony"—of "music" itself), even where (as with "harmony") he has not done so himself. His own precise definitions of "material," "method," "structure," "form," etc.—even where needing some revision or extension to be maximally useful today—can serve as suggestive points of departure for our own efforts.

I propose to examine some of Cage's theoretical ideas a little more closely and then to consider their possible implications for a new theory of harmony. Before proceeding, however, I want to clarify one point. Some of Cage's critics (even friendly ones) seem to think that he is primarily a philosopher rather than a composer—and my own focusing on his contributions as theorist might be misunderstood to imply a similar notion on my own part. This would be a mistake. I believe, in fact, that it is primarily *because of his music*—his very substantial credibility *as a composer*—that we are drawn into a consideration of his philosophical and theoretical ideas. To imagine otherwise is to "put the cart before the horse." In a letter defending the music of Erik Satie, Cage once wrote:

> More and more it seems to me that relegating Satie to the position of having been very influential but in his own work finally unimportant is refusing to accept the challenge he so bravely gave us. (1951)

The same thing can truly be said of John Cage himself.

> Definitions . . . Structure in music is its divisibility into successive parts from phrases to long sections. Form is content, the continuity. Method is the means of controlling the continuity from note to note. *The material of music is sound and silence*. Integrating these is composing. (1949)

Cage's earliest concerns—and his most notorious later innovations—had to do with *method*: "the means of controlling the continuity from note to note." His music includes an astonishing variety of different methods, from one "dealing with the problem of keeping repetitions of individual tones as far apart as possible" (1933–34) and "unorthodox twelve-tone" procedures (1938) through the "considered improvisation" of the *Sonatas and Interludes* and other works of the 1940s to "moves on . . . charts analogous to those used in constructing a magic square" (1951), chance operations based on the *I Ching* (from 1951 to the present), the use of transparent "templates made or found" (1952–), the "observation of imperfections in the paper" on which a score was written (1952–), etc. (1958, 1961). Surely no other composer in the history of music has so thoroughly explored this aspect of composition—but not merely because of some fascination with "method" for its own sake. On the contrary, Cage's frequent changes of method have always resulted from a new and more penetrating analysis of the *material* of music and of the nature of musical activity in general.

Before 1951, Cage's methods (or rather, his "composing means") were designed to achieve two things traditionally assumed to be indispensable to the making of art: on the one hand, spontaneity and freedom of expression (at the level of "content" or "form"), and on the other, a measure of structural control over the musical material. What was *unique* about his compositional procedures stemmed from his efforts to define these things ("form," "structure," etc.) in a way that would be consistent with the essential nature of the musical material and with the nature of auditory perception. These concerns have continued undiminished through his later work as well, but in addition he has shown an ever-increasing concern with the larger *context* in which musical activity takes place:

> The novelty of our work derives . . . from our having moved away from simply private human concerns toward the world of nature and society of which all of us are a part. Our intention is to affirm this life, not to bring order out of chaos nor to suggest improvements in creation, but simply to wake up to the very life we're living, which is so excellent once one gets one's mind and one's desires out of the way and lets it act of its own accord. (1956a)

In this spirit, he had begun, as early as 1951, a series of *renunciations* of those very things his earlier methods had been designed to ensure—first, *expressivity*, and soon after that, *structural controls*. The method he chose to effect these renunciations (after some preliminary work with "moves on charts") involved the use of chance operations, and in writing about the *Music of Changes* (1951) he said:

> It is thus possible to make a musical composition the continuity of which is free of individual taste and memory (psychology) and also of the literature and "traditions" of the art. . . . Value judgments are not in the nature of this work as regards either composition, performance, or listening. The idea of relation (the idea: 2) being absent, anything (the idea: 1) may happen. A "mistake" is beside the point, for once anything happens it authentically is. (1952)

This statement generated a shock-wave which is still reverberating throughout the Western cultural community because it was interpreted as a negation of many long-cherished assumptions about the creative process in art. But there is an important difference between a "negation" and a "renunciation" that has generally been overlooked: to renounce something is not to deny others their right to have it—though it does throw into question the notion that such a thing is universally *necessary*. On the other hand, such things as taste, tradition, value judgments, etc., not only can be but often (and habitually) *are* used in ways that are profoundly negative. Cage's "renunciations" since 1951 should therefore not be seen as "negations" at all but rather as efforts to *give up the old habits of negation*—the old *exclusions* of things from the realm of aesthetic validity, the old *limitations* imposed on musical imagination, the old *boundaries* circumscribing the "art of music." And the result? As he has said:

> Nothing was lost when everything was given away. In fact, everything was gained. In musical terms, *any sounds may occur in any combination and in any continuity.* (1957)

The fact that his own renunciations need not be taken as negations should have been clearly understood when he said, for example:

> The activity of movement, sound, and light, we believe, is expressive, but what it expresses is determined by each one of you. (1956a)

Or again:

> The coming into being of something new does not by that fact deprive what was of its proper place. Each thing has its own place . . . and the more things there are, as is said, the merrier. (1957)

But here, it seems, his critics were not listening.

It should go without saying (though I know it won't) that we don't *need* those old "habits of negation" anymore—neither in life (where they are so often used in ways that are very destructive) nor in art. Still less do we need them in a theory of harmony—and this is one of the reasons I find Cage's work and thought to be essential to new theoretical efforts. His "renunciations" have created an intellectual climate in which it is finally possible to envision a theory of harmony that is both "general" and "aesthetically neutral"—a climate in which a truly *scientific* theory of musical perception might begin to be developed.

> Composing's one thing, performing's another, listening's a third. What can they have to do with one another? (1955)

While the question of method is naturally of interest to a composer—and has been, in Cage's case, the subject of greatest concern to his critics—what is actually *perceived* in a piece of music is not method as such but *material*, *form*, and *structure*. Cage's most radical earlier innovations had involved extensions of material, and these may one day turn out to have more profound implications for theory than his investigations of method. The pieces for percussion ensemble, for prepared piano, and for electrical devices—composed during the late 1930s and 1940s—greatly extended the range of musical materials, first to include *noises* as well as tones, and then *silence* as well as sound.

These extensions were not without precedent, of course. As Cage has said, it was "Edgard Varèse who fathered forth noise into twentieth-century music" (1959b) and who

> more clearly and actively than anyone else of his generation . . . established the present nature of music . . . [which] . . . arises from an acceptance of *all audible phenomena as material proper to music*. (1959b)

But Cage was the first to deal with the *theoretical* consequences of this acceptance. Since "harmony" and other kinds of pitch-organization did not seem applicable to noise,

> the present methods of writing music . . . will be inadequate for the composer, who will be faced with *the entire field of sound*. (1937)

More specifically,

> in writing for these [electrically produced] sounds, as in writing for percussion instruments alone, the composer is dealing with material that does not fit into the orthodox scales and harmonies. It is therefore necessary to find some other organizing means than those in use for symphonic instruments. . . . A method analogous to the twelve-tone system may prove useful, but . . . *because of the nature of the materials involved*, and because their duration characteristics can be easily controlled and related, *it is more than likely that the unifying means will be rhythmic*. (1942)

This statement, which reads like a prediction, was actually a description of the state of affairs that had already prevailed in Cage's work since the *First Construction (in Metal)* of 1939, but it was not until 1948 that the idea took the form of a general principle—even a rather dogmatic one:

> In the field of structure, the field of the definition of parts and their relation to a whole, there has been only one new idea since Beethoven. And that new idea can be perceived in the work of Anton Webern and Erik Satie. With Beethoven the parts of a composition were defined by means of harmony. With Satie and Webern they are defined by means of time lengths. . . . There can be no right making of music that does not structure itself from the very roots of sound and silence—lengths of time. (1948)

A year later this principle was repeated, but with a slightly different emphasis:

> Sound has four characteristics: pitch, timbre, loudness, and duration. The opposite and necessary coexistent of sound is silence. Of the four characteristics of sound, only duration involves both sound and silence. Therefore, a structure based on durations . . . is correct (corresponds with the nature of the material), whereas harmonic structure is incorrect (derived from pitch, which has no being in silence). (1949)

Cage was right, of course, in emphasizing the fundamental importance of time and time-structure in music, but—as compelling and persuasive as this argument is—there is a serious flaw in it. On the one hand, *all* music manifests some sort of temporal structure (including harmonically organized music; Beethoven), and on the other hand, neither Webern nor Satie nor Cage himself had ever managed to "define" the successive parts of a composition purely "by means of time lengths." Such time lengths—in order to be perceived as "parts"—must be *articulated* by some other means, and these means may or may not include the specifically "harmonic" devices of cadence, modulation, etc. In the works of Cage intentionally organized according to this concept of time-structure (as in the music of Satie and Webern), the successive parts in the structure are in fact articulated by various kinds of *contrast*—changes of dynamic level, texture, tempo, pitch-register, thematic material, etc.—and such contrast-devices have *always* been used (with or without the benefit of "harmony") to articulate temporal structure.

We needn't be too concerned, however, with the "dogmatic" aspect of these statements, since it was to be only a few years later that Cage would cease to be concerned with determinate structure at all. What is more important is the way in which he was thinking about *the nature of sound:*

> A sound does not view itself as thought, as ought, as needing another sound for its elucidation. . . . [I]t is occupied with the performance of its characteristics: before it has died away it must have made perfectly exact its frequency, its loudness, its length, its overtone structure, the precise morphology of these and of itself. . . . It does not exist as one of a series of discrete steps, but as transmission in all directions from the field's center. (1955)

This line of thought gradually crystallized into a conception of what Cage calls "sound-space"—that perceptual "space" in which music (*any* music) must exist. His clearest and most complete description of this concept is perhaps the following:

> The situation made available by these [tape-recording] means is essentially a total sound-space, the limits of which are ear-determined only, the position of a particular sound in this space being the result of five determinants: frequency or pitch, amplitude or loudness, overtone structure or timbre, duration, and morphology (how the sound begins, goes on, and dies away). By the alteration of any one of these determinants, the position of the sound in sound-space changes. Any sound at any point in this total sound-space can move to become a sound at any other point. . . . [M]usical action or existence can occur at any point or along any line or curve . . . in total sound-space; . . . [W]e are . . . technically equipped to transform our contemporary awareness of nature's manner of operation into art. (1957)

Note that the list of "four characteristics" given in 1949 has now been increased to "five determinants," and in a later passage a sixth one is added ("an order of succession"; 1958a). Even so, such a list is by no means exhaustive, and important clues regarding the nature of harmonic perception will emerge from a consideration of the "determinants," parameters, or what I will call *dimensions* of "sound-space" that are missing from all of these lists.

By his own definitions (pre-1951), *form* is "content, the continuity," and *method* is "the means of controlling the continuity," i.e., of controlling *form*. After 1951, of course, Cage's methods were no longer intended to "control" form in this same sense, and yet a certain necessary causal relationship still holds between method and form, no matter what the intention. As a result, most of Cage's works since 1951 exemplify an important new formal type that I have elsewhere called "ergodic."[3] I use this term (borrowed from thermodynamics) to mean *statistically homogeneous* at some hierarchical level of formal perception. For example, it can be said about many of Cage's post-1951 pieces (and something like this often *is* said, though usually with negative implications not intended here) that any two- or three-minute segment of the piece is essentially the same as any other segment of corresponding duration, even though the details are quite different in the two cases. I interpret this to mean that certain *statistical properties* are in fact "the same"—or so nearly identical that no distinction can be made in perception.

The relation between the ergodic form and Cage's later methods involving chance and/or indeterminacy is this: an ergodic form will always and inevitably be the result when a range of possibilities (with respect to the sound-elements in a piece and their characteristics) is given at the outset of the compositional process and remains unchanged during the realization of the work. Such a form is quite unlike the dramatic and/or rhetorical forms we are accustomed to in most earlier music and has been the cause of much of the negative response to Cage's music of the last thirty years. A different attitude is obviously required of the listener to be able to enjoy an ergodic piece—and it is perhaps ironic that it is an attitude that most people are able to adopt quite easily in situations outside the usual realm of "art" (e.g., the sounds of a forest). In this respect, many of Cage's pieces represent an "imitation of nature" in more than just "her manner of operation" but in her "forms" (or, as I'm sure Cage would prefer to say, her "processes") as well.

Cage's inclusion of "all audible phenomena as material proper to music" did not mean that distinctions were no longer to be made. On the contrary, it now became possible to distinguish many more varieties of elementary sounds, some of which Cage called "aggregates." In writing about his *Sonatas and Interludes* for prepared piano (1946–48), he says:

> A static gamut of sounds is presented, no two octaves repeating relations. However, one could hear interesting differences between certain of these sounds. On depressing a key, sometimes a single frequency was heard. In other cases . . . an interval [i.e., a dyad]; in still others *an aggregate of pitches and timbres*. Noticing the nature of this gamut led to selecting a comparable one for the *String Quartet*. (1958a)

This concept of the aggregate is, I believe, extremely important for any new theory of harmony, since such a theory must deal with the question: Under what conditions will a multiplicity of elementary acoustic signals be perceived as a "single sound"? When this question is asked about a compound tone containing several harmonic partials, its relevance to the problems of harmony becomes immediately evident.

Aside from their possible implications for a theory of *harmony* as such, Cage's extensions of the range of musical materials to include "all audible phenomena" have created a whole new set of problems for the theorist, but his efforts to understand the *nature* of those materials have also indicated ways in which these problems might be solved. One of his statements about composition might also be applied to theory:

> Something more far-reaching is necessary: a composing of sounds *within a universe predicated upon the sounds themselves* rather than upon the mind which can envisage their coming into being. (1958a)

> When Schoenberg asked me whether I would devote my life to music, I said, "Of course." After I had been studying with him for two years, Schoenberg said, "In order to write music, you must have a feeling for harmony." I explained to him that I had no feeling for harmony. He said that I would always encounter an obstacle, that it would be as though I came to a wall through which I could not pass. I said, "In that case I will devote my life to beating my head against that wall." (1959a)

This metaphor of the wall—and other sorts of boundaries, barriers, or enclosures—is a recurring one in Cage's writings:

> Once a circle is drawn my necessity is to get outside of it. . . . No doubt there is a threshold in all matters, but once through the door—no need to stand there as though transfixed—the rules disappear. (1962)
>
> My philosophy in a nutshell. Get out of whatever cage you happen to be in. (1972)

There were many such walls, but "harmony"—in its narrowest sense (the materials and procedures of traditional, tonal, textbook harmony)—was for Cage a particularly obstructive one:

> Harmony, so-called, is a forced abstract vertical relation which blots out the spontaneous transmitting nature of each of the sounds forced into it. It is artificial and unrealistic. (1954)
>
> Seeking an interpenetration and nonobstruction of sounds . . . a composer at this moment . . . renounces harmony and its effect of fusing sounds in a fixed relationship. (1963)
>
> Series equals harmony equals mind of man (unchanged, used as obstacle . . .). (1966)

Only once does he suggest the possibility of defining the word differently:

> This music is not concerned with harmoniousness as generally understood, where the quality of harmony results from a blending of several elements. Here we are concerned with the coexistence of dissimilars, and the central points where fusion occurs are many: the ears of the listeners wherever they are. *This disharmony*, to paraphrase Bergson's statement about disorder, *is simply a harmony to which many are unaccustomed*. (1957)

Here, Cage was closer than he may have realized to Schoenberg (in the latter's writings, at least, if not in his teaching), as when he had said: "What distinguishes dissonances from consonances is not a greater or lesser degree of beauty, but a greater or lesser degree of *comprehensibility*. . . . *The term emancipation of the dissonance* refers to [this] comprehensibility."[4] What is it, then, in Cage's vision that lies beyond these "walls"? An *open field*—and this is an image that he evokes again and again in his writings:

> I have never gratuitously done anything for shock, though what I have found necessary to do I have carried out, occasionally and only after struggles of conscience, even if it involved actions apparently outside the "boundaries of art." For "art" and "music" when anthropocentric (involved in self-expression), seem trivial and lacking in urgency to me. We live in a world where there are things as well as people. Trees, stones, water, everything is expressive. I see this situation in which I impermanently live as a complex interpenetration of centers moving out in all directions without impasse. This is in accord with contemporary awareness of the operations of nature. I attempt to let sounds be themselves in a space of time. . . . I am more and more realizing . . . that I have ears and can hear. My work is intended as a demonstration of this; you might call it an affirmation of life. (1956b)

This open field is thus life itself, in all its variety and complexity, and an art activity "imitating nature in her manner of operation" only becomes possible when the limitations imposed by "self-expression," "individual taste and memory," the literature and traditions of an "anthropocentric" art—and, of course, "harmony"—have all been questioned so deeply and critically that they no longer circumscribe that activity—no longer define "boundaries." Not that these things will cease to exist, but, "looking back, no wall or doors are seen. . . . *Sounds one hears are music*." No better definition of "music"—for our time—is likely to be found.

The field—thus understood as life or nature—is much more than just music, but the "sound-space" of musical perception is one part of that total field, and Cage would have us approach it in a similar way. Its limits are "*ear-determined only*," the position of a sound within this field is a function of *all aspects of sound*, and

> each aspect of sound . . . is to be seen as a *continuum*, not as a series of discrete steps favored by conventions. (1959b)

This "total sound-space" has turned out to be more complex than Cage could have known, and within it a place will be found for specifically *harmonic* relations—and thus, for "harmony"—but not until this word has been redefined to free *it* from the walls that have been built around it.

Originally, the word "harmony" simply meant a *fitting together* of things in the most mundane sense—as might be applied to pieces of something put together by a craftsman. It was later adapted by the Pythagoreans to serve a much broader philosophical/religious purpose, describing the order of the cosmos. Its specifically musical uses must have been derived from the earlier sense of it, but for the Pythagoreans, the way the tones of a stretched string "fit together" was seen as an instance—in microcosm—of that cosmic order. Even so, it did not refer to simultaneous sounds but simply to certain *relations between pitches*.

Similarly for Aristoxenus: the discipline of "harmonics" was the science of melody considered with respect to pitch (and thus to be distinguished from "rhythmics"—the science of melody with respect to time). These senses of the word "harmony" are carried through in the writings of the medieval theorists. Only after the beginnings of polyphony in about the ninth century did the word begin to carry a different connotation, and since that time its meaning has become more and more restricted. Willi Apel defines it as "the vertical aspect of music," i.e., chord structure and (to a limited extent) relationships between successive chords.[5] But in fact the word has come to imply only a certain limited set of such relationships—a certain *type* of vertical structure. Thus, even in the case of some kinds of music in which tones *are* heard simultaneously (e.g., Indonesian gamelan music), it has been said that "harmony" is not involved. But it is absurd to imagine that the Indonesian musician is not concerned with the "vertical" aspect of his music. The word "harmony" obviously needs to be freed from its implied restriction to triadic/tonal music—but this is not enough. Even in a purely "horizontal" or monophonic/melodic situation, the realities of musical perception cannot be described without reference to *harmonic relations* between tones. Clearly, *a new theory of harmony will require a new definition* of "harmony," of "harmonic relations," etc., and I believe that such definitions will emerge from a more careful analysis of the "total sound-space" of musical perception.

Part II

> This project will seem fearsome to many, but on examination it gives no cause for alarm. Hearing sounds which are just sounds immediately sets the theorizing mind to theorizing, and the emotions

> of human beings are continually aroused by encounters with nature. (1957)
>
> Minimum ethic: Do what you said you'd do. Impossible? (1965)
>
> [More stringent ethic:] . . . make affirmative actions, and not . . . negative . . . critical or polemical actions. (1961)

Cage has always emphasized the *multidimensional* character of sound-space, with pitch as just one of its dimensions. This is perfectly consistent with current acoustical definitions of pitch, in which—like its physical correlate, frequency—it is conceived as a *one-dimensional continuum* running from low to high. But our perception of relations between pitches is more complicated than this. The phenomenon of "octave-equivalence," for example, cannot be represented on such a one-dimensional continuum, and octave-equivalence is just one of several specifically *harmonic relations* between pitches—i.e., relations other than merely "higher" or "lower." This suggests that the single acoustical variable, frequency, must give rise to *more than one dimension* in sound-space—that the "space" of pitch perception is itself multidimensional. This multidimensional space of pitch-perception will be called *harmonic space*.

The metrical and topological properties of harmonic space have only begun to be investigated, but a provisional model of such a space that seems consistent with what we already know about harmonic perception will be outlined here and may eventually help to clarify aspects of harmonic perception that are not yet very well understood. In this model, pitches are represented by points in a multidimensional space, and each is labeled according to its frequency ratio with respect to some reference pitch (1/1). Thus, the pitch one octave above the reference pitch is labeled 2/1, that a perfect fifth below 1/1 is labeled 2/3, etc. But since our perception of pitch intervals involves some degree of approximation, these frequency ratios must be understood to represent pitches within a certain *tolerance range*—i.e., a range of relative frequencies within which some slight mistuning is possible without altering the harmonic identity of an interval. The actual magnitude of this tolerance range would depend on several factors, and it is not yet possible to specify it precisely, but it seems likely that it would vary inversely with the ratio-complexity of the interval. That is, the smaller the integers needed to designate the frequency ratio for a given interval, the larger its tolerance range would be. What Harry Partch called "the language of ratios" is thus assumed to be the appropriate language for the analysis and description of harmonic relations—but only if it is understood to be qualified and limited by the concept of interval tolerance.[6]

For a given set of pitches, the number of dimensions of the implied harmonic space would correspond to the number of *prime factors* required to specify their frequency ratios with respect to the reference pitch. Thus, the harmonic space implied by a "Pythagorean" scale, based exclusively on fifths (3/2), fourths (4/3), and octaves (2/1), is two-dimensional, since the frequency ratios defining its constituent intervals involve only powers of 2 and 3 (see figure 1). The harmonic space implied by a "just" scale, which includes natural thirds (5/4, 6/5) and sixths (5/3, 8/5), is three-dimensional, since its frequency ratios include powers of 5, as well as 2 and 3. A scale incorporating the natural minor seventh (7/4) and other "septimal" intervals would imply a harmonic space of four dimensions, and Partch's "11-limit" scale would imply a harmonic space of five dimensions (corresponding to the prime factors 2, 3, 5, 7, and 11)—if (and only if) we assume that all of its constituent intervals are distinguishable. Whether all such intervals among a given set of pitches are in fact distinguishable depends, of course, on the tolerance range, and it is this that prevents an unlimited proliferation of "dimensions" in harmonic space. That is, at some level of scale-complexity, intervals whose frequency ratios involve a higher-order prime factor will be indistinguishable from

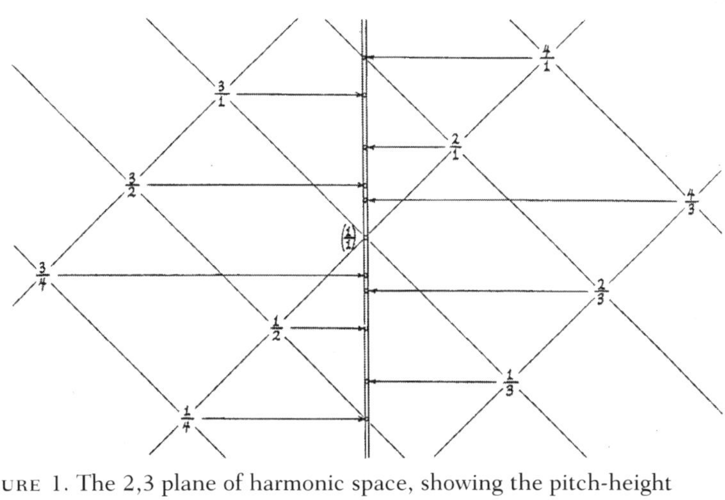

FIGURE 1. The 2,3 plane of harmonic space, showing the pitch-height projection axis.

similar intervals characterized by simpler frequency ratios, and the prime factors in these simpler ratios will define the dimensionality of harmonic space in the most general sense.

The one-dimensional continuum of pitch-height (i.e., "pitch" as ordinarily defined) can be conceived as a central *axis of projection* within this harmonic space. The position of a "point" along this pitch-height axis may be specified, as usual, by the logarithm of the fundamental frequency of the corresponding tone and the distance (or *pitch-distance*) between two such points by the difference between their log-frequency values. That is,

$$PD(f_a, f_b) \propto \log(a) - \log(b) = \log(a/b), \text{ where } f_a \text{ and } f_b$$
$$\text{are the fundamental frequencies of the two tones,}$$
$$a = f_a/\gcd(f_a, f_b),\ b = f_b/\gcd(f_a, f_b), \text{ and } a \geq b$$

Although the pitch-height axis is effectively continuous, harmonic space itself is not. Instead, it consists of a discontinuous network or *lattice* of points. A distance measure that I call *harmonic distance* can be defined between any two points in this space as proportional to the sum of the distances traversed on a shortest path connecting them (i.e., along the line segments shown in the figures). (The "metric" on harmonic space is thus not a Euclidian one but rather a "city-block" metric.) This measure of harmonic distance can be expressed algebraically as follows:

$$HD(f_a, f_b) \propto \log(a) + \log(b) = \log(ab)$$

Here again, the tolerance condition must be kept in mind, and it is useful in this connection to formulate it as follows: an interval is represented by *the simplest ratio within the tolerance range* around its actual relative frequencies, and any measure on the interval is the measure on that simplest ratio.

In this model of harmonic space, octave-equivalence is represented by another sort of projection—of points in a direction parallel to the "2-vectors" (the right-ascending diagonals in figures 1 and 2, the vertical lines in figure 3). Alternatively, it can be conceived as a "collapsing" of the harmonic space in this same direction, yielding a reduced *pitch-class projection space* with one fewer dimension. In a two-dimensional harmonic space, this will be another projection *axis*, as shown in figure 2. In a three-dimensional (2,3,5) harmonic space, the pitch-class projection space will be a two-dimensional (3,5) *plane*, as in figure 3. This pitch-class projection plane can be used to display the primary ("5-limit") harmonic relations of triadic/tonal music. For example, the diatonic major and minor scales appear as shown in figure 4 (using Partch's labeling convention, whereby a given pitch-class is identified by the ratio it has in the first octave above 1/1). With the addition of two scale degrees not included in figure 4 (the minor second and the augmented fourth), these two scales can be combined into a composite structure (similar to what Alexander Ellis called the "harmonic duodene") that shows many of the primary harmonic relations available within the twelve-tone chromatic scale (see figure 5).[7]

In representing what has become an equally tempered version of this chromatic scale with low-integer ratios in harmonic space, we implicitly assume a fairly large tolerance range (on the order of 15 cents or more), but this is precisely what is implied by the use of our tempered scale for triadic/tonal music. Thus, it is no wonder that the evolution of harmony as a clearly functional force in Western music reached a cul-de-sac around 1910. New compositional approaches to harmony will almost certainly involve new "microtonal" scales and tuning systems, and this model of

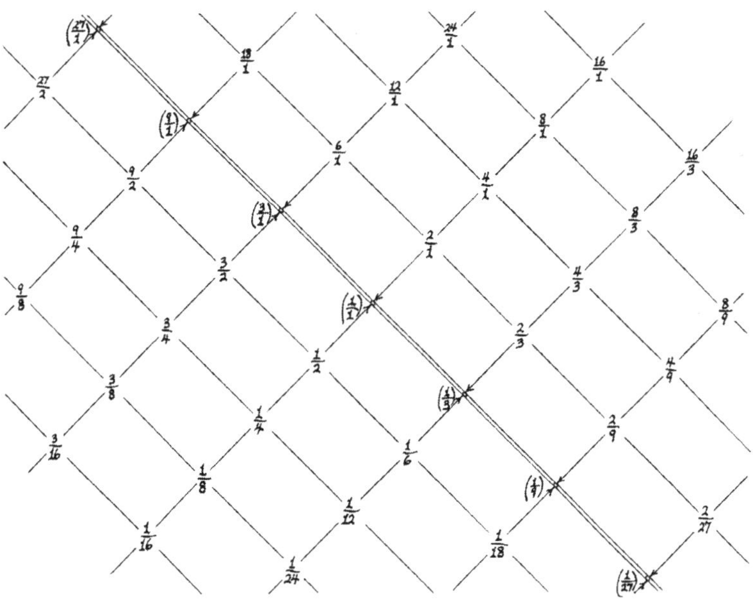

FIGURE 2. The 2,3 plane of harmonic space, showing the pitch-class projection axis.

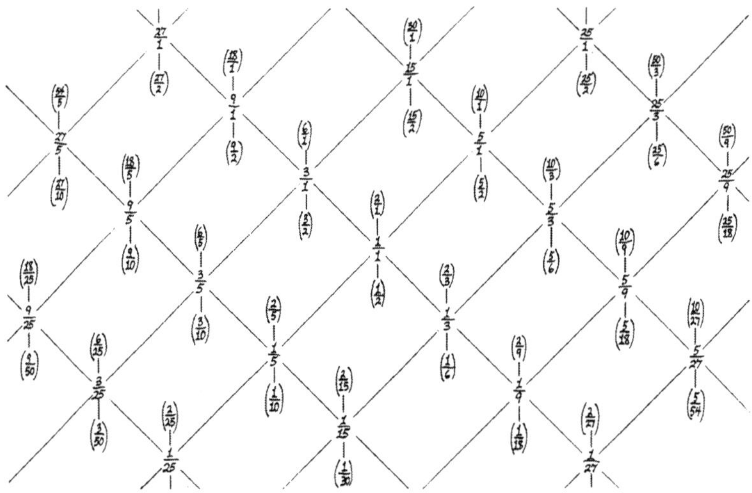

FIGURE 3. The 3,5 plane of harmonic space as a pitch-class projection plane within 2,3,5 space.

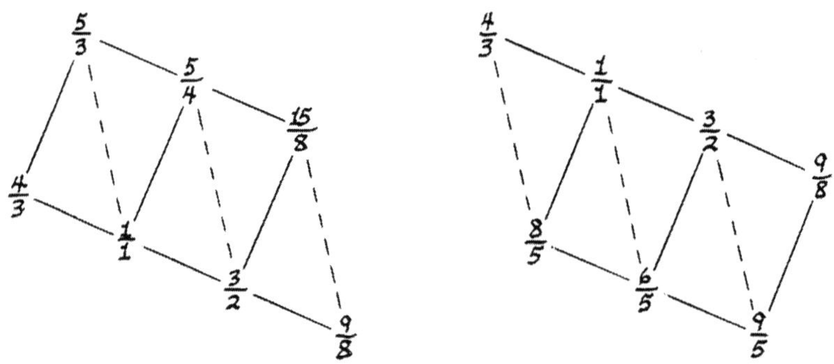

diatonic major diatonic minor

FIGURE 4. Primary harmonic relations within the diatonic scales.

harmonic space provides a useful tool for the design of such systems, as well as for the analysis of old ones. For example, Ben Johnston has for several years now been using what he calls "ratio lattices"—identical in every respect to those described here—for this very purpose of designing new scales and tuning systems. Although he does not use the term "harmonic space" explicitly, he does refer to "harmonic neighborhoods" demonstrated by the lattice structures, and he distinguishes between what he calls the harmonic and the melodic "modes of perception" in a way that is entirely consistent with the concept of harmonic space presented here.[8]

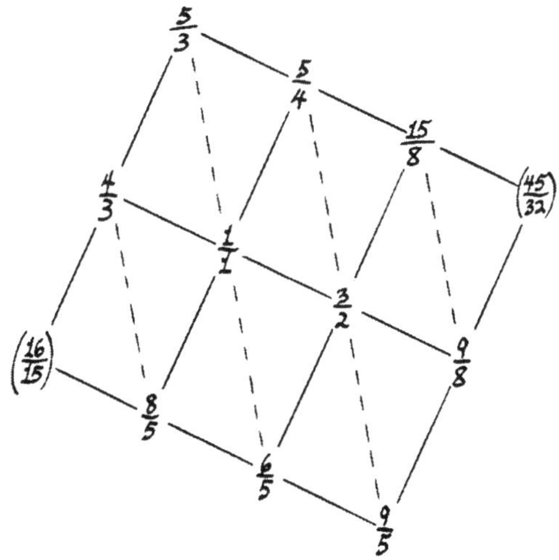

FIGURE 5. Primary harmonic relations within the chromatic scale.

The physiological correlate of the pitch-height projection axis is surely the *basilar membrane* of the inner ear, while that of the surrounding harmonic space (and of the pitch-class projection space) is assumed to be a set of *pitch-processing centers* in the central nervous system (including some form of short-term memory). The functional characteristics of harmonic space will naturally depend on those of its physiological correlate, and a theory of harmonic perception based on this concept requires the elaboration of a viable model of the auditory system. No such model has yet been developed, but preliminary work in that direction suggests the following:

1. Before a point in harmonic space can become activated, the corresponding point on the pitch-height axis must be clearly defined. That is, there must be both pitch-*saliency* and relative *stability* of pitch—and this requires *time*. During the first few hundredths of a second after the onset of a tone, its "image" on the pitch-height axis will not be a well-defined point but will be spread over some considerable portion of the pitch-height axis, above and below the point representing its nominal pitch. With time, the spread of this image will gradually be reduced to an effective point (i.e., a region confined to the tolerance range), and the corresponding point in harmonic space will then be activated.

2. Once activated, a point in harmonic space will remain active for some considerable amount of time after the tonal stimulus has stopped sounding. That is, points in harmonic space are characterized by a certain

persistence (due to a sort of neural "resonance" in short-term memory). The extent of this persistence depends primarily on the number and nature of the sounds that follow the first one.

Note that both of these functional characteristics of harmonic space would involve *time*—and they provide some clues to the question that was asked earlier in regard to Cage's concept of the *aggregate*: Under what conditions will a multiplicity of elementary acoustic signals be perceived as a "single sound"? From a purely physical standpoint, nearly every sound we hear is some sort of "aggregate" made up of a large number of components. But during the first few tens of milliseconds after the onset of a sound it is impossible to distinguish those individual components. As the sound continues, of course, it may gradually become possible to make such distinctions, and these will depend on the separability of these components' "images"—either in harmonic space or on the pitch-height axis alone. There are, however, two common acoustical situations in which a multiplicity of components resists this kind of aural "analysis" almost indefinitely: (1) noise bands and (2) compound tones with harmonic partials.

In the first case—though there may originally have been a large number of individual frequency components (as in a "tone cluster")—their mutual interferences are such that no one of them remains stable long enough to elicit a tonal percept (i.e., long enough for its image to become a well-defined point on the pitch-height axis). Thus, points in harmonic space will not be activated by a noise band, but its image will appear as a cluster of contiguous points (or regions) along the pitch-height axis.

In the second case, the points in harmonic space activated by the several harmonic partials (assuming them to be stable) also form a "cluster of contiguous points" but now projected outward (and upward, in the shape of an inverted cone) from the pitch-height axis into the surrounding regions of harmonic space (see figure 6). What is actually perceived in this case, of course, is a single tone with a pitch corresponding to that of the vertex of the "cone"—whether or not a component of that frequency is actually present in the sound—and a timbre determined by the relative amplitudes of the partials.

On the basis of these examples, the initial question might be answered as follows: a multiplicity of elementary acoustic signals will be perceived as a "single sound"—even long after the initial onset—when their images form *a cluster of contiguous points* either in harmonic space or on the pitch-height projection axis alone.

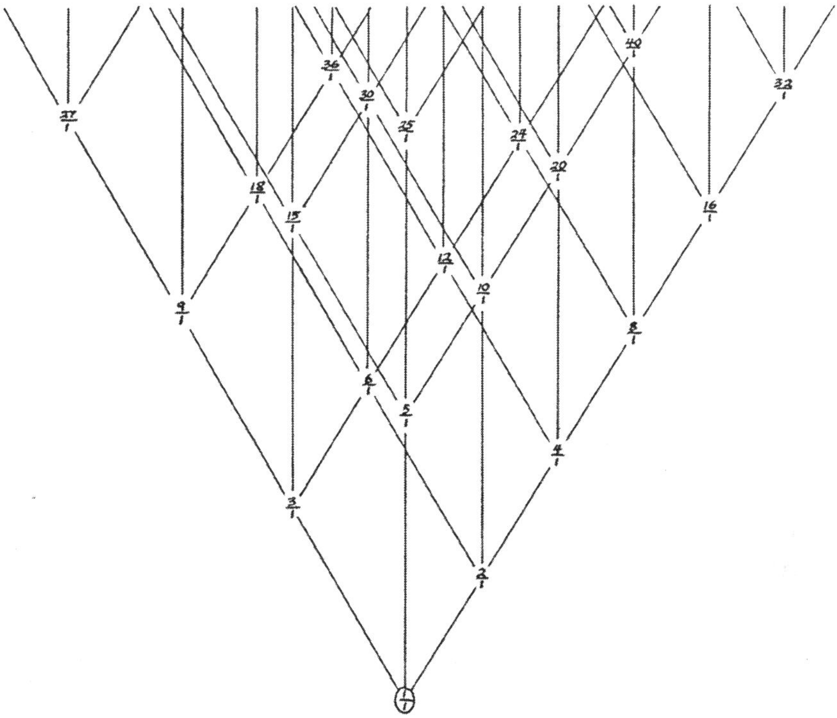

FIGURE 6. The harmonic containment "cone" in 2,3,5 space.

The two most important problems in earlier harmonic theory—regarding the nature of consonance and dissonance and the tonic phenomenon (including the whole question of chord roots)—have not yet been mentioned here. I suspect that harmonic theorists in the future will be far less concerned with these problems than earlier theorists were, but I think the concept of harmonic space may shed some light on them, for what it's worth. The problem of consonance and dissonance has been considerably confused by the fact that these terms have been used to mean distinctly different things in different historical periods.[9] And yet there is one simple generalization that can be applied to nearly all of these different conceptions of consonance and dissonance, which is that tones represented by proximate points in harmonic space tend to be heard as being in a consonant relation to each other, while tones represented by more widely separated points are heard as mutually dissonant. Now this statement serves neither to clarify the distinctions between different senses of consonance and dissonance mentioned above nor to "explain" any one of them. It does, however, indicate an important correlation between consonance and dissonance and what I am calling harmonic space.

Regarding the "tonic phenomenon," our model does not, in itself, suggest either an explanation or a measure of it, but we can incorporate into the model the simple observation that there is a kind of directed "field of force" in harmonic space such that a tone represented by a given point will tend to "become tonic" with respect to tones/points to the "right" of it (in most of my diagrams—i.e., in the 3/2, or "dominant," direction). Such a tone seems capable of absorbing those other tones into what might be called its "tonic field" and of being absorbed, in its turn, into the tonic field of another tone to the "left" of it (i.e., in the 2/3, or "subdominant," direction), or "below" it. This is analogous to the way in which the harmonic partials in a compound tone seem to be absorbed into the fundamental, but this analogy must not be carried too far or taken too literally. The harmonic (or "overtone") series has too often been invoked to explain both consonance and dissonance (e.g., Helmholtz) and the tonic/chord-root phenomenon (e.g., Rameau).[10] But the harmonic series cannot truly explain either of these things (any more than this concept of harmonic space can explain them). Although there is one sense of consonance and dissonance that does depend on the harmonic series (and with respect to this one sense of the terms I believe Helmholtz was essentially correct), there are other senses that remain applicable to tones even in the absence of harmonic partials. And it is not—as Rameau postulated—the *son fondamental* that "generates" the triad but the other way around: when there is a sense that a particular pitch is the root of a chord it is surely the chord itself that creates that sense.

To understand the real relation between the harmonic series and musical perception we must ask the following question: Why is it that a compound tone consisting of many harmonic partials is normally and immediately perceived as a *single tone* rather than as a "chord"? The science of psychoacoustics does not yet provide a satisfactory answer to this question, but I predict that—when it does—it will be seen that it is the nature of harmonic perception in the auditory system that "explains" the unique perceptual character of the harmonic series, not (again) the other way around. The harmonic series is not so much a causal factor in harmonic perception as it is a physical manifestation of a *principle* that is also manifested (though somewhat differently) in harmonic perception. That principle involves the mutual compatibility—as elements in a unitary gestalt or "system" (whether physical-acoustical or psychoacoustical)—of frequencies exhibiting certain rational relations to each other.

We can now define *harmony* as *that aspect of musical perception that depends on harmonic relations between pitches, i.e., relations other than "higher" or "lower."* Thus defined, "harmony" will still include all of those things it now includes—the "vertical aspect of music," chord-structure, etc.—but it is no longer limited to these, and it is certainly not limited to the "materials and procedures of the diatonic/triadic tonal system." It would, for example, also include pitch-relations manifested in a purely melodic or monophonic situation, and—by this definition—nearly *all* music will be found to involve harmony in some way (not just Western "part-music"). In addition, the model of harmonic space outlined here suggests an important "first principle" for a new theory of harmony—that *there is some (set of) specifically harmonic relation(s) between any two salient and relatively stable pitches.*

Yet, by definition, "harmony" does still have some limits in its application, and these are important to recognize. In the case of any music in which no salient and stable pitches occur at all (and there is a great deal of such music in the contemporary literature), harmony—even by this broader definition—would not be relevant. A theory of harmony, therefore, can only be one component in a more general theory of musical perception, and that more general theory must *begin*—as the work of John Cage repeatedly demonstrates—with the primary dimension common to all music: *time.*

References for "John Cage and the Theory of Harmony"

Writings by John Cage

The titles of books in which these articles are currently [as of 1983] to be found (not necessarily where they were first printed) are abbreviated as follows (the page numbers given with these abbreviations are those on which each article begins):

S 1961. *Silence.* Middletown, CT: Wesleyan University Press.

CPC 1962. *Cage/Peters Catalogue.* Ed. Robert Dunn. New York: C. F. Peters.

AYM 1967. *A Year from Monday.* Middletown, CT: Wesleyan University Press.

JC 1970. *John Cage*. Ed. Richard Kostelanetz. New York: Praeger.
M 1973. *M*. Middletown, CT: Wesleyan University Press.
EW 1979. *Empty Words*. Middletown, CT: Wesleyan University Press.
FB 1981. *For the Birds*. In conversation with Daniel Charles. Salem, NH: Marion Boyars.
1937 The Future of Music (S 3)
1942 For More New Sounds (JC 64)
1948 Defense of Satie (JC 77)
1949 Forerunners of Modern Music (S 62)
1951 Satie Controversy (JC 89)
1952 To Describe the Process of Composition Used in *Music of Changes* and *Imaginary Landscape No. 4* (S 57)
1954 45' for a Speaker (S 146)
1955 Experimental Music: Doctrine (S 13)
1956a In This Day (S 94)
1956b letter to Paul Henry Lang (JC 116)
1957 Experimental Music (S 7)
1958a Composition as Process: I. Changes (S 18)
1958b Edgard Varèse (S 83)
1959a Indeterminacy (S 260)
1959b History of Experimental Music in the United States (S 67)
1961 Interview with Roger Reynolds (CPC 45)
1962 Rhythm Etc. (AYM 120)
1963 Happy New Ears! (AYM 30)
1964 Jasper Johns: Stories and Ideas (AYM 73)
1965 Diary: How to Improve the World (You Will Only Make Matters Worse) 1965 (AYM 3)
1966 Seriously Comma (AYM 26)
1967a Diary: How to Improve the World . . . Continued 1967 (AYM 145)
1967b Afterword (to AYM 163)
1968 Diary: How to Improve the World . . . Continued 1968 (Revised) (M 3)
1972 Diary: How to Improve the World . . . Continued 1971–72 (M 195)

CHAPTER 13

Reflections after *Bridge*

(1984)

Since the revolution in aesthetic attitudes wrought by John Cage circa 1951, it has come to pass that virtually anything is possible in music. And yet not everything seems equally urgent or necessary, and, without a sense of necessity, one's musical activities can quickly degenerate into mere entertainment or redundancy. One area of investigation that has that sense of urgency for me now is what I call "harmony"—i.e., that aspect of music that involves *relations between pitches* other than those of sheer direction and distance (up or down, large or small). It has gradually become clear to me that any new development of harmony in this sense will involve more careful considerations of intonation and the design of new tuning systems; the work of Harry Partch has thus taken on a significance quite above and beyond its dramatic (and even heroic) character. It has become, in fact, an indispensable *technical* point of departure, just as Cage's work has provided us with an essential *aesthetic* foundation.

Why do I correlate new developments in harmony with the design of new tuning systems? Consider the history of musical innovations in the early twentieth century. Around 1910 a crisis occurred that profoundly affected subsequent events. Tonality, which had been a primary basis for musical organization for some two hundred years, was seen by many of the more progressive composers of the time as having been exhausted. In response, these composers set out to explore other means of musical organization involving other aspects of music, some of which (like rhythm) had remained nearly static since the very beginnings of the "common practice" period. Harmony, as such, was either ignored or maintained at the same level of development it had reached in 1910. In the absence of some fairly powerful new organizing principles, posttonal music might well have become utterly incoherent. The fact that it did not is evidence that these composers did indeed discover such organizing principles and that—in a more general sense—it is quite possible to make music without "harmony."

Now, however, we find ourselves at a point where these various other aspects of music have all been quite thoroughly explored. Although it would be naive to imagine that nothing new is likely to emerge in these areas, it can certainly be said that none of them has remained "static" in our century. Rhythm, timbre, texture, form, and even the aesthetic premises and social functions of music have all been reexamined and elaborated to an extent without precedent in any earlier period of Western (or perhaps any other) music. What has *not* changed since that watershed year of 1910—at least in any progressive-evolutionary sense—is harmony, and it seems time now to confront this issue again, since it can hardly be ignored indefinitely. It is far too basic (even primitive) an aspect of auditory perception ever to be suspended entirely.

One of the new directions taken by some composers after 1910 did involve the expansion of the pitch resources beyond the 12-tone tempered tuning system (or "12-set") by way of simple subdivisions of that set (the quarter-tones, sixth-tones, etc. of Busoni, Ives, Hába, Carillo, et al.). But where these expansions were not *harmonically based*, they did not—and indeed *could* not—solve the problem that had arisen with the "exhaustion" of tonality. Thus, the music that was written in such tuning systems still required other "organizing principles" in order to maintain coherence. The failure of this music to solve the specifically *harmonic* problem was not due to any lack of skill, talent, or vision on the part of these composers. These qualities most of them had in abundance. Their great expectations of what might be accomplished by such subdivisions of the 12-set were, however, the result of a misunderstanding of the basic nature of the 12-set itself. That is, this pitch set is *not* simply a useful or convenient (much less arbitrary) "division of the octave." More essentially, it is a pitch set that approximates certain just intervals (of the "5-limit") fairly well (although it requires a tolerance range of about a seventh of a semitone for the ear to interpret the tempered major third in a triad as a just third). And the 12-set evolved historically in precisely that way—as a solution to the *harmonic* problem of tuning keyboard instruments in such a way that the important harmonic intervals would be available within a wide range of modulations of the tonic without encountering an intolerable "wolf" at some point. Thus, the 12-tone, equal-tempered scale was originally a harmonically based tuning system, and any extension of this system must also be harmonically based if it is to have any effect on further developments of harmony.

The real problem with the 12-set, of course, is not the relatively small number of pitches it makes available but the fact that a very large tolerance range has to be assumed even for it to be regarded as a "fair approximation" of the basic intervals of the 5-limit—and even greater ranges are involved with those of the 7- and 11-limits. Although some "progressive evolution" of harmony is often suggested or implied in works by early twentieth-century composers using this tuning system, it can only remain mere suggestion or implication. It can neither be made explicit, nor clarified, nor *built upon* without going beyond the confines of the 12-set.

Partch's solution to these problems was to use just intervals only, and his work will stand for a long time as the most important pioneering exploration along the edges of this latest frontier. But other solutions are possible, including other temperaments, *if* these are "harmonically based." In either case, our task now, as I see it, is to investigate the unknown regions *beyond* this "frontier" equipped with the resources already developed by Partch (and a few others: Lou Harrison and Ben Johnston have extended these resources quite considerably and explored some of these regions) while at the same time taking care not to lose sight of the new freedoms already won for us by Cage's "revolution" (otherwise, the results are bound to be regressive in one way or another).

Is a rapprochement between their two worlds possible? Perhaps not. Partch would almost certainly not have given it his blessing, and Cage will probably be at least a little wary of my concern with "relations between pitches." But the sense of what's necessary changes with time (and Cage's own more recent work is itself a demonstration of this, with its renewed use of "chance methods," as distinct from "indeterminacy," and its emphasis on "discipline"). One can even find in his writings another rationale for such an effort, if one is needed, as where he says (in *A Year from Monday*, p. 19): "Where there's a history of organization (art), introduce disorder. Where there's a history of disorganization (world society), introduce order. These directives are no more opposed to one another than mountain's opposed to spring weather. 'How can you believe this when you believe that?' How can I not?"[1] This was written some twenty years ago, and in the interim Cage's numerous and varied introductions of "disorder" into the art of music have taught us to *listen* with ears and minds more open than would earlier have been thought possible. Perhaps it is not too soon to be able to say that art, too, now has a "history of disorder," as well as order, and thus that the question of order versus disorder is no longer the most pressing issue.

CHAPTER 14

Review of *Music as Heard* by Thomas Clifton (1985)

Before his untimely death in 1978, Thomas Clifton developed an approach to music theory intended as a remedy for a problem that he and others had recognized, namely, "the lack of coordination between the activity of analyzing the score and that of analyzing the experience of the music in the score."[1] Near the end of *Music as Heard* Clifton states as one of his primary motivations a desire "to contribute to the effort of reuniting music theory with musical experience."[2] Readers who do not, to begin with, agree with Clifton that such a problem exists at all will probably find little of value in this book—and much to criticize, especially where the author attacks some of the familiar concepts of music theory. But those who do believe that there is an unhealthy disparity between the results of current practice in music theory and the actual experience of listening to music will see this book as an important contribution to the music-theoretical literature.

Music as Heard is difficult: at times brilliant, insightful, and thought-provoking; at other times irritating, exasperating, even embarrassing. While its positive aspects could serve to inject a much-needed element into the ailing body of music theory, there are other aspects that make one wonder if the cure might not be as debilitating as the disease. But whether Clifton has succeeded in his overall effort may not be as important, in the long run, as the fact that he has identified a problem in need of a solution. A new kind of music theory is needed that deals with the question of *what* we actually hear when we listen to a piece of music, as well as *how* or *why* we hear as we do. To the extent that music theory involves the development and application of a descriptive language for music, this means that both the things named and the relations between things described by such a language must be much more precisely correlated than they are now with the things and relations actually perceived or experienced.

Whether music theory as a descriptive language has *ever* really been adequate in this sense is a question that would be difficult to answer. But the discrepancy between language and experience does seem to have become especially critical in our time, particularly with respect to two large bodies of music that have recently attracted an increasing amount of theoretical attention: non-Western musics and twentieth-century Western music. The language of traditional Western music theory is of almost no use at all in describing such music, and more recent theoretical developments—such as those in Schenkerian analysis and set theory—are far too specialized to be applicable beyond the relatively small repertoires for which they were designed. It remains to be seen, of course, whether the "language" developed in *Music as Heard* is any better suited to the task, but it does have a generality that transcends particular styles or compositional grammars. It is significant that a large proportion of the musical examples used in the book are from the literature of twentieth-century music (albeit all of it is Western).

Clifton's "phenomenological" point of departure entails extensive use of the methods, insights, and terminology of Edmund Husserl, Maurice Merleau-Ponty, and Mikel Dufrenne. His earlier articles revealed his fascination with the musical applications of philosophy and his knowledge of its literature, traditions, and methods. His various attempts to apply philosophical concepts to music-theoretical questions demonstrated an understanding of music and musical experience not to be found in the philosophical writings that were so often his sources.[3] But phenomenology, as such, was not explicitly acknowledged in these articles. Since the question "What is phenomenology?" will inevitably arise in the minds of many readers, and since answers to this question are only to be found scattered throughout Clifton's book, it might be useful to precede our review of the book itself with some background on the discipline.

The term "phenomenology"—often defined as "a theory of appearances"—has been used in a variety of ways by writers as diverse in their views as Kant, Hegel, Peirce, Stumpf, Teilhard de Chardin, Heidegger, and Sartre. As a complete philosophical system, however, it has come to be associated primarily with Edmund Husserl (1859–1938). An idea common to many of these different versions of phenomenology is that a deeper understanding of reality can be achieved by a return to "the things themselves"—or rather to the direct experience of these things in consciousness. Husserl repeatedly emphasized that this idea might have important ramifications outside of philosophy per se, particularly in the empirical sciences, although this view seems never to have been taken very seriously by empirical scientists themselves, except for a few in the field of perceptual psychology. For instance, the gestalt psychologist Kurt Koffka wrote: "For us [phenomenology] means as naive and full a description of direct experience as possible." As a rationale for this, he added: "Without describing the environmental field we should not know what we had to explain."[4]

It should be emphasized that the kind of naïveté suggested above is not that of mere "common sense." Even in pre-Husserlian forms of phenomenology, special effort is required to avoid prejudices and presuppositions (whether ideological, systematic, or merely habitual) that might interfere with direct experience or its description. In the words of C. S. Peirce, this effort must "not . . . be influenced by any tradition, any authority, any reason for supposing that such and such ought to be the facts."[5]

Husserl's work involved a radical redefinition of phenomenology that distinguishes it from these more general forms in several ways. His primary focus was on consciousness itself and on its indispensable role in the "constitution" of both meaning and "objective reality." His aim was to describe not just any and all particulars of conscious processes, however, but "essences": aspects of consciousness that remained after the sedimentary layers of presupposition had been cleared away. He developed a strategy for pursuing these essences called variously the "*epoché*," "reduction," or "bracketing" (synonymous with Clifton's term "neutralization"). The process of reduction involved a suspension of belief in virtually everything (the reality of the external world, the "truths" of empirical science and common sense, etc.). But it also involved a considerable reliance on pure *intuition* as a means of locating some bedrock residue of consciousness itself. Latter-day phenomenologists, such as Merleau-Ponty and Dufrenne (and now Clifton), while focusing on different problems and not nearly so concerned with methodology as was Husserl, all seem to share his faith in intuition.

Perhaps no philosophical system has greater potential for solving certain current problems of music theory than phenomenology—or, at least, what has come to be called the "phenomenological attitude," which begins with experience (no matter how far it might extrapolate beyond that starting point) and continually returns to experience as both the foundation and final arbiter of knowledge. Music, after all, is hardly anything more (and it is certainly not less) than its "appearances," in the phenomenological sense. A piece of music is not its score, nor is it the purely physical vibrations that are correlated with a performance of it. It is, as Clifton says, "not a fact or thing in the world, but a meaning constituted by human beings" (5). His view of the nature of music is further clarified when he contrasts it with that of the empiricist:

> If phenomenology criticizes those who . . . attempt to take the measure of music with an empirical eye, it is not because it denies the value of empirical methods, but because the non-empirical status of music is covered up with research on the empirical sounds which are its medium, the empirical techniques which are its means, and the empirical marks (the notation) which are its signs. The sounds, the techniques, and the notation are all vastly important aspects of music, but *they are not music itself.* (36–37, emphasis added)

Clifton would no doubt have agreed that the phenomenological method has great potential not only in music theory but in any of the disciplines requiring verbalizations about music, including criticism and pedagogy. But for this potential to be realized, the method has to be used very carefully, since even "with the best will in the world, it is still deceptively easy to confuse a phenomenological description of music with the poetic ramblings of nineteenth-century criticism" (48). Insofar as phenomenology posits the subjective experience of the observer as a necessary basis for phenomenological description, it is always on the verge of solipsism. Husserl tried to solve this problem by an analysis of "intersubjectivity," but he was not entirely successful in thus exorcising the ghost of solipsism, and the problem remains unresolved in Clifton's work, despite several statements of his that imply that it is merely superficial or easily disposed of. For example, he says that "disagreement about a description simply points to the practical problems of removing ambiguities, choosing clear examples, considering other points of view, and, in general, engaging in intersubjective dialogue" (40). While such "intersubjective dialogue" may not be quite sufficient, it is surely necessary for the development of a viable language for musical description. Clifton may very well not have had the benefit of enough dialogue of this kind in the earlier stages of development of his ideas.

The first three of the book's seven chapters introduce the basic ideas of phenomenology as Clifton interprets them. In the preface, he tells us that "the phenomenological attitude" affords "a way of uttering meaningful statements which are objective in the sense that they attempt to describe the musical object adequately, and subjective in the sense that they issue from a subject to whom an object has some meaning" (viii–ix). To these ends, as he says in chapter 1 ("Introduction: The Point of Departure"): "A phenomenological description concentrates not on facts, but upon essences, and attempts to uncover what there is about an object and its experience which is essential (or necessary) if the object or the experience is to be recognized at all" (9). As an example, Clifton describes a passage from the Gavotte of Bach's G-Minor English Suite and concludes that "time," "space," and "feeling" are three such essences: "In the connection of one event with another, I effect a temporal process which begins and ends with the suite itself, which thus forms a kind of parenthesis in world time. Similarly, I recognize that this music possesses a space, since I indubitably hear an overall descending motion in the upper voice, and if we talk about motion from higher to lower, we are talking about musical space" (13). Furthermore, "there is something about the piece itself which presents a feeling of some kind. . . . I suggest that feeling, like space and time, is a necessary constituent of the musical experience rather than a psychological by-product of the listener" (14). Later in the book an entire chapter is devoted to each of these essences or "essential backgrounds of experience." By that time a fourth, "the element of play," has been added to his list.

Also in this first chapter Clifton gives an "operational definition" of the word "music" as he uses it in his book:

> Music is an ordered arrangement of sounds and silences whose meaning is presentative rather than denotative. This sounds innocuous enough. Perhaps the plot will begin to thicken if I suggest that this definition distinguishes music, as an end in itself, from compositional technique, and from sounds as purely physical objects.

> Furthermore, the definition implies nothing about the intentions of the composer, or indeed, about whether there is a composer. . . . It says nothing about the status of the score or about the nature of the instruments. Both the score and the instruments are as dispensable as the composer. To be more precise, then, I should say that music is the actualization of the possibility of any sound whatever to present to some human being a meaning which he experiences with his body—that is to say, with his mind, his feelings, his senses, his will, and his metabolism. (1)

This definition has several useful aspects. One is that it inextricably involves the listener in the very question of whether a certain collection of sounds is or is not music. Another is that it "says nothing about aesthetic standards which the object of the musical experience is supposed to meet" (5). One might question whether Clifton's inclusion of the word "ordered" in his definition does not imply a kind of "aesthetic standard," but he anticipates the question: "This word is used as a description of an experience which may be independent of, and other than, the kinds of orderings injected into the work by the composer. . . . Order is constituted by the experiencing person, who is just as likely to experience it in a collection of natural sounds, as in . . . a finely wrought fugue" (4).

In chapter 2 ("The Nature of Phenomena and Phenomenological Description") Clifton continues his efforts to explain what the phenomenologist means by "phenomenon," "essence," and "phenomenological description." As a means of clarifying these ideas, he subjects some familiar terms and concepts of music theory to a kind of phenomenological critique in response to the question "How does the vocabulary of traditional music theory imply (or hide) the stratum of intuitive awareness?" The section that follows is one of the weakest in the book. It is flawed by a surprisingly imprecise use of the traditional terms themselves; Clifton seems more concerned with simply denying their "phenomenal validity" than with offering viable alternatives to them or to their interpretations.

For example, he states that "a fairly common interpretation of pitch is as an irreducible atom in the musical universe."

> [However,] from an acoustical point of view, pitch is not a basic stratum, being a function of duration and loudness. From a phenomenological point of view, pitch is also not a basic stratum, for

> two reasons. Pitch is obviously not a basic stratum in the sense that music itself is dependent on discriminable and specifiable frequencies. We could not then account for the roles played by pitchless drums, cymbals, wood blocks, and sirens, not to mention the repertoire of electronic and "found" sounds. More importantly, pitch is "transparentized" in a musical context, which is to say that we experience music *through* the pitch, rather than the pitch itself. More simply, we hear the musical activity of the pitch: it is receding, projecting, emerging, interrupting or being interrupted, changing in tone quality or intensity, glaring, glowing, echoing, etc. (20)

Now, the very existence of so much music for percussion instruments of indefinite pitch confirms the first of his two "phenomenological reasons" why pitch is not a "basic stratum"—if by this he means something without which music cannot exist at all. But aside from this point, there are two basic problems with the passage quoted above. The first is his contention that pitch is "a function of duration and loudness." I can think of only two acoustical or psychoacoustical facts upon which he might have based this statement. One is that in laboratory experiments the perceived pitch of a simple tone of a certain constant frequency can be made to vary as a function of duration (when in the range of very short durations) or of amplitude or intensity (not "loudness"). The other is that pitch is a perceptual quality that is somehow synthesized by the auditory system in response to a physical stimulus that, from a certain point of view, is nothing but a periodic variation of amplitude with time (here neither "loudness" nor "duration" would be accurate). In either case, however—even allowing for a certain imprecision in his use of the terms involved—his statement is simply not true, since "pitch" has a meaning in acoustics and psychoacoustics that is quite independent of both loudness and duration. The other problem in the passage quoted has to do with the second of his "phenomenological reasons" and his discussion of the notion that pitch is "transparentized." Here Clifton uses the word "pitch" in two completely different senses, apparently without being aware of it: that is, on the one hand, as *an attribute* of the tone, and on the other, as *the tone itself*. A "pitch" in the first sense (as the perceptual correlate of a "discriminable and specifiable frequency") does not "recede," "project," and so on, and it certainly cannot "change in tone quality or intensity," whereas a *tone* (i.e., a "pitch" in the second sense) *might* be described as acting in these ways.

Clifton's critiques of "interval," "scale," and "tonality" fare no better, but I leave it to the reader to verify this assertion. In his discussion of "harmony," there is at least the germ of an interesting idea, although it is not very thoroughly developed. He suggests that "consonance as 'sounding-with' implies a homogeneity of space which absorbs individual pitches and intervals. . . . Tones are harmonious with other tones because of their location within, and adherence to, a common space" (23–24). Unfortunately, he has not yet defined, in any precise way, what he means by "space," and even his later discussions of this concept do not quite make clear what he means by a "homogeneity of space" or a "common space." Still, the implication is that "harmony," "consonance," and "dissonance" might be defined in some new and more general way that would allow their application to musical configurations outside the diatonic tonal system. An excerpt from Carter's Piano Concerto is presented as "a much more radical example of phenomenal consonance": "Here, the strings present a thick, opaque band or wall of sound which offers a different instance of spatial homogeneity. Dissonance is experienced as the confrontation of this wall with the piano sounds which seem to bounce off it" (24).

The trouble here is recurrent throughout the book: an unwillingness to consider carefully enough the *objective correlates* of an experience or percept. Such considerations are at least as important as "intersubjective dialogue" in preventing phenomenological descriptions from degenerating into mere exercises in solipsism; if it is not the responsibility of the phenomenologist to investigate the connections between "music as heard" and these objective correlates, it is certainly the responsibility of the music theorist to do so. But a concern with such correlates might involve some consideration of acoustics, psychoacoustics, or the physiological mechanisms of perception, and Clifton seems to have had a positive aversion to these disciplines. The result is that his applications of phenomenology to music completely bypass a certain lower level of analysis at which the phenomenological attitude could be extremely useful. To some extent, of course, Husserlian phenomenology discourages any concern with the "why" or the "how" of things because it involves such an intense focus on the "what" of perception and experience. But in some instances it is very difficult to separate these questions.

In the next section of chapter 2, Clifton develops a set of five criteria for valid descriptive statements of the phenomenological kind. These are (1) that "one must be aware of the actual music" (38); (2) that the description be restricted "to what is given: the composition itself, not facts about it, or bare acoustical data" (38); (3) that the object of the description be "not the materials of a composition . . . or the medium (the sound as such)" but rather "the sense of the sounds: the meaning act, as well as the object of the act" (39); (4) that "the description must be rendered with precision . . . , systematically relevant, and . . . interesting" (39); and finally (5) what he calls a "noninferability criterion"—that "the truth of descriptive statements does not depend on whether something exists empirically or not" (41). Clifton's own descriptions, however, do not always satisfy these criteria, especially numbers 2 and 4: they are by no means always restricted to "what is given," and they are not always "systematically relevant."

After discussing the first four of the five criteria, he says: "So far, none of these criteria will remove the possibility that arguments and disagreements about the accuracy and suitability of descriptive terms are bound to occur. But . . . *when faced with sincere disagreement, the first thing to realize is the nontrivial base of agreement underlying any differences in description*. To disagree over the temporal nature of a certain passage is to implicitly agree about the essential presence of time" (40, emphasis added). This is a crucial point to keep in mind not only in reading Clifton's book but also in reading this review—because, although I often disagree with Clifton, there is usually a "nontrivial base of agreement" that is more important than our differences.

In chapter 3 ("Essential Backgrounds of Experience") Clifton analyzes in more detail the "essences": time, space, play, and feeling. Musical time—a special instance of a more general, phenomenological time—he defines as "the experience of human consciousness in contact with change" (56). Time in this sense is to be distinguished from absolute or clock time. It is inaccurate to speak of time as "flowing"; instead, "it is the experience of objects, events, and other people which is in constant flux. . . . [F]or our purposes, time is not some intrinsic, absolute medium which can be dealt with by quantitative methods, and . . . since time does not flow, it is pointless to say that it is unidirectional and irreversible" (55). With regard to the specifically musical manifestations of phenomenological time, he notes that there exists "a confusion about whether the composition is in time, or whether time is in it. Here we will proceed on the basis that *time is in the composition*" (51). Clifton's definition of time is attractive and seems plausible at first. But it is too broad, since "time" must surely be understood as but one dimension of that experience, and this aspect gives rise to later problems.

In the following section, Clifton discusses what he calls "general time words"—terms and concepts originally developed by Husserl in *The Phenomenology of Internal Time-Consciousness* and other writings.[6] These terms include "horizon" (the "field of presence" of an experienced event, or the temporal boundaries of that field [57]), "retention" (Husserl's "primary remembrance" [59]), and "protention" ("the term for a future which we anticipate, and not merely await" [62]). This marks the first time, to my knowledge, that Husserl's ideas about time have been applied to musical perception, and Clifton does an effective job of explaining these ideas and showing their relevance to musical questions.

In his discussion of "horizon," Clifton comes close to an explicit recognition of the gestalt character of our temporal experience, although he stops just short of attributing to it a central importance: "The horizon refers to the temporal edge of a single field, which itself may enclose a multitude of events interpreted . . . as belonging to this field" (57). He then describes the relation between the temporal field and its content: "The horizon adheres so closely to the object that we may as well say that the object *is* its horizon. I could not experience a melody if it did not also push back the borders of the present to include itself, as a singular event, in a single present" (57–58).

Finally, after noting the similarity in meaning between "horizon" and Heidegger's term *Spanne*, Clifton says: "It seems not unreasonable that we can have spans within spans, horizons within horizons, and that we can speak, with perfect intelligibility, about certain time spans interrupting others, or being interpolated between others, or of alternating with others" (58–59). Not only is it not unreasonable to speak of spans within spans and so forth, but it is absolutely essential that we do so—or at least that we design a descriptive language that *enables* us to do so. The sort of analysis that Clifton is attempting here might provide the basis for the development of such a language, if it were done carefully enough. But there is already some danger of confusion as a result of a blurring of the distinctions between the boundaries of a temporal field, the extent of that field, and its content. While this does not present a problem here, in the earlier stages of Clifton's discussion of time, it will do so later (see commentary below on "time strata").

Clifton's ideas about time are further developed in chapter 4 ("Time in Motion"), which begins with a slightly different formulation of the distinction between musical time and what he now refers to as "world" or "chronological" time: "There is a distinction between the time a piece *takes* and the time which a piece *presents* or *evokes*. It is this kind of time, the time which is *in* the phenomenal world of music, which is the main concern here" (81–82). Note that we have passed, almost imperceptibly, from time as something "in" the music to a time "presented" or "evoked" by it; these will soon be joined by still another sort of time that may be "designated" by the music or that the music may "be about." This proliferation of different kinds of time would be unobjectionable if they were always clearly distinguished, but—as we will see shortly—they are not. Clifton next deals with several instances of "immediate [i.e., unmediated] evocations of time." There are a few insightful comments and some potentially interesting ideas in this chapter, but overall it is somewhat disappointing, especially considering the promise of his earlier discussion of this important essence. A number of problems are evident here: first, he asks the question "What is the essence of beginning?" but doesn't really answer it and instead gets sidetracked trying to explain his perception of a "second beginning" in the first movement of Beethoven's Ninth Symphony (83–87); second, he fails to give clear definitions of some of the special terms he uses, such as "temporal dimensions" (99), "temporal intercut" (110), and "spatial dimensions" (126); third, his analysis of the difference between contrast and interruption (106–110) is superficial; and fourth, his description of a passage in Bach's A-Minor Fugue, *The Well-Tempered Clavier*, vol. 2 (128), is rife with "implied" tones that can only be justified by assumptions derived from traditional harmonic analysis and that have no place in a phenomenological description of the music "as heard."

Perhaps a clearer sense of both the problems and the promise of this chapter can be conveyed by a close look at its last section, which deals with "time strata." Clifton has already stated that "a new or different activity bears a new time within it" (114); continuing with this notion, he says, "We arrive at a consideration of the possibility of experiencing distinct, different, but variously related temporal activities simultaneously" (125). Furthermore,

> two events occurring within a single field of presence may unfold in some chronological order, while nevertheless being *about* a disjunct

> time experience, due to the manner in which the events keep their times from blending. . . . The manner in which these degrees of blend are effected is largely due to the influence of musical activities going on in different spatial dimensions. Multiple appearances of a single idea which are separated in chronological time may create two or more horizontal spaces bonded together by a unity of shape. (125–26)

Clifton's use of language here is disturbingly imprecise. Is the music "*about* a disjunct time experience," or is time "*in* the music"? What are "different spatial dimensions"? And what does he mean by "horizontal spaces"? One can deduce his intended meanings, but his language has made them far from clear. What he apparently has in mind is simply the experience of listening to the relatively independent voices or "strata" in a polyphonic texture. Commenting on a specific example of such a texture, he says: "Phenomenally, we hear four 'nows' of different durations, embedded within the experience of hearing the *whole* sonata *now*. Each of these four 'nows' has its own identifying gesture; each 'now' presents the experience of change somewhat differently" (128). What were described earlier as "distinct, different, but variously related temporal activities" have become four separate "nows." What, after all, does Clifton really mean by phenomenological or musical time? No doubt it is something different from clock time, but it seems improbable that we can experience two or more different times simultaneously. Two or more different durations, rhythmic patterns, tempos, or speeds—yes, but not two different *times*, in the deepest phenomenological sense of the word, which Husserl, Merleau-Ponty, and even Clifton (in other passages in this book) have made virtually synonymous with subjectivity itself.

Why has Clifton chosen the term "time strata" instead of, say, "polyphonic strata"? One reason, of course, is simply that he wishes to focus on the temporal aspect of the musical experience in this chapter. But he could have done this by analyzing the many ways in which the independence of polyphonic strata is maintained by or correlated with differences in their speeds, phrase durations, rhythmic patterns, or other temporal properties. The fact that he does not do this suggests that there is another reason for his choice of words here having to do with his initial definition of time and with a subsequent series of semantic equations, which finally have the effect of erasing all distinctions between the boundaries of a time span, the span itself (as a "stretch" of time), and the perceptual or experiential content of that span. In not qualifying time as but one dimension of "the experience of human consciousness in contact with change," he has already prepared the ground for letting time stand for the events themselves, in all or any of their aspects. Furthermore, he has said that the terms "horizon," "span," and "field of presence" are all intended to mean "more or less the same thing" (59), which blurs the distinction between the boundaries of the field and the field itself. But he has also said that the content of any temporal horizon is determined by the object (58) and that "the object *is* its horizon" (57–58). Thus, the musical "object" (as content) is equivalent to the "horizon" (as boundary), which is equivalent to the span itself (as "field of presence")—and all of these things, finally, are indistinguishable from "time" itself. A great deal of confusion has thus become almost inevitable, and it is all unnecessary. If the definitions of these terms had been formulated more carefully and the necessary distinctions maintained, then a great deal could have been said about the experience of listening to a polyphonic texture that would have been not only clear and unambiguous but also phenomenologically relevant.

Clifton's approach to musical space is strongly influenced by Merleau-Ponty's ideas about motor behavior and synaesthesia as the basis for our experience of (physical) space: "In music we experience straight lines, curved lines, smooth and rough lines because we have carnal knowledge of what these things mean. A straight line cannot be the exclusive acquisition of vision, since my eyes have no existence apart from the body whose property they are" (70). Thus there are analogues in musical perception of features ordinarily associated with visual and tactile perception, but these are not so much features of external objects as they are of the experiences themselves. In fact, Clifton suggests that "in discussing the mutual contributions made by the experiencing subject and the musical object being experienced, we are encouraged to think of space and spatial relations not as properties of objects, but as *fields of action for a subject*" (70, emphasis added).

This might be taken as an implicit definition of musical space—and a useful one at that—if "action" is understood to include perception. In further pursuit of meaningful analogues, Clifton equates space with texture and says that "even the prolongation of a single pitch [i.e., a single *tone* at a constant pitch!] provides a simple type of texture. . . . Texture—or space—is what we experience when we hear durations, registers, intensities, and tone qualities" (69). This equation is not very useful, since "texture" might be better defined as an *aspect* of our perception of sounds in musical space, but it does suggest that such things as "durations, registers, intensities, and tone qualities" might be conceived of as *dimensions* of musical space. Clifton chooses not to make this explicit, but the implication is there.

When we hear a series of tones at different pitches, Clifton says, "We experience the phenomenon of line. The line can be experienced in any number of ways: as smooth, spiky, continuous, broken, receding or advancing, fading in or fading out, or as bifurcating and reuniting" (69). Further, "the notion of texture-as-space must, of course, be developed to include not only line and tone quality, but also the appearance in music of flat surfaces, surfaces revealing varying degrees of relief . . . or masses revealing different degrees of solidity. . . . Masses themselves can dissolve back into tangled webs of lines in three dimensions of musical space. All of these spaces can be discussed without assuming that musical space is anything like the physical spaces which we can see" (69).

In chapter 5 ("Space in Motion") Clifton develops all of these ideas, and there it becomes quite clear that he is *not* able to avoid the assumption of an essential similarity between musical and physical space. The analogies and metaphors so clearly drawn from experience of physical spaces and tactile qualities always remain in the foreground of his descriptions, resulting in an unnecessarily narrow application of the general concept of space to musical perception. Of course, for want of a more precise, aurally based terminology, we are often forced to make use of such analogies and metaphors. The very terms "up" and "down" as used to describe changes of pitch are an obvious example. Such usage need not create a problem, but problems are bound to arise if we forget the metaphorical nature of such terms—or rather, if we extrapolate on the basis of the metaphors themselves. Such an extrapolation is already evident where Clifton speaks of "three dimensions of musical space." There is surely no good reason to limit musical space to just three dimensions—unless, in fact, there *is* some essential similarity between physical and musical space. I would argue that there is not—except in the most general sense implied by Clifton's own phrase "fields of action for a subject"—and that his later analyses fall into difficulties because of a too literal translation from the visual/tactile to the auditory domain.

In the next section of this chapter Clifton elaborates a bit more on the suggestion made in chapter 2 that the element of "play" somehow constitutes an essence of the musical experience as much as do time and space. He realizes that this implies a rather different interpretation of the term "essence": "A consideration of the essential backgrounds of experience entails not only a description of the logical requirements demanded by the materiality of the musical composition, but also the contributions made by the participating listener. To my mind, nowhere does this required fusion between experiencing self and experienced music show itself more clearly than in the notion of play as a musical essence" (71). And he adds: "To say that music is unthinkable without its ludic foundation is a statement that demands careful development on my part, and the suspension of hasty judgments on yours" (71). Even with the most determined effort toward "the suspension of hasty judgments," this notion remains the least convincing of all. This is not because of any implication of a lack of seriousness in Clifton's use of "play." On the contrary, "we should not say that play is outside of, or higher or lower than, reality, but rather, that it is a constitution of reality" (73). But what does this "element of play" have to do with the business at hand—the description of music as heard? Here, perhaps more than anywhere else in this book, Clifton seems to have begun with a set of concepts that recommend themselves in some other domain and then found himself obliged to search for musical examples to which these concepts might be applied. Even aside from the fact that many of these applications have more to do with music as played, studied, or thought about than with the experience of listening, Clifton's whole procedure here, from the standpoint of the phenomenological method, is a striking case of the cart pulling the horse.

One result of this methodological reversal is a singularly unphenomenological proliferation of different descriptive approaches to the same "object." In chapter 6, for example, Clifton distinguishes various forms of play—the "ludic," the "aleatoric," the "agonic," and the "comic"—and within the ludic category he includes "ritual" and "heuristic" behavior. In his discussion of ritual he compares certain musical situations to the phenomena of "status-elevation" and "status-reduction," which have been described by anthropologists as important components of many initiation rites: "It frequently happens that status reduction is exemplified by the giving up of a prominent place in musical space" (218). Later, in his discussion of the "agonic"—after describing an example in which "the space of F major" is eventually "victorious" in its "contest" with the "space" of B♭—he says: "Where there is a victory, there is also a defeat: nothing is acquired without a simultaneous loss" (241). This is followed by an example in which Clifton focuses on the "dissolution and ultimate defeat" of C♯ minor by F♯ minor! Here, the metaphor of status-reduction, which might have applied to this same example, seems to have been forgotten and simply replaced by another metaphor, equally relevant or irrelevant according to one's taste. Although either of these metaphors is perhaps plausible, neither seems really necessary to a phenomenological description of the music, and certainly neither seems deserving of being called a musical essence. These various forms of play, in fact, correspond much more closely to what Clifton has called "induced constructs" than to true phenomenological essences: "The difference between an intuited essence and an induced construct is that the former finds universality within the givenness of a particular situation, while the latter finds it in an intellectual scheme or model imposed *onto* discrete particulars" (49). I would add that, while analogies and metaphors may often seem unavoidable in an effort to describe our intuitive responses to music, they must always be used with the utmost caution and with a sustained awareness of their origins. Otherwise, the results are almost bound to become what Clifton himself has called "poetic ramblings."

Some interesting statements, however, are to be found even in the midst of the most problematic sections. In his discussion of "aleatoric" play, for example, Clifton notes that "we listen to aleatoric music and indeterminate music in essentially the same way we listen to any other kind of music" (237). And: "Purely in terms of the musical experience, it is a matter of supreme indifference to me how a composer went about his task. Let him engage in whatever irrational practice imaginable; if the result is a musical experience, then the result is not irrational" (238). This is an important insight of a kind that is made more accessible by the phenomenological attitude. It is a pity that more contemporary critics do not approach such music in a similar way.

The last of Clifton's "Essential Backgrounds of Experience"—feeling and understanding—is the very heart of his thesis, and it is here that both the strengths and the weaknesses of his point of view emerge most clearly. The strengths include his insistence that music involves a reciprocal relation—a "collaboration"—between the sounds and the listener and his refusal to allow us to forget that "this collaboration cannot be achieved without the necessary constitutive activities of feeling and understanding" (74). As for the weaknesses, we are brought face to face with a profound difficulty with the phenomenological method itself, even when it is followed faithfully. The irony here is that Clifton was clearly aware of its dangers: "By eliminating the critical attitude, we run the risk of submerging our own feelings and confusing the expression in the music with the spontaneity of our own responses" (75). But now if we compare this with one of his earliest discussions of this aspect of the musical experience, we see how perilously close Clifton himself can come to the same point of confusion: "As listeners, what counts as lived musical experiences are such intuited essences as the grace of a minuet by Mozart, the drama of a symphony by Mahler, or the agony of Coltrane's jazz. If we hear the music at all, it is because we hear the grace, the drama, and the agony as essential constituents of, and irreducibly given in, the music itself" (19). One need not take issue with the contention that there is an essential component of feeling involved in the musical experience, or that there is a great variety of such feelings, or even that this way of talking about music is useful. The point, rather, is that in thus naming these feelings we are not in any way identifying an "essential constituent" of a given piece of music, much less describing that music itself (even "as heard"). We are simply projecting—onto the object of our description—some condition that properly belongs to ourselves.

In his final chapter ("The Stratum of Feeling") Clifton tackles this problem again, this time with at least partial success: "Let it be granted that music does not literally contain feeling, emotions, or for that matter, motion or tonality. But when we say that Tamino's first aria in *The Magic Flute* . . . is 'tender and dignified,' these terms are not metaphorically in the music either; and when we say that it is 'tonal,' is it literally or metaphorically tonal?" (281). Then, "to say that all these expressions are metaphorical is still to assume that *there is something in the melody which at least corresponds to the choice of metaphor*, something which the melody 'has,' once and for all" (282, emphasis added). Here again I would add, however, that while it *may* not be the task of the phenomenologist to investigate these correspondences any further (and I am not at all convinced that this is true), it is certainly the task of the music theorist to do this. Calling Tamino's aria "tender" or "tonal" may be an important part of the process of describing this music, but we still need to know what the objective correlates of "tenderness" and "tonality" might be.

Earlier in his book, Clifton describes music theory as "not an inventory of prescriptions or a corpus of systems, but rather, an act: the act of questioning our assumptions about the nature of music and the nature of man perceiving music." He continues: "If we go back to the root meaning of theory—to be a spectator, to observe—then phenomenological reflection is seen not only to lie within the scope of music theory, but to provide it with its foundation" (37). Clifton has, indeed, both questioned our assumptions and argued forcefully for phenomenological reflection as a necessary foundation for any viable music theory. But "the theoretical act will consist not only of observing the music, but also of observing the self observing the music. If music theory wishes to be objective, it can do no better than to ground objectivity in the act of experiencing, and to attempt (at some risk, to be sure) to reveal the geometry of experience" (37).

By his own definition, then, Clifton has done precisely what a music theorist should be doing. But the definition is clearly incomplete. It defines merely a necessary first stage of the theoretical act, and this first stage needs to be followed by others that involve the careful investigation of the correspondences between the music and the observing self. If it is fair to say that current music theory is lacking in this necessary grounding in experience, then it must also be said that although what Clifton offers us here may be a view of the foundation itself, he has not yet revealed "the geometry of experience." What he *has* achieved, however—in spite of the reservations expressed in this review—is a significant contribution toward such a foundation and thus to a new kind of music theory that might be built upon that foundation.

CHAPTER 15

About *Changes: Sixty-Four Studies for Six Harps* (1987)

A. Introduction

My intentions in this work were both exploratory and didactic. That is, I wanted to investigate the new harmonic resources that have become available through the concept of "harmonic space" much more thoroughly than I had in any earlier work. At the same time I wanted to explore these harmonic resources within a formal context that would clearly demonstrate certain theoretical ideas and compositional methods already developed in my computer music of the early 1960s, including the use of stochastic (or constrained-random) processes applied to several holarchical perceptual levels, both monophonically and polyphonically. The references to the *I Ching*, or *Book of Changes*, in the titles of the individual studies derive from correlations that were made partly for poetic/philosophical reasons but also—and perhaps more importantly—as a means of ensuring that all possible combinations of parametric states would be included in the work as a whole. I must confess that I frequently thought of the twenty-four preludes and fugues of J. S. Bach's *Well-Tempered Clavier* as a kind of model for what I wanted to do with the work, although it seems highly unlikely that these studies themselves will ever betray that fact to a listener. A large mainframe computer was used in the composition process to generate coded numerical output, which was then transcribed into standard musical notation. Two separate FORTRAN IV programs were involved, the first dealing with characteristics of the set of sixty-four studies as a whole, the second determining the details of each individual study.

B. General Features

The harps are tuned a sixth of a semitone (16.66 ... ¢) apart, so the ensemble is capable of producing a tempered microtonal set of seventy-two pitches in each octave. This tuning system (which I call the 72-set) provides very good approximations of most of the important just intervals within the 11-limit, with the worst case being the three-cent error for the 5/4 major third (383¢ instead of 386¢). The relations between some of these just intervals and their nearest approximations in the 72-set are shown in table 1 (where interval sizes are rounded off to the nearest cent).

Each of the studies is correlated with (and named after) one of the sixty-four hexagrams in the *I Ching*. This correlation is based on the configuration of adjacent digrams in the hexagram, as follows: of the three disjunct digrams in each hexagram, the lower one is associated with pitch, the middle one with temporal density, and the upper one with

TABLE 1. A comparison of some important just intervals with their approximations in the 72-set.

ratio	size	pc number in 72-set	size	error
8/7	231¢	14	233¢	+2¢
7/6	267¢	16	267¢	±0¢
6/5	316¢	19	317¢	+1¢
11/9	347¢	21	350¢	+3¢
5/4	386¢	23	383¢	−3¢
9/7	435¢	26	433¢	−2¢
4/3	498¢	30	500¢	+2¢
11/8	551¢	33	550¢	−1¢
7/5	583¢	35	583¢	±0¢

(etc.—larger intervals which are octave-complements of these have the same absolute values for error)

dynamic level. Each digram may take one of four different forms, and each of these is interpreted to mean one of four possible "states" in a parameter—low (⚎), medium (⚏), high (⚍), and full (⚌). Thus, for example, the hexagram associated with the fifth study is number 59 ("Dispersion"), which has the following form:

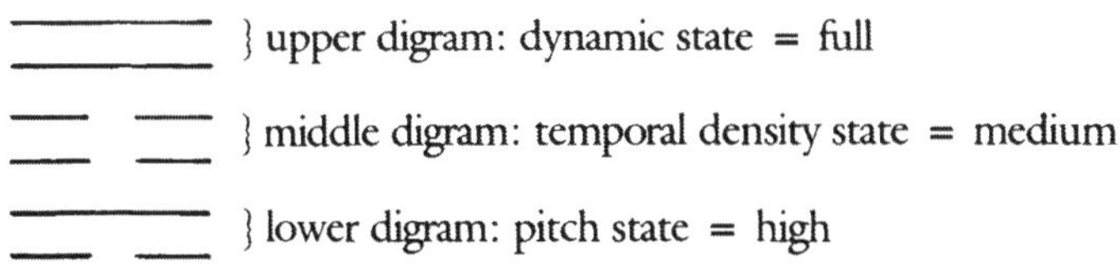

Relative means and ranges corresponding to the four different states are shown in example 1.

Actually, the parametric states of each study are determined by *two* hexagrams—the first one (for which the study is named) corresponding to the parametric states at the beginning of the study, the second to those at the end. Where these terminal states differ in a given parameter, a gradual transition from one to the other is produced by the program using a half-cosine interpolation function. At lower holarchical levels, linear interpolation is also used for such changes of state during the course of a temporal gestalt-unit (or TG). In both cases, two mean-values are used

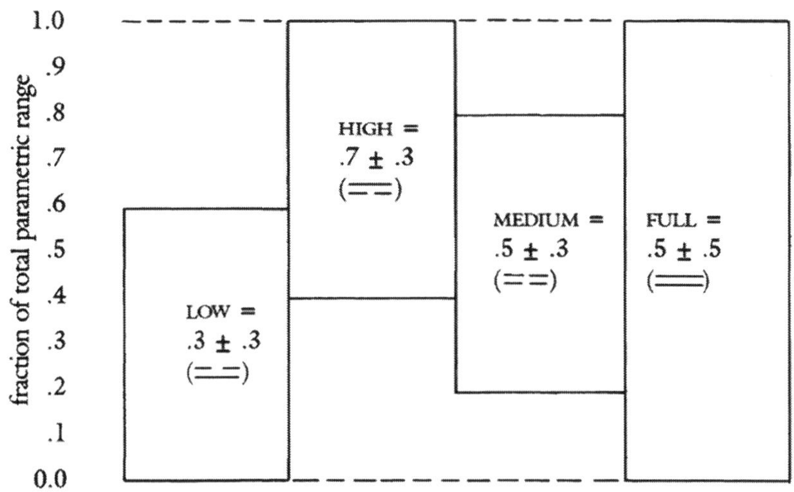

EXAMPLE 1. Relative means and ranges corresponding to the four digram states.

for each TG, an initial one and a final one, and these terminal values are connected by the interpolation function. For this purpose, the following formulae are used:

linear interpolation:

$$v_t = v_1 + (v_2 - v_1) * (t - t_1)/(t_2 - t_1),$$

half-cosine interpolation:

$$v_t = \frac{v_1 + v_2}{2} + \frac{v_1 - v_2}{2}\cos\left(\pi * \frac{t - t_1}{t_2 - t_1}\right),$$

where v_t is the value in the parameter at time t, v_1 the initial value (at time t_1), and v_2 the final value (at time t_2).

The first program generates two nonrepeating random sequences of hexagram numbers, one for initial states, the other for final states, so every possible combination of parametric states occurs once at the beginning of one of the studies and once at the end of (usually) a different one. "Changing lines" for the initial hexagram are then inferred such as would effect its transformation into the final hexagram. Because of this indirect way of deriving changing lines, they occur more often than they do when the *I Ching* hexagrams are obtained in the traditional ways, where the probability of a changing line is one in four, or 25%; here, approximately 50% of the lines are changing.

On the basis of the initial and final parametric states of each study, the first program also determines (1) whether it is to be monophonic or polyphonic and then (2) the average vertical density of its elements, (3) the overall duration of the study, (4) its average clang-duration, and (5) the initial and final tonic locations for the study, as described more fully below. To determine whether a study was to be monophonic or polyphonic, it was first considered *potentially* polyphonic if at least one parameter was in the "full" state either at the beginning or at the end. When this was the case, a weighted random decision was made, with the weighting adjusted in such a way that approximately half of the sixty-four studies would be polyphonic, the other half monophonic.

Both temporal density and vertical density vary exponentially in the studies—i.e., the probable distribution of values in these two parameters will be uniform on a logarithmic scale. Thus, for example, the average temporal density mTd of a TG will be computed as mTd = 2^{mS}, where S is the stochastically controlled variable and *mS* its average value. Similarly for vertical density: mVd = 2^{mZ}. But while the mean values for temporal density depend directly on input data, those for vertical density are determined by a formula that relates them to pitch range, average temporal density, and the number of polyphonic strata, as follows:

$$mZ = .5 + \left(1 - \sqrt{mS/1.6}\right) * \sqrt{nP/195} \, / \sqrt{Nst}$$

where *mS* is the average value of the temporal density exponent and 1.6 is the maximum value it can have in any study; *nP* is one-half of the number of pitches in the range (always ≤195); and *Nst* is the number of polyphonic strata in the study (either 1 or 2). The average vertical density of any study thus varies directly with the pitch-range and inversely with the average temporal density and the number of strata.

The total duration of each study varies directly with the average "volume" of the three-dimensional space outlined by the ranges in the three basic parameters (pitch, temporal density, and dynamic level) and inversely with the average density of events within this space. This volume is proportional to the product of the average ranges in the three parameters and the "density of events" to the product of (average) temporal density, vertical density, and the number of strata, as:

$$\text{Dur} \propto \frac{\text{Volume}}{\text{Density}} = \frac{nP * nS * nL}{mTd * mVd * Nst}$$

where all variables (except *Nst*) are arithmetic averages of the corresponding variables in the initial and final states of the study. The results of this computation are later rescaled to yield a minimum duration of 1'20" and a maximum of 2'40", so the average duration for the studies in the set is about two minutes.

Each study is organized into TGs at two holarchical levels between those of individual elements and the study as a whole—clangs and segments. Here I have deliberately avoided TG-articulations at both the sequence- and section-levels, in an effort to enhance the sense of continuity and the perceptibility of contour at the segment-level and over the whole study. The average clang-durations in individual studies were made to depend (inversely) on their average densities (as defined above) and scaled to yield a minimum duration of $2.4/\sqrt{2} = 1.697$ and a maximum duration of $2.4*\sqrt{2} = 3.394$ seconds.

The harmonic organization of the studies will be described in more detail later, but a brief summary here may help clarify certain other operations carried out by this first of the two programs. The pitch classes (PCs) available within a given clang constitute a "mode" of (usually) seven different PCs, one of which is treated as a local or temporary tonic or root. In monophonic studies, a new root and a new mode are chosen for each new clang. In polyphonic studies—whose clang-boundaries are not, in general, synchronous—a new root and mode are chosen whenever the starting time of a new clang in one stratum is later than halfway through the duration of the concurrent clang in the other stratum, so PCs in the two strata are drawn from the same set more than half of the time. In both monophonic and polyphonic studies, the series of root-progressions is controlled in such a way that each study ends with a dominant-to-tonic "cadence" on the same root (the "global tonic") with which it began. Initial tonic PCs are ordered in a way that distributes the seventy-two PCs given by the tuning system over the sixty-four studies as uniformly as possible by simply omitting every ninth PC in the series from 0 to 71. The final tonic location is determined in a way that will be explained later.

The output of this first program consists of sixty-four blocks of data, each of which is used as input to the second program to generate the details of one of the studies. Each block includes the following data: the numbers of the hexagrams defining initial and final parametric states for the study; its total duration and average clang-duration; its initial tonic PC and the number of unit steps (in harmonic space) to the dominant of the "target tonic"; the number of polyphonic strata; and the initial and final mean values and ranges for pitch, temporal density, dynamic level, and vertical density.

C. Individual Studies

In generating the output data for an individual study, the second program works "from the top down." That is, it first determines the duration and other parametric state values for the first segment, then for the first clang in that segment, and then for successive elements in that clang. When all the elements in the first clang have been generated, it determines the state values for the second clang and for its elements. After the last element of the last clang in this first segment has been generated, the program proceeds to the second segment, its first clang and the latter's successive elements, and so on. In the case of polyphonic studies, these operations are carried out "in parallel" in such a way that successive elements' parametric values are generated alternately from the two polyphonic strata. This was necessary to maintain harmonic coherence between the two strata, since pitches in the two strata were to be drawn from the same set of available pitch classes at any given moment whenever this was possible.

The number of segments in a study is approximately equal to the average number of clangs in a segment, and the average segment-duration approximates the geometric mean of clang- and study-durations, although individual segment durations vary randomly within a range of ±25% of this average duration. For each segment, an initial and final mean value in each of the other parameters—pitch, temporal density, dynamic level, and vertical density—are chosen within the available range around the current "global" mean for the study, which is determined—as explained earlier—by a half-cosine interpolation between the initial and final mean values for that parameter given by the input data for the study. Each of the terminal mean-values for the *segment* is computed as the arithmetic average of two random values, which results in a tendency toward a "triangular" frequency distribution rather than a uniform one, peaking at the current global mean and decreasing linearly toward the upper and lower boundaries of the current range in that parameter. This was done to lower the probability of extreme mean values at the segment level, which would have resulted in overly narrow ranges at the clang level.

The average clang-duration for each study is given in the input data for that study, but—as with segment-durations—the durations of individual clangs were made to vary randomly within a range of ±25% around the average value. Parametric means for each clang are chosen within segment-means in relation to the current mean of the segment—as with segment-means in relation to the current global mean of the study—except that here (a) the current segment-mean is determined by linear (rather than half-cosine) interpolation between the terminal values, (b) only a single value in the parameter is used for a clang (i.e., its parametric mean will be constant throughout the clang), (c) this value is determined by a single random number (so the frequency distribution of clang-means would tend to be uniform), and (d) the clang-mean for temporal density is made equal to the current segment-mean itself, rather than being allowed to vary randomly around that mean, in order to ensure a sufficient range of element-durations within each clang.

In all of my earlier stochastic music, the articulation of successive TGs was effected via the "similarity factor" only—involving differences in mean-values in various parameters. In an effort to incorporate the "proximity factor" as well, in the articulation of successive clangs, a new procedure was used here that interposes a *delay* before the beginning of each new clang (effectively prolonging the duration of the final element in the preceding clang) according to the following formula:

$$\text{Delay} = (\text{Dmax} - \text{Dur}) * (1 - \text{Pdst}/\text{Pdmx}),$$

where Dur is the element-duration, Dmax the maximum element-duration possible in that clang, Pdst the pitch-distance between the two clang-means, and Pdmx the largest value this can have. The magnitude of the delay is thus determined by the relative distance between the pitch-means of the two clangs and by the difference between the duration of the last element in the first clang and the maximum element-duration allowed for that clang (given its temporal density mean and range). The smaller the distance between the pitch-means of the two clangs (relative to the maximum value it could have, given the available range of clang pitch-means within the segment at that moment), the longer the delay is likely to be. Thus, for example, if the distance between the pitch-means of the two clangs happens to be zero (i.e., if the two clangs have the same pitch-mean, which could occur, although it's not very likely), the amount of the delay will be such that the (modified) duration of the last element in the first clang will be equal to the maximum element-duration in that clang. If, on the other hand, this distance happens to be at maximum, the delay will be zero, and the duration of that last element will remain unmodified.

The hierarchical (or holarchical), recursive character of the program, already described for segments and clangs, continues at the element-level, although element-durations are generated more simply than were clang- and segment-durations (as the reciprocal of a temporal density value for the element), and element dynamic levels are made equal to the clang-mean in that parameter (so dynamic levels remain constant throughout a clang). The value derived at this level for vertical density—truncated to the next-lower integer—determines the number of pitches in the element. As with clangs and segments, parametric values (other than dynamics) for an element are drawn from the available range around the clang-mean, but for the pitch-parameter, other, specifically harmonic procedures intervene here to determine a set of available pitch *classes* (or PCs) before the actual pitches are selected. These procedures will be described in the section that follows.

D. Harmonic Procedures

My intentions in this work with respect to harmony included the following:

1. that one of the PCs in every clang should function as a temporary tonic or root in relation to all the other PCs in that clang—which latter are interpreted as a kind of temporary "mode" for that clang;
2. that the root PC would change from clang to clang by means of a root-progression chosen stochastically from a set of possible root-progressions with preset relative probabilities assigned to them;
3. that the PCs in a mode should tend to form relatively compact sets in harmonic space in relation both to the other PCs in that clang and to those in the previous clang; and finally
4. that the "random walk" character of the series of root-progressions should gradually be "focused" in such a way that each study would end with a dominant-to-tonic progression to the same root PC with which it began—and in the same mode.

To achieve these intentions required a careful analysis of the 72-set and its several possible mappings in harmonic space. For example, the PCs in the 72-set can be mapped in pitch-class projection spaces of 2, 3, or 4 (or more!) dimensions, according to the prime-limit being considered. For *Changes*, I decided to assume an 11-limit (five-dimensional) harmonic space for the modes and a 7-limit (four-dimensional) harmonic space for root-progressions and to locate the final "target tonic" on the same 3,5-plane as the initial tonic (which implies a 5-limit, three-dimensional space for this relation between initial and final tonic locations). Examples 2 and 3 show some of these mappings of the PCs in the 72-set in pitch-class projection spaces of two and three dimensions (corresponding to prime-limits of 5 and 7, respectively). Note that, because the 72-set is an equal-tempered system, its lattice structure is *periodic* in harmonic space (no matter what the dimensionality may be of that space into which it is mapped). That is, it repeats itself endlessly in all directions. It was decided to use as the target tonic in each of these studies one of the many locations of that tonic in the 3,5-plane in a direction (in relation to the initial tonic) similar to the direction in which Bach's harmonic progressions tend to move in a mapping of the 12-set in harmonic space—i.e., toward the left along the 3-axis (via descending fifths, e.g., V–I) and upward along the 5-axis (less quickly, and mostly via the descending minor third progression, e.g., I–vi). Example 4 shows the configuration of recurring tonics (in relation to an initial 1/1 or "0") in an abbreviated but extended mapping on the 3,5-plane. The location used for each study was one of the three indicated by the arrows, which one of the three depending on the estimated number of clangs (and thus, the number of root-progressions) in that study. The numbers in parentheses give the number of unit steps along the 3- and 5-axes, respectively, from the initial to the final tonic location.

Each of the sixty-four studies begins (and thus ends) on a different tonic PC, and these form an ascending integer series, beginning with 0 (E↡—read: "three-sixths of a semitone below E") for study no. 1 and ending with 71 (D♯/E♭↟) for study no. 64, skipping every ninth PC in the series. The other PCs of the mode associated with a root are chosen from a set of alternatives—for each of six "scale degrees" (in addition to the tonic)—given as input data to the program (but common to all sixty-four studies). These are arranged in "stacked thirds" order (prime, third, fifth, seventh, ninth, eleventh, thirteenth), and they include from three to five alternatives for each degree above the tonic. These are listed in table 2, which gives both the PC number in the 72-set and the just ratio or ratios most closely approximated by that PC (in parentheses). The most important harmonic relationships among these various alternatives are shown in example 5, representing their locations in harmonic space (or, more precisely, in a pitch-class projection space essentially in 7-limit form, but with the additional ratios of 11 interposed along the 3-axes [and in parentheses]). The choice of a particular PC (or interval-class in relation to a given tonic PC) for each degree is determined by several conditions,

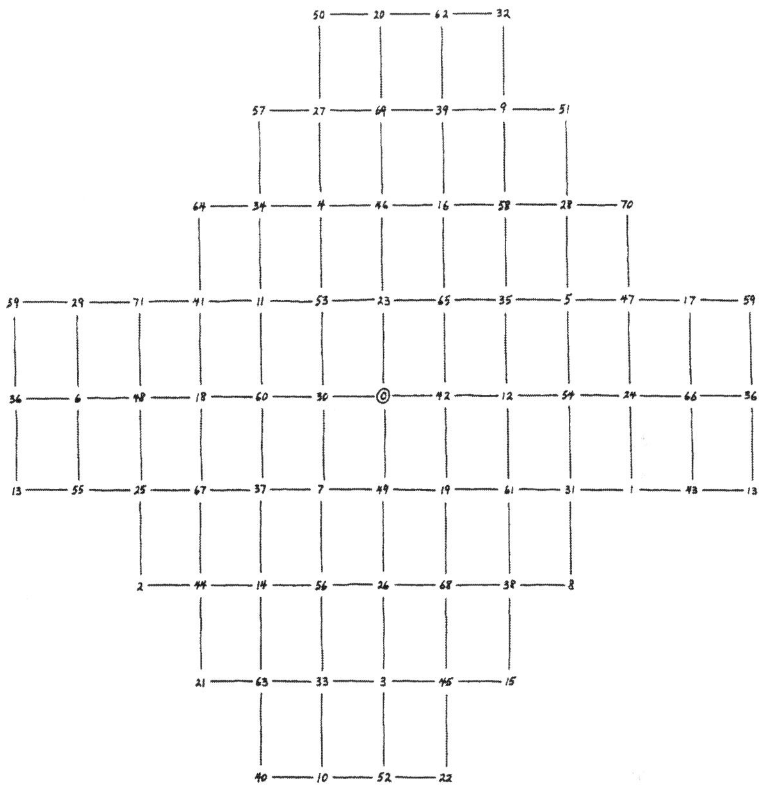

EXAMPLE 2. The 72-set in the 3,5-plane.

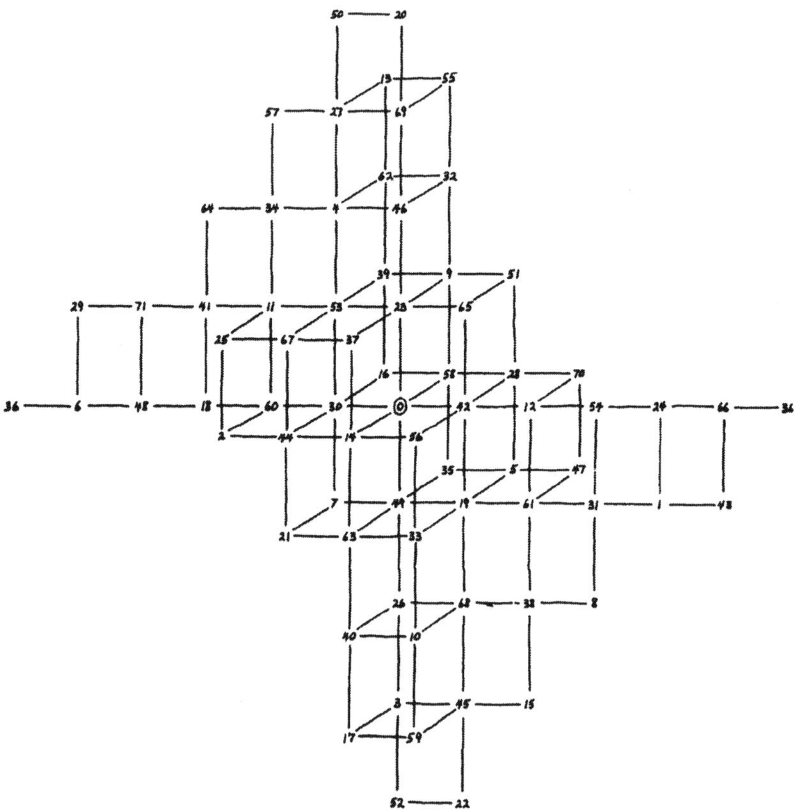

Example 3. The 72-set in 3,5,7-space.

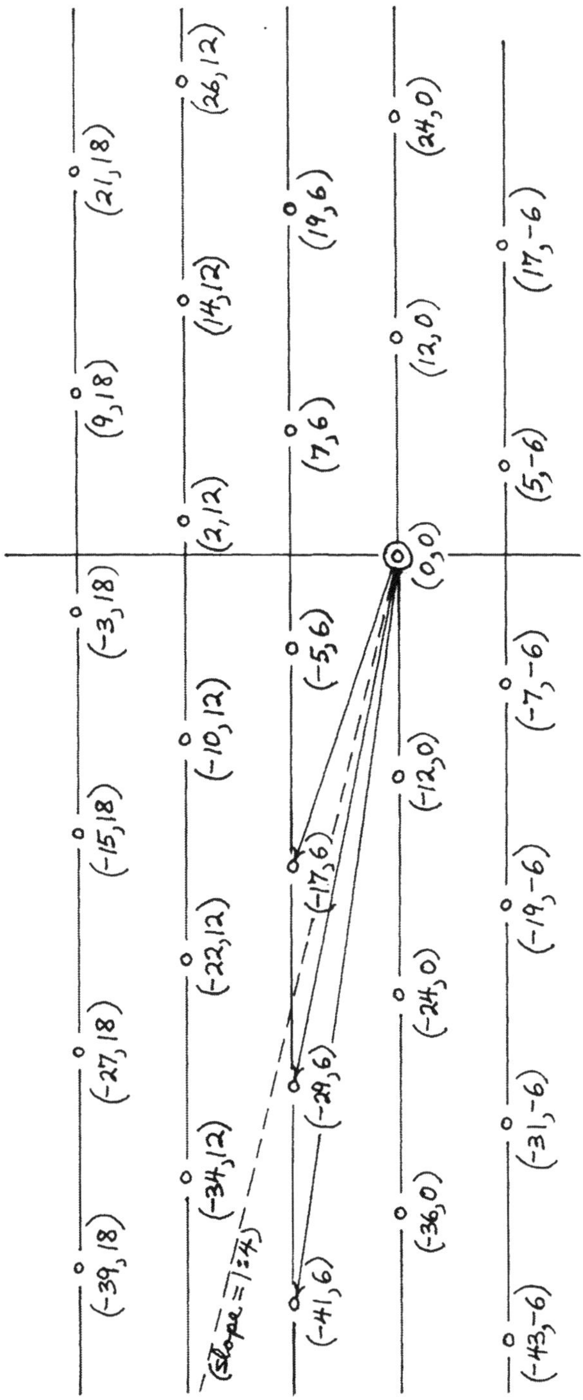

Example 4. Recurring tonics in the 3,5-plane.

some of which might be described as "rules," while others are more statistical in character. The rules include the following:

1. in the initial (and thus also the final) tonic set, the fifth is always made equal to 42 (3/2), and the seventh is allowed to equal 58 (7/4) only if the third (already chosen) equals 16 (7/6);
2. in the dominant set preceding the final ("target") tonic, the third is always equal to 23 (5/4), and the seventh is always equal to 58 (7/4);
3. the various "thirds" between adjacent degrees may vary in size only within specified ranges: from a minimum of 12 (9/8) to a maximum of 26 (9/7) between prime and third or third and fifth, a minimum of 16 (7/6 or 75/64) and a maximum of 30 (4/3) between adjacent degrees above the fifth;
4. no "mistuned fifths" are allowed between nonadjacent degrees (as between the third and seventh, fifth and ninth, etc.); i.e., any such interval must either be precisely equal to 42 (3/2) or differ from it by an interval greater than 3 (a "quarter-tone");
5. no octaves (either exact or "mistuned") are allowed between those nonadjacent degrees that share a common PC or approximate that condition too closely (as between the third and the ninth or eleventh, the fifth and the eleventh or thirteenth); i.e., no "seventh" larger than 68 is allowed, and no "ninth" smaller than 4. Thus, any interval between nonadjacent degrees must differ from an octave by at least 4 (two-thirds of a semitone);
6. if the third equals 19 (6/5), the fifth must equal 42 (3/2), thus disallowing both the "flat" and "raised" fifths when the third is of the ordinary minor form;
7. the raised fifth—46 (25/16)—is only allowed when the third equals 23 (5/4).

TABLE 2. Alternative PCs for a mode.

prime: 0 (1/1)

3rds: 16 (7/6), 19 (6/5), 21 (11/9), 23 (5/4), 26 (9/7)

5ths: 35 (7/5 or 45/32), 42 (3/2), 46 (25/16)

7ths: 58 (7/4), 61 (9/5), 63 (11/6), 65 (15/8)

9ths: 5 (21/20), 7 (15/14, 16/15 or 77/72), 9 (12/11 or 35/32), 12 (9/8), 16 (7/6 or 75/64)

11ths: 28 (21/16), 33 (11/8), 35 (7/5 or 45/32)

13ths: 49 (8/5 or 77/48), 51 (18/11 or 105/64), 53 (5/3), 54 (27/16), 56 (12/7 or 55/32)

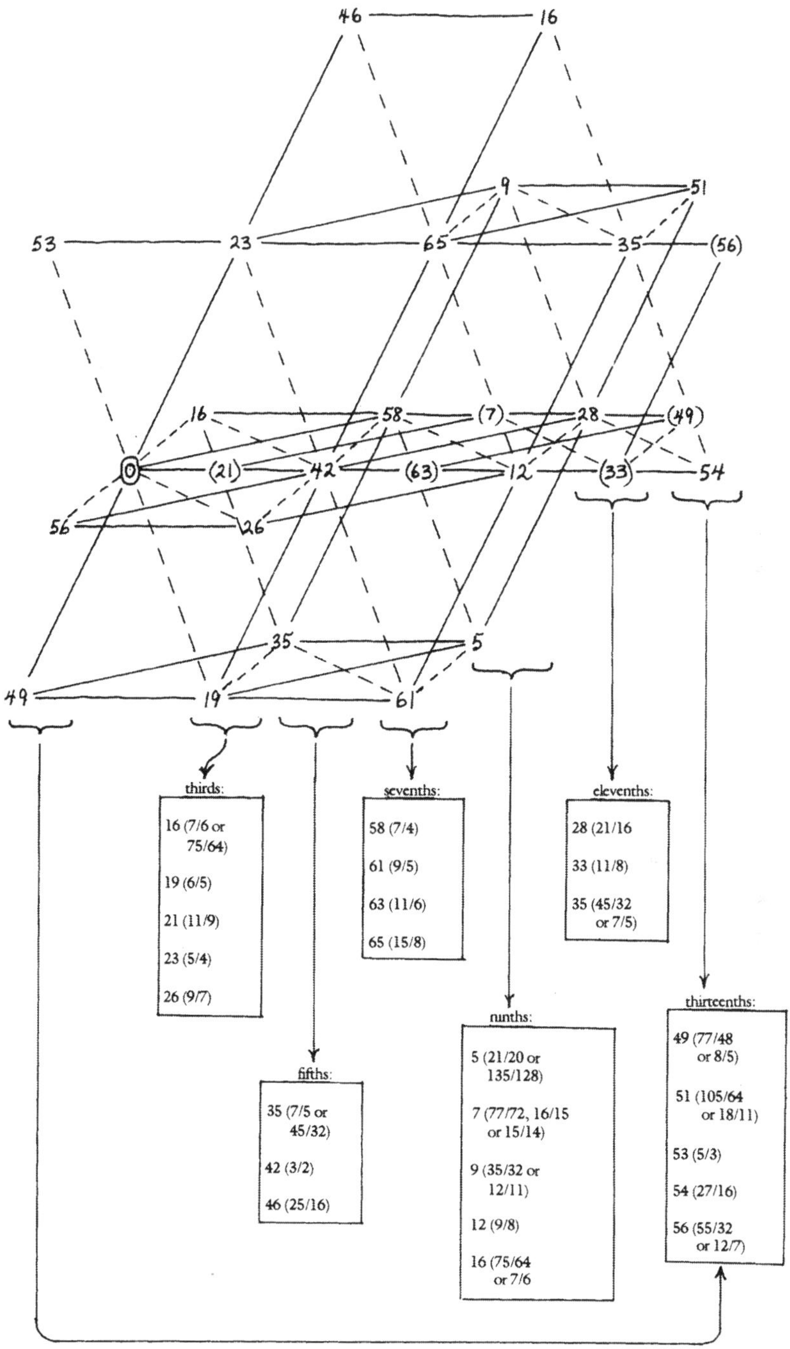

EXAMPLE 5. Harmonic relationships among alternative PCs for the modes.

Some of these rules correspond to similar rules for chord-construction in both traditional and jazz harmonic practice (and I should perhaps add here something that has not been made explicit before: the PCs of a mode are often heard simultaneously as well as successively—as "chords" as well as "melodic lines"—thus the ambivalence [which may have been noticed already] in my use of the terms "tonic" and "root"). Other rules were designed to avoid certain ambiguities and/or conflicts that might otherwise occur in the creation of these modes. Although these rules appear to be quite restrictive, a very large number of modal sets were still possible, but these were further constrained by what I have referred to (above) as "statistical" conditions, as follows:

The PCs that remain available for a given modal degree after testing against the rules just listed are assigned varying probabilities depending on the sums of their harmonic distances to PCs already chosen for that clang—and to the PCs actually occurring in the clang just preceding (I say "actually occurring" because—due to the random process involved in the selection of pitches in a clang—it is always possible that one or more of the PCs constituting the mode will not occur). The relation between these probabilities and harmonic distances varies according to the modal degree in question (the constraint is "tighter" for the higher degrees) and whether this was the first clang in the study or not (the constraint is "looser" for the first clang), but in general that relation is an *inverse* one. That is, the lower the sum of harmonic distances between a PC and the others preceding it, the higher its probability of being chosen—and vice versa. This constraint was made stronger for higher degrees of the mode (arranged in "stacked thirds" order, remember) by raising the harmonic-distance sum to a power corresponding to the "height" of the degree, as follows:

$$\Pr(j) \propto 1/\mathrm{Hdsm}(j)^{n+k-1},$$

where $\Pr(j)$ is the relative probability of the jth PC in the set of still-available PCs for that degree, $\mathrm{Hdsm}(j)$ equals the sum of that PC's harmonic distances to preceding PCs, n is the order-number for the modal degree (i.e., $n = 2$ for the third, 3 for the fifth, 4 for the seventh, etc.), and $k = 1$ for the first clang and 2 for all later clangs. The result of all this is that there will be a tendency for PCs to form relatively *compact sets* in harmonic space, with this tendency becoming stronger for higher modal degrees—and conversely, so there is more freedom for random variation in the lower degrees.

It might be noted that the sets of alternative PCs for modal degrees yield seven different kinds of triads, only four of which are familiar in traditional Western harmony (numbers 2, 4, 6, and 7 below):

1. septimal minor	0 (1/1),	16 (7/6),	42 (3/2)
2. 5-limit minor	"	19 (6/5)	"
3. 11-limit "neutral"	"	21 (11/9)	"
4. 5-limit major	"	23 (5/4)	"
5. septimal major	"	26 (9/7)	"
6. augmented	"	23 (5/4),	46 (25/16)
7. diminished	"	16 (7/6),	35 (7/5)

Another possible form of the diminished triad—0 (1/1), 19 (6/5), 35 (7/5)—was avoided because the most likely seventh degree with such a triad would have been 65 (15/8), and the perfect fourth—30 (4/3)—that this forms with 35 would have introduced an unwanted ambiguity with respect to the root. The sets of alternative PCs for scale degrees were designed to avoid PCs that might compete with the nominal root, and the perfect fifth and fourth—and even the (5-limit) major third and minor sixth, though less strongly—have very clear root-defining effects. Thus, the perfect fourth itself—30 (4/3)—was not included as a possible eleventh in a mode, and 49 (8/5 or 77/48) was only included as a possible thirteenth because of its dual character—and harmonic distance values for this interval were set to correspond to its interpretation as 77/48 rather than 8/5. The same thing was done for the interval formed by PC 26 (9/7) to avoid its interpretation as 32/25, which—because of the way in which I calculated harmonic distances (for an explanation of which, see below)—would have given it more prominence than I thought it should have.

The seventh-chords that can arise by way of this procedure for constructing modes include most of the traditional ones (major, minor, dominant, half-diminished, minor-major, augmented, etc., but not the diminished seventh), plus several others that are of interest, including the one used by Ives as the primary chord in the "Choral" of his *Three Quarter-Tone Pieces*—0 (1/1), 21 (11/9), 42 (3/2), 63 (11/6). Ninth-chords include—again—all of the traditional ones, plus the blues "flat 7, sharp 9," and a very interesting group of new ones with PC 9 as the ninth of the mode. This PC—at the "quarter-tone" position between the 12-set's minor and major seconds—functions in the 72-set most frequently as the major third above the "dominant" seventh; i.e., it can be analyzed as 58 (7/4) + 23 (5/4) = 81 (mod 72) = 9 (35/32). The fact that it occurs in a "dominant"-type PC set more often than the more familiar minor or major ninth is suggestive: perhaps the latter are merely the best approximations available in the 12-set for this interval! Finally, the eleventh-chords include a good approximation of Partch's "otonality hexad": 0 (1/1 ± 0¢), 23 (5/4 – 3¢), 42 (3/2 – 2¢), 58 (7/4 – 2¢), 12 (9/8 – 4¢), and 33 (11/8 – 1¢).

The basic formula for the harmonic distance between any two pitches is $\mathrm{Hd}(a/b) = k\log_x(ab)$, where a/b is the frequency ratio representing the interval (in its maximally reduced, "relative prime" form), and k simply determines the unit of measurement (with base-2 logarithms, if $k = 1$, Hd is in "octaves"). The form used in this program, however, is a bit different in two respects. First, it is a measure of the harmonic distance between pitch-classes rather than actual pitches. Second, since we are dealing here with a tempered system, a *tolerance* rule is invoked, which essentially says that we can assume the *simplest* integer ratio within the tolerance range around the tempered pitch to be the harmonically effective one (that tolerance range is here taken to be ± one-half the size of the smallest step in the tuning system—i.e., ± 1/144 of an octave or 8.33 ... ¢). The first qualification means that we are concerned with a distance not between points in the full, n-dimensional harmonic space itself but rather between points in the $(n - 1)$-dimensional "pitch-class projection space." This, in turn, means that the formula for harmonic distance must be replaced by another of the form $\mathrm{Hd}(a'/b') = k \log_2(a'b')$, where $a' = a/2^i$, $b' = b/2^j$, and i and j are the largest integer exponents which yield integer values of a' and b'. The second qualification means that where there are two or more relatively simple integer ratios defining intervals within the tolerance range of a PC, the one whose ratio-terms' product is smallest determines the harmonic distance value assigned to that PC. It has already been mentioned that two exceptions were made to this procedure involving PCs 26 and 49. Pitch-class 26 (433¢) approximates both 32/25 (427¢) and 9/7 (435¢), while PC 49 (817¢) approximates 8/5 (814¢), 77/48 (818¢), and 45/28 (821¢). While I wanted both of these PCs to be included among the available alternatives (for thirds and thirteenths, respectively), I wanted 26 to be treated as a 9/7 and 49 as a 77/48, so their minimal harmonic distance values were overridden in another part of the program with the higher values. (I see now, in studying the program again, that the value I assigned to 49 was that of 45/28 rather than 77/48—i.e., $\log_2(315) = 8.30$ rather than $\log_2(231) = 7.85$—but fortunately this error turned out to be a small one, with a scarcely noticeable effect on the final results.)

Once the PCs of the mode for a clang have been chosen, the program is almost ready to proceed to the selection of actual pitches within the range already determined for that clang. As at all higher levels, this involves a random process, but at this level the process is further constrained by two kinds of probability distributions, one providing some control over the rate of recurrence of each pitch, the other correlating modal degree with register. The probability of a given pitch being chosen by the random process at any moment was computed as the product of two probability "factors" stored in a two-dimensional array called PPR(N, L), where $N = 1$ or 2, and L is an index for pitch ($L = 1$ for the lowest pitch in the harps' range, $L = 452$ for the highest). For all values of L, PPR(1, L) was initialized at 1, so all pitches began with the same relative probabilities. Just after a pitch is chosen for an element, PPR(1, L) for that pitch is reduced to a very small value and then increased step by step, with the generation of each succeeding element (at any *other* pitch) until it is again equal to 1. The result of this procedure is that the immediate recurrence of a given pitch is made highly unlikely (although not impossible, especially in long and/or dense clangs and in a polyphonic texture), with the probability of recurrence of that pitch gradually increasing over the next several elements until it is equal to what it would have been if it had not already occurred. The other probability factor—PPR(2, L)—is used to effect a correlation between modal degree and register, as shown graphically in example 6. Note that while the root or tonic of the mode has an equal probability of occurring anywhere within the pitch-range of the clang—and all other modal degrees are equally likely at the upper boundary of the clang's pitch-range—the higher modal degrees have low probabilities of occurring in the lower regions of the clang range (and conversely for the lower modal degrees).

Finally, values are determined for the starting-time (or epoch), duration, pitch(es), and dynamic level of each element in the clang. Element-duration is computed as the reciprocal of a temporal density value for that element, and the epoch is given by the sum of epoch and duration values

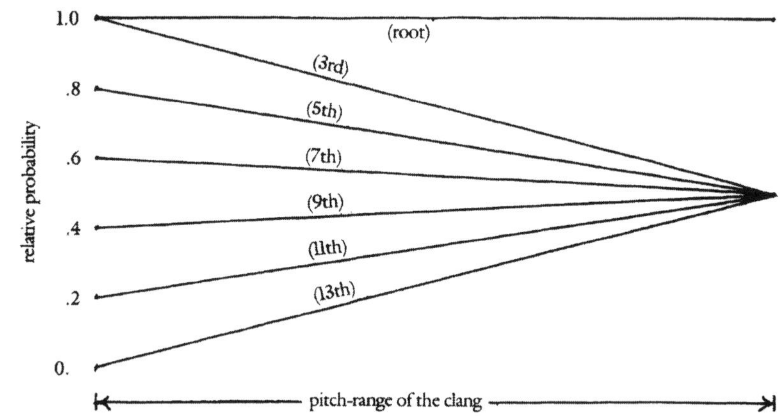

EXAMPLE 6. Correlation of modal degree with register.

for the previous element in the stratum (plus the "delay" described earlier, when the element is the first in a new clang). These time values were initially calculated on a virtually continuous scale—as in *Bridge*—but (unlike *Bridge*) I decided in this work to quantize or "rationalize" these values so they could be represented in the standard metrical rhythmic notation in the score and parts. This was done as follows: for the epoch of each element, the program computes (and prints out with the other parametric values for that element) the absolute differences between the initially calculated value and both the nearest sixteenth note and the nearest triplet eighth note. It is then left up to the person transcribing the numerical output data into musical notation to decide which of the two rational approximations to use, based on the magnitude of the "error" involved and on the epochs and errors for any other elements that may begin within the same quarter note (since the two divisions of the quarter—by 3 and by 4—cannot generally be mixed within a given quarter in our standard system of rhythmic notation). Example 7 shows an example of a page of output data, with the values for a single element boxed and the "error" values just described shown [boxed inside].

When the ending-time of an element equals or exceeds a predetermined ending-time for the clang, the program computes a new root PC for the next clang and a new mode for that clang. The interval-class (IC) between this new root and the root of the previous clang thus defines a root-progression and is determined as follows: an array is used to store an initial set of relative probabilities for allowable root-progressions (these

```
STUDY #25, HEXAGRAMS 54 AND  8; DURATION=  86.56 SECONDS DPR=, 1.875
     231.0 195.0    1.6  1.2    4.0  1.8    0.500  0.500
     231.0 117.0    0.8  1.2    2.8  1.8    0.660  0.660
     IRT= 27  MX= -16  NCP= 41  NST=  2 RANDOM SEED=  1989965660

  INITIAL ROOT-                 0 .00  30 .30  60 .01  11 .05  53 .11  16 .04  58 .02  23 .03  65 .10
  PROGRESSION PROBABILITIES:           42 .10  12 .05  61 .01  15 .01  56 .02  14 .04  49 .10   7 .01

-0.230   0.160   0.000  -0.580   0.350  -0.130   0.290  -0.060   0.060

SEGMENT  1            0.00   12.08   12.08
108.37  72.37     1.53  1.13  4.82  0.98  0.77  0.23
238.33 163.99     0.95  0.58  3.98  1.76  0.49  0.49

                        0          27  53  69  16  39  62   9     -16   6  0       41
                                    0  26  42  61  12  35  54

CLANG  1    0.00     0.30     1.53    1.53
    122.88 112.61    1.46  1.09  3.89  0.17  0.54  0.05

 1: ST=  0.00, DR= 0.63, ET=  0.63,          CMS= 0.3
      0.2.1  0.0.0  0.0.0  0.0.0  0.0.0  0.0.0  0.0.0
         53      0      0      0      0      0      0
      M= 1, Q= 1,    0/3.000    0/4.000        DYN: 3

                                                            SEGMENT  1    0.45   12.22   12.68
                                                            196.51 160.511.62  1.18  4.45  1.35  0.44  0.44
                                                            361.99  59.952.46  0.30  3.80  1.67  0.88  0.14

                                                            CLANG  1     0.00     0.45     1.72    2.18
                                                               268.21 129.79   1.68  1.12  3.42  0.40  0.45  0.39

                                                             1: ST=  0.45, DR= 0.27, ET=  0.72,          CMS= 0.9
                                                                  8.5.3  0.0.0  0.0.0  0.0.0  0.0.0  0.0.0  0.0.0
                                                                     27      0      0      0      0      0      0
                                                                  M= 1, Q=1,    1/3.120    2/4.047        DYN: 3

+-----------------------------------------------------------+
| 2: ST=  0.63, DR= 0.33, ET=  0.97,          CMS= 1.2      |
|      3.3.3  0.0.0  0.0.0  0.0.0  0.0.0  0.0.0  0.0.0      |
|         69      0      0      0      0      0      0      |
|      M= 1, Q= 1,  [2/3.033]  [3/4.116]       DYN: 3      |
+-----------------------------------------------------------+

                                                             2: ST=  0.72, DR= 0.35, ET=  1.08,          CMS= 1.4
                                                                  6.6.2  0.0.0  0.0.0  0.0.0  0.0.0  0.0.0  0.0.0
                                                                     16      0      0      0      0      0      0
                                                                  M= 1, Q=1,    2/3.056    3/4.027        DYN: 3

 3: ST=  0.97, DR= 0.25, ET=  1.22,          CMS= 1.8
      8.3.3  0.0.0  0.0.0  0.0.0  0.0.0  0.0.0  0.0.0
         27      0      0      0      0      0      0
      M= 1, Q= 2,    0/3.032    0/4.032        DYN: 3

                                                             3: ST=  1.08, DR= 0.40, ET=  1.48,          CMS= 2.0
                                                                  5.4.3  0.0.0  0.0.0  0.0.0  0.0.0  0.0.0  0.0.0
                                                                      9      0      0      0      0      0      0
                                                                  M= 1, Q=2,    0/3.075    0/4.075        DYN: 3

 4: ST=  1.22, DR= 0.25, ET=  1.47,          CMS= 2.3
      6.2.2  0.0.0  0.0.0  0.0.0  0.0.0  0.0.0  0.0.0
         16      0      0      0      0      0      0
      M= 1, Q= 2,    1/3.115    1/4.032        DYN: 3

                        0          27  53  69  16  39  62   9     -16   6  0       40
                                    0  26  42  61  12  35  54

CLANG  2    0.38     1.84     2.27    4.12
    172.54  92.33    1.41  1.02  5.36  0.43  0.58  0.15

 1: ST=  1.84, DR= 0.25, ET=  2.09,          CMS= 3.5
      6.2.3  0.0.0  0.0.0  0.0.0  0.0.0  0.0.0  0.0.0
         27      0      0      0      0      0      0
      M= 1, Q= 2,    3/3.156    3/4.094        DYN: 5

                                                             4: ST=  1.48, DR= 0.25, ET=  1.73,          CMS= 2.8
                                                                  3.5.3  0.0.0  0.0.0  0.0.0  0.0.0  0.0.0  0.0.0
                                                                     69      0      0      0      0      0      0
```

EXAMPLE 7. The first two pages of output data for study number 25.

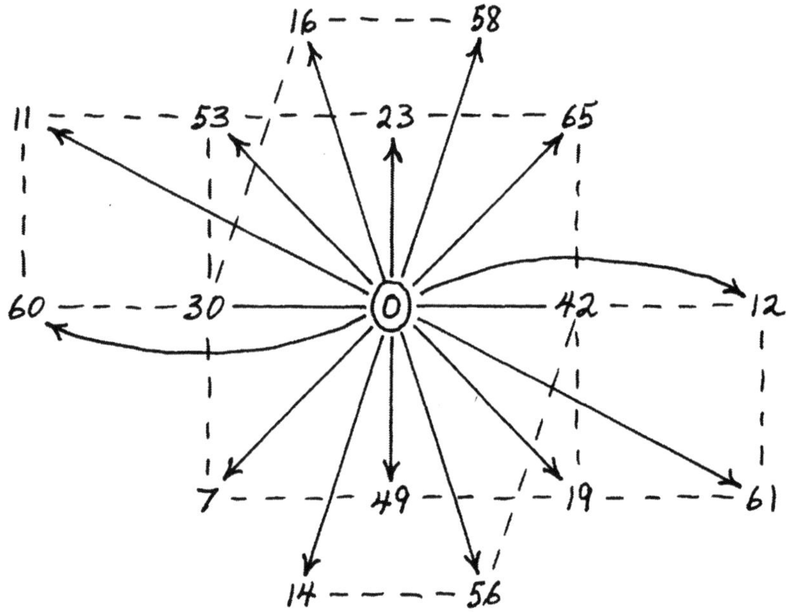

EXAMPLE 8. Available root-progressions.

probabilities are the same for all sixty-four studies), as shown graphically in example 8 and listed in table 3. This set of probabilities is conceived as determining a smaller set of six vector components in a three-dimensional harmonic space, and these, in turn, can be reduced to a single "resultant" vector that indicates the direction and average rate of root-movement through that space—assuming, of course, that a large number of such root-progressions will be involved. The result is a kind of directed "random walk" through the harmonic space.

In order to further ensure not only that this "random walk" will have—over the long run—the appropriate direction and rate in relation to the location of the "target tonic" (or rather, the dominant preceding this tonic) but that the movement will become gradually more "focused" and finally arrive at its goal, the set of individual root-progression probabilities is revised for each new clang according to the actual direction and distance remaining to the target. I won't go into more detail here about the mechanics of this process except to note that this part of the program turned out to be more complicated than I had expected it to be and that it didn't always work! That is, there always remained a certain degree of unpredictability in the final convergence toward the dominant, such that

TABLE 3. Root-progression probabilities.

root-progression *interval-class*	*probability*	root-progression *interval-class*	*probability*
0	.00	30	.30
7	.01	42	.10
11	.05	49	.10
12	.05	53	.11
14	.04	56	.02
16	.04	58	.02
19	.01	60	.01
23	.03	65	.10

the intended target was actually missed in about one out of three runs of the program. When this happened, the output was discarded and the study generated again with a new random seed. Since the total duration and the average clang-duration of each study were considered characteristic features of that study, derived by the first program by operations on its terminal states in the three primary parameters—and not to be altered arbitrarily or contingently—the series of root-progressions was required not only to *arrive* at its target but to arrive there *on time*. Such a percentage of "failures" is therefore not surprising, given the essentially *stochastic* nature of the process. In each study, the program had four chances to succeed: if it arrived at the target dominant at the sixth, fifth, fourth, or third clang from the end, a "cadencing" routine was initiated that kept it rooted on the dominant PC and set the mode in some form of (extended) "dominant seventh" until the next to last (or in some cases, the last) clang, at which point it effected a progression to the final tonic. The similarities between this procedure and what might be inferred from many of the cadential passages in Bach's preludes should be obvious—although profound differences will also be evident to any listener, I am sure.

CHAPTER 16

Darmstadt Lecture

(1990)

If a title had been needed for this lecture, I had thought to call it "Problems of Harmony (II)" because, of course, "Problems of Harmony" I is a wonderful essay by Arnold Schoenberg that was written or published in 1934, the year I was born. My own work with harmony has been motivated by a desire to answer two questions: First, is it possible for the harmonic aspect of music to evolve further without our going back to an earlier language, back to tonality as it was known in the seventeenth, eighteenth, and nineteenth centuries? I believe it is, but how it might be done is not self-evident. The second, parallel question is: Can we develop a theory of harmony that will explicate or illuminate, perhaps even stimulate, that kind of development? I believe that's possible too, and I think of it as a kind of communal or community effort, or at least I would like it to be that. I wish we had in music what physicists and mathematicians and chemists and so forth have, where they are all working with similar problems, and immediately there is a sharing of information, a sharing of new theoretical ideas. Things in those disciplines develop in that communal way. So I throw this out to all of you as an invitation to collaborate with me and with each other on developing a new theory.

Now the more I thought about that title—"Problems of Harmony"—it seemed really to break down into a number of other, smaller problems, and maybe the best way I can give you some sense of my ideas about these things is by talking about each of those smaller problems. These

[Tenney gave this lecture on July 26, 1990, at the Darmstadt Ferienkurse to an audience that included numerous composers.—Ed.]

include, first, the historical problem. Then the problem of the role of theory in general in musical activity. There is what I call the phenomenological problem. The psychoacoustic problem. The semantic problem. And finally what we might call the compositional problem. Now of course composition is not really a problem: we compose. To describe these all as "problems" may make it sound far too negative, but it can be useful anyway. I say composition is not a problem because we go on composing with or without a theory. Maybe in some sense we don't really need a theory. Certainly the existence of music does not depend on it. But I want one anyway, and I think this is a desire that comes out of sheer curiosity. And maybe it would be useful—who knows? So let me say some things about each of those problems.

The historical problem I view in this way: there was a period of harmonic evolution in Western music, the so-called common practice period, which came to a kind of impasse around 1910. I sometimes use the image of this great freight train that is just rattling along until 1910 when crash!—it hits a wall and stops. Now *music* didn't stop, of course. The reason I said a moment ago that maybe we don't need a theory to make music is that clearly the making of music did not stop in 1910. What happened is that the more progressive composers simply went off in ten or twenty different directions and began to explore and develop aspects of music that had pretty much been neglected up to that time.

Schoenberg himself seems to have had the view that he just didn't know what to say about harmony anymore, that is, in relation to his own work, although he had plenty to say about harmony in earlier music in his *Harmonielehre*. I feel very strongly that what he was saying was: "I'm postponing this. It's not that it has come to an end, but we just have to wait and give it some time before it would be appropriate or possible to come back and deal with this aspect of music." So in the period from 1910 until—sometime, I can't give a precise date to it, you know—today, yesterday, thirty years ago, in the twentieth century, an enormous amount of magnificent music has been made, but I still would say that, somehow, harmony has not really gone any place that it hadn't already arrived at in about 1910. I believe some people are going to take issue with me on that point, and that's fine—we can argue about it, and I could well be wrong—but that is my view.

So from this historical consideration we can move right into my second problem, which I define as the *problem of the role of theory* in general.

There has been a very curious change in the relationship between theory and practice in the last few hundred years. Back in the time of Zarlino and Lippius and later Rameau and Carl Philipp Emanuel Bach and Kirnberger most of the theorists were composers, and respectable composers, if not the greatest of their time. In some cases they were as fine as any. And they were formulating their theoretical ideas in a way very closely connected to their compositional practice. By 1910 that situation had changed radically, by a gradual process, I guess, but things were clearly different. In 1910 the theory of harmony was not referring to the current music but only to earlier music. How did that happen? It seems to me that two things were involved: one is the tendency of the conservatory toward self-replication, the fact that teachers teach what they know to students who then go on to teach the same things to their students, et cetera, ad infinitum. The basic curriculum in the conservatory now is virtually identical to the curriculum in the conservatory two hundred years ago, and I think that's very interesting. The other thing is that, when you think about it, in the nineteenth century there were no composer-theorists of any significance. Theory was simply not a respectable thing for a composer to do in the nineteenth century. A composer had to be a poet or something else. Theory just did not fit the romantic image. So these two things together created a very strange situation, this gradual divergence between theory and practice. And it's time to pull that back together. But if we are going to have a new theory, we have to be very careful that we don't build the same box around us that we had before. All of you, I think, probably had the same experience in school that I did, that harmony was something you had to go through even though it was perfectly obvious that it was not relevant to contemporary music. It had nothing to do with the music that you intended to write, but you had to learn it anyway. And then when you did, you found it was a set of rules that told you, like a cookbook recipe, if you mix this with that in certain proportions you'll get this result, which would be music in a certain historical style. I don't think we need rules anymore. I think we need a theory of harmony that is *not* a set of rules, that is not prescriptive, but *descriptive*. And I think we need to think carefully about what the conditions for a useful theory would be. I think that one of these conditions, considering the realities of the world right now, is that a useful theory would have to be one that could be applied to any kind of music from any time and place, not just Western music or Western music of a given period. In addition, it seems to me it should be firmly grounded in acoustics and psychoacoustics and what is known about perceptual and cognitive processes. And a third thing I have already said, but it bears repeating: it should be descriptive, not prescriptive.

The next problem is the one I called the *phenomenological problem*. It seems to me that introspection is necessary in order to make some decisions in the formulation of a new theory, because we'll never be able to prove some things. I don't see any way to prove or demonstrate to what extent certain notions or perceptions we have are innate and to what extent they are culturally determined. The only way you could ever find that out would be by taking somebody completely out of his culture, having him grow up with no cultural influences, and then testing him, and this is such a horrible thought that we can't even consider it. For example, something like the notion of octave equivalence: Is it a real thing, an innate thing, or is it culturally determined? We are always going to be a little bit unsure. People are going to have different opinions about it, and that's fine, but ultimately one has to make a decision, and such decisions often have to be based on introspective considerations: what you really think you hear, what your perception is. Each of us has to ask that: What is my perception? And that is a phenomenological attitude.

The *semantic problem* is very interesting, and although this is a bit of a side issue, it can relate to situations that might arise in other aspects of a new theory of harmony. I did some research a few years ago in the history of music theory because I was interested in understanding better what people had meant by the terms "consonance" and "dissonance" or the various cognates of those words in different languages. And I wrote a book expressing the view that in the course of history there have been at least five distinctly different, or at least separable, meanings of "consonance" and "dissonance."[1] When theorists (who were generally practicing musicians) used those terms or their equivalents, they meant different things in different historical periods. Not necessarily opposing things, but things different enough that you can have very strange anomalous contradictions in theory now. For example, is the perfect fourth a consonance or a dissonance? In one context it's considered a perfect consonance. In another context it's treated as a dissonance. That never made any sense to me until I saw that the idea of the perfect fourth as a dissonance only arose at a certain time in history and was associated with a certain musical situation, in fact, the rise of counterpoint. So we have semantic problems, and they have to be dealt with very carefully. As another example, I suspect that, however many people are in this room, perhaps fifty or sixty, there are that many implicit or unconscious if not explicit and conscious definitions of the word "harmony." Here I'm trying to talk about harmony, and yet I'm aware that we may not understand the word the same way. I'll try to give you my definition of it, but first note that a choice must be made. We can define it any way we choose to, really, if we agree that some redefinition is necessary, and I think it certainly is. What it has come to mean is so much more restricted than what it once meant that it's hardly useful any more, except in the most trivial sense, and think of that as represented by the terminology in commercial music, where you have three different types of instruments: the "rhythm" instruments (the drums), the "melody" instruments (the saxophones and so forth), and the "harmony" instruments (keyboards, or any instrument that can play more than one note at a time). "Harmony" has thus come to mean simply "chords." Well, this doesn't even describe harmony in the common practice period, so it's a terrible restriction in its meaning.

Now, if we go back far enough, it starts to mean more and more things. Before the Pythagoreans it meant simply "a fitting together"—how things fit together. You know, the way a craftsman might put one piece of wood next to another to build a table. "Harmony" basically meant that. The Pythagoreans took that word and applied it to the cosmos in general. I am not inclined to use it in that broad sense, so some decision has to be made. How are we going to use it? I have decided, in the last few years, to use it as referring to certain kinds of pitch relations. Now why do I say "certain kinds of pitch relations"? There are, in fact—shouldn't say "in fact"; this is theory—I believe there are two distinct *aspects* of pitch perception correlated with two distinct *mechanisms*. The one that is not harmony is essentially the one Larry [Polansky] was talking about in his lecture, the one that determines contour. Another manifestation of it is the sense of register as a generalized perception of "higher" or "lower." Contour involves the sense of movement "up" and "down" of larger versus smaller intervals and so forth, but it's not a very precise percept. It's a more generalized aspect of perception, and there is a lot of music in the world that works with that and does not work with what I would call harmonic relations. I have a tape at home of a wonderful set of "Horse Songs" sung by a Navajo Indian singer. And the voice moves so continuously there. The pitch is changing, but the singer never lingers on a pitch. You never can quite identify a pitch. For me, what he is working with is that one aspect of pitch perception I'm calling "contour." The other aspect is much more precise, so we can distinguish between two pitches or intervals that are only very slightly different. The clue that there has to be more than just one aspect to pitch perception seems to me that, if we were listening to a series of intervals [plays the chromatic intervals c–c♯, c–d, c–d♯, etc.], getting bigger, and then [at the octave] something else happens all of a sudden right there. Something doesn't get bigger there, it gets smaller [plays the octave]. The way I think of it, there is a *dimensionality* involved in this relationship that is not generally recognized. If we imagine two dimensions, and the intervals are growing larger in one of those dimensions, and yet at that point [the octave] suddenly there is a collapsing or an approximation, in some original sense of that word, in another dimension. I said I think these two aspects of pitch perception are correlated with different mechanisms, and I mean that quite literally. I think the contour aspect relates to what's happening on the basilar membrane in the inner ear, and this other aspect that I refer to as harmonic I believe relates to the central nervous system's processing of the temporal information that is being transmitted from the basilar membrane.

All right, finally the *compositional problem* [laughs]. What I have found to be most useful, and what for me has become a kind of central concept, is what I call "harmonic space." I don't mean the physical space in which we move but a kind of abstract, perceptual space that is in some ways analogous to physical space. Its structure: first of all, the number of dimensions is determined by the number of prime numbers required to specify the pitches and intervals—to specify their frequency ratios. I should say that I think what Harry Partch called the "language of ratios" is going to be an essential component of any new theory of harmony. I don't see any way around it. For some people it might be a little difficult to relate to these numbers, but the numbers really can come to mean precise perceptual objects. I also believe—although there are very different opinions about this—I believe that *just* intervals are referential for our perceptual systems, and this means two things. One is that whenever we hear an interval in a musical situation we interpret it as though it was the simplest just interval within a certain tolerance region of what we are actually hearing. And this means that although I give a very high importance to just intervals and ratios and so forth, I am not a "just intonationalist," because I think that tempered systems have some very real advantages in certain situations. In fact, I think we tend to forget that this tempered system [pointing to the piano]—I assume this piano is in 12-tone temperament—this tempered system did not develop, historically, because somebody thought it would be nice to divide the octave into twelve parts because twelve is a nice number. It developed out of an evolving effort to find a way to make practical a reasonable approximation to the more important just intervals involved in diatonic-triadic harmony. Twelve-tone temperament has good fifths and fourths. Thirds and sixths are pretty bad, but they are tolerable. And that's how this system arose. Other tempered systems can be extremely useful. You all know that a tempered system has the advantage that it's cyclic, so you can modulate forever and still be within the same small pitch set. But I think it's important to understand or to remember that we're interpreting tempered intervals as approximations of just intervals. An example that I sometimes give is this [draws a circle on the chalkboard]. Do you see that circle? What is that, really? That's an approximation to some ideal circle. It's clearly not even an awfully good approximation, but you don't have any problem with my calling it a circle. So I'm saying that [plays a major third on the piano] my circle is better than that. What we are understanding when we hear that is a five-to-four frequency ratio, an out-of-tune five-to-four, whatever that means harmonically.

What are some other aspects of harmonic space? It has the structure of a *lattice* of discrete points rather than a continuum. Some of you may have seen Ben Johnston's important article on "Rational Structure in Music" where he uses such lattices. Their dimensions are correlated with prime numbers (2, 3, 5, 7, 11, etc.), and he has generally presented them as two- or three-dimensional lattices, depending on the frequency ratios required to specify the pitches and intervals involved. For those of you who like mathematics, I might mention that I've developed a measure of harmonic distance within these lattices in harmonic space. It looks a lot like the measure of pitch distance in the usual one-dimensional sense, but instead of the logarithm of the ratio of two terms (as, for example, the log of five-over-four giving the pitch distance between the tones of a major third), harmonic distance is proportional to the *product* of the two terms. This measure of harmonic distance thus shows how far one would have to go in the lattice to get from one point—say, the 1/1, or reference pitch—to the point representing the interval without cutting across the "empty spaces" in the lattice.

There is a lot of detail that I'm going to skip here, though it may come out later. If anybody is interested in following it up, I'd be very happy to talk to you in other informal situations, but I don't want to get too much into it right here. Just one other thing: it now becomes possible for me to conceive of music in general as *activity in harmonic space*, if harmony is involved at all, and I don't mean just music in which we have already acknowledged harmony to be involved, but music in which it might be, which is to say music in which there are salient and stable pitches. Compositionally, harmonic space becomes a field of operations. One can imagine music moving through this field in various ways, and this can apply to traditional tonal music, it can apply to Schoenberg, it can apply to Stockhausen, it can apply to Cage, it can apply to Indonesian gamelan music, it can apply to anything. In some cases, certain transformations have to be made in order to map tempered systems or other kinds of pitch systems into some form of harmonic space, but I believe that this is quite generally feasible. Harmonic space, plus the other dimensions of sound that Cage elucidated in his earlier articles, finally becomes a fantastically rich field of operations, a field that is completely open. The marvelous thing is, there are no rules, there is no syntax, nothing is necessary and yet everything is possible. Now I hope there are questions, because I'm finished except to try to answer questions.

Voice from the audience: You mentioned at the very beginning of your talk something [with] which I don't really agree, and that is when you spoke of the relationship between theorists or theory and composition. At the same time, you said that there was a gradual dissociation between the two that's unknown. I am not sure that I agree with that, because if you look at the work either of Rameau or Carl Philipp Emanuel Bach . . . I think there is already an extremely clear bit of dissociation. A very simple example is the way Rameau tries to explain minor harmony, where it comes from, in his *Treatise on Harmony*. Major harmony he has no trouble with, as you know, because it's [on the?] monochord. When he gets into minor harmony we find in the history of his, well, in his life, that he went through about four or five different theories and was about as dissatisfied with . . . all of them. He wasn't happy at all, and he gets himself into the most horrible muddles, as anyone knows who has read the book, or the few of them, but anyway . . .

Tenney: But I have read it.

Voice: But the point is, though: Does this have anything to do with what goes on in new music? It's only a very pure reflection of anything. Similarly, Carl Philipp Emanuel Bach wrote that he doesn't even acknowledge the inversion-of-chord principle and goes against harmonics. And there is this surviving letter, just to finish, of Beethoven, where he says that when he gets a new student he sends him out to buy Carl Philipp Emanuel Bach, saying that it's a wonderful work and it has everything you need to know about music. And well, what was Beethoven doing? So I think already there was a dissociation, and what has been happening since is very much along the same lines, and it's not to be wondered at. But there is still the same problem.

Tenney: Well, just because Rameau and Carl Philipp Emanuel Bach were good composers doesn't necessarily mean they weren't going to make mistakes in their theoretical formulations. And certainly Rameau's attempt to explain the minor chord is unsatisfactory, and I think he knew it, and that's why he kept trying. But there is still the sense that he was writing about and trying to say something meaningful and useful about the materials that he was using as a composer, not about the materials that some musical ancestor of his had used as a composer. He was not a musicologist. He was a composer writing about current issues. That's what I'm talking about. In Schoenberg's *Harmonielehre* he's talking about music preceding him. Only when he comes to the last chapter does he begin to try to say something about his own music, but he can't really incorporate it with the other because that theory by then seemed to apply only to that earlier music and not to his own.

Voice from the audience: I want to relate your insistence on a need for clear concepts to something that came up in Eric de Visscher's talk that is very, very important for the future of music: lack of intentionality and indifference to the result. I think there is no possibility of lack of intentionality, there is never anything more than a pretense of indifference to the result, and certainly systematic chance operation neither expresses lack of intentionality nor leads to indifference to the result. I think that's a really important thing to start from in music.

Tenney: Right. I agree with you, but I think Eric had a different connotation in mind for that word "indifference"—a connotation different from yours or mine—because I don't feel indifferent to the result at all.

Voice from the audience: Nor does John.

Tenney: But I don't think Eric meant the kind of indifference that we heard. I think that all he meant was that once you've got it—you know, you've worked out your procedure—you will be able to accept everything that happens. And that's not really indifference at all, not in my sense of the word.

Eric de Visscher: I was really talking about [your] early electronic music pieces in that sense of gradual evolution in which more and more hierarchical levels were left to chance operations.

Tenney: Well, that was the case, but indifference is a difficult word to use, at least in its connotations for me, because it was not from indifference but from a gradual realization that I could really enjoy a result that I hadn't shaped in a precise way, a direct way, that I could let the process go, that if the compositional procedure was properly designed, I could let it go and be pleased with every result that it could have . . .

Voice from the audience: . . . within the process.

Tenney: Yeah.

de Visscher: And I think the choice you are making and surely the absence of indifference and somehow the presence of intention lies at the level of asking questions and the level of setting how the process goes and that afterwards I think the result is depending on that.

Brian Ferneyhough: I was very interested, if I understood you correctly, in [your] talking about a rather Platonic concept of the semanticity of nonjust intervals on the piano. Leaving aside for the moment whether it's really true that we tend to hear modified intervals in the simplest ratio form, as it were . . . I agree with you, of course, [that] the piano has developed historically and that the tuning of the piano came about [for] particular historical, approximational reasons. However, isn't it already true that an instrument is modified by the music that is written for it? And that over the last 150 years or whatever we have come to hear these intervals not as meaning some Platonic divine ratio in its purest form, but we hear the intervals actually in their tempered form on the piano as things in themselves. In that case, how can one apply the concept of the lattice to these particular intervals?

Tenney: Well, I do it by way of a notion that I call "tolerance" and the hypothesis that in harmonic perception we tend to interpret intervals in the simplest way possible within the tolerance range. We do hear in other ways too. Certainly in a lot of contexts I would say I'm not aware of harmonic relations, even though I could be, perhaps. But I think there is a tendency to interpret harmonically in the simplest way possible, and I see this as a result of the very early evolution of the species, as a necessity of information processing, to find the simplest possible interpretation of the thing within reason—"within reason" meaning within some kind of tolerance range. This is very hard to pin down exactly, but we can assume, according to my definitions, that the 12-tone tempered system will imply different tolerance ranges, depending on how it's being used. For example, if we're playing in it with triadic sonorities, it implies a tolerance of about a sixth of a semitone, whereas if you play dominant seventh chords too, then it implies a tolerance of almost a third of a semitone, because I would maintain that we are hearing that tempered minor seventh as a representation of the natural seven-to-four ratio, which is 31 cents smaller than the tempered interval. And be careful with the terms "Platonic" and certainly "divine." There is nothing divine about the ratios, and I'm not a Platonist, but what I meant to demonstrate by drawing the circle is that we work within such tolerances all the time; in our discourse, in our working with materials, and our talking with each other we are constantly doing this. And I think it's a natural activity of the nervous system to do this.

Clarence Barlow: I'm just wondering whether one could also explain it in terms of trying to counteract the tonal feelings within intervals or harmonic drive of intervals by deliberately—for example, by not repeating fifths and things within 12-tone rows, there are such things as more atonal 12-tone rows—fighting the intrinsic tonal radiation of material to produce something that becomes then so neutral in its tonal implications that the other type of theory of high and low, the contour type, takes over. And that a lot of theory of music is pretty [much] based on that other type of theory and not so much on the harmonic theory.

Tenney: Well, yes, I think so. In fact, most of the theory associated with serial music is basically dealing with contour, but it has some elements of the other too. Just as Schoenberg, even in—it might have been "Problems of Harmony" or it might have been another essay where he was explaining the 12-tone method—he says, "How is it possible that one tone can follow another?"[2] His answer is that it's because there are relations between tones already, based on their spectral content. And so in the context of having formulated something that is basically contour-oriented, he's also reminding us that there are these other relationships. And I think the listening situation does vary a lot. If it gets too complicated, we're going to lose it. But I also want to make it clear that when I say that harmonic relations are involved I do not necessarily mean tonality or—what did you say?—"harmonic drive." All these things are possibilities but not necessarily part of it. So I want people to understand that I mean something *larger* than tonality, but something that includes what we know as tonality as well.

Daniel Wolf: Isn't it important to assume that the lattice is independent of a system? A lattice is involved by the music at hand; in other words, people seem to imply a particular kind of musical context that will travel along the lines of . . . a lattice isn't an experimental idea. A lot of models in music have been experimental models, a very deliberate process. The composers that I've been closest to have been exponents of very clear procedural music. And I want to know what comments can you make or what advice do you give composers who operate in a postexperimental model?

Tenney: There is no such thing as postexperimental.

Voice from the audience: Yes there is: academic.

Tenney: My sense of "experimental" is just ongoing research. So I don't understand "postexperimental." But what advice would I give to young composers? Train your ears. Work on hearing things that our standard tuning system has tended to make us not hear. Learn to identify the difference between a natural interval like this one [plays a natural fifth harmonic on a string inside the piano] and its tempered approximation [plays the same note on the keyboard], which in this case is sharp.

Gertrud Meyer-Denkmann: You have said, nothing is necessary but everything is open, like with Cage. And if I have understood this, that you said not to make distinct relations. Would you agree [with] the formulation of Adorno—that the function of musical materials determines the form—that this should not be the case anymore?

Tenney: Well, I'm hung up on your paraphrase of me as having said something about not distinguishing . . .

Meyer-Denkmann: Not in the relationship. Not to make distinct relationships, as we are concerned with the cadence and so on. I know, you haven't said this, but I'm interested about this definition of function in harmony theory.

Tenney: No, I think we have to let go of that. I don't think it's useful, because it's restrictive. There is no harmonic function other than what we choose. That's a choice, a matter of style, culture, and compositional intention. But there are very specific relationships, and when I answered Dan's question I was saying: learn to hear them, but they don't tell us what we have to do. So no, there is no function given. There are relationships that are given. There is a nature there.

Voice from the audience: What is nature?

Tenney: Well, these relationships and the nature of the ear. The acoustical properties of sound and the physiological, neurological properties of the ear. These are real things that are given, as well as what the brain can do with this. But I want to stop short of all the rest, because it's been a burden.

Meyer-Denkmann: And what about the relation of material and form, or, to say in this connection, harmony and form?

Tenney: Well, in the most general sense I view material as form on a microstructural level. So they are basically the same thing at different hierarchical levels. So there is no dualism, there is not form and content. There is form at all levels, or you might say there is content at all levels. And one can choose to deal with them at any level. We're free to focus at any level or at any combination of levels. Not entirely free in perception, because we will generally hear what's there, but as composers we are free to work with or play with these things at any level. Nothing is necessary [laughs] and everything is possible.

Wolf: Maybe the analogy of a cookbook for a harmony textbook was wrong, and you are not opposed to the cookbook, because the cookbook could be very useful to do certain things. For example, in the *Three Indigenous Songs* you had a series of recipes [for simulating] the sonorities [of speech]. It's the *etiquette* book that you are opposed to, how you have to behave in particular situations.

Tenney: Right. That's a much better analogy.

Voice from the audience: I want to ask you [about] some of the definitions of harmony that you mentioned earlier. They seem to be basically related to pitch-oriented systems. Maybe that could be wrong. But would you believe that the definition of harmony could also include noise?

Tenney: Well, as I've said, one has to make a decision. And so far my decision has been to restrict it to certain aspects of relations between pitches. But it's extremely important to understand that I don't define *music* that way, all right? If talk about harmony, it's in this very specific way, that it's one of the aspects of music, and tones are among the materials we may use, but I'm not eliminating noise. So far I haven't found a way to define harmony in a broader sense that is satisfactory to me. Time is an important element here too, and in my article "John Cage and the Theory of Harmony," I tried to make a correlation there [between harmony and time].[3] But I have not so far been able to connect that up with other aspects of sound in a way that satisfies me.

Voice from the audience: You have already implied the insistence of time when you insist on the necessity for pitches in order for the harmonic dimension to arise.

Tenney: That's true. If the tone doesn't last long enough, we don't hear the pitch, or if the sounding object doesn't have enough time to go into a stable vibration, it will be a noise. If you hit a percussion instrument, even a mallet instrument, hit it and damp it right away, all you hear is the noise, right?

Meyer-Denkmann: I just think of a definition in former times of Stockhausen in his lecture "Wie die Zeit vergeht," "As Time Passes," in his early writings.[4] And he is speaking of the relation between *Zeitgerausche*, time noises, and sound color. What do you think about these relationships to your understanding [of] harmony?

Tenney: Well, I view that as a composer's working with materials in an interesting way that is all directed toward the making of a piece. And working with analogies, physically, even mathematically. In some objective way the analogy is there, but I don't believe that such an analogy is actually perceptible. So on one level, yes, you can draw the analogies on paper, you can even make a magnificent piece based on it. But I don't think we hear things that way, that's all. I'm an unregenerate phenomenologist [laughs], and I'm always returning to the question, what do I actually hear? But also I'm quite aware that, as composers, we can think of the wildest schemes that will motivate us, stimulate us to make a piece, right, and the scheme itself may be kind of crazy, but that doesn't mean that the piece will be crazy. We can use all kinds of scaffolds to get up there and build the building.

Meyer-Denkmann: I'm thinking of Boulez and Stockhausen, Boulez also in his thinking of modern music, *Musikdenken*. They tried almost to make relation with the parameters, relation with material and form, relation and relation. And I think you are more open not to make those strict relations, neither between parameters nor between the whole sound material and form, because also I think Boulez was speaking of, if you use noise instruments and very complex rhythm, you have to decide to make relation also to the structure of pitches and so on.

Tenney: It seems to me that that effort was—and I don't mean anything negative by this—it was wishful thinking. It followed the desire to extend Messiaen's generalizations of the idea of the series. And every effort was made to understand or to imagine how one could establish parallels between the situations in these different dimensions, because the musical intention was to try to structure all those different parameters in a similar way. It just seems to me that, well, we are at a different stage in history now, and we can look back at that endeavor and make our own judgment of it. My judgment is that the different parameters involve fundamentally different mechanisms or aspects of the whole mechanism of hearing and that the nature of our perception of different parameters is determined by that hearing process in very important ways, and there are fundamental differences between pitch perception and dynamic perception, for example, fundamental differences between pitch perception and time perception, even though one can generalize from pitch to time and back. In actual perceptual experience, they are totally different things, except sometimes at that interface region of very low frequencies, like in Stockhausen's *Kontakte*, where that tone goes down, down, down, and pretty soon becomes a sequence of pulses. Otherwise they are very different. So my effort now is to try to understand perception as well as possible and relate my thinking about music to that. I don't start off with a stylistic agenda.

Janet Danielson: Regarding your esthetic of different views of consonance and dissonance, you said there were at least five divergent views. How divergent are they? Are there cultures or is there a time in history, for example, in which a minor ninth is considered more consonant than an octave?

Tenney: There are parallels and similarities, but the differences are striking enough that I think a real case can be made for separating them. For example, in the early medieval period, "consonance" and "dissonance" were defined in a certain way, but more significant than the definition was how the theorists listed degrees of relative consonance and dissonance. And there was a very long list of fine distinctions in many categories, you know, from perfect consonance to imperfect consonance and then imperfect dissonance and perfect dissonance. I think there was one theorist that actually had five categories because he had a sort of midrange there in addition to the others. And then, all of a sudden, it seems, in the fourteenth century I believe, you find the theorists saying there are only three categories: perfect consonance, imperfect consonance, and dissonance. And one of the intervals [the perfect fourth] has suddenly migrated from one category to another. Now, you know, that interval wasn't different, the ears weren't different, but the musical textures were different. And my hunch is that the sad fate of the perfect fourth had to do with the fact that a typical form of that time was the polyphonic motet in several languages, and the fourth would create a situation in which the lower voice would obscure a higher voice in the same way the other intervals that were previously considered dissonances did.

Barlow: There are a number of degrees of transposed intervals. There has also been writing in other cultures; for example, in India two thousand years ago, they spoke about three categories: consonance, assonance, and dissonance, and the consonance is the perfect fifth, octave, and perfect fourth; the assonances were thirds and sixths; and the dissonances were the sevenths and seconds, because Indian music also uses twelve notes. So that's an interesting fact. But I also have to point out that one doesn't talk always in terms of consonance and dissonance as phenomena equivalent to harmonicity and inharmonicity. Consonance and dissonance could also be purely physical phenomena of roughness of sound, for example, two trombones in the bass register playing the same interval as a celesta might be more dissonant, a timbral consideration. I recommend the work of Plomp and Levelt, 1965, who did a lot of experiments in this direction about the roughness of sound.[5]

Tenney: Yes, I know their work. It stems from the work of Helmholtz, and it's what I call "timbral" consonance and dissonance, or "CDC-5." It's the fifth in this historical sequence that I found.

Ernstalbrecht Stiebler: I had an experience with the cembalo. We are normally accustomed to the [temperament] on the piano, and we know it, it's not very good, but it's possible. But it's much more difficult with the cembalo. I had invited a cembalo player, and he had tuned the cembalo not in [equal temperament] but what is *mitteltönig*—mean-tone. And I was fifty meters from the studio and the door was open, and I thought, What marvelous sound is that? And that is the problem of the sound spectrum of the cembalo. The thirds, the tempered thirds, [are] thought [of] as the more dissonant, but if you have this old [temperament], mean-tone, then you can't play every key. But it sounds marvelous, and it's a big difference, everybody could hear it.

Voice from the audience: That relationship of tuning . . . to the overtone series I think is very, very important. I think, for instance, it's clear that the anomalous unique tuning systems of Balinese and Javanese gamelans are related to the overtone structure of the bells. I had an interesting experience when I wrote a concerto for harpsichord and gamelan, and I tuned it to the *pelog* scale, and it starts off with an approximate, like a very wide major second and starts off with the harpsichord, and you say, my god, this is awful. Then when you double it in octaves, because the octaves are in tune with each other, you begin to accept it, and as soon as the gamelan comes in it becomes completely normal, acceptable, and everything else. But when you play those intervals with a Western instrument because of the harmonic structure it's unacceptable, and as soon as you bring in the instruments that have a different overtone structure, inherent sound, you don't even notice that there is anything wrong.

Meyer-Denkmann: I think about your different pieces yesterday evening. This marvelous piece of glissando, where harmony is in two dimensions, and this other piece in the Aula that was more melodic, more figurative, more contrapuntal. What about your question about harmony between those two pieces that were for me quite different also in time, time floating and time going more rhythmically and also in another space?

Tenney: Well, I think because I conceive harmony as something that *may* be involved, although it doesn't always *have* to be, that it might become an important element in a piece of music and it might not. And it can become important in several different ways. In some of those pieces yesterday, things are actually related to the harmonic series in one way or another.

Meyer-Denkmann: Which piece?

Tenney: Well, the first and last movements of *Glissade*, all of *Critical Band*, and *Three Indigenous Songs* also is based on the harmonic series. And there are other ways that it can happen, like in the fourth movement of *Glissade*. That's not a harmonic series relation but a very slow divergence of the tones, and at certain points we hear clear, understandable, comprehensible harmonies. And then in between there are these other intervals that we don't understand so well, but you know, harmony is involved all the way along. It's always there, but it goes through an incredible series of different conditions in a piece like that. And then some music . . . You know, the freedom we have now is just extraordinary, once we break away from those old rules, so that we can write music for snare drums [laughs] or a big tam-tam!

CHAPTER 17

The Several Dimensions of Pitch

(1993/2003)

Pitch is usually conceived as a one-dimensional continuum, like frequency. But I suggest that there are, in fact, two different aspects of pitch perception and that one of those aspects can also be thought of as multidimensional. In considering such fundamental questions regarding the nature of auditory perception, it is often useful to think about the evolution of hearing, and I would invoke the image of a primitive hominid trying to survive in the savannah (our ears, after all, surely evolved as a means of survival, not for musical ends). What would the auditory system of this primitive hominid need to be able to do? First, it would have to be sensitive to *changes,* with time, in the properties of a sound, since such changes are indicative of physical processes in the environment. In addition, however, it would need to be able to do two complementary if not contradictory things, namely, (1) distinguish between or among sounds issuing from *different* sound sources and (2) recognize when two or more sounds—though different—actually arise from a *single* sound source. Nature has been very generous to us in this respect, since we have been given two different mechanisms of pitch perception. Fortunately, these two mechanisms work together in such a way that we can scarcely distinguish the two aspects. Thus, although the two mechanisms affect the pitch percept in different ways, they are very easily confused and perhaps for that reason have not previously been distinguished in the literature of psychoacoustics or of music theory. The first mechanism by itself would yield a rather diffuse pitch percept, but it is highly effective in the detection of rapid changes of pitch. The other mechanism lends the pitch percept its more precise, focused quality, but it requires more time to be effective.

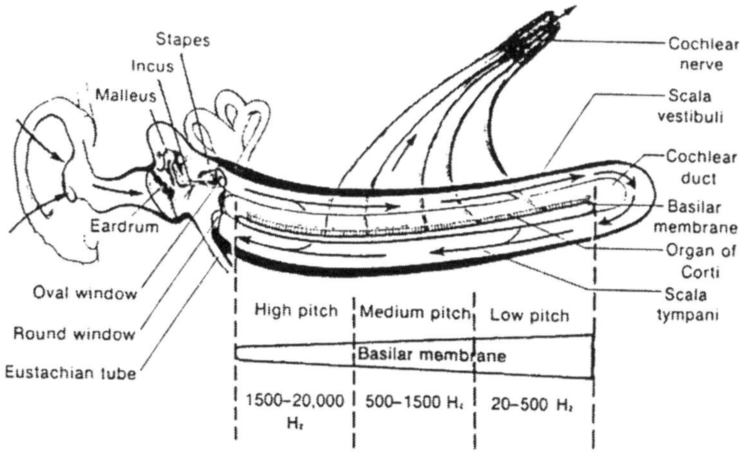

FIGURE 1. Schematic diagram of the "unrolled" cochlea and basilar membrane from Anderson (1976).

The first mechanism is the basis for what I call the *contour* aspect of pitch perception, and I think it is probably correlated with the distribution of mechanical and neural activity on the basilar membrane and the organ of Corti. The inner ear, as we all know, is in the shape of a snail shell (*cochlea* in Latin). If we imagine unrolling that shape, it can be represented schematically as in figure 1. The input to the cochlea is at the oval window, where the vibration generates a traveling wave on the basilar membrane and the organ of Corti. As Georg von Békésy (1960) demonstrated, the envelope of this traveling wave reaches its maximum amplitude at a distance from the oval window determined by the frequency of the vibration—higher frequencies nearer to the oval window, lower ones farther away from it (see figure 2). The vibration of the basilar membrane elicits nerve impulses in hair cells arrayed along the organ of Corti, with a temporal density that varies directly with the amplitude of the traveling wave. A crude form of frequency discrimination is thus effected in the form of a *spatial distribution* of mechanical and neural activity in the cochlea, and this information is transmitted to the central nervous system (CNS) via the auditory nerve in a way that preserves its original spatial order, i.e., tonotopically.

This first mechanism is very sensitive to changes in the properties of a sound and is the basis for our sense of shape in melody and for our sense of register, but it can hardly be what gives the pitch percept its

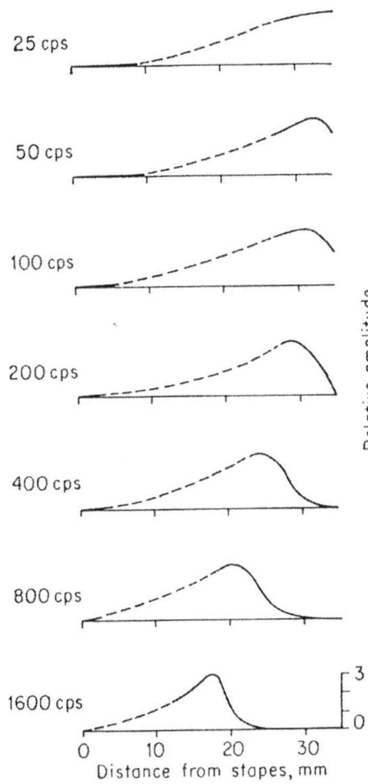

FIGURE 2. Envelopes of traveling waves of various frequencies on the basilar membrane from von Békésy (1960).

"point-like" character, nor is it likely to be the basis for the perception of harmonic relations in music. The amplitude peak of the traveling wave envelope is far too broad to be the primary correlate of this aspect of the pitch percept. Thinking again of the primitive hominid, the first of these aspects of pitch perception tells him about the rushing noise of the lion as it comes through the brush. And it's very useful for establishing the general characteristics of that noise, e.g., its intensity, bandwidth, and approximate pitch. It is also quite sensitive to *changes* in these characteristics. But it is not going to be useful for certain other tasks. For example, it won't help in the determination that the several harmonic partials in the sound of the lion's roar are actually coming from just one lion. For that, something else is needed—a mechanism that can detect any correlations among individual partials in the signal and thus determine when two or more widely separated frequencies are so closely related (in some respect) that they are likely to have been produced by the same sound source.

So what is this other aspect of pitch perception, and what would be its associated mechanism? I believe it has to do with the *temporal ordering* of the neural information. What I have already described involves a spatial ordering: although these nerve impulses are happening in time, their important feature (as far as the first mechanism is concerned) is their spatial distribution—*where* the neural impulses originate. The basis for the other aspect is time—and it is surprising that more hasn't been made of this in the psychoacoustic literature, because the temporal information is there and available to the CNS, and it seems highly unlikely that the evolutionary process would have allowed for an available mechanism to be wasted. If you take any position along the organ of Corti and measure what's happening in the hair cells at that position, any given input frequency produces synchronized pulses in those hair cells and thus in the auditory nerve. Not every hair cell responds to every cycle of the signal, but the input frequency will be represented in the auditory nerve by synchronous nerve firings by groups of cells in "volleys." So time information is being sent to the CNS, and I believe that it is this time information that is the basis for the second mechanism, which, in turn, is responsible for the aspect of pitch perception that I call the *harmonic* aspect.

Now I think the evolutionary reason for the development of a second mechanism of pitch perception is that only in this way could the various harmonic partials in a single vocal sound, whether that of a lion or of another hominid, be correlated and recognized as having been produced by a single sound source. In vowel perception, for example, we don't hear "chords." Rather, the several harmonic partials are somehow correlated with each other so that what we hear is a single tone with a certain pitch, loudness, and timbre. But whatever that correlation process is, I don't think it can be done spatially. I'm aware of the theories that try to explain this in terms of the spatial distribution of activity on the basilar membrane, but I don't think they are workable, because that distribution is not nearly sharp enough.

The distinction I am making between the two mechanisms is rather like the distinction between the rods and the cones in the retina of the eye. The cone cells are specialized to respond to color and in brighter light. In addition, their resolution is better. The rod cells, on the other hand, are more involved in peripheral vision and come into operation when the light is not so bright. And yet they are highly sensitive to movement. The two cell populations are sometimes described as separate visual systems. Even within the auditory system, there is another perceptual mechanism that is generally agreed to be characterized by a similar duality, and that involves binaural localization. Our discrimination of spatial position depends on both temporal and spectral cues, since comparisons are made in the CNS between both the arrival times and the amplitudes (and amplitude distributions) of corresponding neural signals from the two ears.

In an analogous way, I'm suggesting that there are two different aspects of pitch perception based on two different mechanisms. The first mechanism, which determines the contour aspect, is not only very useful but also essential, because it can respond quickly to changes in the frequency and other properties of a sound. But a pitch percept determined by this mechanism alone would not be very precise. The other mechanism, which determines what I'm calling harmonic perception, is much more precise—but it takes time. It takes time because it involves a temporal process. It takes time because there must be some mechanism to correlate these temporal sequences of neural pulses, and that can't be achieved instantaneously.

Before examining harmonic pitch perception in more detail, we should ask what special properties might be associated uniquely with the contour aspect of the pitch percept in addition to its greater diffuseness. These would include the following:

1. It is, in itself, *one-dimensional*, but distances along this dimension would approximately correspond to the "mel scale" rather than the logarithmic scale of harmonic perception. A consideration of the mechanism here proposed as its basis suggests that Eberhard Zwicker's (1970) "psychoacoustic excitation" function might be the appropriate model for exploring contour pitch perception, in which case the appropriate measure of the subjective distance between two pitches would involve Zwicker's "z-scale"—or the rather similar mel scale proposed much earlier by S. S. Stevens (Stevens and Volkman 1940). The units of both of these scales correspond to approximately equal distances along the basilar membrane or to approximately equal numbers of neurons along the organ of Corti.

2. It seems likely that melodic perception would be affected by a kind of *smoothing* of melodic contour, resulting in *interpolative transitions* between pitches, at least for intervals no larger than one or two critical

bandwidths. In figure 3, Zwicker's psychoacoustic excitation pattern is used to show what might happen when a sustained simple tone is heard immediately following another such tone at a different frequency on the assumption that it takes a certain finite amount of time for these functions to build up and to decay and that the changes, with time, of the resultant neural activity on the basilar membrane may be represented by successive sums of the two functions. Note that when—as in figure 3a—the melodic interval is less than or equal to the length of the low-frequency "skirt" of the excitation function (approximately two or three critical bandwidths, depending on absolute frequency), the resultant envelope is unimodal and would appear to involve a continuous interpolation between the conditions represented by the two excitations by

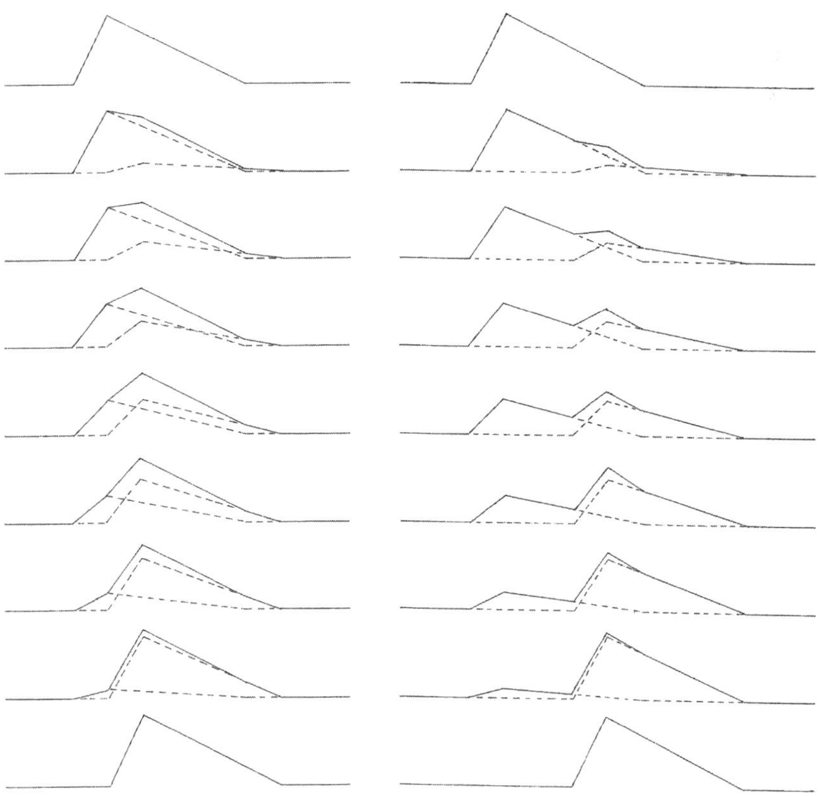

FIGURE 3a. For a small interval ("step"). FIGURE 3b. For a larger interval ("skip").

FIGURES 3a and 3b. Successive sums of two excitations, one rising, the other falling.

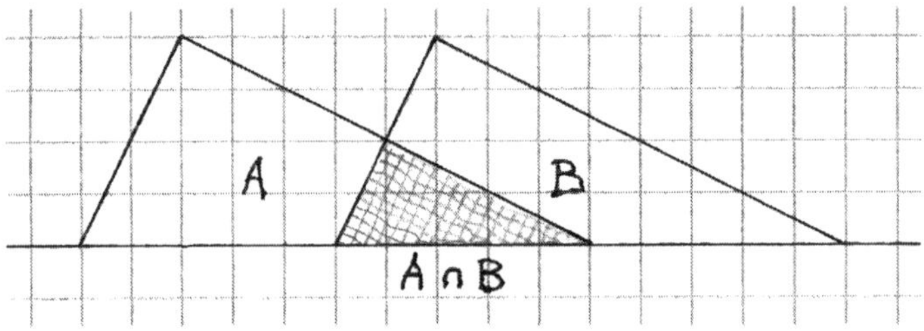

FIGURE 4. A similarity/dissimilarity measure between two excitations.

themselves—and thus, in some sense at least, between the two successive pitches. When, on the other hand, the melodic interval is greater than the length of the low-frequency skirt of the excitation function—as in figure 3b—the resultant envelope is bimodal. The difference between these two conditions corresponds to the distinction that has long been made in traditional music theory between melodic "steps" and "skips"—a distinction that might otherwise seem rather arbitrary.

3. In addition to the distance measure along the mel or *z*-scales (Zwicker 1970) appropriate to this aspect of pitch perception, another kind of "distance" (perhaps, more precisely, "difference") measure might be defined that would involve amplitude—again making use of Zwicker's *z*-scale as follows (see figure 4):

Define the similarity, $S(A,B)$ of two excitation functions (A and B) as

$$S(A,B) = m(A \cap B) / m(A \cup B)\,,$$

where m is area. Then a dissimilarity measure (a "distance"?), $D(A,B)$, might be

$$D(A,B) = 1 - S(A,B).$$

(Whether this might be used as an actual distance measure depends on whether it satisfies the criteria for such a metric—e.g., the triangle inequality—and I'm not sure about this, although my hunch is that it does.)[1]

Musicians have long been skeptical about the mel scale, and understandably so, since it is so very different from the logarithmic scales of musical practice. My proposal would suggest, however, that there need be no conflict between these two types of scales if they are related to two different aspects of the pitch percept, based on two different mechanisms.

I will now propose a model for the *harmonic* aspect of pitch perception that, while not intended to be a picture of what's actually happening in the auditory system, is a useful mathematical construct that can display many of the relations involved in harmonic perception. It takes the form of a lattice structure in what I call *harmonic space*. For a given set of pitches, the dimensions of this space would correspond to the *prime factors* required to specify their frequency ratios with respect to a reference pitch. It is a discrete space, not a continuous one, with the line segment connecting any two adjacent points in a graph of the lattice symbolizing a multiplication (or division) of the frequency ratio by the prime number associated with that dimension. Thus, the first two dimensions of such a lattice structure would involve the prime factors 2 and 3, and a step from one point to an adjacent point in the lattice would mean a shift up or down of one octave (in the 2-dimension) or of a twelfth (in the 3-dimension). What we have then is a two-dimensional harmonic space that would include any combination of octaves and fifths, i.e., any "Pythagorean" pitch set. Note that, if we imagine this lattice structure extended indefinitely outward in all directions, it must eventually include every possible ratio of two numbers whose prime factors are no larger than 3.

The one-dimensional continuum of pitch-height (i.e., "pitch" as ordinarily defined) can be represented as a central *axis of projection* within this harmonic space, as shown in figure 5. The position of a point on this pitch-height axis may be specified, as usual, by the logarithm of the fundamental frequency of the corresponding tone and the distance (or *pitch distance*) between two such points by the difference between their log-frequency values. That is,

$$PD(f_a, f_b) = \log(a/b) = \log(a) - \log(b)$$

where f_a and f_b are the fundamental frequencies of the two tones, and a and b are in maximally reduced or "relative prime" form, i.e., $a = f_a/\gcd(f_a, f_b)$, $b = f_b/\gcd(f_a, f_b)$, and $a \geq b$.

In harmonic space, another measure, which I call *harmonic distance*, can be defined for any interval represented by the frequency ratio $a{:}b$ as

$$HD(a,b) = \log(ab) = \log a + \log b,$$

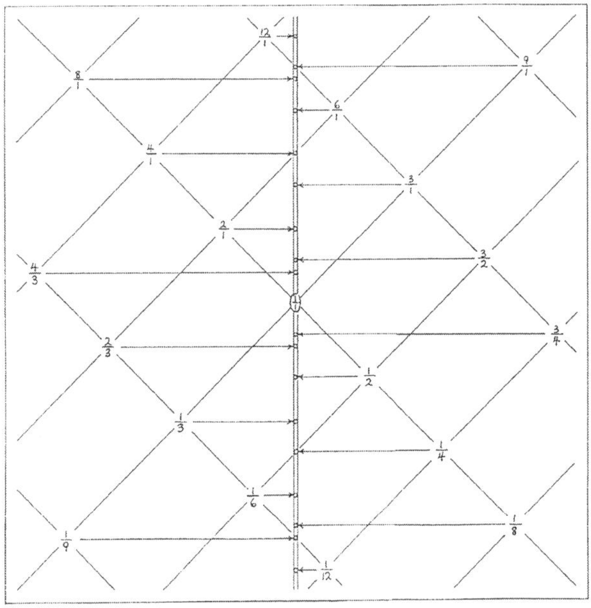

FIGURE 5. A two-dimensional (2,3) lattice in harmonic space, showing the pitch-height projection axis.

where *a* and *b* are again in relative prime form. I should note here that the idea of representing harmonic relations in terms of a multidimensional lattice structure has several important precursors, including the "duodenarium" of Alexander Ellis (in Helmholtz 1954); the "harmonic lattices" of Adriaan Fokker (1969); the "harmonic dimensions" of Longuet-Higgins (1962a, 1962b), who also coined the term *harmonic space*; and the "ratio lattices" of Ben Johnston (1971). The measure of harmonic distance defined above and the notions of a "pitch-height projection axis" and a "pitch-class projection space" (see below) are my own formulations.

In order to go beyond Pythagorean pitch or interval sets, we must introduce one or more new prime factors into our interval ratios and thus new dimensions in our lattice in harmonic space. In figure 6 an extension into a third dimension associated with the prime factor 5 is shown. Again, if such a three-dimensional harmonic space lattice were extended indefinitely in all directions, every possible frequency ratio involving the prime factors 2, 3, and 5 would eventually be included.

If we wish to extend the harmonic space lattice into yet another dimension, we run into the difficulty of representing four dimensions in

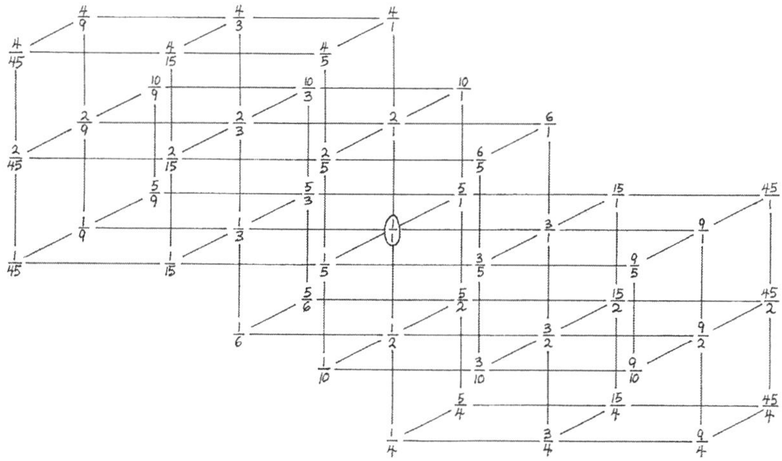

FIGURE 6. A three-dimensional (2,3,5) lattice in harmonic space.

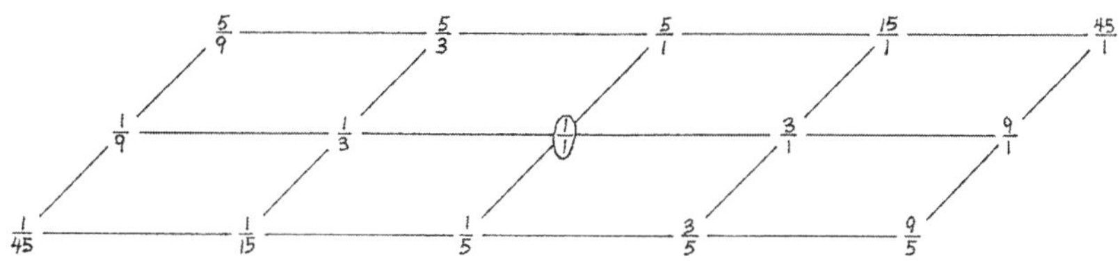

FIGURE 7. The two-dimensional (3,5) lattice in the pitch-class projection space derived from the lattice of figure 6.

a two-dimensional graph, but there is a useful device that can be introduced here that invokes "octave equivalence" and involves collapsing all the points whose labels differ only by a factor of a power of two into a single point, which then represents not a specific pitch (or interval with respect to 1/1) but rather a "pitch class." I call the resulting space, which contains one dimension less than the original lattice, a *pitch-class projection space*. Figure 7 shows the pitch-class projection space derived in this way from the lattice of figure 6. Figures 8a and 8b show the lattice structure for the major and minor diatonic scales (using Harry Partch's labeling convention, whereby a given pitch class is identified by the ratio it has in the first octave above 1/1). The Indian *sruti* system—as described in Sambamoorthy (1963)—would be represented as a two-dimensional lattice in a pitch-class projection space with prime factors 3 and 5, as shown in figure 9.

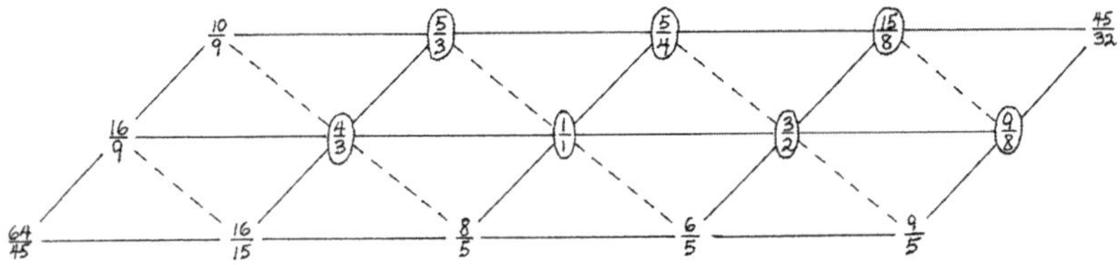

FIGURE 8a. The diatonic major.

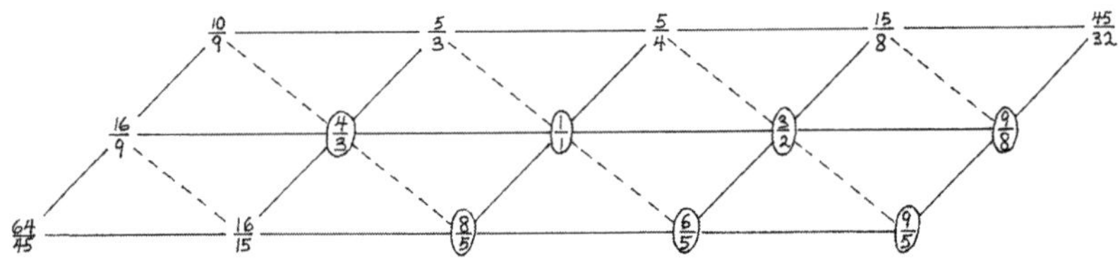

FIGURE 8b. The diatonic minor.

FIGURE 8a. and 8b. The just diatonic major and minor scales, mapped into harmonic space.

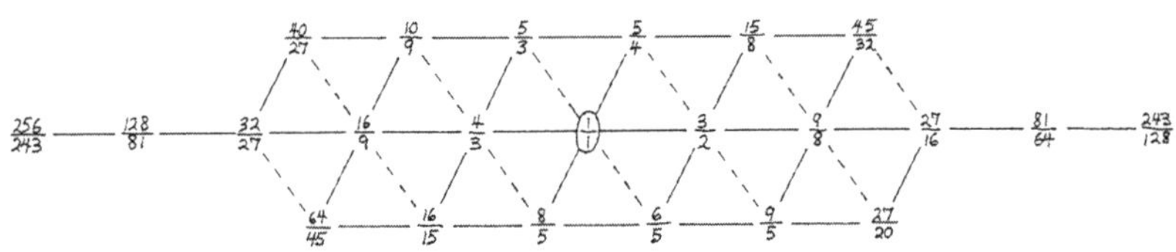

FIGURE 9. The Indian *sruti* system in harmonic space according to ratios given in Sambamoorthy (1963).

So far I have assumed that simple integer or "just" ratios are involved in the specification of a pitch or interval set. The harmonic space concept can be applied to tempered sets as well, but certain new factors must be taken into consideration. The most important is a notion that I call *interval tolerance* or simply *tolerance*: the idea that there is a certain finite region around a point on the pitch-height axis within which some slight mistuning is possible without altering the harmonic identity of an interval. The actual magnitude of this tolerance range would depend on several factors, and it is not yet possible to specify it precisely, but it seems likely that it would vary inversely with the ratio complexity of the interval. That is, the smaller the integers needed to designate the frequency ratio for a given interval, the larger its tolerance range would be. Now I propose as a general hypothesis in this regard that the auditory system would tend to interpret any given interval as thus "representing"—or being a variant of—*the simplest interval within the tolerance range* around the interval actually heard (where "simplest interval" means the interval defined by a frequency ratio requiring the smallest integers). The simpler *just* ratios thus become "referential" for the auditory system—not in any conscious or cognitive way but rather on a very primitive, precognitive, neurological level.

Another hypothesis might be added here that seems to follow from the first one and may help to clarify it: within the tolerance range, a mistuned interval will still carry *the same harmonic sense* as the accurately tuned interval does, although its timbral quality will be different—less "clear" or "transparent," for example, or more "harsh," "tense," or "unstable," etc. I should note that both of these hypotheses are based on a consideration of how the CNS might identify the harmonic interval between two tones. I suggest that this involves a comparison of neural pulse trains synchronous with the fundamental frequencies of the tones and that this comparison is mediated by something like a "coincidence neuron" (or some equivalent neural network) that fires only when two input pulses arrive simultaneously. The output of such a neuron would thus be another neural pulse train with a frequency determined by the common period of the two input pulse trains. But since neural pulses are of finite duration, we must replace the notion of absolute or discrete simultaneity with one of a finite *window of effective simultaneity*. I have no experimental data on which to base an estimate of the duration of such a "window," but a minimum duration—on the assumptions of my model—might be deduced from an estimate of the tolerance range itself. Thus, for example, if our tempered major third is functioning harmonically as a 5/4, the tolerance range must be at least 14 cents (= 400 – 386 cents), and neural pulse trains at these two relative frequencies (the just vs. the tempered) would be as 5/4 versus $\sqrt[3]{2}$, or 1.25/1.2599 = 0.992, so they differ by only eight-tenths of 1 percent! Thus, when we play a major triad on a tempered piano, where the major third is 14 cents larger than the just third, we are "understanding" that third as a 5/4 relationship; i.e., it has the same harmonic sense as a 5/4. It may sound unclear or even out of tune, but it's that particular (5/4) relationship "out of tune."

I introduced my topic by saying that there are two different aspects of pitch perception, both of which are essential not only in our day-to-day experience in the world but in music. And it is important to note that harmonic perception is not always involved in music. It can only occur when there are stable and salient pitches; we must hear a sound as a precise pitch, and it must remain fairly constant long enough for the nervous system to process it. And there is lots of wonderful music that has nothing whatsoever to do with this. To begin with, even in the West the percussion ensemble literature often involves sounds for which it is irrelevant whether they are clear pitches or not. The actual pitch of that wood block doesn't matter to us—we speak of higher or lower. And that's relating to the first aspect of pitch perception that I talked about. It's essential, it's musical, and it's important, but it's different. Many musical cultures make very precise distinctions, as we do in our culture, even when they modify them. For example, I would suggest—though I have no way of proving this—that the Thai 7-tone equal temperament was chosen historically, evolutionarily, because it contains pretty good approximations to perfect fourths and fifths, but there is also a wonderful ambiguity about the thirds. The third is kind of a neutral third (343 cents)—it can function in some ways harmonically like either a major or a minor third. And that ambiguity is important.

Our 12-tone equal temperament developed not because twelve is a nice number to divide things up into (although it is that) or because it has interesting group-theoretical properties (which it does; see Balzano 1980) but because it can function as a fairly good approximation to 5-limit just intervals. Similarly with Indonesian *pelog* and *slendro* scales. I think they were chosen or selected historically because they suggest certain harmonic relationships, but they also carry some ambiguities that are interesting and musically useful. So when I suggest that these simple ratios are *referential*, I'm trying to avoid what I take to be a wrongheaded dogma held in some quarters of the just intonation community—namely, that these simple ratios represent the only proper way to tune instruments. I don't agree with that. I think all kinds of tuning systems are potentially useful, including equal-tempered systems, but I still think that even the tempered relationships are being interpreted by the auditory system, quite unconsciously, as functioning like the simplest ratio within the tolerance range.

I am first of all a composer and only secondarily and occasionally a theorist. This notion of harmonic space is very useful to me as a composer. I can conceive of my music as *activity in harmonic space*—movement in that space. I almost imagine these points like little lights that flash on when the corresponding sound occurs. It's also extremely useful in scale development for working out new pitch sets or new tuning systems. I have, in fact, done several pieces where the tuning of the piece developed out of a lattice, like the diagrams that I've used to illustrate this talk. The problem of applying these ideas to other music is a large one, of course, and I am quite aware that there are many different factors involved there. Even if I am right about the referential character of simple ratios, there are so many other factors that come into play, that are crucial to the final result in a tuning system or what a music sounds like—factors of history, factors of organology, or the factor of ambiguity. This last is extremely important in art—in this context, for example, the ambiguity that can arise when a given tone, precisely because it *is* mistuned, can function harmonically in two or more different ways. It can suggest different relationships without even being changed, just by a change in its context.

References

Anderson, P. D. 1976. *Clinical Anatomy and Physiology for Allied Health Sciences*. Philadelphia: W. B. Saunders.

Balzano, Gerald J. 1980. "The Group-Theoretic Description of 12-Fold and Microtonal Pitch Systems." *Computer Music Journal* 4.4:66–84.

Fokker, A. D. 1969. "Unison Vectors and Periodicity Blocks in the Three-Dimensional (3-5-7) Harmonic Lattice of Notes." In *Proceedings of Koninklijke Nederlandsche Akademie van Wetenschappen* B72.3:153–68.

Helmholtz, Hermann. 1954. *On the Sensations of Tone*. New York: Dover. Translated from the edition of 1877 by Alexander J. Ellis.

Johnston, Ben. 1971. "Tonality Regained." *Proceedings of the American Society of University Composers* 6: 113–19.

Longuet-Higgins, H. Christopher. 1962a. "Letter to a Musical Friend." *Music Review* 23: 244–48.

———. 1962b. "Second Letter to a Musical Friend." *Music Review* 23: 271–80.

Sambamoorthy, P. 1963. *South Indian Music*. Madras: Indian Music Publishing House.

Stevens, S. S., and J. Volkman. 1940. "The Relation of Pitch to Frequency: A Revised Scale." *American Journal of Psychology* 53:329–53.

von Békésy, Georg. 1960. *Experiments in Hearing*. New York: McGraw-Hill.

Zwicker, E. 1970. "Masking and Psychological Excitation as Consequences of the Ear's Frequency Analysis." In *Frequency Analysis and Periodicity Detection in Hearing: Proceedings of the International Symposium held at Driebergen, the Netherlands, June 23–27, 1969*. Ed. Reiner Plomp and G. F. Smoorenburg. Leiden: Sijthoff.

CHAPTER 18

On "Crystal Growth" in Harmonic Space (1993/2003)

It seems clear, intuitively, that a concern for harmonic coherence would lead to the use of relatively compact, connected sets of points in harmonic space, where "connected" simply means that every element is adjacent to at least one other element in the set. How might such compactness be defined more precisely? I have been investigating an interesting algorithm in which sets of points are chosen, one by one, in some n-dimensional harmonic space, under the condition that each new point must have the smallest possible sum of harmonic distances to all points already in the set. That is, at each successive stage in the growth of the lattice, the next ratio added to the set is one whose sum of harmonic distances to each ratio already in the set is minimal. There will be frequent "branchpoints," where two or more ratios have equally minimal HD sums, and here the choice might be random. Thus, for example, in a simple 2,3-space, and always beginning with a reference pitch ("1" in most of the figures below), the first new point chosen (pitch 2) can only be one of the four points marked x and y in figure 1, and since S(x) is less than S(y), that second pitch must be at the octave above or below the reference pitch. If the upper octave is chosen (and it makes no difference to the final result which one is chosen, because the structure will remain invariant), the candidates for pitch 3 are the six adjacent points shown, with their corresponding sums of harmonic distances—S(x), S(y)—in figure 2.

Again at steps 4 and 5, the new pitches will be at the octave above or below those already in the set, because S(x) is still less than S(y) or

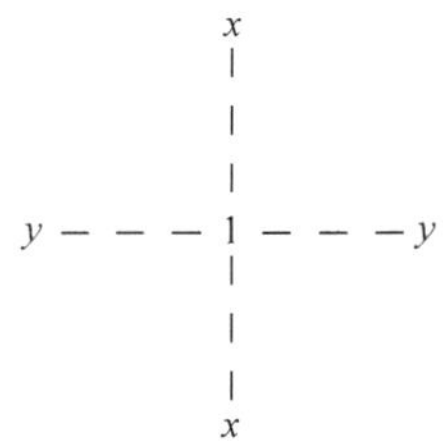

$S(x) = \log_2(2) = 1$

$S(y) = \log_2(3) = 1.585$

FIGURE 1.

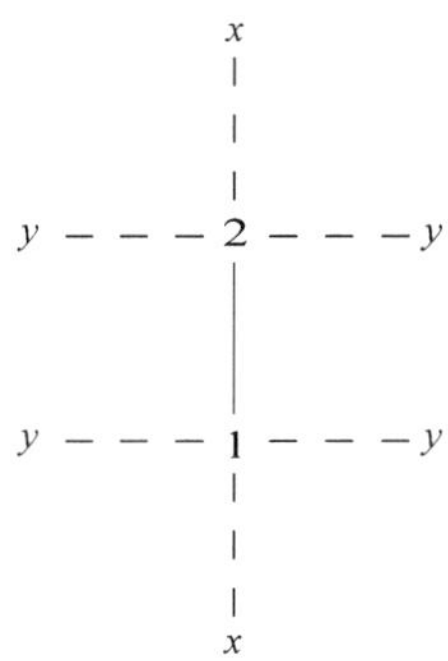

$S(x) = \log_2(2^3) = 3$

$S(y) = \log_2(2 * 3^2) = 4.17$

FIGURE 2.

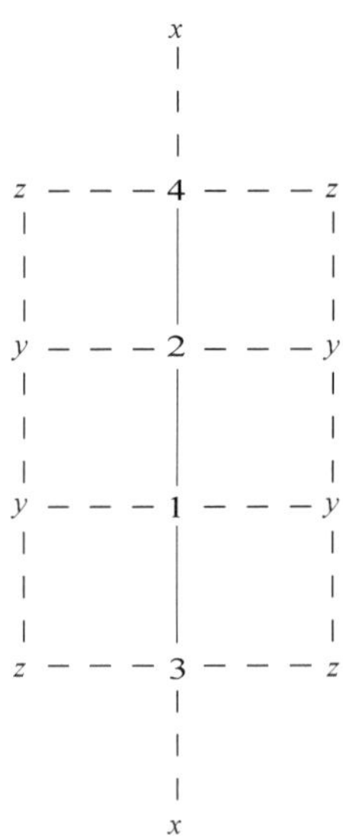

$S(x) = \log_2(2^{10}) = 10$

$S(y) = \log_2(2^4 * 3^4) = 10.34$

$S(z) = \log_2(2^6 * 3^4) = 12.34$

FIGURE 3. Step 5.

S(*z*), as can be seen in figure 3, but at step 6 this process of growth along the 2-axis will be replaced by an extension into the 3-dimension, as shown in figure 4. Note that in figure 3, S(*x*) is still smaller than S(*y*), whereas in figure 4, S(*x*) is considerably larger than S(*y*), suggesting a gradually increasing tendency (as the number of pitches increases) toward extension into the 3-dimension, with a concomitant decrease in the tendency toward continued extension along the 2-axis, finally tipping the balance between the two dimensions at step 6. Figures 5 through 8 show the two-dimensional lattices that result when this process is carried out through 10, 17, 24, and 36 points, respectively.

The symmetry of these sets is a characteristic property of all such "crystals" at certain stages of development and is, in fact, one of the reasons why the analogy with crystal growth suggested itself for this process.

Consider now the specifically musical implications of these structures in 2,3-space: in figure 9 the 17 points of figure 6 are shown again with the numbers representing order of generation replaced by frequency ratios in figure 9a and pitch names in figure 9b (indexed for register, with C_4 meaning middle C), with 1/1 shifted to the center of the lattice

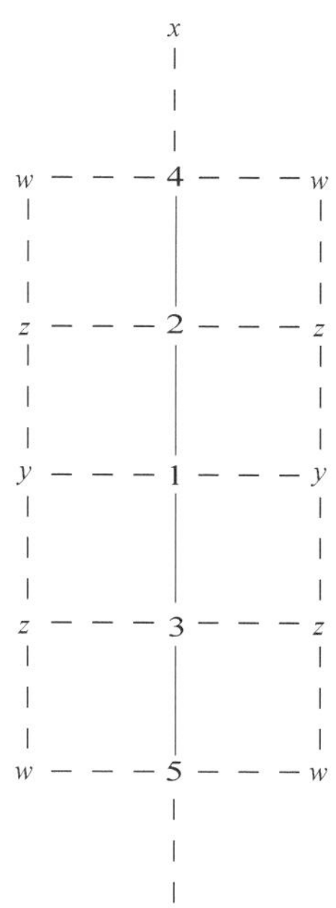

$S(x) = \log_2(2^{15}) = 15$

$S(y) = \log_2(2^6 * 3^5) = 13.92$

$S(z) = \log_2(2^7 * 3^5) = 14.92$

$S(w) = \log_2(2^{10} * 3^5) = 17.92$

FIGURE 4. Step 6.

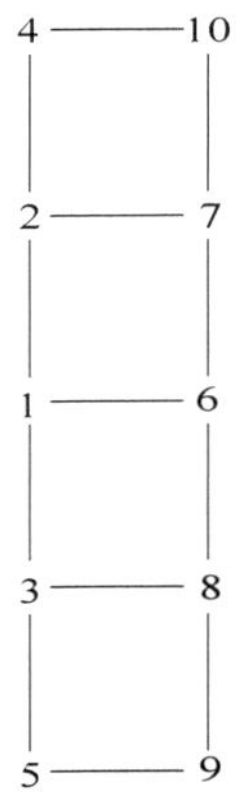

Figure 5. 10 points in 2,3-space.

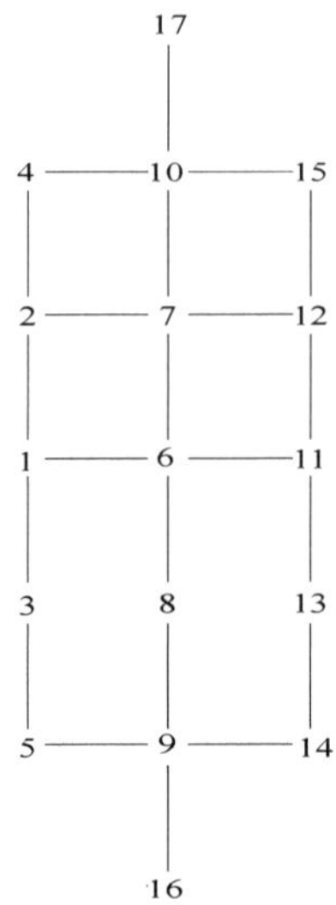

Figure 6. 17 points in 2,3-space.

Figure 7. 24 points in 2,3-space.

FIGURE 8. 36 (and 38) points in 2,3-space.

(the ratio 1/1 is identified here with F_4 for no other reason than to center the whole pitch set with respect to the piano keyboard). In spite of the fairly large difference between $\log_2(2)$ and $\log_2(3)$, the lattice has only extended three octaves above and below the central point, while two new pitch classes have been added to the set. This particular lattice is of special interest because it does not extend beyond the usual range of musical instruments and could thus be mapped onto the piano keyboard (for example).

In the 24-element lattice shown in figures 7, 10a, and 10b, a fourth pitch class has been added to the set, but the range has now been extended somewhat beyond that of the piano (a perfect fifth above and below the range of a Bösendorfer Imperial). It is at least very interesting (even if no more than a coincidence) that four of the five pitch classes of the Pythagorean pentatonic set are generated by this process before the pitch range has greatly exceeded the actual limits of musical perception.

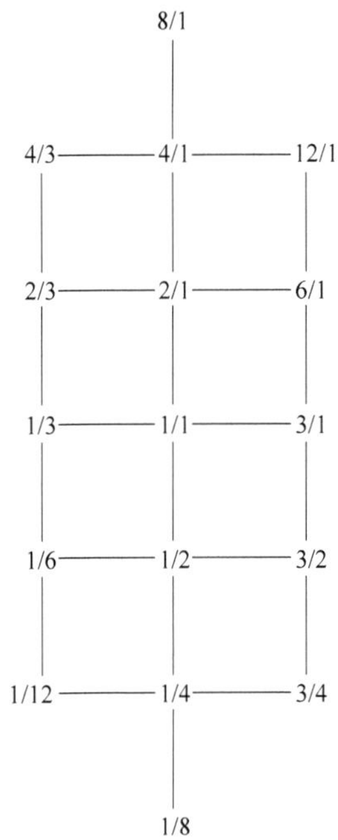

FIGURE 9a.

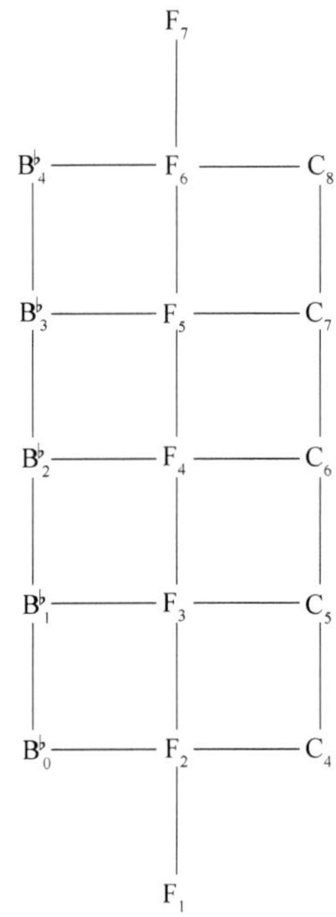

FIGURE 9b.

FIGURE 10a.

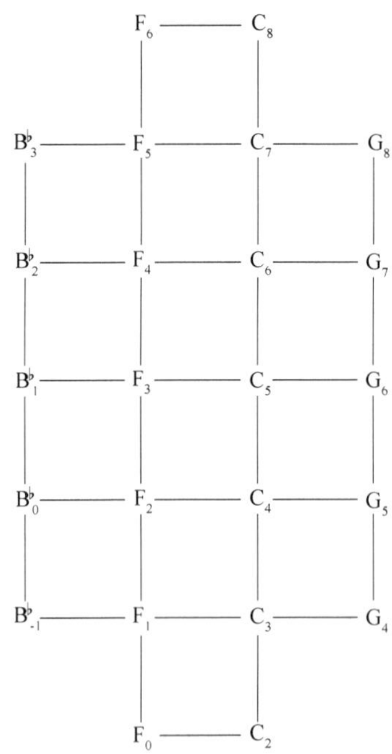

FIGURE 10b.

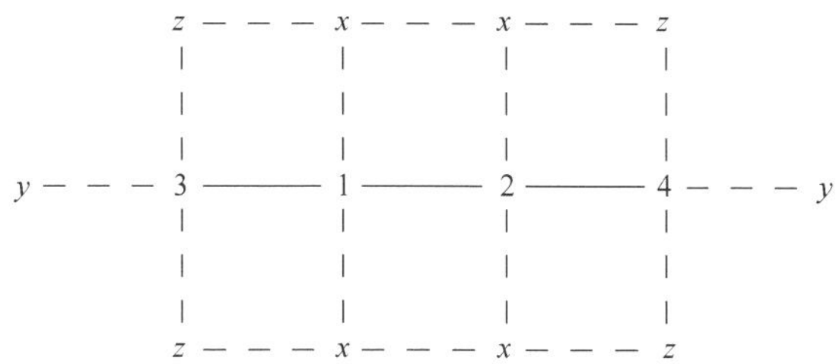

$S(x) = \log_2(3^4 * 5^4) = 15.63$

$S(y) = \log_2(3^{10}) = 15.85$

$S(z) = \log_2(3^6 * 5^4) = 18.80$

FIGURE 11.

These lattices in 2,3-space have been considered here primarily to demonstrate some aspects of the "crystal growth" process in general, even though they may not be particularly significant musically. The musical implications of this process become richer and I believe clearly significant when we study the behavior of such gradually developing "crystals" in various higher-dimensional pitch-class projection spaces. For example, crystal growth in the 3,5-space seems closely related to the historical development of scales and tuning systems in Western music, from Pythagorean 3-limit through 5-limit just systems, and even including our more recent twelve-tone equal temperament. Beginning, as before, with an initial reference pitch, the lattice grows along the 3-dimension, linearly, until four of the five elements of a Pythagorean pentatonic set have been generated, as shown in figure 11 (note: from here on, the 3-dimension is again represented by horizontal axes, but the vertical axes now represent the 5-dimension).

At this stage, there are very nearly equal values of harmonic distance sums for two different sets of candidate pitches, the pair labeled *y* in figure 11, either of which would result in a full pentatonic set, and the four points labeled *x*, any one of which will initiate an extension into the 5-dimension (and it is, of course, one of these that is chosen by the algorithm). If a *y* had been chosen instead of an *x*, the harmonic distance sums at the next stage would have been as shown in figure 12, where

$$S(x) = \log_2(3^6 * 5^5) = 21.12$$

$$S(y) = \log_2(3^{15}) = 23.77$$

$$S(z) = \log_2(3^7 * 5^5) = 22.70$$

$$S(w) = \log_2(3^{10} * 5^5) = 27.46,$$

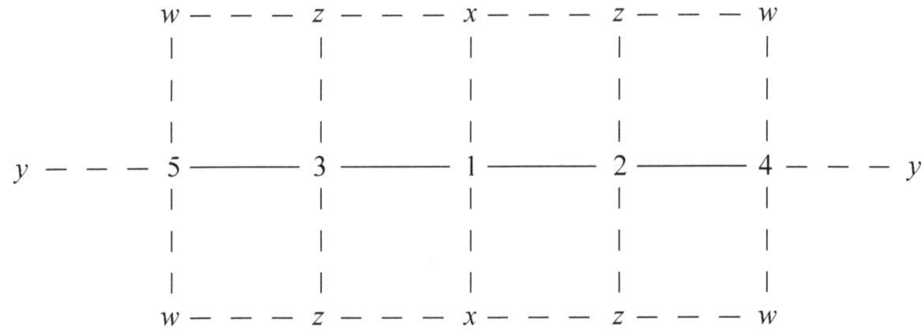

FIGURE 12.

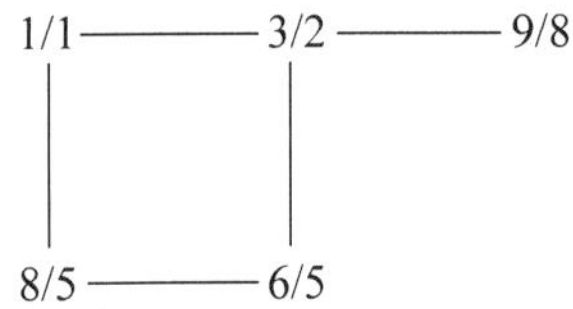

FIGURE 13a.

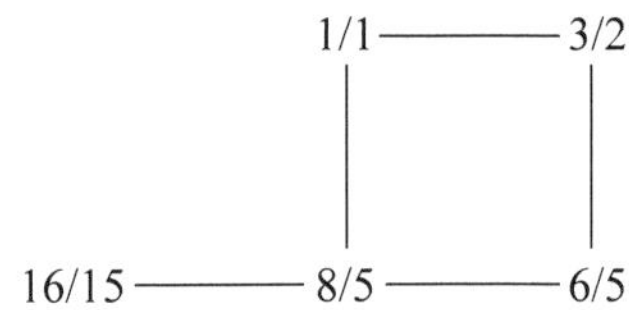

FIGURE 13b.

and it is especially to be noted that even S(z), as well as S(x), is smaller the S(y) (which latter, if it had been chosen, would have extended the Pythagorean set beyond the pentatonic set).

Thus, in addition to other reasons that might be adduced for the ubiquitous manifestations of the Pythagorean pentatonic scale (not only in Western music but in many other cultures as well), this crystal growth model suggests another—specifically harmonic—reason: for a set of pitches arrayed along this single (3-)axis, five pitches constitute a kind of limit beyond which the tendency toward extension into a new dimension (the 5-dimension) becomes decisive. This assumes, of course, that such an extension is not prohibited by Aristotelian dogma, as it evidently was in Western music theory until sometime in the sixteenth century.

The Pythagorean pentatonic set may be conceived as a pitch set that arises when extension into the 3,5-plane is just slightly delayed beyond the point where the algorithm would have begun that extension. Interesting sets also arise when the extension into the 3,5-plane occurs "prematurely," as shown in figures 13a and 13b, below. Note that these represent the two Japanese *koto* scales, *hirajoshi* and *kumoijoshi* (Malm), and the latter might even be taken as approximated by the Balinese five-tone *pelog* scale (McPhee).[1]

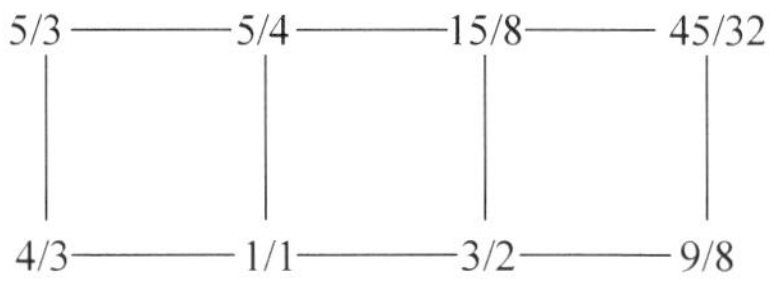

FIGURE 14. 8 points in 3,5-space. Note that this contains both major and minor diatonic sets; major on 1/1 (if 45/32 is omitted) and minor on 5/4 (if 4/3 is omitted).

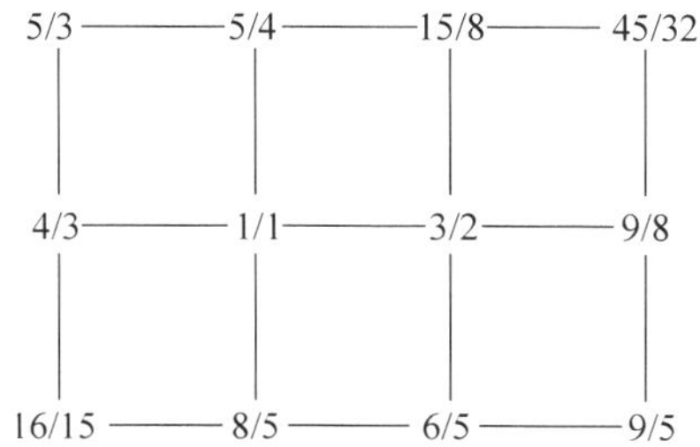

FIGURE 15. 12 points in 3,5-space. This contains both the major and the minor sets simultaneously, both built on 1/1 (the two upper rows minus 45/32 for the major; the two lower rows minus 16/15 for the minor).

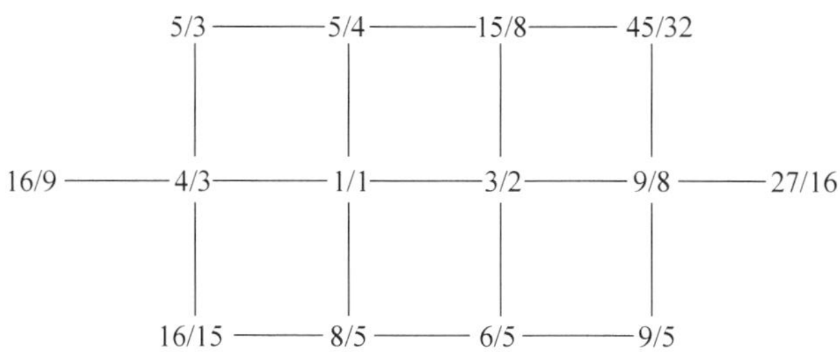

FIGURE 16. 14 points in 3,5-space (adding to the 12-set of figure 15 two of the most frequently needed "alternative tunings," for the major sixth—27/16 [as the fifth of a secondary dominant] in addition to 5/3 [the submediant]—and the minor seventh—16/9 [as the subdominant of the subdominant] in addition to 9/5 [the third of a dominant minor]).

Once the lattice (as generated by the algorithm) has begun to move into the 3,5-plane, the following symmetrical configurations are generated, containing 8, 12, and 14 pitch classes, respectively (figures 14–16).

At this stage in the "crystal growth" process, if ratio-generation is not constrained to remain within the 5-limit, the next element chosen by the algorithm will be one of the 7-ratios indicated by the points labeled x in figure 17, so the 14-element 3,5-lattice appears to be approaching some kind of natural limit for 5-limit lattice structures, just as the 4-element Pythagorean set seemed to be doing for 3-limit structures. Figures 18 and 19 show symmetrical lattices of 18 and 22 points, respectively, in 3,5,7-space.

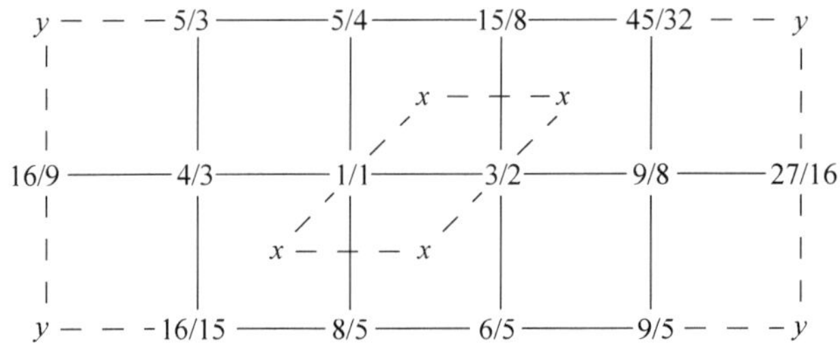

FIGURE 17. Candidates for the next element to be added to the lattice of figure 16, where S(x) = 84.82, S(y) = 87.98.

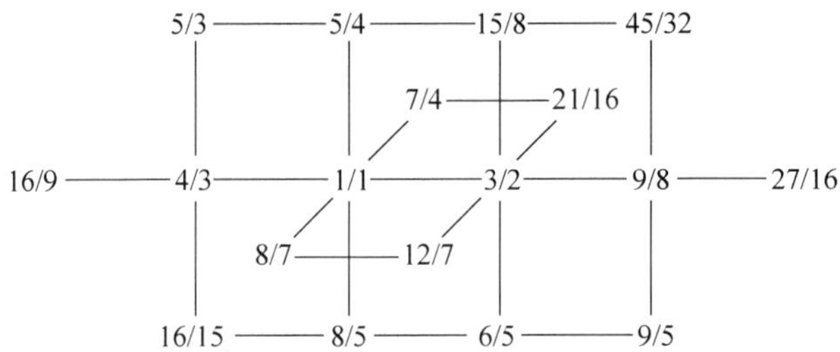

FIGURE 18. 18 points in 3,5,7-space.

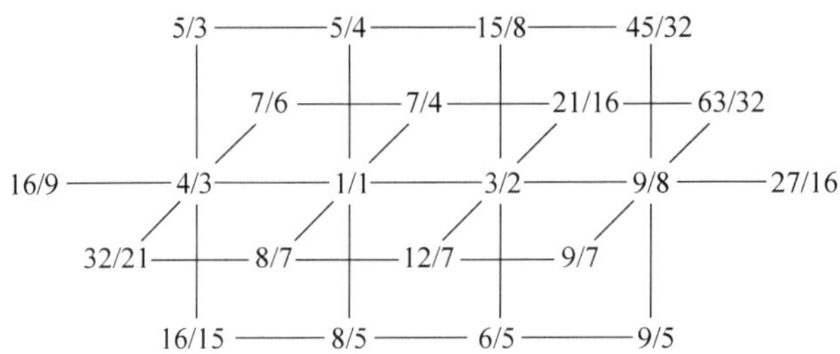

FIGURE 19. 22 points in 3,5,7-space.

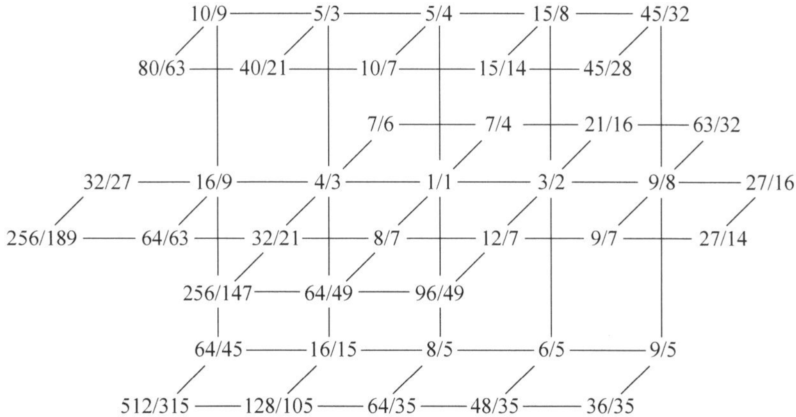

FIGURE 20. 41 points in 3,5,7-space.

Continuing in this way, larger and larger lattices will be built up, but for some reason it appears that none of them are completely symmetrical again until 76 points have been generated, although a few of them are very nearly symmetrical. After 50 elements have been generated in 3,5,7-space—if ratio-generation is not constrained to remain within the 7-limit—the next element chosen by the algorithm will be one involving the next-higher prime number—11—thus initiating growth in a new dimension.

CHAPTER 19

About *Diapason*

(1996)

From Greek *(he) dia pason (chordon symphonia)* . . . (the concord) through all (the notes) . . . "a burst of harmonious sound . . . a full deep outburst of sound" (*Webster's*) . . . also an organ stop, and (earlier) the octave; (still earlier) the set of pitches that might "fill" an octave (i.e., a scale or mode). Here I am using it to refer to a band of seventeen adjacent harmonic partials of a very low fundamental (a B♭ at approximately 29 Hz). This band is not stationary but moves very gradually from one pitch position to another within the harmonic series, and as it moves, the bandwidth changes as well. For example, near the beginning and the end of the piece, the "diapason" includes harmonics from the forty-eighth through sixty-fourth (thus defining an interval of a perfect fourth), whereas at the dynamic climax of the piece (at about two-thirds to three-quarters of the way through), it includes the first through the seventeenth partials (a little more than four octaves). The harmonic sense of the work depends to a great extent on how precisely these pitches are tuned, and since most of the partials in the harmonic series do not coincide with pitches of the standard 12-tone equal-tempered scale, some unusual procedures are required to perform the piece. These include the following: (1) all of the string instruments are retuned in an elaborate *scordatura*, such that the pitches of every open string and its natural harmonics correspond to some subset of the harmonic partials of the same low B♭; (2) wind players are free to choose from the set of pitches being played at any moment by the string players nearest to them, carefully matching their pitches to the string tones by ear but timing their entrances in a quasi-improvisational way; and (3) to facilitate this process, each wind player is seated between two string players or is, in fact, surrounded by from four to six string players whose pitches can thus be matched in this way.

One might well ask why we should go to such extraordinary lengths to produce these unusual pitches, and my answer is that I believe we have entered a new music-historical era during which there will be a resumption of the evolutionary development of *harmony*, a development that had reached an impasse in Western art music in about 1910 because the specifically *harmonic* resources of 12-tone equal temperament had been exhausted. And whereas the hegemony of 12-tone equal temperament had begun to be undermined by work with quarter tones (and other equal divisions of the octave) at about the same time (ca. 1910) by composers like Hába, Carrillo, Ives, Wyschnegradsky, and others, it was not until the pioneering work by Harry Partch, beginning in the 1930s, and the aesthetic revolution brought about by John Cage in 1951 that the harmonic limitations of 12-tone equal temperament began to be understood and a way could be imagined in which *harmony* could serve other—nonsyntactical—purposes than it had during the preceding three and a half centuries. For Partch, the crucial factor was *just intonation*—i.e., using pitches tuned in such a way that the intervals between them may be characterized by relatively small *integer ratios* between frequencies. For reasons that are both theoretical and practical, I have come to the conclusion that a certain amount of *tolerance* must be assumed, with respect to both the precision with which it is possible to tune acoustical instruments in the "real world," and the acuity of our auditory systems in distinguishing small pitch differences, although the size of the tolerance range I have come to accept (about 5 cents, or one-twentieth of a tempered semitone) is much smaller than that which I believe is implied by the performance of triadic-diatonic music of the common practice period on a tempered piano (at least 15 cents, and sometimes—as in the case of the dominant seventh chord—as large as 31 cents, or nearly a third of a tempered semitone).

I have written elsewhere (in "Reflections after *Bridge*," 1984) that while Partch's contribution to this new situation in which we find ourselves was primarily technical, Cage's contribution was primarily aesthetic.[1] I would now suggest that the aesthetic revolution wrought by John Cage in 1951 is absolutely essential to any truly progressive evolution of harmony, because without its decisive shift of focus from *the thoughts and feelings of the composer*—and their "communication" to a relatively passive audience—to *the immediate auditory experience of the listener*—which may be said to be "occasioned" by the work of the composer but assumes an active, participatory audience—the future of music would remain mired in the past. Before harmony can evolve, the *role of music itself* must evolve. Otherwise we will simply be replaying an earlier scenario with minor, "cosmetic" changes in the details.

While celebrating the profound influence on my own work of both Harry Partch and John Cage, I should also mention some aspects of much of my music—and *Diapason* in particular—that are peculiarly my own. The first involves my fascination not only with just intervals but with a particular subset of these—the *harmonic series*. It is perhaps the only thing given to us by nature (as distinct from culture) and is intimately involved in our perception of the vowels of speech as well as the timbre of musical instruments. What I have done that may be new is to find a number of different ways to use the harmonic series as the basis for an entire piece (first in *Clang* for Orchestra, 1972). The second involves my concern with *form* not as a rhetorical device (as in the sonata) or as a means to ensure "comprehensibility" (Schoenberg's motivation) but simply as another *object of perception*—like the sounds themselves but at a larger holarchical level. In *Diapason*, the form is determined primarily by the changes in the pitch-boundaries of the band of adjacent harmonics and secondarily by changes in dynamic level, both as a function of time, as shown in the figure below.[2]

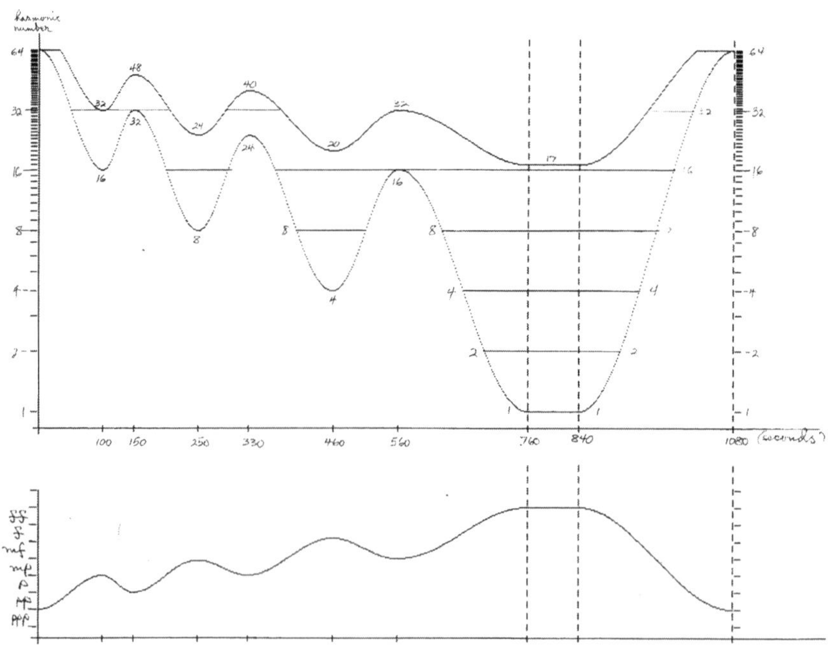

APPENDIX 1

Pre–*Meta ≠ Hodos*

(December, 1959)

[What follows are a series of early efforts to develop a new theory "from scratch", before writing *Meta ≠ Hodos* in 1961. The influences of John Cage and Gertrude Stein are pretty clear; apparently my efforts to attain some clarity with respect to these theoretical issues sometimes drove me to "poetry," when not to tears.[1]]

I. The necessary thing now is to start if possible at the very beginning, to clear the mind of loose ends whose origins are forgotten; loose ends and means become habits. What do we hear when we listen; if we really listen what do we really hear when listening. This means too, what do we hear first and what later after learning after words. (1) *The substance of it is SOUND, the essence, TIME*. Sound and Time. Sound in time sounding time. "A sound is a sound, a man is a man" (Cage, meaning the 5th Symphony (or whatever) is *not* Beethoven (or whomever)—is only itself and should not be confused with another). But further, a sound is one, and any one sound is like another in its being one, a unit, one equals one in this sense, and a sine-tone may be a complex-tone may be a chord may be a melodic-figure or a click may be a noise (white or not) may again be a sine-tone and often is. The differences are in the hearing not in the making as such. Thus we begin with (2) *the sound perceived as a unit*—whether point, line, plane or volume; image, object, word, shot, stroke, gesture, form, figure, shape—in short, a *Gestalt*; a *CLANG*. And this unitary perception of the sound must be understood as prior to, and preceding our analysis of it into the categories or characteristics that follow. The question which comes next in these beginnings, the (timeless) sound or the (soundless) time, is not asked in principle, the answer being arbitrary—the two are reciprocal functions (both are egg, inside and outside) and only separable artificially—that is by definition. Except perhaps that there may not be (timeless) sound, while there may very well be (soundless) time, i.e., *SILENCE* ("ambient noise", Cage). So, taking first the aspect of time, we know we have (3) *DURATION* (whether of sound or of silence) and to begin with, *long-short*, (primary), and its reciprocal—by accumulation in succession—*slow-fast*, (also primary but derived from above). More of this later, when the definitions become more precise. Next must be the sound itself, in the most general terms. What have been called the "secondary characteristics" are here primary, i.e., most immediate. (4) The clang has a certain VOLUME ("weight" or "mass") which is a (subjective) measure of its quantity and to some extent quality. Physics can show this measure to depend upon—to be a function of—relative frequency, intensity, timbre, duration, etc., but the ear does not know this immediately, and the fact of its being related to changes in each of the parameters—or any of them, argues for its being more a fundamental property than any one of these parameters by itself. By analogy with (3) then, we may say that the measure *large-small* must correspond to the primary character of the sound, and that further differentiations will all derive from this: in pitch (register) *low-high*, in loudness *loud-soft*, (and within this, include *near-distant* of spatial distribution), and in duration, as above, *long-short*. All this seems obvious, and it is—so obvious that we tend to take it for granted and thereby forget that these rough distinctions can be and have been used as the basic form-building factors in music. (See, i.e., *hear* Schoenberg's op. 11, #3, where it is precisely these factors and hardly anything else that define its form).

To go back. It is necessary now to go back. I have spoken of "definitions" and have defined nothing. Description is hard enough (to be real) but definition is still more difficult. Perhaps impossible. What *is* sound? And time. And silence. The first has been defined for us—many times. By physics (a disturbance of the air) and by anatomy (a disturbance of the inner ear—of the basilar membrane), which sends nerve-impulses to the brain, creating . . .), by psychology (sensations of sound). Preceding these and presupposed by them—an activity, a manipulation (of the instrument) and/or (when non-electronic) the compositional process. This last is at the beginning and the end of a circle, since the sound is more than a "sensation", it is "the substance" of the matter. Activity—disturbance—sensation—substance—activity—etc. Let this

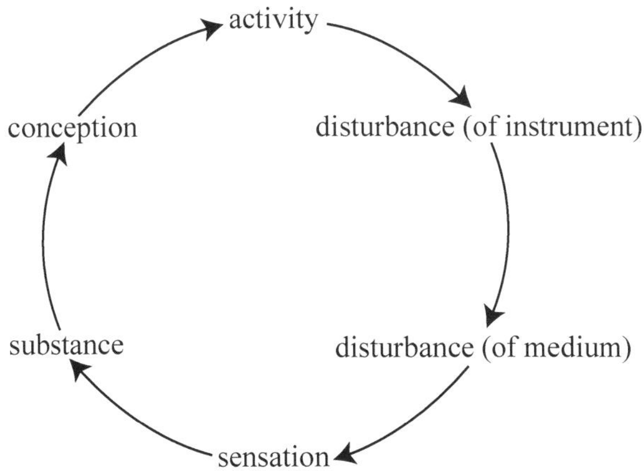

then be our provisional definition. For time, we can give no definition except in terms of what happens in it. It is (is it?) the field wherein sound exists. Rather, it is one dimension of that field. There are others. The field is perhaps silence. Consider silence the field, and time one dimension of that field. We may say that sound is (a disturbance) *in* the field, or [better] (a disturbance) *of* the field, since sound is a disturbance *of* air, and *of* the basilar membrane (inert air—inert membrane, as analogs of silence).

To continue. It is necessary to continue. More or less fine distinctions may be made as to pitch, loudness, timbre, duration, etc., and there is little consistency in differentiability of these different features. Our perception of pitch is the most refined, and next to that, duration. That is, in these we can grasp *relations* somewhat beyond the "more-or-less", perceivable in loudness. This does not necessarily mean finer distinctions, but the possibility of realizing *proportions*. Very fine distinctions can be made in terms of both loudness and timbre, but we are not equipped to realize exact proportions. It is in this respect that our pitch-perception is "most refined", and the capacity to hear subtle relationships has been the basis for much of the development of western music. But it is important to remember that we also hear less subtle relations of pitch, the aspect of *direction* which produces what may be called "pitch-shape", and may be and has been the basis for certain ("non-harmonic") formal processes. The exact pitch-relations may be altered, without substantially altering the "shape" of the figure—and the shape may be completely changed (by octave transposition of parts of it) without altering the "harmonic" constitution of the figure. This ambivalence of pitch-relations may be partly responsible for the importance the pitch-factors have had in western music for so long.

Here we have implied another basic aspect of sound—(5) *SHAPE*—the clang has a certain shape in time (this should really precede questions of individual parameters). And if it has no particularly articulate shape in time (i.e., if it is "rectilinear"), it will at least have *QUALITY*, which might be understood as "shape" independent of time (thus, steady-state timbre may be represented graphically as intensity vs. pitch), that is, quality is shape which does not change in time—or conversely, shape is quality which changes in time—again, reciprocal. At this point, I am no longer able to rely on simple verbal intuition for the development of the definitions and descriptions. The very notion of shape is an analogy from the visual realm, and to describe the various relations of shape it is necessary to resort to graphic representation. Ideally, any clang could be graphed in several ways, and each way will produce a picture of the "shape" of one of its parameters in terms of another. Thus, with respect to time, there will be a pitch-shape, an intensity-shape, etc. In addition, time may be graphed "against" itself, as duration vs. sequence, yielding a rhythmic shape. As I said above, timbre may be graphed as pitch vs. intensity, although this is only a partial representation of timbre (which changes in time too) and cannot represent transients, etc. Other non-temporal graphs can show harmonic disposition (intensity vs. pitch in the larger structure, or pitch vs. timbre). The actual "shape" of the clang is in some sense perhaps the sum of all these different "shapes" and yet probably more than this too, since we are working only with an analogy, and cannot get at the sound itself (except by listening to it!).

Upon reflection it becomes clear that there may very well be a time without sound but there may not be a sound without time, and thus our point (2) is premature perhaps when what needs definition is time without sound or no sound that is silence. And yet how can time be defined it cannot be except in terms of what may exist in it or can it be. And how can silence be heard as anything other than nothing in time that is empty time when sound is not. But think a moment. Think of a moment when there is no sound that is sound surrounding us the ear still the ears still hear within this stillness something still within the ear ("two tones, one the blood and one the nerves", Cage). And it is said that if the ear were any more sensitive than it is we would hear the dance of air molecules called white (thermal) noise. I wonder do we not hear this already (listen carefully on a warm summer night). With the eyes it is just so; when we close them it is not black inside but grey. Thus Cage again: for silence, "ambient noise". It is instructive now to imagine the inner ear, the basilar membrane and its thousands of tiny hairs all within a fluid wherein vibrations may be set up and localized on the membrane by resonance. Here "silence" is the condition of least activity. There may never be no activity, but there are times of least activity. This we call silence, and it has extension in (at least) one dimension which we call time and it may be defined as the basic, primary aural condition corresponding to the basic primary manifestations of the life process itself, that is the vibrations of the nervous system and the circulation of the blood. Our definition of time is then physiological and simpler than that it cannot be. Our definition of silence is then physiological also and is the simplest condition that may be. It is in a very real way the field within which sound occurs—the continuum of the audible realm from which everything else may be derived and to which everything else will be related. Sound itself is no more nor less than a disturbance within this field, a disturbance of the field, of its "flatness"—that is a distortion or a warping of the continuum. I said distortion but "shaping" is better. Sound is a shaping of the continuum, a shaping of the field of silence, a shaping of silence. Silence is simply the simplest sound. Silence is the "flat" sound the "grey" sound, and sound is simply a shaping of the field wherein silence is simply the sound with the least shape, in time. In time, we come back to time since whenever we say shape we must remember always that such a shape is always a time-shape and this must not be forgotten since shape is a borrowed word, borrowed from the visual realm where shape is seen as independent of time, that is it is seen as a shape in space. Here we have a shape in time (there can also be a shape *of* time, but this later). This is especially difficult to remember that our sound-shapes are time-shapes and not of space. Especially difficult to remember since to some extent we have learned to hear changes in pitch as movements in space. And to some extent this may be because changes in pitch are registered in the inner ear as changes in position in space (that is on the basilar membrane). And we say a sound is "high" or "low" in pitch which is of course by analogy with high or low in space, but curiously the expressions "high pitched" and "keyed up" etc., do not mean anything spatial and are very nearly accurate descriptions of the real sensations of pitch-difference. The essential things here are *speed* and *tension* which are dynamic and not at all spatial but temporal. Then there is the question of notation and this perhaps is where we (musicians at least) lose the sense of time-shape as such and come to think of it in terms of space. What is forgotten then is that the symbols of our notation are not at all symbols of the sound, not this but rather symbols of the act or operation or movement designed to produce the sound. What is needed then is to remember that sound (and silence) is a shape and that it is first of all a time-shape. Only then can we pretend (as Varèse does) that it is space we are concerned with—and proceed to explore the possibilities of movement and change within this "space" which is really not space at all but by pretending that it is (after first knowing that it isn't) one is committed to the task of exploring many more possibilities than before since it means a realization of a multi-dimensional continuum, a complex field of forces inherent in the nature of sound in the nature of silence. He (Varèse) "pretends" that it is space that is involved and this is not the same as others who have simply forgotten that it is *not* space that is involved. He knows very well that space is space and not time and uses space as space like no other before or after him. He uses time as time as well like no other before or after, even when he calls it space. He knows very well. (But then, what *is* space, if not simply the field in which we perceive objects—that property which separates one from another, *etc.?*).

II. Sound and Silence are conditions of the field. I said that the field is silence. The field is not silence. Silence is a special condition of the field. Sound is a special condition of the field. Time is one dimension of the field. Any sound is a particular shaping of the field and silence is a particular shaping of the field unique in its being the least shaping possible, that is "flat". Sound is a particular curvature of the field where silence has curvature zero (or nearly zero, that is, the least curvature).

It is necessary really to begin at the beginning. In the beginning is living. In the beginning is listening and in this beginning listening is living, is listening to this living. When there is nothing more than this still there is always this living we are hearing and this is called silence. In this very beginning of living and listening to this living there is always at least what we call silence and this silence is not nothing, not at all nothing. We know this. We know that when listening we are hearing something and this is living and this is the first sound we are always making in living and this is the first sound we are always hearing in listening and we call this sound silence and know that this is not by any means nothing. It is the sound we make in listening.

[end of typed page 6; on the back the following *typed* text:][2]

The one measure common to both sound and silence is (as Cage has said), DURATION, and from this say that the primary definition of anything sounding or anything silent is its duration, and to begin with simply long or short. This is a "binary" description of it, and will correspond to other binary descriptions which will follow. A consideration of the differences between sound and silence will lead to these other primary definitions. It is already demonstrated above that the essential difference is one of shape. There is also a difference in "size" that is AMPLITUDE or loudness. Clearly silence has amplitude of (nearly) zero since it is the least amplitude possible and any other sound must be of greater amplitude. Thus our next primary measure is amplitude and its binary description as loud or soft.

Thus we deduce: from Living, LISTENING and HEARING, and from these SILENCE & SOUND. From Silence and Sound, SHAPE, from Shape, CHANGE and thus TIME. From Time, DURATION and from Change of Shape in Time, EXTENSITY & ACUITY (and perhaps Direction?). From Extensity and Acuity, AMPLITUDE, PITCH, and (again) Duration. The reciprocal of Duration is SPEED (or Temporal Density). From Pitch (in micro-structure) and thus Speed or Tempo (in macro-structure) we deduce PERIODICITY, and from Periodicity, RELATION or PROPORTION. From Silence, Sound, and Shape, I derive CLANG. And from all of the above I derive the FIELD, Silence and Sound being particular Conditions of the Field. There are Three Unique Conditions of the Field, viz., SILENCE (minimal), WHITE NOISE (maximal) and TONE (harmonic division)—(that is, three unique conditions in terms of the pitch-dimension, independent of time). Alternately, all three conditions might be considered in terms of Tone (as in Fourier analysis) in which case White Noise would be the continuous band of harmonics of an infinitely low frequency, and Silence the situation of an infinitely high frequency (or one simply out of audible range) (this last is not actually derived from Fourier analysis, but rather a logical point).

[the following "insert" is from a separate sheet marked simply "Illinois", but seems to belong here][3]

The sound-material must be made "plastic", and for this the piano does not serve. Nor will the electronic equipment unless I avoid at the very beginning using single tones of definite pitch. It will be necessary to find some new means of working that will lead me directly to more or less complete clangs. This means: that all proportional relations will be irrelevant at the start. It will be "rough" shapes and qualities that *are* relevant—any "relations" being secondary.

THE CRUCIAL THING ABOUT CLANG COMPOSITION IS THAT IT IS NO LONGER CONCERNED WITH RELATIONS IN THEMSELVES BUT WITH THE SOUNDS. THE SOUNDS IN THEMSELVES, NOT THE RELATIONS BETWEEN THEM EXCEPT IN SO FAR AS THESE RELATIONS CREATE SHAPE OR FORM OR QUALITY. SHAPE AND FORM AND QUALITY ARE PRIMARY, RELATIONS SECONDARY. IT SEEMS THAT MOST MUSIC HAS HAD TO DO WITH THE RELATIONS, OR MOST MUSICIANS THINK OF IT SO.

III. What is wanted now and what is attempted here is to find a beginning to our thinking about the matter of music which is not to be found in our thinking but in our feeling or in our feeling and thinking as one thing which is the act of listening or the fact of hearing. I am not concerned with feeling or thinking as such but with feeling and thinking as hearing and listening that is as living. What do we hear when we listen, if we really listen what do we really hear when listening. It is necessary really to begin at the beginning. In the beginning is living [living struck out and replaced by listening]. In the beginning is listening [listening replaced by living].[4] In this beginning in the very beginning listening is living. In this very beginning listening is living, listening is hearing living, hearing is listening to this very living. In this beginning to our thinking about the matter of hearing we are listening and knowing that our listening is living and feeling that. Hearing and feeling that. Listening and hearing that. Living and listening and knowing that living. Is hearing that. Is feeling that. Is listening. Is listening to that. Is listening to that what. To that which is. This is that which is. SILENCE. We call it silence. It is not nothing but it is silence. It is feeling being. It is hearing living. It is listening and it is the sound we are hearing in listening, it is the sound we are making in living. It is the sound we make. Living it is the first sound we make listening we can hear it if we listen. Really listen. We call it silence. When there is nothing more there is still this we call silence. When there is nothing more than this there is always still this and this we call silence. There is always this still. Still always this the sound we make in listening to the sound we make in living knowing it is not nothing no it is something hearing it calling it the first sound calling it silence. Here is our beginning then we have found the beginning in this the beginning is SILENCE and it is the first SOUND. Not the sound we make in doing but the sound we make in being unless listening is doing and it is and it is not. It is not being or doing alone but being *and* doing. It is the first sound we make and the second sound is singing which is doing more than being and doing more than listening but this is another matter. The matter now is being or doing which is listening or hearing and what we hear when we listen. Singing is another matter. It is surely some of the matter of music and so are playing and moving and dancing some of its matter but they are all mostly doing and I am concerned here more with being which is listening being mostly hearing being. There is also hearing doing and that is surely next in these beginnings. First is hearing being and next is hearing doing and this whether one's own doing or another one's. These are the same in the sound they make. They are not the same but the sound may be the same and the next matter is *any* sound. One sound is silence but any other sound is a sound and the question is what is it. What do we hear when we really listen. We have heard the first sound which is silence. Now we hear any other sound which is not silence and the question is what has happened. At some point something has happened that is it began. It had a beginning and that beginning was the end of silence. Suppose now it ends, the sound has an end at a point and the silence begins at that point. At a point when. At a point in TIME. A point in time is the beginning of one sound (or silence) and the ending of another sound (or silence). Any beginning and any ending means a point in time. Between these points is a sound or a silence and the common measure of both is DURATION. Duration is a measure and a dimension. Dimension is direction and extension. Dimension is definition and description. Our first definition is this then the measure in common of any sound and thus of sound or silence. Time is our first dimension and duration our first measure. Silence is our first sound and duration our first measure of any sound. But there are others. There must be others because any sound is not like any silence except in this way of duration. They are different in some ways and this means other measures and other definitions and thus other dimensions. Other dimensions means that we can imagine a FIELD or co-ordinate system. Co-ordinate system is abstract, but field is not. Field is when and where a sound may be. Field is the range of possibilities. Field is the inner ear or the brain where there may be many possibilities. It is geometry but it is more than geometry. Geometry is measuring but measuring is distinguishing and distinguishing is not just geometry. So we have a field, and the question is what are the dimensions of that field. We have one dimension, Time. What are the others.

Think of a sound as an audible SHAPE. Not as something *having* a shape but as something which *is* a shape. Not having a shape so much as *being* a shape. Then silence is simply the most flat shape, the least shaped. Or think of sound as a curvature of the field. Then silence is the condition of least curvature of the field. It is a question here of relative not absolute "zero" (in nature there is no absolute zero, no absolutely perfect vacuum), and thus a reference level like zero decibels. The changes in time which define the Shape are changes firstly of EXTENSITY (for Volume, Size, Weight, Mass, etc.—i.e. Quantity) and ACUITY (for Quality, Intensity, etc.).

IV. December 25, 1959

Let these be the new assumptions:

The first fact is the act of listening, which, when nothing more, is living, and listening to this living, which we know as SILENCE. This is not an absolute zero, but is rather the least SOUND, the sound with minimal extension in every dimension except Time, that is, it has DURATION. Any Sound may have this in common with any Silence, and only this—Duration. In any other respect any Sound will differ from Silence, and these other respects are first, volume, size, or EXTENSITY*, and quality, acuity, or INTENSITY*. These are general, statistical features of any sound, simple or complex, and may serve to define and distinguish similarities and differences between any two sounds on a large scale. They are both functions of the three variables, Amplitude, Duration, and Frequency, as well as combinations of these (Timbre, etc.), and they are reciprocal in every respect except Amplitude. That is, they are both proportional to the amplitude, while Extensity is proportional to the duration but inversely proportional to the frequency; Intensity is inversely proportional to the duration and directly proportional to the frequency. Changes in any of the variables will affect both the Extensity and the Intensity, and such changes, in any one or all the variables, produce SHAPE.

* Note: define EXTENSITY as the reciprocal of INTENSITY in all respects except Amplitude.[5]

Thus Extensity $\propto$ D, A, 1/P [where D = duration, A = amplitude, P = pitch]
and Intensity $\propto$ 1/D, A, P
Let D = duration, A = amplitude, P = pitch, T = timbre,
then Extensity is directly proportional to D, A, T, and inversely proportional to P
Intensity is directly proportional to A, T, P, and inversely proportional to D
or, letting $\propto$ mean proportional to,
then $EXT_a \propto INT_a \mid EXT_t \propto INT_t \parallel EXT_p \propto 1/INT_p \mid EXT_d \propto 1/INT_d$
or $EXT = f(D,A,T,1/P)$ and $INT = f(P,A,T,1/D)$

Thus we have, in Time, Sound and Silence, Extensity and Intensity, and Shape. Implicit in the above are Duration, Amplitude and Pitch, Timbre and other second-order combinations of these, and one more factor included in Pitch (and Timbre) which remains to be defined, i.e., Interval Quality, or Harmonic Relation (Proportion), which derives from the phenomenon of octave-equivalence (or relates to it). If we add to this certain facts of perception, such as the tendency to perceive Gestalten—unitary, bounded sound-forms—which I call Clangs, we have, I believe, the basic material of a system that is neither mystical nor arbitrary, but natural and capable of a great richness of possibilities.

APPENDIX 2

On Musical Parameters

(ca. 1960–1961)

[The following pages must have been written at about the same time as parts of *Meta ≠ Hodos* (1961) and may have originally been intended to be a part of that book (probably meant to occur between sections I and II). Although I evidently decided not to include it in the book, I see now that it contained at least the seeds of several important ideas that were not developed fully until some years later.[1]]

In order to describe a thing, whether it be an object that is apprehended aurally, visually, or through some other mode of perception, certain assumptions have to be made as to the number of distinct characteristics or attributes in terms of which one such object might differ from another. A complete description would then be one that left no doubt about the object's properties with respect to any of these attributes, serving thus to distinguish it from every other object of the same general category. The distinct attributes of sounds and sound-configurations will be called *parameters,* and I shall give a provisional definition of it now as *any distinctive attribute of perceived sound, in terms of which one sound may differ from another, and which is therefore necessary to specify a sound—to characterize it uniquely, or describe it completely*. In this paper, seven of these parameters will be referred to—*pitch, loudness, timbre, duration, amplitude/time-envelope, temporal density*, and *vertical density*.

It is essential to make a very careful distinction between the characteristic parameters of the musical object as it is *perceived* and the parameters of the physical signal that is the objective counterpart and source of that "object." These latter parameters—viz., frequency, amplitude, and time—will be called *acoustic parameters* and must not be confused with those attributes of the perceived object that constitute the various "dimensions" of the musical experience itself. In this paper, the word *parameter,* when used alone in this way, will always mean the "subjective" or *musical parameter*. Thus, the parameters that are the subjective counterparts of the acoustic parameters named above (frequency, amplitude, and time) are primarily *pitch*, *loudness*, and *duration*. But—as is shown in every book on acoustics or psychoacoustics—there is no one-to-one correlation between the "objective" and the "subjective" properties thus defined. As measuring instruments, the ear and brain are decidedly "nonlinear" in their responses to the acoustic parameters of a sound-signal, although the magnitude and direction of this nonlinearity can be determined—at least statistically—and have been so determined for pitch and loudness, if not for duration, by psychological tests.

But for the purposes of musical analysis or description, these three parameters are not sufficient to "uniquely characterize" a sound, even after their differences from the acoustic parameters are accounted for. There are many attributes of perceived sound that are irrelevant to the physicist (the acoustician), because the objective factors responsible for them are—for his purposes—satisfactorily measurable (or definable) in terms of the same three basic acoustic parameters—frequency, amplitude, and time. Timbre, for example, whose physical correlate is often (and I think loosely) defined as "waveform," does not require for its specification any new acoustic parameters, because the description of waveform can be reduced to a specification of certain values of frequency, amplitude, and time (phase-relations) in that particular sound-vibration—and this is unquestionably the most efficient way for him (the physicist) to record his description. A *musical* definition of timbre, however, cannot be similarly "reduced" to pitch, loudness, or duration. From the standpoint of the actual perception of sound, this attribute is effectively independent of the others and constitutes a musical parameter that is as unique and autonomous as are the other three.

The first problem, then, is to determine what the real and effective parameters are in the musical perception of sound and only secondarily to define the interdependence of one of these parameters with others in perception and with the acoustic parameters involved in the *production* of a sound. This is no easy problem to solve in a way that is likely to be agreed upon by every musician or every listener to music. The number of "distinctive attributes" required by one person to "uniquely characterize" a musical sound may not represent a complete description to another person, and the disparity becomes more significant as one moves farther along the temporal scale to larger and larger perceptual levels—as from the element to the clang to the sequence.

At the sequence level, for example—if we hold to the definition of the word *parameter* suggested above ("any distinctive attribute," etc.)—a very great variety of factors may be encountered "in terms of which one sound (i.e., one clang) may differ from another." A consistent application of my definition would thus have to include many other attributes than those which I shall actually describe here, but these other features—these "large-scale" parameters—will be dealt with in a later section of the paper rather than here because they pertain to matters of sequence-structure and musical form in general that have yet to be developed. Instead I shall restrict my descriptions of musical parameters to those that are likely to be particularly relevant at the level of the *clang*, involving therefore the question as to how one element (which might be either a single sound or a sound-configuration) may be distinguished from another element within a clang. The word *parameter* will thus be used in this more restricted way, but with the understanding that it could very meaningfully be extended to the higher-order percepts that may emerge at the larger levels of the sequence, group, and beyond.

Four parameters have already been mentioned as "unique and autonomous" dimensions of musical perception—pitch, loudness, duration, and timbre. It will be recognized that these four are the basic parameters that have traditionally been involved in the analysis and description of music (though they have seldom been given equal attention by theorists nor even a consideration that is in proportion to their relative significance in music). In addition, each of these four parameters is usually assumed to be an irreducible aspect of musical perception, defining, in each case, a single attribute of sound. It has not generally been recognized that each one of these parameters involves at least two subordinate factors that define relatively independent (or at least partially independent) attributes of musical sound relating to separately distinguishable aspects of perception. I shall try to clarify this statement by considering, one by one, the four main parameters, pitch, loudness, duration, and timbre, showing the ways in which they may be divided into what will here be called "subparameters," for want of a better term.

Two basic subparameters within the one dimension of pitch may be distinguished. One of these I shall call "pitch-height" or "pitch-distance" and the other "pitch-chroma" or "chromatic quality." The first terms refer to that aspect of pitch-perception that depends upon the existence of a *continuous range* of pitch-values, from the lowest to the highest regions of audibility. The second factor, on the other hand, relates to the fact that—owing to the phenomenon of "octave equivalence"—this continuous range is at the same time *cyclic*, virtually returning to its starting-point in the move from one octave to the next in the range. This is well represented by a kind of spiral trajectory in the pitch-space—or rather, a *helix*, not a spiral, as in the figure below (adapted from *[Introduction to t]he Psychology of Music* by Géza Révész), in which every C, for example, is located at some point on a vertical line that skips from octave to octave.[2] The continuous scale of the pitch-height subparameter is represented by the helical curve itself.

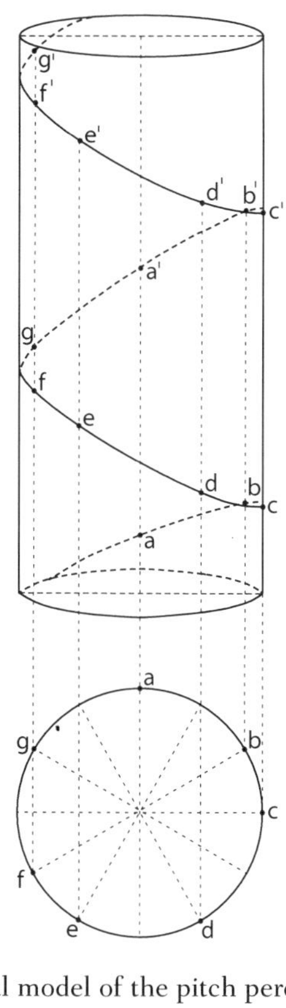

FIGURE 1. Révész's helical model of the pitch percept.

The capacity for "absolute pitch" discrimination has been related (by Révész and others) to the second of these attributes of pitch, suggesting that the ability to specify the precise *chroma of a tone* (its "C-ness" as distinct from another's "D-ness") is not simply a refinement of the more general perception of pitch-height, but that these represent two distinct attributes or qualities of the pitch-phenomenon itself. But even without this ability, pitch-chroma may be perceived as a distinct quality of pitch-perception whenever more than one pitch is involved—when we are considering, that is, the perception of *intervals* rather than of single tones. Any interval, whether its constituent tones are heard in melodic succession or in "harmonic" simultaneity, will have these two unique characteristics, and a description of it should include a specification of both the distance between the tones and the chromatic quality that pertains to the interval. And in the case of tones sounding simultaneously, there will be yet a third factor involved, which I will call the *acoustic quality*, so that we finally have at least three subparameters within the single realm of pitch-perception. And although these subparameters are not absolutely independent, one from another, they are relatively independent in their possibilities of deployment in the musical fabric.

Pitch-distance is perhaps the most immediately perceptible of the three, but it is also of such an imprecise nature that a scale of "equal increments" can only be determined statistically on the basis of the results of a number of psychological tests. This has been done, however, and it is represented graphically as a function of frequency in the so-called mel scale proposed by S. S. Stevens and shown in the figure below.[3] As can be seen in the graph, equal musical intervals (e.g., octaves or fifths) do not have, in this scale, the same subjective width in different registers, so that there is no one-to-one correlation between what I am calling pitch-distance and the interval types as defined in music. The latter correspond more closely to the second subparameter—pitch-chroma. But it is pitch-distance that primarily determines melodic shape or contour, as this is usually defined.

Chromatic quality is the characteristic of pitch-perception that has had the most attention in music theory and might be defined precisely in terms of the *ratios* between the frequencies of two tones. It is that "harmonic relation" between pitches by which a major third, for example, is considered virtually identical to a minor sixth or major tenth, or a minor second to a major seventh or minor ninth, etc. This "chromatic identity"

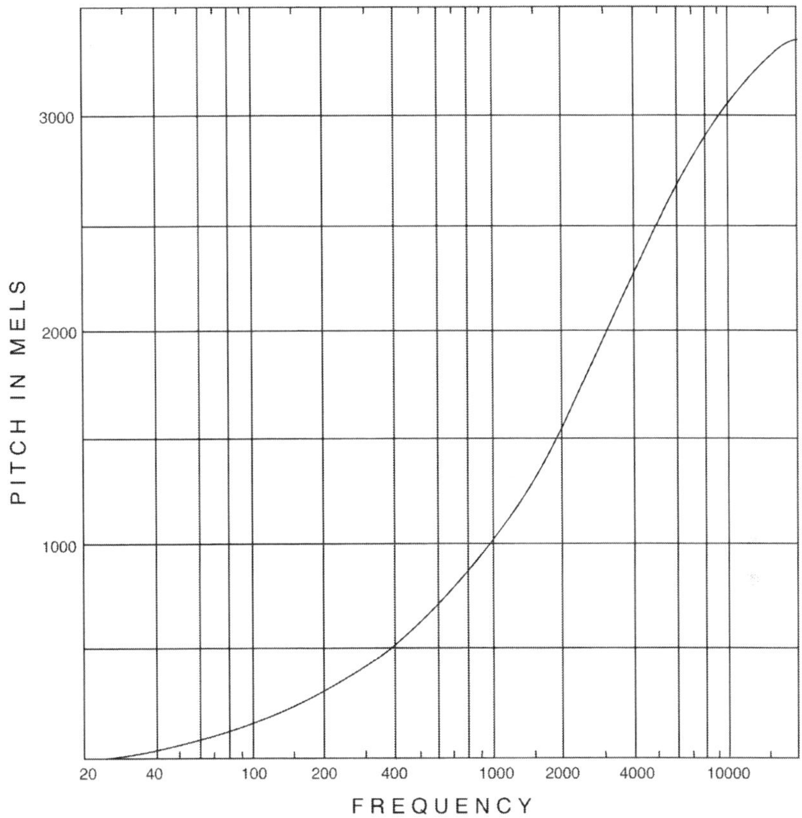

FIGURE 2. The "mel scale" proposed by S. S. Stevens.

is thus implicit in the process of inversion and expansion of an interval by means of an octave-transposition of one of its component tones. And this identity-relation is apparent in the similarity of the frequency-ratios that define the above intervals (as they would be in *just intonation*, not in equal temperament): 5/4, 8/5, and 5/2 for the third, sixth, and tenth, respectively; and 16/15, 15/8, and 32/15 for the second, seventh, and ninth. It may be seen that "octave equivalence" or octave transposition (corresponding to division or multiplication of one of the terms of the above ratios by 2) is the basis of this relation—just as it was said to be for pitch-chroma itself.

The third characteristic of pitch-intervals mentioned above—*acoustic quality*—may be a result of the relative distribution of the harmonic (and/or inharmonic?) partials in the two tones forming the interval, and in some cases it may also be conditioned by the presence of combination-tones produced by actual distortion in the ear. This factor therefore depends to a great extent on the other parameters, loudness and timbre, but it is an attribute whose results we generally ascribe to the pitch-intervals themselves, so that for practical purposes it is appropriate to include it as an aspect of pitch-perception. Incidentally, it may be of interest to note that it is this characteristic of our perception of pitch-intervals that leads Ernst Krenek to the classification of intervals according to their "degrees of tension," and it would seem that Paul Hindemith's attempt to explain traditional harmony on the basis of combination-tones and harmonic partials fails primarily because he confuses *chromatic quality* with *acoustic quality*.[4]

That these three characteristics of pitch-intervals are relatively independent attributes of the pitch phenomenon is shown by the fact that an alteration in one of the constituent tones of an interval does not affect them all equally or in the same way. Thus, a change from a major third to a minor sixth will show an increase in pitch-distance and a very noticeable change in acoustic quality, while the chromatic quality may remain the same. On the other hand, in the change from a perfect fifth to a diminished fifth, the pitch-distance is altered only slightly, while both the acoustic quality and the chromatic quality of the sound are changed considerably.

It should be clear, then, that in order to specify completely even the simplest melodic configuration in terms of pitch alone, both pitch-distance and pitch-chroma will have to be considered and that any simultaneously sounding elements in the configuration will involve acoustic quality, in addition to the first two. It is curious that these distinctions have never been made explicit in music theory, although they must always have been at least implicit in musical practice. The 12-tone method, for example, assumes the identity of only those transformations of a "basic shape" (viz., octave transpositions and mirror-forms) that preserve the pitch-chroma relations in the original series, and yet—in actual practice—Schoenberg himself frequently employs devices that involve the assumption of identity after transformations of another sort and that preserve only the general profile of a "basic shape" while altering the actual chromatic relations in the original.

The pitch-parameter is thus seen to contain at least three subparameters, and the description of any moderately complex clang in terms of its pitch characteristics ought really to include the specification of conditions pertaining to all three. This becomes especially true when we shift our attention to the level of the sequence, since the *morphological relations* between clangs—which constitute one of the primary determinants of *form* in the sequence—may be associated with either pitch-distance-relations or pitch-chroma-relations, if not with both of them together, and, to a lesser extent perhaps, acoustic quality.

A fourth aspect of pitch should be mentioned here, though it is not a subparameter of pitch in the same sense that the other three are. It is rather a subparameter of timbre or tone-quality, deriving from rapid changes of pitch such as in vibrato and other, less regular pitch fluctuations. They affect tone-quality by way of a phenomenon that Carl Seashore called "sonance," meaning the perceptual *fusion* of these variations into a more or less steady and homogeneous sound.[5] But sonance includes not only variations in pitch but also fluctuations in loudness, and these may occur both in the perceived fundamental of a tone and/or in each of its partials, this last resulting in variations in the shape of the spectrum of the tone, or what Seashore calls its "timbre" (note that I do not restrict the meaning of the word in this way; and I don't mean it to refer exclusively to compound tones but to any sound). Sonance, then, is an aspect of tone-quality, and the part played in this by pitch should be considered along with the other subparameters of timbre.

Time—Duration, Tempo, and Temporal Density

Subjective, musical, or "experiential" time (the last being a translation of Stockhausen's "erlebnisse Zeit") is in many ways the most important single parameter in music. The fact that music can only occur in time—and that its elements are made perceptible in a (more or less) determinate order in time—is something that is characteristic of only a few other arts, such as spoken poetry and drama, dance, and film, and distinguishes it from the nontemporal art-forms in a rather profound way. It is not necessary to go so far as to define music itself as "time—experienced through sound," as does Stockhausen,[6] or to say, with John Cage, that (because the only measure of a silence is duration) "any valid structure involving sounds and silences should be based . . . rightly on duration," etc.,[7] in order to recognize the significance of the time-parameter in music. The very fact that such composers have found it necessary or meaningful to formulate such definitions is an indication of the enormous importance this parameter has come to have in contemporary music. The analyses of the various factors influencing our perception of the clang and the sequence, which will be found throughout later portions of this paper, nearly always involve the consideration of the variations of some parameter *with time*—I see no other way to do it that is meaningful. And in some cases, one aspect of time-perception may even be plotted "against itself" (or rather, one aspect against "physical time") in order to show the structural functioning of a particular temporal factor in the course of the music. The singular importance of the temporal aspect of musical perception justifies its being called the *primary dimension of music*, just as space might be called the primary dimension of the visual arts of painting and sculpture.

The lack of a one-to-one correspondence between the physical, "acoustic" parameter and the musical parameter is perhaps even more crucial in the time-dimension than in any of the other parameters that have been mentioned. Pierre Schaeffer has pointed out that one's estimation of relative duration in a sound or sound-configuration is conditioned—to an extent that is nearly incredible—by the variations in what he calls the "information density" of the sound from one moment to the next.[8] Specifically, he found (in a series of experiments) that a higher degree of information density in one part of a sound (as in the attack) was correlated with a longer sense of subjective duration (indicated by an overestimation of duration) for that part of the sound—and vice versa. He says, "Musical duration is a direct function of information density" (67). Subjective time, then, like pitch (and loudness, as will be shown later), is not a simple, linear function of physical time, but the extent and nature of the differences between the two has not been determined in any way that would correspond to the mel scale described earlier in connection with pitch. Both Abraham Moles and before that Stockhausen have suggested that the relation between physical and psychological duration corresponds approximately to a *logarithmic* relation (this is consistent with the so-called Weber/Fechner Law of sensation and has been found to hold at least in an approximate way for other parameters of sound and in other modes of perception), although there is not, as far as I know, any conclusive experimental evidence to substantiate this assertion.[9] There is, however, an introspective basis for it that rests on the observation that one's perception of duration is generally in terms of *proportions*, rather than absolute values or absolute differences. *Rhythmic perception*, at least, is directed to the relative proportions of one duration-value to another—and the appropriate measure of such proportional relations is on a logarithmic scale.

But all of these problems relate to merely one aspect of the musical time-parameter—namely, the perception of *duration*—and there are two other time-factors in musical perception that I think deserve to be considered as separate subparameters along with duration, and these are *tempo* and *temporal density*. These two attributes (or subparameters) are closely related to each other, the only real difference between them being that the first—tempo—arises only when there is a perceptible *periodicity* in the sound-articulation—tempo is, in fact, the frequency of that periodicity. Temporal density, on the other hand, does not depend on any such regularity or periodicity and is a much less specific or precise aspect of perception. From the *physical* standpoint, the two are analogous to chromatic quality and pitch-height. Here again, the one is related to precise "measures" of a periodic phenomenon, the other is less contingent on this.

Again, as was the case with the pitch-parameter, a single acoustic parameter is the source of more than one musical attribute ("in terms of which one sound [or in this case, one elementary sound-configuration] may differ from another"). One can easily conceive of a simple sound-configuration that serves merely as an element in a larger sound-configuration or clang that is characterized by a certain tempo or temporal density—in addition to its overall duration. An obvious example of such an element would be a trill, string tremolo, or quick repeated-note pattern. And in order to describe this element—in terms of its temporal features only—it would be necessary to specify not only the duration of the element as a whole but also the number of discrete attacks (pulsations in loudness, in this case) occurring within that duration—i.e., its temporal density. Now it is evident that—from the standpoint of the physical or acoustic time-parameter—these two attributes would only involve the one measure of duration. That is, the temporal density of the element is (physically) a function of these smaller durations between the attacks—the one is (again "reducible" to the other, as I noted earlier in connection with timbre). But this should not lead us to conclude that our temporal perception is necessarily so singular, nor make us forget that, in musical practice, duration and tempo have always been *treated* as separate and distinct parameters. The perception of tempo is obviously some kind of integration of an aggregate of smaller durations, but what I am suggesting here is that tempo is much more than a mere aggregate of durations and rather constitutes a separate *percept* that is almost as different from duration as it is from pitch.

Most musicians are probably familiar by now—either from acoustic demonstrations or from writings on acoustics—with the phenomenon of the gradual transformation of a series of separate pulses or clicks, in which a tempo can be perceived, into a continuous tone of low pitch, the transformation being brought about simply by increasing the rate of pulsation from something less than ten to twenty per second to something more than twenty to thirty per second. This transformation can be reversed, of course, beginning with what is perceived as a steady tone and, by gradually decreasing the frequency, becoming a discrete series of pulses again, in which one no longer hears a salient pitch but rather a "speed" of pulsation—a *tempo*. If now the rate of pulsation is decreased still further, until the time-interval between pulses approaches five, ten, or perhaps fifteen seconds, any sense of a tempo as such will have become so attenuated that it is virtually nonexistent, from a subjective point of view. The only relevant temporal characteristic that remains in one's perceptual image of this sound-configuration is now *duration*—the length of the time-interval between separate pulses. There is, of course, a rather extensive region in this scale of pulsation rates within which *both* tempo and duration are very real attributes of one's perception of the sounds. But at the upper and lower extremes of this scale there are regions within which only one is of any importance—in fact, at the limits, only one is *possible*. This suggests that what is involved here is indeed an overlapping of two separate subparametric scales in the middle regions. And if this is so, it is important to recognize the distinctions between the two factors and to consider their respective functions in musical organization and perception.

These differences between the perception of duration and the perception of tempo and temporal density correspond very closely to the differences, noted many years ago by Josephine Nash [Curtis] between what she called "duration" and "progression," and I want to quote here some of the conclusions she derived from a series of psychological experiments on the estimation of time-durations by a number of subjects and from their introspective statements about the temporal experience.[10]

> We have evidence that the tones can be taken in either one of two ways. The duration may be either "static" or "moving," may be

> either length or progression . . . [and] there are two ways of taking the temporal experience, as progression and as length. *These stand at quite different levels*, and are the results of quite different attitudes toward the experience [emphasis mine]. A sensation taken as it comes immediately to one, as it comes under a merely existential determination, progresses. The determination to compare or to estimate, however, tends to result in a taking of the experience as a length. Progression is the more ingrained, the more vital aspect of the experience; without progression, length is impossible. Length is something that may or may not be added on afterward and does not belong to the sensation as such. That is, the sensation has length only in retrospect, has length only after it is over, while it has progression while it is going on.

Both pitch-chroma and tempo are musical parameters in which we are able to perceive relatively precise relations or *proportions*, and in this respect they are unique among all the parameters of sound. The objective basis for this perceptibility of proportional relations is the fact that both of the corresponding acoustic parameters are *periodic* phenomena, defined by a *frequency*—and our perceptive faculties are able to compare two frequencies and detect relatively small differences in "phase" between them.[11] This is so even when they do not occur simultaneously but rather follow one another in time—although one's precision in the perception of "phase differences" is far greater when the two frequencies occur simultaneously. In the consideration of the other parameters—loudness and timbre—the fact that these latter are *not* based on periodic phenomena in this sense is perhaps the first thing that should be noted about them. From the standpoint of musical perception, there can be no "proportional relations" between two values in either of these parameters. In fact, the concept of "proportion" is quite devoid of any meaning in relation to loudness and timbre. And it is perhaps for this reason that these two parameters have not—until quite recently—been given much attention in music theory or been included in any systematic or "rationalized" compositional method. They resist such rationalization, and perhaps this is in some way related to the fact that they do not include the possibility of *ratio-relation* (i.e., *proportion*), which is contained in the very word *rational*.

But it should be pointed out that only one aspect of each of the parameters, pitch and time, is really subject to such precise proportional relations anyway—viz., pitch-chroma and tempo—and that the other aspects of these parameters—pitch-distance and acoustic quality, as well as duration and temporal density—are all comparable to loudness and timbre, with respect to this limitation in the degree of precision with which they may be perceived. Furthermore, the actual awareness of a specific ratio or proportion between two "frequencies"—that is, the ability to *name* the ratio—pertains only to tempo. It is not something that is implicit in one's actual perception of pitch-chroma but rather something that may be *learned*.

The conclusion that seems inevitable to me—although I cannot expect any very general agreement here—is that the proportional relations that are involved in pitch-chroma and tempo pertain more to the *physical* characteristics of these parameters—inherent features of the acoustic parameters that correspond to them—rather than constituting any very significant aspect of the musical parameters per se. It is for this reason that I have adopted for this paper a procedure whereby every parameter or subparameter is represented by an *ordinal* scale (see Stevens) that indicates merely a rank-ordering of parametric values and does not purport to show precise differences or proportions between them. I shall say more about these *parametric scales* in a later part of this section of the paper after loudness and timbre have been examined.

Loudness—like pitch-height—is a parameter in which there is an approximately logarithmic relation between the physical or acoustic parameter (amplitude) and the musical or subjective correlate. And here again, this relation has been determined (for simple sine-tones at least) and may be represented by the graph shown on the following page.[12] A strictly logarithmic measure of amplitude—called the intensity-level, and measured in *decibels*—is the basis for comparison in this graph. The unit of measure of loudness (as opposed to intensity-level) is called the *phon*.

But there is one other manifestation of this parameter that is of very great importance in music. This is the dynamic "time-envelope," which I have mentioned before. The amplitude envelope of a tone—the particular shape of its attack and decay, as well as of its steady-state portion—might almost be considered a fifth "basic parameter" (in addition to pitch, time, loudness, and timbre), so influential is it in the "unique characterization" of a sound. But I think it is appropriate to consider it either as a special manifestation of the loudness-parameter or else as a subparameter of timbre, because it is a determining factor in one's impression of

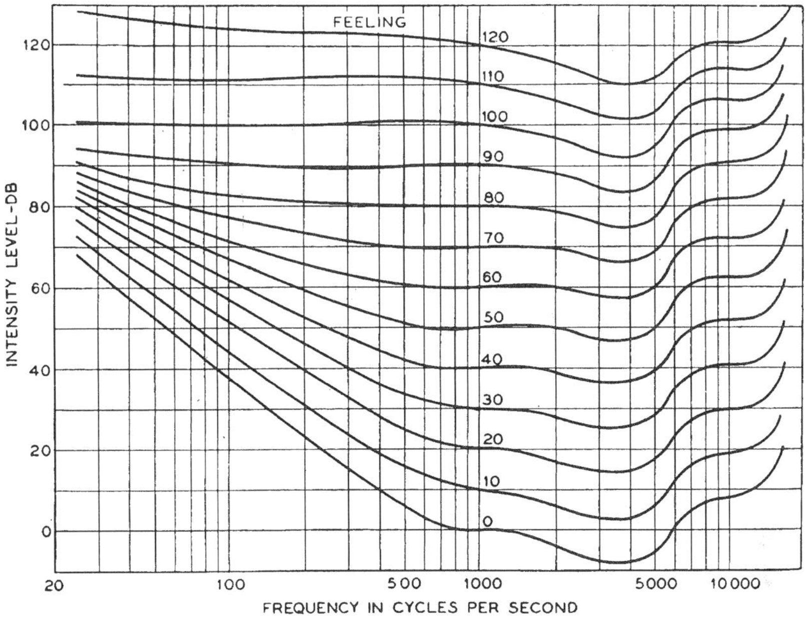

FIGURE 3. Loudness Level Contours versus Intensity Level

"tone-quality," often being the *essential* and decisive factor in the characterization of the timbre of an instrument. It has often been pointed out that—in certain cases—if the attack portion of a recorded instrumental tone is removed by cutting, one is no longer able to recognize the instrument that produced the original tone. This suggests that, for some tones at least, one's perception of timbre is more conditioned by the dynamic envelope of the tone than it is by the spectrum of the steady-state portion. And it is not just the attack of the tone that is influential in this. Schaeffer has shown (op. cit.) that it is the *total shape* of the dynamic envelope of the sound that determines the impression of quality, not simply the beginning of the tone. And although one usually refers to this feature as the "time-envelope," the time-element in it is often a matter of the physical signal only and is not relevant to (not even present in) the actual perceptual characteristics of the sound.

The above remarks refer principally to tones with little or no "steady-state" portion. But another aspect of dynamic envelope is often prominent in (i.e., within) more or less "steady" sustained tones of an instrument or voice in the form of regular (or irregular) pulsations ("sonance") in loudness, or *tremolo*. Seashore has analyzed this factor very thoroughly, and the most instructive illustrations of its importance in music are to be found in his book. Like the attack and decay characteristics of tones, tremolo probably belongs in the category of timbre—rather than to the loudness parameter itself—but it is nevertheless a manifestation of the loudness parameter, merely referred to a more microscopic level of perception.

There is, then, this point of overlap between the two parameters, loudness and timbre. But timbre obviously includes other factors—other subparameters—and I shall try to describe these here. I must admit, however, that I am much less prepared to give any very conclusive or even coherent analysis of the factors involved in timbre-perception. This parameter is the most complex of all those we have been considering because it is a compound of the other three, from the acoustic standpoint, and, in addition, the very term "timbre" is one that has come to include more different attributes of perception than have any of the others. The word is a kind of universal "catch-all" for anything that cannot be conveniently included in one of the other parametric categories, and it should not be surprising if we find many different subparameters involved within the larger concept of timbre or "tone-quality." Schoenberg seemed to be expressing a similar (though not identical) idea when he wrote: "The distinction between tone color and pitch, as it is usually expressed, I cannot accept without reservations. I think the tone becomes perceptible by virtue of tone color, of which one dimension is pitch. Tone color is, thus, the main topic, pitch a subdivision. Pitch is nothing else but tone color measured in one dimension."[13]

The attempt to differentiate between more or less distinct subparameters in this case must be approached from a slightly different direction than was employed for pitch and time. With pitch, for example, the decisive question seems to be: In how many distinct ways is the musical event changed by an alteration in the acoustic parameter, frequency? For the time-parameter this becomes: How many distinct perceptual attributes are engendered by a given articulation in (physical) time? For timbre, on the other hand, the question would seem to be this: In how many distinct ways can a change in timbre be produced by alterations in one or more features of a sound, measured with respect to any of the other three parameters, pitch, loudness, or time. But there are several ways in which the timbre of a sound may be effectively altered during its sustained portion. The conventional definitions of the acoustic determinants of timbre generally refer to the number, distribution, and relative strengths of *partials* in a tone, but this is not a very precise answer to our question. It does suggest, however, that there are several factors involved.

One might begin by distinguishing between sounds in which a more or less definite *pitch* is heard and those that do not have any salient pitch. These latter would be characterized, acoustically, by a very broad and rather *continuous* spectrum of partial tones (continuous, i.e., also *dense*). The "noisy" quality of these sounds is what constitutes their characteristic timbre, and there is very little further differentiation that can occur within this class of sounds. The larger class of (at least partially) pitched sounds may likewise be subdivided into two types. On the one hand are those whose spectrum consists of discrete pitches, or very sharp peaks. On the other are sounds whose spectrum is more continuous, but (unlike the "noisy" sounds described above) there are resonance peaks that are sharp enough to give the sound some pitch-character. I make this last distinction in order to account for the difference between the tone of a single instrument and that of a whole group of instruments playing (approximately) in unison—and also to include certain speech sounds, for example, in which some pitch-quality may be heard, though it is not as clear as when the same words are sung. Finally, one can distinguish—among pitched sounds (whose spectra may be either discrete or continuous, according to the last distinction)—between compound tones whose partials are integral multiples of the fundamental (constituting a "harmonic series") and those in which the partials are not simply related to a fundamental, as in bell tones, for example, and the tones of most pitched percussion instruments.

APPENDIX 3

Excerpt from *A History of 'Consonance' and 'Dissonance'* (1988)

Section VI. Summary and Conclusions: Toward a New Terminology

In an effort to unravel the tangled knot of confusion that currently exists regarding the meanings of 'consonance' and 'dissonance,' I have traced the historical development of the consonance/dissonance concept [CDC] from Pythagoras and Aristoxenus through Rameau and Helmholtz. It has been shown that five different conceptions of consonance and dissonance emerged in the course of that development and that (with the possible exception of the last one, CDC-5) each of these was closely related to musical practice for an extended period during which it was the prevailing form of the CDC. And yet—since in most cases an earlier form of the CDC was carried over into the following period and continued to exist along with the newly emergent form—each has survived, in one manifestation or another, to the present.

In the earliest form of the CDC—which I have called CDC-1—the terms 'consonance' and 'dissonance' had an essentially *melodic* connotation, referring to a sense of affinity or *relatedness* between the pitches forming an interval. The consonances were those intervals that

[This appendix consists of the final section of Tenney's 1988 book *A History of 'Consonance' and 'Dissonance'* (New York: Excelsior), a major work by Tenney not reprinted in this collection. The final section is included here because some of its conclusions and ideas provide a useful context for other writings in this collection.—Ed.]

were *directly tunable*: the perfect fourth, fifth, octave, and the octave-compounds of these. All other intervals were considered dissonant. The fact that such consonant intervals involved simple integer ratios between string lengths was an essential element in the Pythagorean tradition, but even Aristoxenus—in spite of his anti-Pythagorean stance regarding the relevance of such ratios to musical perception—held the same melodic conception of consonance and dissonance and classified the same intervals as consonant. Although the terms 'consonance' and 'dissonance' are seldom used in this way today, the aspect of musical perception involved in this earliest form of the CDC survives in the contemporary musical vocabulary as, for example, "relations between tones."

With the advent of polyphony in about the ninth century, a new conception of consonance and dissonance emerged—CDC-2—that had to do with an aspect of the *sonorous character* of simultaneous dyads. In its earliest manifestations, this new form of the CDC was only barely distinguishable from its predecessor, because in the earliest forms of polyphony only the consonances of CDC-1 were used to form simultaneous aggregates. With the increasing melodic independence of the added voice or voices in the tenth, eleventh, and twelfth centuries, however, the category of consonances was gradually expanded to include thirds and (by the same process of expansion, though not until sometime later) sixths. In addition, finer distinctions began to be made with respect to this new dimension of musical perception, leading to more elaborate systems of interval classification in the thirteenth century. John of Garland, for example, distinguished six degrees of consonance and dissonance, rank-ordering the intervals along a continuum that ranged from "perfect consonances" at one end (the unison and octave) to "perfect dissonances" at the other (the minor second, major seventh, and tritone), with varying shades of "intermediate" and "imperfect" consonances and dissonances in between. The definitions of these terms given by the major theorists of this period (including Franco of Cologne and Jacobus of Liège, as well as John of Garland) suggest that "consonance" meant something similar to the concept of "fusion" advocated by the nineteenth-century theorist Carl Stumpf—i.e., the degree to which a simultaneous dyad sounded *like a single tone*. Although the theorists of this period were all strictly Pythagorean in viewpoint, their rank-orderings of intervals did not simply follow the order that would be derived from a consideration of the complexity of their Pythagorean ratios. This suggests that these theorists were carefully listening to the sounds of these dyads and basing their classification systems on perceived qualities rather than theoretical doctrine.

New developments in polyphonic practice in the later thirteenth and early fourteenth centuries, including what came to be called the "art of counterpoint," eventually led to a new system of interval classification and a new conception of consonance and dissonance that I have called CDC-3. This form of the CDC seems to have been shaped by two factors: (1) a tendency to reduce the number of distinctly labeled categories to a smaller set that would have an *operational correspondence* to the rules of counterpoint, and (2) the emergence of a *new criterion* for the evaluation of consonance and dissonance. As a result of the first of these factors, the five or six perceptually distinct categories in CDC-2 were reduced to three operationally distinct categories: "perfect consonances" (octaves and fifths), "imperfect consonances" (thirds and sixths), and "dissonances" (all others, including perfect fourths). Although in most other respects the new classification system looks simply like a reduced version of those in the thirteenth century, the change in status of the fourth cannot be explained in this way, and thus the second factor listed above is invoked—the emergence of a new criterion involving another aspect of the sonorous character of simultaneous dyads. Among several hypotheses that might be advanced to account for the peculiar status of the fourth in CDC-3, the most likely one would involve the perceptual effect of an upper voice in a two-part texture on the melodic and/or textual *clarity* of the lower voice.

CDC-3 remained the prevailing conception of consonance and dissonance even after the new "rationalization" of thirds and sixths as consonances in Zarlino's *senario*, the emergence of the triadic concept, and the profound stylistic innovations of the *seconda prattica* in the late sixteenth and early seventeenth centuries. But in the new notation and descriptive language of seventeenth-century figured-bass practice, an ambiguity developed whereby "a consonance" or "a dissonance" might refer not only to the dyad formed with the bass by the note figured but to that note itself. In the writings of Rameau, beginning with the *Treatise on Harmony* of 1722, what had been merely a kind of verbal shorthand in the language of figured-bass treatises was reinterpreted in a way that became what I call the *dissonant-note concept*. This was central to a new conception of consonance and dissonance—CDC-4. In this form of the CDC, any note that is related to the harmonic root of an aggregate as prime, third, or fifth—i.e., any note that is a triadic component—is a consonance (or consonant note), while any note that is not thus related to the harmonic root is a dissonance (or dissonant note). Because the consonant or dissonant status of a note depends on the identity of the harmonic root of the chord in which it occurs, any ambiguity regarding that root affects the status of every other note in the chord, and such ambiguities can only be resolved by a consideration of context and function. Since the property associated with consonance or dissonance in CDC-4 can no longer be simply some aspect of "sonorous quality" (or "character"), it is assumed to be its *obligation to resolve* (in the case of a dissonance) or the lack of any such obligation (in the case of a consonance). And since "obligation" later becomes "tendency," *motion* is implied. Thus, in CDC-4, consonance and dissonance no longer have any direct or necessary connection to "sonorous qualities," and definitions are possible in which such qualities are not involved at all—'consonance' and 'dissonance' can become purely "functional." With certain modifications instituted by Kirnberger, CDC-4 has become an essential element in twentieth-century formulations of the theory of "common practice" harmony.

Finally, in response to the increasingly chromatic character of the harmonic language during the first half of the nineteenth century, to the radical extensions of pitch-registral, dynamic, and timbral ranges made possible by the growth of the orchestra, and to the increasing use of contrast in these parameters to serve some of the functions of formal articulation previously carried (in the diatonic/triadic tonal system) by harmony alone, a new conception of consonance and dissonance emerged that I have designated CDC-5. In this form of the CDC—first clearly articulated by Helmholtz in 1862—the dissonance of a dyad or larger simultaneous aggregate is defined as equivalent to its "roughness," and this turns out to be dependent on pitch register, timbre, and intensity, as well as on its constituent intervals. In addition, it becomes appropriate to ascribe consonance/dissonance values to single tones (although *not* in the sense of CDC-4), as well as to dyads and larger tone-combinations. Although the relevance of CDC-5 to musical practice has frequently been questioned (especially by music theorists concerned with more "functional" definitions of "consonance" and "dissonance"), it is the form of the CDC implicit in most psychoacoustical studies that have been done since the work of Helmholtz and is probably the basis for the prevailing colloquial uses of the terms (even by many musicians).

Thus, in the course of the two and a half millennia since Pythagoras, the entitive referents for 'consonance' and 'dissonance' have changed from *melodic intervals* (in CDC-1), to *simultaneous dyads* (in CDC-2 and CDC-3, eventually extended to larger aggregates as well), then to *individual tones* in a chord (in CDC-4), and finally to virtually *any sound* (in CDC-5). The qualitative referents have changed correspondingly from *relations between pitches*, through aspects of the *sonorous character* of dyads (and then larger aggregates), to the *tendencies toward motion* of individual tones, and then again to still another aspect of the *sonorous character* of simultaneous aggregates. The implicit definition of 'consonance' has gone through a sequence of transformations from *directly tunable* (in CDC-1), to *sounding like a single tone* (in CDC-2), to a condition of *melodic/textual clarity* in the lower voice of a contrapuntal texture (in CDC-3), to *stability as a triadic component* (in CDC-4), and finally to *smoothness* (in CDC-5), with 'dissonance' meaning the opposite of each of these. In only one instance did the semantic transformation involved in the transition from one form of the CDC to another result in a clear replacement of one set of meanings by another, and that was with the shift from an essentially "horizontal" orientation in CDC-1 to a "vertical" one in CDC-2. In all other cases the process was cumulative, with the newly emergent set of meanings simply being added to the earlier ones and thus contributing to the current confusion. This brief summary of the general evolution of the CDC is represented schematically below.

With the possible exception of Riemann (and his definitions of 'consonance' and 'dissonance' can easily be treated as a variant or extension of CDC-4), no theorist of the nineteenth century appears to have held a conception of consonance and dissonance that differed in its basic assumptions from one of the five forms of the CDC described above. Nor does any really new form seem to be expressed in the writings of the most prominent theorists of the first half of the twentieth century, although other aspects of harmonic theory were developed by them in important new directions. The references to consonance and dissonance by Schoenberg, Schenker, Hindemith, et al. can usually be identified as manifestations of one or more of these earlier forms of the CDC, although the distinctions I have made between these forms are not generally made explicit in their writings.

One obvious reason for the current semantic confusion and disagreement regarding the meaning of 'consonance' and 'dissonance' is simply that these same two words are continually being used to mean different

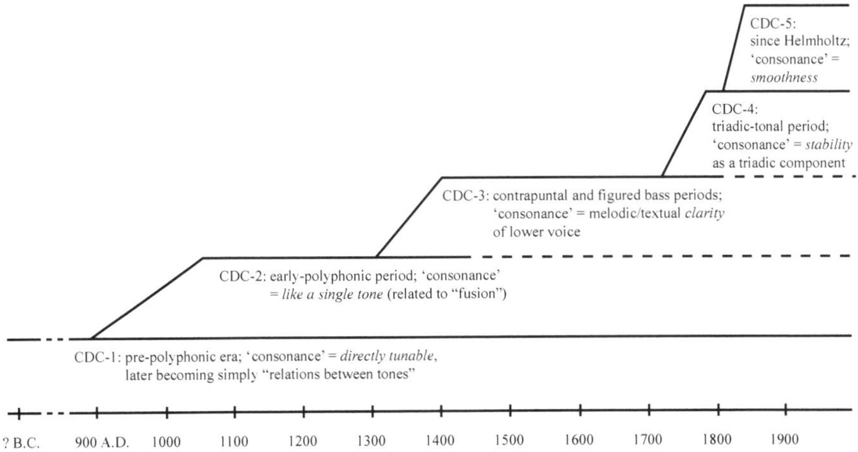

FIGURE. The evolutionary sequence of the five basic conceptions of consonance and dissonance.

(though perhaps equally important) things, often without any apparent awareness or explicit acknowledgment that this is the case. The obvious remedy for this would be to *qualify* these terms in some way that would clarify which of these several meanings is intended. Another source of confusion and disagreement has been the inclination on the part of some recent theorists to *redefine* 'consonance' and 'dissonance' in ways that are completely different from every semantic or lexical tradition preceding the twentieth century or to insist on the *exclusive* use of these terms in a purely functional sense. For example, Cogan and Escot (in *Sonic Design*, 1976) have proposed what they call a "consonance-dissonance system," which they define as follows: "A consonance-dissonance system . . . is a *context* that creates a hierarchy of intervals . . . some of which are *predominant* (consonances), and some *subordinate* (dissonances). In such a system the dissonances are handled specially so that they do not intrude upon the basic sonority that is established, predominantly, by the consonances" (128). The conception of consonance and dissonance implied here appears to be essentially *statistical*, and a distinction between "predominant" and "subordinate" intervals would of course be very useful as a means of describing the characteristic sonority of a piece—or of a whole style period. But the use of such statistical measures as criteria for *defining* "consonance" and "dissonance" clearly puts the cart before the horse. Consonant aggregates do indeed "predominate" in Western music from the ninth through the nineteenth centuries, but it is not this fact in itself that makes them "consonant." On the contrary, they were used "predominantly" *because they were considered to be consonant*—according to one or more criteria having little if anything to do with statistical frequency—and consonant textures were clearly preferred by composers of that period. On the other hand, many twentieth-century composers evidently prefer *dissonant* textures, but in accordance with such a "consonance-dissonance system" the ubiquitous seconds, sevenths, and ninths in the music of Schoenberg, Webern, Ruggles, or Varèse would have to be called "consonances" and the less frequent octaves, fifths, etc., "dissonances." This is certainly not the way these composers would have described the various aggregates in their own music; Schoenberg's "emancipation of the dissonance" was surely never interpreted by any of them as an occasion for the semantic *reversal* of the consonance/dissonance polarity.

To a great extent, of course, the natural evolution of a language inevitably involves some radical semantic transformations, and these will often include what Lewis Rowell has aptly called "semantic casualties" (1979, esp. 68). But in Cogan and Escot's "consonance-dissonance system" (and even in Riemann's "extrapolation" of CDC-4) the words 'consonance' and 'dissonance' have been appropriated to mean something quite different from any of their earlier meanings—and something, incidentally, that could be expressed quite adequately by terms like "predominant" and "subordinate" (or "stability" and "instability" in relation to a tonic, in Riemann's case). These terms are invariably invoked in order to explain what is *meant* by 'consonance' and 'dissonance' in these new formulations anyway, so there is really no need to use these older words at all.

One of the most outspoken advocates of an exclusively "functional" definition of 'consonance' and 'dissonance' has been Norman Cazden, who recommends the term *euphony* for this nonfunctional form of the CDC—or rather, for *all* of the various nonfunctional aspects of "sonorous quality" that might be invoked in the description of tone-combinations (1975, 9). Similarly, Richard Bobbitt has insisted that "studies in music theory should no longer use the terms 'consonance' and 'dissonance' when describing the quality of isolated, non-functional intervals" (178). He would simply substitute the term "intervallic quality." But neither Cazden nor Bobbitt seems to be aware that the use of the words 'consonance' and 'dissonance' in a nonfunctional sense is supported by a long and venerable historical tradition—beginning in the ninth century, remaining essentially unchallenged after the transition from CDC-2 to

CDC-3 in the fourteenth century, and surviving in some manifestations right through to the present day. Although I am not the first to have noted some of the distinctions between the several forms of the CDC that have been discussed in the book, I would seem to be alone in suggesting that it is not these nonfunctional senses of consonance and dissonance that are in need of a new terminology but rather the purely functional or contextual senses that have arisen only since the seventeenth century.

That a new, more precise terminology is urgently needed, however, is beyond dispute, and the distinctions that have been made here on the basis of a historical analysis might be useful in developing such a terminology. The inelegant acronyms used in this book to designate the different conceptions of consonance and dissonance ("CDC-n") were chosen deliberately for their neutral and essentially uninformative character, and I never expected or intended that they should be adopted for use outside of this present context. But the distinctions between the qualitative referents in the various forms of the CDC—and between their implicit definitions of 'consonance' and 'dissonance'—suggest one possible approach to the solution of this problem of terminology. That is, qualifying words or phrases might be used that reflect the different meanings more clearly, and I will suggest the following: for CDC-1, monophonic or *melodic* consonance and dissonance; for CDC-2, *diaphonic* consonance and dissonance; for CDC-3, polyphonic or *contrapuntal* consonance and dissonance; for CDC-4, *triadic* consonance and dissonance (this form is often called "functional," but this is not altogether accurate either and might better be reserved for the more *purely* functional conception articulated by Riemann, although his might also be called *tonic* consonance and dissonance if not simply "stability/instability"); and finally, for CDC-5, *timbral* consonance and dissonance.

Such a use of qualifying terms is one possibility suggested by the results of the historical investigations reported in this book. As a lasting solution to the terminological problem, however, it is not as attractive to me as another, more radical one that is also made possible by these results. That is, having made these distinctions between basically different conceptions of consonance and dissonance, it has at last become feasible to search for acoustical (or, better, psychoacoustical) *correlates* of each of these forms of the CDC. And if such correlates can be found, they might themselves suggest a terminology that is more precise than any that can be derived from historical data alone. The research outlined in this book was originally motivated by a desire to clarify certain questions that arose during just such a search for acoustical correlates of consonance and dissonance. That effort reached an impasse at a certain point with the realization that the various theoretical disagreements regarding consonance and dissonance were not merely disagreements about their physical (or other) basis but much deeper ones having to do with the very nature of the perceptual phenomenon signified by the terms themselves. Quite obviously, then, any search for "correlates" (whether physical, psychological, or other)—and thus any effort to develop an explanatory *theory* of consonance and dissonance—was doomed to failure almost before it began, since there was no common consensus as to what it was that such a theory would need to "explain."

One of my initial assumptions was that, although many of the important aspects of harmonic practice would not be amenable to a purely acoustical analysis, at least *some* of them might be, and that it is merely a question of isolating these from the plethora of facts and concepts associated with various periods in the history of harmonic practice that could *not* be dealt with acoustically. I am now convinced, however, that *acoustical correlates can be found for each of the five forms of the CDC* that have been identified here. It is beyond the scope of this book, however, to even begin to present the theoretical analysis from which such correlates might be derived, and that analysis will therefore be presented elsewhere.

There are many similarities between what I have called in this book "conceptions of consonance and dissonance" and the concept of "paradigms" developed by Thomas Kuhn in *The Structure of Scientific Revolutions* (1962). Like each of the major paradigms in the history of science, each form of the CDC provided an effective conceptual framework for musical practice (for what Kuhn calls "normal science") during some extended historical period, although it could not have answered every question that arose during that period. As Kuhn says: "To be accepted as a paradigm, a theory must seem better than its competitors, but it need not, and in fact never does, explain all the facts with which it can be confronted" (ibid., 17–18). That "normal" activity (whether scientific or musical) may even contain the seeds of a subsequent conceptual "revolution," since "research under a paradigm must be a particularly effective way of inducing paradigm change. That is what fundamental novelties of fact and theory do. Produced inadvertently by a game played under one set of rules, their assimilation requires the elaboration of another set" (ibid., 52). For a time however, such novelties or "anomalies" may not give rise to paradigm change because of a natural and valuable cultural inertia:

> In the normal mode of discovery, even resistance to change has a use. . . . By ensuring that the paradigm will not be too easily surrendered, resistance guarantees that scientists will not be lightly distracted and that the anomalies that lead to paradigm change will penetrate existing knowledge to the core. The very fact that a significant scientific novelty so often emerges simultaneously from several laboratories is an index both to the strongly traditional nature of normal science and to the completeness with which that traditional pursuit prepares the way for its own change. (ibid., 65)

Partly because of the inevitable emergence of such novelties or anomalies—and perhaps partly because of the elusive nature of reality itself—a period of "crisis" eventually occurs: "When . . . the profession can no longer evade anomalies that subvert the existing tradition of scientific practice—then begin the extra-ordinary investigations that lead the profession at last to a new set of commitments, a new basis for the practice of science. The extra-ordinary episodes in which that shift of professional commitments occurs are the ones known . . . as scientific revolutions" (ibid., 6). During such periods of crisis and impending revolution, many candidates for a new paradigm may be proposed—and many may possess some measure of viability, since

> philosophers of science have repeatedly demonstrated that more than one theoretical construction can always be placed upon a given collection of data. History of science indicates that, particularly in the early developmental stages of a new paradigm, it is not even very difficult to invent such alternates. But that invention of alternates is just what scientists seldom undertake except during the pre-paradigm stage of their science's development and at very special occasions during its subsequent evolution. So long as the tools a paradigm supplies continue to prove capable of solving

> the problems it defines, science moves fastest and penetrates most deeply through confident employment of those tools. The reason is clear. As in manufacture so in science—retooling is an extravagance to be reserved for the occasion that demands it. The significance of crises is the indication they provide that an occasion for retooling has arrived. (ibid., 76)

What finally does emerge from such a period of crisis will usually be radically different from its predecessors:

> The transition from a paradigm in crisis to a new one from which a new tradition of normal science can emerge is . . . a reconstruction of the field from new fundamentals, a reconstruction that changes some of the field's most elementary theoretical generalizations as well as many of its paradigm methods and applications. During the transition period there will be a large but never complete overlap between the problems that can be solved by the old and by the new paradigm. But there will also be a decisive difference in the modes of solution. When the transition is complete, the profession will have changed its view of the field, its methods, and its goals. (ibid., 84–85)

The parallels between this aspect of the history of science and the emergence of new conceptions of consonance and dissonance in the history of music are remarkable. Equally remarkable is the fact that in both fields there is a tendency toward a distortion of the real history of these changes, a distortion especially noticeable in textbooks, which, as Kuhn says,

> being pedagogic vehicles for the perpetuation of normal science, have to be rewritten . . . in the aftermath of each scientific revolution, and, once rewritten, they inevitably disguise not only the role but the very existence of the revolutions that produced them. . . . Textbooks thus begin by truncating the scientist's sense of his discipline's history and then proceed to supply a substitute for what they have eliminated. . . . [T]he textbook-derived tradition in which scientists come to sense their participation is one that, in fact, never existed. . . . *Scientists are not, of course, the only group that tends to see its discipline's past developing linearly toward its present vantage*

> [my emphasis]. The temptation to write history backward is both omnipresent and perennial. (ibid., 137–38)

Indeed they are not! But the analogies between scientific and music theoretical textbooks are much closer than Kuhn seems to realize when he says: "In music, the graphic arts, and literature, the practitioner gains his education by exposure to the works of other artists, principally earlier artists. Textbooks . . . have only a secondary role" (ibid., 165). I think this underestimates the extent to which a music student's attitudes toward "the works of . . . earlier artists" are conditioned by the textbooks that purport to explain the theoretical premises of their music.

If such distortions of history are questionable in science, how much more so they should be in music, where a quest for "truth" has not generally been considered to be the fundamental motivating force. And yet—as the many parallels between the histories of science and music suggest—these two disciplines may have more in common than has been supposed since the demise of the medieval *quadrivium*. The very fact that it now seems possible to develop a new terminology for "consonance" and "dissonance" that is relevant to each of the five historical forms of the CDC but is based strictly on objective physical or structural characteristics of musical sounds is persuasive evidence that there has always been an intimate connection between musical perception, practice, and theory, on the one hand, and on the other—what Rameau and the philosophers of the Enlightenment chose to call "nature." One wonders now how it could ever have been thought otherwise. To a far greater extent than has hitherto been recognized, the Western musical enterprise has been characterized by an effort to *understand* musical sounds, not merely to manipulate them—to *comprehend* "nature" as much as to "conquer" her and thus to *illuminate* the musical experience rather than simply to impose upon it either a willful personal "vision" or a timid imitation of inherited conventions, habits, assumptions, or "assertions." In this enterprise, both composers and theorists have participated, although in different, mutually complementary ways—the former dealing with what might be called the "theater" of music and the latter with its theory. A conception of these as indeed mutually complementary aspects of one and the same thing is suggested by the fact that both *theory* and *theater* derive from the same etymological root, the Greek verb *theasmai*, which was used (I am told) by Homer and Herodotus to mean "to gaze at or behold with wonder."

References

Bobbitt, Richard. "The Physical Basis of Intervallic Quality and Its Application to the Problem of Dissonance." *Journal of Music Theory* 1 (1959): 173–235.

Cazden, Norman. "The Definition of Consonance and Dissonance." Unpublished manuscript, 1975.

Cogan, Robert, and Pozzi Escot. *Sonic Design*. Englewood Cliffs, NJ: Prentice-Hall, 1976.

Kuhn, Thomas S. *The Structure of Scientific Revolutions*. Chicago: University of Chicago Press, 1962.

Rowell, Lewis. "Aristoxenus on Rhythm." *Journal of Music Theory* 23.1 (1979): 63–79.

PUBLICATION HISTORY

On the Development of the Structural Potentialities of Rhythm, Dynamics, and Timbre in the Early Nontonal Music of Arnold Schoenberg (1959)

Unpublished. It is likely that this was a paper Tenney wrote as a graduate student at the University of Illinois.

Meta ≠ Hodos *(1961) and* META Meta ≠ Hodos *(1975)*

First written as an MA thesis at the University of Illinois in 1961. First published by the Inter-American Institute for Musical Research, Tulane University, New Orleans, 1964. *META ≠ HODOS (A Phenomenology of 20th-Century Musical Materials and an Approach to the Study of Form) and META Meta ≠ Hodos* (Lebanon, NH: Frog Peak Music, 1986; 2nd ed., 1988).

"META *Meta ≠ Hodos*" was published in the *Journal of Experimental Aesthetics* 1.1 (1977). For many years, prior to the Frog Peak publication, *Meta ≠ Hodos* and "META *Meta ≠ Hodos*" were circulated in manuscript form.

Computer Music Experiences (1964)

Electronic Music Reports, no. 1 (Utrecht: Institute of Sonology, 1969). Substantial portions of this article were reprinted in quotation in the monograph "The Early Works of James Tenney" (Polansky 1983) in *Soundings 13: The Music of James Tenney*, ed. Peter Garland (Santa Fe, NM: Soundings Press, 1984), 119–297; and also in the liner notes to the CD *James Tenney: Selected Works 1961–1969*, Frog Peak Music/Artifact 1001/1007 CD, 1992; and in the reissue of that CD (with the same name) on New World Records, NW 80570, 2003.

On the Physical Correlates of Timbre (1965)

Gravesaner Blätter 26 (1965): 106–9.

An Experimental Investigation of Timbre—the Violin (1966)

Unpublished. Originally part of a grant proposal. Robert Wannamaker conferred with Tenney on the content of this article in preparation for its publication in this collection, and he has served as its technical editor in consultation with the other editors.

Form in Twentieth-Century Music (1969–70)

Tenney (from the revised manuscript used here): "An edited version of this text was published in the *Dictionary of Contemporary Music* in 1971. What follows is my original version." This complete version is published here for the first time. A shorter version, titled "Form," was published in *Dictionary of Contemporary Music*, ed. John Vinton (New York: E. P. Dutton, 1971).

The Chronological Development of Carl Ruggles's Melodic Style (1977)

Perspectives of New Music 16.1 (1977): 36–69.

Hierarchical Temporal Gestalt Perception in Music: A Metric Space Model (with Larry Polansky) (1978)

Journal of Music Theory 24.2 (1980): 205–41. Another version of this article that included data, source code, and an extended text was privately circulated in booklet form before the *Journal of Music Theory* publication.

Introduction to "Contributions toward a Quantitative Theory of Harmony" (1979)

Unpublished. This was originally planned as part of a book that also would have contained "The Structure of Harmonic Series Aggregates" (a separate article in this current volume); what later became *A History of 'Consonance' and 'Dissonance'*; Tenney's late, unfinished article called "A Multiple Pitch Perception Algorithm"; and some other unfinished material.

The Structure of Harmonic Series Aggregates (1979)

Unpublished. Robert Wannamaker conferred with Tenney on the content of this article in preparation for its publication in this collection, and he has served as its technical editor in consultation with the other editors.

John Cage and the Theory of Harmony (1983)

In *Soundings 13: The Music of James Tenney*, ed. Peter Garland (Santa Fe, NM: Soundings Press, 1984), 55–83. Reprinted in *Musicworks* 27 (1984): 13–17. Reprinted in German in *MusicTexte* 37 (December 1990): 45–53. Reprinted in *Writings about John Cage*, ed. Richard Kostelanetz (Ann Arbor: University of Michigan Press, 1993), 136–61.

Reflections after **Bridge** *(1984)*

Originally written for the New Music America premiere in Hartford, Connecticut, 1984, and printed in the program booklet. Reprinted as the liner notes to *James Tenney: Bridge & Flocking*, hat ART CD 6193, 1996.

Review of **Music as Heard** *by Thomas Clifton (1985)*

Journal of Music Theory 29.1 (1985): 197–213.

About **Changes: Sixty-Four Studies for Six Harps** *(1987)*

Perspectives of New Music 25.1–2 (1987): 64–87. Tenney's contribution to the special edition dedicated to his work.

Darmstadt Lecture (1990)

Published in German as "'Nichts ist nötig und alles ist möglich': Über Probleme der Harmonik (Darmstadt Vortrag)," *MusikTexte* 37 (1990): 11–18.

The Several Dimensions of Pitch (1993/2003)

Edited version of a lecture given at the Royal Conservatory, The Hague, December 1992. First published in *The Ratio Book: A Documentation of the Ratio Symposium*, ed. Clarence Barlow, Feedback Papers 43 (Cologne: Feedback Studio Verlag, 1999), 102–15. The content of this article is different in some respects from the version published in *The Ratio Book*. Robert Wannamaker conferred with Tenney on the content of this article in preparation for its publication in this collection, and he has served as its technical editor in consultation with the other editors.

On "Crystal Growth" in Harmonic Space (1993/2003)

First published in German in *MusikTexte* 112 (February 2007): 75–79. Reprinted in *Contemporary Music Review* 27.1 (2008): 79–89.

About **Diapason** *(1996)*

First publication in English. Originally written (and printed in German) for the program booklet of Donaueschinger Musiktage premiere of the piece, October 18, 1996.

*Appendix 1: Pre–*Meta ≠ Hodos *(1959)*

Unpublished.

Appendix 2: On Musical Parameters (ca. 1960–61)

Unpublished.

Appendix 3: Excerpt from A History of 'Consonance' and 'Dissonance' *(1988)*

A History of 'Consonance' and 'Dissonance' (New York: Excelsior Music Publishing, 1988). This book is out of print.

NOTES

1. On the Development of the Structural Potentialities of Rhythm, Dynamics, and Timbre in the Early Nontonal Music of Arnold Schoenberg

1. Arnold Schoenberg, *Style and Idea* (New York: Philosophical Library, 1950). Unless otherwise noted, all quotations from Schoenberg are taken from this source.

2. Ernst Krenek, *Music Here and Now* (New York: W. W. Norton, 1939); René Leibowitz, *Schoenberg and His School* (New York: Philosophical Library, 1949); Erwin Stein, *Orpheus in New Guises* (London: Rockliff, 1953); Josef Rufer, *Composition with Twelve Notes,* trans. Humphrey Searle (New York: Macmillan, 1954).

3. [The manuscript for this article has no extant musical examples. We have left the references for these examples in the text to show their intended locations. With the exception of example 1, the musical references to Schoenberg scores are unambiguous.—Ed.]

4. Rufer, *Composition with Twelve Notes.*

5. It is ironic that Schoenberg was unable to convince Mahler of the validity of the concept of the *Klangfarbenmelodie,* according to an account of a conversation between the two composers in Alma Mahler Werfel's *And the Bridge Is Love* (New York: Harcourt, Brace, 1958), especially since we know that Schoenberg's treatment of orchestral sonority was influenced by Mahler's work.

2. *Meta ≠ Hodos*. A Phenomenology of Twentieth-Century Musical Materials and an Approach to the Study of Form

1. Schoenberg, *Style and Idea*, 216–17.

2. Note that the parameters listed here are specifically *musical parameters*—attributes of perceived sound that are the "subjective" counterparts of the physical or *acoustic parameters* (frequency, amplitude, wave-form, etc.). The word *parameter*, when used by itself in this way, will always

refer to the musical parameter rather than to the corresponding acoustic parameter.

3. This is not intended to mean that there is always a faster rate of change in the music but rather simply that faster changes can and do often occur.

4. Schoenberg, *Style and Idea*, 240.

5. Koffka, *Principles*, 175.

6. Wolfgang Köhler, "Physical Gestalten," in Ellis, *A Source Book*, 17.

7. Especially Schaeffer, *À la recherche d'une musique concrète*.

8. Max Wertheimer, "Laws of Organization in Perceptual Form," in Ellis, *A Source Book*. This edited collection also includes some early papers by Köhler that are of interest from a theoretical standpoint.

9. See the listings for these authors in the bibliography.

10. An ordinal scale represents a "rank ordering" of relative magnitudes of some attribute, an ordering that involves the distinctions "greater than" and "less than" (indicated on the scale by displacements up or down, respectively), but does not purport to show how much greater or how much less one point on the scale may be than another point.

11. Koffka, *Principles*, 186–209.

12. The relationships that can be described show characteristics that indicate that some kind of "field-theory" might provide a basis for the definition of the essential features of this factor—more specifically, some of the concepts of the "topological field" introduced into psychology by Köhler, Koffka, and Lewin. The concepts of information theory might also provide such a basis, perhaps even in combination with the field-concept, and this could be correlated with the other cohesive factors in ways suggested on page 44, section II. All this is pure speculation on my part, of course, but it is sometimes meaningful to point out possibilities in the way of larger relationships, even though these have not yet been clearly formulated.

13. For a review of this theory and of the concepts of information theory in general, see Cherry, *On Human Communication*.

14. Cf. the implications of "segregation" in section II and the following remarks by Wertheimer ("Laws of Organization," 88): "When an object appears upon a homogeneous field there must be stimulus differentiation (inhomogeneity) in order that the object may be perceived. A perfectly homogeneous field appears as a total field [Ganzfeld], opposing subdivision, disintegration, etc."

15. The term *parametric interval* will be used here to refer to an approximate measure of the difference between two values (in any parameter, not just pitch)—especially when the change from one value to the other is *discontinuous*. A parametric interval would thus be defined by both a relative magnitude and a "sense" or direction, i.e., up or down on that parametric scale. The word *gradient* will refer to *continuous* changes, also specified by both a magnitude (the rate of change or "slope") and a direction (positive or negative) exhibited by a given segment of a parametric profile.

16. This transposability of a melodic figure was in fact one of the principal attributes of this particular *Gestaltqualität* (shape or form) noted in the 1890s by von Ehrenfels, a precursor of Wertheimer and Köhler in the early development of gestalt psychology. For a description of von Ehrenfels's contribution to gestalt theory, see Köhler, *Introduction to Gestalt Psychology*, 102–4.

17. Heinrich Schenker's concept of "middleground" (and perhaps also "background") could be considered a special type of morphological outline "at the sequence-level," involving the pitch-parameter and representing one of the many possible measures of "statistical differences" between successive musical configurations, which determine the shape of the next larger configuration.

18. If such a sound were separated—by silences—from the sounds that immediately precede and follow it, it might very well be perceived as a complete clang, but in this case the silences must be interpreted as real elements of that clang, so that its actual duration will no longer be outside of the normal range of durations within which aural gestalts can be perceived as such.

3. Computer Music Experiences, 1961–1964

1. ["Sound Generation by Means of a Digital Computer," *Journal of Music Theory* 7, no. 1 (1963): 24–70.—Ed.]

2. [*Music from Mathematics*, Decca DL 9103, 1962.—Ed.]

3. [DL stands for "difference limen," which is more or less synonymous with the more currently common "just noticeable difference."—Ed.]

4. [James C. Tenney, "Discriminability of Differences in the Rise Time of a Tone," *Journal of the Acoustical Society of America* 34, no. 5 (1962), abstract. Only the abstract was published, and to the best of our knowledge the body of the paper is not extant. None of the scientific papers that Tenney wrote at Bell Labs are included in this present publication.—Ed.]

5. [This article was never published.—Ed.]

6. [The RANDH function picked a new random number and "held" it for some number of samples (specified by 512 divided by an input value), similar to the "sample and hold" function on analog synthesizers.—Ed.]

7. [PLF was the Fortran "call subroutine" function implemented by Mathews. In the manuscript, Tenney sometimes referred to his "subroutines" (composing programs) with hyphens, sometimes not. In this edition we have regularized them to the nonhyphenated forms.—Ed.]

8. [Tenney uses the term *gruppetto* to refer to a tuplet.—Ed.]

9. [Variant versions of the second clause of this sentence exist. It is possible that "units" should be singular and, consequently, that the word "the" was omitted in the original manuscript, in which case the sentence would read: "The printout showed the number of metrical units in the clang, the number of the gruppetto unit, and of the smaller unit in that gruppetto unit on which the note ended."—Ed.]

10. [CVT refers to the data conversion routine for a given unit generator.—Ed.]

11. [Max Mathews's CON function returned values of a piecewise linear function whose breakpoints were specified by the programmer.—Ed.]

12. [Tenney used the term "music compiler" twice in this paper, the first time in lowercase, the second time (here) capitalized. For simplicity's sake, we have made them both lowercase, but the term "Music Compiler" (uppercase) was used early at Bell Labs to refer to the first music synthesis programs.—Ed.]

4. On the Physical Correlates of Timbre

1. [Dayton C. Miller, *The Science of Musical Sounds* (New York: Macmillan, 1922), 62. Tenney inserted the word "phenomena."—Ed.]

5. Excerpts from "An Experimental Investigation of Timbre" (1966)

1. [Note that *LF*, *AM*, *WF*, and *HF* are each real-valued functions of a real argument (time). P, Z_t, and FM_t, on the other hand, are all operators whose arguments and values are themselves *functions*—not real numbers, as this expression might suggest. Tenney described the expression as serving a *mnemonic* purpose. Where t appears as a subscript it indicates an operator that is time-varying.—Ed.]

2. Probably the best procedure for carrying out step 1 would be as follows:

   1. Fourier-analyze the steady-state region of the tone and compute spectral envelopes;
   2. compute an average center-frequency and an average bandwidth for each of the major peaks in these spectral envelopes (parameters 1–6); and
   3. use digital band-rejection filters (with fixed parameters) to flatten these peaks (thus compensating for the effect of any fixed resonances in the instrument). This would be done throughout the whole tone, not just the steady-state region.

3. The procedure for determining Z_t would be as follows:

   1. Fourier-analyze the whole (already fixed-filtered) signal ($S_1(t)$), compute spectral envelopes (again, as in step 1.2, above), and compute a best estimate of zero-positions for each period (e.g., assuming periodic spacing of the zeros in the spectrum, find the frequency-factor that, with its multiples, touches the lowest points in the spectral envelope);
   2. derive two functions, $ZF(t)$ and $ZB(t)$, representing the variations in time of the "frequency-factor" (from step 2.1, above) and the (average) bandwidth, respectively, of the zeros in the spectrum. Since these characteristics should be slowly varying, linear (ramp) functions (derived by computing a least-squares best fit to the sets of points in $ZF(t)$ and $ZB(t)$) should be sufficient in precision (this step will specify parameters 7–10); and
   3. use emphasis-filters (i.e., digital bandpass filters) with variable parameters to remove the zeros and flatten the spectrum still further than in step 1.3, thus compensating for the effect of the bow (reed, lip, etc., depending on the instrument). In some cases (e.g., the flute), physical considerations might eliminate any necessity for locating zeros in the spectrum, and these steps could be skipped.

4. [At the time when he was reviewing this manuscript for publication in this volume, Tenney was aware of an error in the two expressions for $C_i(t)$ here and the one for $Q(t)$ below, but he did not complete their revision. If the frequency of $C_i(t)$ is specified by the given linear

interpolation function F_i then the total phase (the argument of the cosine) will be given by an antiderivative of F_i multiplied by 2π. This yields $C_i(t) = A_i \cos\left[\phi + 2\pi\left(f_{1_i} + \frac{t - t_i}{2T_i}(f_{2_i} - f_{1_i})\right)(t - t_i)\right]$ where A_i is as given. Similarly, $Q(t) = \left(A_1 + \frac{t}{T}(A_2 - A_1)\right)\cos\left[\phi + 2\pi\left(F_1 + \frac{t}{2T}(F_2 - F_1)\right)t\right]$ below.—Ed.]

5. It might be asked why two separate functions ($C(t)$ and $Q(t)$) are involved in the analysis and how one can justify subtracting a function ($C(t)$) that is different from the function ($Q(t)$) that will later be used in the synthesis of the envelope. The answer is that some such procedure seems both necessary and sufficient. Necessary, because if the simpler function ($Q(t)$) were the one subtracted from $M(t)$ (in step 3, above), there would be, in general, some of this quasi-periodic modulation left in the random modulation function, $R(t)$ (wherever phase-differences occurred); sufficient, because any differences between $C(t)$and $Q(t)$ should be scarcely perceptible in a synthesized tone. This is not an arbitrary assumption but is based on experiments in sound-synthesis with various kinds of enveloping on the quasi-periodic modulation parameters, where it was found that surprisingly large differences in the temporal evolution of these modulation parameters in two tones were imperceptible. However, if the procedure eventually proved to be inadequate, still another level of analysis could be undergone to approximate the actual fluctuations in these parameters (probably by way of slower random functions). Such a further degree of complexity does not seem necessary now, however. It should also be noted that some of the discrepancies between $C(t)$ and $Q(t)$—in terms of the general *type* of fluctuation they represent—will be compensated for by the random modulation. That is, the relative regularity of $Q(t)$ will be more or less distorted by the random function-generator output, the input parameters for which are derived in the next few steps of the analysis.

6. Form in Twentieth-Century Music

1. [We are unable to locate an unambiguous source for this statement; an interested reader might examine Henry Cowell's analysis of the "Emerson" movement in Henry Cowell and Sidney Cowell, *Charles Ives and His Music* (New York: Oxford University Press, 1955), 190–95.—Ed.]

8. The Chronological Development of Carl Ruggles's Melodic Style

1. Steven E. Gilbert, "The 'Twelve-Tone System' of Carl Ruggles: A Study of the Evocations for Piano," *Journal of Music Theory* 14, no. 1 (1970):

68–91; Gilbert, "Carl Ruggles (1876–1971): An Appreciation," *Perspectives of New Music* 11, no. 1 (1972): 224–32; Gilbert, "An Introduction to Trichordal Analysis," *Journal of Music Theory* 18, no. 2 (1974): 338–62.

2. John Kirkpatrick, "The Evolution of Carl Ruggles," *Perspectives of New Music* 6, no. 2 (1968): 146–66.

3. "Dissonant relations" will be used here to mean, exclusively, the relations of the minor second, major seventh, and minor ninth.

4. Partly because of the complexly contrapuntal nature of certain parts of *Sun Treader* and partly because whole long sections of the piece are nearly identical to earlier sections, I have used only the first half (mm. 1–118) for input data. I am convinced, however, that this will in no way lessen the significance—or even the effective "accuracy"—of my results.

5. The differences between fourths and fifths in this respect, mentioned above, *might* be merely a special case of this more general condition, but I believe the harmonic consideration I have suggested to explain it is, at the very least, an important contributing factor.

6. Henry Cowell, *New Musical Resources*, 2nd ed. (New York: Something Else Press, 1969), 41–42.

7. Charles Seeger, "Carl Ruggles," *Musical Quarterly* 18, no. 4 (1932): 578–92.

8. Arnold Schoenberg, "Composition with Twelve Tones (2)," *Style and Idea*, 2nd ed. (New York: St. Martin's Press, 1975), 246.

9. Seeger, "Carl Ruggles," 588.

10. The points marked x in figure 27—and the numbers in parentheses following the value for ALSD in the tables at the top of figures 1–18—are values attained when the "phrase-reiterations" Seeger refers to are deleted from the input data. ALSD naturally increases somewhat when this is done, but the general trends in Ruggles's melodic style are well represented even without these deletions.

11. Charles Seeger, "In Memoriam: Carl Ruggles (1876–1971)," *Perspectives of New Music* 10, no. 1 (1972): 171–74.

9. Hierarchical Temporal Gestalt Perception in Music. A Metric Space Model (with Larry Polansky)

1. W. D. Ellis, ed., *A Source Book of Gestalt Psychology* (London: Routledge and Kegan Paul, 1955); W. Köhler, *Introduction to Gestalt Psychology* (New York: New American Library, 1959); K. Koffka, *Principles of Gestalt Psychology* (New York: Harcourt, Brace, 1935).

2. J. Tenney, *Meta ≠ Hodos—a Phenomenology of 20th-Century Music and an Approach to the Study of Form*, privately circulated monograph, 1961, published in 1964 by the Inter-American Institute for Musical Research, Gilbert Chase, editor.

3. J. Tenney, "Form," in *Dictionary of Contemporary Music*, ed. John Vinton (New York: E. P. Dutton, 1971); J. Tenney, "META *Meta ≠ Hodos*," *Journal of Experimental Aesthetics* 1 (1977): 1–10.

4. Some of these problems were noted by Wayne Slawson in his review of *Meta ≠ Hodos* in the *Journal of Music Theory* 10 (1966): 156.

5. Tenney, "META *Meta ≠ Hodos*."

6. [The square brackets around "and" are Tenney's; the ellipses have been inserted by the editors.—Ed.]

7. F. Attneave, "Dimensions of Similarity," *American Journal of Psychology* 63 (1950): 516–56; R. N. Shepard, "Attention and the Metric Structure of the Stimulus Space," *Bell Telephone Laboratories Technical Memorandum*, October 1962; Shepard, "The Analysis of Proximities: Multidimensional Scaling with an Unknown Distance Function," *Psychometrika* 27 (1962).

8. See E. Beckenbach and R. Bellman, *An Introduction to Inequalities* (New Mathematical Library, 1961). It should be noted that Shepard uses the term "proximity" for what is here being called "distance."

9. Compare Attneave, "Dimensions of Similarity," and Shepard, "The Analysis of Proximities."

10. The Euclidean and city-block metrics are themselves special cases of a more general class of distance-functions sometimes called the Minkowski metric, which (in two dimensions) is of the form

$$d = [(x_2 - x_1)^R + (y_2 - y_1)^R]^{1/R} \text{ for } R \geq 1.$$

Note that when $R = 1$, this becomes the city-block distance-function, and when $R = 2$, it is equivalent to the Euclidean metric. It would be of interest to experiment with this parameter of the equation in the context of the current algorithm. In particular, it might turn out that a value of R somewhere *between* 1 and 2 would be even more appropriate to the "space" of musical perception.

11. Compare Tenney, "META *Meta ≠ Hodos*."

12. Note that the sum of the weightings used to compute boundary-distances is always less than 1 but approaches this value as a limit when higher levels are being considered (i.e., $1/2 + 1/4 + 1/8 + \ldots < 1.0$).

13. A detailed description of the program with a complete documentation of the relevant input and output data is contained in an earlier research report written by this author (in collaboration with Larry Polansky) entitled "Hierarchical Temporal Gestalt Perception in Music: A 'Metric Space' Model," August 1978. [Privately printed.—Ed.] See also L. Polansky, "A Hierarchical Gestalt Analysis of Ruggles' *Portals*," July 1978.

14. A. S. Bregman and J. Campbell, "Primary Auditory Stream Segregation and Perception of Order in Rapid Sequences of Tones," *Journal of Experimental Psychology* 89 (1971): 244–49.

15. S. S. Stevens, "Mathematics, Measurement, and Psychophysics," in *Handbook of Experimental Psychology* (New York: John Wiley and Sons, 1951).

16. Jean-Jacques Nattiez, *Densité 21.5 de Varèse: Essai d'analyse sémiologique*, Groupe de Recherches en Sémiologie Musicale, Faculté de Musique, Université de Montréal, Québec, 1975.

17. Leopold Spinner, "Analysis of a Period," *Die Reihe* 2 (English ed.) (1958).

18. For "ergodic," see Tenney, "META *Meta ≠ Hodos*."

10. Introduction to "Contributions toward a Quantitative Theory of Harmony"

1. [Some of the proposed contents of this uncompleted work became part of papers or larger works. CDC means "consonance/dissonance concept." See appendix 3, "Excerpt from *A History of 'Consonance' and 'Dissonance'* (1988)."—Ed.]

2. [Arnold Schoenberg, "Composition with Twelve Tones (I)," in *Style and Idea: Selected Writings*, ed. Leonard Stein (1941; Berkeley: University of California Press, 1975), 218.—Ed.]

3. Note: What followed this introduction was an early version of what later became *A History of 'Consonance' and 'Dissonance.'* [Tenney added this note later during the preparation of this collection.—Ed.]

11. The Structure of Harmonic Series Aggregates

1. [Tenney follows Helmholtz (1954) in referring to a tone with multiple harmonics as a "compound tone" rather than a "complex tone."—Ed.]

2. [In this essay, a forward slash or a colon in the argument to a function assumes the role of separating arguments that is conventionally played by a comma. Tenney assumes throughout that frequencies are

positive integers, in which case his LCM and GCD have their familiar mathematical meanings. Note that any finite set of rationally related frequencies can be expressed as positive integer multiples of a frequency unit equaling the reciprocal of their lowest dommon denominator. The reader should also see Tenney's discussion below of the "effective value" for a frequency ratio.—Ed.]

3. [Tenney states some formulas without detailed development. For the benefit of the reader, the editors' annotations include sketches for selected possible derivations. For ease of reference, some notations, identities, and definitions are collected in the Editors' Appendix at the end of this paper.—Ed.]

4. [$(a,b) = 1$ whenever a and b are relatively prime, so that equation 1.2 follows from the identity $[a,b] = ab / (a,b)$.—Ed.]

5. [From equation 1.2, the harmonic period of the dyad a/b is $HP(a/b) = [a,b] = ab$. Within that harmonic period, the number of harmonics of tone a is $[a,b] / a = b$, while the number of harmonics of tone b that coincide with a harmonic of tone a is one. Therefore, within one harmonic period, the ratio of the number of harmonic coincidences to the number of harmonics of tone a is $I(a : b) = 1 / b$, which is equation 1.3. Equation 1.4 may be derived similarly.—Ed.]

6. [In actuality, harmonic roots are not addressed in the sequel.—Ed.]

7. [The second-to-last expression in equation 1.14 follows from the preceding expression after substituting the identity $[f_a,f_b] = f_a f_b / (f_a,f_b)$. The final expression in equation 1.14 then follows from the definitions of a and b that precede equation 1.2.—Ed.]

8. [By definition, the geometric mean of two values a and b is $\sqrt{ab}$. Note that $\log\left(\sqrt{ab}\right) = \left(\log(a) + \log(b)\right)/2$, which is an average of pitch values corresponding to the frequencies a and b, as indicated in the figure.—Ed.]

9. [Regarding the concept of "effective value," the reader is also referred to Tenney's discussion of "interval tolerance" in his essays "John Cage and the Theory of Harmony" and "The Several Dimensions of Pitch," both of which are reprinted in this volume.—Ed.]

10. [Tenney herein refers to any collection of three distinct pitches as a "triad."—Ed.]

11. [The last equality in equation 1.16 is an identity for the least common multiple of three integers (see the Editors' Appendix).—Ed.]

12. [The third expression in equation 1.17 corresponds to an identity for the least common multiple of three integers with the substitution

$(a,b,c) = 1$ (see the Editors' Appendix). The final expression in equation 1.17 reduces to $[a,b,c]$ after substituting the definitions $f_a = (f_a,f_b,f_c)a$, $f_b = (f_a,f_b,f_c)b$, and $f_c = (f_a,f_b,f_c)c$ into the numerator and then applying the identity $(ma,mb,mc) = m(a,b,c)$ where, in this case, $m = (f_a,f_b,f_c)$.—Ed.]

13. [With respect to the triad $a/b/c$, equation 1.18 for $I(a : b/c)$ expresses the proportion of the harmonics in tone a that coincide with a harmonic in either tone b or tone c. Consider a single harmonic period $[a,b,c]$ of the triad. For each harmonic period $[a,b]$ of the dyad a/b there is one coincidence between a harmonic of tone a and a harmonic of tone b, so the number of such coincidences in one harmonic period of the triad is $[a,b,c] / [a,b]$. Similarly, in one harmonic period of the triad there are $[a,b,c] / [a,c]$ coincidences between harmonics of tone a and tone c. The total number of harmonics in tone a in one harmonic period of the triad is $[a,b,c] / a$, so the fraction of tone a's harmonics that coincide with a harmonic in either tone b or tone c is

$$\left(\frac{[a,b,c]}{[a,b]} + \frac{[a,b,c]}{[a,c]} - 1\right) \Big/ \left(\frac{[a,b,c]}{a}\right),$$

where one must be subtracted in the first parenthesis so that the single harmonic coinciding between all three tones is not counted twice. Simplification yields the middle expression in equation 1.18. The last expression in equation 1.18 follows from the preceding one by substituting equation 1.17 and the identities $[a,b] = ab/(a,b)$ and $[a,c] = ac/(a,c)$. Equations 1.19 and 1.20 arise analogously.—Ed.]

14. [With respect to the triad $a/b/c$, equation 1.28 for $I(b/c : a)$ expresses the proportion of the distinct harmonics in the dyad b/c that coincide with a harmonic in tone a. (This may be compared with equation 1.18 for the proportion of the harmonics in tone a that coincide with a harmonic in the dyad b/c.) Consider a single harmonic period $[a,b,c]$ of the triad. Proceeding as in the derivation of equation 1.18, the number of harmonics in tone a that coincide with a harmonic of either tone b or tone c is

$$\frac{[a,b,c]}{[a,b]} + \frac{[a,b,c]}{[a,c]} - 1 .$$

In one harmonic period of the triad, the total number of distinct harmonics in the dyad b/c is $[a,b,c]/b + [a,b,c]/c - [a,b,c]/[b,c]$, where the last subtraction prevents harmonics that coincide between tones b and c from being counted twice. Thus the fraction of the harmonics in the dyad b/c that coincide with some harmonic in tone a is

$$\left(\frac{[a,b,c]}{[a,b]}+\frac{[a,b,c]}{[a,c]}-\frac{[a,b,c]}{[a,b,c]}\right)\Big/\left(\frac{[a,b,c]}{b}+\frac{[a,b,c]}{c}-\frac{[a,b,c]}{[b,c]}\right)$$
$$=\left(\frac{1}{[a,b]}+\frac{1}{[a,c]}-\frac{1}{[a,b,c]}\right)\Big/\left(\frac{1}{b}+\frac{1}{c}-\frac{(b,c)}{bc}\right),$$

where the identity $[b,c] = bc/(b,c)$ has been employed. Combining the terms in the last parenthesis over a common denominator yields equation 1.28. Equations 1.26 and 1.27 arise analogously.—Ed.]

15. [In equation 1.43, Tenney writes $[a,b]$, even though this simply equals ab (since a and b are relatively prime for a dyad). He may have done this in order to render apparent to the eye a structural parallelism between equations 1.43 and 1.42. Beginning from equation 1.9 and using $[a,b] = ab$, the number of distinct harmonics in one harmonic period of the dyad a/b can be written as

$$N(a/b)=\frac{[a,b]}{a}+\frac{[a,b]}{b}-1=[a,b]\left(\frac{1}{a}+\frac{1}{b}-\frac{1}{[a,b]}\right).$$

As Tenney points out following equation 1.45, the expression in parentheses is a form of equation 1.24 for the intersection ratio between a dyad and a complete harmonic series on its own GCD:

$$I\big((a,b):a/b\big)=\frac{a+b-1}{ab}=\frac{1}{a}+\frac{1}{b}-\frac{1}{ab}=\frac{1}{a}+\frac{1}{b}-\frac{1}{[a,b]}.$$

Note, by the way, that the final expression in equation 1.43 follows from the preceding line by applying the definitions of a and b and the identity $[mp,mq] = m[p,q]$ in the form

$$[f_a,f_b]=[a(f_a,f_b),\, b(f_a,f_b)]=(f_a,f_b)[a,b]\text{—Ed.]}$$

16. [This reference to *A History of 'Consonance' and 'Dissonance'* (Tenney 1988) was apparently a late addition to this manuscript. For further discussion of CDCs (consonance/dissonance concepts), the reader is referred to appendix 3.—Ed.]

17. [Schügerl's assumption of a "large number of harmonics" appears to serve a purpose similar to that of Tenney's assumption that his f_{max}

corresponds to an integral number of harmonic periods. In both cases, these simplifying assumptions allow the writer to ignore any fractional harmonic period that may reside near the upper frequency limit of a spectrum.—Ed.]

18. [Tenney's manuscript for "The Structure of Harmonic Series Aggregates" originally comprised three sections. The second section, entitled "Harmonic Density," is not published here because Tenney marked it for deletion when he was preparing the manuscript for publication. The original third section, "Harmonic Distance and Pitch Mapping," appears as the second section of the essay, with equations and figures renumbered accordingly.—Ed.]

19. [Tenney included no proof that *HD* constitutes a metric. One is supplied below, but the notation of the metric conditions differs from that appearing in Tenney's text. In the text, the triangle inequality is stated in terms of arguments *a*, *b*, and *c*, which are letter names that Tenney has previously reserved for reduced frequency values, i.e., $a = f_1/(f_1,f_2,f_3)$, etc. However, the *HD* function can be regarded as effectively reducing its arguments anyway, and doing so *pairwise*. Thus any assumption that its arguments are reduced is unnecessary, and, furthermore, the notational implication that they are reduced is potentially confusing since, even if they are relatively prime as a triple, they may not be *pairwise* relatively prime. Therefore the following proves that *HD* is a metric on the space of positive integer (frequency) values without any assumption that the values are a priori reduced in any way. To make this notationally clear, f_1, f_2, f_3 appear below as arguments to *HD* rather than *a*, *b*, *c*.

THEOREM:

$\mathrm{HD}(f_1,f_2) = \log_2(ab)$ is a metric on the space of positive integers, where a/b equals f_1/f_2 in lowest terms.

PROOF:

Symmetry: $HD(f_1,f_2) = \log_2(ab) = \log_2(ba) = HD(f_2,f_1)$

Nonnegativity: Since $a \geq 1$ and $b \geq 1$, $ab \geq 1$ so that $HD(f_1,f_2) = \log_2(ab) \geq 0$.

Nondegeneracy: If $f_1 = f_2$, then $a = b = 1$, in which case $HD(f_1,f_2) = \log_2(1) = 0$. On the other hand, $\log_2(ab) = 0$ only if $ab = 1$, which requires $a = b = 1$ so that $f_1 = f_2$.

Triangle inequality: The proof relies on the prime factorization

$$f_i = \prod_p p^{\upsilon_p(f_i)},$$

where the sum is over all prime integers. Now

$$(f_i, f_j) = \prod_p p^{\min(\upsilon_p(f_i), \upsilon_p(f_j))},$$

so that

$$\frac{f_i}{(f_i, f_j)} = \prod_p p^{\upsilon_p(f_i) - \min(\upsilon_p(f_i), \upsilon_p(f_j))} = \prod_p p^{\max(0, \upsilon_p(f_i) - \upsilon_p(f_j))}$$

and

$$\begin{aligned} HD(f_i, f_j) &= \log_2\left(\frac{f_i}{(f_i, f_j)} \frac{f_j}{(f_i, f_j)}\right) \\ &= \log_2\left(\prod_p p^{\max(0, \upsilon_p(f_i) - \upsilon_p(f_j)) + \max(0, \upsilon_p(f_j) - \upsilon_p(f_i))}\right) \\ &= \log_2\left(\prod_p p^{|\upsilon_p(f_i) - \upsilon_p(f_j)|}\right) \\ &= \sum_p |\upsilon_p(f_i) - \upsilon_p(f_j)| \log_2 p. \end{aligned}$$

(This expression shows that *HD* is a form of "city-block metric," as Tenney indicates below.) Using the triangle inequality for real numbers, $|x_1| + |x_2| \geq |x_1 + x_2|$, we then have

$$\begin{aligned} HD(f_1, f_2) + HD(f_2, f_3) &= \sum_p \left(|\upsilon_p(f_1) - \upsilon_p(f_2)| + |\upsilon_p(f_2) - \upsilon_p(f_3)|\right) \log_2 p \\ &\geq \sum_p |\upsilon_p(f_1) - \upsilon_p(f_3)| \log_2 p \\ &= HD(f_1, f_3). \end{aligned}$$

—Ed.]

20. [Note that, if *a*/*b* is in lowest terms, then at least one of m_a and m_b is zero so that either $a' = a$ or $b' = b$ (or both). Also, in equation 2.15, $i = m_a + m_b$.—Ed.]

21. [Figure 9 was a late addition, and Tenney left no caption for it. The upper portion furnishes an example illustrating that, for simple tones, *GD* can be considered as the sum of pitch-distances between the GCD of their frequencies and the lowest whole-number octave-equivalents of

each of those tones. The lower portion illustrates that it is also the sum of the pitch-distances between each of the two octave-reduced fundamentals and the lowest octave-equivalent of the point of harmonic intersection in the combined spectrum. This conclusion follows from equation 2.14: $\log_2(a'b') = \log_2(a') + \log_2(b') = PD(a',1) + PD(b',1)$.—Ed.]

22. [The lowest point of harmonic intersection in the combined spectrum is *ab*, whose lowest octave-equivalent (using equation 2.15) is $ab/2^i = a'b'$. Then Tenney's sum of pitch-distances is $PD(a'b',a') + PD(a'b',b') = \log_2 b' + \log_2 a' = \log_2(a'b') = GD(a,b)$, as he indicates. $a'b'$ is actually present in the harmonic series aggregate because, if a/b is in lowest terms, then either $a' = a$ or $b' = b$, in which case either $a'b = a'b$ or $a'b' = ab'$ so that $a'b'$ is a multiple of one of the fundamentals (either *a* or *b*).—Ed.]

23. [Tenney made a marginal note in the manuscript of this essay that, while he planned and sketched such an auditory model, he never completed or published it.—Ed.]

24. [The concept of a *pitch-height projection axis* lends importance to this angle, but Tenney does not introduce that concept in this paper; see "John Cage and the Theory of Harmony" and "The Several Dimensions of Pitch," both of which are reprinted in this volume.—Ed.]

12. John Cage and the Theory of Harmony

1. Arnold Schoenberg, *Theory of Harmony*, trans. Roy E. Carter (Berkeley: University of California Press, 1978), 389.

2. *Webster's New Collegiate Dictionary* (Toronto: Thomas Allen & Son, Ltd., 1979).

3. James Tenney, "Form," in *Dictionary of Contemporary Music*, ed. John Vinton (New York: E. P. Dutton, 1971).

4. Arnold Schoenberg, "Composition with Twelve Tones (I)" (1941), in *Style and Idea* (New York: St. Martin's Press, 1975), 216–17.

5. Willi Apel, *Harvard Dictionary of Music* (Cambridge, MA: Harvard University Press, 1953), 322.

6. Harry Partch, *Genesis of a Music* (Madison: University of Wisconsin Press, 1949).

7. Hermann Helmholtz, *On the Sensations of Tone* (1862), translated from the edition of 1877 by Alexander J. Ellis (New York: Dover, 1954).

8. Ben Johnston, "Tonality Regained," in *Proceedings of the American Society of University Composers* 6 (1971).

9. James Tenney, *A History of 'Consonance' and 'Dissonance'* (New York: Excelsior Music Publishing, 1988).

10. Helmholtz, *On the Sensations of Tone*; Jean-Philippe Rameau, *Treatise on Harmony* (1722), trans. Philip Gosset (New York: Dover, 1971).

13. Reflections after *Bridge*

1. [John Cage, "Diary: How to Improve the World (You Will Only Make Matters Worse)," in *A Year from Monday: New Lectures and Writings* (Middletown, CT: Wesleyan University Press), 19–20.—Ed.]

14. Review of *Music as Heard* by Thomas Clifton

1. Thomas Clifton, "Some Comparisons between Intuitive and Scientific Descriptions of Music," *Journal of Music Theory* 19 (1975): 73.

2. Thomas Clifton, *Music as Heard* (New Haven, CT: Yale University Press, 1983), 296. Hereafter cited in the text.

3. Clifton, "Some Comparisons"; "Music and the A Priori," *Journal of Music Theory* 17 (1973): 66–85.

4. Kurt Koffka, *Principles of Gestalt Psychology* (New York: Harcourt, Brace, 1935), 73.

5. Charles Sanders Peirce, "The Principles of Phenomenology," in *Philosophical Writings of Peirce*, ed. Justus Buchler (New York: Dover, 1955), 75.

6. Edmund Husserl, *The Phenomenology of Internal Time-Consciousness*, trans. James S. Churchill (Bloomington: Indiana University Press, 1969).

16. Darmstadt Lecture

1. [*A History of 'Consonance' and 'Dissonance,'* an excerpt of which is reprinted in this collection as appendix 3.—Ed.]

2. [Arnold Schoenberg, "Problems of Harmony," in *Style and Idea: Selected Writings*, ed. Leonard Stein (1934; Berkeley: University of California Press, 1975), 270.—Ed.]

3. ["John Cage and the Theory of Harmony" is reprinted in this collection.—Ed.]

4. [Karlheinz Stockhausen, ". . . wie die Zeit vergeht . . ." *Die Reihe* 3 (1957): 13–42, translated by Cornelius Cardew as ". . . How Time Passes . . ." *Die Reihe* 3 (1959): 10–40.—Ed.]

5. [R. Plomp and W. J. M. Levelt, "Tonal Consonance and Critical Bandwidth," *Journal of the Acoustical Society of America* 38 (1965): 548–60.—Ed.]

17. The Several Dimensions of Pitch

1. [List item 3 involves a conjecture for a distance function on amplitude envelopes (or excitation functions). The conjecture proved mathematically problematic to Tenney, and in preparing the manuscript for this publication Tenney inked a box around list item 3 and marked "delete" inside the box. He may have intended to delete this list item due to issues with the model, but it is possible that he intended this marking to apply to only part of the list item. Uncertain what Tenney's ultimate intentions were for list item 3, we have retained it.—Ed.]

18. On "Crystal Growth" in Harmonic Space

1. [William P. Malm, *Japanese Music and Musical Instruments* (Rutland, VT: C. E. Tuttle, 1959), 178; and Colin McPhee, *Music in Bali: A Study in Form and Instrumental Organization in Balinese Orchestral Music* (New Haven, CT: Yale University Press, 1966), 47.—Ed.]

19. About *Diapason*

1. [Reprinted in this collection.—Ed.]
2. [The diagram used here was reconstructed from the version published in the program booklet for the premiere of *Diapason* on October 20, 1996, at Donaueschinger Musiktage.—Ed.]

Appendix 1. *Pre–Meta ≠ Hodos*

1. [Added to the manuscript by Tenney in 2005 in preparation for this publication.—Ed.]
2. [These two square-bracketed comments were inserted many years later as a comment on his original typescript.—Ed.]
3. [This square-bracketed comment was inserted many years later as a comment on his original typescript.—Ed.]
4. [These square-bracketed comments were inserted many years later as a comment on his original typescript.—Ed.]
5. [In notes made while preparing this collection, Tenney indicated that where he originally wrote "is proportional to" or used the mathematical symbol for proportionality, he really meant "increases with." Similarly, by "inversely proportional to," he apparently meant "decreases with." He also indicated an intention to further clarify his notation, as well as his remarks about timbre, and to provide a citation for the concepts of "extensity" and "intensity," but these changes were never made.—Ed.]

Appendix 2. On Musical Parameters

1. [Added to the manuscript by Tenney in preparation for publication.—Ed.]

2. [Géza Révész, *Introduction to the Psychology of Music* (London: Longmans, Green and Co., 1953), 67.—Ed.]

3. [S. S. Stevens and J. Volkman, "The Relation of Pitch to Frequency: A Revised Scale," *American Journal of Psychology* 53 (1940): 329–53.—Ed.]

4. [Ernst Krenek, *Studies in Counterpoint; Based on the Twelve-Tone Technique* (New York: G. Schirmer, 1940), 7; Paul Hindemith, *The Craft of Musical Composition*, rev. ed. (New York: American Music Publishers, 1945).—Ed.]

5. [Carl E. Seashore, *Psychology of Music* (New York: Dover Publications, 1967).—Ed.]

6. [Karlheinz Stockhausen, "Structure and Experiential Time," *Die Reihe* 2 (1958): 64–74.—Ed.]

7. [John Cage, "Experimental Music: Doctrine," in *Silence: Lectures and Writings* (Middletown, CT: Wesleyan University Press, 1961), 13–17.—Ed.]

8. [Pierre Schaeffer, "Note on Time Relationships," *Gravesaner Blätter* 17 (1960): 41–77.—Ed.]

9. [Abraham Moles, *Théorie de l'information et perception esthétique*, 2nd ed. (Paris: Flammarion, 1958); Karlheinz Stockhausen, ". . . wie die Zeit vergeht . . ." *Die Reihe* 3 (1957): 13–42, translated by Cornelius Cardew as ". . . How Time Passes . . ." *Die Reihe* 3 (1959): 10–40.—Ed.]

10. [Josephine Nash Curtis, "Duration and the Temporal Judgment," *American Journal of Psychiatry* 27, no. 1 (1916): 1–46.—Ed.]

11. [Understood to mean that when two frequencies are slightly different, we hear that difference not so much as a frequency difference but in the "phasing" of beats.—Ed.]

12. [Graph not included here. Harvey Fletcher, *Speech and Hearing in Communication* (New York: Van Nostrand, 1953), 188.—Ed.]

13. [Arnold Schoenberg, *Theory of Harmony* (*Harmonielehre*), trans. Roy Carter (1911; Berkeley: University of California Press, 1978), 421.—Ed.]

INDEX

James Tenney was a prolific and important experimental composer, theorist, writer, and performer.

Larry Polansky is Professor of Music at the University of California, Santa Cruz, and Emeritus Strauss Professor of Music at Dartmouth College.

Lauren Pratt is the associate producer of music at REDCAT (Roy and Edna Disney/CalArts Theater) and executor of the Tenney estate.

Robert Wannamaker is Associate Dean at the California Institute of the Arts, where he teaches music composition, theory, history, and literature.

Michael Winter is a composer and founder and director of the wulf. in Los Angeles.

The University of Illinois Press
is a founding member of the
Association of American University Presses.

University of Illinois Press
1325 South Oak Street
Champaign, IL 61820-6903
www.press.uillinois.edu